The SAGE
Handbook *of*

Workplace Learning

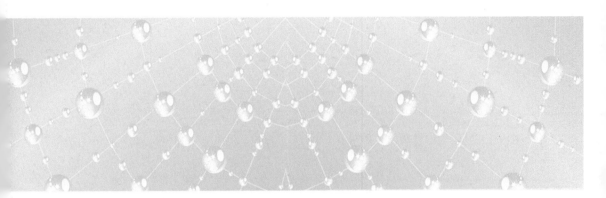

The SAGE Handbook *of*

Workplace Learning

Edited by
Margaret Malloch
Len Cairns
Karen Evans
Bridget N. O'Connor

Los Angeles | London | New Delhi
Singapore | Washington DC

Introduction and editorial arrangement © Margaret Malloch, Len Cairns, Karen Evans and Bridget N. O'Connor 2011

Chapter 1 © Len Cairns and Margaret Malloch 2011
Chapter 2 © Paul Hager 2011
Chapter 3 © Knud Illeris 2011
Chapter 4 © Alison Fuller and Lorna Unwin 2011
Chapter 5 © Stephen Billett 2011
Chapter 6 © Len Cairns 2011
Chapter 7 © Yrjö Engeström 2011
Chapter 8 © Per-Erik Ellström 2011
Chapter 9 © Darlene Russ-Eft 2011
Chapter 10 © Nicholas Allix 2011
Chapter 11 © Karen Evans, David Guile and Judy Harris 2011
Chapter 12 © Peter H. Sawchuk 2011
Chapter 13 © Michael Eraut 2011
Chapter 14 © Victoria Marsick, Karen Watkins and Bridget N. O'Connor 2011
Chapter 15 © Nicky Solomon and David Boud 2011
Chapter 16 © Hans Gruber and Christian Harteis 2011
Chapter 17 © Sang-Duk Choi 2011
Chapter 18 © Gerhard Naegele and Alan Walker 2011
Chapter 19 © Richard D. Lakes 2011.
Chapter 20 © Allie Clemans and Peter Rushbrook 2011
Chapter 21 © John M. Dirkx 2011
Chapter 22 © Martin Mulder and Judith Gulikers 2011
Chapter 23 © Tara Fenwick 2011
Chapter 24 © Robert G. Brookshire, Kara M. Lybarger and Lynn B. Keane 2011
Chapter 25 © Brenda R. Beatty 2011
Chapter 26 © Karen Evans, Edmund Waite and Natasha Kersh 2011
Chapter 27 © Margaret Harris and Colin Chisholm 2011
Chapter 28 © David Guile 2011
Chapter 29 © Carol Costley 2011
Chapter 30 © Amy Lui-Abel 2011
Chapter 31 © Bridget N. O'Connor and Doug Lynch 2011
Chapter 32 © Elizabeth Regan and Chester Delaney 2011
Chapter 33 © Jingli Chen, Su Jin Son and Curtis J. Bonk 2011
Chapter 34 © Craig E. Johnson 2011

First published 2011
This paperback edition first published 2013

SAGE Publications Ltd
1 Oliver's Yard
55 City Road
London EC1Y ISP

SAGE Publications Inc.
2455 Teller Road
Thousand Oaks, California 91320

SAGE Publications India Pvt Ltd
B 1/I 1 Mohan Cooperative Industrial Area
Mathura Road
New Delhi 110 044

SAGE Publications Asia-Pacific Pte Ltd
3 Church Street
10-04 Samsung Hub
Singapore 049483

Library of Congress Control Number: 2009939507

British Library Cataloguing in Publication data

A catalogue record for this book is available from the British Library

ISBN 978-1-84787-589-1
ISBN 978-1-4462-7052-3 (pbk)

Typeset by Glyph International Ltd
Printed by MPG Printgroup, UK
Printed on paper from sustainable resources

Contents

About the Editors

Margaret Malloch, PhD, is a Reader in the Cass School of Education, University of East London. She is an Executive Committee Member and past Chair of the Workplace Learning Special Interest Group of the American Educational Research Association and a member of the VETNET Board for the European Educational Research Association. Margaret's research encompasses the NCVER projects: *Capable Organisation: Implications for Vocational Education and Research* and *Getting the job done: How employers use and value accredited training leading to a qualification*. This Handbook was initiated whilst Margaret coordinated postgraduate education programs emphasising workplace learning at Victoria University, Australia.

Len Cairns, PhD, is Associate Professor and Associate Dean (Development) in the Faculty of Education at Monash University, Australia. He also holds an ongoing Visiting Professor position in the Institute of Work-Based Learning at Middlesex University in London. He teaches in the Master of Organisational Leadership and Master of School Leadership programmes at Monash, and is researching and writing in the fields of Workplace Learning, Capability and Leadership. Recent published studies have focused on developing capability through leadership, intercultural capability in management education and the impact of NVQs (and related competency-based qualifications) on learning in organisations. A recent volume with Professor John Stephenson is, *Capable Workplace Learning*. Len has recently completed a four-year research and development programme on Educational Leaders with Professor Peter Gronn funded by the Australian and Victorian State governments. Len is a past Chair of the Workplace Learning Special Interest Group of the American Educational Research Association.

Karen Evans, PhD, is Chair in Education (Lifelong Learning) at the Institute of Education, University of London; Co-Director of the Centre for Excellence in Work-Based Learning for Education Professionals; and past Head of the School of Lifelong Education and International Development. She has directed numerous international research studies on workplace learning and on learning in life and work transitions. Her previous books include *Learning, Work and Social Responsibility* (Springer, 2009); *Improving Workplace Learning* (Routledge, 2006); *Reconnection: Countering Social Exclusion through Situated Learning* (Springer, 2004); *Working to Learn: Transforming Learning in the Workplace* (Routledge, 2002) and *Learning and Work in the Risk Society* (Palgrave, 2000). Her international interests are also reflected in her editorship of the journal of international and comparative education *COMPARE*, between 2004 and 2009.

Bridget N. O'Connor, PhD, is Professor of Higher Education and Business Education at New York University. She is the co-author of *Learning at Work* (HRD Press, 2007), *End-user Information Systems: Implementing Individual and Group Technologies* (Prentice Hall, 2002), and *Training for Organizations* (South-Western, 2002). She is a past president of the Organizational Systems Research Association and was Chair of its two national model curriculum projects and editor of its journal, *Information Technology, Learning and Performance Journal*. She is a Past Chair of the American Educational Research Association's Special Interest Group, Workplace Learning. She is also a past Chairperson of the New York University Faculty Senators Council. In 2006, she was a Fulbright Senior Specialist at Victoria University in Melbourne, Australia.

Notes on Contributors

Amy Lui Abel is Director of Leadership Development, Morgan Stanley University, specializing in organizational needs assessment, leadership and competency development, performance improvement, design and delivery of learning programmes, and change management. Her New New York University doctoral dissertation won the 2009 AERA SIG Workplace Learning Outstanding Dissertation Award. She serves on the Board of the New York City Chapter of the American Society for Training and Development (ASTD).

Nicholas M. Allix lectures and researches in organisational leadership, capability, and learning at Monash University Faculty of Education, Australia. Nicholas has worked in the commercial, public and private health and vocational sectors in general business management and administration, corporate human resource management and development; educational administration, and knowledge management.

Brenda R. Beatty researches and teaches at the University of Melbourne on the emotions of leadership, leadership development, school improvement, collaborative cultures, organisational change, student connectedness with school and the use of interactive web-based technologies to support development of professional learning communities. *Leading with Teacher Emotions in Mind*, with Leithwood, was recently published by Corwin Press.

Stephen Billett (Professor, Griffith University, Australia) investigates learning through and for work. He publishes in journals, sole authored books (*Learning Through Work: Strategies for Effective Practice*; *Work, Change and Workers*) and edited *volumes* (*Work, Subjectivity and Learning, Emerging Perspectives of Work and Learning*, and is Editor in Chief of *Vocations and Learning*.

Curtis J. Bonk is a former accountant and CPA who received his Master's and PhD degrees in educational psychology from the University of Wisconsin. Dr Bonk is currently Professor of Instructional Systems Technology at Indiana University and adjunct in the School of Informatics. Curt is President of CourseShare and SurveyShare.

David Boud is Professor of Adult Education at the University of Technology, Sydney. His research in recent years has been on learning in workplaces, particularly informal learning and the many ways learning has been taken up in organisational practices.

Robert G. Brookshire is Professor and Director of the Technology Support and Training Management Program at the University of South Carolina. He holds qualifications from the University of Georgia, Georgia State University, and a PhD from Emory University. He is editor of the *Information Technology, Learning, and Performance Journal*.

Jingli Cheng is an instructional designer and learning programme manager at Executive and Leadership Development, Hewlett-Packard Company, while completing his PhD degree in

Instructional Systems Technology from Indiana University Bloomington. His research interests include work place learning, knowledge management, organisational behaviour and strategic management.

Colin Chisholm, Emeritus Professor, Glasgow Caledonian University, led the establishment of a multilevel postgraduate Framework in Work-Based Learning. In research and publications he applies work-based learning concepts to Lifeplace learning and environments. He has worked with the UNESCO International Centre for Engineering Education, Monash University, Australia, for innovative engineering education.

Sang-Duk Choi is the Director, Office of HRD and Lifelong Education Research, Korean Educational Development Institute. His main research interest is lifelong learning policies in higher education. He is a member of the Advisory Committee of the Ministry of Education, Science and Technology, and contributed to the Presidential Commission on Education Innovation.

Allie Clemans is a Senior Lecturer in the Faculty of Education at Monash University in Australia. Her research programme focuses on adult education practices in a range of learning spaces such as workplaces and communities. Her research work invites a critical reading of contemporary adult learning and development approaches.

Carol Costley is Professor and head of the Work-Based Learning Research Centre at Middlesex University. She has developed the Work-Based Learning and Doctorate in Professional Studies programmes. Her research interests are on work-based learning and issues of trans-disciplinarity, equity, ethics and the insider as researcher. Carol convenes the Universities Association for Lifelong Learning, Work-Based Learning network.

Chester Delaney worked for 24 years in New York's Financial District, starting as a programmer at the Federal Reserve and ending as a manager of technology training and Human Resources at Chase Manhattan. He published widely in the fields of technical and management training. Now retired, he resides in Massachusetts. He is the co-author of *Learning at Work* (HRD Press, 2007).

John M. Dirkx is Professor of Higher, Adult and Lifelong Education at Michigan State University. He is co-author of *A Guide to Planning and Implementing Instruction for Adults: A Theme-Based Approach*, the editor of *Adult Learning and the Emotional Self*, and is the editor for the *Journal of Transformative Education*.

Per-Erik Ellström, MA, MSc, PhD, is Professor of Education at Linköping University, Sweden. He is also Director of the HELIX Excellence Centre (www.liu.se/helix) at the same university. His research interests include studies of workplace learning, adult education, vocational education and training, practice-based innovation, and interactive research.

Yrjö Engeström is Professor of Adult Education and Director of the Center for Research on Activity, Development and Learning, University of Helsinki. His theory of expansive learning and interventionist methodology of developmental work research is well known. *From Teams to Knots: Activity-Theoretical Studies of Collaboration and Learning at Work*, was published in 2008.

Michael Eraut's interest in workplace learning developed in the 1980s and stretches across a wide range of professional and vocational sectors: business, education, engineering, healthcare and management. He has researched work placements in degree courses, early career learning and mid-career learning, and the nature and epistemology of practice.

Tara Fenwick is a Professor of Professional Education at the Stirling Institute of Education, University of Stirling, Scotland. Her recent research focuses on professional knowledge and learning, with particular interest in issues of materiality, identity, and transition.

Alison Fuller is Professor of Education and Work and Head of the Post-compulsory Education and Training Research Centre in the School of Education, University of Southampton. Research interests include changing patterns of participation in education, training and work; education – work transitions; apprenticeship; and workplace learning. She has recently (with Felstead, Unwin and Jewson) published *Improving Working as Learning*.

Hans Gruber is Professor of Educational Science at the University of Regensburg (Germany). Main research interests are professional learning, expertise, workplace learning, social network analysis, higher education. He is a member of the Review Board "Education Sciences", of the German Research Foundation and of the Executive Committee of the EARLI.

David Guile, Reader in Education, Institute of Education, University of London, is a founding member of the Education and Social Research Centre for Learning and Lifechances in the Knowledge Economy/Society. Research interests include Professional, Vocational and Workplace Learning. David's book *The Learning Challenge of the Knowledge Economy* is in press.

Judith Gulikers, PhD, is researcher at the chair group of Education and Competence studies at the Wageningen University in the Netherlands. Her expertise is on competence-based or authentic assessment at pre-vocational, vocational and higher education.

Paul Hager is Professor of Education at University of Technology, Sydney. His main scholarly interest is the emerging field of philosophy of adult and vocational education. His work centres on topics such as informal workplace learning, professional practice, and the role of generic skills in work.

Judy Harris is Learning Adviser in the Centre for Learning and Teaching at Bishop Grosseteste University College, Lincoln. Research interests are recognition of prior learning, work-based learning and widening participation in higher education, particularly curricular and pedagogic implications. Judy has roles with the Open University, England and Thompson Rivers University, Canada.

Margaret Harris is a Senior Teaching Fellow at the University of Aberdeen. Her research area is adult lifelong learning, including work-based and lifeplace learning. She publishes extensively in these areas. She holds a Doctorate and Masters in Education and Learning and qualifications in research, management and teaching in tertiary education.

Christian Harteis holds a senior researcher position at the Institute of Educational Science of the Regensburg University (Germany). His research field is on workplace learning and professional development. He has conducted several German and international research projects on individual and organizational features of work-related learning.

Knud Illeris is Professor of Lifelong Learning at The Danish University of Education (part of Aarhus University). He is internationally known for his comprehensive theory of learning, published in the book *How We Learn* (Routledge 2007), and recently edited *Contemporary Theories of Education and International Perspectives on Competence Development* (Routledge, 2009).

Craig E. Johnson is Professor of Leadership Studies and director of the Doctor of Management Program at George Fox University, Oregon, teaching leadership, management and ethics courses. Research interests include leadership ethics, organisational ethics, and leadership education with several publications. Extensive international projects with nonprofit organisations have been undertaken.

Lynn B. Keane is Director of the Business Education Program at the University of South Carolina. She previously taught business education, computer applications, and information technology courses at Lehman College (1999–2005), Pace University (1992–2006), and New York University. She has authored four books in the John Wiley *Getting Started* series.

Natasha Kersh, Research Officer at the Faculty of Policy and Society, Institute of Education, University of London, researches workplace learning, employability and post-compulsory education and adult literacy. She is a member of the Economic and Social Research Council Centre for Research into Learning and Life Chances in Knowledge Economies and Societies.

Richard D. Lakes is Professor of Educational Policy Studies at Georgia State University, Atlanta. He researches the impact of globalisation on education for work, and writes about neoliberal policy formulations in vocational education. He recently co-authored "Disciplining the Working Classes: Neoliberal Designs in Vocational Education," in *Pedagogies: An International Journal.*

Kara M. Lybarger is a graduate student at the University of South Carolina-Columbia for her MA in Art History. She holds a graduate assistantship with the Department of Technology Support and Training Management and is the Assistant Editor of the *Information Technology, Learning, and Performance Journal.*

Doug Lynch is Vice Dean, Graduate School of Education, University of Pennsylvania. Current research, teaching and activities focus on learning in the context of educational innovation and entrepreneurship. Building on a career of innovation and prestigious awards, Doug serves on the American Enterprise Institute's Future of Education Project and the International Standard's Organization.

Victoria J. Marsick is Professor of Adult Learning and Leadership and Co-Director of the J.M. Huber Institute for Learning in Organisations in the Organisation and Leadership Department of Teachers College, Columbia University. Her teaching, research and consulting focus on informal and transformative learning at the individual, group and organisational levels.

Martin Mulder, PhD, is Full Professor and Head of the Department of Education and Competence Studies at Wageningen University, the Netherlands. He leads a research programme on competence development and published over 400 articles, chapters and books with his co-workers. He is editor, chairman, and member of various peer reviewed journals.

Gerhard Naegele, Professor and Director of the Institute of Gerontology, Dortmund University, conducts qualitative and quantitative research into socio-political issues and policies of ageing, older workers, labour market, pensions, caring and life-course developments. He is a member of the German Society of Gerontology and Geriatrics and the Gerontological Society, America.

Elizabeth Regan is Professor and Chair of the Information Systems Department at Morehead State University. She also chairs the Northeast Kentucky Regional Health Information

Organisation Board of Directors. She has 16 years of industry management experience. Current research interests include IT innovation and health systems transformation. She is co-author of *End-User Information Systems* (Prentice Hall 2002).

Peter Rushbrook is Senior Lecturer in the School of Education at Charles Sturt University, Australia, Wagga Wagga campus. Before beginning a career as a university academic he worked for twenty-five years in Victorian junior technical schools, Technical and Further Education (TAFE) institutes and a range of adult learning centres.

Darlene Russ-Eft, PhD, is Professor and Chair of Adult Education and Higher Education Leadership at Oregon State University. Her research and publications focus on evaluation, learning, development, and competency. She is president-elect of the Academy of Human Resource Development and director of the International Board of Standards for Training, Performance, and Instruction.

Peter H. Sawchuk is Professor of Sociology & Equity Studies in Education at the University of Toronto. He specialises in the area of work, learning and social control. His books include *Adult Learning and Technology in Working-Class Life* (2003); *Workplace Learning: A Critical Introduction* (2004); *Critical Perspectives on Activity* (2006).

Nicky Solomon is Professor of Education at the University of Technology, Sydney. Her research on work and learning has contributed to understandings of the worker as learner as well as the complexities in naming and managing everyday learning at work.

Su Jin Son recently earned her PhD in Human Resource Education (HRE) at University of Illinois at Urbana-Champaign. She received an EdM in Educational Technology from Kyung Hee University in Korea. Her research interests include mentoring relationships, implementation of technology for learning, and programme evaluation in corporate settings.

Lorna Unwin is Professor and Chair in Vocational Education at the Institute of Education, University of London, and is also Deputy Director of the ESRC-funded LLAKES Research Centre. Her recent books include: *Improving Working for Learning*, 2009; and *Communities of Practice*: *Critical Perspectives*, 2008, both published by Routledge.

Edmund Waite is a researcher at the Department of Lifelong and Comparative Education, Institute of Education, London University. His research interests and publications relate to the study of adult literacy in the United Kingdom and international contexts as well as the anthropological study of education in Muslim societies.

Alan Walker is Professor of Social Policy and Social Gerontology, University of Sheffield, UK. He currently directs the UK's largest research programme on ageing, The New Dynamics of Ageing, and the European Research Area in Ageing.

Karen E. Watkins is Professor of Lifelong Education, Administration and Policy at the University of Georgia. Watkins is the author/co-author of an extensive number of articles, chapters and books and the organisational survey, *Dimensions of the Learning Organization Questionnaire [DLOQ]*, which has been used in over 70 published studies worldwide.

General Introduction

This *SAGE Handbook* provides a state-of-the art overview of the field of Workplace Learning Internationally. The assembled authors are all well-placed theoreticians, researchers and practitioners in this burgeoning field of educational endeavour which is now across higher education, vocational education and training, post-compulsory secondary schooling and lifelong education.

The premise of the volume is that it is both timely and necessary for a broad based, yet incisive analysis of the range of theory, research and practical developments in this now prominent field of educational activity.

This volume presents a comprehensive study of work and workplace learning in its many manifestations and contested areas. This *Handbook* draws together the three essential areas of Theory, Research and Practice, and Issues in the field of Workplace Learning and is structured accordingly. The final chapters focus on issues, future developments, and directions, with recommendations for further development.

In recent years, the idea that learning in the workplace is a significant area for study, and theorisation as well as intervention in and examination of practice, has emerged strongly as world-wide interest amongst scholars and has gathered momentum. Key researchers and writers in the field have approached workplaces as the base of learning about work, that is, work-based learning. As well, there has been emerging interest in such variations of the idea as, learning *about*, *through* and *at* work. Many of the theoretical discussions have centred on adult learning and some on learners' managing their own learning with emphasis on aspects such as communities of practice, activity systems and self-directed learning.

Early work in the field was often linked to the foundations of Vocational Education and Training (VET) traditions with concerns around skills, competencies and "on the job" learning. In fact, much of the leading work in the field has been carried out by researchers and writers who have their base in either VET or Adult Learning, often in education faculties or related sections of universities and sometimes affiliated with National Vocational Research Centres or international groups in the area (e.g. Cedefop, VETNET in Europe, AERA in the United States).

The idea that learning and workplaces had more to do with real lifelong and life-wide aspects than the traditional "training" regimen has emerged in the last decade through the untiring efforts of researchers and writers such as Jack Mezirow, Victoria Marsick in the United States, and David Boud in Australia and the UK. The field has, since the mid 1990s, grown enormously as an area of theory, research and practical work which has not only expanded the interest but more "legitimised" the area as a field of study, reflection and progress.

Dichotomies such as "informal" versus "formal" learning and the notions surrounding learning at workplaces versus learning in formal training or vocational institutions became debatable areas of some contentiousness. Various theories associated with the nature and specificity of learning in work situations began to draw in scholars and writers to debate the very nature and conditions of what "work" was, how one learned at work and today even debates about the brave new world of work where the very essence of employment and work for remuneration as the underlying assumption about place are being questioned.

Internationally, many USA scholars in this field either work within the adult learning or organisational development arena. Others have pursued the aspects of post-compulsory learners preparing for "work" through school-related activities. Some have sought to apply learning theories from the adult learning tradition and relate theories such as Vygotskian understandings of children learning to the new dynamics of adults learning about work. Interest in the workplace as a learning environment and an understanding of the role of work in the lifespan is another focus.

There was also an apparent differentiation in the field in the USA where another group of writers on the "work-based" learning focused heavily on adolescent-age school children learning about the "world of work" through supervised internships and other school-to-work initiatives that help students explore careers and learn job skills and develop interpersonal relationship skills.

In Europe, apprenticeships, models of young people better developing a sense of vocation and studies of learning by adults in different sites, appeared to dominate the area for some time. Recent theories of learning and work relations have emerged and gained considerable strength in the European scene. Some have been psychological (Illeris) others have been socio-cultural (Engeström), while others have attempted sociological explanations of wider societal trends (Beck), or adopted an industrial relations perspective on learning and human relations in workplaces. Also in the UK there has been a flurry of research activity built around work-based learning in skills and literacy aspects as well as "higher end" work on professional doctorates and the design of ways to "credit" or recognize prior work-related learning at professional levels and for part of formal qualifications.

In Australia, New Zealand, and to some extent in Canada, writers and researchers appeared to be fascinated by the way people in workplaces got together and shared expertise and learnt about skilled practice. In addition, research on aspects such as competency-based education and training across the VET sector and the way work and learning can be mutually reinforcing as people learn through their work activities.

In Asia and South East Asia, there has been a concern with advancing technological and manufacturing skill bases in India and China and with engaging with Western management and globalisation ideas in the former "tiger" economies. There are also moves, as shown in some of the chapters in the theory section, to translate Eastern philosophical positions on knowledge, self and learning places for Western enlightenment.

A dominant concern across the Western world in the past twenty years, which became known as "situated learning theory" (Lave and Wenger) and its applicability across a range of work sites and types of interaction in groups or "communities of practice" features in a number of the chapters. This set of ideas became one of the major theory into practice approaches of the 1990s and into the early twenty-first century, and it is both explained and critiqued in the Handbook's chapters.

Research in this new century has expanded to question the learning that is engaged in and the respective positions of both the organisation and the individual. Ranging across the notions of the individual bounded by the workplace, to moving beyond the workplace to cross "boundaries", or turn at "intersections", contrasts between formal and informal, tacit, implicit and explicit learning, generic skills and specific skills, team learning, and lifespace learning, have all been explored, theorised and examined. Each aspect (often presented in dichotomies and with metaphorical emphases as has emerged in the literature) has been explicated, with cases supporting and attacking various positions.

Organisations are interested in return on investment in learning, in how and whether to be a 'learning organisation.' Governments address the skilling of a dwindling and aging population, identifying apparent skills shortages, particularly in areas traditionally regarded as 'the trades'. At the same time there is wide concern and almost a pre-occupation with the promise or threat and effects of globalisation. These aspects, when viewed against the theories of Beck, for example, and his prediction of the emergence in the West of a "Brazilianisation" of work and the flow on from that for learning, provide a fascinating backdrop to current debates.

This *Handbook* draws together a wide range of views, theoretical dispositions and assertions, and provides a leading edge presentation by key writers and researchers with insight into the field and its current state as well as a glimpse at possible futures. Many of the contributors to this *Handbook*, are the developers and key writers in the field as to the leading edge work on Workplace Learning, and their contributions offer a close examination of their theories and work from the proverbial 'horse's mouth'.

This *SAGE Handbook of Workplace Learning* should serve as a basic source for researchers and serious academics who are interested in the scope and breadth of the Workplace Learning area and what theory, research and practice has to offer for its understanding and creating its future.

The first section of the *Handbook* explores the **Theory and Theoretical Frameworks** relating to Workplace Learning. There has been a shift from a behaviourist approach to the training for specific skills in specific workplaces to a consideration of people as learners operating in workplaces and beyond. There is a questioning of what learning is engaged in and therefore a reconsideration of the positions of the organisation, the employee and the person who is learning in and through work and within and across groups at work.

The theoretical underpinnings and models of Workplace Learning and their implications for research and practice are traced, developed, challenged and explicated in this section of the *Handbook*.

Section 2 of the *Handbook* focuses on **Research and Practice** in the field and offers a range of views and practical research that explores how, where, why, and for what ends people work and learn at and through work activities. This synthesis of current and recent research and practice should provide researchers and other readers with a comprehensive examination of many of the key aspects of Workplace Learning.

Section 3 of the *Handbook* examines **Issues and Futures** in the area of Workplace Learning in a set of chapters where key current and potential future issues and ideas abound. This section should establish a set of ideas about where the field of Workplace Learning is going over the 21st century and what issues we face now and in the future as we move forward in these exciting times.

Theory

INTRODUCTION

This section of the *SAGE Handbook of Workplace Learning* presents a set of eleven chapters which address a wide range of theoretical positions, models, theories and their implications for the field under consideration in the Handbook.

The influences of psychological theories, sociological, situated, and postmodern thinking on the possible theories of how people learn and respond in and through workplace activity is dealt with in detail. There is a range of frameworks and positions adopted by the set of authors who show a variety of international backgrounds and orientations.

Initially, Cairns and Malloch explore new ideas and directions for the concept of Workplace Learning arguing for a broader conceptualisation in this, the beginning of a new century. Work is defined as more than employment for remuneration, and the considerations of place as more than a physical location for learning and work open a set of possibilities for much broader concerns and issues to be examined. A set of future prospects is also considered as a way to look forward to what might be pressing challenges for work, place and learning in the twenty-first century.

Hager, in Chapter 2, provides an historical overview of major theories relevant to workplace learning in order to take the reader to the present and future. The discussion covers the many views of workplace learning theories and their underlying philosophical positions to show how theories of workplace learning have evolved and emerged to their significant place in current research and practice across the field.

Illeris offers a chapter that examines changes and development in learning and workplace learning and he presents a model of workplace learning and 'working life as a space for learning'. Illeris sees workplace learning as a matter of what takes place in the interaction of the learner's work identity with workplace practices. A key focus for Illeris in this chapter is on learning as competence development, which he elaborates and positions as a central idea.

Fuller and Unwin take on the aspect of organisations and their place in a consideration of workplace learning. In this chapter they discuss, amongst other aspects, the various forms of work organisations (including high performance work and management of high performance organisations). The chapter also offers a detailed discussion of the workplace as a site for learning and presents an interesting exemplar of the 'expansive' and 'restrictive' ends of their earlier developed idea of the 'expansive restrictive continuum'.

Billett suggests strongly that it is time for the significance of personal agency and self to figure more prominently in theories of Workplace Learning and he presents his theoretical stance on the interactions and 'affordances' that operate between individual 'cognitive experience' and social experience and how these are negotiated in the workplace. Central to Billett's case are the elements of learning *through* and *for* work and how individual engagement is based on what he calls 'relational interdependence with social agency' in workplaces. His conclusion relates to individuals being active participants in 'remaking cultural practices' which arise and are involved in work and workplaces.

Cairns suggests that the influential model of *communities of practice,* as developed and popularised by Lave and Wenger, may have, to some extent, outlived its relevance as an explanatory model of learning in the workplace, even though its impact and significance has been immense. Cairns surveys a range of critiques of the idea and its application over the past twenty years and offers some additional thoughts on ways to think differently about the intersections that individual learners face in workplace learning situations and how societal elements may be included in the way workplace learning takes place. There is also a link to the following chapter by Engeström amongst the suggestions for different thinking about ensembles and self in learning in the workplace.

Engeström offers a clear and very useful update on his Activity theory and its relationship to studying workplaces and workplace learning. By presenting his 'expansive theory' and the concept of 'knotworks' within the context of broad-based professionals in medical treatment groups with collaborative work and learning to better offer treatment, Engeström shows some very insightful and different views as he moves towards a co-configuration model.

Ellström, in Chapter 8 discusses Informal Learning at Work and takes on the points made elsewhere by critics who see the informal-formal dichotomy to be unhelpful as he argues that informal learning is a significant and pervasive learning mode in a range of contexts, including schools. Ellström also discusses the differences between adaptive and developmental learning as he examines what he calls 'enabling' and 'constraining' learning environments. Ellström's journey through his theoretical chapter, which also covers a four-level model of action and reflection, suggests that while structural conditions are important in learning at work, so too are subjective factors; he also reminds readers that micro, macro and meso levels of analysis are necessary elements in any consideration of learning in the workplace.

Russ-Eft sets out to identify, through various theories and considerations, what she calls a 'meta theory,' which is her constructed theoretical framework based on implications from the range of theories and views she has charted. This review of various theories and their underlying conceptualisation locates a range of views and will assist the reader to reconsider what learning theories suit application and development in the arena of workplace learning.

Allix, in Chapter 10 addresses the significant area of Knowledge with a detailed tour of the various theoretical areas and influences including work on mind and cognition that have arisen from more recent brain sciences and how learning relates to these views. Again, Allix comes down to a conclusion that learning is *both* 'a profoundly individual *and* social phenomenon' which resonates with the positions of a number of the authors in this section (albeit in slightly differing forms and with different bases and emphases).

Finally, in this first section, Evans, Guile and Harris present a case for rethinking work-based learning and start with some points about workplace and work-based differences and similarities and how work-based learning has, in the UK, been 'appropriated' as a different concept akin to basing qualifications in higher education on work assignment and other 'learning opportunities'. They continue to argue for a more inclusive stand and understanding of work-based learning to enhance learning *for* and *through* work, aspects that resonate throughout this Handbook. The suggestions for a model of recontextualisation of content, workplace, pedagogy and learner as the four 'modes' offers a cogent case for this to be a core aspect of any rethinking of work-based learning and they add that it also avoids transfer issues in other models.

This first section of *The SAGE Handbook of Workplace Learning* sets the theoretical scene and presents the reader with a range of views, models and theories and yet with some elements of convergence amongst the very broad church of the international group of authors. There are issues, challenges and positions suggested that should, in turn, challenge the field to rethink and reconsider a number of positions and theoretical orientations to better develop the study of Workplace Learning.

1

Theories of Work, Place and Learning: New Directions

Len Cairns and Margaret Malloch

INTRODUCTION

The first decade of the twenty-first century may or may not be the harbinger of incredible change and global difference among the many peoples and nations that saw such advances that were achieved in the twentieth century. Globalization, that late twentieth century spectre of either connected intercultural and cross-cultural development, or the single greatest threat to harmony and autonomy, for example, may in fact be a non-event by the mid twenty-first century. To some, this last statement may be heretical, yet early in this century we have seen the financial markets melt down in late 2008 and various other effects of too great an interconnectedness, as the world notes that 'thinking global' is not always an advantage to all.

Other current trends and directions may be, as was the case in previous generations, just perceptions that this era is one of great change like never before seen, rather than some normal progression stage. As Sir John Adams wrote in the introduction to his 1922 volume on *Modern Developments in Educational Practice*:

> It seems inherent in human beings to regard their own period as one of notable change. We are continually telling each other that this is a critical time, that we are at the parting of the ways, that vital issues lie in our hands at the present moment (p. 2).

This chapter sets out to explore new ideas and directions for the concept of Workplace Learning. It suggests that the three terms included in the composite, that is, Work, Place and Learning, each need to be considered more broadly than has been the case in the last 50 years and that the combination of the three should invoke some new thinking in this 'ultramodern' age of the twenty-first century. In addition, the chapter presents a number of suggested challenges which could necessitate different approaches to a wide range of workplace learning thinking and activities as this twenty-first century unfolds.

We are suggesting, contrary to Sir John Adams' rather dismissive rebuff, that this era *is* one of critical importance and change, not just a possible misperception of normality.

This chapter explores, from a theoretical perspective, the three terms that together constitute Workplace Learning: Work, Place and Learning, and how there should be broader consideration given to these terms in the twenty-first century. In addition, the chapter offers some insights and ideas for new directions in the area of Workplace Learning.

Beginning with the term Work, the chapter suggests that a much broadened understanding of this word is needed to include the many areas of civic service (Beck, 2000) and household activities (including child rearing) that have previously been discounted as actual work in most Western societies (Chisholm and Davis, 2005). We argue that work is a more generalized notion than employment or an activity taking place in a specific site that involves production for remuneration.

We were recently reminded that John Dewey, in his seminal work *Democracy and Education* (1916), wrote about the differences and similarities among children with regard to work and play. That play and work could be further extended more broadly is summed up by the following:

> It is important not to confuse the psychological distinction between play and work with the economic distinction. Psychologically, the defining characteristic of play is not amusement nor aimlessness. It is the fact that the aim is thought of as more activity in the same line, without defining continuity of action in reference to results produced. Activities as they grow more complicated gain added meaning by greater attention to specific results achieved. Thus they pass gradually into work. Both are equally free and intrinsically motivated, apart from false economic conditions which tend to make play into idle excitement for the well to do, and work into uncongenial labor for the poor. Work is psychologically simply an activity which consciously includes regard for consequences as a part of itself; it becomes constrained labor when the consequences are outside of the activity as an end to which activity is merely a means. Work which remains permeated with the play attitude is art – in quality if not in conventional designation (p. 205–206).

The discussion of the nature of work also embraces the concept of place, in relation to situated theories of learning and issues of transferability and generalizability of capable learners. There is also a need to consider, with regard to learning places in this definitional and conceptualization debate, where it may be that one learns in the individual sense and in the psychological examination of the learning process. The *Workplace*, in our discussion, then becomes a more potentially personal and negotiated location than where one is employed by a third party or organization. The central role personal agency can play in this conceptualization is then emphasized as significant. Consideration of the socio-cultural theories of the learning place and more sophisticated models of adult learner-managed learning as evidenced in the PAM model (Cairns, 2003) will be included in this discussion.

The third term in the Workplace Learning descriptor, which is the major reason and core of what this volume is about, *Learning*, evokes a wide range of theories and ideas which lead to a range of contested and often contradictory positions amongst theorists and researchers (Illeris, 2009). In this chapter we shall argue that learning, as an activity that involves change and development in individuals and organizations, is a process that impinges on all humans at all times. Engagement in learning, however, is an aspect that requires individuals to take some agency and decisions about how, when, where and why they engage.

WORK

There is no doubt that the word work and what it stands for across the world seems to raise considerable interest, and the notion of what work constitutes in an individual's life (whether this is conceived as a lifecourse, lifeplace or lifespace) has been a historically significant definer of who and what people do in society.

This trend to define or identify one's self through what we work at has emerged over many years to be a singularly significant aspect of life in the late twentieth century.

Identifying self through work

Work is an activity where individuals alone and together participate in productive endeavours to complete tasks or to achieve outcomes which are either self set or set by others and which may or may not be remunerated. Work is also a process whereby individuals engage in activity from which they gain some satisfaction on completion which may or may not be recognized by others. (Cairns and Malloch, 2006).

We frequently identify ourselves through our work. In social settings we introduce ourselves by name and when the question comes 'and what do you do?' the response is an identification, primarily in terms of what we do for paid employment (almost 'I work therefore I am'). If no longer in paid work, then 'I work as a volunteer', or 'I am retired', or 'I was a 'specific occupation' is proffered. This has occurred throughout history: for example, in English, with names of occupations identifying individuals, such as fletcher, farmer, fisher, butcher, baker, knight, smith, and so on. We are identified officially by occupations, by our work in travel, social security, health, insurance, and financial documents. This century the notion of what people do, associated with the term 'work', is how people tend to define themselves. Later, as one of the Challenges for the Future and how societies will respond, this aspect will be raised as a serious potential shift in the twenty-first century.

Exploring the concept of work

In definitional terms, the word, 'work', can have many meanings, ranging from the traditional meaning (and we would suggest in the twenty-first century a simplistic definition) as an activity carried out to produce a product or outcome remunerated by an employer. It can also be the place where individuals are employed. 'Work' is therefore utilized as a term for the place and the activity carried out in that place. Work and workplace are seen as distinct from home and places for recreation. Work has become a place where one goes to carry out labour distinct from one's home. (Cairns and Malloch, 2008, p. 4). We wish to suggest that for the twenty-first century, this conceptualization of work is too narrow and we shall offer some broadening ideas and draw together some critical thinking as to why such a broadening is necessary.

Birch and Paul (2003), tell us that in ancient Greece, work was seen as 'interfering with the duties of citizens, distracting them from the important pursuits of politics, art, philosophy and what they called leisure' (p. 21). Interestingly, leisure was 'skhole' from which we derive the word school. Birch and Paul also tell us that the republican Romans had a similar view.

The Romans of the Republic period adopted a similar attitude. The Latin for 'work', *labor*, means 'extreme effort associated with pain' (p. 21).

It is apparent that in history, 'work' was not seen as a positive element of social need and activity. How work was subsequently defined may have been part of this perceived attitude.

Existing theories of work are strongly influenced by historical and economic developments. Class and status linked to work roles are influential in the development of theories of work, place and learning. Historians have written of work from the perspective of a shift from agrarian to industrial to post-industrial societies. In analyses of the division of labour, employers and workers have been identified as separate entities, separate in role and class and power status (Braverman, 1974). Within most Western societies, the statistical data on employment as percentages of persons in paid work has become a key measure of national economic success (Cairns and Malloch, 2008, p. 4). Unemployment is seen as a measure for economic difficulties and a weakened economy in any nation where the figures are high.

Babbage (1835; in Davis and Taylor, 1972, p. 23) writing in the time of the Industrial Revolution, argued that '(p)erhaps the most important principle upon which the economy of a manufacture depends, is the *division of labour* amongst the persons who perform the work'. Work in the Industrial Revolution had brought about a shift from the agrarian, more 'home' based work to the development of separate places of employment, such as mills and, eventually, factories, which by the twentieth century featured assembly lines and mass production, referred to as the Fordist and Post Ford eras. In the longer-term consideration of history, this view of 'work' is relatively recent and somewhat out of place with the traditions of work as what each person and family completed at home, be it their workshop shed, farm or cottage.

Workers' rights and needs were fought over in the nineteenth and twentieth centuries with unionism supporting workers in what in many cases was a struggle between capitalism and socialism, characterized as money versus the people. In the twenty-first century, with unionism somewhat disempowered, workers have again been subjected to diminished rights and conditions. Western economies have moved manufacturing, in particular, offshore to cheaper, more populous, less protected workforces in the east and south east of the European centric global mapping terms.

Beck (1999; 2000; 2004) challenged prevailing ideas and theories in the field of work and its place in society, suggesting that Western societies were heading to become 'risk societies' where only one out of two people will be employed in the current sense. Beck presents an alternative view for the defining of work, bringing in formal recognition for the unpaid, voluntary work carried out by citizens.

> For me, the antithesis of the work society is boosting the political society of individuals, the active citizen's society on the spot. This society can find and develop in miniature, local answers to the challenges of the Second Modernity. However, this is tied up with a few preconditions. Work time would have to be shortened for all on the full-employment labour market. Everyone – women and men – should be able to have one leg in gainful employment. Parent's work, i.e. work with children, would have to be equally recognized by society as would be artistic, cultural and political civic work by, for example, claims for pensions and health care being granted to both categories – parental and civic. In the final analysis, simultaneous commitment to gainful employment and civic work will therefore presuppose family obligations being redistributed between men and women as well (2004, p. 2).

The study of work (or more specifically 'the world of work') and what it involves has a history that Statt (2004) claims only goes back to the late nineteenth and twentieth centuries (p. 5).

As he later examines the trends in work and what he calls 'non-work' he comes to an interesting conclusion:

> Paid work in the form of a job is one of the central aspects of our identity, though the relationship between work and employment is not always clear-cut. A great many activities that would normally be described as work may not be paid and a lot of employed time may not be spent working (p. 156).

In another detailed examination of the idea and definition of work, Noon and Blyton (2002) also suggest that the differences in this new era between work and non-work may be blurred and somewhat confused. After opting for a definition taken from Thomas (1999) which focuses on three elements: (1) work achieves something, (2) work involves a degree of obligation or challenge and (3) work involves effort and persistence, Noon and Blyton suggest that many leisure activities fit these three points as well as paid employment (p. 4). They conclude, significantly we believe:

> What is needed is to strike a balance that gives greater recognition to the different activities that constitute people's work. Further, such a balance is necessary not only because of the scale of the different spheres of work but also because of the key links that exist between the different aspects of paid and unpaid, visible and hidden work (p. 4).

There are now a number of ways of viewing work and its meanings across society. Some may see it as labour, others as a job, and many as employment. Our point is that work needs, in this twenty-first century period of what we describe as ultramodernity (Beck also uses this and 'second modernity'), to be conceived of as a broader-based activity across a very wide range of ambits of social interaction and self-motivated action. This is necessary because the ways and means of action people take in order to exist, play and earn is currently shifting in a paradigmatic manner from paid actions by an employer to a broader range of activities that may lead to some remuneration amidst other activities (often by direct choice) where pay is not a factor, and where work is still carried out in significant ways. In addition, the modes of action, be they direct physical exertion, knowledge development and application or virtual actions in a cyberspace, all have differing work connotations.

Elsewhere we have defined this new conception of work as:

> We see work more as an enabled purposive effort by an individual to initiate activity or respond to an issue or problem in a range of situations for some perceived (by them) productive end. This emphasises that the action is intentional engagement by an individual (Cairns and Malloch, 2008).

Work is intentional engagement. Work is an application of effort. Work has a purpose and is an intentional or purposive act and finally, work may or may not be a matter of employment or remunerated activity.

PLACE

We now turn to the second element in the composite term Workplace Learning, that of Place.

The term *place* also has a range of meanings and connotations. These range across the obvious physical location, through the more esoteric spiritual location and to the more recent virtual location. Place, we are told, in a serious and scholarly examination of the intersection of place and education by Hutchison (2004), has many reference points:

> The term "place" conjures up visions of locality, spatial representations of those places with which we are familiar, and those places the unfamiliarity of which intrigues us. We reside in places, go to work and recreate in places, travel daily through places that are sometimes meaningful to us and other times ignored or taken for granted. We identify with those places that played some formative (if still illusive) role in our childhood years, those places that are associated with good times or bad. The term 'place' is imbued with emotion, defined by the boundaries it imposes on space, and informed by the utility to which space is put in our lives. Place can be understood as an individually constructed reality – a reality informed by the unique experiences, histories, motives, and goals that each of us brings to the spaces with which we identify (p. 11).

When we discuss place and places in this chapter we are seeking to open up many of the areas Hutchison has cited and more. We seek to enable a broader consideration of place in the sense of the composite term Workplace Learning. There are two aspects of the relationship between place and the other two terms in this expression. There are places of work and there are places of learning.

The simple and most common connotation for workplace, is that of a physical location. Be it a factory, an office or a bench space at home or at some other location, it is a space where one works. This first order concept of place as related to work is the most frequently utilized aspect of workplace in common language about the idea, but the idea of places as a range of different orders of location and being have emerged more recently.

Places can also be heavily spiritually significant, as it is argued it is with indigenous Australians. The identification with the land is clearly summed up by Hardy in her book *Lament for the Barkindji*, about the tribes along the great Darling River in Australia (1976):

> They were spiritually akin to every natural feature and to every growing thing that clothed the hillsides or roamed the plains or drank deeply from the waterholes. They and the land were one, and it was a wholeness designed to endure in the natural order of things (p. 1).

Place has effects and is an affective link between humans and their origins as well as something of significance in relation to where they live, work and play. People will ask for their ashes to be spread over their old school grounds, the place where they had enjoyable holidays or where they played football in a local park. The reference to locations (places) as where one's 'roots' are, abounds in everyday talk and in literature.

In addition to both physical and spiritual places of significance in life, there are aspects of psychological place which are important, particularly in the context of workplace learning. Psychological place may be a consideration of identification as well as some concern with 'mind' as a place where we think, dream and consider ourselves. This is not the Cartesian mind/body dichotomy but rather the cognitive psychology consideration of where learning might take place. How human experience and cognition come together is the basis of much of the work of Varela and his colleagues Thompson and Rosch (1993).

In their examination of the contributions of Educational Psychology to Adult Learning and Development, Smith and Pourchot (1998) concluded that a new field of Adult Educational

Psychology was needed and that the way lifelong learning and development for adults proceeded was a major necessary study area for advancement. Their book dealt with a wide range of ideas and approaches, including Bonk and Kim's (1998) case for the extension of socio-cultural theory (especially the concepts of the Zone of Proximal Development (ZPD) and scaffolding) to adult learning. Whilst we have resonance with the ideas of socio-cultural theory and the important foundations of Vygotskian thinking, we believe it should be remembered that Vygotsky was working with and theorizing about children and their learning. We have also argued elsewhere (Cairns and Malloch, 2008) that sophisticated adult learners may operate as self-scaffolders or even without any necessary scaffolding as it is currently conceptualized. We also contend that whilst the idea of the ZPD may have some relevance as a place of learning activity, the notions of more capable others (be they peers or teachers) in the adult worker situation may be quite different from the research-base work with children. Aspects of the Japanese thinking on **Ba** and **Basho** (see Nishida, 1987a, 1987b; Nonaka and Takeuchi, 1995; Von Krogh, Nonaka and Nishiguchi, 2000) where Ba is a 'shared mental place for emerging relationships' (Nonaka, Reinmoeller and Senoo, 2000), are also worthy of consideration in this debate area. Western ideas of place and space and their relationship to thinking and mind may need a considerable shake-up for better clarity to emerge.

Place, in relation to learning and cognition, can cover a very wide range of ideas and situations. It can refer to physical or spiritual locations and also relate to spaces in which we see ourselves as people and learners. Place can also refer to where it is that we think we operate cognitively as we think and learn (Intra-Personal Place). There is no doubt that the social interaction aspect of learning in a multitude of (Inter-Personal Place) offers some useful thought for the consideration of how and where workplace learning occurs (see Figure 1.1).

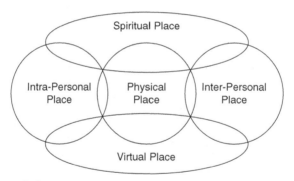

Figure 1.1   Concepts of place

LEARNING

Of all the areas involved in this discussion, the field described by the term 'Learning' has the most definitional and research-based models and theories (Jarvis, 2001; Jarvis et al., 1998; Smith and Pourchot, 1998; Vaill, 1996; Illeris, 2009). We all 'know' what we mean when we use the term 'learning', but there are variations and aspects that require comment and debate.

Among the more contentious aspects of dealing with Learning and Learning theories is the commonsense equation of the *learning* idea with *schooling* or the broad term *education*.

There has developed a binary of education and training, where education is seen as more comprehensive and extending and training more specific and bounded. Wenger (1998, p. 263) provides a definition of these two aspects of learning:

Education, in its deepest sense and at whatever age it takes place, concerns the opening of identities – exploring new ways of being that lie beyond our current state. Whereas training aims to create an inbound trajectory targeted at competence in a specific practice, education must strive to open new dimensions for the nego-tiation of the self. It places students on an outbound trajectory toward a broad field of possible identities. Education is not merely formative – it is transformative.

As Wenger also suggests, education can be a process of lifelong renewal.

Vocational learning can also be more community oriented. Writing in 2000 about 'non-Western' educational traditions and cultural elements, Reagan presents an examination of learning for vocational purposes positioned within traditions as part of normal life and 'civic education'. The community is the centre for learning preparing young learners to be effective members of society. Reagan points to the significant differences between the patterns and approaches to vocational learning in the West and non-Western societies.

> In modern capitalist societies in general, and in American society in particular, educational institutions are often expected to serve the needs of the economy (or, more accurately, of employers) rather than the needs of individual workers. To be sure, one could suggest that these two sets of needs ought to be, at least in the ideal, very similar, but they are by no means the same. In the cases examined in this book, the emphasis placed on vocational preparation is largely an empowering one, with greater emphasis placed on the needs and aptitudes of the individual rather than the needs of the employer (pp. 207–208).

Learning is an interaction between an agentic individual's mind and a socially constructed community of practice. There does not need to be an 'either or' approach to being situated within a social context and process versus being an individual's construction of meaning (Cairns and Malloch, 2008, p. 10). Learning is therefore viewed as the outcome of an enabled active intentional interactional engagement in experience and thinking. In their book on facilitating learning organizations, Marsick and Watkins (1999, p. 64) refer to people learning all the time, everywhere and as self-managed learners:

> People often have, want and are expected to take more control of their learning. Learning infrastructures have grown up around these new needs. Learning takes place around the clock. Learning is frequently integrated with work. People learn what they need to do their job just-in-time as they face challenges that require new knowledge or skills. Knowledge is often created in action rather than before action. Classroom activities are still part of a learning infrastructure. But learners often choose the courses that they want with less direction from the organization. They might even choose how they want to learn. Learning could still be delivered through a workshop, but it might also arise through on-the-job training, personal reading and study, interaction with peers or coaches, or through internet-based activities.

Whilst this is in many ways an 'ideal' situation, it does point to possibilities of a broader and deeper view of adult learning and learning in the workplace. Marsick and Watkins envisage this as a 'continuous learning system' with 'structured educational practices, informal work and learning practices, rewards, and technology to support formal and informal learning' (1999, p. 69). Their model of continuous learning consists of an inner cycle of learning without changing assumptions and values and an outer cycle of learning considering the context from a range of perspectives and to operate more critically and differently (1999, p. 75). They take the position that '(W)ork can be designed so that learning takes place as and when it is needed: in order to better understand and frame problems, to generate alternative solutions to each problem or challenge, to gain skills needed to implement solutions, and to understand the results so that adjustments can be made in the cycle' (1999, pp. 74–75).

Wenger provides a more organic view of learning proclaiming that 'Learning cannot be designed. Ultimately it belongs to the realm of experience and practice. It follows the negotiation of meaning; it moves on its own terms. It slips through the cracks; it creates its own cracks. Learning happens, design or no design'. He adds the proviso though that we do however need 'to design social infrastructures that foster learning' (1998, p. 225).

Learning, as the essence of change in people, can largely be a matter of individual or personal change, or can also be a matter of 'ensemble' or group change and development. Argyris and Schon (1978, 1996) posed the question with regard to their proposition that organizations may learn as 'What is An Organization That it May Learn?' In their discussion the argument emerged that 'evidence of change in organizational theory-in-use' was the basis for their case that an organization can and does 'learn'. Today, after 30 plus years, the idea that an organization might 'learn' is definitely seen as less dramatic than it did when Argyris and Schon first postulated the concept.

Learning has become a concept that has reached into new realms, as Jarvis (2001) has stated:

> Learning has come to the forefront of the educational agenda in many countries of the world – the knowledge society, the learning society, the learning organization and so forth are now all common terms. The terms appear in policy and strategy papers of the European Union and of many countries in and beyond the European community. Traditional views about education appear to be threatened as it becomes a commodity in the learning market. Learning has itself become a contested concept and the discourse about it is being captured by the world of work (p. vii).

We would not be as concerned as Jarvis was at this stage of the term Learning being 'captured' by the world of work. We believe and argue that learning in the workplace is a significant and inspiring element of the whole dimension of learning.

We take the view that Learning is a process of change in an individual or group through activity. It is temporal as well as mindful and generally follows some agentic intent by the individual or group. With this in mind we now turn to the specifics of workplace learning.

LEARNING IN THE WORKPLACE

As a response to the late twentieth century globalized influence, there has been an emphasis in the developed West over the past two decades in particular on the need for a multiskilled, flexible workforce able to work anywhere, at any time on a range of tasks. Western countries have strongly linked in policy rhetoric the need for a well-trained, skilled populace for economic prosperity and high productivity, a goal only partially achieved. The idea of work has been seen as a means to an end in socio-economic terms. Preparation for work, predominantly through vocational education and training, has been conducted mostly through formal institutional systems and apprenticeship models.

Earlier studies of workplace learning situate the learner very narrowly in specified settings, for example, in Stevenson's (2002) study of motel front desk operations in which he concluded that the knowledge construction was not generic. The learning in motel reception work is described as being related to the specific context and not transferable. Much research on vocational learning (which tended to be the predominant model of workplace learning) focused on skills and knowledge acquisition and these aspects were fairly tightly defined and delineated for training. In fact the whole set of contested theories and ideas surrounding workplaces and the learning that took place there became part of the dualistic debate about models of acquisition versus models of participation and related concepts of cognition versus socio-cultural situativity.

Australia, for example, still delivers vocational education and training through a competency-based system whereby specified job skills are narrowly defined and developed as behavioural, demonstrable actions that can be seen and assessed. Whilst the views and definitions of what 'competence', 'competences', 'competencies' and 'competency' might mean vary across different nations and systems, there is a healthy debate (Mulder et al., 2009; Hughes and Cairns, 2009).

Vocational training programmes are designed to be, wherever possible, delivered in the workplace. Delivery elsewhere, such as in a classroom, is a support, or an alternative, if required. The importance of the workplace as a site for learning is constantly reiterated in such approaches, not so much as the learning process element but more as the demonstration site.

Place, in this argument, is important for the learning of skills for specific work. Salary levels, status, roles, all are impacted upon by the qualifications gained. If additional learning is required for a job, then the workplace is the preferred site of delivery. Place therefore has become interpreted as the employment workplace and this is perceived as providing relevance, authenticity and validation as a preferred site for learning; learning relevant for specific tasks in their paid work.

Policies support the workplace as the site for training through the funding to employers to conduct training and assessments, the de-regulation and privatization of organizations able to deliver vocational education and training, the cutting back of apprenticeship time and the focus on assessment rather than training.

The strong reiteration of the workplace as the site for learning means that 'workers' can be locked into specific strands of learning and into a narrowing of learning opportunities. There is a focus on the immediate requirements of the specified job and the workplace in the here and now, and not on future possibilities for the individual or the organization. The concepts of lifelong and lifewide learning, in these interpretations, have not been registered.

The situated theorists of the 1990s (Lave and Wenger, 1991; Wenger, 1998) saw learning as socially located, with people learning in communities of learners. More recently, the argument has developed that agency and the social are interactive, with the individual learner having more control as an agentic being in interaction with the social environment and with others to 'learn' (Bandura, 2001).

A number of unfortunate binaries that frequently dominate discussions and explanations surrounding workplace learning have emerged in the field. These 'binaries that bind' as we characterize them, have the effect of locking in debate and possible thinking about the whole field of workplace learning. These dichotomous approaches that have been raised in writing, thinking and research across the broad field of workplace learning and associated areas (be it work-based, work located or just work research and writing) have, we suggest, influenced thinking in a manner that has been singularly unhelpful over the decades (see Table 1.1).

Table 1.1 Binaries that bind (and should be discounted)

Informal	versus	Formal
Experiential	versus	Theoretical
Education	versus	Training
Physical	versus	Intellectual
Explicit	versus	Implicit
Tacit	versus	Explicit
Pure	versus	Applied
Action	versus	Theory
The Academy	versus	The Factory
Lived	versus	Studied
Classroom	versus	Workplace

The binaries listed in Table 1.1 offer a reference point for the many debates that can be seen across the workplace learning field. We do not intend to flesh out each binary and the implications of each as to the impact on discussions about workplace learning they might have. What we suggest is that discarding many of these positions might assist the field to develop in a less bounded manner. We would also suggest that reading the chapters in this *Handbook*, with an eye to discounting the binaries might be a useful way to proceed.

WORKPLACE LEARNING – THE FUTURE

Workplace learning should no longer be viewed and implemented through the binaries of formal and informal learning. McCormack (2000, p. 398) supports the notion of the concept of workplace learning being able to provide a 'common currency' and means to 'navigate the set of orthodoxies that permeate education, training, and development'.

Raelin (2008, 65) argues that in workplace learning we need a model integrating 'the many traditions underlying its construction', and need to incorporate the theory and practice modes of learning and explicit and tacit forms of knowledge.

With such suggestions in mind, and following our own quest in this chapter to broaden and suggest a re-consideration of the terms *Work, Place* and *Learning* as they come together in *Workplace Learning*, we now move to the future. What might be some of the effects of trends over the remaining years of the twenty-first century in and on workplaces and workplace learning?

CHALLENGES FOR THE TWENTY-FIRST CENTURY

The twenty-first century, like many eras that have come before, appears to us as we are living through its early years to be an era of immense change and rapid development. Within this context, very much in the arena of unfamiliar situations where we also face unfamiliar problems (see Capability 'Z' Zone in Cairns and Stephenson, 2009), there are a number of specific potential challenges that we will need to consider and face in a range of ways if we are to sustain learning in the lifespace, sustain the planet and develop the children and have a future viable world.

These challenges may not eventuate the way we are suggesting. Of course that will depend on how and in what ways we operate in the new 'Spaceship Culture' that the Australian futurist, David Ellyard claims will be the dominant ideology by 2020 (Ellyard, 2001). In this scenario, we will need to thrive, not just drive change and reactions to it.

Ellyard sets up an interesting contrast between what he says was the Cowboy Culture of Modernism of the 1960s with the necessary Spaceship Culture/Planetism of 2020 in Table 1.2.

In this comparison, the Cowboy Culture of the past is very much an unsustainable culture and the coming Spaceship Culture as a sustainable society. Ellyard used the Spaceship metaphor as a way to suggest that we are all aboard the Spaceship Earth and we need to be conscious of our roots in the total planet, not just part of it if the spaceship is to be able to continue along its journey and not fail.

We have taken this metaphor as a starting point and we now postulate a few 'trends' that we predict might impact on the world during this new century.

Table 1.2

The Cowboy Culture /Modernism (1960)	The Spaceship Culture/Planetism (2020)
Individualism	Communitarianism
Independence	Interdependence
Autocracy	Democracy
Humanity against nature	Humanity part of nature
Unsustainable production and consumption	Sustainable production and consumption
Patriarchy	Gender equality
Intercultural and inter-religious intolerance	Intercultural and inter-religious tolerance
Conflict resolution thru confrontation	Conflict resolution thru negotiation
Reliance on Defence	Reliance on Security

Source: Elllyard, 2001, pp. 6–7

Challenge 1: Work and workplace change in the lifespace

If Beck and others are correct (and there appears to be some reasonable likelihood that we are heading in those directions) then the 'brazilianization' of the world of work and workplaces, jobs and employment as we know it, is happening rapidly. No longer will people have a career for life, nor will we continue to define ourselves by what we do as the shifts and changes in occupations, and work opportunities move to be less significant in our lives. Who we are and where we live will become, once again, defining characteristics of people. Work, as an employment, will be but one aspect of our activity in the lifespace, and periods of so-called 'unemployment' will be the norm, not the stigma as is currently.

Humanity working together for some common goals with support for civic participation and a recognition that the previous 200 years of industrial work were something of an aberration as the world developed, will become more recognizable.

Challenge 2: Technological sustainability

There is no doubt that the whole nature of the so-called Technological Revolution has a rapidity and rate of change built into the industry and its manifold applications that suggest that we are yet to see many of the major advances. It seems to many of us that the Internet, with all its joys, uses and vices, is a new and recent development. Think back to how people thought of a similar world-changing technological development at the start of the last century, the automobile, and look where it has taken us! We are almost certainly at the very early stages of the 'T Model Ford' in the way we employ and develop the World Wide Web and associated technological aspects in these early years of the new century. We already have people advocating in 2008–2009 that a Web 2 has emerged.

The challenge for all of us in this new era will be to be flexible and adaptable enough to not only try keeping up with the rapid changes, but also to see the potential and to prepare and work with the future generations in our care to enable them to both drive and then thrive amidst such magical developments. Ellyard, in the paper mentioned earlier, claims that '70% of the job categories, products and services for the year 2020 have yet to be invented' (p. 9). It is hard to estimate with any real basis other than trend projections and a whole range of fantastic assumptions how such changes might affect us. However, many people in the past would never have predicted the Internet, the WWW, and the idea of cloning and many other biotechnological advances that are currently happening. The whole issue of *Sustainability* (in its many manifestations and areas, and not just environmentally) will continue to dominate late twenty-first century thinking and, hopefully, action by governments and individuals.

The impact of these ideas and 'advances' (for they may not be such) on what constitutes work and workplaces and, of course workplace learning, will be both fascinating and challenging to much of what we know and believe.

Challenge 3: Globalization dominance and loss of cultural relevance

There is no doubt that the rapidity of information exchanges, the effects of some of the media developments internationally and the way globalized products and organizations have developed over the past 50 or so years, that we are facing major cultural and national challenges to both preserve and maintain traditional differences and values. The so-called McDonaldization of the world, the corporatization of many universities and other social institutions, the way certain products and lifestyles have pervaded the far corners of the globe does alarm many people. All of these 'influences' have been leading towards a more homogenized world order. There are, in many places, movements to stem this development, as if it is a tide that can be stopped or at least turned in its impact in some areas. As we mentioned above, the financial consequences in the early years of this new century have shown some of the explicit dangers of this trend. Whatever the response in some nations and cultures, there is a strong challenge to work, sustainability and social order in this trend and influence.

Challenge 4: Travel restriction due to fuel and environmental issues

We are all acutely aware that fossil fuels and our carbon-based world are under increasing pressure and that the lifestyles associated with this history are changing and need to change for global sustainability. There may be a number of consequences of this necessary change scenario that may restrict travel as we know it. Unless we can change the way we move around the globe in terms of what vehicles we utilize, we will see travel and tourism as historical anachronisms. We simply will not be permitted to travel just for the fun and change of scenery ideals. This potential constraint on freedom of movement and international interaction could have grave consequences for social order and the style and scope of much 'work' that we currently assume and take somewhat for granted.

This is a potential challenge that many will reject as fanciful, but it already appears to be emerging. In 50 years will we be travelling internationally at the rate and for the purposes we currently do?

Challenge 5: Loss of personal autonomy in the new work order

Associated with the previous challenge and partially influenced by the second on technology, the rapidity and complexity of change and development across the world may see some case being built for increases in the loss of personal autonomy as societies move to more complex work orders. Ulrich Beck (2000), the German sociologist, has written about the 'Risk Society' and how there is emerging a 'Brave New World of Work' where modern Western societies are finding work is not just a career for life and that not all people can be employed in the traditional earning sense and two out of three people may be unemployed in the traditional sense with many people becoming 'work nomads' seeking small jobs here and there.

There is no doubt, as we have presented earlier in this chapter, that we need to re-define what we mean by the word 'work' and as this rapidly changing society that is the total world moves on through this century, we will find that we need to be much more flexible and adaptable than we have needed to be in past centuries.

Challenge 6: New world order in world power relationships

There is also an evident shift underway in the world as to power relationships. The former centuries of some dominance in commerce and industry by Europe and the Americas is shifting at an ever-increasing rate towards an Asian centric global influence. This is not about ethnic nor religious elements, but rather about where economic and social power will reside in an international sense. The huge population base across the Indian, Chinese and South-East Asian part of the world, the so called former 'Tiger' economies and the adoption and mastery of modern technologies, bio-technologies and communications in this part of the world has seen significant rates of growth and development which are shifting the hubs of many industries and thinking towards this sector of the globe. The changing relationship between the USA as the world's largest economy and former loan-granting state to one of the world's largest borrower states (mainly from China) is one evident base for this shift.

The rise of power-bases in the past rested often on military might. This now seems to be changing and economic power, social activity and communication, rather than military power is showing up as a new order. There is no doubt that some of the military might remaining may influence which direction this power shift will take. Friedman (2009) argues, again as a 'futurist' that there will be major conflict as these shifts begin to 'bite' in the next 100 years.

These Challenges for the future all have implications for the way workplace learning is seen, defined and might operate in the future. That there are new directions and deep and meaningful challenges in these broad scenarios is self-evident. Whether our theories and practices of workplace learning can accommodate or even keep up with the rapidity and breadth of such change and challenge is, in itself, the main game as to where and how we progress this field of work, study and learning. We are optimistic about the way work and workplace learning is developing as a field and a site for study, theorizing, development and future sustainability.

REFERENCES

Argyris, C. and Schon, D.A. (1978) *Organizational Learning*. Reading, Massachusetts: Addison-Wesley.

Argyris, C. and Schon, D.A. (1996) *Organizational Learning 11*. Reading, Massachusetts: Addison-Wesley.

Bandura, A. (2001) 'Social Cognitive Theory: An Agentic Perspective', *Annual Review of Psychology*, 52: 1–26.

Beck, U. (1999) 'Ulrich Beck on Insecurity and Re-defining Work', from the Jobs Letter No. 102/30 June, www.jobsletter.org.nz/jb110211.htm (accessed 23.3.06).

Beck, U. (2000) *The Brave New World of Work*. Cambridge: Polity Press.

Beck, U. (2004) 'Brave New Work World', Living at Work Series, (Part 15) ChangeXPartner Forum, 04.16.2004, www.changeX.de (accessed, 23.3.06).

Birch, C. and Paul, D. (2003) *Life and Work: Challenging Economic Man*. Sydney: UNSW Press.

Bonk, C.J. and Kim, K.K. (1998) 'Extending Sociocultural Theory to Adult Learning', Chapter 4 in M.C. Smith and T. Pourchot (eds), *Adult Learning and Development: Perspectives from Educational Psychology*. Lawrence Erlbaum Associates. Mahwah: New Jersey.

Braverman, H. (1974) *Labour and Monopoly Capital: The Gradation of Mark in the Twentieth Century*. New York and London: Monthly Review Press.

Cairns, L.G. (2003) 'Examining Place, Agency and Mindfulness in Learners Managing Their Own Learning', Visiting Professorial Lecture, International Centre for Learner Managed Learning, Middlesex University: London.

Cairns, L.G. and Malloch, M.E. (2006) 'Can Self-Managed Learners Jump Puddles?', Paper at *Annual Meeting of the American Educational Research Association*, San Francisco.

Cairns, L.G., Malloch, M.E. and Burns, G. (2006) 'Learning Work', *International Journal of Technology and Engineering Education*, 3(2): 91–105.

Cairns, L.G. and Malloch, M.E. (2008) 'Learning, Work and Places: Exploring Workplace Learning'. Unpublished Manuscript under review.

Cairns, L.G. and Stephenson, J. (2009) *Capable Workplace Learning*. Rotterdam/Boston/Taipei: SENSE Publishers.

Chisholm, C. and Davis, M. (2005) 'Extending the Models for Work-Based Learning into the Lifeplace', *American Educational Research Association Annual Meeting*, Montreal.

Davis, L.E. and Taylor, J.C. (eds) (1972) *The Design of Jobs*. Harmondsworth, Middlesex: Penguin Modern Management Readings.

Dewey, J. (1916/1944) *Democracy and Education*. New York: The Free Press.

Ellyard, D. (2001) 'Learning and Innovating for Thrival and Thrivability in a Planetist Future'. Background Paper for the School Libraries Association of Victoria Conference, March, Melbourne.

Friedman, G. (2009) *The Next 100 Years; A Forecast for the 21st Century*. New York: Anchor Books.

Hardy, B. (1976) *Lament for the Barkindji*. Adelaide: Rigby Limited.

Hutchison, D. (2004) *A Natural History of Place in Education*. New York and London: Teachers College Press.

Hughes, L. and Cairns, L.G. (2009) 'Competency-Based Training: Nostradamus's Nostrum: What Happened and Where Might We "Capably" Go?'. Paper presented at the *European Conference on Educational Research*, Vienna, Austria.

Illeris, K. (2009) (ed). *Contemporary Theories of Learning*. Abingdon: Routledge.

Jarvis, P. (2001) (ed). *The Age of Learning*. London: Kogan Page.

Jarvis, P., Holford, J. and Griffin, C. (1998) *The Theory and Practice of Learning*. London: Kogan Page.

Lave, J. and Wenger, E. (1991) *Situated Learning: Legitimate Peripheral Participation*. Cambridge: Cambridge University Press.

Malloch, M., Cairns, L. and Hase, S. (1998) 'Learning in the Workplace: Implications of the Capability Learning Model', American Education Research Association Annual Meeting, San Diego.

Marsick, V.J. (ed.), (1987) *Learning in the Workplace*, Beckenham. London: Croom Helm.

Marsick, V.J. and Watkins, K.E. (1990) *Informal and Incidental Learning in the Workplace*. London: Routledge.

Marsick, V.J. and Watkins, K.E. (1999) *Facilitating Learning Organisations*. Publishing Limited, England: Gower.

McCormack, B. (2000) 'Workplace Learning: A Unifying Concept?' Review Article, *Human Resource Development International* 3(3): 397–404.

Mulder, M., Weigel, T. and Collins, K. (2009) 'The Concept of Competence in the Development of Vocational Education and Training in Selected EU Member States: A Critical Analysis', *Journal of Vocational Education and Training*, 59(1): 67–88.

Nishida, K. (1987a) *An Inquiry into the Good* (translated by Masao Abe and Christopher Ives). New Haven and London: Yale University Press.

Nishida, K. (1987b) *Last Writings: Nothingness and the Religious Worldview* (translated by David A Dilworth). Honolulu: University of Hawaii Press.

Nonaka, I. and Takeuchi, H. (1995) *The Knowledge Creating Company*. New York: Oxford University Press.

Nonaka, I., Reinmoeller, P. and Senoo, P. (2000) 'Integrated IT Systems to Capitalize on Market Knowledge', in G. Von Krogh, I. Nonaka and T. Nishiguchi (eds), *Knowledge Creation: A Source of Value*. London: Macmillan Press.

Noon, M. and Blyton, P. (2002) *The Realities of Work*. New York: Palgrave.

Raelin, J.A. (2008) *Work Based Learning: Bridging Knowledge and Action in the Workplace*. San Francisco: Jossey-Bass.

Reagan, T.G. (2000) *Non-Western Educational Traditions: Alternative Approaches to Educational Thought and Practice*. (2nd edn) Mahwah, NJ: Lawrence Erlbaum Associates.

Scharmer, C.O. (2000) 'Organizing Around Not-Yet Embodied Knowledge', Chapter 2 in G. Von Krogh, I. Nonaka and T. Nishiguchi (eds), *Knowledge Creation: A Source of Value*. London: Macmillan Press.

Smith, M.C. and Pourchot, T. (1998) *Adult Learning and Development*. Mahwah, NJ: Lawrence Erlbaum Associates.

Statt, D.A. (2004) *Psychology and the World of Work* (2nd edn). Basingstoke: Palgrave Macmillan.

Stevenson, J. (2002) 'Concepts of Workplace Knowledge', *International Journal of Educational Research*, 37: 1–15.

Thomas, K. (ed.) (1999) *The Oxford Book of Work*. Oxford: University Press.

Vaill, P.B. (1996) *Learning as a Way of Being*. San Francisco: Jossey-Bass.

Varela, F.J., Thompson, E. and Rosch, E. (1993) *The Embodied Mind: Cognitive Science and Human Experience*. Cambridge, MA: The MIT Press.

Wenger, E. (1998) *Communities of Practice, Learning, Meaning, Identity*. New York: Cambridge University Press.

2

Theories of Workplace Learning

Paul Hager

INTRODUCTION

Theories of workplace learning have evolved dramatically over the last two decades. An initial focus on individual, mainly formal, learning has expanded to encompass both formal and informal learning, and multiple types of learning, such as organizational, group and individual learning. The theoretical resources employed have outstripped standard concepts such as vocational education, vocational learning, on-the-job training, and skill and competency acquisition by individuals to invoke more complex, multi-layered considerations that include adult learning, relations, communication, meaning-making, and identity formation. Accompanying these developments has been a gradual discernment of the mistaken nature of the formerly prevalent assumption that all of the learning needed for successful performance in an occupation can be specified in advance and imparted in a formal course. The result has been that at all levels of vocational preparation, including professions, there has been increasing concern to make formal courses align better with the practice of the occupation, even though exact alignment appears to be unattainable. Ongoing concerns to minimize this gap are evident in initiatives as diverse as competency-based training, improvements to practicums, sandwich courses, internships, mandatory periods of practice prior to being granted full status, and a burgeoning of mandatory continuing education requirements. All of these, in different ways, reflect acceptance that traditional formal preparation courses, by themselves, are not sufficient to produce long-term proficient practitioners. This growing realization of the inherent limitations of front-end vocational education is itself a major factor behind the growing interest in workplace learning.

In a sense this realization is a rediscovery of the past, since if we go back far enough in human history, before the advent of formal education or of formal trade training arrangements, then all vocational learning was on-the-job/in the workplace. Indeed, so self-evident was it to our distant forebears that the right place to learn performance of work was in the workplace itself, that early formal vocational education centred on moral development and liberal education. The aim was to provide general education for 'workers' who by definition had either left school early or never attended school. So, learning at and from work in the shape of informal apprenticeships was the norm for most of human history. It was, of course, the Industrial Revolution that led to formal education being established on a wide scale, including the gradual rise of pre-service occupational courses designed to prepare people for generic aspects of particular occupations. Preparation for professions was gradually absorbed into higher education institutions. Apprenticeships gradually came to include off-the-job components at formal vocational education institutions. In all of this, there developed gradually a focus on the learning for work performance being able to be delivered in formalized classrooms or training rooms. With apprenticeships a perennial concern soon arose: how to make the formal offerings more relevant to work practice. For professions the equivalent perennial problems have been: how to make the practicum meaningful. How to reliably assess the practicum. Along with this, has dawned a gradual realization that some important learning for practice can only being gained from practicum experiences, i.e. workplace learning assumes a significant role. In this sense, we have returned to the understandings of our ancestors about the importance of informal apprenticeships.

In providing an historical tracing of the development of theory in this field, this chapter will discuss a range of psychological, socio-cultural and postmodern theories relating to learning and work. In the process of briefly spanning the history and development of the field of workplace learning via a discussion of influential theories, a series of key trends and ongoing issues will be identified and analysed. By providing an overview of these key trends and issues this chapter sets the scene for the Theory section of the *Handbook*.

HISTORICAL TRACING OF THE DEVELOPMENT OF THEORY IN THE FIELD OF WORKPLACE LEARNING

1 Theories mainly influenced by psychological theories

Behaviourism was a major influence on vocational education in the decades prior to the emerging interest in workplace learning. It was grounded in the supposedly scientific idea that learning should be understood and explained only in terms of what is directly observable. The result of this flawed assumption is that learning is to be thought of solely in terms of observable behaviours, since other terms commonly associated with learning, such as thinking, knowing, and understanding, refer to activities that are inaccessible to direct observation (for more detailed discussion see e.g. Kalantzis and Cope, 2009). Applying this perspective to learning to perform work, behaviourism requires that the job be specifiable as a series of behaviours that can be minutely codified and workers trained to perform correctly. The implication is that the required learning can be acquired in training rooms in advance of joining the workplace. Trainers merely need to set up the appropriate stimuli and reinforcement schedules for prospective workers to learn the specified behaviours. The major problem here is that most work is not minutely codifiable or predictable as required by the theory. This has become increasingly apparent as social, economic and technological changes have accelerated in recent decades. Indeed, interest in workplace learning, as a topic in its own right, can be said to have been stimulated in large part by the gradual realization that, increasingly, proficient practice requires ongoing learning on-the-job. Yet the notion that job performance can be fully specifiable in advance remains a seductively attractive one. This false hope has underpinned much of the support that competency-based training has garnered in recent times. As will become apparent in what follows, one feature of behaviourism that survived the demise of that theory was the idea that learning is a thing or entity, albeit one that is no longer observable.

The recognition that behaviourism, whatever its strengths, was severely limited as an account of human learning, led to a resurgence of cognitive theories of learning that invoked unobservable mental terms such 'thinking', 'reflection' and 'understanding'. Some of the earliest notable investigations of workplace learning stemmed from this development. Chris Argyris and Donald Schön carried out major work that was strongly influenced by organizational psychology and management theory. In a series of key texts (e.g., Argyris and Schön, 1974, 1978), they introduced some enduringly influential distinctions and concepts, such as single loop learning (in which the learner exhibits reactive behaviour in order to adapt to changing circumstances) vs. double loop learning (in which the learner reflectively amends or adds to previous learning in selecting a suitable course of action to deal with a challenging situation). They also emphasized that a practitioner's theory-in-use (inferred from what is actually done in a particular situation) frequently diverges dramatically from the practitioner's espoused theory (the one that they claim is exemplified by their actions). Argyris carried out further influential work on theories in action, while Schön (1983, 1987) went on to immortalize the notion of the 'reflective practitioner'. Schön's 'reflective practitioner' engages in 'knowing-in-action' and 'reflecting-in-action'. According to Schön, knowing-in-action depends on 'reflecting-in-action' or 'reflecting-in-practice'. In turn, these capacities are underpinned by spontaneous episodes involving practitioners in 'noticing', 'seeing' or 'feeling' features of their actions and consciously or unconsciously correcting their practice accordingly. In effect, this is Schön's account of workplace learning. With the focus on knowing occurring during the heat of practice actually happening, together with underpinnings that are spontaneous and, in part, unconscious, Schön advanced an innovative epistemology of professional practice. His account was intended to confront traditional understandings that portrayed professional practice as application of theory. In particular, he rejected *technical rationality*, the view that professional practice consists essentially of practitioners employing standard disciplinary knowledge to analyse and solve the sequence of problems posed in their daily work practice. Instead he emphasized holistic performance and the challenges of problem identification. However, his central notion of *reflective practice* still focuses firmly on the rational, cognitive aspects of performance.

Another landmark contribution to theorizing workplace learning was provided by Marsick and Watkins (1990). Their work offered a very influential account of 'informal learning', together with its supposed sub-set 'incidental learning'. The Marsick and Watkins analysis of informal and incidental learning featured 'experience' and 'reflection' as central concepts, but also incorporated other diverse, but related, ideas such as 'learning from experience, learning by doing, continuous learning for continuous improvement, accidental learning, self-managed learning or the learning organization' (Watkins and Marsick, 1992, p. 287). For them, the 'defining characteristics' of informal learning were that it is 'experience-based, non-routine and often tacit' (1990, pp. 15–24). Importantly, they highlighted a diverse and complex range of conditions that either delimit or enhance informal learning. Significant delimiters included problem-framing capacity and intellectual ability. Prominent enhancers included 'proactivity', 'critical reflectivity', and 'creativity' (Marsick and Watkins, 1990, pp. 24–31). Further, they recognized the role of particular contextual factors, such as 'the organization's culture' (1990, p. 29).

The examples of workplace learning theories discussed thus far have some themes in common:

- The focus is on individual learners.
- The rational, cognitive aspects of workplace performance are stressed.
- Performance of work is represented as thinking (or reflection) followed by the application of this thinking or reflection. (This theme is especially evident in Schön's work.)
- The concept of learning is simply assumed to be unproblematic. Learning is treated as a 'thing'. As Elkjaer (2003) noted, the effect of this is that these theories tend to treat workplace learning as akin to formal learning. Among other things, this means that they also employ the acquisition and transfer metaphors unproblematically.
- The significant role of social, cultural and organizational factors in workplace learning is underestimated. Though some of the theorists discussed above do allow a role for such factors, they serve as a backdrop against which workplace learning occurs. Later theories of workplace learning provide much more decisive roles for social, organizational and cultural factors in shaping workplace learning and performance.

There have also been various other research contributions, which have enhanced understanding of workplace learning whilst sharing some, but not all, of the five themes just outlined. One such example was major work in cognitive psychology that investigated the development of expertise (for good summaries of this work see Athanasou, 2008; Tennant and Pogson, 1995). This literature helped to place the topic of workplace learning onto wider agendas, as it suggested that learning in the form of mental schemas gained from the early years of practice served to displace much of the types of knowledge that practitioners acquired in their undergraduate training.

However, later work criticized this expertise research for its claims that expertise is located in individual rational minds that are separate from arenas of practice (see, e.g. Wertsch, 1998). But not all work on expertise has this limitation. Hubert Dreyfus and his brother Stuart (Dreyfus and Dreyfus, 1986) developed a well-known five-stage model of skill acquisition in which 'expertise' is the final stage. (In later work (Dreyfus, 2001), Hubert extended the original model to a seven-stage one which features 'practical wisdom' as the seventh stage). Whilst being clearly applicable to learning in the workplace, the Dreyfus model is intended to have wider scope than that. It is claimed to specify:

> .... the stages in which a student learns by means of instruction, practice, and, finally, apprenticeship, to become an expert in some particular domain and *in everyday life* (Dreyfus, 2001, p. 32, emphasis added).

However, from the perspective of workplace learning, the key point here is that the role of informal experiential learning, occurring over extended time periods, becomes increasingly important in the later stages of this seven-stage model. All stages of the Dreyfus model are *activity-and experience-based*. This feature serves to suggest the *contextuality* of the informal learning, centred on judgement and practices. Taken together, the seven stages highlight the range of complex dimensions involved in this key feature of informal learning. For Dreyfus, skills and practices are non-representational; they are passed on through society to individuals without conscious thought necessarily being involved. The social character of skills and practices means that they can be developed through conformism. So while it is perfectly possible, and common, to teach skills and practices, they will develop naturally in situations where *learning is not the main intention*. According to Dreyfus' skill model, experts engaging in practice are very likely to learn. But usually, they are not engaging in practice in order to learn. So informal learning will commonly occur in situations that were *not initiated by teachers/ trainers*. Dreyfus' insistence on the social nature and origin of skills and practices illuminates the *often collaborative/collegial* character of such informal learning. However, the Dreyfus model is still focused on individuals as learners.

Another theory that has been of relevance for workplace learning is the widely influential model of knowledge creation developed by Nonaka and Takeuchi (1995). Nonaka and Takeuchi claimed to be offering a more profound Japanese understanding of knowledge to replace traditional Western concepts. However, as Bereiter (2002, pp. 175–176) has convincingly demonstrated, their work actually relies closely on a common 'folk theory' of learning as a thing (or product) located in the mind of the learner. The accuracy of Bereiter's critique is evident from the fact that their theory exemplifies each of the first four of the five themes commonly found in early workplace learning theories as discussed above.

So far, this chapter has discussed representative accounts of workplace learning that belong to the first main category of such theories, ones that have been strongly influenced by the fields of organizational and cognitive psychology and management theory. The strengths of these theories discussed so far are, firstly, that they increasingly develop a richer account of work than that portrayed by behaviourism. Secondly, they increasingly recognize the importance of learning by practice (doing). Before moving on to consider other categories of workplace learning theories, it will be useful to consider briefly some key issues that will recur throughout this chapter. These issues serve to highlight some of the main differences between the several categories, and, in some cases, even between theories within the same category. These issues also point to the main limitations of the theories discussed so far.

Issue 1: The individual as the unit of analysis for understanding learning

It is a common unquestioned assumption in most literature about learning that the individual learner is the appropriate unit of analysis. This is so whether learning is being theorized as a product to be acquired or as the process by which the product is acquired.

Making the individual learner the focus in turn ushers in a cluster of closely connected assumptions about learning that easily go unnoticed, as they seem to reflect 'common sense', once the primacy of the individual learner is accepted. In fact, as the discussion of more recent theories of workplace learning will show, these taken-for-granted assumptions are each highly debatable. A very important example of these 'common sense' sub-assumptions is the notion that learning has a specific location, namely in the individual learner's mind or body. Locating learning in this way neatly complements the most commonly favoured learning metaphors, that is, acquisition and transfer. On this account, the task of the teacher, for example, is to impart (or transfer) learning to individuals. Success consists in them acquiring (and, hence, possessing) the learning. However, for typical cases of human possessions, such as a car, a block of land, or a wine collection, it is not the case that individuals contain these possessions. This would suggest that even if learners do possess their learning, it does not follow that it is located inside of them. Why does common sense think otherwise in the case of learning? It seems that this sub-assumption gains plausibility because we believe learning to be real in some sense, yet it is not something that can be directly observed or touched. Hence, locating it inside of the learner appears to offer a common-sense explanation of this inaccessibility. Similar considerations are sometimes applied to other abstract entities, such as rights or duties.

Once thinking about learning is focused on individuals' minds and bodies acquiring knowledge and skills, a second important sub-assumption becomes almost irresistible. This is the notion that people's minds have particular mental powers (or faculties) with individual differences in how well individuals are endowed with such powers. There is an equivalent assumption for people's bodies that endows them with skills (or capacities) that are once again distributed differently across populations of individuals. Of course, educational thought, at least since the classical Greeks, has been dominated by a mind/body dualism that regards the mind as superior to body. Thus the assumption about mental powers has received most educational attention. So common-sensical does this sub-assumption appear to be, that it comes as a shock to realize that it is actually a conceptual rather than an empirical matter whether or not we should posit such things as mental powers (Davis, 2005).

Issue 2: Learning as a product or 'thing'
Another outcome of the acquisition and transfer metaphors being so influential in our understandings of learning is that they ensure that learning comes to be viewed as a 'thing' or product. The mind becomes a 'container' of 'knowledge as a type of substance' (Lakoff and Johnson, 1980). Thus, *acquisition* of knowledge, i.e. learning, becomes movement of entities into a container, out of which they can be *transferred* as required (cf. Freire 1972 on 'banking education').

> Under the influence of the mind-as-container metaphor, knowledge is treated as consisting of objects contained in individual minds, something like the contents of mental filing cabinets (Bereiter 2002, p. 179).

The container metaphor helps to make sense of a whole web of related common-sense notions about learning such as the idea that as well as in minds, learning can be stored in other suitable receptacles (books, libraries, CD ROMs, etc). This seeming capacity of learning as a thing to be located in a variety of receptacles gives rise to the important sub-assumption of the independence of learning. This takes it as a given that what is learnt is a product, a thing or substance that is independent both of the learner and of the context in which the learning occurs. So the assumption is that, just as many people can read the same book, so the various learners in a group can each achieve identical learning, i.e. their minds can each acquire the same something that is independent of any one of them. Thus learning as an independent thing can move across space and through time. This independence notion fits well with traditional disciplinary models of knowledge (or learning), e.g. mathematics has often been viewed as a world independent of the world of humans. Later it will be shown that more recent workplace learning theorizing maintains that there are important kinds of learning for which this independence assumption does not apply.

There is a parallel popular discourse about skills as independent things to be learnt, e.g. 'gaining skills', 'passing skills on from one generation to the next', 'either use them or you lose them'. The independence of skills from the learner is shown supposedly by the fact that different learners can all acquire the same skill. Certainly, early accounts of workplace learning were strongly influenced by this learning as a product view and its associated sub-assumptions.

Issue 3: Learning as independent of context

Once learning is thought of as a thing or substance that is independent of the learner, it seems natural to also view it as independent of context. Thus there has been the widespread assumption that what is learnt is separate from and independent of the context in which it is learnt. The popularity of this assumption is evident from the current enthusiasm for generic skills. As nations have sought to respond to globalization by enriching, expanding and better recognizing the skills profiles of their labour force, policies to promote and reward so-called 'generic skills', such as employability skills, key skills, and learning to learn skills, have become common at all levels of education systems. Once acquired, it is assumed that these skills can be transferred unproblematically by learners to diverse situations. Yet as contemporary theoretical and research-based accounts of learning at work suggest (Hager and Holland, 2006), the contextuality of actual work processes severely curtails naive expectations of unproblematic generic transfer. It seems that this assumption, that what is learnt is independent of the context in which it is learnt, underpins common attempts to specify occupations in terms of a list of competence statements. Such competence statements have proliferated in recent years, but the results of their use have been mixed at best (Hager, 2004). It seems that skilful practice of occupations is both holistic and significantly contextual, rather than atomistic and context-free, as is assumed by naive use of competence statements.

Of course, nobody denies that context has *some* influence on the process of learning and its quality. Learners with excellent mentors will learn better than those without. Likewise, provision of quality resources can greatly enhance learning. However, whilst accepting this, *weak contextuality* can be characterized as the claim that the content of learning is ultimately independent of context. This means that while context can influence the *process* of learning, and thus how well it occurs, the *content* that is learnt is something that is not altered by context. This view connects with several of the assumptions and sub-assumptions discussed above. The assumption that the learner is an individual in whose mind (or body) the learning resides immediately disconnects learning from context, since context is regarded as something external to the learner. Hence learning is portrayed as learners acquiring novel attributes, which are independent of their surroundings. That is, the learning within an individual's mind (or body) is constituted solely with respect to attributes (or properties) that obtain within the individual. It is identifiable without reference to anything outside of the individual. This point links to the philosophical distinction between *narrow content* and *wide content* (for discussion see Davis, 2005). The narrow content of a belief is content that is what it is regardless of the environment of the belief's owner. In contrast, wide content depends at least in part on features of the believer's environment. According to this take on weak contextuality, a particular instance of learning can have been acquired in any number of environments but the same internal properties will result in the learner, as long as the external environment does not actually prevent the learning from occurring. As we will see later, more recent theories of workplace learning agree with the contrary view expressed by Davis that

> there are many beliefs relating to performances supposedly manifesting mental powers for which a wide content reading is essential. That is, the belief content cannot be characterized adequately without making essential reference to the social environment in which the believer is situated (2005, p. 642).

Weak contextuality also connects with another assumption discussed above, namely that learning is an independent thing or substance that can move across space and through time. This independence assumption, in conjunction with the acquisition and transfer metaphors, depicts products of learning as stable, unchanging entities that are basically the same whatever the details of the particular context in which they happen to be located at some given time.

These, then, are the senses in which weak contextuality asserts that context is ultimately passive in relation to learning. In the next section, some theories of workplace learning that posit strong contextuality will be considered. Strong contextuality claims that, in many instances of learning, the nature of what is learnt is significantly marked by the features of the context in which the learning occurs. Workplace learning is a paradigm of such learning because, strong contextualists argue, both the nature of work processes, as well as the performance standards that are applicable to those processes, are significantly shaped by contextual influences. On this kind of view, the same occupation carried out on different sites will entail significant differences in the learning required to be a proficient practitioner at each site. Of course there will also be some similarities in the required learning, but overall it is not context-free. Also, according to these views the notion of *context* is itself very complex, as will be discussed in the next section.

Overall, the assumptions about learning that underpin the theories in the first category of workplace learning theories are problematic and limiting in a number of respects, privileging human consciousness and intention, and portraying a learner that is atomized and, incidentally, conservative.

2 Socio-cultural theories

The second broad group of workplace learning theories, socio-cultural theories, were strongly influenced by work in sociology and social anthropology. By rejecting many of the main assumptions of the first broad grouping, they provide alternative perspectives that have received increasing attention in theorizing work-related learning in its various forms. For instance, they offer fruitful angles for re-thinking the nature of continuing professional learning (see, e.g. Cevero, 2001; Hodkinson et al., 2008).

These socio-cultural theories differ from the first broad grouping in how they deal with the three key learning issues just discussed. For Issue 1, they elevate the various social aspects of learning to a new prominence, thereby rejecting the idea that the individual learner should be the focus of analysis. In some instances, attention is directed exclusively onto the social. In others, an account is offered that encompasses both individual and social learning. This latter point is important since, at first glance, it may be tempting to simply align the individual learner acquiring learning as product with human capital theory and to contrast this with group learning as a participatory process based on social capital theory. But the reality is more complex than this because some significant socio-cultural learning theories challenge the idea that learning has to be exclusively either individual or social. These theories accept that, although all learning is social in some significant sense, this situation is still compatible with some instances of learning being individual learning, and other instances being group or community learning. So at least some of the social learning theories to be discussed later include a place for learning by individuals that is different from pure communal learning. Thus, with reference to workplace learning in particular, it is a plausible claim that individual and social learning are both important dimensions of it (see, e.g., Hodkinson et al., 2008).

For Issue 2, these socio-cultural theories emphasize learning as an ongoing process of participation in suitable activities, thereby rejecting the primacy of learning as a product. Here the focus is more on learners developing by actively engaging in the ongoing processes of workplaces, rather than by acquiring a series of specific products. Whereas learning as product dovetails neatly with the acquisition and transfer metaphors, learning as process accords with the metaphor of participation.

For Issue 3, these socio-cultural theories reject the supposed independence of learning from context. They support strong contextuality by insisting that workplace learning and performance are significantly shaped by social, organizational, cultural and other contextual factors. Thus, their accounts extend well beyond considerations of the individual and its properties.

As well as taking distinctive positions on the first three key issues about learning, the theories within this second broad grouping of workplace learning theories have various other commonalities. They include:

- A recognition that workplace learning and performance are embodied phenomena. (Thus they reject mind-body dualism and related dichotomies).
- A recognition that workplace learning and performance seamlessly integrate a range of human attributes that is much wider than just rationality. So context becomes the causal background of the learning.
- A tendency to problematize the concept of learning and to seek to re-theorize it. As such they pose a challenge to mainstream understandings of learning.

The first two of these points represent a tendency to holism that is common in socio-cultural theories. From this, it is evident that various earlier general learning theorists, such as Dewey (1916) and Vygotsky (1978), have been significant influences on much of this work.

Lave and Wenger (1991) were a particular landmark in workplace learning theorizing as, for the first time, it offered understandings that were definitely not centred on learning as a 'thing' located in individual minds. Specifically they put into wide currency notions that became very influential, such as workplaces as 'communities of practice' and 'legitimate peripheral participation' as the social learning process that novices go through to become full members of the community of practice. Rather than viewing the learning as acquisition of discrete items, whether propositions or skills, their specifically relational account views the novice as learning how to function appropriately in a particular social, cultural and physical environment. This means that the learning ('situated learning') is something outside of the individual's head, or even body. Rather it occurs in a framework of participation, in a network of relations. It is clear, then, that on each of the three key issues related to learning, Lave and Wenger offer distinctive socio-cultural alternatives to traditional assumptions.

However, despite its widespread influence, their work has attracted cogent criticism. As Hodkinson and Hodkinson (2004a) point out, Lave and Wenger (1991) left the key notion of community of practice rather vague, but wished it to have wide applicability as an account of learning. For instance, taking their famous example of Liberian tailors, on some occasions the community of practice appears to be the tailors working in a particular shop; on other occasions it is all tailors in Liberia, or even all tailors in the world. Seeking to remedy this, Wenger (1998) gives a tighter account of what identifies a community of practice, but at the cost of reducing the incidence of such communities. As Hodkinson and Hodkinson (2004a) note, this in turn deflates the original Lave and Wenger claim to have developed a general socio-cultural account of learning. A further deficiency of the Lave and Wenger theory is that its strong reliance on the participation metaphor means that it is largely silent about the individual's learning as their personal identity changes from that of novice to full participant (see, e.g., Elkjaer, 2003; Guile and Young, 1999).

Another very influential socio-cultural theory of workplace learning is cultural-historical activity theory. Its major proponent, Engeström (1999, 2001), views workplaces as activity systems that comprise a range of components, including items such as workplace rules, the division of labour, and mediating artifacts. Engeström regards learning as occurring as work proceeds within such activity systems, because they continually throw up contradictions and tensions that need to be resolved. In doing so, the system as a whole changes, usually as a result of either internal or external contradictions or tensions. Thus, the context in which individuals and groups work and learn changes, and, thereby, they change with it. Engeström's account of workplace learning finds places for social, organizational and cultural factors within the activity system.

However, it might be questioned whether all learning at work occurs from contradictions and tensions within the system. Engeström also posits a dialectical interplay between the learner and the activity system. To what extent is the learner a locus of learning as against the system being the locus? The learner/system locus issue remains unresolved. In more recent work (Tuomi-Gröhn and Engeström, 2003), Engeström has proposed the concept of 'boundary crossing' as a different and better way to understand transfer of learning. However, others have cast strong doubt on the ongoing value of the transfer metaphor. They argue that rather than relying on the transfer metaphor that characterized early theories of workplace learning, more productive metaphors, such as 'becoming' can be derived from socio-cultural accounts of learning (see, e.g. Hager and Hodkinson, 2009).

Both the Lave and Wenger focus on situated learning and Engeström's activity systems approach have stimulated a surge of recent research and conceptual innovation on learning at work (e.g. see Rainbird et al., 2004). For instance, Fuller and Unwin (2003, 2004) have developed a new conceptual framework, the *expansive-restrictive continuum*, for analysing the incidence and quality of workplace learning. In particular, the *expansive-restrictive continuum* aims to characterize the key features of different learning environments. It centres on two broad sets of features: those relating to organizational context and culture, and those relating to learning opportunities arising from various forms of participation in workplaces. Their framework is intended specifically to remedy deficiencies that Fuller and Unwin identify in the Lave and Wenger account of learning. In particular, their framework adds fresh dimensions to understandings of what the widely employed, but under-theorized, participation metaphor might entail.

Guile and Young (2003) drawing on the sociological distinction between vertical, generalizable academic knowledge and horizontal workplace knowledge, have developed an account of boundary crossing and transfer as a development within cultural-historical activity theory. Similarly, Guile and Okumoto (2007) have developed an account of knowledge generation within vocational practice that they maintain supplies a missing dimension to cultural-historical activity theory.

A range of other authors have put forward accounts of learning at work that incorporate at least some main features of this second broad category of accounts of workplace learning. Some, such as Eraut and colleagues (e.g. Eraut, 2000; Eraut et al., 2000; Eraut, 2004; Eraut and Hirsh, nd) are difficult to classify as their work combines prominent themes from both categories of workplace learning theories. This is evident from considering their position in relation to the three key issues discussed earlier. There is a strong commitment to the individual learner as the unit of analysis for understanding learning (Issue 1). In most cases this is a taken-for-granted assumption. Even where there is explicit consideration of group or organizational learning, the assumption is that such learning is no more than the sum of the individual learnings of the group or organizational members. Though there is acceptance that combining these learnings of the several individuals can result in a 'combined capability of a team ... greater than that of its members acting only individually' (Eraut and Hirsh, nd, p. 42). There is also a strong tendency to treat learning as a thing (Issue 2), as evidenced by pervasive reliance on the acquisition and transfer metaphors. However, a distinction is emphasized between codified and personal knowledge. The latter is specified as being often tacit (in various senses – Eraut, 2000) and can also be significantly contextual. Thus, on Issue 3 (learning as independent of context), Eraut and colleagues are closer to the second broad category of accounts of workplace learning. The result is that Eraut views transfer as a much more complex process than its portrayal in earlier theories. In fact he regards transfer as a five-stage learning process in which the knowledge being 'transferred' is transformed and re-contextualized in several distinct ways (Eraut, 2004, p. 212 ff.). Overall, Eraut's work can be read as a plea that accounts of workplace learning in the second category should not jettison all of the resources of the first category.

The idea that much workplace learning has tacit dimensions recurs in much of the literature. However, the notion of 'tacit' is multiply ambiguous. Some aspects of workplace know-how may be, in principle, unable to be expressed in words. Yet, for other aspects it may simply be the case that they have so far not been subject to the requisite detailed investigation that would elucidate them. Various political and power considerations have also helped to decide that certain types of skills have been codified and elaborated, whereas others have been largely ignored. In this latter vein Evans and colleagues have carried out valuable research that has documented the vocational relevance and wide applicability of a range of skills that are gained from experiences of work that are typically either unpaid or lowly paid (e.g., Evans, 2002; Evans et al., 2004).

Billett is another writer who has been dissatisfied with the vagueness of the participation metaphor as deployed in socio-cultural theories of learning. He has proposed a range of concepts, such as 'agentic activity', 'invitational qualities', and 'workplace affordances', to better describe the ways in which practitioners continually reshape their practice as they engage in it (Billett, 2002). Billett has also been critical of the tendency for the role of individuals to be subsumed into the social in the early socio-cultural theories of learning, thereby being rendered invisible. He argues that the role of personal agency seems to be left out of these accounts. In a series of publications (Billett, 2001, 2004, 2008a, 2008b; Billett and Somerville, 2004), Billett has sought to develop a theory of workplace learning that centres on the relational inter-dependencies between individual and social agency, between the engagement of the worker and the affordances of the work environment. He proposes a similar relational theory of expertise, locating it in the dynamic activities of social practices. This theory:

> .... proposes how individuals come to know and act by drawing on cognitive, sociocultural and anthropo-logical conceptions, and through an appraisal of the ontological premises of domains of knowledge. The inter-psychological processes for developing expertise are held to be constituted reciprocally between the affordance of the social practice and how individuals act and come to know in the social practice (Billett, 2001, p. 432).

So, rather than being a capability of the individual practitioner, expertise resides, on Billett's account, in particular social practices and their related knowledge domains.

Hodkinson and Hodkinson (2004b) agree with Billett that in integrating the individual learner into a social participatory process, there is a danger that the sense of the individual life history, dispositions and agency of each learner, is lost. However, they question whether it is desirable to view the individual as an entity clearly separated from and interacting with the social situations in which they work and learn. They see Billett as following Engeström (1999) in positing a sharp separation of, and even opposition between distinct entities, the individual and social structures, with the two interacting dialectically. Rather than regarding the individual and the social as separate entities that interact, the Hodkinsons follow Bourdieu (1984) in viewing individual persons as reciprocal parts of the social context in which they learn, and vice versa. On this account, the embodied individual is constructed through the positioned social life that the person leads, including their work. Here Bourdieu (1984) is deploying an Aristotelian concept of habitus, which comprises a largely internalized, sub-conscious battery of socially acquired but relatively stable dispositions, that orientate a person's actions in any situation (Bourdieu and Wacquant, 1992). For Bourdieu, rather than individuals being influenced by and in turn influencing the social structures around them, the social structures are themselves represented through individual persons, in their habitus. Thus, habitus becomes a way of expressing the unitary integration of social structures and individual persons, and agency and structure both have significant, but complementary roles.

Other work by Hodkinson and Bloomer (2002) and Hodkinson and Hodkinson (2004a, 2004b) also deserves attention. Their contributions to the socio-cultural theorizing of workplace learning seek to enrich the notion of 'community of practice' by employing Bourdieu's concepts of habitus, capital and field. As well, they stress the importance for workplace learning of individuals' previous learning biographies. This suggestive conceptual work is illustrated and supplemented by an impressive range of evidence drawn from diverse case studies.

In discussion of the first category of workplace learning theories, those largely inspired by psychology, it was a common assumption that learning was located inside of the learner, in their body if not in their head. By contrast, for socio-cultural theories, learning becomes a process located in the framework of participation, rather than some thing in an individual mind. Here, learning appears to be distributed among the group of co-participants. This suggests the possibility that groups, teams, communities, and even organizations can intelligibly be said to learn. Collective learning is an important addition to the notion of individual learning. It has been under-theorized and under-researched, but is now starting to receive significant attention (see, e.g., Boreham, 2004; Boreham and Morgan, 2004; Garavan and McCarthy, 2008). However, as was noted above, it is a mistake to assume that collective learning replaces notions of individual learning. Rather, the dimensions of the concept of learning have been expanded.

Much of the above work in the second category of workplace learning theories can be said to follow a modernist agenda, i.e. the theories seek to understand and explain workplace learning so that the conditions that support and enhance quality learning can be identified and implemented. Thus, while much of this theorizing accepts that contextual factors in particular are diverse and complex, the aim is for sound theorizing to enable workplaces to be structured so as to bring about quality learning. It is the hope that decidable and predictable systems can be designed and implemented. We turn now to recent theorizing of workplace learning that questions this modernist assumption.

3 Postmodern theories

A third category of workplace learning theories has emerged relatively recently. It is still too soon to estimate what their overall impact on the field will be. However, these theories seem to raise a new key issue that is significant enough to be highlighted in the way that the earlier three key issues were. This issue concerns whether and in what senses workplace learning can be said to be emergent.

Issue 4: Workplace learning as emergent

The theories in this third category accept that learning should be viewed as an ongoing process, i.e. it is characterized by temporal change. But as well, they view this change as not fully decidable in advance. This means that learning is emergent from its context in unanticipated and unpredictable ways. Thus context transforms learning in an ongoing creative process. The modernist aims of decidability and predictability are unrealistic according to these theories. So the directions of workplace learning can only be characterized in broad, general terms. The kind of control that might be desired by policymakers is not feasible. According to the theories in this third category, there is an ineliminable temporal dimension to workplace learning as it emerges from ever-changing, complex contexts.

If emergence becomes an accepted feature of learning then we will require new metaphors to advance our understanding. The two most influential metaphors of learning, *acquisition* and *participation*, that Sfard (1998) argues underpin most educational thought, are clearly limited once the temporal dimension is acknowledged. Metaphors such as engagement, (re)construction, emergence or becoming, all look to be more promising.

Although, until recently, much theorizing in the humanities and social sciences has resisted the idea of emergence, it has now gained increasing credibility. For example, the philosophical theory known as 'critical realism', stemming from the work of Roy Bhaskar, is one that attributes emergent properties to social reality. Social reality is agreed to be dependent on human activity. But some social structures are emergent properties, which have causal powers and persist, even though those who were originally responsible for their emergence are long since dead. However, these social structures also exhibit the temporal dimension that accompanies emergence, since they are 'relations into which people enter (which) pre-exist the individuals who enter into them, and whose activity reproduces or transforms them . . .' (Archer, 1998, p. 359). Archer quotes Bhaskar's position that 'society may . . . be conceived as an articulated ensemble of such relatively independent and enduring structures' (Archer, 1998, p. 368). Practices would appear to be good examples of such social structures, thereby having causal powers and persisting over time whilst gradually being transformed by their practitioners. If practices can have emergent properties, then why should not the same apply to the learning that accompanies their transformation? Whilst the theories of workplace learning discussed above focused, respectively, on the individual learner and on the socio-cultural context in which the learner is located, this third category of workplace learning theory assigns a significant role in learning to the 'sociomaterial' (Fenwick, 2009).

Theories of workplace learning that fall under this third category include ones influenced by complexity theory and actor network theory. It is also likely that some variants of cultural-historical activity theory will fit here. For instance, complexity figures in Engeström's most recent work (Engeström, 2008). This will not be surprising, given the strong influence of Marx's historical materialism on cultural-historical activity theory and its progenitors. Just as there are more and less deterministic interpretations of Marx, the same is likely also for different versions of cultural-historical activity theory.

Complexity theory in its various guises has been proposed as offering afresh and nuanced understanding of learning. Learning is viewed as emerging in complex adaptive systems as humans interact with their environment in ongoing dynamic processes that mutually reconstruct both the environment and the human actors (see, e.g., Davis and Sumara, 2006; Osberg and Biesta, 2007). This approach puts an emphasis on learning as an increasing capacity for acting in flexible, constructive and innovative ways appropriate to the challenges of ever-changing circumstances. Such learning is emergent in the strong sense that its growth out of continuous and non-linear interactions is not predictable from an understanding of the structures that preceded it. Some writers, particularly in the field of organizational studies, have begun to apply complexity theory to understanding workplace learning (e.g., Stacey, 2005; Stacey and Griffin, 2005; Tsoukas, 2005; Tsoukas and Chia, 2002).

Actor network theory (ANT) provides another novel approach to understanding learning. Fenwick characterizes its central idea as follows:

> ANT takes knowledge generation to be a joint exercise of relational strategies within networks that are spread across space and time and performed through inanimate – e.g. books, mobile phones, measuring instruments, projection screens, boxes, locks – as well as animate beings in precarious arrangements. Learning and knowing are performed in the processes of assembling and maintaining these networks, as well as in the negotiations that occur at various nodes comprising a network (Fenwick, 2009, p. 5).

The, so far, few writers on workplace learning who have drawn on actor network theory include Edwards and Nicoll (2004); Mulcahy (2007) and Gherardi and Nicolini (2000).

Other authors whose work fits broadly into this third category (postmodern theories of workplace learning) include Gherardi (2006); Shotter (2008); Nicolini et al. (2003), and Usher and Edwards (2007). Usher and Edwards (though they would probably prefer the appellation 'post-structuralist') claim that in a postmodern world almost any activity can be valorized as 'learning'. They view learning as something that 'is neither invariant nor unchanging because "learning" is a socio-culturally embedded set of practices' (2007, p. 2). Noting that 'the boundaries between leisure, entertainment and learning are increasingly blurred (Usher and Edwards, 2007, p. 30), they point out that the same activity may be described differently. When, for example, is someone learning music and when are they actually playing it? When is work learning? Could any activity be described as learning in the right context? 'Who then has the authority or power to rename practices as learning…?' (Usher and Edwards, 2007, p. 167). Are all forms of learning equally worthwhile?

'Practices' is the key notion in the Usher and Edwards theorization of learning:

> . . . learning is embedded in practices, we learn through participation in these practices (Usher and Edwards, 2007, p. 6).

However, it is perhaps noteworthy that they do not say what they understand by their key notion of a practice. Yet they use this term ubiquitously throughout their book, seemingly at a bewildering multiplicity of levels of description. Thus at different places in the book we meet truth-telling practices, meaning making practices, confessional practices, discursive practices, vocational practices, homemaking practices, and more. However, the Usher and Edwards argument can usefully serve to alert us to the great diversity within learning. This is sometimes lost in the deployment of generic labels such as 'workplace learning'. Perhaps research can benefit by recognizing the diversity within workplace learning, and engaging in closer investigation of particular types of workplace learning. An example of this is the Beckett and Hager (2002) proposal, (extended further by Hager and Halliday, 2006), that the development of judgement via experience of practice is a key instance of workplace learning. The development of this kind of judgement making is highly contextual. It usually involves both learning that can be understood at the level of the individual, and also some learning that is inherently at the level of the group or community of practitioners.

CONCLUSION

Theorizing of workplace learning has evolved significantly since it began to emerge as a significant topic. This chapter has outlined the major theories that have contributed to this evolution, as well as some key issues that continue to reshape this field of study. At present, newer theories, that posit emergence as a characteristic feature of workplace learning, are beginning to take hold. It remains to be seen to what extent they will continue to reshape this field. In the meantime, policies that relate to workplace learning too often reflect uncritical acceptance of individualistic learning as product assumptions. The result is that they fail to connect in any significant way with the very activities they are supposed to influence and support. Remediation of this unsatisfactory situation will require a major rethink by policy makers of their understanding of workplace learning.

REFERENCES

Archer, M. (1998) 'Realism and Morphogenesis', in R. Bhaskar, A. Collier, T. Lawson and A. Norrie (eds) *Critical Realism*. London: Routledge.

Argyris, C. and Schön, D.A. (1974) *Theory in Practice: Increasing Professional Effectiveness*. San Francisco: Jossey-Bass.

Argyris, C. and Schön, D.A. (1978) *Organizational Learning: A Theory of Action Perspective*. Reading, MA: Addison-Wesley.

Athanasou, J.A. (ed.) (2008) *Adult Educational Psychology*. Rotterdam: Sense Publishers.

Beckett, D. and Hager, P. (2002) *Life, Work and Learning: Practice in Postmodernity*. Routledge International Studies in the Philosophy of Education 14. London and New York: Routledge.

Bereiter, C. (2002) *Education and Mind in the Knowledge Age*. Mahwah, NJ/London: Lawrence Erlbaum Associates.

Billett, S. (2001) 'Knowing in Practice: Re-Conceptualising Vocational Expertise', *Learning and Instruction* 11: 39–58.

Billett, S. (2002) 'Workplace Pedagogic Practices: Co-participation and Learning', *British Journal of Educational Studies* 50(4): 457–481.

Billett, S. (2004) 'Learning through Work: Workplace Participatory Practices', in Rainbird, Fuller and Munro (eds) *Workplace Learning in Context*. London: Routledge, pp. 109–125.

Billett, S. (2008a) 'Learning Throughout Working Life: A Relational Interdependence Between Personal and Social Agency', *British Journal of Educational Studies* 56(1): 232–240.

Billett, S. (2008b) 'Learning through Work: Exploring Instances of Relational Interdependencies', *International Journal of Educational Research* 47: 232–240.

Billett, S. and Somerville, M. (2004) 'Transformations at Work: Identity and Learning', *Studies in Continuing Education* 26(2): 309–326.

Boreham, N. (2004) 'A Theory of Collective Competence: Challenging the Neo-Liberal Individualisation of Performance at Work', *British Journal of Educational Studies* 52(1): 5–17.

Boreham, N. and Morgan, C. (2004) 'A Sociocultural Analysis of Organisational Learning', *Oxford Review of Education* 30(3): 308–325.

Bourdieu, P. (1984) *Distinction: A Social Critique of the Judgement of Taste*. London: Routledge and Kegan Paul.

Bourdieu, P. and Wacquant, L.J.D. (1992) *An Invitation to Reflexive Sociology*. Cambridge: Polity Press.

Cevero, R.M. (2001) 'Continuing Professional Education in Transition, 1981–2000', *International Journal of Lifelong Education* 20(1–2): 16–30.

Davis, A. (2005) 'Learning and the Social Nature of Mental Powers', *Educational Philosophy and Theory* 37(5): 635–647.

Davis, B. and Sumara, D.J. (2006) *Complexity and Education: Inquiries into Learning, Teaching and Research*. Mahwah, NJ: Lawrence Erlbaum.

Dewey, J. (1916) *Democracy and Education*. New York: Macmillan.

Dreyfus, H. (2001) *On the Internet*. London: Routledge.

Dreyfus, H.L. and Dreyfus, S.E. (1986) *Mind over Machine: The Power of Human Intuition and Expertise in the Era of the Computer.* New York: Free Press.

Edwards, R. and Nicoll, K. (2004) 'Mobilizing Workplaces: Actors, Discipline and Governmentality', *Studies in Continuing Education* 26(2): 159–173.

Elkjaer, B. (2003) 'Organizational Learning with a Pragmatic Slant', *International Journal of Lifelong Education* 22(5): 481–494.

Engeström, Y. (1999) 'Activity Theory and Individual and Social Transformation', in Y. Engeström, R. Miettinen and R. Punamaki (eds), *Perspectives on Activity Theory.* Cambridge: Cambridge University Press, pp. 19–38.

Engeström, Y. (2001) 'Expansive Learning at Work: Towards an Activity-Theoretical Reconceptualisation', *Journal of Education and Work* 14(1): 133–156.

Engeström, Y. (2008) *From Teams to Knots: Activity-Theoretical Studies of Collaboration and Learning at Work.* Cambridge: Cambridge University Press.

Eraut, M. (2000) 'Non-Formal Learning and Tacit Knowledge in Professional Work', *British Journal of Educational Psychology* 70: 113–136.

Eraut, M. (2004) 'Transfer of Knowledge between Education and Work Settings', in Rainbird, Fuller and Munro (eds), pp. 201–220.

Eraut, M. and Hirsh (no date) *The Significance of Workplace Learning for Individuals, Groups and Organisations,* ESRC Centre on Skills, Knowledge and Organisational Performance (SKOPE – Oxford and Cardiff Universities), available at www.skope.ox.ac.uk/WorkingPapers/Eraut-Hirshmonograph.pdf (accessed 22 Sept 2009).

Eraut, M., Alderton, J., Cole, G. and Senker, P. (2000) 'Development of Knowledge and Skills at Work', in F. Coffield (ed.) *Differing Visions of a Learning Society: Research Findings,* Vol. 1. Bristol: The Policy Press, pp. 231–262.

Evans, K. (2002) 'The Challenge of "Making Learning Visible"', in K. Evans, P. Hodkinson and L. Unwin (eds), *Working to Learn: Transforming Learning in the Workplace.* London: Kogan Page.

Evans, K., Kersh, N. and Sakamoto, A. (2004) 'Learner Biographies: Exploring Tacit Dimensions of Knowledge and Skills', in Rainbird, Fuller and Munro (eds), *Workplace Learning in Context.* London: Routledge, pp. 222–241.

Fenwick, T. (2009) 'Re-Thinking the "Thing": Sociomaterial Approaches to Understanding and Researching Learning at Work'. Paper presented at *The 6th International Conference on Researching Work and Learning.* Roskilde University, Denmark, June 28–July 1 2009.

Freire, P. (1972) *Pedagogy of the Oppressed.* Harmondsworth: Penguin.

Fuller, A. and Unwin, L. (2003) 'Learning as Apprentices in the Contemporary UK Workplace: Creating and Managing Expansive and Restrictive Participation', *Journal of Education and Work* 16 (4): 407–426.

Fuller, A. and Unwin, L. (2004) 'Expansive Learning Environments: Integrating Organisational and Personal Development', in Rainbird, Fuller and Munro (eds) *Workplace Learning in Context.* London: Routledge, pp. 126–144.

Fuller, A., Hodkinson, H., Hodkinson, P. and Unwin, L. (2005) 'Learning as Peripheral Participation in Communities of Practice: A Reassessment of Key Concepts in Workplace Learning', *British Educational Research Journal* 31(1): 49–68.

Garavan, T.N. and McCarthy, A. (2008) 'Collective Learning Processes and Human Resource Development', *Advances in Developing Human Resources* 10(4): 451–471.

Gherardi, S. (2006) *Organizational Knowledge: The Texture of Workplace Learning* (with the collaboration of D. Nicolini). Malden, MA: Blackwell.

Gherardi, S. and Nicolini, D. (2000) 'To Transfer Is to Transform: The Circulation of Safety Knowledge', *Organization* 7(2): 329–348.

Guile, D. and Young, M. (1999) 'Beyond the Institution of Apprenticeship: Towards a Social Theory of Learning as the Production of Knowledge', in P. Ainley and H. Rainbird (eds) *Apprenticeship: Towards a New Paradigm of Learning.* London: Kogan Page, pp. 111–128.

Guile, D. and Young, M. (2003) 'Transfer and Transition in Vocational Education: Some Theoretical Considerations', in T. Tuomi-Gröhn and Y. Engeström (eds), *Between School and Work: New Perspectives on Transfer and Boundary-Crossing.* Amsterdam: Elsevier Science, pp. 63–81.

Guile, D. and Okumoto, K. (2007) 'Developing Vocational Practice in the Jewelry Sector Through the Incubation of a New "Project-Object"', *International Journal of Educational Research* 47(4): 252–260.

Hager, P. (2004) 'The Competence Affair, or Why VET Urgently Needs a New Understanding of Learning', *Journal of Vocational Education & Training* 56(3): 409–433.

Hager, P. and Halliday, J. (2006) *Recovering Informal Learning: Wisdom, Judgement and Community.* Dordrecht: Springer (re-issued in paperback 2009).

Hager, P. and Holland, S. (eds) (2006) *Graduate Attributes, Learning and Employability.* Dordrecht: Springer.

Hager, P. and Hodkinson, P. (2009) 'Moving Beyond the Metaphor of Transfer of Learning', *British Educational Research Journal* 35(4): 619–638.

Hodkinson, P. (2004) 'Theoretical Constructions of Workplace Learning: Troubling Dualisms and Problems of Scale'. Paper Presented at the ESREA Adult Education and the Labour Market Conference, Northern College, Barnsley, UK, 12–14 November.

Hodkinson, P. and Bloomer, M. (2002) 'Learning Careers: Conceptualizing Lifelong Work-based Learning', in K. Evans, P. Hodkinson and L. Unwin (eds), *Working to Learn: Transforming Learning in the Workplace*. London: Kogan Page, pp. 29–43.

Hodkinson, H. and Hodkinson, P. (2004a) 'Rethinking the Concept of Community of Practice in Relation to Schoolteachers' Workplace Learning', *International Journal of Training and Development* 8(1): 21–31.

Hodkinson, P. and Hodkinson, H. (2004b) 'The Significance of Individuals' Dispositions in Workplace Learning: A Case Study of Two Teachers', *Journal of Education and Work* 17(2): 167–182.

Hodkinson, P., Biesta, G. and James, D. (2008) 'Understanding Learning Culturally: Overcoming the Dualism Between Social and Individual Views of Learning', *Vocations and Learning* 1(1): 27–47.

Kalantzis, M. and Cope, B. (2009) *New Learning: Elements of a Science of Education*. Cambridge: Cambridge University Press.

Lakoff, G. and Johnson, M. (1980) *Metaphors We Live By*. Chicago: University of Chicago Press.

Lave, J. and Wenger, E. (1991) *Situated Learning*. Cambridge: Cambridge University Press.

Marsick, V. and Watkins, K. (1990) *Informal and Incidental Learning in the Workplace*. London: Routledge.

Mulcahy, D. (2007) '(Re)working Relations of Strategy and Spatiality in Education', *Studies in Continuing Education* 29(2): 143–162.

Nicolini, D., Gherardi, S. and Yanow, D. (eds) (2003) *Knowing in Organizations: A Practice-Based Approach*. Armonk, NY: M.E. Sharpe.

Nonaka, I. and Takeuchi, H. (1995) *The Knowledge-Creating Company: How Japanese Companies Create the Dynamics of Innovation*. Oxford and New York: Oxford University Press.

Osberg, D. and Biesta, G. (2007) 'Beyond Presence: Epistemological and Pedagogical Implications of "Strong" Emergence', *Interchange* 38(1): 31–51.

Rainbird, H., Fuller, A. and Munro, A. (eds) (2004) *Workplace Learning in Context*. London: Routledge.

Schön, D.A. (1983) *The Reflective Practitioner*. New York: Basic Books.

Schön, D.A. (1987) *Educating the Reflective Practitioner*. San Francisco: Jossey-Bass.

Sfard, A. (1998) 'On Two Metaphors for Learning and the Dangers of Choosing Just One', *Educational Researcher* 27(2): 4–13.

Shotter, J. (2008) 'Dialogism and Polyphony in Organizing Theorizing in Organization Studies: Action Guiding Anticipations and the Continuous Creation of Novelty', *Organization Studies* 29(4): 501–524.

Stacey, R. (2005) *Experiencing Emergence in Organizations: Local Interaction and the Emergence of Global Pattern*. London: Routledge.

Stacey, R. and Griffin, D. (eds) (2005) *A Complexity Perspective on Researching Organizations: Local Taking Experience Seriously*. London: Routledge.

Tennant, M. and Pogson, P. (1995) *Learning and Change in the Adult Years: A Developmental Perspective*. San Francisco: Jossey-Bass.

Tsoukas, H. (2005) 'Afterword: Why Language Matters in the Analysis of Organizational Change', *Journal of Organizational Change Management* 18(1): 96–104.

Tsoukas, H. and Chia, R. (2002) 'On Organizational Becoming: Rethinking Organizational Change', *Organization Science* 13(5): 567–582.

Tuomi-Gröhn, T. and Engeström, Y. (2003) (eds) *Between School and Work: New Perspectives on Transfer and Boundary-Crossing*. Amsterdam: Elsevier Science.

Usher, R. and Edwards, R. (2007) *Lifelong Learning – Signs, Discourses, Practices*. Dordrecht: Springer.

Vygotsky, L.S. (1978) *Mind in Society: The Development of Higher Psychological Processes*. Cambridge, MA: Harvard University Press.

Watkins, K. and Marsick, V. (1992) 'Towards a Theory of Informal and Incidental Learning in Organizations', *International Journal of Lifelong Education* 11(4): 287–300.

Wenger, E. (1998) *Communities of Practice: Learning, Meaning and Identity*. Cambridge: Cambridge University Press.

Wertsch, J.W. (1998) *Mind as Action*. Oxford and New York: Oxford University Press.

3

Workplaces and Learning

Knud Illeris

WHY LEARNING AT WORK?

During the 1990s 'workplace learning', 'work-based learning' and the like became popular slogans in the context of vocationally oriented education and personnel development. Considerable interest has arisen on many sides – in practice, in theory, in politics, locally, nationally and internationally – for placing rising emphasis on the vocationally oriented learning and development that take place directly at the workplace, because such learning and development meet a number of current challenges to the qualification of the staff perhaps better than learning at courses and in educational institutions.

This situation is fundamentally paradoxical, because as a point of departure workplace learning has precisely been the general and obvious form of vocationally oriented learning and qualification ever since a distinction began to be made between working life and the rest of life. Historically there has been a clear tendency for increasingly larger parts of qualification being transferred from the workplaces to formalized types of school, education and course activity, as working life and the rest of society gradually have become more and more complex. And there have, of course, been important reasons for this. Expensive school and educational systems are not established and developed if they would make no difference.

This development got under way first and foremost with the breakthrough and spread of industrialization and capitalism up through the nineteenth century, and it has been proved time and again that the decisive dynamism in this development lay in the need for fundamental and gradually more and more differentiated socialization and qualification for the requirements of wage labour (cf. e.g. Masuch, 1972). On a basic level, this requires a certain attitude that is not inborn: selling oneself as labour and loyally performing work determined by others within certain time frames.

Ever since wage labour became the general type of work relation, the requirements concerning wage labourers' qualifications, practical as well as personal, have grown and grown. They have become increasingly differentiated and it has become increasingly more difficult for workplaces to undertake up-to-date training.

Originally, apprenticeships in Denmark lasted for seven years and periods at school were not included. In time, the apprenticeship was cut to three to four years and evening schools provided a supplement. Starting in 1956, one weekly school day was introduced, and since 1972 lengthy periods of schooling have been built into all types of apprenticeships, while the time at the workplace has been reduced. In other European countries there has been a similar development. Today we must reckon with the need for both vocational basic training courses and workplace training having to be brought up to date to a considerable extent with supplementary training or direct retraining outside the workplace.

The trend in this has been absolutely clear: more and more schooling and less and less educational training at the workplaces. How can it be then that it is precisely now that a significant counter trend has arisen that wishes to 'return' as much learning as possible to working life?

The cause of all of this should primarily be sought in the extensive and profound developments and changes in the structures of society that have been described as the transition to late modernity, post modernity, cultural liberation, the knowledge society, the information society and the like, and which encompass the breakthrough of market management, globalization and the new technologies (cf. e.g. Giddens, 1990; Beck, 1992; Bauman, 1998).

This process of change has included two key development trends in the area of learning and education. In the first place, there has been a shift away from the notion that education and qualification were something that essentially belonged to childhood and youth, something that could be finished when a certain vocational competence had been acquired upon which one could base one's activity for a forty to fifty year career, if necessary with occasional updating. This notion was well matched by a school and educational system that could deliver such vocational competences and could be expanded and differentiated in step with developments. But it is clear that this situation no longer prevails. Everyone must be prepared for their working functions changing constantly and radically during the whole of their working lives. Therefore, what is needed today is what is typically called 'lifelong', 'lifewide' and 'lifedeep' learning (cf. e.g. EU Commission, 2000; Illeris, 2004), and the extent and the way it best takes place and the role the school and the educational system can play in this context are open questions.

Secondly, 'what is to be learned' has changed in nature. At one time the learning targets of the school and education programmes were referred to in categories such as knowledge, skills, attitudes, or more generally, qualifications. All of this is, naturally, still necessary. But at the same time it must necessarily be updated, developed, reorganized and recreated constantly to fit new situations, so that it quickly and flexibly can be used in changed contexts that are not known at present but which we know with certainty will come. This is the essence of the current concepts of competences and competence development (cf. e.g. Beckett and Hager, 2002; Illeris, 2004, 2009b). And it is obviously a huge challenge to the school and education system to supply competences for the solution of problems and situations that are unknown at time of learning. How is this to be done?

It is first and foremost on the basis of these matters that the new ideas about workplace learning have emerged and have gained ground. Would it not be easier, less expensive and more efficient if such development and constant adaptation of competences were to take place where the competences are to be utilized and where there is always first-hand knowledge of what is new? In the case of vocationally oriented competences, this would, after all, be directly in the workplaces, or in networks and organizations where the workplaces are partners that can ensure that the processes are always up-to-date.

And would this not also be more democratic? After all, in this way those who are directly affected can always know what is going on and play a part in deciding what is to take place and how. And is there not also a broad interest on the part of society at one and the same time to ensure in this way an up-to-date competence development and co-decision for ordinary people, which can be far more wide-ranging and direct than when learning takes place in schools and institutions that have their own agenda and modes of functioning?

There would seem to be many good arguments for the idea of workplace learning from the point of view of learning theory, efficiency and democracy. This is why it also has obtained many strong adherents. Interest has not least been expressed in the supranational expert organizations such as the OECD, the EU and the World Bank as a key element in the lifelong learning that at one and the same time can lead to economic growth, personal development for the individual and increased social balance, nationally and internationally (cf. e.g. OECD, 2000, 2001). But other interests are also at stake that cannot be disregarded if a full perception of the new trend is to be obtained.

In the first place, it is clear that the steadily growing education requirements are expensive, and the state has, therefore, an obvious interest in some of the burden being moved out of the institutions – but not all of it, because the state also has overall responsibility for the level of education and training of the workforce as an important prerequisite for economic growth and global competitiveness. If vocationally oriented training is left completely to the labour market, the qualification could easily become too short-sighted and narrow. Therefore the state will quite generally aim for interaction between institutionalized vocationally oriented education and workplace learning and seek to get the business sector and the participants to undertake as great a part of the financing as possible.

The enterprises/employers will naturally be reluctant to undertake this. They are basically interested in education being publicly financed unless it is significantly personal or enterprise specific in nature. But on the other hand, workplace learning would give the enterprises more influence over what is learned and how, and a lot of general education in which the individual enterprise can see no direct interest could be reduced in step with learning taking place directly in the workplace. Here also the attitude would in principle be dual, but would very largely tend to welcome more workplace learning, especially if it were linked with some or other type of financial compensation.

The workers and their organizations would also be largely positive. It would be necessary, to a lesser degree, for the workers to 'go back to school': on the individual level the great majority think that they learn better in informal contexts and at their work than in institutionalized education (cf. e.g. CEDEFOP, 2003). And the trade unions would also find it easier to influence the way in which it takes place. On the other hand, it is obvious that formalized education is in general better at ensuring the workforce a good, well-documented level of education, and the unions can perhaps exert more influence when the representatives of the state play a part in decision making than they can achieve in direct interaction with the employers.

Finally, it should not be forgotten that the institutions and the teachers have a strong self-interest in maintenance of the formalized study programmes. Even though there are at present some experiments involving teachers coming out to the enterprises and taking part in organizing interactively oriented courses, this can hardly make up for the safe incomes ensured by permanent courses at the schools.

There are thus many and very different interests at play when it comes to learning in working life, and it is also part of late modern market society that one should not believe all one hears. Today goods, ideas and attitudes are marketed professionally on the basis of interests that are not always immediately visible.

But there are also some quite fundamental problems in connection with workplace learning that are not very much in focus right now. First and foremost, the overall aim of the workplaces is to produce goods and services and not to produce learning. And even though in many cases it would make good economic sense to invest in upgrading the employees' qualifications, there is an unmistakable tendency that when a pressed situation arises – and this seems frequently to be the case in late modern market society – learning measures will often be downgraded in prioritization in relation to current short-term needs.

This is why there is so much focus on the learning that can take place more or less 'by chance' in direct connection with the performance of the work and which thus in principle neither costs anything nor must be prioritized – the learning that in a manner of speaking comes 'by itself' (cf. Marsick and Watkins, 1990; Garrick, 1998). The problem is, however, that precisely this kind of learning, to a far greater extent than learning in working life that is structured and planned, tends to be narrow and lacking in theory. When it takes place in direct connection with the work, one can easily focus on what can create improvements here and now, while the broad lines and the wider contexts are omitted and with them the possibility of the learning having a wider application value in new situations and in connection with a more general understanding and an overview, which is decisive for what we call competence (cf. Billett, 2001; Beckett and Hager, 2002; Illeris et al., 2004 for a broader discussion of these matters).

The great current interest in workplace learning is thus not as unambiguous as it often purports to be. But on the other hand there are clearly also some current matters pulling the picture in this direction, and there is good reason to expect workplace learning to play a greater role in the educational scene in the future. I shall therefore in the following sections first try to develop a more structured conception of the main features of such learning. Next, I shall discuss workplace learning in relation to different theoretical approaches and point out some basic features that must be considered. Finally, I shall relate learning in working life to the concept of competence development, which seems to be the kind of learning that is especially intended or hoped for in this connection.

SOME BASIC ISSUES AND CONCEPTS ON LEARNING

The most fundamental condition of human learning is that all learning includes two essentially different types of process: an external interaction process between the learner and his or her social, cultural and material environment, and an internal psychological process of elaboration and acquisition in which new impulses are connected with the results of prior learning.

The criteria of the interaction process are of a social and societal character, i.e. they are determined by time and place. The individual is in interaction with an environment that includes other people, a specific culture, technology and so on, which are characterized by their time and society. In the late modern globalized world, this is all mixed up in a giant and rapidly changing hotchpotch that offers unlimited, and to a great extent also unstructured, possibilities for learning. Hence, the often formulated need for learning to learn, i.e. creating a personal structure or a value system to sort out what is worth learning from what is not. This is also the background for understandings such as those of the social constructionists, focusing on the needs, difficulties and prevalence of this interaction process in late modernity (e.g. Gergen, 1994).

But no matter how dominant and imperative the interaction process has become, in learning there is also always a process of individual acquisition in which the impulses from the interaction are incorporated. As discussed by such scholars as Piaget (e.g. 1952) and Ausuble (1968), the core of this process is that the new impressions are connected with the results of prior learning in a way that influences both. Thus, the outcome of the individual acquisition process is always dependent on what has already been acquired, and ultimately the criteria of this process are of a biological nature and determined by the extensive, but not infinite, possibilities of the human brain and central nervous system to cope with, structure, retain and create meaning out of impressions as perceived by our senses.

However, learning, thinking, remembering, understanding and similar functions are not just cognitive or content matters, although they have generally been conceived of as such by traditional learning psychology. Whether the frame of reference is common sense, Freudian psychology, modern management or brand new results of brain research, there is lots of imperative evidence that all such functions are also inseparably connected with emotions and motivation. The Austrian-American psychologist Hans Furth (1987), by combining the findings and theories of Piaget and Freud, has unravelled how cognition and emotions during the preschool years gradually separate as distinctive but never isolated functions, and the Portuguese-American neurologist Antonio Damasio (1994) has explained how this works in our brain and what disastrous consequences it has when the connections between the two are cut by damage to the brain, even when neither of the functions in themselves has been affected. Thus the acquisition process also necessarily always has both a cognitive and an emotional side, or more broadly spoken: a *content* and an *incentive* side.

Consequently, all learning always includes three dimensions which must always be considered if an understanding or analysis of a learning situation is to be adequate: the content dimension of knowledge, understandings, skills, abilities, attitudes and the like; the incentive dimension of emotion, feelings, motivation and volition; and the social dimension of interaction, communication and cooperation – all of which are embedded in a societally situated context. The learning processes and dimensions may be illustrated by Figure 3.1.

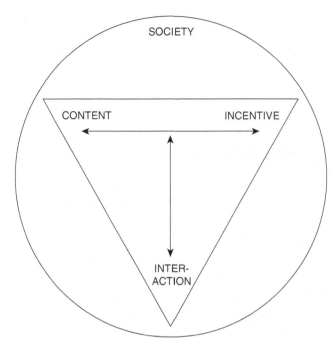

Figure 3.1   The basic processes and dimensions of learning

A model of workplace learning

When it comes to the issue of workplace learning the point of departure should be taken in what characterizes workplaces and working life as a space for learning. If this is seen in relation to the learning triangle, it is obvious that it has mainly to do with the interaction dimension. The workplace also includes management, colleagues, the organization and its relations and role in society. From this point of view a triangle depicting the workplace as a learning space and matching the learning triangle can be drawn in the following way (Jørgensen and Warring, 2003; Illeris et al., 2004).

Parallel to the division of the acquisition process of learning the workplace environment also contains two fundamentally different elements which can be termed the technical-organizational learning environment and the social-cultural learning environment. The technical-organizational learning environment is about matters such as work content and division of labour, the opportunities for autonomy and using qualifications, the possibilities of social interaction and the extent to which the work is a strain on the employees. The social-cultural learning environment concerns social groupings and processes at the workplace and matters such as traditions, norms and values and covers communities of work, cultural communities and political communities.

The third dimension of the learning environment is about the interaction between the environment as a whole and the learners. It is, so to say, the same interaction process as the one which is involved in the learning triangle, but seen as part of the learning life and not as part of the learners as individuals. It involves in general such elements as the workers' or employees' social and cultural backgrounds, their actual life situations, and their future perspectives, and specifically in relation to the single learner such elements as their family background and school and work experience.

In the book entitled *Learning in Working Life* (Illeris et al., 2004), these dimensions were merged with the learning triangle into what was termed 'a double perspective on learning in working life' in the 'holistic model' shown in Figure 3.2.

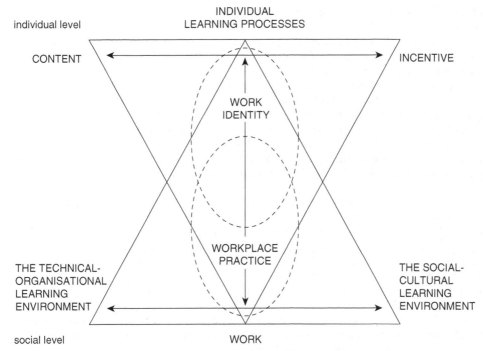

Figure 3.2   Learning in working life (after Illeris et al. 2004, p. 69)

It should be noted that in addition to the dimensions of the two triangles each of them here also includes a central focus area round the meeting point of the double arrows. In the learning triangle this focus area is the learner's personal *identity*, which psychologically is where all that is learnt sums up into the individual experience of 'who I am' and 'how I am experienced by others' (Illeris, 2003, 2007) and especially the parts of the identity which comprise the personal relations to working life and therefore constitute the 'work identity' (Andersen et al., 1994). In the workplace environment triangle the central focus area is the *workplace practice*, which comprises the work activities including all the tools and artefacts, the work patterns and personal and social relations, positions, power conditions, etc.

In this way the model shows that the essential general workplace learning takes place in the interaction between workplace practice and the learner's work identity – and it is also this learning that takes on the character of competence development (to which I shall return later). But there is also in the model space for less essential learning processes that more or less circumvent these core fields, such as the acquisition of certain technical skills that can take place in a more limited interaction anchored between the workplace's technical-organizational learning environment and mainly the content dimension of the learner's acquisition, but naturally also can be related to the model's other elements to a greater or lesser extent.

Different approaches to workplace learning

On the more concrete level, there are a number of approaches to what is central in connection with the understanding of workplace learning. In line with a classic learning understanding, most of these approaches place main emphasis on the individual acquisition process, corresponding to the horizontal double arrow at the top of the model in Figure 3.2.

This applies, in the first place, to the so-called industrial sociological approach, which in particular has interested itself in the qualification requirements the work has of the employees and how the qualifications are developed, now also including to a high degree what has been termed the 'process independent' or later the 'generic qualifications'.

Next, it applies as point of reference to the management-anchored approach also, which is termed 'organizational learning'. Americans Chris Argyris and Donald Schön have been key figures here for a generation, and they have emphasized, *inter alia*, that the employees' learning is crucial to the development of the enterprises and that a distinction must be made between single-loop learning, which remains within, and double-loop learning, which exceeds the existing frames of understanding (cf. Argyris and Schön, 1978, 1996; Argyris, 1992).

Finally, it also refers to the approach that has roots in general adult education, mostly to individual learning when it, typically on a humanistic basis, interests itself in the employees' experience and interest in learning (cf. e.g. Weil and McGill, 1989; Marsick and Watkins, 1990; Boud and Garrick, 1999; Billett, 2001; Ellström, 2001; Evans et al., 2002; Rainbird et al., 2004).

In contrast are the approaches that very largely focus on the workplace as learning environment and the development or 'learning' of the workplace, i.e. on the bottom horizontal double arrow in Figure 3.2. This primarily concerns the approach that goes under the name of 'the learning organisation'. This is originally a branching out of the organizational understanding of learning, but with the decisive difference that here the focus is on what is understood as the organization's 'learning' that is made independent as something different and more than the sum of the employees' learning. A key work here is Peter Senge's book about 'the fifth discipline' (Senge, 1990). It must be clear, however, that with the learning concept which has been introduced here one cannot say that the organization can learn – and much of what is marketed under the term 'the learning organization' in my opinion has more to do with management and sometimes smart formulations than with learning.

Also the approach that was launched with the book, *Situated Learning*, by Jean Lave and Etienne Wenger (Lave & Wenger, 1991) and later continued by Wenger in *Communities of Practice* (Wenger, 1998), must be said to be mainly oriented towards the workplace as the focal point of learning. This is the case despite the fact that to a large extent it has its roots in the Russian cultural-historical tradition and Vygotsky's understanding of learning, which is quite classically oriented towards the individual acquisition process. In Lave and Wenger's work, it seems almost to be the case that when the individual has first entered a community of practice, by means of a learning process he or she will automatically move from 'legitimate peripheral participation' towards a more central and competent position. A more individual oriented formulation of Vygotsky's approach can, however, be found in Finnish Yrjö Engeström, who, though he may work with learning in organizations, does so with a high degree of focus on the individuals (cf. e.g. Engeström, 2009).

I am thus on the way towards the third major approach to workplace learning, namely the approach that primarily focuses on the interaction between the social and the individual level, i.e. on the vertical double arrow in the middle of the model in Figure 3.3. Here there is reason to note the approach that has its roots in the 'critical theory' of the German-American so-called Frankfurt school. The best-known representative of this school is the German sociologist and philosopher Jürgen Habermas (1984–87) – but in relation to workplace learning other names are more important (although they have generally published only in German). They have focused mainly on the social conditions and their significance for the consciousness formation of the individual, in particular with Oskar Negt's work concerning 'Sociological Imagination and Exemplary Learning' (Negt, 1968; cf. Illeris, 2007). But an important contribution is also to be found in the work of Ute Volmerg concerning the significance of the employees' opportunities for organizing their own work, for communication with others at work and for applying the qualifications they have acquired as the three decisive focal points for their learning possibilities in working life (Volmerg, 1976). Finally there should be mention of Birgit Volmerg et al.'s study of 'The Life World of Private Enterprises', i.e. the way in which the employees seek and utilize the possibilities of the workplace for a free space to set their own agenda (Volmerg et al., 1986; Leithäuser, 2000).

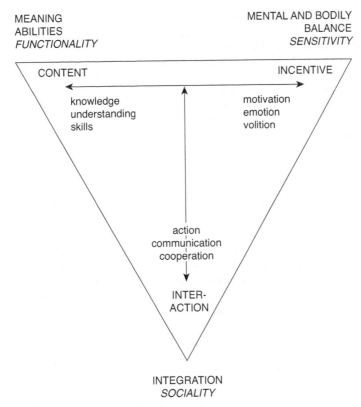

MEANING
ABILITIES
FUNCTIONALITY

MENTAL AND BODILY
BALANCE
SENSITIVITY

CONTENT

knowledge
understanding
skills

INCENTIVE

motivation
emotion
volition

action
communication
cooperation

INTER-
ACTION

INTEGRATION
SOCIALITY

Figure 3.3   Learning as competence development

It is basically also this type of approach I have followed in my work although I simultane-ously include the individual acquisition process to a high degree (Andersen et al., 1994, 1996; Illeris et al., 2004; Illeris, 2005, 2007, 2009c).

General features of workplace learning

If one tries to cut across all these approaches, it is possible in general to extract a number of possibilities and problems that especially characterize workplace learning. Quite fundamen-tally, a huge amount of learning takes place in direct connection with the performance of the work, and as mentioned earlier, the employees typically experience that this learning is of greater importance for them than learning in institutionalized education (CEDEFOP, 2003). Viewed from the outside it must, however, be maintained that this learning is accidental in nature and that it is usually narrow and without theoretical foundation.

However, by systematically building up a learning-oriented environment this learning can be strengthened considerably – this is the main idea behind the approaches called 'organizational learning' and 'the learning organization', although they do not agree when it comes to the rela-tion between the individual and the organization. Nonetheless the risk will still remain of the learning obtaining a certain accidental flavour and an inadequate structure and systematics. Moreover, there is a tendency for the employees who are already best qualified to profit more from this procedure. But it is also possible to try to counteract this by introducing such types of activities as self-directed groups, projects or action learning programmes for all employees (cf. Illeris et al., 2004).

Another possibility – which can very well be combined with organizational learning – is to aim at targeted learning measures in close connection with the work. This can take place by means of personal backing for the individual employee in the form of instruction, pedagogic mentoring, partner guidance, mentor schemes or coaching, through broadly based support from so-called 'ambassadors', 'super users' or 'gardeners', who are especially used in the ICT field, or through access to consultant assistance, and it can take place through teaching activities in close connection with the work. All of this can be backed up by means of regular staff development interviews or the like (cf. Illeris et al., 2004).

Finally, there can be emphasis on more general measures, such as internal or external networks and experience groups or job exchange and job rotation schemes, where there is also a possibility for involving all staff organizationally (cf. Illeris et al., 2004).

Under all circumstances there are three important issues that exist to one extent or another. The first is that workplace learning, to an even higher degree than learning by means of institutionalized education, has a tendency to especially favour those who already have the best education (the so-called "Matthew effect": "For whoever has to him shall be given and he shall be caused to be in abundance" (Matthew 13:12). The second is that the necessary work will always receive higher priority than learning-oriented measures. The third is that learning measures can have a disturbing effect on the targeted work which is the purpose of the workplace.

These issues can be dealt with to a certain degree by workplace learning being combined with courses and education programmes, for example such as those that take place in the so-called alternating education programmes in the apprentice and professional fields where there is alternation between school and work experience periods.

Learning as competence development

In relation to the workplace it is today also important to discuss how such learning in theory and practice can obtain the qualities of what is termed 'competence development' as this to a great extent seems to be what could be a main advantage of learning in more or less direct connection to the workplace. I shall start this discussion by examining, in slightly more detail, some general matters to do with each of the three learning dimensions, namely what we generally – consciously or unconsciously – aim at achieving within each of the three dimensions when we learn something, and what the overall result could be.

As already mentioned, the content dimension is about what we learn. In this dimension the learner's *knowledge, understanding, skills* and generally his/her ways of dealing with life are developed and through this we attempt to generate *meaning,* i.e. a coherent understanding of the different matters in existence (cf. e.g. Bruner, 1990; Mezirow, 1990, 1991; Wenger, 1998), and also to develop *abilities* that enable us to tackle the practical challenges of life. To the extent that we succeed in this endeavour, we develop out *functionality* as a whole, i.e. our capacity to function appropriately in the various contexts in which we are involved. This appropriateness is directly linked to our placing and interests in the current situation in relation to our qualifications and future perspectives, but as such quite general, just as learning as a whole is related to the survival possibilities of the individual and the species.

As mentioned before, it is very largely the content dimension that learning research traditionally has concerned itself with, and it is also this dimension that is in direct focus when one speaks about learning in everyday language. But the learning triangle points to other matters being at stake in connection with learning.

Acquisition has also an incentive dimension covering the motivational, the emotional and the volitional – or what can be summed up as the motive forces or engagement of learning. This dimension is concerned with mobilization of the mental energy required by learning, and we fundamentally engage ourselves in this mobilization in order to constantly maintain our *mental and bodily balance.* In so doing, through this dimension we simultaneously develop our *sensitivity* in relation to ourselves and our environment.

These two dimensions are activated simultaneously and in an integrated fashion by impulses from the interactive process between the individual and the environment. The content that is learned is therefore, as previously mentioned, always marked or 'obsessed' by the nature of the mental engagement that has mobilized the mental energy necessary for the learning process to take place. On the other hand, the incentive basis is also always influenced by the content with which the learning is concerned. For instance, a new understanding or an improved skill alters our emotional and motivational and also perhaps our volitional patterns.

Learning psychology has traditionally studied the acquisition of content independent of the incentive dimension – but there have also been learning researchers who have strongly emphasized the connection, for example Lev Vygotsky (1986 [1934]) and Hans Furth (1987), and this has later been conclusively supported by brain research, e.g. Antonio Damasio (1994).

Finally, there is the interaction dimension of learning, which is concerned with the individual's interaction with his/her social and material environment on two levels: on the one hand the close, social level in which the interactive situation is placed, for example in a classroom or a working group, and on the other hand the general societal level that establishes the premises for the interaction.

This dimension promotes the individual's *integration* in relevant social contexts and communities and by this contributes to the development of the learner's *sociality*, i.e. ability to become engaged and function appropriately in various forms of social interaction between people. The development itself of sociality, however, takes place through the two dimensions of the acquisition process and is thereby marked by what concerns the interactive process and the nature of our relationship to it.

It is now possible to elaborate the learning triangle in Figure 3.1 into a new triangle as shown in Figure 3.3 by entering the signal words used to qualify the nature of each of the three dimensions, and outside each of the angles to place the key words for what we aim at (upright) and what we generate (italics). What then emerges is that in our learning as a whole we attempt to develop meaning, skills, mental and bodily balance and social and societal integration, and in this way we simultaneously develop our functionality, sensitivity and sociality.

Such a general characterization means that learning as a whole can promote the development of what in modern parlance is called the learner's *competence*. Or the other way around: that if learning is to be in the nature of competence development, it must contribute to the generation of relevant functionality, sensitivity and sociality which are the main general characteristics of competences. The widespread popularity of this concept is precisely due to its embracing the total scope of the learning dimensions – in contrast to the more limited focus on the content dimension of traditional educational thinking.

Workplace learning and competence development

It is not so very many years ago that competence was mainly a formal and legal matter, something that gave a person a legal right to make decisions in a certain area, especially in the public administration. However, over the last two decades the use of the word has permeated the educational area, working life, management and politics as a modern expression for what a person is actually able to do or achieve.

Thus, in recent years the concept of competences has taken a central position and more or less displaced the concept of qualifications – and this is not merely a chance or indifferent linguistic innovation. On the contrary, it could be said that this linguistic change has pointed to some features which are significant for contemporary learning demand. A very useful definition of the concept, which draws attention precisely to how it surpasses terms as abilities, skills and qualifications, has been given by a Danish social psychologist and member of the former 'Danish Competence Council':

> The concept of competence refers [...] to a person's being qualified in a broader sense. It is not merely that a person masters a professional area, but also that the person can apply this professional knowledge – and more than that, apply it in relation to the requirements inherent in a situation which perhaps in addition is uncertain and unpredictable. Thus competence also includes the person's assessments and attitudes, and ability to draw on a considerable part of his/her more personal qualifications (Jørgensen, 1999: 4).

Competence is thus a unifying concept that integrates everything it takes in order to perform in a given situation or context. The concrete qualifications are incorporated in the competence rooted in the personality – or to be more accurate, the work identity – and one may generally also talk of the competence of organizations and nations, including the pattern of personal competences and how they work together.

Where the concept of qualifications historically has its point of departure in requirements for specific knowledge and skills, and to an increasing degree has been used for pointing out that this knowledge and these skills have underlying links and roots in personality, the perception in the concept of competence has, so to speak, been turned upside down. In this concept, the point of departure lies at the personal level in relation to certain contexts, and the more specific qualifications are something that can be drawn in and contribute to realization of the competence. So the concept of qualifications took its point of departure in the individual elements, the individual qualifications, and gradually developed towards a more unified perception, whereas the concept of competence starts with a unity, e.g. the type of person or organization it takes to solve a task or fulfil a job, and on the basis of this points out any possible different qualifications necessary.

It is characteristic that the concept of competence does not, like the concept of qualifications, have its roots in industrial sociology (cf. Braverman, 1974), but in organizational psychology and modern management thinking. This has made it more adequate in relation to modern working life, but it has also given it a dimension of 'smartness' which makes it easier to 'sell' politically and tend toward a superficiality which in this context seems to characterize large parts of the management orientation (cf. Argyris, 2000). Some problems have also developed because a number of national and supranational bodies have taken over the concept and sought to implement it as a tool to govern educational institutions. Wide-ranging work has been initiated to define a number of competences that the various education programmes should aim at and to make these measurable in order to make it possible to judge whether the efforts succeed (cf. Illeris, 2004, 2009c).

However, at the same time it is difficult to deny that the concept of competence captures something central in the current situation of learning and qualification. It is ultimately concerned with how a person, an organization or a nation is able to handle a relevant, but often unforeseen and unpredictable problematic situation, because we know with certainty that late modern development constantly generates new and unknown problems, and the ability to respond openly and in an appropriate way to new problematic situations is crucial in determining who will manage in the globalized market society.

So I find it very important to maintain a broad and holistic understanding of competence both on the general level and *vis-à-vis* a technocratic understanding which is rapidly becoming the horse dragging a carriage of narrow economically oriented control interests that empty the concept of the liberating potential springing from the place of the competences as relevant contemporary mediators between the societal challenges and individual ways of managing them.

The concept of competence can thus be used as a point of departure for a more nuanced understanding of what learning efforts today are about – with a view of reaching a theoretically based and practically tested proposal concerning how up-to-date competence development can be realized for different people in accordance with their possibilities and needs, both within and outside of institutionalized education programmes. Such an approach has, in my opinion, far better and more well-founded possibilities for contributing to real competence development, at the individual level as well as the societal level, than the measuring and comparing approach that has been mentioned above. However, it will to a much higher degree be oriented towards experiments and initiatives at practice level than the top-down control approach inherent in the measuring models.

Quite concretely it is about the fact that competence development may be promoted in environments where learning takes place in connection with a (retrospective) actualization of relevant experience and contexts, that (at the same time) interplay between relevant activities and interpretation of these activities in a theoretical conceptual framework, and a (prospective) reflection and perspective, i.e. a pervasive perspective in relation to the participants' life or biography, linked with a meaning and conception-oriented reflection and a steady alternation between the individual and the social levels within the framework of a community (cf. Illeris, 2004).

It is precisely these qualities that make competences so important and attractive in the modern ever-changing world, and at the same time constitutes an immense challenge to education and training of any kind. How can people be educated or trained to function appropriately in situations that are unknown at the time of the acquisition?

This is actually a question that undermines a lot of traditional educational thinking which starts by formulating precise objectives and then tries to deduce educational measures from this. Fundamentally, it must be realized that competences are not something that can be produced like commodities, but precisely something that must be *developed* in and by the person, hence the concept of 'competence development'.

In general it is obvious that the concept of competences captures something that is essential in relation to education and training today, precisely because it relates to how a person, an organization or a nation is able to manage in the constantly changing globalized market society. Thus, the societal changes that fostered this concept and other linked concepts such as 'the learning society', 'the learning organization' and 'lifelong learning' imply a new conception of the relation between learning and education/training with increased focus on informal learning possibilities outside the educational institutions in daily life and in working life especially.

But to capture the impact of this change of perspective it is not enough just to refer to 'practice learning' or 'workplace learning' as has often been the case. It is obvious that the school and education system will still be the 'State Apparatus' which is constructed to be the fundamental public means of providing the competences demanded. Moreover, it will inevitably – also in the future – be in the practical and economic interests of both the private and the public sector that as many competences as possible should be developed outside the workplace and without placing a strain on the economy and daily work conditions of companies and organizations.

Therefore competence development cannot be a means of ensuring savings on public education budgets, which some politicians seem to imagine. On the contrary, it is a challenge demanding increased cooperation between education and training institutions and private as well as public workplaces. In all likelihood this will lead to increased costs for both parties if the promises of adequate and up-to-date competence development are to be met – which is regarded as a key factor in future competitiveness.

Finally, it must also be stressed that a decisive factor in all this will be that competence development programmes are set up in accordance and cooperation with the persons and groupings that are to implement the competences. Whereas qualifications to some extent could be understood and dealt with as "objective" qualities, it is inherent in competences that they include personal and collective motivations, emotions and engagement, and their practical value to a great extent is dependent on a positive interest and attitude. From this point of view competence development could be an important democratizing factor in working life and society in general. But this is by no means always the case.

So, it is a persistent question whether the great commitment to the idea of competence development will be able to meet the positive prospects that it most certainly implies. Like other keywords from the same vocabulary, the concept of competence development seems to have a double impact and to demonstrate tension between a very promising and useful interpretation of significant demands of modern societies and a buzzword, which, behind the tempting surface, hides new smart means of human and economic exploitation of labour (Illeris, 2009b).

REFERENCES

Andersen, V., Illeris, K., Kjærsgaard, C., Larsen, K., Olesen, H. S., and Ulriksen, L. (1994) *Qualifications and Living People.* Roskilde: The Adult Education Research Group, Roskilde University.

Andersen, V., Illeris, K., Kjærsgaard, C., Larsen, K., Olesen, H. S., and Ulriksen, L. (1996) *General Qualification*. Roskilde: The Adult Education Research Group, Roskilde University.

Argyris, C. (1992) *On Organizational Learning*. Cambridge, MA: Blackwell.

Argyris, C. (2000) *The Next Challenge in Organizational Learning: Leadership and Change*. Paper presented at the Learning Lab Denmark Opening Conference, Copenhagen, 6 November.

Argyris, C. and Schön, D. (1978) *Organizational Learning: A Theory of Action Perspective*. Reading, MA: Addison-Wesley.

Argyris, C. and Schön, D. (1996) *Organizational Learning II – Theory, Method, Practice*. Reading, MA: Addison-Wesley.

Ausuble, D. P. (1968) *Educational Psychology: A Cognitive View*. New York: Holt, Rinehart and Winston.

Bauman, Z. (1998) *Globalization: The Human Consequences*. Cambridge, UK: Polity Press.

Beck, U. (1992 [1986]) *Risk Society: Towards a New Modernity*. London: Sage.

Beckett, D. and Hager, P. (2002) *Life, Work and Learning: Practice in Postmodernity*. London: Routledge.

Billett, S. (2001) *Learning in the Workplace: Strategies for Effective Practice*. Crows Nest, NSW: Allen & Unwin.

Boud, D. and Garrick, J. (eds) (1999) *Understanding Learning at Work*. London: Routledge.

Braverman, H. (1974) *Labor and Monopoly Capital*. New York: Monthly Review Press.

Bruner, J. (1990) *Acts of Meaning*. Cambridge, MA: Harvard University Press.

CEDEFOP (European Centre for the Development of Vocational Training) (2003) *Lifelong Learning: Citizens' Views*. Luxembourg: Office for Official Publications of the EU.

Damasio, A. R. (1994) *Descartes' Error: Emotion, Reason and the Human Brain*. New York: Grosset/Putnam.

Ellström, Per-Erik (2001) Integrating Learning and Work: Conceptual Issues and Critical Conditions. *Human Resource Development Quarterly*, 4: 421–436.

Engeström, Y. (2009) 'Expansive Learning: Toward an Activity-Theoretical Reconceptualization', in Knud Illeris (ed.), *Contemporary Theories of Learning*. London: Routledge.

EU Commission (2000) *Memorandum on Lifelong Learning*. Brussels: EU.

Evans, K., Hodkinson, P. and Unwin, L. (eds) (2002) *Working to Learn – Transforming Learning in the Workplace*. London: Kogan Page.

Furth, H. G. (1987) *Knowledge as Desire*. New York: Columbia University Press.

Garrick, J. (1998) *Informal Learning in the Workplace: Unmasking Human Resource Development*. London: Routledge.

Gergen, Kenneth, J. (1994) *Realities and Relationships*. Cambridge, MA: Howard University Press.

Giddens, A. (1990) *The Consequences of Modernity*. Stanford, CA: Stanford University Press.

Habermas, J. (1984–87 [1981]) *The Theory of Communicative Action*. Cambridge, UK: Polity Press.

Illeris, K. (2003) 'Learning, Identity and Self Orientation in Youth', *Young – Nordic Journal of Youth Research*, 4(11): 357–376.

Illeris, K. (2004) *Adult Education and Adult Learning*. Copenhagen: Roskilde University Press/Malabar, FL: Krieger Publishing.

Illeris, K. (2005) 'A Model for Learning in Working Life', *Journal of Workplace Learning* 8(16): 431–441.

Illeris, K. (2007) *How We Learn: Learning and Non-Learning in School and Beyond*. London: Routledge.

Illeris, K. (ed.) (2009a) *Contemporary Theories of Learning*. London: Routledge.

Illeris, K. (ed.) (2009b) *International Perspectives on Competence Development*. London: Routledge.

Illeris, K. (2009c) 'From Learning to Competence Development', in Knud Illeris (ed.) *International Perspectives on Competence Development*. London: Routledge.

Illeris, K. and Associates (2004) *Learning in Working Life*. Copenhagen: Roskilde University Press.

Jørgensen, C. H. and Warring, N. (2003) 'Learning in the Workplace: The Interplay Between Learning Environments and Biographical Learning Trajectories', in Christian Helms Jørgensen and Niels Warring (eds), *Adult Education and the Labour Market VII B*. Copenhagen: Roskilde University Press.

Jørgensen, Per Schultz (1999) 'Hvad er Kompetence?', [What is Competence?]. *Uddannelse*, 9, pp. 4–13.

Leithäuser, T. (2000) 'Subjectivity, Life World and Work Organization', in Knud Illeris (ed.), *Adult Education in the Perspective of the Learners*. Copenhagen: Roskilde University Press.

Marsick, V. J. and Watkins, K. E. (1990) *Informal and Incidental Learning in the Workplace*. London: Routledge.

Masuch, M. (1972) *Politische Ökonomie der Ausbildung*. [The Political Economy of Education]. Reinbek: Rowohlt.

Mezirow, J. (1990) 'How Critical Reflection Triggers Transformative Learning', in Jack Mezirow and Associates (eds), *Fostering Critical Reflection in Adulthood*. San Francisco, CA: Jossey-Bass.

Mezirow, J. (1991) *Transformative Dimensions of Adult Learning*. San Francisco, CA: Jossey-Bass.

Negt, O. (1968) *Soziologische Phantasie und Exemplarisches Lernen*. [Sociological Imagination and Exemplary Learning]. Frankfurt A.M.: Europäische Verlagsanstalt.

OECD (2000) *Knowledge Management in the Learning Society*. Paris: OECD. Centre for Educational Research and Innovation.

OECD (2001) *Cities and Regions in the New Learning Economy*. Paris: OECD. Centre for Educational Research and Innovation.

Piaget, J. (1952 [1936]) *The Origin of Intelligence in Children*. New York: International Universities Press.

Rainbird, H., Fuller, A. and Munro, A. (eds) (2004) *Workplace Learning in Context*. London: Routledge.

Senge, P. (1990) *The Fifth Discipline: The Art and Practice of the Learning Organization*. New York: Doubleday.

Volmerg, B., Senghaas-Knobloch, E. and Leithäuser, T. (1986) *Betriebliche Lebenswelt: Eine Sozialpsychologie industrieller Arbeitsverhältnisse.* [Life World at Work: A Social Psychology of Work Conditions in Industry]. Opladen: Westdeutscher Verlag.

Volmerg, U. (1976) 'Zur Verhältnis von Produktion und Sozialisation am Beispiel industrieller Lohnarbeit', in Thomas Leithäuser and Walter Heinz (eds), *Produktion, Arbeit, Sozialisation.* [Conditions of Production and Socialization in Industrial Wage Labour] Frankfurt a.M.: Suhrkamp.

Vygotsky, L. (1986 [1934]) *Thought and Language.* Cambridge, MA: MIT Press.

Weil, S. W. and McGill, I. (eds) (1989) *Making Sense of Experiential Learning: Diversity in Theory and Practice.* Buckingham: Open University Press.

Wenger, E. (1998) *Communities of Practice: Learning, Meaning and Identity.* Cambridge MA: Cambridge University Press.

4

Workplace Learning and the Organization

Alison Fuller and Lorna Unwin

INTRODUCTION

Any attempt to understand learning at work has to consider the wider context in which a particular workplace exists. The primary function of any workplace (in both the private and public sectors) is not learning, but the production of goods and services (Rainbird et al., 2004). Furthermore, organizations have to function within the boundaries of a broader political economy (Unwin et al., 2007; Hall and Soskice, 2001; Ashton, 2004). These factors influence the extent to which organizations feel they are more or less constrained in their approach to workforce development, including, for example, whether they should commit to long-term programmes such as apprenticeships. Such considerations pose considerable challenges to national vocational education and training (VET) systems which rely heavily on the sustained participation of employers. National systems are also faced with the challenges posed by the impact of globalization through, for example, such practices as relocating production from the developed to emerging economies. Brown et al. (2004) argue that policy-makers still have choices to make in the way they react to the strategies of businesses, including multinational companies (MNCs). For example, they suggest that, in Germany, globalization might be treated as a threat to its long-established dual system of apprenticeship, whereas the UK would see globalization as a rationale to further champion the need for flexible labour markets.

Research interest in learning at work has been accelerating over the past 20 years or so and its study engages researchers across the fields of work psychology, labour economics, labour process, organizational studies, human resource development/management and, more broadly, education and sociology. There are three main reasons for this growing attention: first, new forms of work organization have been viewed as potential catalysts for learning; second, the workplace is firmly recognized as a site for learning; and, third, governmental concern to increase workforce skills and capacity for innovation to compete in the global marketplace.

This chapter is organized in six sections in order to explore a range of themes raised by these factors. The first section focuses on the importance and nature of workplace context. The second section discusses the relevance of changing forms of work organization to understandings of learning at work. The third section concentrates on the workplace as a site for learning and introduces theorizations of workplace. This is followed in the fourth section by a discussion about the role of the individual, and in the fifth section by a focus on organizational learning. The final section provides a concluding discussion.

WORKPLACE LEARNING IN CONTEXT

The factors shaping the workplace are wide-ranging: they include the underpinning political and economic context, sectoral characteristics and institutional arrangements, as well as organizational features such as size, ownership, history and culture (Fuller et al., 2003). Conditions underpinning the workplace reflect the economic model employed by the state. In the case of advanced industrial countries this relates to the form of capitalism being pursued and the extent to which competitive trends in production are shifting patterns of work organization from and between Fordist and post-Fordist models (*inter alia* Ashton and Green, 1996; Brown et al., 2001; Ashton, 2004). The Anglo-Saxon model of capitalism, often characterized in terms of short-termism, skill polarization and flexible (often casualized) labour markets, has been linked to the prevalence of organizations in the UK that compete successfully within what Finegold and Soskice (1988) termed a 'low skills equilibrium' (see also, Keep and Mayhew, 1999).

Ashton (2004) distinguishes three different ways in which the relations between state, capital and labour are configured ('free market', 'corporatist' and 'developmental state'). He argues that these can be associated with the ways in which nation states create their VET systems and, by extension, the ways in which workplaces organize work and their production structures. The extent to which the state plays an interventionist/developmental state (e.g. Singapore), supportive/corporatist (e.g. Germany) or *laissez-faire/free market* (e.g. US, UK) role in the creation and shaping of the VET system, is seen, on one level, to reflect the model of capitalism in operation. On another level, it can be seen as an indicator of how far the state reaches into organizations themselves. For example, and in contrast with the US and UK, the state in Singapore:

> … retains a high degree of autonomy from both capital and labour … the power of capital is fragmented and does not form a coherent block that can exert continuous pressure on the government. Labour has been co-opted by the government into supporting the government's agenda (Ashton, 2004: 32).

Ashton goes on to explain that this agenda includes the will to create a virtuous economic circle generated through high added value industries, forms of production and work organization and facilitated by a highly skilled workforce. Focusing on the organizational level, Keep and Mayhew (1999) draw attention to the relationship between management decisions and employers' demand for skills. They distinguish between 'first order management decisions' relating to competitive strategy and product market, and 'second order management decisions' relating to work organization and job design. This focus is relevant to understanding the workplace, as the level and pattern of employers' demand for skills is an important influence on the nature and culture of the organization and, hence, how it is experienced by employees. The identification of product- (or relatedly service-) market strategy is also useful in that it draws attention to a dimension of decision-making with which all managements have to engage. However, the rationale for and nature of product-market decisions will be structured by the sector and organizational context within which they are operating. For example, sectors may set regulatory conditions with which organizations have to comply, and organizations themselves will be subject to the requirements of their owners.

In their study of workplace learning across eleven sectors of the UK economy, Felstead et al. (2009) highlighted the importance of locating workplaces (and their corresponding groups of workers) within their productive systems in order to build a much more holistic picture of the factors shaping the relationship between workplaces and learning. The concept of a productive system comprises all the constituent stages and structures of production (see Wilkinson, 2002). The stages of production (spread out across a horizontal axis) in a typical manufacturing plant, for example, would include the raw materials, the processes involved in turning those materials into products, the packaging of the products, the marketing and advertising required for display, the distribution and sale of the products, and, ultimately, the consumption of the products by customers. The structures of production (spread across a vertical axis) would start at the top with the owner of the plant (e.g. an MNC, government, or a family) and flow through such levels as 'head office', regional offices, departments, and so on. The more complex the ownership and activities of an organization, the more intricate will be their productive system. Felstead et al. (2009) argue that researchers who want to investigate workplace learning in relation to particular groups of workers need to locate those workers within the productive system of their organization in order to appreciate the extent to which their particular workplace has the discretion to create optimal conditions for learning. It may be, for example, that a particular workplace is under considerable pressure to meet certain targets, demonstrate it is meeting externally imposed quality assurance requirements, or is having to adapt changing demands from customers or a new owner.

FORMS OF WORK ORGANIZATION

A debate about 'high' and 'low' performing work organizations and what distinguishes them has grown out of broader analyses of trends in contemporary capitalism, and questioning of whether there has been a paradigm shift in the nature of contemporary economies (Lloyd and Payne, 2004). Visions associated with such a shift to a 'knowledge economy' (*inter alia* Guile, 2003; Foray and Lundvall, 1996; and Florida, 1995) include post-Fordism (Amin, 1994), flexible specialization (Piore and Sabel, 1984), and the information society (Castells, 1996). Such developments are seen to have occurred in response to increasing global competition and technological innovation particularly in the areas of information and communication technologies. In relation to competitive pressures, advanced industrial economies are viewed as vulnerable to the cheaper labour costs available in developing countries and so need to find new ways to compete based on high added-value production and services. The introduction of new technology is seen as key to increasing competitiveness and as providing opportunities for the reorganization of capital and labour to produce competitive edge over 'lower tech' rivals.

One strand of the academic debate has revolved around whether new forms of production are leading to the upskilling or deskilling of the workforce (Warhurst et al., 2004). Another is around employee management, particularly the extent to which new forms of working foster employee involvement and are: (a) central to improved organizational performance; and (b) are experienced as empowering and developmental by (sections of) the workforce. In this regard the debates relate, on the one hand, to the relationship between the organization of work and production, the way employees are managed and organizational outcomes and, on the other hand, to the nature of the workplace from the perspective of those who work in it. Butler et al. (2004) have reviewed the conceptual and empirical literature in these areas. In terms of the relationship between forms of work organization and performance the assumption is that a 'high performance management' approach will lead to improved organizational outcomes. As Butler et al. observe, there is little agreement about what specific practices constitute such a management model, but there is a growing consensus that it requires the implementation of 'clusters' or 'bundles' of practice (McDuffie, 1995). The goal of implementing such bundles of human resource management practices is to facilitate new forms of working which are associated with better organizational performance. Butler et al. explain:

> Here [in relation to work organisation] it is argued, there has been a trend towards production activities based on knowledge, cognition and abstract labour. The *sine qua non* of this aspect of the new model is team working, the medium whereby tacit knowledge shared amongst the work group is developed into explicit knowledge (Butler et al., 2004: 4).

It follows from the point made by Butler et al. that a workplace in which knowledge is distributed, shared, and jointly created requires a model of employee relations in which workers feel committed to a joint organizational purpose and enjoy a high level of trust within and between teams. The assumption is that under new technological and global conditions, organizations need to reconfigure their work processes and management styles so as to engender much greater emphasis on employee involvement, the development of higher levels of skill and knowledge creation, and their capacity to innovate.

A very different model of employee management is associated with workplaces organized along what are termed, 'Taylorist' lines, where knowledge is seen to reside at the level of management and technical specialists, and jobs are designed to maintain a highly fragmented division of labour. These ideas, based on the scientific management theories developed in the late nineteenth and early twentieth centuries by the American industrialist, F.W. Taylor, were widely adopted in the twentieth century in the UK and the US. Their aim is to increase workforce and production efficiency through economies of scale, which was pursued with vigour by Henry Ford in his car manufacturing plants. The term 'Fordism', came to epitomize a style of management and production that reduced work tasks to strict routines that could be performed day in, day out on assembly lines, and, hence, deskilled workers (see Braverman, 1974). This was the antithesis of the high-performance model's focus on the facilitation of problem solving and knowledge creation (key components of high performance) through flatter hierarchies, teamworking and highly involved and committed workers. In this model, the style of employee management and quality of worker–manager relations are perceived to have a significant influence on organizational performance.

In their review of the relationship between high-performance management practices and organizational performance, Ashton and Sung found strong empirical evidence to support the link: 'Put plainly, investment in these practices and the skills associated with them pays off on the bottom line' (2002: 17). However, while Butler et al.'s (2004) literature review of the area revealed support for Ashton and Sung's conclusion, they listed a number of caveats including: (a) ambiguity about the notion and practice of teamworking; (b) the direction of causality – is it that organizational success allows the introduction of such innovative HR practices?; and (c) the generalizability of the finding from its base in manufacturing industry to other sectors. Drawing on Wood (1999), they suggest: 'the debate is whether high-performance systems will *universally* outperform all other systems or whether the optimal system is relative to the circumstances of the firm' (Butler et al., 2004: 13, original emphasis). Put another way, the effectiveness of the high performance management model is likely to be contingent on the organizational context. An important aspect of this is the relationship between the organizational context and the way in which employees experience new forms of working.

The logic of the high-performance narrative assumes what is referred to as a unitarist understanding of the interests of managers and workers. In other words, that managers and workers share the same goals and assumptions about work. The strength of the labour process perspective has been its critique of this assumption. Hence, writers such as Smith and Thompson (1999) and Edwards (2001) acknowledge that new forms of working can lead to productivity and performance gains, but that these are achieved by finding new ways of squeezing more effort from the workforce. From this perspective the superficially benign rhetoric surrounding teamworking is reinterpreted as work intensification leading to increased stress and responsibility (usually without any accompanying improvement in remuneration). The (only) positive outcome following reorganization is that the worker still has a job. Rainbird et al.'s (2004) case study of a housing department confirms the relevance of this analysis to a group of public sector workers.

Much of the evidence base for the benefits of High Performance Working (HPW) is in the form of case studies. More longitudinal research is required to assess the extent to which causality can be established in the light of the considerable number of variables involved and the different interpretations of the actual practices themselves (see Wall and Wood, 2005; Vidal, 2007). Evaluation is also problematic due to the differing lists of the practices and their adoption in an *ad hoc* incremental manner (see EEF and CIPD, 2003). A distinction needs to be made between high-performance work organizations (HPWOs) and high-performance work practices. The former implies the integration of the practices as opposed to using them in a more piecemeal way, without the level of integration and mutually reinforcing properties found in HPWOs.

In summary then, the high-performance work organization literature has found that the way work is organized contributes to organizational performance and materially affects how the workplace is experienced by employees. The debate about the universality and direction of the high-performance workplace and its 'laggardly' low-performing counterpart continues. Much more research is needed on the workplace contexts in which different models of performance management have been introduced and how these are experienced by employees, and on methods for assessing the causal relationship between forms of management, employees' experiences and outcomes. The labour process/political economy perspective finds that the way work is organized can contribute to productivity gains and the development of skills, but has emphasized the (inevitably) negative experience of change for workers. This is an important antidote to the optimism of the high-performance management model, but it needs to be tested to distinguish how experiences of employee groups may differ and to uncover the organizational and sectoral conditions influencing their negative or more positive perceptions.

THE WORKPLACE AS A SITE FOR LEARNING

Given the stress in the previous sections on the importance of context, it is clear that workplaces create different types of environments for learning. In using the term 'workplace', we have to be aware of the changing ways in which people carry out their work. There has been growing research interest in recent years of the impact that new technologies are having on people's ability to work on the move (for example, on trains and from hotel rooms) and from their homes (see Felstead et al., 2005a). From the educational perspective, the workplace is increasingly being seen as an important and interesting location in which learning occurs. Theoretical and research interest revolves around questions of why, what and how people learn at work and the ways in which this differs from the learning that takes place in formal educational settings or other non-specialist educational settings, for example, in the community and in the home. This focus is drawing on social and situated theories of learning, and builds on the work of writers such as Lave and Wenger (1991) to theorize learning processes. The metaphor of 'learning as participation' reflects this conceptual perspective. Of particular interest to researchers (see *inter alia* Billett, 2001; and Fuller and Unwin, 2003, 2004) is the extent and type of opportunities to participate available in contrasting workplaces.

Learning at work arises from, and is embedded within, everyday workplace activity and the technical and social relations of production (Hoyrup and Elkjaer, 2006; Billett, 2001; Lave and Wenger, 1991). It can take many forms, including structured training away from the site of production, instruction on-the-job and the sharing of knowledge and techniques between colleagues. The degree of separation between on-the-job and off-the-job varies, with some workplaces blurring the boundary through the use of methods such as e-learning, portfolio building, and guided learning. External regulation (including 'license to practice') can promote learning, particularly in the professions (e.g. law, accountancy and medicine) where regular updating is required (Fuller et al., 2003).

For those whose primary interest is in theorizing learning, any putative relationship between learning and organizational performance is likely to be seen as of lesser concern, or at least as being problematic. The difficulties relate in particular to the methodological challenge of capturing and then measuring the effectiveness of workplace learning (Colley et al., 2003, Hodkinson and Hodkinson, 2004). More positively, Stasz (2001) suggests that finding ways of assessing what and how people learn at work could provide an important counterweight to the conventional economists' focus on quantifiable 'attainments', which ignore the contribution of learning through 'everyday' participation in work. Stasz (2001) suggests the potential of the socio-cultural perspective on learning to provide a new approach to assessing the effectiveness of learning at work. This approach provides a framework for capturing the complex pattern of social relations and organizational factors which influence how people learn at work and how this learning is valued, fostered or limited. The 'measurement challenge' has been taken up by Felstead et al., (2005b) who are seeking both to better understand the nature of workplace learning and its relationship to forms of work organization. They have recently developed a module of questions designed to capture 'everyday' workplace learning in a survey of adult workers. Their paper presents and discusses the promising results of this 'experiment' to generate quantitative data on how and the extent to which different groups of employees learn at, and through participation in the social relations of work.

In recent years, learning theorists with backgrounds including cultural historical activity theory (e.g. Engeström) and cognitive anthropology (e.g. Lave), as well as education, have been developing what may be summarized as a 'social theory of learning'. An important motive underpinning this effort has been dissatisfaction with cognitive and behaviourist theories (Beckett and Hager, 2002). Engeström (2004), for example, indicates that cognitivist explanations for the development of expertise are grounded in assumptions of individualism (the individual as autonomous learner) and stability (the acquisition of codified and stable bodies of knowledge and skills). Following Lave and Wenger (1991), he goes on to argue that the 'proper unit of analysis of skilled human activity is a community of practice rather than an isolated individual' (ibid., p. 147). Lave and Wenger's work has challenged conventional learning theories in at least two important ways. In using the insights gained from research in to apprentice learning, they have used the metaphor of 'participation' to draw attention to the importance of learning processes and the umbilical link between learning and identity formation. In so doing, they question the conventional view of learning as product, where individuals acquire 'packages' of skills and knowledge.

Second, their analysis of apprentice learning drew attention to the social and relational character of the learning process. Hence, they argued that newcomers become mainstream members of a 'community of practice' (e.g. workforce, sport club, hobby group) by having the opportunity to learn through participating in the social relations of the community. For Lave and Wenger, then, the 'proper unit of analysis' becomes the community of practice, consisting of the social relations of production, in which learning by and through the collective, is embedded. Eraut (2000, 2004; Eraut et al., 2000) has also argued strongly for a situated learning perspective that conceives learning as a process which is embedded within the activities, tasks and social relations that constitute social settings (such as the workplace). He has pointed out that from the situated learning perspective the idea of learning transfer between settings is problematic. He argues that explicit support should be given to people (e.g. newly qualified professionals) entering the workforce to help them contextualize the knowledge gained in one setting (e.g. specialist educational institution) in the new setting (e.g. the workplace).

Conceiving learning as a social process is powerful not only because it can account for learning which takes place in diverse settings but also because it provides a basis for understanding learning at the collective level. This is particularly important in relation to studies of workplace learning where the extent and quality of the opportunities for participation (learning) available are influenced by the character and structure of the social relations being produced and reproduced by the organizational context.

Fuller and Unwin (2004) have characterized this diversity of environments in the form of an 'expansive restrictive continuum' which encompasses approaches to work organization and to workplace pedagogical practices. Their continuum (see Table 4.1) identifies a set of features that, when taken together, indicate the extent to which a workplace can be said to sit more towards one end of the expansive-restrictive range than the other.

It can be seen from Table 4.1 that the continuum provides a framework for analyzing and critiquing the nature of workplaces as learning environments. It presents two broad categories of expansive and restrictive features: (a) those that arise from understandings about organizational context and culture (e.g. job design, organization of work, and distribution of knowledge and skills; and (b) those which relate to understandings of how employees learn through different forms of participation. As such, the framework provides a broader conceptualization of participation than that described by Lave and Wenger (1991) as it foregrounds both pedagogical and organizational features as being of relevance to the creation of expansive and restrictive learning environments.

More expansive learning environments are ones that allow for 'substantial horizontal, cross-boundary activity, dialogue and problem-solving' (Fuller and Unwin, 2004: 136), and which

Table 4.1 Characteristics of workplaces as learning environments

Expansive	Restrictive
Participation in different communities of practice is encouraged – job/team boundaries can be crossed	Participation restricted to immediate work team/area – boundary crossing discouraged
Primary community of practice has shared 'participative memory'	Primary community of practice operates without reference to cumulative expertise
Vision of workplace learning – career progression	Short-termism – get the job done
Recognition of and support for workers as learners – newcomers (including trainees) given time to become full members of the community	Workers seen only as productive units – fast transition from newcomer/trainee to fully productive worker
Workforce development used as vehicle for aligning goals of the organization and of the individual	Workforce development used only to tailor individual capability to organizational goals
Skills widely distributed though workplace – multi-dimensional concept of expertise	Polarized distribution of skills – knowledge/expertise regarded as being confined to key workers
Planned time off-the-job for reflection and deeper learning beyond immediate job requirements	All training on-the-job and limited to immediate job requirements
Managers given time to support workforce development and facilitate workplace learning	Managers restricted to controlling workforce and meeting targets
Workers given discretion to make judgements and contribute to decision-making	Discretion limited to key workers – no employee involvement in workplace decisions

generate multi-dimensional, heterogeneous and reflexive forms of expertise. In contrast, more restrictive environments have little diversity. Participation in learning is limited to a narrow range of homogeneous tasks, knowledges and locations. In these circumstances, learners acquire confined, hierarchical and unreflexive forms of expertise. Furthermore, restrictive environments are associated with the concept of learning as a top-down process, in which legitimate knowledge is transmitted to novices by designated 'experts'.

In an expansive environment, effective pedagogy (on-the-job) treats learning as part of work, supported by supervisory and managerial processes such as mentoring and coaching, and embedded within appraisal and other review procedures. Fuller and Unwin (2004: 127) argue that '*expansive* rather than *restrictive* environments foster learning at work and the integration of personal and organizational development'. Thus, expansive environments do not separate personal and organizational goals, but see them as integrated within a symbiotic relationship.

THE ROLE OF THE INDIVIDUAL

The previous section emphasized the importance of context to our understanding of workplace learning and the ways in which workplaces create different types of learning environment. Those environments are, of course, shaped by the individuals who work in them, just as much as they, in turn, are affected by the context. The actions of each individual in the workplace will be partly influenced by their life history and their prior experiences in and outside work. Each individual will, therefore, exert their individual agency in terms of how far they decide to participate in (and help to shape) the opportunities that the workplace offers to them (see Field and Malcolm, 2006; Billett, 2004; Hodkinson and Hodkinson, 2004). The recognition of the role of individual agency should not, however, be seen as existing in tension with the contextual perspective, but rather to remind us that the behaviour of human beings cannot be taken for granted.

Fuller and Unwin (2004) argue that every individual has, and has had, access to a unique set of learning opportunities that comprise what they term, a 'learning territory'. Each territory is divided into 'regions'. For example, one region of an individual's learning territory would cover their classroom-based learning experiences and qualifications, whilst another would cover their learning in a social environment (for example, as a member of a sports team or a neighbourhood club). It follows, therefore, that the workplace will be a key region for those employees in some form of organized work (paid or unpaid). For employees working in a very restrictive workplace environment, there may be a considerable disconnect between their learning regions as they may find they cannot utilize their true capabilities in the workplace region. These ideas suggest that managers and supervisors in workplaces should be aware that they may be ignoring their employees' skills and knowledge through workplace practices that render them invisible.

The dangers of treating employees as a homogeneous group who can be expected to respond in a certain way to managerial expectation are highlighted in Kakavelakis et al.'s (2008) study of the training of sales staff in a chain of private fitness clubs in the UK. All new sales staff are sent on a five-day training course to learn how to sell annual gym membership to the general public. The researchers found that, despite the strict demands from their trainers to follow the company's sales rules, several of the trainees refused to accept or use what they saw as 'hard sell' routines. They regarded these techniques as unethical, but also inefficient as a means of persuasion. Kakavelakis et al. argue that one explanation for this reaction lies with the dispositions of the individual sales staff. Hence, those sales staff who came to the course with prior experience gained in a more ethical or 'service' based sales environment rejected the techniques being pushed on the course.

As the above example illustrates, training (whether on or off-the-job) has to be responsive to the trainees' existing expertise and professional values. It has long been known that off-the-job training has variable success, depending on the perceived relevance and on the extent to which employees feel they have been 'sent' for either 'punishment' or 'reward' reasons. In recent years, e-learning (broadly defined as the use of connected Information and Communication Technologies) has been promoted as a way to enable employees to participate in additional learning in ways that are more convenient for them and their employers, and for widening access to learning in the workplace. Wright (2006) has argued, for example, that in relation to the National Health Service (NHS) in the UK, involvement in e-learning could help to 'anchor' the learner in workplaces that are highly dynamic, stressful and fragmented. The use of 'virtual tutors' and mechanisms such as e-portfolios and blogs would make it easier for learners to record evidence for accredited courses and to relate to other learners through virtual communities of practice. The increased availability and use of ICTs in the workplace and in everyday life may mean that employees are increasingly more likely to accept e-learning than in the past. Interestingly, in terms of workplace practices to promote well-being, teleworking (using technology to work more flexibly, including from home) has been shown to be the most commonly used (Fauth, 2007).

Yet research shows that e-learning has not been used for work-based learning as widely as was forecast. There is evidence that learner satisfaction correlates strongly with the quality of materials and support, but research sample sizes are regarded as too small for robust conclusions to be made about e-learning's overall effectiveness (Lain and Aston, 2005). For e-learning to become more widely used and to increase an individual's effectiveness, it has to be integrated with wider management and business strategies in the same way as any approach to workplace learning (see Wynarczyk, 2005).

ORGANIZATIONAL LEARNING

Taking an organizational perspective raises the question of how workplaces can be reconfigured to foster more effective 'organizational learning' (*inter alia* Argyris and Schon, 1978; Marsick and Watkins, 1990). The focus on organizational learning links to the assumption touched on earlier, that that there is a (positive) association between certain forms of work organization, learning and improved organizational outcomes. We suggest that an approach which seeks to combine insights from a social learning theory with a socio-cultural approach to organizational analysis could provide a fruitful way of re-conceptualizing the workplace as site for both performance and learning.

Originating in organizational psychology and management, the concept of organizational learning is highly relevant to this discussion in that, potentially, it helps to build conceptual bridges between learning in the workplace and organizational performance. It also foregrounds the collective nature of workplace activity which echoes the earlier discussion of learning as a collective process:

> Most contemporary researchers define *learning as organisational* to the extent that it is undertaken by members of an organisation to achieve organisational purposes, takes place in teams or other small groups, is distributed widely throughout the organisation and embeds its outcomes in the organisation's system, structures and culture (Boreham and Morgan, 2004: 308).

Influential organization theorists such as Argyris and Schön (1974, 1978) and Marsick and Watkins (1990) have directly addressed the question of what kinds of learning people engage in at work and the extent to which this learning is 'effective'. The well-known distinction made by Argyris and Schön is between single and double loop learning. In the former, the learner (worker) simply reacts and adapts to organizational change, whereas in the latter, the learner uses reflection to engage with change to develop novel solutions or to create new knowledge. Engeström (2001) has built on the work of organizational theorists, including Argyris and Schön, as well as cultural historical activity theory to develop his expansive theory of organizational learning. The important insight contained in Engeström's argument is the connection he makes between new ways of configuring the social relations of production and new forms of (organizational) learning. In this regard, the hallmark of organizations (or work groups) exhibiting expansive learning is the fostering of innovative collective endeavour achieved by bringing together people with different disciplinary and professional backgrounds to address (common) problems. Expansive organizational learning has been achieved where work practices and procedures have been transformed. Such transformations are embedded in, and evidenced by, the group's production of new tools, concepts and processes to respond (more effectively) to the situations that were seen as problematic.

In some similarity with the concept of high performance management (which assumes more effective organizational learning), the concept of organizational learning also calls for critique. First, it is overly reliant on a benign view of management – employee relations and on the idea that workers throughout an organization or work group have or want to have shared interests and purposes. There has also been relatively little elaboration of what the learning processes actually consist (what is learned); how learning processes are distributed throughout the workforce, and how they are experienced by (different groups) of employees. Put simply, there is a need for more detailed studies: (a) into the contested nature of organizational learning; (b) how organizational learning takes place; and (c) for research which gives voice to the experiences of employees (at all levels and in different types of organizational context).

Boreham and Morgan (2004) use a socio-cultural analysis of organizational learning to address some of these issues. They have extended the application of socio-cultural theory beyond its use as a theory of learning, to focus on its relevance to understanding the relationship between organization, organizational learning and performance. They employ the perspective to analyse the findings from an empirical study of an 'oil refinery and petrochemicals manufacturing complex'. The study presents rich qualitative evidence on the organizational context, culture and character of the workplace which sheds light on the opportunities for learning that are created by this company. It also links the analysis to the changing forms of work organization that have been introduced and hence provides much needed empirical evidence on the relationship between work reorganization, learning and performance.

One promising feature of this study and the detailed theoretical discussion, in which it is grounded, is the connection Boreham and Morgan make between organizational learning theory and the analysis of organizational change. They conclude that 'there must be a common object of its [the organization's] collective activity' for organizational learning to occur (2004: 321). This condition exists in the case study they report:

> ... the 850 company employees had adopted the common object of improving their collective performance against the targets in the site plan (this was a genuinely 'common object' because all levels of employee participated in setting the targets) (Ibid).

The example of organizational learning presented by Boreham and Morgan is enabled by employees' shared collective purpose and was embedded in, and fostered by, workplace interaction or 'dialogue'. The dialogue through which organizational learning occurs was structured within explicit relational practices, such as the involvement of *all* employees in rewriting the company's standard operating procedures. Employees at all levels were able to link the new forms of working (and opportunities for dialogue) tracked in the research to improvements in organizational outcomes.

However, the implication of Boreham and Morgan's work is that learning 'as an organization' cannot occur without the harmonious cultural and organizational conditions and reinforcing social practices their research highlights. Given the frequently conflictual nature of the workplace, it is questionable whether many cases of genuine (whole organization) organizational learning may be found. Research is needed to investigate whether the conditions for 'organizational learning' outlined in Boreham and Morgan's study are applicable to smaller workgroups sharing a common purpose but located within contested organizational contexts.

DISCUSSION AND CONCLUSION

This chapter has provided a broad introduction to some of the influential concepts and theories used by researchers to study workplace learning and organization. It has argued that the workplace is a more understandable phenomenon when it is perceived in relation to the context in which it has emerged. In this regard the multiple factors influencing the character of the workplace context are seen as central. Hitherto, interest has focused particularly on the relevance of macro political and economic features, including models of capitalism and on debates about the transformation to new models of production and the implications for skills. At the more micro levels, there has been some attention to the relationship between forms of production, models of management and performance, but these have been largely conducted within the manufacturing sector. There is scope for much more empirical research into the nature of these relationships in contrasting product and service sectors, in organizations of different sizes and forms of ownership, and with different product/service – market strategies.

This discussion and analysis of the workplace also reinforces our view that empirical work is needed which gives voice to the employee perspective (from all grades and levels within the workplace). Without this, it is too easy to read off the employee experience from the assumptions which contrasting perspectives (e.g. knowledge economy optimists and sceptics) make about the changing relationship between forms of work organization, skills and learning. In this regard, Adler (2004) contrasts what he terms the 'new-marxist' and 'palaeo-marxist' perspectives on the forces of production. The Neo-Marxist perspective hypothesises that given the (inevitably) exploitative effects of capitalist modes of production, that (all) employees will experience the changing nature of work as a source of deskilling (reduced task complexity and individual autonomy) and work intensification/exploitation. In contrast, the Palaeo-Marxist perspective hypothesises that there are progressive forces underlying the social relations of production and, consequently, at least some employees will be experiencing the changing nature of work (e.g. teamwork) as a source for increasing their skills and collective autonomy (e.g. via self-directed teams). This perspective chimes with that advanced by Hennessy and Sawchuk (2003) in their analysis of the way Canadian public sector employees developed new skills though they subverted the instructions for using new technologies introduced by management to reorganize their work process. Whereas this reorganization appeared on the surface to be leading to deskilling, Hennessy and Sawchuk found that both deskilling and upskilling were happening in tandem.

Researchers working in the disciplinary tradition of the sociology of work have long drawn attention to the ways workers subvert management through the work process. Through his ethnographic studies of manufacturing plants in the US, Darrah (1996) showed that in order to perform their jobs, progress, and survive in the workplace, employees have to gain an understanding about the cultural norms, sources of power, accepted levels of behaviour, and other invisible, but highly important, characteristics of their organization. This learning may lead employees into practices which, in an industrial relations sense, are of benefit to them (e.g. making sure no-one works too quickly) and which might mean poor and inefficient ways of working are sustained and reproduced as workers come and go. By agreeing to acquiesce in such practices, employees acknowledge their loyalty may be more to their fellow workers than to the organization. In this sense, there may be a number of communities within an organization, each with its own culture and characteristics. These communities may reveal their differences through such activities as initiation and 'rites of passage' rituals, which are still found in workplaces, from manufacturing plants to hospitals and offices. Their underlying purpose is to socialize the new recruit or graduating apprentice into becoming a fully accepted member of the workplace community. As Vaught and Smith (2003) show, through their study of American coal mines, these events, which can often be degrading for the victim, also reinforce the sense of worker solidarity, particularly in occupational settings which are highly pressurized and dangerous.

There is relatively little research on the role of the trade unions *vis-à-vis* workplace and organizational learning. In the UK, researchers have contested the extent to which there is evidence to suggest that employees are more likely to have access to formalized training in unionized workplaces. Recently, Kersley et al. (2006) have argued there is evidence, whereas Hoque and Bacon (2008) say it is, at best, weak. Stroud and Fairbrother (2007) argue that trade unions should show an interest because there are benefits to be gained (for both employees and organizations) when the skills of any workforce are improved and expanded. These benefits relate to greater security of employment and improvements of the organization's position in product or service markets. As Stroud and Fairbrother (2007: 9) acknowledge, however, unions have not always been willing or able to set the agenda when it comes to learning at work. Firstly, unions are faced with 'an employment and educational terrain that is largely defined by the employer'. Secondly, unions have tended to show more interest in labour (trade union) education rather than workplace learning. From their research into the activities of trade unions across Europe, Stroud and Fairbrother (2007) are concerned that they are failing to influence workplace-learning agendas and, hence, are not serving their members' needs at a time when the importance of learning in the workplace is at the forefront of policy and economic agendas.

We also need to understand more about the nature of the learning in which employees are engaged. Here, the research evidence is much more limited. Work organization and job design affect the extent to which employees have access to knowledge and are able to create new knowledge in the process of their work (Boreham et al., 2002; Nonaka and Takeuchi, 1995). Activity theorists such as Engeström (2001) have developed the concept of *boundary crossing* as a means for employees from different professional backgrounds (e.g. in the health and finance sectors) to acquire new levels of professional knowledge by collaborating on a horizontal level (within and between agencies and organizations in the same sectors), rather than regarding the acquisition of new knowledge as a process of *vertical* advancement. Thus, knowledge is not just deployed, but is also acquired and created in workplaces (see also Eraut, 2004).

The use of so-called 'soft' skills and emotional labour, particularly in the personal services sectors, demands new thinking about the meaning of vocational knowledge (Hughes, 2005). Also, new theories reflecting the relationship between knowledge creation and innovation in the contemporary workplace are required (for a detailed review, see Guile, 2003).

Workplaces are dynamic, multi-faceted organisms that adapt to and are changed by a number of economic, political and social forces, some of which are out of their control. They constitute rich environments for learning, but our understanding of the nature of that learning is still in its infancy. In order to enhance and expand that understanding, we need to develop more sophisticated research methods to enable researchers to unlock the secrets of places and spaces whose primary purpose is to produce goods and services. This primary purpose means that the researcher who is interested in learning has to engage closely with and develop an understanding of the production processes in order to 'see' the learning that they engender.

As Hoyrup and Elkjaer (2006: 29) note: 'In a workplace the most important sources of learning are the challenges of work itself, the organisation of work and the social interactions at work'.

REFERENCES

Adler, P. (2004) 'Skill Trends under Capitalism and the Socialisation of Production', in C. Warhurst, I. Grugulis and E. Keep (eds), *The Skills That Matter*. Basingstoke: Palgrave Macmillan.

Amin, A. (ed.) (1994) *Post-Fordism: A Reader*. Oxford: Blackwell.

Appelbaum, E., Bailey, T. and Berg, P. (2000) *Manufacturing Advantage: Why High Performance Systems Pay Off*. New York: ILR Press.

Argyris, C. and Schön, D. (1974) *Theory in Practice: Increasing Professional Effectiveness*. San Francisco: Jossey-Bass.

Argyris, C. and Schön, D. (1978) *Organizational Learning: A Theory of Action Perspective*. Reading, MA: Addison-Wesley.

Ashton, D. (2004) 'Political Economy of Workplace Learning', in H. Rainbird, A. Fuller and A. Munro (eds), *Workplace Learning in Context*. London: Routledge, pp. 21–37.

Ashton, D. and Green, F. (1996) *Education, Training and the Global Economy*. London: Edward Elgar.

Ashton, D. and Sung, J. (2002) *Supporting Workplace Learning for High Performance Working*. Geneva: International Labour Office.

Beckett, D. and Hager, P. (2002) *Life, Work and Learning: Practice in Postmodernity*. London: Routledge.

Billett, S. (2001) *Learning in the Workplace: Strategies for Effective Practice*. Crows Nest NSW: Allen & Unwin.

Billett, S. (2004) 'Learning Through Work: Workplace Participatory Practices', in H. Rainbird, A. Fuller and A. Munro (eds), *Workplace Learning in Context*. London: Routledge, pp. 109–125.

Boreham, N. and Morgan, C. (2004) 'A Sociocultural Analysis of Organizational Learning', *Oxford Review of Education*, 30(3): 307–325.

Boreham, N., Samurcay, N.R. and Fischer, M. (eds) (2002) *Work Process Knowledge*. London: Kogan Page.

Braverman, H. (1974) *Labor and Monopoly Capital: The Degradation of Work in the Twentieth Century*. New York: Monthly Review Press.

Brown, P., Green, A. and Lauder, H. (2001) *High Skills, Globalization, Competitiveness and Skill Formation*. Oxford: Oxford University Press.

Brown, P., Lauder, H., Ashton, D. and Tholen, G. (2004) 'Towards a High-skilled, Low-waged Economy? A Review of Global Trends in Education, Employment and the Labour Market', in S. Porter and M. Campbell (eds), *Skills and Economic Performance*. London: Caspian Publishing, pp. 55–90.

Butler, P., Felstead, A., Ashton, D., Fuller, A., Lee, T., Unwin, L. and Walters, S. (2004) 'High Performance Management: A Literature Review', 'Learning as Work' Research Paper, No. 1, Centre for Labour Market Studies, University of Leicester.

Castells, M. (1996) *The Rise of the Networked Society*, Oxford: Blackwell.

Colley, H., Hodkinson, P. and Malcom, J. (2003) *Informality and Formality in Learning: A Report for the Learning and Skills Research Centre*. London: LSDA.

Darrah, C. N. (1996) *Learning and Work: An Exploration in Industrial Ethnography*. London: Garland Publishing.

Edwards, P. (2001) 'The Puzzle of Work: Autonomy and Commitment Plus Discipline and Insecurity'. *SKOPE Research Paper*, No. 16, University of Warwick.

EEF and CIPD (2003) *Maximising Employee Potential and Business Performance: The Role of High Performance Working*. London: EEF and CIPD.

Engeström, Y. (2001) 'Expansive Learning at Work: Toward an Activity-Theoretical Reconceptualization', *Journal of Education and Work*, 14: 133–156.

Engeström, Y. (2004) 'The New Generation of Expertise: Seven Theses', in H. Rainbird, A. Fuller and A. Munro (eds), *Workplace Learning in Context*. London: Routledge.

Eraut, M. (2000) 'Non-formal Learning and Tacit Knowledge in Professional Work', *British Journal of Educational Psychology*, 70: 113–136.

Eraut, M. (2004) 'Transfer of Knowledge Between Education and Work Settings', in H. Rainbird, A. Fuller and A. Munro (eds), *Workplace Learning in Context*. London: Routledge.

Eraut, M., Alderton, J., Cole, G. and Senker, P. (2000) 'Development of Knowledge and Skills at Work', in F. Coffield (ed.), *Differing Visions of a Learning Society*. Bristol: The Policy Press.

Fauth, R. (2007) *Workplace Trends: 2003 to 2006*. London: Work Foundation.

Felstead, A., Fuller, A., Jewson, N. and Unwin, L. (2009) *Improving Working as Learning*. London: Routledge.

Felstead, A., Jewson, N. and Walters, S. (2005a) *Changing Places of Work*. Basingstoke: Palgrave Macmillan.

Felstead, A., Fuller, A., Unwin, L., Ashton, D., Butler, P. and Lee, T. (2005b), 'Surveying the Scene: Learning Metaphors, Survey Design and the Workplace Context', *Journal of Education and Work*, 18: 359–383.

Field, J. and Malcolm, I. (2006) *Learning, Identity and Agency in the New Economy: Social and Cultural Change and the Long Arm of the Job*, Learning Lives Working Paper, http://www.learninglives.org/

Finegold, D. and Soskice, D. (1988) 'The Failure of Training in Britain: Analysis and Prescription', *Oxford Review of Economic Policy*, 4(3): 21–53.

Florida, R. (1995) 'Towards the Learning Region', *Futures,* 27: 527–536.

Foray, D. and Lundvall, B.-A. (1996) *The Knowledge-Learning Economy: from the Economics of Knowledge to the Learning Economy.* Paris: Organization for Economic Cooperation and Development.

Fuller, A. and Unwin, L. (2003) 'Learning as Apprentices in the Contemporary UK Workplace: Creating and Managing Expansive and Restrictive Participation', *Journal of Education and Work*, 16(1): 5–25.

Fuller, A. and Unwin, L. (2004) 'Expansive Learning Environments: Integrating Organizational and Personal Development', in H. Rainbird, A. Fuller and A. Munro (eds) *Workplace Learning in Context*, London: Routledge.

Fuller, A., Ashton, D., Felstead, A., Unwin, L. and Walters, S. (2003) *The Impact of Informal Learning on Business Productivity.* London: Department of Trade and Industry.

Guile, D. (2003) 'From 'Credentialism' to the 'Practice of Learning': Reconceptualising Learning for the Knowledge Economy', *Policy Futures in Education*, 1: 83–105.

Hall, P.A. and Soskice, D. (2001) 'An Introduction to Varieties of Capitalism', in P.A. Hall and D. Soskice (eds), *Varieties of Capitalism.* Oxford: Oxford University Press, pp. 1–70.

Hennesy, T. and Sawchuk, P.H. (2003) 'Worker Responses to Technological Change in the Canadian Public Sector: Issues of Learning and Labour Process', *Journal of Workplace Learning,* 15(7/8): 319–325.

Hodkinson, P. and Hodkinson, H. (2004) 'The Significance of Individuals' Dispositions in Workplace Learning: A Case Study of Two Teachers', *Journal of Education and Work*, 17: 167–182.

Hoque, K. and Bacon, N. (2008) 'Trade Unions, Union Learning Representatives and Employer-Provided Training in Britain', *British Journal of Industrial Relations*, 46(4): 702–731.

Hoyrup, S. and Elkjaer, B. (2006) 'Reflection: Taking it Beyond the Individual', in Boud, D., Cressey, P. and Docherty, P. (eds), *Productive Reflection at Work.* London: Routledge.

Hughes, J. (2005) 'Bringing Emotion to Work: Emotional Intelligence, Employee Resistance and the Reinvention of Character'. *Work, Employment and Society*, 19: 603–625.

Kakavelakis, K., Felstead, A., Fuller, A., Jewson, N. and Unwin, L. (2008) 'Making a Sales Advisor: the Limits of "Instrumental Empathy"', *Journal of Vocational Education and Training*, 60(3): 209–221.

Keep, E. and Mayhew, K. (1999) 'The Assessment: Knowledge, Skills and Competitiveness', *Oxford Review of Economic Policy*, 15(1): 1–15.

Kersley, B., Alpin, C., Forth, J., Bryson, A., Bewley, H., Dix, G. and Oxenbridge, S. (2006) *Inside the Workplace: Findings from the 2004 Workplace Employment Relations Survey.* London: Routledge.

Lain, D. and Aston, J. (2005) *Literature Review of Evaluation of E-Learning in the Workplace.* Brighton: IES.

Lave, J. and Wenger, E. (1991) *Situated Learning: Legitimate Peripheral Participation.* Cambridge: Cambridge University Press.

Lloyd, C. and Payne, J. (2004) 'The Political Economy of Skill: A Theoretical Approach to Developing a High Skills Strategy in the UK', in C. Warhurst, I. Grugulis and E. Keep (eds), *The Skills That Matter.* Basingstoke: Palgrave Macmillan.

Marsick, V. and Watkins, K. (1990) *Informal and Incidental Learning in the Workplace.* New York: Routledge.

McDuffie, J. (1995) 'Human Resource Bundles and Manufacturing Performance', *Industrial and Labor Relations Review* 48(2): 197–221.

Nonaka, I. and Takeuchi, H. (1995) *The Knowledge-Creating Company: How Japanese Companies Create the Dynamics of Innovation.* Oxford and New York: Oxford University Press.

Piore, M.J. and Sabel, C. (1984) *The Second Industrial Divide.* New York: Basic Books.

Rainbird, H., Fuller, A. and Munro, A. (eds) (2004) *Workplace Learning in Context.* London: Routledge.

Smith, C. and Thompson, P. (1999) 'Reevaluating the Labor Process Debate', in M. Wardell, T.L. Steiger, P. Meiskins (eds), *Rethinking the Labor Process,* Albany: Albany State University of New York Press.

Stasz, C. (2001) 'Assessing Skills for Work: Two Perspectives', *Oxford Economic Reports*, 3: 385–405.

Stroud, D. and Fairbrother, P. (2007) 'Workplace Learning: A Trade Union Failure to Service Needs', *Journal of Workplace Learning*, 20(1): 6–20.

Unwin, L., Felstead, A., Fuller, A., Bishop, D., Lee, T., Jewson, N. and Butler, P. (2007) 'Looking inside the Russian Doll: The Interconnections between Context, Learning and Pedagogy in the Workplace', *Pedagogy, Culture & Society* 15: 333–348.

Vaught, C. and Smith, D.L. (2003) 'Incorporation and Mechanical Solidarity in an Underground Coal Mine', in D. Harper and H.M. Lawson (eds), *The Cultural Study of Work.* Oxford: Rowman and Littlefield.

Vidal, M. (2007) 'Lean Production, Worker Empowerment, and Job Satisfaction: A Qualitative Analysis and Critique', *Critical Sociology,* 33: 247–278.

Wall, T.D. and Wood, S. (2005) 'The Romance of Human Resource Management and Business Performance and the Case for Big Science', *Human Relations* 58: 429–462.

Warhurst, C., Grugulis, I. and Keep, E. (eds) (2004) *The Skills That Matter.* Basingstoke: Palgrave Macmillan.

Wilkinson, F. (2002) *Productive Systems and the Structuring Role of Economic and Social Theories.* ESRC Centre for Business Research, University of Cambridge, Working Paper No. 225.

Wood, S. (1999) 'Human Resource Management and Performance', *International Journal of Management Review*, 1(4): 367–413.

Wright, A. 2006. *E-learning and Widening Participation for NHS Staff: Expert Paper for the Strategy Task Groups.* Available from: http://www.wideningparticipation.nhs.uk/pages/expertpapers.html

Wynarczyk, P. 2005. 'The Impact of Connectivity Technologies on E-flexible Working Practices of Small and Medium-sized Enterprises in the North East of England', *New Technology, Work and Employment*, 20: 234–247.

5

Subjectivity, Self and Personal Agency in Learning Through and for Work

Stephen Billett

The central role and significance of the self and personal agency is now being accounted for within explanations of workplace learning. Here, these contributions to understanding workplace learning are identified and discussed. In particular, this chapter elaborates a view of learning premised upon individuals' construal (i.e. perception or making meaning of) and construction of (i.e. generating knowledge) what is afforded them in workplace settings. This process is explained as comprising a relational interdependence between personal and social factors and contributions. This elaboration is aimed to inform both workplace pedagogies and personal epistemologies at and for work. The key argument is that what constitutes work is negotiated between institutional facts (Searle, 1995) and other social forms (Valsiner, 1998) that constitute the social experience (Harré, 1995), on the one hand, and individuals 'cognitive experience' on the other. Given this, it is necessary to identify and elaborate the bases of these negotiations and their role in what constitutes learning through work and the remaking of that work. So, these personal-social processes have both personal and social legacies: individual development and cultural remaking and transformation. The processes are held to be interdependent: each requiring the other. However, rather than mutual or equally exercised in the negotiations, the relationship is relational, with different emphases and contributions being afforded in different ways by the exercise of individual and social agency.

> … personality becomes socially guided and individually constructed in the course of human life. People are born as potential persons, the process of becoming actual persons takes place through individual transformations of social experience (Harré, 1995: 373).

LEARNING THROUGH AND FOR WORK

The purpose of this chapter is to elaborate the personal contributions to the experiencing of work and working life as a process of individual learning and the remaking of practice. It emphasizes the salience for considering the subjective qualities of learning through and for work. These qualities include the role of personal agency and subjectivity in negotiating between the social and individual contributions that constitute engaging in and learning through work and throughout working life. In all, learning through work is proposed as a duality comprising a relational interdependence between personal and social contributions (Billett, 2008). The interdependence within this duality is founded in the needs of the social world and also those of persons. The social world requires individuals' agency to actively remake and transform its practices, while individuals need the social world to provide access to knowledge that is sourced in history, cultural practices (i.e. occupations) and manifested in particular instances of the practice of that work (i.e. work settings).

Neither the social suggestion, nor individuals' agency alone is sufficient to account for the processes of engaging in the simultaneous process of learning and remaking the cultural practices that constitute work. One dimension of this duality – the social experience (Harré, 1995) or social suggestion – comprises societal norms, practices and values, and their enactment, which constitute the requirements for work and are shaped by local factors. However, the social suggestion encountered in workplaces is never unambiguous, complete or comprehensive enough to secure the unquestioned and unquestionable transfer of knowledge to workers. Berger and Luckman (1967) propose that the social suggestion is never so compelling as to lead to socialisation. Indeed, if the social world could express its message unequivocally and unambiguously, there would be little need to communicate because understanding would be implicit, not requiring further communication for that message to be construed and comprehended (Newman et al., 1989). Instead, depending upon their intents, individuals engage with what is suggested through norms and practices and interactions with greater or lesser degrees of interest and receptiveness (Valsiner, 2000). Yet, even when receptive to social experiences, individuals are required to be active in interpreting what is being suggested because of the limits of its projection. So, beyond the suggestion of the social, individuals will necessarily construct their views about work, workplace participation and requirements for performance. This construction will be premised upon what they know: their cognitive experience. This construction will be personally particular in certain ways, because that learning arises through a unique set of personal experiences. Hence, the duality that comprises engaging in and learning through work has personally relational bases that are referred to elsewhere as inter-psychological processes. In this way, the processes of negotiations between the social and personal contributions are relational, and premised on social suggestion and individuals' construal and construction.

Importantly, the processes of thinking, acting and learning occur simultaneously (Lave, 1993; Rogoff, 1995) and include the formation of working identities or subjectivities (Lave and Wenger, 1991). For instance, Lave (1993) concludes that wherever you encounter practice, you also identify learning. Others emphasise participation in activities and interactions as constituting learning (Billett, 2002; Rogoff, 1995; Sfard, 1998). Across these views, and consistent with cognitive theorising (e.g. Anderson, 1993), the consequences or legacies of individuals' engagement in goal-directed activities are more than completing those activities' goals (e.g. work tasks). There is also a cognitive legacy: change in cognitive structures or individuals' knowledge that is shaped by engagement in these activities (Anzai and Simon, 1979; Newell and Simon, 1972). Such theories also suggest that the scope and kind of learning that arises is influenced by the degree of novelty that an activity poses for individuals and the effort they elect to deploy when engaging in these activities (Newell and Simon, 1972). That is, activities that are novel to individuals lead to new learning, while activities that are familiar serve to reinforce and refine what the individual knows, including assisting transforming conceptual into procedural knowledge (Anderson, 1982).

Constructivist theories hold that everyday conscious thought is active in seeking to make sense of what is encountered (Van Lehn, 1989; von Glasersfeld, 1987). Giddens (1991), in ways analogous to Piaget's conception of equilibrium, refers to individuals seeking to secure ontological security: reconciling what they encounter with their own goals and interests. Importantly, this drive to secure equilibrium or ontological security energises and directs individuals' learning, albeit shaped by their intents and prior knowledge. In both social (e.g. Vygotskian) and individual (e.g., Piagetian) constructivist perspectives, cognitive change (i.e. learning) is held to occur through individuals' deployment of their cognitive resources when engaging in tasks and interactions (Billett, 1996). So the kind of problem or impasse that constitutes the task for individuals and their responses shapes the character and extent of their learning (Van Lehn, 1989). As noted, two kinds of legacies – individual change and the re-making of the cultural practices that constitute work – emerge from these processes.

Both of these forms of development are central to understanding performing and learning in and for work. The knowledge required for occupational practice has its origins in cultural practices and historical precedents (Scribner, 1985), in response to meeting culturally derived needs that have been refined over time through its enactments. Consequently, accessing this socio-historically derived knowledge requires engaging and negotiating with the social world. When individuals engage with this knowledge and deploy it they engage in the active remaking of cultural practices through performing that comprise paid work at a particular point in time, and in negotiation with particular kinds of social suggestion and different kinds of access to it (Billett and Somerville, 2004). Importantly, given that individuals play an active role in constructing meaning from what they encounter, their learning through and for work is both shaped by and shapes their agency and intentionality. Indeed, studies across a range of industry sectors identify the learning of work skills through participating in everyday work activity in ways that rely upon both individuals' engagement in work activities (i.e. observation, engagement, monitoring, etc.) and the direct and indirect social guidance available in work settings (Billett, 2001b). These active and negotiated processes of learning and remaking culture are not mere enactments of knowledge sourced elsewhere. Instead, of necessity, individuals' engagement with and construction of those practices is premised on the agency of individuals' construing, negotiating and remaking the practice of work, which is premised in their subjectivities and mediated by the exercise of social and cultural norms and practices.

PERSONAL SUBJECTIVITY AND AGENCY AT WORK

In recent theoretical accounts of learning, many derived from research in workplace settings, there has been a privileging of both the immediate social (i.e. situational) and cultural contributions to cognition (e.g. communities of practice, activity systems). Yet, given what has been proposed above, there are at least four premises to now bring individual subjectivities and agency to the forefront of explanations about work and learning through work and working life.

Firstly, as new culturally derived needs arise, the exercise of personal agency is essential in transforming the cultural practices that have developed to respond to those needs (Giddens, 1984), including paid work. This transformation requires the effortful engagement buoyed by interests and intentionality (Malle et al., 2001; Baldwin, 2001), and possibly, in the absence of socially derived exemplars. So, realising changing requirements for work will be premised (in part) on individuals' agency and intentionality.

Secondly, individuals' participation and learning through work are person-dependent to some degree. Individuals' construal of what they encounter is uniquely socially shaped throughout their life histories or ontogenies, and as a product of myriad, on-going, situationally peculiar and personally realised negotiations with social forms and practices (Billett, 2003). These experiences shape individuals' thinking and acting through moment-by-moment or microgenetic developmental processes that contribute to their ontogenetic development (Rogoff, 1990). From the earliest age and through inter-psychological interactions and for purposes that Piaget (1968) refers to as securing equilibrium and von Glasersfeld (1987) as maintaining viability, individuals engage in and enact an enduring personal epistemological venture of making sense of what they experience in the social and brute worlds. Individuals' ontogenetic development arises through personally agentic epistemological processes. This influences how individuals engage with new experiences. Yet, as the construal of these experiences is likely to be in some ways peculiar to individuals, their process of knowledge construction and their remaking of cultural practices will be in some ways personally unique (Billett, 2003).

Thirdly, because of this personal ontogenetic legacy, individuals' earlier or pre-mediate experiences shape how and what they learn. These epistemologies both shape and are shaped by individuals' conceptions and subjectivities, which in turn direct the initiation, intensity and intentionality of their activities and interactions as they work, remake and transform the practices that comprise paid work. Consequently, even the most apparently uniform social experience will be subject to interpretation, construal and construction. So ontogenetic development comprises the legacy of individuals' prior social experiences, and as such stands as an important premise for how individuals engage with brute and social worlds beyond them and learn.

It follows, therefore, and fourthly, that the relationship between individuals and the social world is relational. Just as the social world exercises its suggestion either more or less strongly, so too individuals' engagement with the workplace's social suggestion can be more or less intense, and focused in particular ways and engaged with to different degrees of intentionality. For instance, individuals may be selective in their reading of a particular social suggestion or simply be unaware of it, thereby not explicitly engaging with it (Billett, 2006). The prospect is very remote for individual and social agency (i.e. personal agency and social suggestion) being enacted in equal parts or ways that are equally shared. Therefore, the relations between social and individual agency are likely to be relational in character.

The contributions and interdependences outlined above suggest that it is essential to include the personal in the forms of self and subjectivity in explanations of learning through and for work.

PREMISES FOR NEGOTIATING BETWEEN THE OBJECTIVE AND SUBJECTIVE

It follows that considerations of relations between agency and structure help explain the negotiation between the objective and subjective phenomena that comprises learning through work, and the place of the social and the personal in all this. Helpfully, these issues have long been discussed within psychology, sociology and philosophy.

Psychological accounts

Some psychological accounts take the individual as the starting and focus point for explaining how humans make sense of, engage in and learn through activities such as work. From this perspective, social practices, such as workplaces, are seen as mere contexts in which individuals think and act, engage with to achieve their work goals, and learn. Certainly, cognitive psychology and information processing perspectives emphasise individuals' capacity to manipulate their own cognitive structures (Chi et al., 1981; Chi et al., 1982) when engaging in activities such as paid work. So, in its origins and at its firmest, the cognitive perspective downplays the contributions of the social world to thinking and acting, and thereby granting significant agency to the individual in cognition. Such perspectives are consistent with earlier views about educational purposes associated with a belief in general thinking capacities that are not situation-dependent. For instance, both Bartlett (1958) and Bruner (1966) propose education should free the individual from the constraints of a particular time and place. The legacy of such views is to focus on the development of intelligence and general thinking processes that are held to be applicable to any situation despite the problematic nature of such a claim (Brown et al., 1989).

However, in response to the earlier individual focus within much of the psychology literature, the last two decades have seen a strong emphasis on the cultural and social contributions to human cognition. This is evident in cultural-historical activity theory, and interest in activity systems, communities of practice and distributed cognition. Approaches such as activity theory (Cole, 1998; Leontyev, 1981; Scribner, 1985) provide a means to understand the social geneses of work and the knowledge required for performance in work activities and workplaces, which, in some instances, includes how individuals' learning arises socially. Moreover, these social and cultural perspectives have dominated recent accounts and have emphasised strong associations between individuals' thinking and acting and the circumstances in which they are situated (e.g. Collins et al., 1989; Engeström, 1993; Wenger, 1998). Some of these accounts infer situational determinism, that is, the situation determines individuals' thinking and acting (Pea, 1993). Indeed, some of these accounts hold that individuals play a limited role in their thinking, acting and learning (Pea, 1993), because cognition is directed by social factors or because the self is socially-saturated (Gergen, 2000). These perspectives are, in many ways, analogous to structural accounts from within sociology, where social factors and forms determine cognition. They grant considerable agency and certainty to social forms and structures. An inherent quality of these accounts is that the knowledge for work that individuals need to learn has cultural and social geneses: its source is elsewhere and in the past. This knowledge also reflects proven practices that have evolved over time as new demands emerge and technologies change. Such historically derived knowledge constitutes much of the occupational knowledge that is exercised through work. However, as more recent accounts suggest, socially sourced knowledge needs to be engaged with by individuals for their contributions to be exercised.

Such theoretical positions are understandable corrections to the earlier individual-focused perspectives within cognitive psychology (Bruner, 2001). However, their explanatory power is weakened by over-emphasising the contributions of the social suggestion. Moreover, the capacity of socially derived knowledge to address new situations or circumstances is questionable. Cole (2002), a principal advocate of cultural historical activity theory, acknowledges this limitation of the historical and cultural genesis of knowledge and its social transition. He suggests that individual agency stands as a necessary prerequisite for the successful deployment of historically derived knowledge, particularly to novel circumstances. Hence, in the face of constant changes in the requirement for work the contributions from the past will only be partially helpful. It will be individuals' agency that will adapt that knowledge in new ways and to novel circumstances in workplaces, thereby remaking and transforming those practices, as they learn themselves.

Therefore, collectively, psychological accounts are helpful in understanding how individuals' learning through work progresses and what contributions are made by both the individual and the social world. The social world provides much of the knowledge to be learnt, its valuing and purposes as well as its tried and tested practices and conceptions. The personal contribution is through engagement with, making sense of and enacting the socially derived knowledge about work, at particular moments in time and in particular work situations. Sociological and philosophical accounts also offer explanations.

Sociological and philosophical accounts

The relations between structure and agency have long been theorised within sociology and philosophy. Both of these disciplines offer accounts that emphasise the key role of social structures in which individual agency and autonomy is seen as illusory (e.g. Bourdieu, 1977, 1991; Foucault, 1979), accounts that grant individual autonomy (e.g. Goffman, 1990; Rousseau, 1968), and those that acknowledge interactions between the two (e.g. Berger and Luckman, 1967; Bhaskar, 1998; Giddens, 1991). Highly structured views, such as Foucault's earlier work, position individuals as mere placeholders in social networks (Mansfield, 2000) because their personal autonomy is diminished through being so enmeshed in social structures. Such views see workers as being driven by changes to work, or at best being only reactive to these changes. For instance, Bourdieu (1991) refers to the socially constraining nature of individual action, citing how social practice determines dialects. That is, the social world is so pervasive as to determine the patterns and enunciation of an individual's speech. Similarly, Foucault (1979) positions individuals as being subject to pervasive social press and 'placed under' or subjected to the influence of societal norms and practices encountered earlier within their life histories. Therefore, in these views, individuals' socially derived subjectivities determine their behaviour and cognition (Davies, 2000), including what is experienced in and learnt through experiences in the workplace. It is possible to identify situations that illustrate the extent of social suggestion as proposed in these accounts. For instance, coalminers who lived in coalmining communities reported how the pervasiveness of both the cultural milieu and immediate social press were involved in shaping miners' work and work habits. Work practices in mine sites are shaped by the masculine culture of the workplace and mining community. This is manifested in dangerous and unsafe workplace practices (Somerville and Abrahamsson, 2003). Such is the pervasiveness of the mining culture that miners' subjectivities appear captured by the social suggestion of the community in which they live and work. Only when significant personal events (e.g. severe accidents, severe ill-health) occur in coalminers' lives do they question the hegemonic masculine culture of the mine sites. Even then, those miners affected by these accidents stand astonished at their inability to influence other miners' behaviours and practices, despite the obvious and visible evidence they present. So these findings offer instances where social factors operate in a highly deterministic way in work- related activities.

However, other perspectives view the concept of structure as being more personally enabling. Giddens (1984) proposes a key role for human agency in the social structuring of knowledge through his concept of structuration. Through acknowledging intersections and interactions (interdependence) between social structures Giddens links individuals' intentionality with their subjectivities. In ways analogous to the Piagetian concept of equilibrium, Giddens (1991) suggests the self seeks to maintain its security in circumstances that threatens its stability and is driven to locate reference points for stability. Yet, he offers a significant role and agency for individuals in securing that security, even within highly structured social circumstances. Indeed, the coalmining and aged care sectors offer evidence of individuals' exercise of autonomy in the face of social subjugation (Somerville and Abrahamsson, 2003). For instance, some aged care workers challenged and transformed existing practices in aged care facilities that they believed were inappropriate. Certainly, the exercise of personal agency at work is easier for some workers than others. Owners and managers of hairdressing salons seemed more able and likely to offer treatments outside of those normally provided by the salon, whereas apprentices and junior hairdressers were not permitted such discretion (Billett, 2003). The other workers held views about and preferences for hairdressing that were different from those privileged in their workplaces. Indeed, they exercised them when they had the discretion to do so. Yet, in hairdressing salon's public space there were constraints on how the personal preferences could be enacted, in ways Evans (2002) describes as bounded agency. Analogously, small-business operators were often less constrained by workplace norms and practices, because they were quite likely to be those who established and monitored the work practices, yet were constrained by other factors, such as customer demands and need for profitability which comprised their wage (Billett et al., 2003).

The more structured views proposed above, suggest that workplace factors (i.e. norms, practices and values) determined the degree of discretion afforded workers. However, there were also opportunities for individuals to create discretionary spaces for themselves. That is, workers are still able to exercise their agency and intentionality. Referring to desire, Foucault (1986) proposed that no amount of constraint or surveillance will be sufficient to extinguish individuals' personal beliefs and values. Similarly taking up Bourdieu's (1991) claim about language, individuals' accents are shaped by the social milieu in which spoken language is practised and learnt. However, the ideas and meanings that sit behind and comprise their language, are not necessarily shared (Billett, 2003; Newman et al., 1989).

Indeed, others suggest individuals are less constrained or even unconstrained by these structural factors (e.g. Rousseau, 1968). Of course, this view is strongly refuted by structuralists (e.g. Ratner, 2000) who claim that individuals are unable to separate themselves from the social world. Central to considerations of the extent and role of human agency are individuals' intentions when engaging with the social world. Children learn from an early age to expect inconsistency when dealing with the social world, and the need to be selective when engaging with it (Baldwin, 1898). Indeed, structuralists' generalised claims about the worth of work and its generation of anxiety and disempowerment might not be so universal or universally applicable.

What constitutes 'good work' for individuals might not be consistent with the assumed social worth or status that others might ascribe to what constitutes worthwhile work (Billett et al., 2005). Therefore, a more personally relative approach about what constitutes worthwhile work is warranted.

Each of the theoretical orientations is quite distinctive in their advocacy of the relative purchase of individual or social agency. Moreover, each orientation can explain particular workplace circumstances. Therefore, there may well be workplace situations that are more or less pervasive, and there will always be space for human consciousness and intentionality, although the degree by which it can be openly exercised will vary. This is perhaps what Evans (2002) refers to as bounded agency. Indeed, sometimes, the exercise of consistency and limits to work agency is legitimated through the need for strict adherence to particular practices (e.g. air-traffic controllers). In all, an explanation for how individuals respond to changing work requirements throughout their working lives is probably best provided by acknowledging the conduct of work and its learning as comprising both social and personal practices whose enactment is premised in relationships between the two. This exercise of socially structured institutions remains incomplete without acknowledging how individuals engage with them. It is through a consideration of relationships between the personal and workplace practices that learning through work can best be explained.

To advance this explanation, the concept of workplace participatory practices is now elaborated.

WORKPLACE PARTICIPATORY PRACTICES

Workplace participatory practices constitute a means to understand individuals' participation and learning in the workplace (Billett, 2002). They comprise a duality between the affordance of the workplace and the individual's engagement with what they are afforded. These two concepts and their interdependence are now elaborated in turn.

Workplace affordances

Workplace affordances comprise the degree by which individuals are invited to participate in and learn through work practices. The kinds of activities individuals are afforded through their work are the products of the workplaces' micro-social processes (Engeström and Middleton, 1996): their norms and practices. Although reflecting historically and culturally-derived practices, the knowledge to be constructed for effective work performance, the kinds of problems to be solved and what constitutes an acceptable solution constitute workplace requirements and participatory practices (Billett, 2001a). These practices are shaped by situational factors and local negotiations (Engeström and Middleton, 1996; Suchman, 1996; Wenger, 1998).

When individuals are paid to engage in workplace activities, they are invited and expected to engage in ways that contribute to their continuity. This includes maintaining or improving the standing and employment of individuals or cohorts of individuals in the workplace. Consequently, opportunities are likely afforded in ways that are intended to sustain or extend the work practice and/or particular interests in the workplace. Because workplaces are contested (e.g. Bernhardt, 1999; Darrah, 1996; Hull, 1997), the distribution of workplace affordances is far from being benign. Instead, the distribution is influenced by workplace hierarchies, group affiliations, personal relations, workplace cliques and cultural practices that distribute opportunities to act and interact there (Billett, 2001c). Put baldly, opportunities to participate in and access support and guidance are distributed in ways that reflect workplace political and power relationships (Bierema, 2001; Solomon, 1999). In coalmines, skilled workers would not assist the participation in learning of a worker unaffiliated with their union (Billett, 1995), as this would violate workplace affiliations and demarcations, including the standing of the particular union. Similarly, to safeguard their own employment, full-time retail workers in pharmacy chain stores restricted the activities and learning of part-time employees (Bernhardt, 1999). Then, there are the ongoing tensions between labour and management, and resistance to divisions of labour that assists management's control over the workplace (Danford, 1998). Across advanced industrial economies, employers are also more likely to provide opportunities for and expend funds on the development of younger and well-educated workers than older and less-educated workers (Bishop, 1997), and more likely to support those workers who are white than of colour (e.g. McBrier and Wilson, 2004).

In these ways, workplace norms and practices shape the distribution of affordances to workers. The kinds of participation individuals are afforded and elect to engage in have cognitive consequences (i.e. learning). Individuals denied support and inclusion may have more limited learning opportunities than those invited to participate and supported by experienced co-workers. Yet, there may be consequences beyond opportunities for skillfulness, when affordances are weak or belligerent. For instance, individuals may well learn that workplaces are not to be trusted, nor equitable, or they may learn the importance of acting in ways that align themselves to powerful individuals to protect their own interests, their standing or the interests of those with whom they are affiliated. However, whether these affordances are developmental, helpful or lead to abuse of the self, they are a product of negotiation between the individual's and the workplace's affordances.

Yet, the affordances are dynamic. The situational factors and local negotiations that constitute workplaces' social practices and their enactment are constantly transforming due to changes in those factors (e.g. Skinner, 2004). Equally, workplace affordances are subject to constant change, in terms of tasks, goals, interactions, participants and relations (Billett et al., 2005). This dynamic quality reinforces the salience of understanding the ongoing negotiated relations between individuals and the social practice. This is because these negotiations constitute a key element of workplace participatory practices, as both the bases for realising workplace continuity and individuals' learning. More than being once-off sources of knowledge that result in some fixed cognitive legacy, inter-psychological processes are necessarily ongoing (Vygotsky, 1978). Moreover, individuals' activities and interactions in workplace settings do much to change the practices that constitute transformation to workplace requirements. The other key element is how individuals elect to engage with what is afforded them.

Individual engagement

Individuals' engagement in the workplace comprises the other element of workplace participatory practices (Billett, 2002) that constitute the duality between the social and personal contributions to work and learning through and for work. Despite the goal-directed activities and interactions that comprise the observable elements of work and their distribution being shaped by social norms and practices, individuals also exercise their agency in determining how they construe, construct and engage in work. This agentic action and its exercise, as noted, are shaped by individuals' personal histories or ontogenies and are constituted in the form of subjectivities and identities (Somerville and Bernoth, 2001). Individuals participate simultaneously in a number of social practices (Lave and Wenger, 1991), such as workplaces. However, the quality of their engagement in these practices will not be uniform. Full-bodied participation in one social practice can be contrasted by reluctance in another. The quality of individuals' efforts to engage is influenced by their values, beliefs and socio-cultural background. Workers of a South Vietnamese heritage rejected teamwork in an American manufacturing plant, believing this work practice reflected the very communal, indeed communist values and practices they had fled Vietnam to avoid (Darrah, 1996). So, central to these local negotiations and participatory practices are individuals' subjectivities and agency that shape how they engage with what is afforded them. This agency is, as noted, guided by the learners' identities and subjectivities, and are themselves socially derived through unique personal histories. Therefore, learning through engagement in social practices, such as workplaces, is not a unidirectional process leading to socialisation or enculturation with the outcome being the reproduction of situational values and practices. Instead, individuals' personally subjective interpretation and quality of their engagement in workplaces will always be unique in some ways to their personal history and subjectivities (e.g. Valsiner and van der Veer, 2000). So, there is interdependence between what is afforded individuals by social practice, and how they elect to engage with and construct what is afforded them by that social practice is relationally shaped through subjectivities and agency.

INDIVIDUAL ENGAGEMENT IS PREMISED ON RELATIONAL INTERDEPENDENCE WITH SOCIAL AGENCY

It follows, therefore, that the process of individual engagement in workplaces is premised on a relational interdependence between the individual and the social world. Dewey (1887, cited in Valsiner and van de Veer, 2000) proposes individuals' experience is the product of their intellect engaging with sensations, those arising through the social world as well as through the brute world. However, this explanation of experience as intentional and active engagement needs to include the subtle, yet ubiquitous, social suggestions that are encountered almost unconsciously in the conduct of daily life. These are analogous to what Bourdieu (1991) refers to as habitus: the battery of clues, cues and models that suggest and guide conduct. Habitus can have legacies in terms of personal dispositions that shape how individuals engage with the social world, to what extent and with what intent (Bloomer and Hodkinson, 2000). Yet, there are different kinds of relations between individuals and the social world. This battery of social suggestion is experienced in different ways and/or construed differently by different individuals (Newman et al., 1989). Foucault (1979) suggests that individuals become subjected to the social world through the discourses and discursive practices of the social, primarily through language. Yet worker subjectivities have particular relationships to learning. The subjectivity of coal miners was found to be constituted within a strong hegemonic masculine culture of aggression, competitiveness and risk-taking which was at odds with the company's new training in safe work practices (Somerville, 2002). These work practices are handed down inter-generationally in mining communities. The mines as workplaces are described as 'closed communities' where workplace practices are highly regulated by the social pressure of subjugation. A particular culture of masculine competitiveness has been characteristically cultivated in mining workplaces because of its relationship to production (Somerville, 2002). However, masculine peer pressure supports unsafe work behaviours, preventing workers from expressing problems and admitting mistakes or weakness. While the social press for mine workers was strongly supportive of hegemonic masculine work practices, there were nevertheless some mineworkers who persisted in asserting their difference, either through natural inclination or through a self-conscious process of transformation (Billett and Somerville, 2004).

In these ways, the kinds of social interactions that shape learning can be of the close interpersonal or proximal kind. That is, the kind often referred to as teaching or guided learning. In intentional teaching activities, this kind of interaction is often directed to secure inter-subjectivity or shared understanding between a more-experienced and less-experienced social partner. However, they can comprise a pervasive form of social suggestion that individuals are subjected to and represent potentially pervasive social press. These have been conceptualised as habitus (Bourdieu, 1991) or subjectification (Foucault, 1979). Yet, it is these forms of social suggestion that individuals relationally elect to appropriate, transform or ignore. Linking this proposition to learning and remaking practice, it seems that both close guidance and the more distal forms of social suggestion do more than shape behaviour in the immediate circumstance. They also have a cognitive legacy in the form of permanent or semi-permanent change in individuals, that is: learning. Yet, beyond learning, these processes also constitute the process of remaking practice.

WORKPLACE TRANSFORMATIONS AND INDIVIDUALS' REMAKING OF PRACTICE

Key imperatives for cultural practices, such as occupations, are their transmission and remaking across time and place. These processes are not achieved through some uniform wave of socially driven change that propels each new generation of practitioners, because the social processes are not that strong or unambiguous. Instead, individuals actively remake and refine these cultural practices as they confront work tasks and adopt new technologies and requirements in doing so. So, cultural heritage is transmitted and remade incrementally, individually, yet in ways that may well constitute patterns of change. At the heart of this process are changing environments, requirements and technologies that are products of evolving history. Of course, structuralist views suggest that the society determines change and directs the locus of new learning or change. However, other views suggest that individuals act in shaping responses to these changing circumstances that constitute the vanguard of cultural transformation (Leontyev, 1981; Rogoff, 1990; Valsiner, 1998). There are examples of workers electing to participate in and transform practices because they are inconsistent with their values and beliefs. The dramatic experience of an aged care nurse, through a back injury, led her to focus upon improving work practices in that industry sector (Somerville, 2003). She exercised energy and intentionality in her efforts to improve (transform) practice. Taking another example, in one aged care facility, the practices of dealing with the deceased was transformed by the agency of one worker, who raised issues of sensitivity as practice in that aged care setting. In a mortuary that performs coronial autopsies, one counsellor succeeded in changing the processes of counselling the next of kin that transformed the operation and practice not only of the counsellors, but also other workers in the facility (Billett et al., 2004). That individual's belief about appropriate counselling, the opportunity to advance his view, and an invitational environment in which he was afforded professional standing all contributed to his transforming the counselling activity in the workplace. These instances of changing practices illuminate the possibilities for individuals to make significant changes to the conduct of their work that are the requirements for work performance.

Changes in practice may represent instances of processes that occur in workplaces. For instance, in an inquiry that elaborated five workers' working lives, it was found that they all experienced significant change in their working lives over a period of about seven months (Billett and Pavlova, 2003). Against what is often reported about the de-skilling, marginalisation and alienation of contemporary working life brought about by such changes, each worker had managed these changes well. In four of the five instances, the changes were actually consistent with and buttressed the workers' career trajectories. That is, these changes provided the vehicle by which they could enact their preferences, gain greater security in their work, practice fulfilling and personally rewarding work and direct energies into projects that were closely associated with their identity and values. Of course, others associated with these participants were identified as not faring so well. However, the changes provided the context for individuals to play a constructive role in changing of practice. Leontyev (1981) identified this process of remaking culture as being a product of an individual's active engagement in and appropriation of particular cultural practices and values. He proposed that:

> ... through activity, human beings change the environment, and through that change they build their own novel psychological functions ... (1981: 195).

Similarly, in small business operators' efforts to learn about the new goods and service tax, it was found that the key basis for directing their learning, who they consulted, how the consultation occurred and the degree of effort sustained in learning about the new tax was dependent upon their identity and intentionality (Billett and Pavlova, 2003). The response to this uniform initiative was diverse in its scope, attention and enactment. Even when compelled to conform to particular practices, it was individuals who decided how they would respond which included their construction of the initiative.

All this suggests that rather than being wholly subject to change, individuals are actively engaged in remaking cultural practices, such as those required for effective work practice. The change or learning that arises from everyday and novel events is associated with how individuals direct their intentionalities and agency when engaging with what they experience through these events. Individual experiences in social practices, such as workplaces, will incrementally, and at times, transformationally contribute to changes in their ways of knowing and sense of self. Moreover, individuals' subjectivity shapes the kind of changes that occur and is shaped by events, particularly singularly dramatic events, because it shapes response to those events. Perhaps as Rogoff (1990) suggests, it is the engagement of individuals in solving novel problems that are generated by culturally and historically derived knowledge confronting new circumstances through which culture and cultural practices are remade.

REFERENCES

Anderson, J.R. (1982) 'Acquisition of Cognitive Skill', *Psychological Review*, 89(4): 369–406.
Anderson, J.R. (1993) 'Problem Solving and Learning', *American Psychologist*, 48(1): 35–44.
Anzai, Y. and Simon, H.E. (1979) 'The Theory of Learning by Doing', *Psychological Review*, 86: 124–140.
Baldwin, J.M. (1898) 'On Selective Thinking', *The Psychological Review*, V(1): 1–24.
Bartlett, F.C. (1958) *Thinking: An Experimental and Social Study*. New York: Basic Books.
Berger, P.L. and Luckman, T. (1967) *The Social Construction of Reality*. Harmondsworth, Middlesex: Penguin Books.
Bernhardt, A. (1999) 'The Future of Low-Wage Jobs: Case Studies in the Retail Industry', *Institute on Education and the Economy Working Paper*, 10 (March).
Bhaskar, R. (1998) *The Possibility of Naturalism*. London: Routledge.
Bierema, L.L. (2001) 'Women, Work, and Learning', in T. Fenwick (ed.), *Sociocultural Perspectives on Learning Through Work*. San Francisco: Jossey-Bass/Wiley, pp. 53–62.
Billett, S. (1995) *Skill Formation in Three Central Queensland Coalmines: Reflections on Implementation and Prospects for the Future*. Brisbane: Centre for Research into Employment and Work. Griffith University.
Billett, S. (1996) 'Situated Learning: Bridging Sociocultural and Cognitive Theorising', *Learning and Instruction*, 6(3): 263–280.
Billett, S. (2001a) 'Knowing in Practice: Re-Conceptualising Vocational Expertise', *Learning and Instruction*, 11(6): 431–452.
Billett, S. (2001b) *Learning in the Workplace: Strategies for Effective Practice*. Sydney: Allen & Unwin.
Billett, S. (2001c) 'Learning Throughout Working Life: Interdependencies at Work', *Studies in Continuing Education*, 23(1): 19–35.
Billett, S. (2002) 'Workplace Pedagogic Practices: Co-Participation and Learning', *British Journal of Educational Studies*, 50(4): 457–481.
Billett, S. (2003) 'Sociogeneses, Activity and Ontogeny', *Culture and Psychology*, 9(2): 133–169.
Billett, S. (2006) 'Relational Interdependence Between Social and Individual Agency in Work and Working Life', *Mind, Culture and Activity*, 13(1): 53–69.
Billett, S. (2008) 'Learning Throughout Working Life: A Relational Interdependence Between Social and Individual Agency', *British Journal of Education Studies*, 155(1): 39–58.
Billett, S. and Pavlova, M. (2003) '*Learning Through Working Life: Individuals' Agentic Action, Subjectivity and Participation in Work*. Paper presented at the 11th Annual International Conference on Post-Compulsory Education and Training: Enriching Learning Cultures, Gold Coast.
Billett, S. and Somerville, M. (2004) 'Transformations at Work: Identity and Learning', *Studies in Continuing Education*, 26(2): 309–326.
Billett, S., Barker, M. and Hernon-Tinning, B. (2004) 'Participatory Practices at Work', *Pedagogy, Culture and Society*, 12(2): 233–257.
Billett, S., Ehrich, L. and Hernon-Tinning, B. (2003) 'Small Business Pedagogic Practices', *Journal of Vocational Education and Training*, 55(2): 149–167.
Billett, S., Smith, R. and Barker, M. (2005) 'Understanding Work, Learning and the Remaking of Cultural Practices', *Studies in Continuing Education*, 27(3): 219–237.
Bishop, J.H. (1997) 'What We Know About Employer Provided Training: A Review of the Literature', *Research in Labour Economics*, 16, 19–87.
Bloomer, M. and Hodkinson, P. (2000) 'Learning Careers: Continuity and Change in Young People's Dispositions to Learning', *British Education Research Journal*, 26(5): 583–598.
Bourdieu, P. (1977) *Outline of a Theory of Practice*. New York: Cambridge University Press.
Bourdieu, P. (1991) *Language and Symbolic Power* (edited by J.B. Thompson). Cambridge: Polity Press.

Brown, J.S., Collins, A. and Duguid, P. (1989) 'Situated Cognition and the Culture of Learning', *Educational Researcher,* 18(1): 32–34.

Bruner, J.S. (1966) 'On Cognitive Growth II', in J.S. Bruner, R.R. Oliven and P.M. Greenfield (eds), *Studies in Cognitive Growth* (pp. 30–67). New York: Wiley.

Bruner, J. (2001) 'Foreword', in B. F. Malle, L. J. Moses and D. A. Baldwin (eds), *Intentions and Intentionality: Foundations of Social Cognition.* Cambridge, MA: The MIT Press, pp. ix–xii.

Chi, M.T.H., Feltovich, P.J. and Glaser, R. (1981) 'Categorisation and Representation of Physics Problems by Experts and Novices', *Cognitive Science,* 5: 121–152.

Chi, M.T.H., Glaser, R. and Rees, E. (1982) 'Problem-Solving Ability', in R. J. Sternberg (ed.), *Advances in the Psychology of Human Intelligence* (Vol. 1). Hillsdale, NJ: Erlbaum, pp. 7–76.

Cole, M. (1998) 'Can Cultural Psychology Help Us Think About Diversity?', *Mind, Culture and Activity,* 5(4): 291–304.

Cole, M. (2002) *Building Centers of Strength in Cultural Historical Research.* Paper presented at the Annual Meeting of the American Education Research Association, New Orleans.

Collins, A., Brown, J.S. and Newman, S.E. (1989) 'Cognitive Apprenticeship: Teaching the Crafts of Reading, Writing and Mathematics', in L. B. Resnick (ed.), *Knowing, Learning and Instruction: Essays in honour of Robert Glaser.* Hillsdale, NJ: Erlbaum and Associates, pp. 453–494.

Danford, A. (1998) 'Teamworking and Labour Regulation in the Autocomponents Industry', *Work, Employment & Society,* 12(3): 409–431.

Darrah, C.N. (1996) *Learning and Work: An Exploration in Industrial Ethnography.* New York: Garland Publishing.

Davies, B. (2000) *A Body of Wrtiting 1990–1999.* New York: Altamira Press.

Engeström, Y. (1993) 'Development Studies of Work as a Testbench of Activity Theory: The Case of Primary Care Medical Practice', in S. Chaiklin and J. Lave (eds), *Understanding Practice: Perspectives on Activity and Context.* Cambridge, UK: Cambridge University Press, pp. 64–103.

Engeström, Y. and Middleton, D. (1996) 'Introduction: Studying Work as Mindful Practice', in Y. Engeström and D. Middleton (eds), *Cognition and Communication at Work* Cambridge, UK: Cambridge University Press, pp. 1–15.

Evans, K. (2002) 'Taking Control of their Lives? Agency in Young Adult Transitions in England and the New Germany', *Journal of Youth Studies,* 5(3): 245–269.

Foucault, M. (1979) *Discipline and Punishment.* New York: Vintage Books.

Foucault, M. (1986) *The Care of the Self: The History of Sexuality,* Vol. 3 (translated by R. Hurley). Harmondsworth: Penguin.

Gergen, K.J. (2000) *The Saturated Self: Dilemmas of Identity in Contemporary Life.* New York: Basic Books.

Giddens, A. (1984) *The Constitution of Society.* Cambridge: Polity Press.

Giddens, A. (1991) *Modernity and Self-identity: Self and Society in the Late Modern Age.* Stanford: Stanford University Press.

Goffman, E. (1990) *The Presentation of Self in Everyday Life.* London: Penguin Books.

Harré, R. (1995) 'The Necessity of Personhood as Embedded Being', *Theory and Psychology,* 5: 369–373.

Hull, G. (1997) 'Preface and Introduction', in G. Hull (ed.), *Changing Work, Changing Workers: Critical Perspectives on Language, Literacy and Skills.* New York: State University of New York Press, pp. 3–39.

Lave, J. (1993) 'The Practice of Learning', in S. Chaiklin and J. Lave (eds), *Understanding Practice: Perspectives on Activity and Context.* Cambridge, UK: Cambridge University Press, pp. 3–32.

Lave, J. and Wenger, E. (1991) *Situated Learning – Legitimate Peripheral Participation.* Cambridge, UK: Cambridge University Press.

Leontyev, A.N. (1981) *Problems of the Development of the Mind.* Moscow: Progress Publishers.

Malle, B.F., Moses, L.J. and Baldwin, D.A. (2001) 'Introduction: The Significance of Intentionality', in B.F. Malle, L.J. Moses and D.A. Baldwin (eds), *Intentions and Intentionality: Foundations of Social Cognition.* Cambridge, MA: The MIT Press, pp. 1–26.

Mansfield, N. (2000) *Subjectivity: Theories of the Self from Freud to Haraway.* Sydney: Allen & Unwin.

McBrier, D.B. and Wilson, G. (2004) 'Going Down? Race and Downward Occupational Mobility for White Collar Workers in the 1990s', *Work and Occupations,* 31(3): 283–322.

Newell, A. and Simon, H.A. (1972) *Human Problem Solving.* Englewood Cliffs, NJ: Prentice-Hall.

Newman, D., Griffin, P. and Cole, M. (1989) *The Construction Zone: Working for Cognitive Change in Schools.* Cambridge, UK: Cambridge University Press.

Pea, R.D. (1993) 'Practices of Distributed Intelligence and Designs for Education', in G. Salomon (ed.), *Distributed Cognitions.* New York: Cambridge University Press, pp. 47–87.

Piaget, J. (1968) *Structuralism* (translated and edited by C. Maschler). London: Routledge & Kegan Paul.

Ratner, C. (2000) 'Agency and Culture', *Journal for the Theory of Social Behaviour,* 30: 413–434.

Rogoff, B. (1990) *Apprenticeship in Thinking – Cognitive Development in Social Context.* New York: Oxford University Press.

Rogoff, B. (1995) 'Observing Sociocultural Activity on Three Planes: Participatory Appropriation, Guided Participation, Apprenticeship', in J. W. Wertsch, A. Alvarez and P. del Rio (eds), *Sociocultural Studies of Mind.* Cambridge, UK: Cambridge University Press, pp. 139–164.

Rousseau, J.J. (1968) *The Social Contract.* London: Penguin.

Scribner, S. (1985) 'Vygostky's Use of History', in J.V. Wertsch (ed.), *Culture, Communication and Cognition: Vygotskian Perspectives*. Cambridge, UK: Cambridge University Press, pp. 119–145.

Searle, J.R. (1995) *The Construction of Social Reality*. London: Penguin.

Sfard, A. (1998) 'On Two Metaphors for Learning and the Dangers of Choosing Just One', *Educational Researcher, March*: 4–13.

Skinner, C. (2004) 'The Changing Occupational Structure of Large Metropolitan Areas: Implications for the High School Educated', *Journal of Urban Affairs*, 26(1): 67–88.

Solomon, N. (1999) 'Culture and Difference in Workplace Learning', in D. Boud and D. J. Garrick (eds), *Understanding Learning at Work*. London: Routledge, pp. 119–131.

Somerville, M. (2002) *Changing Masculine Work Cultures*. Paper presented at the Envisioning Practice – Implementing Change, Gold Coast.

Somerville, M. (2003) *Who Learns?: Enriching Learning Cultures in Aged Care Workplaces*. Paper presented at the 11th Annual International Conference on Post-Compulsory Education and Training: Enriching Learning Cultures, Gold Coast.

Somerville, M. and Abrahamsson, L. (2003) 'Trainers and Learners Constructing a Community of Practice: Masculine Work Cultures and Learning Safety in the Mining Industry', *Studies in the Education of Adults*, 35(1): 19–34.

Somerville, M., and Bernoth, M. (2001) *Safe Bodies: Solving a Dilemma in Workplace*. Paper presented at the Knowledge Demands for the New Economy. 9th Annual International Conference on Post-compulsory Education and Training, Gold Coast, Queensland.

Suchman, L. (1996) 'Constituting Shared Workspaces', in Y. Engeström & D. Middleton (eds), *Cognition and Communication at Work*. Cambridge: Cambridge University Press, pp. 35–60.

Valsiner, J. (1998) *The Guided Mind: A Sociogenetic Approach to Personality*. Cambridge, MA: Harvard University Press.

Valsiner, J. (2000) *Culture and Human Development*. London: Sage Publications.

Valsiner, J. and van der Veer, R. (2000) *The Social Mind: The Construction of an Idea*. Cambridge, UK: Cambridge University Press.

Van Lehn, V. (1989) 'Towards a Theory of Impasse-Driven Learning', in H. Mandl and A. Lesgold (eds), *Learning Issues for Intelligent Tutoring Systems*. New York: Springer-Verlag, pp. 19–41.

von Glasersfeld, E. (1987) 'Learning as a Constructive Activity', in C. Janvier (ed), *Problems of Representation in the Teaching and Learning of Mathematics*. Hillsdale, NJ: Lawrence Erlbaum.

Vygotsky, L.S. (1978) *Mind in Society – The Development of Higher Psychological Processes*. Cambridge, MA: Harvard University Press.

Wenger, E. (1998) *Communities of Practice: Learning, Meaning, and Identity*. Cambridge, UK: Cambridge University Press.

6

Learning in the Workplace: Communities of Practice and Beyond

Len Cairns

INTRODUCTION

The ideas and approaches to people learning to take their place in a workplace as a 'fully fledged' participant has been described and located, over the past two decades, as a process of joining a 'community of practice' (Lave and Wenger, 1991; Wenger, 1998; Wenger, 2000a, 2000b; Wenger et al., 2002). This terminology has become quite pervasive across the writing in the field of work and related learning (Eraut, 2002; Hodkinson and Hodkinson, 2004). The concept has, however, also been the subject of some critique and discussion (Fuller et al., 2005; Fuller, 2007). This chapter seeks to argue a case that while the concepts associated with 'communities of practice' which underpin the related 'legitimate peripheral participation' have been useful as starting points for some reconsideration of theory and practice elements across workplace learning, movement 'beyond' these ideas is necessary if the field of theory and research in workplace learning is to progress further in the twenty-first century.

There is little doubt that in the twenty-first century, the concern with learning located in sites other than what has formally and formerly been seen as educational institutions (be they schools or colleges or other institutes, including universities) has emerged from behind the facade of 'learning on the job' or experience whereby there was an element of the second-rate, or less than sophisticated approach, in these real-world situations. Learning and Work have become, as we have promoted in this *Handbook*, inextricably linked and reinforcing each other as genuine areas of endeavour for second or ultra modern people and needs. Attempts to theorise and understand the ways in which people engage and develop their skills, hone their attitudes and seek advancement in work and learning across their lifespace activities, whether for paid employment or other rewards or satisfactions, have fascinated researchers over the past years (Marsick, 1987; Boud, 1998; Boud and Garrick, 1999; Marsick and Watkins, 1990; Evans et al., 2002; Noon and Blyton, 2002; Cairns et al., 2006; Cairns and Stephenson, 2009).

SITUATED LEARNING

This chapter discusses the trend, in the late twentieth century, to move from the previously alleged dominant model of learning theory associated with informal or work-related learning as a largely cognitive individualistic model towards the assertion that all learning was socially situated (Lave and Wenger, 1991). Much of the case developed in the late twentieth century related to the perception of a former dominant model of learning, largely based on American psychological ideas (influenced by positivist philosophies and approaches) and emerged as an alternative view of learning (especially in workplaces) which emphasised the legitimacy of participation in communities and re-asserted, or as Lave and Wenger claimed (p. 29), 'rescued' the idea of apprenticeship.

> Learning viewed as situated activity has as its central defining characteristic a process that we call *legitimate peripheral participation*. By this we mean to draw attention to the point that learners inevitably participate in ·communities of practitioners and that mastery of knowledge and skill requires newcomers to move toward full participation in the sociocultural practices of a community (p. 29).

The general theoretical position within which the idea of *communities of practice* emerged in the early 1990s has become referred to as *situated learning theory*. This view of learning and how it may be theorised, arose through the work of Lave (1988) and Brown et al., (1989) and has been further developed and enhanced by Lave and Wenger (1991) as well as a number of other commentators such as Kirshner and Whitson (1997).

Any brief discussion of the situated theory of learning, as this conceptualisation has become known, is fraught with the accusation that to do so in a few short paragraphs does not do the field and its many advocates justice. However, this introduction to the area attempts to locate the related or derived concept of *communities of practice* as the main focus of this chapter, not the entire writings on situatedness.

Nevertheless, there are some key elements of the Lave and Wenger presentations that need some referencing here to avoid any misconceptions of their theoretical case. A much quoted aspect of Lave and Wenger's 1991 book appears at the end of their Chapter 1, which set out their basic concept of *legitimate peripheral participation* and, as such, emphasised the contrast between their emerging model and theory and the more traditional individualistic emphasis.

> In conclusion, we emphasize the significance of shifting the analytic focus from the individual as learner to learning as participation in the social world, and from the concept of cognitive process to the more-encompassing view of social practice (p. 43).

This view (albeit almost at the start of their case in the volume) has been interpreted as a key (if not a cornerstone aspect) of their theory (Hara, 2009) and has led to a range of views that have been characterised as a 'participation' approach which sought to replace the then dominant 'acquisition' approach (Sfard, 1998; Mason, 2007; Vosniadou, 2007). (More will be said in the section on Dualism on page 76).

Of particular interest for this author, at this stage of the chapter, is the fact that while Lave and Wenger do assert the primacy of practice and social interactions as the basis for understanding learning and cognition; they are not excluding (as some who followed their work over-emphasised) that the individual's agentic behaviour had little or no place. As they clearly put their position in 1991:

> Briefly, a theory of social practice emphasizes the relational interdependency of agent and world, activity, meaning, cognition, learning, and knowing. It emphasizes the inherently socially negotiated character of meaning and the interested, concerned character of the thought and action of persons-in-activity. This view also claims that learning, thinking, and knowing are relations among people in activity in, with, and arising from the socially and culturally structured world (p. 50).

In addition, in Chapter 2 of their 1991 book, significantly titled *Practice, Person and Social World,* Lave and Wenger argue that the person is still central to their theory but as a person in the world, a 'whole person' interacting in social communities. They even discuss the possible sense of 'contradiction between efforts to "decenter" the definition of the person and efforts to arrive at a rich notion of agency in terms of "whole persons"', and conclude that their approach "implies that changing memberships in communities of practice, like participation, can be neither fully internalised nor fully externalised"' (p. 54).

It is certainly an approach to theorising learning that has had a major impact over the past twenty years (Sfard, 1998; Vosniadou, 2007; Salomon, 1993; Kirshner and Whitson, 1997) and that there have been attempts at seeking some interplay or even reconciliation between the extremes of *situativity* ideas and theoretical stances and the more traditional *cognitive* views (though these terms are almost stereotypic in their attempt to group or classify the many variations along the dimensions inclined in each theoretical direction) (Billett, 1996; Alexander, 2007; Vosniadou, 2007; Hodkinson et al., 2008).

The whole enterprise of the theorising and applicability to workplace learning of the situated theories of learning, knowledge and the relationships among knowledge, agency and mind and society led to the approach which came to be known as the *communities of practice* view of how people learn in life and workplaces.

COMMUNITIES OF PRACTICE: THEORY AND APPLICABILITY

We now turn to exploring the concept of 'communities of practice' and its essential projection as the centre piece of a social theory of learning as propounded by Wenger (1998) and its subsequent adoption and use across the Workplace Learning field over the next two decades (Wenger et al., 2002; Hara, 2009). The chapter will critique the concept and its applicability and suggest additional considerations in the twenty-first century. There have been a wide range of opinions, critiques and extremely useful analyses of the concept and its usefulness to the field of workplace learning theory and practice implications over recent years (Eraut, 2002; Hodkinson and Hodkinson, 2004; Fuller et al., 2005; Edwards, 2005; Barton and Tusting, 2005; Fuller, 2007; Hughes et al., 2007).

At the outset, the initial explication of the notion of 'communities of practice' was set out in the Lave and Wenger book on Situated Learning in 1991.

> The concept of community of practice underlying the notion of legitimate peripheral participation, and hence of "knowledge" and its "location" in the lived-in world, is both crucial and subtle. The community of practice of midwifery or tailoring involves much more than the technical knowledgeable skill involved in delivering babies or producing clothes. A community of practice is a set of relations among persons, activity, and world, over time and in relation with other tangential and overlapping communities of practice (p. 98).

A significant element of this quotation is the term 'lived-in-world' which is an aspect that is not elaborated by Lave and Wenger in detail but which pervades their conceptualisation of the concept of communities and their functioning. This element of activity and practice is discussed by Engeström and Cole (1997) in terms whereby they suggest that '(s)o the notion of situatedness leads to the primacy of practice – a whole new landscape for the study of cognition' (p. 301). The nesting of situated theory in practice and real world or lived in world practice resonated well with theory in workplaces and workplace learning and much of the Lave and Wenger evidential base for their theorising arose from anthropologically influenced studies of workers in various sites and groups such as Mayan midwives, Vai and Gola tailors in Liberia, butchers in US supermarkets and reformed alcoholics in AA (p. 65ff, Lave and Wenger, 1991) (which all led to the 'communities' idea).

Writing his own volume specifically dedicated to the idea and its theory in 1998, Wenger suggests that he is proposing a social theory of learning through the concept of communities of practice. Wenger argues that his theoretical stance sees learning as a matter of social participation (p. 4), and that communities of practice are pervasive, often not explicit and 'are an integral part of our daily lives' (p. 7).

Definitionally, Wenger (1998) suggests that there are three characteristics or 'dimensions' that constitute a community of practice. These are 'mutual engagement' in a set of activities or practice, a 'joint enterprise' and a 'shared repertoire' (p. 73). Wenger is at pains to point out that his idea for such a community is not a synonym for a group, a team or a network (p. 74). Further, he presents a set of what he calls 'indicators' that a community of practice has formed. These 14 indicators are presented by Wenger as follows:

1 sustained mutual relationships-harmonious or conflictual
2 shared ways of engaging in doing things together
3 the rapid flow of information and propagation of innovation
4 absence of introductory preambles, as if conversations and interactions were merely the continuation of an ongoing process
5 very quick setup of a problem to be discussed
6 substantial overlap in participants' descriptions of who belongs
7 knowing what others know, what they can do, and how they can contribute to an enterprise
8 mutually defining identities
9 the ability to assess the appropriateness of actions and products
10 specific tools, representations, and other artifacts (sic)
11 local lore, shared stories, inside jokes, knowing together
12 jargon and shortcuts to communication as well as the ease of producing new ones
13 certain styles recognised as displaying membership
14 a shared discourse reflecting a certain perspective on the world (p. 125ff).

Wenger argues that these 14 characteristics, when evident, indicate that the three dimensions of the concept 'are present to a substantial degree' (p. 126).

By 2002, however, Wenger and his colleagues, McDermott and Snyder, had broadened the idea of a community of practice to be defined as:

Communities of practice are groups of people who share a concern, a set of problems, or a passion about a topic, and who.deepen their knowledge and expertise in this area by interacting on an ongoing basis (p. 4).

As indicated by Barton and Tusting (2005) in their introduction to their volume on moving 'beyond communities of practice', the concept 'has been used, applied, criticised, adapted and developed by a wide range of researchers' (p. 1). The idea and its applicability has been open to considerable debate and further consideration and critique over the past decade (Eraut, 2002; Hodkinson and Hodkinson, 2004; Edwards, 2005; Barton and Tusting, 2005; Fuller et al., 2005; Hughes et al., 2007).

It is clear that the idea of an entity such as 'communities of practice' has had both impact and effect across the areas of learning approaches, theory and practice, particularly in non-formal learning sites such as the workplace. What follows is an examination of a number of aspects of relevance to this discussion of the place of *communities of practice*.

The discussion needs to start with a brief side-piece about the dualism element in the debate about the theory and underlying assumptions of the concept and its application over the past twenty years.

DUALISM AND ITS PITFALLS AS A BASIS FOR CONCERN IN THE DISCUSSION

A central concern with many of the models of learning and development of learners in work-places and in relation to the work enterprise has been the way writing and descriptions have 'dichotomised' what takes place in work settings as either 'informal' or 'work-related' as opposed to more 'formal' and scholarly or institutionalised learning sites and activities. This dichotomy has been underpinned by what appears to be an assumption (albeit implicit at times) that learning activities more associated with the world of work were somehow inferior or of lesser standing than more formal institutional learning. This dichotomy echoes the 'dualism' that has come to dominate many scholars and approaches to the field of learning and its under-standing over the past four to five hundred years in the Western world.

Certainly the famous Cartesian dualism (mind–body) is the one idea in this vogue that comes into play in most discussions (Nonaka and Takeuchi, 1995; Kim, 2006). There is however, a more interesting and broad basis to dualism in this area and it is argued in this chapter that the situational learning (and by extension the related concept of 'communities of practice') is another dualism in the field that needs addressing and possible redressing. At least, there needs to be either a reconciliation, re-consideration or what Billett called, in 1996, a 'bridging' of the two apparently opposing camps of individually motivated cognitive theories and the socially located 'situated' theories and their attendant assumptions and implications for work and workplace learning to make sense of the field and the implications for practice and development.

Writing in 1998, Sfard argued quite convincingly that two metaphors for learning had dominated thinking in much writing and debate. She characterised these as the *acquisition* metaphor and the *participation* metaphor. This dualistic interpretation of the major thrust of debate circulating through the late twentieth century exemplified the fact that the long and often heated debate about dualism was still evident in theories and their implications for practice and interpretation of learning and life. Sfard suggested, in her conclusion that 'one metaphor is not enough' and she suggested that 'we can live neither with nor without either of them' (p. 10).

Dualism ('any view that postulates two kinds of thing in some domain' p. 105, Oxford Dictionary of Philosophy, Blackburn, 2008) has its roots in the West through Cartesian philosophy and has been one of the burning issues in the field (Ryle, 1968; Heil, 2004; Carruthers, 2004; Kim, 2006). The differentiation of 'mind' from 'body', in its simplest applications led many to proffer what relationship this had to the personal and the logistics of the social. Educational writers, from Comenius, through Dewey and beyond (see Murphy, 1995; Prawat, 1998), have emphasised the faults with such dualism and emphasised the holistic and experiential aspects of learning theories. (Comenius actually reported meeting with Descartes around 1642, and he reported that whilst they respected each others' differing theories and basic philosophical positions, they talked for some four hours, but did not agree (Comenius, quoted in Murphy, 1995, pp. 29–30).

What is interesting is that such views of mind are not held in the same way in the Eastern thinking of India, Japan and China, and this will be taken up below as another potential way forward in our thinking.

The situated models of learning (originally developed by Brown et al., 1989), before being more popularised by Lave and Wenger, became identified as a learning model apposite from the more traditional cognitive (acquisition) approaches and advocates clearly considered that all learning was socially situated as a truism. The situated model of learning, as this approach became known, led to contrasts with the previously dominant cognitive models and what emerged as a consequence of this newer model and thinking were some attempts to reconcile (or possibly reassert) the significance of the individual learner with the emerging emphasis on the social (or 'ensemble') aspect of learning. As Kirshner and Whitson (1997) stated, their book was an attempt to expound a situated cognition which might redress some of the perceived excesses of the situated theory's 'misuses' to better position thinking about mind and learning theories for practical applicability. Similar gradual attempts to provide bridges or reconciliations have emerged (Salomon, 1993; Billett, 1996; Vosniadou, 2007; Hodkinson et al., 2008).

Certainly, through the 1990s and into the beginning of the twenty-first century, the ideas associated with situated learning and communities of practice (and more flexible uses such as learning communities and professional communities (Roberts and Pruitt, 2009; Hough and Paine, 1997) in different contexts, became central within the learning literature. That these elements resonated strongly with the workplace learning thinking was also very evident (Fuller, 2007; Hara, 2009).

While there was a pervasive influence there have been critical reactions to the ideas of *communities of practice*, as mentioned above. The next section will outline, albeit briefly, some of these critical points, and the chapter will conclude with some ideas about where the field might go 'beyond' the concept.

CRITIQUES OF COMMUNITIES OF PRACTICE

Aspects of the concept and the theorisation of *communities of practice* that have attracted critique and discussion have included the following:

1 Definitional issues surrounding the idea of *community* and how the concept is interpreted in different workplace settings or contexts (Eraut, 2002; Hodkinson and Hodkinson, 2004; Gee, 2005).
2 How communities of practice deal with learning something new (Edwards, 2005; Hughes et al., 2007).
3 The model seems to be concerned with what is done as learning rather than approach what is actually learnt (Edwards, 2005; Hughes et al., 2007).
4 The way the exposition of Lave and Wenger sees the learning in a community of practice to be moving inwards rather than expansive, and what is the level of the unit of analysis in exploring such communities? (Fuller, 2007: Engeström, 2001).
5 The need for additional consideration of the place of language in the theory of communities of practice (Barton and Tusting, 2005).
6 The place of individual agency within the model (Billett, 1996; Hughes et al., 2007).

These six areas raise some of the comments, issues and questions that critics and supporters alike have written about in response to the communities of practice expositions. Most of those mentioned write from a perspective of acknowledging that the ideas and surrounding theory of the communities of practice notion have impacted significantly and in ways that have opened up debate and some re-considerations of human learning and its social interactivity elements.

Eraut, presenting at an American Educational Research Association (AERA) conference in New Orleans in 2002 questioned the concept and the 'appropriation' of the term community by Lave and Wenger for what he described as their 'particular theoretical perspective' (p. 3). As part of his discussion, Eraut sought to explore issues he saw in the concept as proposed in terms of diversity of professional practice and the balance between diversity and commonality within such a 'community'. He also questioned how the concept, as developed, handled dysfunctional groupings and what the role of agency was in these communities. Eraut's comments were offered within the context of his own research and that of others into professional learning in the workplace, and he offered a number of studies as examples to indicate the complexities of learning trajectories and social interaction whilst working with groups such as nurses, junior doctors and 'a diabetes ward team' of mixed health professionals. Eraut's conclusion was that the two terms, *learning community* and *community of practice,* did not offer much added value to the discussion, and while he suggested that Wenger's three dimensions of participation, mutual engagement and joint enterprise could be identified within some of the examples he presented, they could be so discussed 'without needing to refer to the problematic concept of a community of practice' (p. 12).

James Gee (2005) also questions the term 'community', and as a linguistics scholar offers an interesting and very different way to examine a learning space. He starts with an outline of what he terms a Semiotic Social Space and uses examples from computer games to make his points. He then proposes what he calls Affinity Spaces as a better descriptor than community, and outlines eleven characteristics or features of an affinity group or space and argues that these actually define the affinity space concept.

Writing in 2004 as part of the reporting of a study of schoolteachers and their schools and departments within them, Hodkinson and Hodkinson suggest that the concept of *communities of practice* has offered a useful movement away from traditional models of learning (or the 'standard paradigm' Beckett and Hager, 2002) which emphasised the acquisition of knowledge through a transmission or transfer approach towards a more socially centred understanding of human learning. Hodkinson and Hodkinson criticise the Lave and Wenger concept as being somewhat ambiguous in different stages of its development and definition, particularly with reference to its applicability across small ('close-knit') groups versus larger and broader groupings of practitioners.

In their study, Hodkinson and Hodkinson report four accounts of differing secondary school subject departments and their patterns of work and learning. Two schools each had one department characterised as 'collaborative' in its learning approach and one that was more 'individualistic' (p. 29). They concluded that there were some issues with the way Wenger, in particular, had subsequently defined and worked on the concept from a perspective more at the level of what Hodkinson and Hodkinson call the 'narrower meaning' (the closer tighter groups idea) which, while applicable to some of the teacher departmental analysis, was not so where a broader conceptualisation (the wider model) was needed. As they emphasised:

> Thus, it is useful to apply this tighter form of community of practice to the small coherent subject departments in our study. It provided a valuable intermediate level of analysis, between the broader occupational and organisational context and the dispositions of individual workers. Both the departmental scale and the national scale have explanatory value for understanding teacher learning and no account is complete without incorporating both (p. 30).

This experience with their study led Hodkinson and Hodkinson to arrive at a set of suggestions about the terminology needed for such workplace learning studies of socially situated learning by groups:

> This suggests the following use of terminology: *Situated learning*, or *learning as social participation*, are better terms than communities of practice to capture the underlying essence of Lave and Wenger's (1991) theoretical approach. The *field of practice*, or *learning field*, following Bourdieu, may be better terms than community of practice to represent the view that learning is ubiquitously social. *Community of practice* may be better preserved for the narrower, more cohesive types of social relations that characterise Lave and Wenger's examples. Such a community of practice implies a smaller scale of focus than 'field', and can be useful where such narrower communities can be clearly identified.

Edwards, writing in 2005, sets her comments on the ideas and theoretical underpinnings of *communities of practice* within her discussion of 'learning by participating' taking her start from the examination of a set of Teaching and Learning Research Programme (TLRP) funded studies in the UK. She utilises the metaphor of participation from Sfard and notes that this view was more common in TLRP projects concerned with post-compulsory education and training than school-based or related projects. She argues that her concern in her paper is with Learning, and similar to Hodkinson and Hodkinson's earlier paper, she draws parallels with Bourdieu's concepts of habitus, field and practice (p. 57).

Edwards offers four aspects of critique about *communities of practice*, taking her position as one whose concern is about 'what learning is'. She sees 'limitations in the view offered by Lave and Wenger' (p. 57), but softens her comments to say she is 'not criticizing that work, simply suggesting that perhaps too much has been read into it'.

Edwards' four points, all made quite briefly, are:

1 That there is a need to question the idea of a *community of practice*. She says that the three aspects of joint enterprise, mutual engagement and a shared repertoire set as key defining features by Wenger, could also apply across such diverse activities as being in a traffic jam or bottleneck at the same time and place each evening, or holding a department store's loyalty card. She suggests that "the concept needs tighter boundaries".

2 The second critical point concerns the fact that the concept does not appear to deal with how a community learns something new. The main thrust of the *communities of practice* descriptions and examples is how apprentices are socialised into a working community and move from a novice to an "old timer" through a centripetal journey. Edwards suggests here that a solution is to turn to Engeström's "expansive learning" ideas.

3 Edwards' third point is a simple, yet very significant line that "(f)inally, and perhaps most importantly, it does not tell what is learnt, only what is done" (p. 57). (This point is also taken up by Hughes, Jewson and Unwin, 2007).

4 At the end of her brief set of critical points Edwards also suggest that whilst Vygostky is an apparent source or possible linked inspiration for Lave's views, and he was most concerned with the place of language, it is a pity that this element has not been a major focus in the *communities of practice* works (she does acknowledge that this is a bit unfair as a criticism of Lave). This element forms a good deal of the case being made across the Barton and Tusting (2005) book.

In what are quite comprehensive and detailed works examining a wide range of elements in the debate about *communities of practice*, the two volumes by Barton and Tusting (2005) and Hughes et al., (2007) offer possibly the best teasing out of issues and needs with this concept.

Barton and Tusting, in their introduction to the ten chapters they commissioned for the book, present a clear case that this volume, entitled *Beyond Communities of Practice*, is intended to both take the concept further and to also suggest areas where it may be strengthened by additional thinking. The authors are mostly coming to the concept from backgrounds in the areas of language and literacy (though not exclusively). The editors sum up the work and its critique neatly at the end of their introduction:

> Across these chapters, three sets of common themes emerge, identifying areas in which we need to move beyond the current theory of communities of practice. Firstly, there is a call to incorporate a model of language-in-use, covering language, literacy and discourse; this is argued both on a theoretical level and with reference to a variety of examples. Secondly, there is the call for attention to issues of power and conflict within communities. This is expressed in different ways in different chapters (risk and stigma, diversity, equity, legitimation conflicts) but emerges throughout much of the work. Thirdly, there is the need to incorporate the broader social context in some way when researching communities of practice (p. 12).

In the Hughes, Jewson and Unwin (2007) volume, there are a number of chapters which again take up many of the issues raised above, including Jewson examining 'community' in the concept, Billett discussing 'the missing subject', the personal within the community and a comprehensive review of the theories of learning and communities of practice by Fuller.

Fuller (2007) in Chapter 2 of the Hughes, Jewson and Unwin volume raises some significant additional issues with the concept of *communities of practice*, which she terms 'an underdeveloped concept' (p. 20). Starting with the sobering thought that *communities of practice* can lead to 'less than benign effects' and that this element has been overlooked by many advocates of the idea but was seen by Lave and Wenger as a possibility, Fuller reminds her readers that workplaces have often been sites of conflict and disputations and are not only to be seen as positive joint enterprises as in most of the Lave and Wenger examples. She goes on to raise issues with the participation element and raises points made by Hager (2005) which emphasised that participation in such a community could be seen as inherently conservative as it leads to reproduction and continuity rather than transformation (p. 22). Fuller cites the Hodkinson and Hodkinson issues and those raised by Edwards (above). Fuller, in discussing the Hodkinson and Hodkinson suggested delineation of communities, suggests that there is an 'intractable problem' which is what she terms the 'container notion' of context. This aspect about 'boundaries' will be returned to below.

Fuller also offers criticisms (some of which echo her earlier work with Unwin and the Hodkinsons, Fuller et al., 2005), about the inadequacy of communities of practice to transform, the difficulties of the novice–expert notion encapsulated in the 'old timers' and 'newcomers' terminology, and the need for differing learning trajectories from the dominant version of the inward inherent in the model (though she does point out that Wenger has attempted some modification of this element in 1998) and how learning across communities might take place.

Hughes et al. (2007) conclude their excellent volume of essays with an overview of the critiques and their main points in a conclusion they subtitle 'Further developments and unresolved issues'. These developments and issues are placed clearly to suggest that while the concept of *communities of practice* was 'a noble project with humane objectives' (p. 171), it raised many issues and problematic aspects that have been canvassed in this section. They do conclude, however, that 'the idea is one which is rich, complex, multi-stranded and deserves to be the focus of intensive further theoretical analysis and empirical research (p. 176).

BEYOND COMMUNITIES OF PRACTICE?

This final section of the chapter offers, after a consideration of much of the preceding commentary and critique, what can be viewed as a way to move forward in the consideration of how learning in the workplace can be theorised and examined as an experience by individuals within socially situated activities and in a reciprocal interactive manner.

First, it is apparent from what has been canvassed within this chapter that any dualistic approach of an 'either or' model of learning is flawed and will not lead to any useful long-term progress in the understanding of workplace learning theories and applicability. Accordingly, there is a need to consider re-inserting what Billett (2007) called the 'personal' into community or as Hughes et al. put it in their conclusion that 'a number of authors seek to rescue proactive, creative, purposeful, reflexive agents from over-deterministic structural perspectives in learning theory' (p. 172). This resonates with Sfard's idea of a necessary 'middle way' and the writings of others who suggest differing models of learning that do not lean too far in either the 'acquisition' or the 'participation' directions of the old dualism. This also fits with earlier attempts to build other thinking into the *communities of practice* literature such as Fox's marriage of Foucault and Actor-Network theory (Fox, 2000) and the more recent case for a 'cultural theory of learning' and a 'theory of learning cultures' as suggested by Hodkinson et al. (2008).

It seems essential that whatever learning models and theories we develop and apply to workplace learning there needs to be a consideration of the social situatedness of that learning and the agency of the individual in the learning process. Whether the notion of a 'community' is still useful has been raised with a movement to suggest that it may seem to be both too rigid as a metaphor for what we are examining and also vague in its definition and interpretation.

The matter of multiple communities of practice and the way learners move across and between them has exercised some writers as mentioned above (e.g. Fuller). There is a serious need to account for the way people move around in their learning and particularly in relation to workplace learning. If we accept that work and place need wider and more contemporary considerations as to their meaning in our ultramodern world (see Chapter 1, Cairns and Malloch, this volume) then the concepts about what social ensembles, people (workers), learn among and between should be conceived of as a far more fluid and intersecting concept than the 'community' image projects. What has emerged from this somewhat rigid image of the community is the notion of crossing boundaries between communities (sometimes also referred to as borders).

Engeström, (2001 and also this volume Chapter 7) has a different view of boundary crossing in his theory of what he calls expansive learning. For Engeström, boundary crossing is about 'stepping into unfamiliar domains' (Engeström et al. (1995) and also involved what he terms network building. In more recent work (see Chapter 7 this volume) he has proposed a concept called 'knotworking', which refers to a group coming together in a manner that can metaphorically resemble a knot which is tied and untied at different stages and which is somewhat spontaneous like an improvised collaboration amongst 'loosely connected actors and activity systems' (Engeström, Engeström and Vahaaho, 1999 as cited in Chapter 7; also see Engeström (2008).

Whilst this has offered an interesting site for debate and the notion of learners in some instances as boundary crossers may have some academic appeal, the operation of most learners is more a matter of trajectory tracing along a journey with intersection choices and cultural influences at different stages or points along that trajectory. Some intersections lead to different social influences and cultural impacts, others lead to rejections and potential conflicts and may lead to retreat and retracing steps and different intersection choices. The learner engages and is engaged with the choices and the consequences. The learner is not outside the system and is fully operational on, in and with the social situations and people in those systems. Learning is *through* involvement and interaction of an agentic learner with the social system and its influences and features.

Places where learning occurs can be any of interpersonal, intrapersonal, physical, spiritual and even virtual (also see Chapter 1) and there is much to be gained from some differing perspectives of place and the role of people in places and how this relates to learning.

The Japanese philosopher, Nishida, offered a concept termed *Basho* (also written of as *Ba*) which may be useful in considering a different lens to examine where we may move beyond *communities of practice* (Nishida 1987a, 1987b). For Nishida, *Basho* refers to a field or space where there are shared emerging relationships. It is not, we are reminded by Scharmer (2000), an object or a subject. Nonaka, and his colleagues, who write of *Ba* as the same aspect from Nishida's theory, describe this concept as 'a shared mental place for emerging relationships' (p. 93, Nonaka et al., 2000). Underlying this concept is a more wholistic notion which Wargo (2005) writing on Basho, describes as resembling 'the notion of a domain of discourse' (p. 96), but he suggests this is too simplistic as an explanation of the meaning of the term. The philosophical understanding of just what Nishida meant by his term Basho is gone into in great detail by Wargo, and his concluding points may assist us in this understanding.

A key aspect is that Nishida rejects Descartes and the dualism inherent in that thinking which Nonaka and Takeuchi (1995) argue has dominated Western thinking for years.

Wargo sums up his explanations as follows:

The logical characteristics that basho shares with the domains of discourse are these:

1 the 'is' of existence and the 'is' of prediction are intimately related;
2 existence is determined by being in a basho;
3 a change of basho means a change of entities; and
4 from the point of view of elements in a basho, it is nonsensical to say that basho either exists or does not exist.

The primary epistemological and ontological characteristics are these:

5 basho determines itself;
6 basho reflects things and itself;
7 the elements in basho are a part of basho;
8 the elements in basho are images of basho;
9 there is a final basho; and
10 basho contains its own principle of individuation.

Such positioning philosophically, to some, may sound like a circular and non-practically relevant argument. Scharmer, however, has applied Nishida's thinking and his three levels of basho to the argument about implicit knowledge and the way knowledge that is 'not yet embodied' can be better understood. He argues that there are three types of knowledge: explicit knowledge, embodied tacit knowledge, and not-yet-embodied tacit knowledge. He continues his case by suggesting that Nishida's three levels of basho reflect the three levels of knowledge. First is the basho Nishida calls the 'universal of self consciousness' (Scharmer says this corresponds to explicit knowledge). The second basho is, according to Scharmer, equivalent to tacit embodied knowledge and envelops the first basho. The third basho is referred to as 'the intelligible universal' and Scharmer suggest that '(t)he third corresponds with the epistemology of self-transcending knowledge'. In another interesting connection made by Scharmer, he suggests that the first two Basho are similar to Schon's ideas of reflection-on-action and the third relates to reflection-in-action or what he says Nishida called 'action-intuition' (p. 42).

Nonaka and his colleagues have taken their version of this thinking and developed what they called the SECI Model (Socialization, Externalization, Combination and Internalization) which offers a model of how knowledge is converted from explicit to new and more complex explicitness, from tacit to explicit and so on. In Nonaka's thinking about SECI and his work on knowledge creation he draws on the notion of *Ba* (Basically Nishida's Basho) and suggests that:

Ba can be thought of as a shared mental place for emerging relationships. This place can be physical (for example, an office, or a dispersed business place), virtual (such as e-mail, teleconferencing, web chat rooms) or mental (shared experiences, ideas, ideals) (p. 93).

For Nonaka, Reinmoller and Senoo, 'knowledge is embedded in *Ba* (in these shared mental places) where it is acquired through one's own actions or reflections on the experiences of others' (p. 94). Nonaka and his colleagues have also developed what they call four types of Ba which underpin and support the SECI process. This process involves 'originating Ba, dialoguing Ba, systemizing Ba and exercising Ba' all of which assist the 'conversions' that Nonaka and his colleagues argue lead to knowledge creation. As they acknowledge:

> *Ba* is the world where an individual realises itself as a part of the environment on which its life depends. Such *ba* of knowledge can emerge in individuals, working groups, or on the shop floor. It is such *ba* where the knowledge embedded in the ambient affords specific conversions (p. 94).

This Japanese based thinking about place and how knowledge is created and related to a self-transcending process offers a very different perspective on how learning may operate in the interaction around self and society.

Another significant approach to thinking differently from the *communities of practice* notion is that work which has been developed and written about by Engeström (2001) as his theory of what he calls 'expansive learning'. Coming from a Vygostkian influenced theoretical position Engeström has elaborated his theory and offers what he suggests is a third metaphor for learning beyond Sfard's dichotomy of *acquisition* versus *participation* mentioned above. Engeström locates his theory clearly within the cultural-historical traditions and moves his activity theory to more complex levels of analysis to account for examples of collaborative work in medical workplaces. While this approach offers a different and original view of how individuals and groups may come together and influence their learning as members of a knotwork and within activities which are 'expansive' it has some critics. Hager (Chapter 3 this volume), for example, raises the issue of 'whether all learning at work occurs from contradictions and tensions within the system' which appears to be a key elements of the Engeström approach. This point was also raised by Young (2001) in his brief response to Engeström's exposition of his expansive learning model or theory.

It is not the intention in this chapter to subject the reader to further expansions and orientation to the Engeström theory as it is well presented in the following chapter by Engeström himself. What is being suggested here is that there is strong appeal in the Engeström ideas and how this may work in workplaces and that the added dimension of the knotworking metaphor may offer a definite move beyond *communities of practice.*

CONCLUSION

This chapter has presented a series of issues and developments based around the concept of *communities of practice* which has been influential in thinking about the theory of workplace learning for over twenty years. The chapter has suggested that there are some issues inherent in this model of learning, has canvassed a number of critiques from the literature, and has suggested some possible different thinking and platforms for theorising approaches to future understanding of learning, especially in workplaces, that could move *beyond communities of practice.*

REFERENCES

Alexander, P.A. (2007) 'Bridging Cognition and Socioculturalism within Conceptual Change Research: Unnecessary Foray or Unachievable Feat?', *Educational Psychologist,* 42(1): 67–73.

Barton, D. and Tusting, K. (2005) *Beyond Communities of Practice; Language, Power, and Social Context.* Cambridge: Cambridge University Press.

Beckett, D. and Hager, P. (2002) *Life, Work and Learning: Practice in Postmodernity.* London: Routledge.

Billett, S. (1996) 'Situated Learning: Bridging Sociocultural and Cognitive Theorising', *Learning and Instruction,* 6(3): 263–280.

Blackburn, S. (2008) *Oxford Dictionary of Philosophy.* Oxford: Oxford University Press.

Boud, D.J. (ed.) (1998) *Current Issues and New Agendas in Workplace Learning.* NCVER: Adelaide.

Boud, D. and Garrick, J. (1999) (eds) *Understanding Learning at Work.* Routledge: London and New York.

Brown, J.S., Collins, A. and Duguid, P. (1989) 'Situated Cognition and the Culture of Learning', *Educational Researcher,* 18(1): 32–42.

Cairns, L.G. and Stephenson, J. (2009) *Capable Workplace Learning.* Rotterdam/Boston/Taipei: SENSE Publishers.

Cairns, L.G., Malloch, M. and Burns, G. (2006) 'Learning Work', *International Journal of Engineering Education,* 3(2): 91–105.

Carruthers, P. (2004) *The Nature of The Mind.* New York: Routledge.

Dewey, J. (1916) *Democracy and Education.* New York: The Free Press.

Edwards, A. (2005) 'Let's Get Beyond Community and Practice: The Many Meanings of Learning by Participating', *The Curriculum Journal,* 16(1): 49–65.

Engeström, Y. (2001) 'Expansive Learning at Work: Toward an Activity Theoretical Reconceptualization', *Journal of Education and Work,* 14(1): 133–156.

Engeström, Y. (2008) *From Teams to Knots: Activity-Theoretical Studies of Collaboration and Learning at Work.* Cambridge: Cambridge University Press.

Engeström, Y. and Cole, M. (1997) 'Situated Cognition in Search of an Agenda', Chapter 12 in Kirshner, D. and Whitson, J.A. (eds), *Situated Cognition Social, Semiotic, and Psychological Perspectives.* Mahwah: Lawrence Erlbaum Associates.

Engeström, Y., Engeström, R. and Karkkainen, M. (1995) 'Polycontextuality and Boundary Crossing in Expert Cognition: Learning and Problem Solving in Complex Work Activities', *Learning and Instruction,* 5: 319–336.

Eraut, M. (2002) 'Conceptual Analysis and Research Questions: Do the Concepts of "Learning Community" and "Community of Practice" Provide Added Value?'. Paper presented at AERA Annual Meeting, New Orleans.

Evans, K., Hodkinson, P. and Unwin, L. (eds) (2002) *Working to Learn: Transforming Learning in the Workplace.* London: Kogan Page.

Fox, S. (2000) 'Communities of Practice, Foucault and Actor-Network Theory', *Journal of Management Studies,* 37(6): 853–867.

Fuller, A. (2007) 'Critiquing Theories of Learning and Communities of Practice', Chapter 2 in Hughes, J., Jewson, N. and Unwin, L. (eds), *Communities of Practice: Critical Perspectives.* London and New York: Routledge.

Fuller, A., Hodkinson, H., Hodkinson, P. and Unwin, L. (2005) 'Learning as Peripheral Participation in Communities of Practice: A Reassessment of Key Concepts in Workplace Learning', *British Educational Research Journal,* 31(1): 49–68.

Gee, J.P. (2005) 'Semiotic Social Spaces and Affinity Spaces', chapter 10 in Barton, D. and Tusting, K. (eds), *Beyond Communities of Practice.* Cambridge: Cambridge University Press.

Hager, P. (2005) 'Current Theories of Workplace Learning: a Critical Assessment', chapter in Bascia, N., Cumming, A., Dannow, A., Leithwood, K. and Livingstone, D. (eds), *International Handbook of Education Policy.* Dortrecht, Boston and London: Kluwer.

Hara, N. (2009) *Communities of Practice: Fostering Peer-to-Peer Learning and Informal Knowledge Sharing in the Work Place.* Berlin: Springer-Verlag.

Heil, J. (2004) *Philosophy of Mind* (2nd edn). New York: Routledge.

Hichman, L.A. and Alexander, T.M. (1998) (eds), *The Essential Dewey: Volume 1, Pragmatism, Education and Democracy.* Bloomington, IN: Indiana University Press.

Hodkinson, H. and Hodkinson, P. (2004) 'Rethinking the Concept of Community of Practice in Relation to Schoolteachers' Workplace Learning', *International Journal of Training and Development,* 8(1): 21–31.

Hodkinson, P., Biesta, G. and James, D. (2008) 'Understanding Learning Culturally: Overcoming the Dualism Between Social and Individual Views of Learning', *Vocations and Learning,* 1(1): 27–47.

Hough, M. and Paine, J. with Austin, L. (1997) *Creating Quality Learning Communities.* South Melbourne: Macmillan Education Australia.

Hughes, J., Jewson, N. and Unwin, L. (2007) (eds), *Communities of Practice: Critical Perspectives.* London: Routledge.

Kim, J. (2006) *Philosophy of Mind* (2nd edn), Cambridge, MA: Westview Press.

Kirshner, D. and Whitson, J.A. (1997) (eds), *Situated Cognition: Social, Semiotic, and Psychological Perpectives.* Mahwah: Lawrence Erlbaum Associates.

Lave, J.H. (1988) *Cognition in Practice: Mind, Mathematics and Culture in Everyday Life.* Cambridge: Cambridge University Press.

Lave, J. and Wenger, E. (1991) *Situated Learning: Legitimate Peripheral Participation.* Cambridge: Cambridge University Press.

Marsick, V.J. (ed) (1987) *Learning in the Workplace.* Beckenham: Croom Helm.

Marsick V.J. and Watkins, K.E. (1990) *Informal and Incidental Learning in the Workplace.* London: Routledge.

Mason, L. (2007) 'Introduction: Bridging the Cognitive and Sociocultural Approaches in Research on Conceptual Change: Is it Feasible?', *Educational Psychologist,* 42(1): 1–7.

Mercer, N. (2007) 'Commentary on the Reconciliation of Cognitive and Sociocultural Accounts of Conceptual Change', *Educational Psychologist,* 42(1): 75–78.

Murphy, D. (1995) *Comenius: A Critical Reassessment of His Life and Work.* Dublin: Irish Academic Press.

Murphy, K.P. (2007) 'The Eye of the Beholder: The Interplay of Social and Cognitive Components of Change', *Educational Psychologist,* 42(1): 41–53.

Murphy, P. and Hall, K. (eds) (2008) *Learning and Practice: Agency and Identities.* London: Sage and The Open University Press.

Nishida, K. (1987a) *An Inquiry into the Good* (translated by Masao Abe and Christopher Ives). New Haven and London: Yale University Press.

Nishida, K. (1987b) *Last Writings: Nothingness and the Religious Worldview* (translated by David A. Dilworth). Honolulu: University of Hawaii Press.

Nonaka, I. (1994) 'A Dynamic Theory of Organizational Knowledge Creation', *Organization Science,* 5(1): 14–37.

Nonaka, I. and Takeuchi, H. (1995) *The Knowledge Creating Company.* New York: Oxford University Press.

Nonaka, I., Reinmoeller, P. and Senoo, P. (2000) 'Integrated IT Systems to Capitalize on Market Knowledge', in G. Von Krogh, I. Nonaka and T. Nishiguchi (eds), *Knowledge Creation: A Source of Value.* London: Macmillan Press.

Noon, M. and Blyton, P. (2002) *The Realities of Work* (2nd edn). Basingstoke: Palgrave.

Prawat, R.S. (1998) 'Current Self-Regulation Views of Learning and Motivation Viewed through a Deweyian Lens: The Problems with Dualism', *American Educational Research Journal,* 35(2): 199–224.

Roberts, S.M. and Pruitt, E.Z. (2009) *Schools as Professional Learning Communities* (2nd edn). Thousand Oaks, CA: Corwin Press.

Ryle, G. (1968) *The Concept of Mind.* Harmondsworth: Penguin Books.

Salomon, G. (1993) (ed.), *Distributed Cognitions: Psychological and Educational Considerations.* Cambridge: Cambridge University Press.

Scharmer, C.O. (2000) 'Organizing Around Not-Yet-Embodied Knowledge', chapter 2 in von Krogh, G. Nonaka, I. and Nishiguchi, T. (eds), *Knowledge Creation: A Source of Value.* London: Macmillan Press.

Sfard, A. (1998) 'On Two Metaphors for Learning and the Dangers of Choosing Just One', *Educational Researcher,* 27(2): 4–13.

Stevenson, J. (1994) (ed.) *Cognition at Work.* Adelaide: NCVER.

Stevenson, J. (2002) 'Concepts of Workplace Knowledge', *International Journal of Educational Research,* 37: 1–15.

Vosniadou, S. (1996) 'Towards a Revised Cognitive Psychology for New Advances in Learning and Instruction', *Learning and Instruction,* 6(2): 95–109.

Vosniadou, S. (2007) 'The Cognitive-Situative Divide and the Problem of Conceptual Change', *Educational Psychologist,* 42(1): 55–66.

Wargo, R.J.J. (2005) *The Logic of Nothingness: A Study of Nishida Kitaro.* Hawaii: University of Hawaii Press.

Wenger, E. (1998) *Communities of Practice: Learning, Meaning and Identity.* Cambridge: Cambridge University Press.

Wenger, E. (2000a) 'Communities of Practice and Social Learning Systems', *Organization,* 7(2): 225–246.

Wenger, E. (2000b) 'Communities of Practice: The Organizational Frontier', *Harvard Business Review,* January–February: 139–145.

Wenger, E., McDermott, R. and Snyder, W.M. (2002) *Cultivating Communities of Practice.* Boston: Harvard Business School Press.

Young, M. (2001) 'Contextualising a New Approach to Learning: Some Comments on Yrjö Engeström's Theory of Expansive Learning', *Journal of Education and Work,* 14(1): 157–161.

7

Activity Theory and Learning at Work

Yrjö Engeström

INTRODUCTION

Anna Sfard (1998) suggested two basic metaphors of learning that compete for dominance today: the *acquisition* metaphor and the *participation* metaphor. The key dimension underlying Sfard's dichotomy is derived from the question: Is the learner to be understood primarily as an individual *or* as a community? This is an important dimension, largely inspired by the notion of community of practice put forward by Lave and Wenger (1991; Wenger, 1998). However, an attempt to construct a one-dimensional conceptual space for the identification, analysis and comparison of theories is bound to eliminate too much of the complexity of the field of learning. The potential and significance of cultural-historical activity theory in general and the theory of expansive learning (Engeström, 1987) in particular calls for a more multi-dimensional treatment (for a concise introduction to activity theory as a living movement, see Sannino et al., 2009).

To locate the theory of expansive learning more adequately in the conceptual field of learning theories, three additional dimensions may be usefully employed:

1 Is learning primarily a process that transmits and preserves culture or a process that transforms and creates culture?
2 Is learning primarily a process of vertical improvement along some uniform scales of competence or horizontal movement, exchange and hybridization between different cultural contexts and standards of competence?
3 Is learning primarily a process of acquiring and creating empirical knowledge and concepts or a process that leads to the formation of theoretical knowledge and concepts?

The theory of expansive learning puts the primacy on communities as learners, on transformation and creation of culture, on horizontal movement and hybridization, and on the formation of theoretical concepts. This theory does not fit into either one of the two metaphors suggested by Sfard (1998). From the point of view of expansive learning, both acquisition-based and participation-based approaches share much of the same conservative bias, having little to say about transformation and creation of culture. Both acquisition-based and participation-based approaches depict learning primarily as one-way movement from incompetence to competence, with little serious analysis devoted to horizontal movement and hybridization. Acquisition-based approaches may ostensibly value theoretical concepts, but their very theory of concepts is quite uniformly empiricist and formal (Davydov, 1990). Participation-based approaches are commonly suspicious if not hostile toward the formation of theoretical concepts, largely because these approaches, too, see theoretical concepts mainly as formal 'bookish' abstractions.

So the theory of expansive learning relies on its own metaphor: expansion. The core idea is qualitatively different from both acquisition and participation. In expansive learning, learners learn something that is not yet there. In other words, the learners construct a new object and concept for their collective activity, and implement this new object and concept in practice. This shift in metaphors has been noted by Paavola et al. (2004) who suggest knowledge creation as a new, third metaphor, and by Fenwick (2006b) who suggests participation, expansion, and translation as relevant alternative and complementary metaphors for theorizing work-based learning.

The theory of expansive learning was initially formulated some 20 years ago (Engeström, 1987). Especially in recent years, it has been used in a wide variety of studies and interventions. The topics range from adult mathematics learning in workplaces (FitzSimons, 2003) and hybrid educational innovations (Yamazumi, 2008) to the impact of ICT reforms on teacher education (Rasmussen and Ludvigsen, 2009). The theory has been used in studies of the development of a conflict-monitoring network (Foot, 2001) and multi-organizational change efforts in an industry (Hill et al., 2007). These studies also deal with learning in and for interagency working with youngsters at-risk of exclusion with special educational needs (Daniels, 2004), as well as with the uses of weblogs in e-learning (Makino, 2007), and learning among nurses and adult educators who function as 'portfolio professionals' contracting their services to multiple employers and organizations (Fenwick, 2004). The theory has been used as framework in a study of simulated clinical experience in university nursing education (Haigh, 2007), in a study of learning as boundary crossing in a school–university partnership (Tsui and Law, 2007), and in a study of promoting new types of transfer between school and workplace (Konkola et al., 2007). The work of Gutiérrez and her colleagues on expanded 'third spaces' for learning and literacy development has been influenced by the theory of expansive learning (Gutiérrez and Larson, 2007; Gutiérrez, 2008; Vossoughi and Gutiérrez, 2010). Although necessarily incomplete, the list indicates that the theory of expansive learning has been found particularly useful in analyses of learning in non-traditional, hybrid multi-organizational and multi-cultural settings.

SOCIETAL AND HISTORICAL DEMAND FOR A NEW KIND OF LEARNING

In *Learning by Expanding*, the emergence of expansive learning activity was seen as a consequence of historical transformations in work:

> The increasingly societal nature of work processes, their internal complexity and interconnectedness as well as their massive volumes in capital and capacity, are making it evident that, at least in periods of acute disturbance or intensive change, no one actually quite masters the work *activity* as a whole, though the control and planning of the whole is formally in the hands of the management. This creates something that may be called 'grey zones', areas of vacuum or 'no man's land', where initiative and determined action from practically any level of the corporate hierarchy may have unexpected effects (Engeström, 1987, pp. 113–114).

The inner contradictions of capitalist production and organization of work have remained at the center of research on expansive learning. Many of these studies have been carried out within a research program called developmental work research (for earliest studies, see Engeström and Engeström, 1986 and Toikka et al., 1986). Most of these empirical studies and interventions have been conducted in workplace settings (for recent representative collections, see Engeström, 2005 and Engeström, Lompscher et al., 2005).

The basic argument is that traditional modes of learning deal with tasks in which the contents to be learned are well known ahead of time by those who design, manage and implement various programs of learning. When whole collective activity systems, such as work processes and organizations, need to redefine themselves, traditional modes of learning are not enough. Nobody knows exactly what needs to be learned. The design of the new activity (externalization) and the acquisition of the knowledge and skills it requires (internalization) are increasingly intertwined. In expansive learning activity, they merge (Engeström, 1999a).

Pihlaja (2005) adds to this argument the important aspect of historically changing types of generalizing in work processes. Generalization is at the root of learning. Generalization is based on identifying and mastering variation. In mass production, what needed to be mastered was variation in the ways different workers performed the same tasks. This led to standardization of key actions and action sequences. In flexible mass production or 'lean production', what needs to be mastered is variation in the form of deviations from an optimal streamlined process, that is, breaks, disturbances and waste. This leads to continuous process optimization.

Today the life cycles of entire product, production and business concepts are rapidly becoming shorter. Correspondingly, the rhythm of overall concept-level transformations is accelerated. In other words, what needs to be mastered is variation in the sense of constantly shifting product, production, and business concepts. This is no longer achievable by means of technical optimization of isolated actions and processes. Accelerated concept-level changes in work and organizations require generalization and learning that expand the learners' horizon and practical grasp up to the level of collective activity systems.

There are two additional factors that add weight to the societal need for expansive learning. The first one is the emergence and escalation of social production or peer production (Benkler, 2006) that utilizes the interactive potential of the Internet, or Web 2.0. This opens up a field of possibilities for the formation of new types of activities and use values with huge expansive potentials, such as Linux and Wikipedia.

The second factor is the emergence and increasing presence of global threats and risks, or 'runaway objects' (Engeström, 2008b), exemplified by global warming, new pandemic diseases and global financial disasters. This opens up a field of tremendous challenges for concept formation and practical redesign in a scale that has to exceed the boundaries of any single discipline, profession or organization.

THEORETICAL ROOTS OF THE CONCEPT OF EXPANSIVE LEARNING

The theory of expansive learning builds on foundational ideas put forward by four key figures in Russian cultural-historical school: Vygotsky, Leont'ev, Il'enkov, and Davydov. Six ideas developed by these scholars form the conceptual basis of the theory of expansive learning. Two additional roots come from Bateson and Bakhtin. I will briefly characterize each of these eight roots.

(1) It may be argued that for Vygotsky, the unit of analysis was mediated action (Zinchenko, 1985). Leont'ev (1981) demonstrated how the emergence of division of labor within a community leads to the separation of action and activity. In a tribal hunt, for example, certain participants chase the game away, toward other participants who wait in ambush and kill the game. These two groups perform different actions (chasing, killing) in the collective activity of hunting. The half-life on an action is finite; an action has a definite beginning and an end. A collective activity, on the other hand, reproduces itself without a predetermined endpoint by generating seemingly similar actions over and over again. Yet there is continuous and at times dramatically discontinuous change in the activity. The very idea of expansive learning is built on this theoretically consequential *distinction between action and activity*. Expansive learning is movement from actions to activity.

The essence of [expansive] learning activity is production of objectively, societally new activity structures (including new objects, instruments, etc.) out of actions manifesting the inner contradictions of the preceding form of the activity in question. [Expansive] learning activity is *mastery of expansion from actions to a new activity*. While traditional schooling is essentially a subject-producing activity and traditional science is essentially an instrument-producing activity, [expansive] learning activity is an *activity-producing activity* (Engeström, 1987, p. 125).

(2) Vygotsky's concept of the *zone of proximal development* is another important root of the theory of expansive learning. Vygotsky (1978, p. 86) defined the zone as '*the distance between the actual developmental level as determined by independent problem solving and the level of potential development as determined through problem solving under adult guidance or in collaboration with more capable peers.*' In *Learning by Expanding*, Vygotsky's individually oriented concept was redefined to deal with learning and development at the level of collective activities:

> It is the *distance between the present everyday actions of the individuals and the historically new form of the societal activity that can be collectively generated as a solution to the double bind potentially embedded in the everyday actions* (Engeström, 1987, p. 174).

In effect, the zone of proximal development was redefined as the space for expansive transition from actions to activity (Engeström, 2000).

(3) Being an application of activity theory, the theory of expansive learning is foundationally an *object*-oriented theory.

> Properly, the concept of its object (*Gegenstand*) is already implicitly contained in the very concept of activity. The expression 'objectless activity' is devoid of any meaning. (…) the object of activity is twofold: first, in its independent existence as subordinating to itself and transforming the activity of the subject; second, as an image of the object, as product of its property of psychological reflection that is realized as an activity of the subject(…) Leont'ev (1978, p. 52).

In other words, the object is both resistant raw material and the future-oriented purpose of an activity. The object is the true carrier of the motive of the activity. Thus, in expansive learning activity, motives and motivation are not sought primarily inside individual subjects – they are in the object to be transformed and expanded. As Leont'ev (1978, p. 186) pointed out, motives cannot be taught, they can only be nurtured by developing 'the content of actual vital relations' of the learners. Expansive learning is a process of material transformation of vital relations.

(4) Activity theory is a dialectical theory, and the dialectical concept of *contradiction* plays a crucial part in it. Following Il'enkov (1977, 1982), the theory of expansive learning sees contradictions as historically evolving tensions that can be detected and dealt with in real activity systems. In capitalism, the pervasive primary contradiction between use value and exchange value is inherent to every commodity, and all spheres of life are subject to commoditization. This pervasive primary contradiction takes its specific shape and acquires its particular contents differently in every historical phase and every activity system. Most importantly, contradictions are the driving force of transformation. The object of an activity is always internally contradictory. It is these internal contradictions that make the object a moving, motivating, and future-generating target. Expansive learning requires articulation and practical engagement with inner contradictions of the learners' activity system.

(5) Il'enkov's dialectics were powerfully translated into learning theory by Davydov (1990) whose theory of learning activity is based on the dialectical method of *ascending from the abstract to the concrete*. This is a method of grasping the essence of an object by tracing and reproducing theoretically the logic of its development, of its historical formation through the emergence and resolution of its inner contradictions. A new theoretical idea or concept is initially produced in the form of an abstract, simple explanatory relationship, a 'germ cell'. This initial abstraction is step-by-step enriched and transformed into a concrete system of multiple, constantly developing manifestations. In learning activity, the initial simple idea is transformed into a complex object, into a new form of practice. Learning activity leads to the formation of theoretical concepts – theoretically grasped practice – concrete in systemic richness and

multiplicity of manifestations. In this framework, abstract refers to partial, separated from the concrete whole. In empirical thinking based on comparisons and classifications, abstractions capture arbitrary, only formally interconnected properties. In dialectical-theoretical thinking, based on ascending from the abstract to the concrete, an abstraction captures the smallest and simplest, genetically primary unit of the whole functionally interconnected system (see Il'enkov, 1977; Davydov, 1990; also Bakhurst, 1991; Falmagne, 1995).

Ascending from the abstract to the concrete is achieved through specific epistemic or learning actions. According to Davydov (1988, p. 30), an ideal-typical sequence of learning activity consists of the following six learning actions: (1) transforming the conditions of the task in order to reveal the universal relationship of the object under study, (2) modeling the identified relationship in a material, graphic, or literal form, (3) transforming the model of the relationship in order to study its properties in their 'pure guise', (4) constructing a system of particular tasks that are resolved by a general mode, (5) monitoring the performance of the preceding actions, (6) evaluating the assimilation of the general mode that results from resolving the given learning task. In the theory of expansive learning, Davydov's concept of learning activity is developed further, to deal with the challenges of learning outside the school and the classroom (see the next section).

(6) Vygotsky and his colleagues saw the essence of human psychological functioning in the mediation of action by means of cultural tools and signs. Traditional experimental methods largely excluded cultural mediation from their analyses. But the human subject always 'imports' into an experimental setting a set of psychological instruments in the form of signs that the experimenter cannot control externally in any rigid way (Van der Veer and Valsiner, 1991, p. 399).

> The person, using the power of things or stimuli, controls his own behavior through them, grouping them, putting them together, sorting them. In other words, the great uniqueness of the will consists of man having no power over his own behavior other than the power that things have over his behavior. But man subjects to himself the power of things over behavior, makes them serve his own purposes and controls that power as he wants. He changes the environment with the external activity and in this way affects his own behavior, subjecting it to his own authority (Vygotsky, 1997, p. 212).

In other words, the subject's agency, his or her ability to change the world and his or her own behavior, becomes a central focus. Vygotsky built his interventionist methodology of *double stimulation* on this insight. Instead of merely giving the subject a task to solve, Vygotsky gave the subject both a demanding task (first stimulus) and a 'neutral' or ambiguous external artifact (second stimulus) the subject could fill with meaning and turn into a new mediating sign that would enhance his or her actions and potentially lead to reframing of the task. Expansive learning typically calls for formative interventions based on the principle of double stimulation (Engeström, 2007c).

(7) The theory of expansive learning also owes a great deal to the innovative thinking of the anthropologist Gregory Bateson (1972). His conceptualization of levels of learning, particularly the notion of *Learning III* and the associated concept of *double bind*, must be identified as the seventh theoretical root of the theory of expansive learning. Bateson's *Learning III* is basically the same as expansive learning activity. Within the theory of expansive learning, Bateson's notion of double bind may be interpreted as 'a social, *societally essential dilemma which cannot be resolved through separate individual actions alone – but in which joint co-operative actions can push a historically new form of activity into emergence*' (Engeström, 1987, p. 165).

(8) Finally, Mikhail Bakhtin's (1982) idea of *multi-voicedness,* or heteroglossia, needs to be included among the roots of the theory of expansive learning. 'Applied in expansive learning and research, this means: *all the conflicting and complementary voices of the various groups and strata in the activity system under scrutiny shall be involved and utilized.* As Bakhtin

shows, this definitely includes the voices and non-academic genres of the common people. Thus, instead of the classical argumentation within the single academic speech type, we get clashing fireworks of different speech types and languages' (Engeström, 1987, pp. 315–316). Expansive learning is an inherently multi-voiced process of debate, negotiation and orchestration.

CENTRAL TENETS OF EXPANSIVE LEARNING

The theory of expansive learning focuses on learning processes in which the very subject of learning is transformed from isolated individuals to collectives and networks. Initially individuals begin to question the existing order and logic of their activity. As more actors join in, a collaborative analysis and modeling of the zone of proximal development are initiated and carried out. Eventually the learning effort of implementing a new model of the activity encompasses all members and elements of the collective activity system (see Figure 7.1).

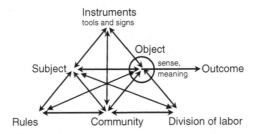

Figure 7.1 General model of an activity system (Engeström, 1987, p. 78)

The circle around the object in Figure 7.1 indicates at the same time the focal role and inherent ambiguity of the object of activity. The object is an invitation to interpretation, personal sense making, and societal transformation. We need to distinguish between the generalized object of the historically evolving activity system and the specific object as it appears to a particular subject, at a given moment, in a given action. The generalized object is connected to societal meaning, the specific object is connected to personal sense.

As activity systems are increasingly interconnected and interdependent, many recent studies of expansive learning take as their unit of analysis a constellation of two or more activity systems that have a partially shared object. Such interconnected activity systems may form a producer–client relationship, a partnership, a network, or some other pattern of multi-activity collaboration.

Obviously this kind of extension of the unit of analysis makes it more demanding to identify and give voice to the actual flesh-and-blood human subjects in each activity system. The theory of expansive learning cannot be reduced to the learning of abstract organizations without concrete human subjects. Movement between a system's view and a subject view is of crucial importance: 'The system view of an organization is blatantly insufficient when the researchers try to understand and facilitate qualitative changes by means of expansive learning. Changes must be initiated and nurtured by real, identifiable people, individual persons and groups. The interventionist researcher must find within the activity system flesh-and-blood dialogue partners who have their own emotions, moral concerns, wills, and agendas. Organization must necessarily be translated back into a workplace inhabited by human beings' (Engeström and Kerosuo, 2007, p. 340).

Contradictions are the necessary but insufficient engine of expansive learning in an activity system. In different phases of the expansive learning process, contradictions may appear (a) as emerging latent primary contradictions within each and any of the nodes of the activity system, (b) as openly manifest secondary contradictions between two or more nodes (e.g., between a new object and an old tool), (c) as tertiary contradictions between a newly established mode of activity and remnants of the previous mode of activity, or (d) as external quaternary contradictions between the newly reorganized activity and its neighboring activity systems. Conflicts, dilemmas, disturbances, and local innovations may be analyzed as manifestations of the contradictions.

Contradictions become actual driving forces of expansive learning when they are dealt with in such a way that an emerging new object is identified and turned into a motive: 'the meeting of need with object is an extraordinary act' (Leont'ev, 1978, p. 54). The motive of collective activity becomes effective for an individual by means of personal sense: 'sense expresses the relation of motive of activity to the immediate goal of action' (Leont'ev, 1978, p. 171).

Expansive learning leads to the formation of a new, expanded object and pattern of activity oriented to the object. This involves the formation of a theoretical concept of the new activity, based on grasping and modeling the initial simple relationship, the 'germ cell', that gives rise to the new activity and generates its diverse concrete manifestations (Davydov, 1990). The formation of an expanded object and corresponding new pattern of activity requires and brings about collective and distributed agency, questioning and breaking away from the constraints of the existing activity and embarking on a journey across the uncharted terrain of the zone of proximal development (Engeström, 1996). In other words, the 'what' of expansive learning consists of a triplet: expanded pattern of activity; corresponding theoretical concept; and new type of agency.

Ascending from the abstract to the concrete is achieved through specific epistemic or learning actions. Together these actions form an expansive cycle or spiral. An ideal-typical sequence of epistemic actions in an expansive cycle may be described as follows (Engeström, 1999b, pp. 383–384):

- The first action is that of questioning, criticizing or rejecting some aspects of the accepted practice and existing wisdom. For the sake of simplicity, I will call this action *questioning.*
- The second action is that of *analyzing* the situation. Analysis involves mental, discursive or practical transformation of the situation in order to find out causes or explanatory mechanisms. Analysis evokes 'why?' questions and explanatory principles. One type of analysis is *historical-genetic;* it seeks to explain the situation by tracing its origins and evolution. Another type of analysis is *actual-empirical;* it seeks to explain the situation by constructing a picture of its inner systemic relations.
- The third action is that of *modeling* the newly found explanatory relationship in some publicly observable and transmittable medium. This means constructing an explicit, simplified model of the new idea that explains and offers a solution to the problematic situation.
- The fourth action is that of *examining the model,* running, operating and experimenting on it in order to fully grasp its dynamics, potentials and limitations.
- The fifth action is that of *implementing the model* by means of practical applications, enrichments, and conceptual extensions.
- The sixth and seventh actions are those of *reflecting* on and evaluating the process and *consolidating* its outcomes into a new stable form of practice.

These actions bear a close resemblance to the six learning actions put forward by Davydov (1988; see above). Davydov's theory is, however, oriented at learning activity within the confines of a classroom where the curricular contents are determined ahead of time by more knowledgeable adults. This probably explains why it does not contain the first action of critical questioning and rejection, and why the fifth and seventh actions, implementing and consolidating, are replaced by 'constructing a system of particular tasks' and 'evaluating' – actions that do not imply the construction of actual culturally novel practices.

The process of expansive learning should be understood as construction and resolution of successively evolving contradictions. The entire ideal-typical expansive cycle may be diagrammatically depicted as in Figure 7.2. The thicker arrows indicate expanded scope of and participation in the learning actions. The cycle of expansive learning is not a universal formula of phases or stages. In fact, one probably never finds a concrete collective learning process which would cleanly follow the ideal-typical model. The model is a heuristic conceptual device derived from the logic of ascending from the abstract to the concrete. Every time one examines or facilitates a potentially expansive learning process with the help of the model, one tests, criticizes and hopefully enriches the theoretical ideas of the model.

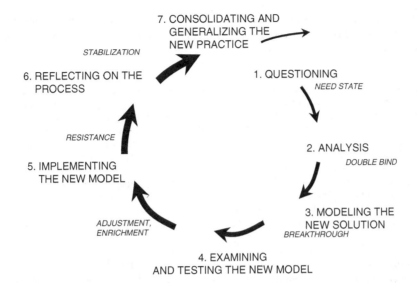

Figure 7.2 Sequence of learning actions in an expansive learning cycle

The key ideas of the theory of expansive learning are enriched and developed further in empirical and interventionist studies. I will now examine a series of themes developed in such studies.

EXPANSIVE LEARNING AS TRANSFORMATION OF THE OBJECT

Traditionally we expect that learning is manifested as changes in the subject, i.e., in the behavior and cognition of the learners. Expansive learning is manifested primarily as changes in the object of the collective activity.

In her study of teacher teams, Kärkkäinen (1999) analyzed changes in the object as qualitative *turning points*. She followed a primary school teacher team which embarked on a process of learning to design and execute new kinds of thematic curriculum units that cut across multiple school subjects, went beyond the physical boundaries of the classroom and the school, and lasted longer than the usual single lesson.

Kärkkäinen analyzed the design and implementation of a thematic unit called 'Local Community'. The object evolved in three phases. The first four meetings of the teacher team produced the idea of the work on themes that cut across subjects. The next meetings produced a plan for the 'Local Community' theme. The final five meetings monitored the execution of the plan and evaluated the realization of both the specific theme and the work on themes more generally. Each turning point was characterized by clusters of discursive disturbances (misunderstandings, disagreements, conflicts, and minor dilemmas), phases of questioning, and concentrations of different voices or perspectives (Kärkkäinen, 1999, pp. 111–116). Moving through these phases and turning points, the object evolved from a general notion of cross-subject 'theme working' into a specific theme focused on the local community and finally into a relatively complex multi-faceted constellation of the main theme and its sub-themes.

The expansion of the object proceeds in multiple dimensions. Engeström (2000) and Hasu (2000) identified four dimensions: the social-spatial ('who else should be included?'), the anticipatory-temporal ('what previous and forthcoming steps should be considered?'), the moral-ideological ('who is responsible and who decides?'), and the systemic-developmental ('how does this shape the future of the activity?'). Engeström, Puonti et al. (2003) compared three studies of expansive learning focusing on the socio-spatial dimension on the one hand and the temporal dimension on the other hand. They concluded that space and time are not the whole story; there moral-ideological dimension of power and responsibility is always also at stake. This third dimension was discussed by Puonti (2004) in her study of the investigation of economic crimes:

> A case under investigation consists of a constant interplay of the crime and its investigation. The case, however, is never merely unique: the crime under investigation constitutes a part of economic crime in general, and the investigation is part of economic crime prevention. The interplay between the crime and its investigation can be viewed at two levels: at the specific case level and at the general level. Expansion is a twofold movement: the crime is expanded by the criminal perpetrators, and the investigators have the opportunity to expand the object in their investigation. The self-movement of the object generates the *potential for expansion*, but the efforts to expand the object of investigation have remained insufficient.
>
> Expansion is commonly understood as positive development. My empirical setting, however, shows the dark side of expansion as well. It may be seen as a shift of a contradictory phenomenon from one developmental phase to another. There is a constant battle between the criminals and the authorities: Which side is able to move first to the next phase of development? The investigation is not merely in the hands of the investigators, but the crime 'strikes back' and forces the investigators to adopt new ways of action (Puonti, 2004, p. 82).

Puonti's observation is a useful reminder of the fact that expansion is not reducible to the efforts of learners aimed at emancipation and empowerment. Expansion is also generated from within the object, and it is never only a benign process.

EXPANSIVE LEARNING AND THE ZONE OF PROXIMAL DEVELOPMENT

In the theory of expansive learning, criteria and yardsticks of learning are built by means of historical analysis. Such an analysis aims at identifying the contradictions that need to be resolved and charting the zone of proximal development that needs to be traversed in order to move beyond the existing contradictions. This calls for effective ways of articulating and depicting the historically possible zone of proximal development.

Haavisto (2002) studied expansive learning efforts of a Finnish district court implementing locally the general guidelines of a nationwide court reform. She followed, recorded and analyzed three civil trials before the reform and another three after the reform. The Finnish court proceedings were traditionally very formal and non-interactive, based on lengthy written briefs read aloud in front of the judge. At the same time, the judges traditionally allowed the attorneys to decide what issues to cover and the timeframe for the exchange of briefs. In other words, the old proceedings were both formal and unrestricted, which often meant multiple hearings extended over a period of several months. The new legislation aimed at proceedings based on informal oral discussion yet actively controlled and guided by the presiding judge. The aim is for a compact process addressing all points of view in one hearing. This transformation is intertwined with a transition from the traditional notion of justice as material truth to the idea of negotiated justice and pragmatic compromise.

In Haavisto's study, expansive learning took place by means of modest incremental steps led by 'spearheads' such as trials in which the clients (not attorneys) began to take active initiatives and proceedings in which the judges intervened actively to promote settlement between the parties. In these spearheads, new ways of talking emerged, such as instructional talk of the judge directed at lay clients taking initiatives in the hearing. Simultaneously, new tensions also emerged, such as the tension between increased client initiatives made possible by the informality and the increased emphasis on active control and leadership on the part of the judge.

EXPANSIVE LEARNING AS CYCLIC PROGRESSION OF LEARNING ACTIONS

The expansive cycle of learning actions depicted in Figure 7.2 has been used as framework of interpretation in studies of relatively large-scale and lengthy processes of transformation.

Seppänen (2004), for example, used the expansive cycle to interpret the significant steps in the learning of two farms in transition from traditional to organic farming over a period of a decade. Nilsson (2003) analyzed three successive expansive cycles in the integration of preschool, leisure-time center and elementary school in Sweden, the first cycle spanning from 1981 to 1999, the second from 1998 to 2000, and the third from 2000 on, being incomplete at the time of the analysis. Similarly, Foot (2001) analyzed the development of a monitoring network of ethnic conflicts (EAWARN) over a period of several years, identifying two successive cycles. The cycle model forces the analyst to make sense of events in terms of epistemic learning actions. This often leads to important insights, as exemplified by Foot (2001, p. 74):

> Viewing the two cycles next to each other reveals that, chronologically, there is a partial overlap between them. As spiraling cycles, the second is contingent upon the first, though not strictly successive to it. The introduction of the indicator model [a new tool for the network] occurred in the evaluation phase of the first cycle and in the analyzing phase of the second cycle. In other words, the introduction of the indicator model was an action with dual meaning. On the one hand, it was an action of evaluation and consolidation. On the other hand, it was an action that led to the modeling of a new form of activity.

What initially looks like an expansive transformation may in the end become something else. In analyzing the development of a nursing home over 25 years, Mäkitalo (2005, p. 179) concluded that at a certain point the cycle began to narrow. While this is certainly plausible, it may also be problematic to use the cycle to cover excessively long periods. In other words, it is important to articulate and argue the criteria of the starting and end points of a cycle. The logic of the expansive cycle is such that a new cycle is assumed to begin when an existing, relatively stable pattern of activity begins to be questioned. Correspondingly, the cycle ends when a new pattern of activity has become consolidated and relatively stable. It might be argued that a narrowing cycle emerges if one interprets the questioning and increasingly aggravated contradictions typical to the beginning of a new cycle merely as end phases of the previous cycle. On the other hand, it is indeed to be expected that many transformations in activity systems are not predominantly expansive. Mäkitalo's (2005, p. 99) tentative distinction between expansive, narrowing, repetitive, and divided cycles is therefore warranted and needs to be developed further in empirical analyses.

Large-scale cycles involve numerous smaller cycles of learning actions. Such a smaller cycle may take place within a few days or even hours of intensive collaborative analysis and problem solving. Careful investigation may reveal a rich texture of learning actions within such temporally short efforts. But can such a miniature cycle be called expansive? This question was addressed in a study focused on miniature cycles of learning actions in team meetings of an industrial plant (Engeström, 1999b):

> Miniature cycles of innovative learning should be regarded as *potentially* expansive. A large-scale expansive cycle of organizational transformation always consists of small cycles of innovative learning. However, the appearance of small-scale cycles of innovative learning does not in itself guarantee that there is an expansive cycle going on. Small cycles may remain isolated events, and the overall cycle of organizational development may become stagnant, regressive, or even fall apart. The occurrence of a full-fledged expansive cycle is not common, and it typically requires concentrated effort and deliberate interventions. With these reservations in mind, the expansive learning cycle and its embedded actions may be used as a framework for analyzing small-scale innovative learning processes (Engeström, 1999b, p. 385).

In the study of the team meetings, expansive learning actions did not strictly follow the order presented in the ideal-typical cyclic model of Figure 7.2. For instance, in one of the meetings modeling the new solution was attempted at the very beginning, and later completed after actions of analysis and questioning. Among the expansive actions, there were also some non-expansive learning actions, such as reinforcing the existing practice (Engeström, 1999b, pp. 390–391). The entire miniature cycles were socially distributed accomplishments. Thus, in one of the meetings, seven successive expansive learning actions were initiated by six different participants (Engeström, 1999b, p. 401). A larger sample of potentially expansive miniature cycles of learning actions was subsequently analyzed by Lambert (1999).

The Change Laboratory interventions (Engeström et al., 1996, Engeström, 2007c) occupy an intermediate position between multi-year macro cycles and miniature cycles that may last a couple of hours. A Change Laboratory intervention often takes place as a series of six to twelve weekly meetings of a pilot unit of an organization, plus one or two follow-up meetings several months later. This kind of intervention attempts to accelerate and intensify the expansive learning process by introducing successive tasks that require specific expansive learning actions. Expansive learning cycles and learning actions generated with the help of Change Laboratory interventions have been analyzed by Engeström (2001a), Ahonen and Virkkunen (2003), Virkkunen and Ahonen (in press), Pihlaja (2005), and Hyrkkänen (2007), among others. The studies show that the learning actions taken by participants do not necessarily correspond to the intentions behind the tasks assigned by the interventionist. Time and again, the participants take over the leading role in the intervention process, rejecting and reformulating tasks and performing actions that change the plans of the interventionist. This dialectic between planned and actually realized courses of expansive learning is of great importance in future research.

EXPANSIVE LEARNING AS BOUNDARY CROSSING AND NETWORK BUILDING

Important processes of innovation and learning are increasingly occurring in collaborative constellations and networks of multiple activity systems. In studies of expansive learning, this was first taken up in a paper that put forward boundary crossing as a serious theoretical concept (Engeström et al., 1995). Boundary crossing was characterized as 'horizontal expertise where practitioners must move across boundaries to seek and give help, to find information and tools wherever they happen to be available' (p. 332).

Lambert (1999) examined boundary crossing in the field of vocational teacher education. Traditional teacher education can take standard practices of classroom teaching for granted. The culmination of Finnish vocational teacher education has been the 'proof lesson' given by the student teacher to demonstrate her ability to teach in practice. In such a model, the new challenges and development efforts of the work organizations that eventually employ the students of vocational education are all but completely absent. Teacher education is an encapsulated world of its own.

In her experimental program, Lambert replaced the proof lessons with a boundary-crossing arena called Learning Studio. The student teachers in the program were already working as teachers in vocational education in the field of health care and social welfare; they attended the teacher education program in order to acquire a full formal teacher qualification. The student teachers were asked to conduct development projects in the workplaces, aimed at improving their curricula and teaching practices. Each student teacher presented a project report in the Learning Studio. The participants of the studio included (a) representatives of the teacher education institute, (b) teachers and students of the vocational training school in which the student teacher worked, and (c) representatives of one or more employer organizations (in this case, health care and social welfare service delivery organizations) for which the specific project was relevant. In the studio session, the participants discussed the student teacher's project as a possible shared innovation. In other words, the studio sessions required discursive crossing of multiple boundaries. This led to reciprocal exchange and adoption of ideas driven by a shared, potentially expansive object – a process called 'developmental transfer'.

Lambert's analysis of eleven Learning Studios as processes of expansive learning and boundary crossing led to findings that successful boundary crossing and developmental transfer were largely dependent on the employment of appropriate tools. In particular, 'boundary objects' (Star and Griesemer, 1989), such as forms, knowledge repositories, and graphic models, played an important role in the expansion of the shared object.

The idea of developmental transfer as an outcome of boundary crossing in an expansive learning process has been developed further in a number of subsequent studies (Tuomi-Gröhn and Engeström, 2003; Konkola et al., 2007). In these, the focus has moved to the practice periods or internships of students of vocational and professional education. The practice periods or internships are jointly redesigned as development projects aimed at meeting real needs and challenges in workplaces. The student or group of students may act as a crucial change agent, carrying, translating and helping to implement new ideas between the educational institution and the workplace.

The relatively general idea of boundary crossing was further developed in a series of studies of expansive learning in the medical care of chronic patients with multiple illnesses, using multiple care providers (Engeström, 2001a, 2001b, 2003; Engeström et al., 2003, Saaren-Seppälä, 2004; Kerosuo, 2006). The learning challenge in such fields of activity is to acquire a new, negotiated way of working in which patients and practitioners from different caregiver organizations will collaboratively plan and monitor the patient's trajectory of care, taking joint responsibility for its overall progress. The key concept developed in these studies is negotiated knotworking.

The notion of knot refers to rapidly pulsating, distributed and partially improvised orchestration of collaborative performance between otherwise loosely connected actors and activity systems. Knotworking is characterized by a pulsating movement of tying, untying and retying together otherwise separate threads of activity. The tying and dissolution of a knot of collaborative work is not reducible to any specific individual or fixed organizational entity as the center of control. The center does not hold. The locus of initiative changes from moment to moment within a knotworking sequence. Thus, knotworking cannot be adequately analyzed from the point of view of an assumed center of coordination and control, or as an additive sum of the separate perspectives of individuals or institutions contributing to it. The unstable knot itself needs to be made the focus of analysis (Engeström et al., 1999, pp. 346–347).

Knotworking is the emerging mode of collaboration in work settings that move toward co-configuration, a form of production aimed at the creation of customer-intelligent products or services which adapt to the changing needs of the user and have very long life trajectories, requiring that the customer becomes a real partner with the producer (Victor and Boynton, 1998; Engeström, 2004b). In the health care studies the expansive learning process led to the creation of new tools for negotiated care. The key tool was called 'care agreement'. It was complemented by the care map and the care calendar. Together these were aimed at generating a new instrumentality for negotiated knotworking (Kerosuo and Engeström, 2003; Engeström et al., 2005).

The concept of knotworking has been found useful in recent studies on learning in such diverse contexts as university–school partnerships (Fenwick, 2006a), knowledge sharing among globally distributed anti-doping experts (Kazlauskas and Crawford, 2007), and collaboration between speech therapists and school staff (Martin, 2008).

Boundary crossing has also been analyzed in activity-theoretical studies of technological innovations. In a study of the implementation of a complex technological device in clinical use, Hasu and Engeström (2000) observed that bridging the gap between the developers and users may require new types of software tools: 'software agents must operate as boundary-crossing agents that facilitate interaction and mutual intelligibility between the perspectives' (p. 86).

Learning in organizational networks is commonly depicted as horizontal movement of information between organizational units. This view easily forgets that networks are also hierarchies. In other words, learning is also vertical movement and boundary crossing between different organizational levels. This aspect of expansive learning was the focus of Toiviainen's (2003) study. Toivainen analyzed learning in a small-firm network, initially at four levels: the network-ideological, the project, the production, and the worker levels. The longitudinal study revealed that the different levels were activated one by one as the expansive cycle progressed. The interplay between the levels eventually led to the formation of an entirely new level of functioning and learning located between the project level and the production level – a partnership between several firms in the original network.

the emergence of the fifth level of learning, 'the partnership level', was decisive for the dynamics of learning across the levels. It was an intermediate level that was needed, above all, to bridge the gap between the visions and ideals of networking and the practices of production across the firms. On the threshold of the new cycle of expansive learning, the major learning challenge pointed at the partnership level and its capability of encouraging learning-from-below – transforming the creative actions of production units into contributions to the entire network's learning (Toiviainen, 2007, p. 353).

FORMATIVE INTERVENTIONS

Vygotsky's methodological principle of double stimulation leads to a concept of formative interventions which are radically different from the linear notion of intervention embedded in the traditional idea of controlled experiment. The crucial differences may be condensed in three points (Engeström, 2008a).

(1) *Starting point*: In linear interventions, the contents and goals of the intervention are known ahead of time by the researchers. In formative interventions, the subjects (whether children or adult practitioners, or both) face a problematic and contradictory object which they analyze and expand by constructing a novel concept, the contents of which are not known ahead of time to the researchers.
(2) *Process*: In linear interventions, the subjects, typically teachers and students in school, are expected to execute the intervention without resistance. Difficulties of execution are interpreted as weaknesses in the design that are to be corrected by refining the design. In formative interventions, the contents and course of the intervention are subject to negotiation and the shape of the intervention is eventually up to the subjects. Double stimulation as the core mechanism implies that the subjects gain agency and take charge of the process.
(3) *Outcome*: In linear interventions, the aim is to control all the variables and to achieve a standardized solution module, typically a new learning environment, that will reliably generate the same desired outcomes when transfered and implemented in new settings. In formative interventions, the aim is to generate new concepts that may be used in other settings as frames for the design on locally appropriate new solutions. A key outcome of formative interventions is agency among the participants.

In the mid-1990s, University of Helsinki researchers developed a new intervention toolkit under the generic name of *Change Laboratory* (Engeström, Virkkunen et al., 1996). Variations of this toolkit have been used in a large number of intervention studies in settings ranging from post offices and factories to schools, hospitals, and newsrooms. The Change Laboratory serves as a microcosm in which potential new ways of working can be experienced and experimented with (Engeström, 1987, pp. 277–278).

A Change Laboratory is typically conducted in an activity system that is facing a major transformation. This is often a relatively independent pilot unit in a large organization. Working practitioners and managers of the unit, together with a small group of interventionist-researchers, conduct six to twelve successive Change Laboratory sessions, often with follow-up sessions after some months. When feasible, customers or patients are invited to join Change Laboratory sessions in which their particular cases are analyzed in detail. Change Laboratories are also conducted as boundary crossing laboratories with representatives from two or more activity systems engaged in collaboration or partnership.

The Change Laboratory is built on ethnographic data from the activity setting in which it is conducted. Critical incidents, troubles, and problems in the work practice are recorded and brought into Change Laboratory sessions to serve as *first stimuli*. This 'mirror material' is used to stimulate involvement, analysis, and collaborative design efforts among the participants.

To facilitate analysis and resolution of the problems, interventionists typically introduce conceptual tools such as the triangular models of activity systems (see Figure 7.1) as *second stimulus*. Commonly the conceptual models offered by the interventionists are replaced or combined with mediating conceptualizations or models formulated by the participants.

The participants are challenged to use the mediating second stimulus as an instrument in the design of a *new concept* for the activity they are trying to transform. Implementation of the designed new solution is usually initiated while the Change Laboratory sessions are still running, in the form of pilot experiments. The implementation typically leads to a richer and more articulated concept.

In the analysis and design, the participants are asked to move between the past, the present, and the future. This means that historical origins of the current problems are dug up and modeled, and the ideas toward a future concept are played with in anticipatory simulations such as role play. The laboratory sessions themselves are videotaped for analysis and used as stimuli for reflection. The procedure allows for the collection of rich longitudinal data on the actions and interactions involved in deliberately induced cycles of expansive learning.

While numerous studies and dissertations (many discussed here) have been published based on data collected in Change Laboratory interventions, relatively little research has as yet been done on the methodology as such (see, however, Engeström, 2000, 2007c; Cole and Engeström, 2007; Sannino, 2008b; Virkkunen, 2004; Virkkunen and Ahonen, in press). Pihlaja (2005) describes and analyzes the very first Change Laboratory process conducted in the Finnish postal services. Teräs (2007) analyzes a Change Laboratory process (called Culture Laboratory) aimed at the empowerment of immigrant students in a vocational training college. Ahonen (2008) gives a comprehensive analysis of a Change Laboratory process (called Competence Laboratory) aimed at proactive development of the competences of the employees and teams of a telecommunications company. Bodrozic (2008) proposes a broad historical perspective for the analysis and future shaping of post-industrial interventions.

FUTURE CHALLENGES

The most important outcome of expansive learning is agency – participants' ability and will to shape their activity systems. A major challenge for the study of expansive learning is to conceptualize and characterize empirically the new forms of agency involved in expansive processes (see Edwards, 2009; Nummijoki and Engeström, 2009; Sannino, 2008b; Virkkunen, 2006a, 2006b; Yamazumi, 2009). In formative Change Laboratory interventions, I have tentatively identified the following five interconnected forms of participants' emerging agency which seem to be quite specific and characteristic to this type of interventions: (1) resisting the interventionist or the management, (2) explicating new possibilities or potentials in the activity, (3) envisioning new patterns or models of the activity, (4) committing to concrete actions aimed at changing the activity, (5) taking consequential actions to change the activity (Engeström, 2008a). In Change Laboratory processes, the consequential change actions are mostly taken after and in between the laboratory sessions. To record and reflect on such actions, various kinds of follow-up data are collected and specific follow-up sessions are included in the longitudinal intervention process.

Expansive learning is a process of concept formation. This framework suggests that the very idea of concepts needs to be redefined. As Hall and Greeno (2008, p. 213) point out, 'concepts and their meanings develop and evolve in settings of practice and are maintained in practices because they are useful in conducting the community's activities.' In this perspective, concepts are consequential for the lives of those who work with them. Such concepts are embodied, embedded, and distributed in and across human activity systems equipped with multi-layered and multi-modal representational infrastructures or instrumentalities (Engeström, 2007a). Of particular interest are 'possibility concepts' (Engeström, 2007b) and 'perspectival concepts' (Engeström et al., 2005) which explicate time-bound collective intentions or visions of future development and change.

In a recent series of studies on expansive learning in organizations moving toward co-configuration work (Engeström, 2007a), a recurring gap was observed between the highly motivated modeling phase in which participants designed a new concept for their work, and the implementation phase in which numerous obstacles and persistent inertia tended to take over. This gap was momentarily overcome in episodes in which the participants put themselves into imagined, simulated and real situations which required personal engagement in actions with material objects and artifacts (including other human beings) that followed the logic of the anticipated or designed future model of the activity.

The concept of experiencing, as put forward by Vasilyuk (1988), seems promising as a bridge between design and implementation. According to Vasilyuk (1988, p. 10), experiencing is 'particular internal work by means of which a person overcomes and conquers a crisis, restores lost spiritual equilibrium, and resurrects the lost meaning of existence.' In other words, Vasilyuk defines experiencing as the working out of contradictions human beings encounter in maintaining their activities.

If one had to use one word only to define the nature of such situations one would have to say that they are situations of *impossibility*. Impossibility of what? Impossibility of living, of realizing the *internal necessities* of life. The struggle against impossibility, the struggle to realize internal necessities – that is experiencing. Experiencing is a repair of a 'disruption' of life, a work of restoration, proceeding as it were at right angles to the line of actualization of life. If the psychological theory of activity studies, figuratively speaking, the way in which a human being travels life's road, then the theory of experiencing studies the way in which he or she falls and rises again to continue the journey (Vasilyuk, 1988, p. 32).

Practitioners facing major transformations in their work activities are indeed working out contradictions and struggling to overcome the impossible. 'The process of experiencing does not lead the participant directly to realize his or her needs. It leads to restoring the psychological possibilities to carry on the activity required for the realization of these needs. In other words, experiencing may be seen as a process through which individual disposition to act is prepared' (Sannino, 2008b, p. 241). Interventions such as Change Laboratories aimed at expansive learning may be fruitfully analyzed as 'discourse- and activity-centered processes of experiencing' (Sannino, 2008b, p. 253). In future intervention studies of expansive learning, participants' autobiographical accounts of critical conflicts may be used as an important type of 'mirror material' for experiencing (Sannino, 2008a).

Perhaps the biggest challenge for future studies and theorizing in expansive learning comes from the emergence of what is commonly characterized as social production or peer production (Benkler, 2006). In social production or peer production, activities take the shape of expansive swarming and multi-directional pulsation, with emphasis on sideways transitions and boundary-crossing. Recently I have suggested the notion of wildfire activities to point out that there are activities that have important characteristics similar to those of peer production but predate Internet and take place mainly outside the sphere of digital virtuality (Engeström, 2009). Learning in wildfire activities is learning by swarming that crosses boundaries and ties knots between actors operating in fractured and often poorly charted terrains. These characteristics call for a reworking of Vygotsky's (1978) foundational concept of the zone of proximal development, and of the collective and expansive redefinition of this concept (Engeström, 1987).

The ultimate test of any learning theory is how it helps us to generate learning that penetrates and grasps pressing issues the humankind is facing today and tomorrow. The theory of expansive learning currently expands its analysis both up and down, outward and inward. Moving up and outward, it tackles learning in fields or networks of interconnected activity systems with their partially shared and often contested objects. Moving down and inward, it tackles issues of subjectivity, experiencing, personal sense, emotion, embodiment, identity, and moral commitment. The two directions may seem incompatible. Indeed, there is a risk that the theory is split into the study of collective activity systems, organizations, and history on the one hand and subjects, actions, and situations on the other hand. This is exactly the kind of split the founders of activity theory set out to overcome. To bridge and integrate the two directions, serious theoretical and empirical efforts are needed.

REFERENCES

Ahonen. H. (2008) *Oppimisen kohteen ja oppijan vastavuoroinen kehitys: Teleyrityksen asiakaspalvelun työyhteisöjen oppimiskäytäntöjen uudistaminen osana teknologis-taloudellista kumousta* (*Reciprocal Development of the Object and Subject of*

Learning: The Renewal of the Learning Practices of Front-Line Communities in a Telecommunications Company as Part of the Techno-Economical Paradigm Change). Helsinki: University of Helsinki, Department of Education (in Finnish).

Ahonen, H. and Virkkunen, J. (2003) 'Shared Challenge for Learning: Dialogue Between Management and Front-Line Workers in Knowledge Management', *International Journal of Information Technology and Management*, 2(1–2): 59–84.

Bakhtin, M.M. (1982) *The Dialogic Imagination: Four Essays by M.M. Bakhtin.* Austin: University of Texas Press.

Bakhurst, D. (1991) *Consciousness and Revolution in Soviet Philosophy: From the Bolsheviks to Evald Ilyenkov.* Cambridge: Cambridge University Press.

Bateson, G. (1972) *Steps to an Ecology of Mind.* New York: Ballantine Books.

Benkler, Y. (2006) *The Wealth of Networks: How Social Production Transforms Markets and Freedom.* New Haven: Yale University Press.

Bodrozic, Z. (2008) *Post-industrial Intervention: An Activity-Theoretical Expedition Tracing the Proximal Development of Forms of Conducting Interventions.* Helsinki: University of Helsinki, Department of Education.

Cole, M. and Engeström, Y. (2007) 'Cultural-Historical Approaches to Designing for Development', in J. Valsiner and A. Rosa (eds), *The Cambridge Handbook of Sociocultural Psychology.* Cambridge: Cambridge University Press.

Daniels, H. (2004) 'Cultural Historical Activity Theory and Professional Learning', *International Journal of Disability, Development and Education*, 51(2): 185–200.

Davydov, V.V. (1988) 'Problems of Developmental Teaching: The Experience of Theoretical and Experimental Psychological Research. Excerpts (Part II)', *Soviet Education*, 30(9): 3–83.

Davydov, V.V. (1990) *Types of Generalization in Instruction: Logical and Psychological Problems in the Structuring of School Curricula.* Reston, VA: National Council of Teachers of Mathematics.

Edwards, A. (2009) 'From the Systemic to the Relational: Relational Agency and Activity Theory', in A. Sannino, H. Daniels and K. Gutiérrez (eds), *Learning and Expanding with Activity Theory.* Cambridge: Cambridge University Press.

Engeström, Y. (1987) *Learning by Expanding: An Activity-Theoretical Approach to Developmental Research.* Helsinki: Orienta-Konsultit.

Engeström, Y. (1996) 'Development as Breaking Away and Opening Up: A Challenge to Vygotsky and Piaget', *Swiss Journal of Psychology*, 55: 126–132.

Engeström, Y. (1998) 'Reorganizing the Motivational Sphere of Classroom Culture: An Activity-Theoretical Analysis of Planning in a Teacher Team', in F. Seeger, J. Voigt and U. Waschescio (eds), *The Culture of the Mathematics Classroom.* Cambridge: Cambridge University Press.

Engeström, Y. (1999a) 'Expansive Visibilization of Work: An Activity-Theoretical Perspective', *Computer Supported Cooperative Work*, 8: 63–93.

Engeström, Y. (1999b) 'Innovative Learning in Work Teams: Analyzing Cycles of Knowledge Creation in Practice', in Y. Engeström, R. Miettinen and R-L. Punamäki (eds), *Perspectives on Activity Theory.* Cambridge: Cambridge University Press.

Engeström, Y. (2000) 'From Individual Action to Collective Activity and Back: Developmental Work Research as an Interventionist Methodology', in P. Luff, J. Hindmarsh and C. Heath (eds), *Workplace Studies.* Cambridge: Cambridge University Press.

Engeström, Y. (2001a) 'Expansive Learning at Work: Toward an Activity Theoretical Reconceptualization', *Journal of Education and Work*, 14(1): 133–156.

Engeström, Y. (2001b) 'Making Expansive Decisions: An Activity-Theoretical Study of Practitioners Building Collaborative Medical Care for Children', in C.M. Allwood and M. Selart (eds), *Decision Making: Social and Creative Dimensions.* Dordrecht: Kluwer.

Engeström, Y. (2003) 'The Horizontal Dimension of Expansive Learning: Weaving a Texture of Cognitive Trails in the Terrain of Health Care in Helsinki', in F. Achtenhagen and E.G. John (eds), *Milestones of Vocational and Occupational Education and Training. Volume 1: The Teaching-Learning Perspective.* Bielefeld: Bertelsmann.

Engeström, Y. (2004a) 'Managing as Argumentative History-Making', in R.J. Boland Jr. and F. Collopy (eds), *Managing as Designing.* Stanford: Stanford Business Books.

Engeström, Y. (2004b) 'New Forms of Learning in Co-Configuration Work', *Journal of Workplace Learning*, 16: 11–21.

Engeström, Y. (2005) *Developmental Work Research: Expanding Activity Theory in Practice.* Berlin: Lehmanns Media.

Engeström, Y. (2007a) 'Enriching the Theory of Expansive Learning: Lessons from Journeys Toward Coconfiguration', *Mind, Culture, and Activity*, 14(1–2): 23–39.

Engeström, Y. (2007b) 'From Stabilization Knowledge to Possibility Knowledge in Organizational Learning', *Management Learning*, 38: 271–275.

Engeström, Y. (2007c) 'Putting Vygotsky to Work: The Change Laboratory as an Application of Double Stimulation', in H. Daniels, M. Cole and J.V. Wertsch (eds), *The Cambridge Companion to Vygotsky.* Cambridge: Cambridge University Press.

Engeström, Y. (2008a) *From Design Experiments to Formative Interventions.* Paper presented at the ISCAR conference, San Diego, September.

Engeström, Y. (2008b) *From Teams to Knots: Activity-Theoretical Studies of Collaboration and Learning at Work.* Cambridge: Cambridge University Press.

Engeström, Y. (2009) 'Wildfire Activities: New Patterns of Mobility and Learning', *International Journal of Mobile and Blended Learning*, 1(2): 1–18.

Engeström, Y. and Engeström, R. (1986) 'Developmental Work Research: The Approach and an Application in Cleaning Work', *Nordisk Pedagogik*, 6(1): 2–15.

Engeström, Y. and Kerosuo, H. (2007) 'From Workplace Learning to Inter-Organizational Learning and Back: The Contribution of Activity Theory', *Journal of Workplace Learning*, 19: 336–342.

Engeström, Y., Engeström, R. and Kärkkäinen, M. (1995) 'Polycontextuality and Boundary Crossing in Expert Cognition: Learning and Problem Solving in Complex Work Activities', *Learning and Instruction*, 5: 319–336.

Engeström, Y., Engeström, R. and Kerosuo, H. (2003) 'The Discursive Construction of Collaborative Care', *Applied Linguistics*, 24: 286–315.

Engeström, Y., Engeström, R. and Vähäaho, T. (1999) 'When the Center Does Not Hold: The Importance of Knotworking', in S. Chaiklin, M. Hedegaard and U.J. Jensen (eds), *Activity Theory and Social Practice: Cultural-Historical Approaches*. Aarhus: Aarhus University Press.

Engeström, Y., Kerosuo, H. and Kajamaa, A. (2007) 'Beyond Discontinuity: Expansive Organizational Learning Remembered', *Management Learning*, 38(3): 319–336.

Engeström, Y., Lompscher, J. and Rückriem, G. (eds) (2005) *Putting Activity Theory to Work: Contributions from Developmental Work Research*. Berlin: Lehmanns Media.

Engeström, Y., Pasanen, A., Toiviainen, H. and Haavisto, V. (2005) 'Expansive Learning as Collaborative Concept Formation at Work', in K. Yamazumi, Y. Engeström and H. Daniels (eds), *New Learning Challenges: Going Beyond the Industrial Age System of School and Work*. Kansai: Kansai University Press.

Engeström, Y., Puonti, A. and Seppänen, L. (2003) 'Spatial and Temporal Expansion of the Object as a Challenge for Reorganizing Work', in D. Nicolini, S. Gherardi and D. Yanow (eds), *Knowing in Organizations: A Practice-Based Approach*. Armonk: Sharpe.

Engeström, Y., Virkkunen, J., Helle, M., Pihlaja, J. and Poikela, R. (1996) 'The Change Laboratory as a Tool for Transforming Work', *Lifelong Learning in Europe*, 1(2): 10–17.

Falmagne, R.J. (1995) 'The Abstract and the Concrete', in L.M.W. Martin, K. Nelson and E. Tobach (eds), *Sociocultural Psychology: Theory and Practice of Doing and Knowing*. Cambridge: Cambridge University Press.

Fenwick, T.J. (2004) 'Learning in Portfolio Work: Anchored Innovation and Mobile Identity', *Studies in Continuing Education*, 26(2): 229–245.

Fenwick, T. (2006a) 'Organisational Learning in the "Knots": Discursive Capacities Emerging in a School-University Collaboration', *Journal of Educational Administration*, 45(2): 138–153.

Fenwick, T. (2006b) 'Toward Enriched Conceptions of Work Learning: Participation, Expansion, and Translation Among Individuals With/in Activity', *Human Resource Development Review*, 5(3): 285–302.

FitzSimons, G.E. (2003) 'Using Engeström's Expansive Learning Framework to Analyse a Case Study in Adult Mathematics Education', *Literacy and Numeracy Studies*, 12(2): 47–63.

Foot, K. (2001) 'Cultural-Historical Activity Theory as Practical Theory: Illuminating the Development of a Conflict Monitoring Network', *Communication Theory*, 11(1): 56–83.

Gutiérrez, K. (2008) 'Developing a Sociocritical Literacy in the Third Space', *Reading Research Quarterly*, 43(2): 148–164.

Gutiérrez, K. and Larson, J. (2007) 'Discussing Expanded Spaces for Learning', *Language Arts*, 85(1): 69–77.

Haavisto, V. (2002) *Court Work in Transition: An Activity-Theoretical Study of Changing Work Practices in a Finnish District Court*. Helsinki: University of Helsinki, Department of Education.

Haigh, J. (2007) 'Expansive Learning in the University Setting: The Case for Simulated Clinical Experience', *Nurse Education in Practice*, 7: 95–102.

Hall, R. and Greeno, J.G. (2008) 'Conceptual Learning', in T. Good (ed), *21st Century Education: A Reference Handbook*. London: Sage. (pp. 212–221).

Hasu, M. (2000) 'Blind Men and the Elephant: Implementation of a New Artifact as an Expansive Possibility', *Outlines*, 2: 5–41.

Hasu, M. and Engeström, Y. (2000) 'Measurement in Action: An Activity-Theoretical Perspective on Producer-User Interaction', *International Journal of Human-Computer Studies*, 53: 61–89.

Hill, R., Capper, P., Wilson, K., Whatman, R. and Wong, K. (2007) 'Workplace Learning in the New Zealand Apple Industry Network: A New Co-Design Method for Government "Practice Making"', *Journal of Workplace Learning*, 19(6): 359–376.

Hyrkkänen, U. (2007) *Käsityksistä ajatuksen poluille: Ammattikorkeakoulun tutkimus- ja kehitystoiminnan konseptin kehittäminen* (*From Conceptions to Cognitive Trails: Developing the Concept of Research and Development Activity for the University of Applied Sciences*). Helsinki: University of Helsinki, Department of Education (in Finnish).

Il'enkov, E.V. (1977) *Dialectical Logic: Essays in Its History and Theory*. Moscow: Progress.

Il'enkov, E.V. (1982) *The Dialectics of the Abstract and the Concrete in Marx's 'Capital'*. Moscow: Progress.

Kärkkäinen, M. (1999) *Teams as Breakers of Traditional Work Practices: A Longitudinal Study of Planning and Implementing Curriculum Units in Elementary School Teacher Teams*. Helsinki: University of Helsinki, Department of Education.

Kazlauskas, A. and Crawford, K. (2007) 'Learning What is Not Yet There: Knowledge Mobilization in a Communal Activity', in I. Verenikina, P. Kell and G. Vogl (eds), *Learning and Socio-cultural Theory: Exploring Modern Vygotskian Perspectives*. Workshop proceedings. Wollongong: University of Wollongong. ISBN 978–1–74128–138–5. E-version: http://ro.uow.edu.au/llrg.

Kerosuo, H. (2006) *Boundaries in Action: An Activity-Theoretical Study of Development, Learning and Change in Health Care for Patients with Multiple and Chronic Illnesses*. Helsinki: University of Helsinki, Department of Education.

Kerosuo, H. and Engeström, Y. (2003) 'Boundary Crossing and Learning in Creation of New Work Practice', *Journal of Workplace Learning*, 15: 345–351.

Konkola, R., Tuomi-Gröhn, T., Lambert, P. and Ludvigsen, S. (2007) 'Promoting Learning and Transfer Between School and Workplace', *Journal of Education and Work*, 20(3): 211–228.

Lambert, P. (1999) *Rajaviiva katoaa: Innovatiivista oppimista ammatillisen opettajankoulutuksen, oppilaitosten ja työelämän organisaatioiden yhteistyönä [Boundaries Fade Away: Innovative Learning Through Collaboration Between Vocational Teacher Education, Training Institutes, and Work Organizations]*. Helsinki: Helsingin ammattikorkeakoulu (in Finnish).

Lave, J. and Wenger, E. (1991) *Situated Learning: Legitimate Peripheral Participation*. Cambridge: Cambridge University Press.

Leont'ev, A.N. (1978) *Activity, Consciousness, and Personality*. Englewood Cliffs: Prentice-Hall.

Leont'ev, A.N. (1981) *Problems of the Development of the Mind*. Moscow: Progress.

Makino, Y. (2007) 'The Third Generation of E-Learning: Expansive Learning Mediated by a Weblog', *International Journal of Web Based Communities*, 3(1): 16–31.

Mäkitalo, J. (2005) *Work-Related Well-Being in the Transformation of Nursing Home Work*. Oulu: Oulu University Press.

Martin, D. (2008) 'A New Paradigm to Inform Inter-Professional Learning for Integrating Speech and Language Provision into Secondary Schools: A Socio-Cultural Activity Theory Approach', *Child Language Teaching and Therapy*, 24(2): 173–192.

Nilsson, M. (2003) *Transformation Through Integration: An Activity Theoretical Analysis of School Development as Integration of Child Care Institutions and Elementary School*. Karlskrona: Blekinge Institute of Technology.

Nummijoki, J. and Engeström, Y. (2009) 'Towards Co-Configuration in Home Care of the Elderly: Cultivating Agency by Designing and Implementing the Mobility Agreement', In H. Daniels, A. Edwards, Y. Engeström, T. Gallagher and S. Ludvigsen (eds), *Activity Theory in Practice: Promoting Learning Across Boundaries and Agencies*. London: Routledge.

Paavola, S., Lipponen, L. and Hakkarainen, K. (2004) 'Models of Innovative Knowledge Communities and Three Metaphors of Learning', *Review of Educational Research*, 74: 557–576.

Pihlaja, J. (2005) *Learning In and For Production: An Activity-Theoretical Study of the Historical Development of Distributed Systems of Generalizing*. Helsinki: University of Helsinki, Department of Education.

Puonti, A. (2004) *Learning to Work Together: Collaboration Between Authorities in Economic-Crime Investigation*. Vantaa: National Bureau of Investigation.

Rasmussen, I. and Ludvigsen, S. (2009) 'The Hedgehog and the Fox: A Discussion of the Approaches to the Analysis of ICT Reforms in Teacher Education of Larry Cuban and Yrjö Engeström', *Mind, Culture, and Activity*, 16(1): 83–104.

Saaren-Seppälä, T. (2004) *Yhteisen potilaan hoito: Tutkimus organisaatiorajat ylittävästä yhteistoiminnasta sairaalan, terveyskeskuksen ja lapsipotilaiden vanhempien suhteissa (The Care of a Shared Patient: A Study of Collaboration across Organizational Boundaries between Hospital, Health Center and Parents of Child Patients)*. Tampere: University of Tampere.

Sannino, A. (2008a) 'Experiencing Conversations: Bridging the Gap Between Discourse and Activity', *Journal for the Theory of Social Behaviour*, 38(3): 267–291.

Sannino, A. (2008b) 'From Talk to Action: Experiencing Interlocution in Developmental Interventions', *Mind, Culture, and Activity*, 15: 234–257.

Sannino, A. and Nocon, H. (2008) 'Introduction: Activity Theory and School Innovation', *Journal of Educational Change*, 9(4): 325–328.

Sannino, A., Daniels, H. and Gutierrez, K. (2009) 'Activity Theory Between Historical Engagement and Future-Making Practice', in A. Sannino, H. Daniels and K. Gutiérrez (eds), *Learning and Expanding with Activity Theory*. Cambridge: Cambridge University Press.

Seppänen, L. (2004) *Learning Challenges in Organic Vegetable Farming: An Activity-Theoretical Study of On-Farm Practices*. Helsinki: University of Helsinki, Institute for Rural Research and Training.

Sfard, A. (1998) 'On Two Metaphors of Learning and the Dangers of Choosing Just One', *Educational Researcher*, 27(2): 4–13.

Star, S.L. and Griesemer, J.R. (1989) 'Institutional Ecology, "Translations" and Boundary Objects: Amateurs and Professionals in Berkeley's Museum of Vertebrate Zoology', 1907–39, *Social Studies of Science*, 9: 387–420.

Teräs, M. (2007) *Intercultural Learning and Hybridity in the Culture Laboratory*. Helsinki: University of Helsinki, Department of Education.

Toikka, K., Hyötyläinen. R. and Norros, L. (1986) 'Development of Work in Flexible Manufacturing', *Nordisk Pedagogik*, 6(1): 16–24.

Toiviainen, H. (2003) *Learning Across Levels: Challenges of Collaboration in a Small-Firm Network*. Helsinki: University of Helsinki, Department of Education.

Toiviainen, H. (2007) 'Inter-Organizational Learning Across Levels: An Object-Oriented Approach', *Journal of Workplace Learning*, 19(6): 343–358.

Tsui, A.B.M. and Law, D.Y.K. (2007) 'Learning as Boundary-Crossing in School–University Partnership', *Teaching and Teacher Education*, 23: 1289–1301.

Tuomi-Gröhn, T. and Engeström, Y. (eds) (2003) *Between School and Work: New Perspectives on Transfer and Boundary-Crossing*. Amsterdam: Pergamon.

Vasilyuk, F. (1988) *The Psychology of Experiencing*. Moscow: Progress.

van der Veer, R. and Valsiner, J. (1991) *Understanding Vygotsky: A Quest for Synthesis*. Oxford: Blackwell.

Victor, B. and Boynton, A. (1998) *Invented Here: Maximizing Your Organization's Internal Growth and Profitability*. Boston: Harvard Business School Press.

Virkkunen, J. (2004) 'Developmental Interventions in Work Activities: An Activity Theoretical Interpretation', in T. Kontinen (ed.), *Development Intervention: Actor and Activity Perspectives*. Helsinki: Center for Activity Theory and Developmental Work Research and Institute for Development Studies, University of Helsinki.

Virkkunen, J. (2006a) 'Dilemmas in Building Shared Transformative Agency', *Activités revue électronique*, 3(1).

Virkkunen, J. (2006b) 'Hybrid Agency in Co-Configuration Work', *Outlines*, 8(1): 61–75.

Virkkunen, J. and Ahonen, H. (in press) 'Supporting Expansive Learning Through Theoretical-Genetic Reflection in the Change Laboratory', *Journal of Organizational Change Management*.

Vossoughi, S. and Gutiérrez, K. (2010) 'Lifting off the Ground to Return Anew: Mediated Praxis, Transformative Learning, and Social Design Experiments', *Journal of Teacher Education*, 61(1–2): 100–117.

Vygotsky, L.S. (1978) *Mind in Society: The Development of Higher Psychological Processes*. Cambridge: Harvard University Press.

Vygotsky, L.S. (1997) 'The History of the Development of Higher Mental Functions', In R.W. Rieber (ed.), *The Collected Works of L.S. Vygotsky. Vol. 4: The History of the Development of Higher Mental Functions*. New York: Plenum.

Wenger, E. (1998) *Communities of Practice: Learning, Meaning and Identity*. Cambridge: Cambridge University Press.

Yamazumi, K. (2008) 'A Hybrid Activity System as Educational Innovation', *Journal of Educational Change*, 9(4): 365–373.

Yamazumi, K. (2009) 'Expansive Agency in Multi-Activity Collaboration', in A. Sannino, H. Daniels and K. Gutiérrez (eds), *Learning and Expanding with Activity Theory*. Cambridge: Cambridge University Press.

Zinchenko, V.P. (1985) 'Vygotsky's Ideas about Units for the Analysis of Mind', in J.V. Wertsch (ed.), *Culture, Communication, and Cognition: Vygotskian Perspectives*. Cambridge: Cambridge University Press.

8

Informal Learning at Work: Conditions, Processes and Logics

Per-Erik Ellström

INTRODUCTION

Over the last two decades, there has been an increasing interest in research on learning in work and the workplace as a site for learning (e.g. Boud and Garrick, 1999; Evans et al., 2002; Nijhof and Niuwenhuis, 2008). In spite of this development, it is clear that the field of workplace learning still has a diverse and in certain respects contested character (e.g. Fenwick, 2006). However, there are also converging lines of research within the field. One example is the interest in research on the integration of work and learning, and a focus on workplace learning, not as activities that are separated from work, but rather as a more or less conscious and deliberate aspect of work activities (Barnett, 1999; Ellström, 2001; Evans and Rainbird, 2002). As succinctly formulated by Zuboff (1988: 395) based on her studies of complex work processes: 'Learning is not something that requires time out from productive activity; learning is the heart of productive activity.'

Zuboff's (1988) early and at the time somewhat visionary view of workplace learning has in general terms received considerable support from later research. This is attested to not least by the influential ideas of situated learning and learning as participation in social practices (Lave and Wenger, 1991), or as change and development in activity systems (Engeström, 1987). There are also a large number of other researchers who have addressed issues about the integration between work and learning and the learning potential of the workplace (e.g. Billett, 2001, 2004; Ellström et al., 2008; Evans, 2002; Evans et al., 2004; Eraut, 2000, 2004; Fuller and Unwin, 2004; Gustavsson, 2007; Nieuwenhuis and van Woerkom, 2008). Taken together, these and other studies on learning in work have led to considerable advances in our knowledge about workplace learning. Among the important insights from these studies is that learning at work is dependent on interactions between characteristics of the workplace as a learning environment and a range of individual factors, including biographical characteristics, motivation, self-efficacy and previous acquired knowledge and skills.

Pursuing this line of research, the aim of this chapter is to propose a framework for analyzing informal learning in work and the learning potential of the workplace. However, contrary to much current research in this field, learning in work is conceptualized neither as a social process inseparable from work practices nor as a purely cognitive process. Rather, learning is viewed as mediated by individual actions and interactions in dealing with different tasks and situations at work. Hopefully, this framework can help to further our understanding of the workplace as a learning environment, how it shapes and is shaped by individual actions and interactions at work, and how learning occurs through these processes. Furthermore, by proposing a distinction between two organizational logics, an attempt is made to conceptualize the workplace as a learning environment in a broader institutional perspective.

The chapter is organized in five sections. In the following section, the concept of informal learning is defined, and a distinction is made between two modes of learning in work: adaptive and developmental learning. In the third section, the workplace as a learning environment is discussed with a focus on the relations between structural and subjective conditions of learning and how learning environments constrain and enable learning in work. In the fourth section, there is a more direct focus on learning processes and how learning can be understood in terms of interplay between different levels of action and reflection in the performance of work activities. In the fifth section, two organizational logics, called the logic of production and the logic of development, are distinguished. These two logics are viewed as institutionalized patterns of practice that shape the learning environment in an organization. Finally, in the concluding section, the main arguments presented in this chapter are summarized and some of the implications for theory and research are highlighted.

LEARNING IN WORK: ADAPTIVE VERSUS DEVELOPMENTAL LEARNING

The focus of this chapter concerns informal learning at work. Some would argue (e.g. Billett, 2004) that the notion of informal learning should be avoided on the grounds that it is defined in negative terms, i.e. in terms of what it is not, implying that it is inferior to learning in educational institutions. However, there is of course no necessity to define informal learning in this way. On the contrary, as used here, the notion of informal learning is defined in positive terms as referring to learning that occurs regularly in work as well as in everyday life, but subordinated to other activities (e.g. work practices) in the sense that learning is not their primary goal. Such learning may occur without the awareness or intention to learn (implicit learning), or it may involve a more or less deliberate effort to learn (cf. Eraut, 2000; Marsick and Watkins, 1990). Basically, the relations between a learning subject (e.g. an individual or a work team) and its learning environment are assumed to be reciprocal. Thus, learning is viewed both as an adaptive process that is shaped by environmental conditions and as a process that contributes to the shaping of these conditions. This reciprocity is an important aspect of the distinction between adaptive and developmental learning that is made below.

There is considerable evidence in support of the significance, or even the necessity, of informal learning, not only in work contexts, but also in schools and in the community at large (Coffield, 2000; de Grip, 2008). Considering informal learning in work contexts, the latter author presents data that indicate that informal learning activities account for more than 90 per cent of the time that Dutch workers are involved in learning activities on the job. However, the emphasis that is put here on the importance of informal learning in work and everyday life does not entail some kind of degradation of formal learning, i.e. learning within the formal education system. Rather, an integration of formal and informal learning appears to be essential in order to create desirable competencies, both from an individual and an organizational perspective (Barnett, 1999; Svensson et al., 2004).

Another important point of departure for this chapter is a distinction between two qualitatively different but complementary modes of learning called adaptive and developmental learning (Ellström, 1997; 2001). Adaptive learning has its focus on the mastery of certain given tasks, or situations, or on the improvement of task performance or routines in an organization. It has its role primarily in the formation of competencies for handling routine tasks or problems, or tasks that recur quite frequently. This is in contrast to developmental learning, where the focus is on individual/collective development, and/or on more radical changes of a prevailing situation. Developmental learning is assumed to occur when individuals or groups within an organization begin to question and explore existing working conditions or established definitions of the problems and tasks at hand, and act to develop new ways of handling the duties and often complex problems involved in a job. Thus, the notion of developmental learning used here has links to Dewey's (1933) notion of inquiry, as well as to such different traditions as Engeström's (1987) activity theory based model of expansive learning and Argyris' et al. (1985) model of investigative learning.

To further clarify the distinction between adaptive and developmental learning, a few additional points should be made. First, the distinction does not concern two types of learning that are mutually exclusive. Rather, they represent two complementary modes of learning, where one or the other of these modes can be dominant or relatively inconspicuous depending on the conditions that prevail in a specific situation. Second, the two modes of learning are viewed here as two extremes on a continuum where it is also possible to define other categories of learning between the two extremes. These 'middle forms' may be seen as representing more incremental modes of learning between adaptation or improvement and more radical change. One example is the notion of productive learning proposed by Engeström (1987) and used also by Ellström (2001). However, for the purposes of this chapter it is sufficient to use only the two main categories of adaptive and developmental learning.

Third, although adaptive learning might be perceived as having mainly negative connotations, for example, focusing on people adjusting themselves to an aversive reality, the significance of this kind of learning should not be depreciated. Newcomers' socialization to a workplace and their attempts to master existing norms, social practices, and routines can be mentioned as prime examples of the importance of this mode of learning (Fenwick, 2003). Conversely, developmental learning, although the connotations are perhaps mainly positive, may nevertheless entail negative aspects. For example, too strong an emphasis on flexibility, the transformation of prevailing practices and the creation of new solutions, might create negative stress and feelings of anxiety and insecurity. Under favourable conditions, however, developmental learning might also be a driving force for change and innovation in an organization. In line with this, and as indicated by a large number of studies in different areas (e.g. Brown and Duguid, 1991; Olsen and Rasmussen, 1989; Zuboff, 1988), both modes of learning distinguished here are at least potentially required in many jobs. Thus, there is often a requirement to deal alternately with well-known, routine problems and new or unknown problematic situations, and, thereby, being able to alternate between an adaptive and a developmental mode of learning. This distinction between adaptive and developmental learning will be further elaborated in the fourth section.

ENABLING AND CONSTRAINING LEARNING ENVIRONMENTS

As assumed here, and in line with previous research (e.g. Billett, 2001; Ellström, 2001; Fuller et al., 2007), learning in work is a matter of design. That is, it is a matter of organizing the workplace, not only for production of certain goods or services, but also for supporting learning. Following Billett (2001), a workplace is designed for learning – has a learning readiness – to the extent that it affords opportunities for individuals to engage in and be supported for learning.

How, then, can the learning readiness of a workplace be conceptualized? In the following, this is done by using the concept of a learning environment (Billett, 2001, 2004; Ellström, 1997, 2001; Fuller and Unwin, 2004). Specifically, we will make a distinction between two types of learning environment: enabling and constraining. By an enabling learning environment we refer to working conditions and practices that are likely to promote a balance between adaptive and developmental learning, i.e. an environment where individuals are able to alternate between these two modes of learning. In contrast, in constraining learning an environment refers to conditions and practices that are likely to constrain both adaptive and developmental learning, or to promote adaptive learning at the expense of developmental learning. The two types of learning environment are viewed here as two extremes on a continuum, while in practice we are likely to encounter cases with both constraining and enabling characteristics (cf. Fuller and Unwin, 2004; for empirical examples, see also Ellström et al., 2008).

As already indicated, this distinction between two types of learning environment is to some extent parallel to the distinction between expansive and restrictive learning environments proposed by Fuller and Unwin (2004). However, an important difference between the two distinctions concerns their underlying views of learning. Fuller and Unwin's (2004) distinction has its roots in a sociocultural perspective on learning that equates learning with participation in work practices (Lave and Wenger, 1991). A problem with this view of learning, is that it makes it difficult, if not impossible, to analytically separate learning from organizational conditions and practices. By implication, this makes it difficult to analyse empirical relationships between environmental characteristics (e.g. work conditions) and learning and, thereby, also to empirically substantiate statements about the restrictive (constraining) or expansive (enabling) character of a learning environment. The distinction proposed here, on the other hand, builds on a conception of learning in work as analytically independent of the learning environment, including the forms of participation that it offers. Thus, the participation in work practices is considered as one among several important conditions for learning, but one that cannot be equated with learning.

This notion of learning does not, however, entail a view where isolated individuals are the locus of the learning process, i.e. some version of methodological individualism. On the contrary, building on critical realist theory (e.g. Archer, 1995; Bhaskar, 1989), individual subjectivity, actions and interactions are viewed as constrained and enabled by pre-existing structural conditions of the workplace, conditions which in their turn are shaped (reproduced or transformed) by individual actions and interactions.

The pre-existing structural conditions – comprising material factors including time and other resources, social-organizational factors (e.g. norms, routines, division of labour), and cultural factors, including concepts, ideas and theoretical knowledge – constitute important aspects of the learning environment of a workplace and are assumed to determine its learning potential at a certain point in time. As argued elsewhere (Ellström, 2001), the learning potential of a workplace is the result of a complex interplay between a range of factors, including: (a) task characteristics, for example, task complexity, variety and control; (b) opportunities for feedback, evaluation and reflection; (c) the type and degree of formalization of work processes; (d) organizational arrangements for employee participation in problem handling and developmental activities; and (e) learning resources in terms of, for example, time for analysis, interaction and reflection.

These and other structural conditions constitute the opportunities for learning afforded by a workplace (e.g. Billett, 2001, 2004). Typically, though, the opportunities for learning are not homogeneous across individuals or groups of individuals in an organization. On the contrary, a learning environment may be assumed to represent an access structure (March and Olsen, 1976) that, formally or informally, regulates the rights to participate in different work and learning activities, i.e. who is invited to participate in what activities. As indicated by previous research, participation in workplace learning may differ along lines of job position, occupational status and roles, where blue-collar workers report the lowest rates of participation (Rubenson, 2006; cf. Felstead et al., 2000).

However, we have also to consider a range of subjective factors that influence how the structural conditions are experienced, understood and valued by an individual. These factors are assumed to influence the capacity to identify and take advantage of the structural conditions (Ellström, 2001) or, in the words of Billett (2001), the extent to which individuals 'elect to engage' in the learning opportunities afforded by the workplace. Thus, the learning processes and outcomes of different people placed in the same task or job with the same learning opportunities will be expected to differ depending on personal background and subjective factors.

As shown by Fenwick (2003), subjective factors appear to be at least as important as favourable structural conditions. Specifically, her findings point to the importance of employee awareness of the learning opportunities that are encountered as part of the daily work, combined with self-awareness of their own way of handling these opportunities. As argued by Ellström (2001), subjective factors of this kind constitute the learning readiness of an individual. However, this readiness is not only related to individual knowledge and understanding of learning opportunities, but also to a number of individual and social factors such as identities, previous experience, self-confidence, motivation, formal education, interpersonal relationships, family structure and so forth (Evans et al., 2004; Ellström et al., 2008; Fuller and Unwin, 2004; Gorard et al., 2001).

The argument so far implies that more advanced learning at work – learning beyond simple adaptation – presupposes a workplace designed to promote learning, as well as employees that are able to identify and make sense of the experiences and opportunities for learning encountered at work, i.e. employees with a certain learning readiness. Thus, structural factors are necessary but not sufficient conditions for learning. Furthermore, the relations between structural and subjective factors are assumed to be neither deterministic nor unidirectional. On the contrary, an individual has the capacity (competence) – within constrains – to reflect and to act upon her/his environment and thereby to shape it to a certain extent. This capacity, which may be interpreted in terms of the concept of bounded agency proposed by Evans (2007), is viewed here as an important dimension of an individual's learning readiness, specifically her/his readiness for developmental learning.

In the next section, these ideas will be explored from an action theory perspective. Specifically, it will be argued that the learning potential of a task or a set of tasks (a job), as well as the actual learning that occurs, can be understood and defined in terms of the levels of action and reflection that are exercised in performing the task (or job). Thus, the focus is moved from the workplace as the unit of analysis to that of the task or the job. This appears reasonable, not least in the perspective that most workplaces comprise a number of jobs and an even large number of tasks with different learning potentials.

LEARNING POTENTIALS AND PROCESSES

This section focuses on learning in work as a result of actions and interactions of individuals engaging in certain work practices. People perform tasks, solve problems and cooperate with others, based on knowledge and skills resulting from previous learning. While such actions are under certain conditions clearly deliberate and reflective, they are under other conditions best described as automatic or routinized (e.g. Bargh and Chartrand, 1999). Furthermore, the intentionality of actions does not necessarily mean that the actor has clear intentions, or goals *before* acting (e.g. Searle, 1980; Weick, 1979). On the contrary, intentions, motives and goals may sometimes be viewed as reconstructions that are discovered during or after an action. In fact, reconstructions of this kind may themselves be viewed as a result of learning (March and Olsen, 1976). In the following, these aspects of practical action will be developed and used as a framework for conceptualizing learning in work (see also Ellström, 2006a).

Levels of action and reflection

The framework presented below, which is based on theory and research within the field of cognitive action theory (e.g. Frese and Zapf, 1994; Klein et al., 1993; Norman, 1988; Rasmussen, 1986), portrays learning in work as interaction between individuals, streams of action and changing contextual conditions, but also as an interplay between different levels of action in carrying out a task or job. Specifically, the four-level model of action presented here is an elaboration of the action models proposed by Rasmussen (1986) and Frese and Zapf (1994). The model is based on a distinction between four levels of action called:

- skill-based (routinized) action;
- rule-based action;
- knowledge-based action;
- reflective action.

A basic assumption behind this model is that the four levels of action entail different levels of knowledge use and reflection (Bargh and Chartrand, 1999; Frese and Zapf, 1994). The concept of reflection as used here is broadly defined as a more or less deliberate and conscious process of interpreting and making sense of experience. More specifically, a process of reflection may be described and analysed as connected cognitive and emotional processes involved in the planning, monitoring or evaluation of action. Although the levels of action are organized hierarchically, reflection and action at one level do not exclude parallel or integrated activity at other levels. In practice, the optimal handling of a certain task may require performance at a specific level of action, or performance at different levels, in sequence or in parallel (Olsen and Rasmussen, 1989).

Skill-based action

At this level, actions are typically performed smoothly and with little subjective effort, conscious attention and control. Generally, actions at this level are governed by implicit (tacit) knowledge, or what Schön (1983) calls knowing-in-action. Typically, the acting subject cannot verbally report the knowledge the actions are based on (cf. Berry and Broadbent, 1988). Although performance is automatized and governed by implicit knowledge, routinized actions are not performed passively or 'mindlessly'. On the contrary, higher-level cognitive functions are assumed to monitor ongoing actions and to anticipate upcoming problems and demands in the environment (Olsen and Rasmussen, 1989). Consistent with this observation, Giddens (1984) talks about the 'reflexive monitoring of action' to indicate the active character of routine actions. As also argued by Giddens (1994), the consolidation of thought and action patterns as routines or habits is also a way of coping with the daily flow of events, problem situations and contradictory demands, while maintaining a sense of security and stability in life (Giddens, 1984).

Performance at the level of skill-based, routinized actions is the result of explicit and implicit processes of learning (Anderson, 1982; Berry and Broadbent, 1988). However, once established, routinized actions are very difficult to change and 'unlearn', especially if one relies on intellectual and verbal forms of education and training (Frese and Zapf, 1994). People function well at a routinized level of action until problems or surprises of one kind or another arise (Gersick and Hackman, 1990). This is clearly in line with Dewey's (1933) view of reflection as a process that begins with a perceived difficulty or disturbance in the routinized way of handling a certain task or situation. However, at the same time routinization may easily impede our detection and management of contextual changes or disturbances (Gersick and Hackman, 1990) and, as a consequence, we tend in many situations to ignore or misinterpret changes in our surroundings in order to maintain existing structures and patterns of thought and action.

Rule-based action

In contrast to the level of skill-based action, the rule-based level of action is characterized by a greater flexibility and a higher degree of conscious control. At this level, a subject is assumed to be able to handle familiar situations or problems in accordance with stored and ready-made rules that can usually also be reported (Anderson, 1982). Furthermore, actions are performed on the basis of a rule or procedure that is based on experience from previous occasions of a similar character, communications from other people, or that has been developed through a process of problem solving and experimentation in the situation at hand (Miner et al., 2001). However, the boundary between this level and the level of skill-based action is not distinct.

Learning at the level of rule-based action is typically linked to the interpretation and application of rules and procedural knowledge ('know-how'). This is far from a simple mechanical process. On the contrary, this process is critically dependent on the subject's ability to fill in the openness and incompleteness that characterize most rules. In many respects, reflection at this level of action comes close to the way Schön (1983) uses the notion of reflection-in-action: it is driven by unexpected outcomes of actions ('surprises') and it gives rise to experiments in order to revise the rules of thumb or procedures currently in use. However, contrary to Schön's (1983) emphasis on the critical and analytical character of reflection-in-action, experiments conducted at the rule-based level of action appear to be based on observed empirical correlations of successful acts and their outcomes, rather than on an analytical diagnosis of the situation (Olsen and Rasmussen, 1989; see also Eraut, 1995, 2002 for a critical discussion of the notion of reflection-in-action).

Knowledge-based and reflective action

At the knowledge-based level, the actions are consciously controlled, generated and selected on the basis of analyses of tasks and goals, previous experience and environmental conditions. The knowledge base for action may comprise factual knowledge and/or more general theoretical and explanatory knowledge (cf. Eraut, 2004; Evans et al., in Chapter 11 this volume). This is the level of action that people move to when they encounter novel or unfamiliar situations for which no rules or procedural knowledge (know-how) are available from previous experience. Performance is controlled by goals and based on explicit knowledge, i.e., knowledge that we in principle are able to articulate and codify.

At this level of action, there is both the scope for and a need for reflective exploration, interpretation and problem solving. However, in contrast to the rule-based level, there is also scope for the analytical diagnosis of a situation, and for what Mezirow (1991) calls the critical assessment of the content and processes of activities.

The main difference between the knowledge-based and the reflective levels of action is that the latter level refers to actions based on evaluations and reflections concerning not only the performance and consequences of actions, but also reflections concerning the task and the goals themselves. That is, what Mezirow (1991) calls critical reflection or reflection on the premises of action. One of the crucial elements of this reflection process is to make explicit, and thereby testable, the often implicit and taken for granted premises of our actions. This requires that the actor is able to consider alternatives and to critically analyse underlying assumptions and other conditions of action. Thus, the concept of reflection relevant at this level comes close to Schön's (1983) notion of reflection-on-action. What seems to be essential to such a process is that it is guided by explicit knowledge that can be used in the analysis of the task and goal of action, its underlying assumptions, and in interpreting and evaluating the consequences of the action. In this kind of reflective process, logical inconsistencies as well as self-reflection become of focal concern, which also makes a reliance on meta-cognitive knowledge necessary, i.e., knowledge about oneself and one's own knowledge, its scope and limits, strengths and weaknesses (e.g. Eraut, 2004; Flavell, 1979).

Learning as an interplay between routinized and reflective levels of action

Now, as illustrated in Figure 8.1, the distinction made previously between adaptive and developmental learning (see Section Two) can be interpreted and elaborated in terms of the different levels of action and reflection that were presented above.

Considering first the process of adaptive learning, it can be conceptualized as a process of learning in which the learning subject manages to handle a certain task or situation at the skill-based level of action, i.e. in a routinized (automatized) way. Adaptive learning thus entails a learning process in which the learning subject 'moves' from a reflective or knowledge-based level of action to levels of action founded on experience-based, implicit knowledge (cf. Anderson, 1982; Berry and Broadbent, 1988), i.e. to a skill-based level of action. However, this process could also begin at the level of rule-based learning, or even directly at the skill-based level. As argued by Rasmussen (1986), the skill-based level of action has a relative autonomy in relation to the other 'higher' levels, and performance on this level can be learnt without previous leaning at a rule-based or knowledge-based level, i.e. through processes of imitation and trial and error (Olsen and Rasmussen, 1989).

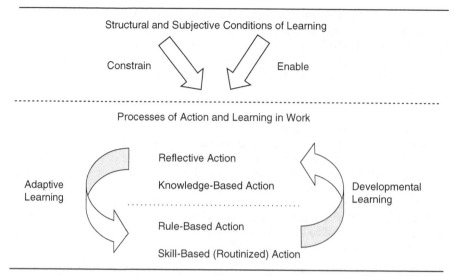

Figure 8.1   Adaptive and developmental learning as an interplay between four levels of action and reflection constrained and enabled by structural and subjective conditions of learning at a workplace

Contrary to this process of adaptive learning, the process of developmental learning is based on our ability to question established practices, to break our way out of routinized actions ('unlearn'), and to develop new patterns of thought and action through processes of reflection and problem solving. This could be described as an 'upward movement' from the level of skill-based (routinized) action to the levels of knowledge-based or reflective action. As argued above, these latter levels require conscious analytical thinking, reflection on previous experience and access to theoretical knowledge of the object and task at hand. Thus, in accordance with Dewey (1933), it could be argued that developmental learning requires the cultivation (through previous learning) of habits of reflection, i.e. 'habits of critical examination and inquiry' (p. 29).

This type of developmental learning sequence could be expected if an individual (or group), while working at a routinized level of action, encounters an unfamiliar problem or a new situation for which there is no ready-made rule or solution available (cf. Gersick and Hackman, 1990). In such a situation, the alternative to seek a solution through trial-and-error is to engage in a process of problem solving at a knowledge-based or reflective level of action.

Now, considering a complete cycle of action and learning as portrayed in Figure 8.1, it may, in idealized terms, start with the mastery of a certain task through adaptive learning, continue with a routinized performance of this task for some time, followed by disturbances or problems that trigger questioning and unlearning, and eventually learning of new ways of handling the task or problem at hand. Thus, as conceptualized here, informal learning at work means a cyclical interplay between routinized and reflective actions, and between adaptive and developmental learning. Of course, the actual process of learning is likely to be fuzzier compared to this idealized model.

In practice, the actual scope for adaptive and developmental learning and the possibilities to alternate between these two modes of learning critically depend on a range of structural and subjective factors (Ellström, 2001, 2006b). In terms of the action model presented above (see Figure 8.1), both the learning potential and the learning processes that are possible in a given learning environment can be defined in terms of the extent to which the demands of the task (the job) require the individual to move between levels of action and to perform the task not only at a skill- and rule-based level of action, but also at 'higher' levels. However, the individual must also have sufficient discretion (control) and what we earlier called a subjective learning readiness to deal with the requirements of the task, and, thus, to perform the task at the different levels of action that are required. To the extent that these requirements involve performance at a knowledge-based and/or reflective level of action, this presupposes that the individual has access to theoretical knowledge about the task at hand as well as meta-cognitive knowledge and reflective skills (cf. Eraut, 2004).

This line of reasoning can be related to the demand-control model proposed by Karasek (1979). According to this model, jobs with high demand and high control are likely to have a high learning potential (cf. Ashton, 2004b). More recently, Weststar (2009) was able to show that the degree of worker control, i.e., their discretion to shape and perform their own work, was positively related to their opportunities to engage in learning activities. In line with this, the proposal made here is that the concepts of demand and control can be given a theory-based interpretation and definition in terms of the levels of action and reflection outlined above. Thus, related to the demand-control model, the four-level model of action presented here makes it possible to arrive at a theory-based interpretation of the concepts of demand and control, and thereby to provide a platform for an integration of theory and research on workplace learning and work-related health and well-being (e.g. Karasek and Theorell, 1990).

ORGANIZING FOR LEARNING AT WORK

As was argued above, more advanced learning in work presupposes a workplace designed to promote learning. This is also very much in line with recent research in this field (e.g. Ashton, 2004a,b; Ellström et al., 2008; Fuller et al., 2007; Skule, 2004). These and other studies have provided detailed knowledge about conditions that are likely to constrain and enable learning at work. However, there is a lack of more systematic knowledge about the relations between different conditions of learning, as well as about why certain conditions are likely to prevail in an organization.

In this section, this issue is addressed by identifying and exploring two different organizational logics, called the logic of production and the logic of development (see also Ellström, 2006b), that are assumed to shape, more or less deliberately, the learning environment in an organization. This distinction is inspired by the distinction made by March (1991) between activities based on the use and refinement of established knowledge ('exploitation') and those based on the development of new knowledge and innovations ('exploration'). The two logics are viewed here as patterns of practice – with strong roots at an institutional level and in established traditions for organizing work.

Two organizational logics

It is important from the beginning to underline that the two logics distinguished here have the character of ideal typic reconstructions of actual practices that will not be found in pure form in real life. Thus, the distinction is made here for analytical purposes. In actual practice, the two logics will appear as more or less conspicuous patterns in the flow of practice within an organization. However, making this analytical distinction will hopefully help us to observe and analyse the interplay between the two logics in organizational practices.

The logic of production

If we look at the logic of production first, there is a focus on promoting efficient, effective and reliable task performance that, as far as possible, is also relatively stable over time. In order to accomplish this, it is necessary to *reduce variation* in performance within and between individuals in an organization, i.e. to promote homogeneity. In line with this orientation, the logic of production puts a strong emphasis on goal consensus, standardization, stability and the avoidance of uncertainty. The underlying idea is that people involved in an activity should quickly learn the 'codes' and 'the prevailing rules', i.e. how one 'should' or 'must' act in different situations. Thus, there is a strong focus on the implementation and mastery of prescribed methods and routines ('best practices'). Of course, in its basic principles this logic has affinities with Taylorist models for organizing work (Ashton, 2004a), but the logic of production transcends the boundaries of the Taylorist model and it is in certain respects more general.

In terms of learning, the logic of production entails adaptive learning, with a focus on establishing and maintaining well-learned and routinized action patterns, i.e. a focus on the elimination of errors (cf. Argyris and Schön, 1978). Problems are handled through the application of given rules/instructions. Thinking and reflection, although in practice an integral aspect of most work processes (Hirschhorn, 1984; Schön, 1983), are in this logic officially recognized and valued only to the extent that they are instrumental in promoting efficient action. Thus, in terms of the levels of action discussed in the previous section, this logic tends to emphasize task performance at a skill-based or rule-based level of action.

In line with this, the formal demands on the individual with respect to knowledge and skills as well as her/his degree of control over work activities are quite limited. However, as argued by Ashton (2004a), there is also an informal workplace culture, which might be at variance with the formal way of organizing work according to the logic of production. This informal side of an organization may provide opportunities for problem solving and substantial creativity in the actual carrying out of work (cf. Barley and Kunda, 2001; Hirschorn, 1984; Zuboff, 1988). At the same time, the logic of production with its emphasis on skill-based, routine action may become a way to maintain a feeling of security and stability. Somewhat paradoxically, however, it may also relieve the burden on individuals and free mental resources for other purposes, including creative and developmental activities (Ellström, 2001; Klein et al., 1993).

The logic of development

In contrast to a striving for a stable implementation of 'best practices', the logic of development is characterized by a focus on practice as a source of new thinking and knowledge development, i.e. a focus on promoting innovativeness in ways of defining and carrying out an activity. It is assumed that this innovativeness will be based on the variation that always exists in the performance of work. Accordingly, this logic has a focus not on reducing variation and attaining uniformity but, rather, a focus on promoting and exploring *variation and diversity* in thought and action (heterogeneity). Thus, the logic of development entails action and learning that calls for risk-taking, the acceptance of failures and a capacity for critical reflection, together with sufficient scope and resources for experimenting with and testing alternative ways of acting in different situations.

Contrary to the logic of production, this logic requires a movement away from a routinized level of action towards a knowledge-based or reflective level of action (see Figure 8.1) through processes of developmental learning. This entails a capacity for distancing, alternative thinking and critical reflection. In line with this orientation, there is a strong emphasis on the subjects' capacity for self-management and their preparedness to question, reflect upon and, if necessary, transform established practices in the organization into new solutions or ways of working (cf. Dewey, 1933; Engeström, 1999). Thus, conflicts and ambiguity are viewed not as threats to learning or to efficient performance, but rather as potentials for triggering developmental learning processes.

Balancing the two logics

As is clear from the descriptions of the two logics given above, they both entail learning as a basic mechanism for furthering, in the one case, efficient performance and, in the other case, innovativeness. In line with this, the two logics also entail different organizational conditions and practices, which are assumed to constrain or enable learning in work (Ellström, 2006b). However, in spite of these seemingly contradictory orientations, the two logics are viewed not as mutually exclusive but, rather, as complementary patterns of practice. That is, both are regarded as necessary for the long-term continuation and development of an organization. In practice, though, the two logics compete for scare resources, and organizations make choices between them based on, among other things, beliefs about their costs in relation to expected returns (March, 1991). Thus, the two logics may, in the short and medium terms, be contradictory in that they entail different ways of using available resources in an organization.

Now, depending on how the learning environment of a workplace is designed in terms of these logics, we can expect a situation where there would be more or less scope for adaptive and developmental learning. Of course, in reality we hardly encounter a simple either-or situation with respect to these two logics, but rather a more complex mix of learning conditions. Thus, the challenge is to find a suitable balance and assign priorities between measures that bring about stability, efficiency and short-term results, in accordance with the logic of production, and to promote long-term development and innovation in accordance with the logic of development.

Here, we touch on a tension between time for production and time for exploration, learning and innovation that has long attracted the attention of researchers who have studied learning in organizations (March, 1991; March and Simon, 1958). More deliberative learning activities focusing on the content, processes and outcomes of actions require time – time to observe, time to think and time to exchange ideas with others (Ellström, 2002; Eraut, 2002). However, as argued by March (1991), one difficulty in establishing these priorities is that the value of learning activities in terms of increased innovativeness and long-term survival is both more remote in time and less reliable than the more easily calculated value of measures to boost day-to-day production. Furthermore, the decisions made when it comes to allocating resources for workplace learning are highly related to prevailing views concerning management strategies and leading actors' perceptions of the possible, desirable and, for the time being, appropriate way of managing a production system (Ellström and Kock, 2009).

Of course, this does not imply that simply providing time for learning and reflection would mean that this time would also be used for learning activities. Thus, even if time is a necessary condition for learning, it is not a sufficient condition (for an extended discussion of these and related issues, see Ellström, 2006b).

CONCLUDING REMARKS

The arguments presented in this chapter were developed in four main steps. In the first step, a distinction was made between two modes of learning in work: adaptive and developmental learning. In the second step, this duality of learning was used as a point of departure for distinguishing between two types of learning environment: constraining and enabling. The notion of learning environment was defined in terms of structural factors. However, as was also argued, the learning potential of a workplace as well as the actual learning that takes place cannot be understood as a function of structural conditions alone. Rather, the learning potential of a task (a job or a workplace) as well as the actual learning that occurs is viewed as a function of structural as well as subjective factors.

In the third step, a conceptual framework – a four-level model of action and reflection – was proposed. This model was used to interpret and elaborate the distinction between adaptive and developmental learning as an interplay between four different levels of action and reflection. In the fourth and final step, there was a focus on the institutionalized patterns of practice that are assumed to shape the workplace as a learning environment and, thereby, the conditions for learning in an organization. Two such patterns were distinguished: the logic of production and the logic of development.

Now, turning to the implications of these arguments for theory and research in the field of workplace learning, at least the following three points can be made. First, while the focus in this chapter has concerned conditions for learning in work at the level of the task, the job or the workplace, i.e. factors at a micro-level of analysis, it is often also important to relate micro-level factors to factors at a meso- or a macro-level of analysis (e.g. Ellström and Kock, 2009; Fuller et al., 2009). In line with this, Kock et al. (2008) were able to show how strategies for competence development in organizations were determined by an interaction between external organizational conditions (e.g. competitive pressure) and internal factors such as management support and opportunities for learning. The need to go beyond the level of the workplace in analyses of learning environments is also made clear by the arguments presented above concerning how learning environments are shaped by patterns of practice that have their roots at an institutional level.

Second, the concept of learning proposed in this chapter emphasizes the importance of theoretical knowledge as a condition of learning (cf. the four-level model of action and reflection presented in the fourth section). The access to and use of concepts and theoretical knowledge as resources from outside the workplace makes it possible for the individual to think beyond a specific situation, task or work process, to understand the work process in a comprehensive perspective, and to reflect upon and question existing practices within an organization (Eraut, 2004; Evans et al., in Chapter 11 of this volume; Svensson et al., 2004; Young, 2004). Considering the role of formal learning in organizations, it can in this perspective be viewed as one of several ways to 'import' external, codified knowledge into an organization in order to support informal learning at work (Eidskrem, 2009).

Third, the concept of learning proposed in this chapter entails a distinction between four dimensions in which learning in work may occur: (i) *the subjective dimension*, i.e. different aspects of the capacity or competence of the learning subject, including knowledge, understanding, skills, and attitudes (Ellström, 1997); (ii) *the action dimension*, i.e. the actions performed by an individual in handling a specific situation or task or solving a problem; (iii) *the social dimension*, i.e. the interactions and social relations of individuals within and between groups; (iv) *the structural dimension*, i.e. different aspects of the learning environment (social, cultural and material aspects) that shape the learning process, but that also may be shaped by individual actions and interactions as part of the learning process. Taken together, these dimensions constitute a four-dimensional learning space in terms of which it might be possible to position and define many current approaches to and theories of workplace learning. Furthermore, it is possible to define conditions, processes and/or outcomes of learning in terms of one or more of these dimensions.

Considering, for example, the issue of how to conceptualize the relations between individual and organizational learning. As argued elsewhere (Ellström, 2001), organizational learning can be defined as changes in organizational knowledge and practices that are mediated through individual learning and knowledge creation. In terms of the four-dimensional learning space proposed here this mediation process can be interpreted as a matter of the relations between dimensions (i) and (ii), on the one hand, and dimensions (iii) and (iv), on the other. In line with this, workplace learning can be viewed as a process of knowledge production that may contribute to the articulated and codified knowledge base of an organization (or in the terminology of Archer, 1995, its cultural system), and also in this sense to organizational learning (Zollo and Winter, 2002).

REFERENCES

Anderson, J.R. (1982) 'The Acquisition of Cognitive Skill', *Psychological Review*, 89: 369–406.
Archer, M.S. (1995) *Realist Social Theory: The Morphogenetic Approach*. Cambridge: Cambridge University Press.
Argyris, C. and Schön, D.A. (1978) *Organizational Learning*. Reading: Addison-Wesley.
Argyris, C., Putnam, R. and McLain Smith, D. (1985) *Action Science: Concepts, Methods, and Skills for Research and Intervention*. San Francisco: Jossey-Bass.

Ashton, D.N. (2004a) 'The Impact of Organizational Structure and Practices on Learning in the Workplace', *International Journal of Training and Development*, 8(1): 43–53.

Ashton, D.N. (2004b) 'The Political Economy of Workplace Learning', in H. Rainbird, A. Fuller and A. Munro (eds), *Workplace Learning in Context*. London: Routledge, pp. 21–37.

Bargh, J.A. and Chartrand, T.L. (1999) 'The Unbearable Automaticity of Being', *American Psychologist*, 54: 462–479.

Barley, S.R. and Kunda, G. (2001) 'Bringing Work Back In', *Organization Science*, 12(1): 76–95.

Barnett, R. (1999) 'Learning to Work and Working to Learn', in D. Boud and J. Garrick (eds), *Understanding Learning at Work*. London: Routledge, pp. 29–44.

Berry, D.C. and Broadbent, D.E. (1988) 'Interactive Tasks and the Implicit–Explicit Distinction', *British Journal of Psychology*, 79: 251–272.

Bhaskar, R. (1989) *Reclaiming Reality: A Critical Introduction to Modern Philosophy*. London: Verso.

Billett, S. (2001) 'Learning Through Work: Workplace Affordances and Individual Engagement', *Journal of Workplace Learning*, 13(5): 209–214.

Billett, S. (2004) 'Learning Through Work: Workplace Participatory Practices', in H. Rainbird, A. Fuller and A. Munro (eds), *Workplace Learning in Context*. London: Routledge, pp. 109–125.

Boud, D. and Garrick, J. (eds) (1999) *Understanding Learning at Work*. London: Routledge.

Brown, J.S. and Duguid, P. (1991) 'Organizational Learning and Communities of Practice: Towards a Unified View of Working, Learning, and Innovation', *Organization Science*, 2: 40–57.

Coffield, F. (ed.) (2000) *The Necessity of Informal Learning*. Bristol, UK: The Policy Press.

Dewey, J. (1933) *How We Think: A Restatement of the Relation of Reflective Thinking to the Educative Process*. Boston: D.C. Heath.

Eidskrem, I.B. (2009) *Integrating Formal and Informal Learning in the Workplace – a Resituative Learning Approach*. Paper presented at the 6th International Conference on Researching Work and Learning, Roskilde University, Roskilde, Denmark, June 28 to July 1. Website: http://rwl6.ruc.dk

Ellström, E., Ekholm, B. and Ellström, P.-E. (2008) 'Two Types of Learning Environment: Enabling and Constraining: A Study of Care Work', *Journal of Workplace Learning*, 20(2): 84–97.

Ellström, P.-E. (1997) 'The Many Meanings of Occupational Competence and Qualification', *Journal of European Industrial Training*, 21(6/7): 266–274.

Ellström, P.-E. (2001) 'Integrating Learning and Work: Conceptual Issues and Critical Conditions', *Human Resource Development Quarterly*, 12(4): 421–435.

Ellström, P.-E. (2002) 'Time and the Logics of Learning', *Lifelong Learning in Europe*, 2: 86–93.

Ellström, P.-E. (2006a) 'The Meaning and Role of Reflection in Informal Learning at Work', in D. Boud, P. Cressey and P. Docherty (eds), *Productive Reflection. An Anthology on Reflection and Learning at Work*. London: Routledge, pp. 43–53.

Ellström, P.-E. (2006b) 'Two Logics of Learning', in E. Antonacopoulou, P. Jarvis, V. Andersen, B. Elkjær and S. Høyrup (eds), *Learning, Working and Living: Mapping the Terrain of Working Life Learning*. London: Palgrave Macmillan, pp. 33–49.

Ellström, P.-E. and Kock, H. (2009) 'Competence Development in the Workplace, Concepts, Strategies and Effects', in K. Illeris (ed.), *International Perspectives on Competence Development*. London: Routledge, pp. 34–54.

Engeström, Y. (1987) *Learning by Expanding: An Activity Theoretical Approach to Development Research*. Helsinki, Finland: Orienta Konsultit Oy.

Engeström, Y. (1999) 'Innovative Learning in Work Teams: Analyzing Cycles of Knowledge Creation in Practice', in Y. Engeström, R. Miettinen and R.-L. Punamäki (eds), *Perspectives on Activity Theory*. New York: Cambridge University Press, pp. 19–38.

Eraut, M. (1995) 'Schön Shock: a Case for Reframing Reflection-In-Action', *Teachers and Teaching*, 1(1): 9–22.

Eraut, M. (2000) 'Non-Formal Learning, Implicit Learning and Tacit Knowledge in Professional Work', in F. Coffield (ed.), *The Necessity of Informal Learning*. Bristol, UK: The Policy Press, pp. 12–31.

Eraut, M. (2002) 'Menus for Choosy Diners', *Teachers and Teaching*, 8(3/4): 371–379.

Eraut, M. (2004) 'Transfer of Knowledge Between Education and Workplace Settings', in H. Rainbird, A. Fuller and A. Munro (eds), *Workplace Learning in Context*. London: Routledge, pp. 201–221.

Evans, K. (2002) 'The Challenges of Making Learning Visible: Problems and Issues in Recognizing Tacit Skills and Key Competences', in K. Evans, P. Hodkinson and L. Unwin (eds), *Working to Learn. Transforming Learning in the Workplace*. London: Kogan Page, pp. 79–94.

Evans, K. (2007) 'Concepts of Bounded Agency in Education, Work and Personal Lives of Young Adults', *International Journal of Psychology*, 42(2): 1–9.

Evans, K. and Rainbird, H. (2002) 'The Significance of Workplace Learning for a Learning Society', in K. Evans, P. Hodkinson and L. Unwin (eds), *Working to Learn: Transforming Learning in the Workplace*. London: Kogan Page, pp. 7–28.

Evans, K., Hodkinson, P. and Unwin, L. (eds) (2002) *Working to Learn: Transforming Learning in the Workplace*. London: Kogan Page.

Evans, K., Kersh, N. and Sakamoto, A. (2004) 'Learner Biographies: Exploring Tacit Dimensions of Knowledge and Skills', in H. Rainbird, A. Fuller and A. Munro (eds), *Workplace Learning in Context*. London: Routledge, pp. 222–241.

Felstead, A., Ashton, D. and Green, F. (2000) 'Are Britain's Workplace Skills Becoming More Unequal?', *Cambridge Journal of Economics*, 24: 709–727.

Fenwick, T.J. (2003) 'Professional Growth Plans: Possibilities and Limitations of an Organization Wide Employee Development Strategy', *Human Resource Development Quarterly*, 14(1): 59–77.

Fenwick, T.J. (2006) 'Tidying the Territory: Questioning Terms and Purposes in Work-Learning Research', *Journal of Workplace Learning*, 18(5): 265–278.

Flavell, J.H. (1979) 'Metacognition and Cognitive Monitoring. A New Area of Cognitive-Developmental Inquiry', *American Psychologist*, 34(10): 906–911.

Frese, M. and Zapf, D. (1994) 'Action as the Core of Work Psychology: A German Approach', in H.C. Triandis, M.D. Dunnette and L.M. Hough (eds), *Handbook of Industrial and Organizational Psychology*. Palo Alto, CA: Consulting Psychologists Press, Inc, pp. 271–340.

Fuller, A. and Unwin, L. (2004) 'Expansive Learning Environments: Integrating Organizational and Personal Development', in H. Rainbird, A. Fuller and A. Munro (eds), *Workplace Learning in Context*. London: Routledge, pp. 126–144.

Fuller, A., Unwin, L., Felstead, A., Jewson, N. and Kakavelakis, K. (2007) 'Creating and Using Knowledge: An Analysis of the Differentiated Nature of Workplace Learning Environments', *British Educational Research Journal*, 33(5): 743–761.

Fuller, A., Kakavelakis, K., Felstead, A., Jewson, N. and Unwin, L. (2009) 'Learning, Knowing and Controlling the Stock: The Nature of Employee Discretion in a Supermarket Chain', *Journal of Education and Work*, 22(2): 105–120.

Gersick, C.J.G. and Hackman, J.R. (1990) 'Habitual Routines in Task-Performing Groups', *Organizational Behavior and Human Decision Processes*, 47: 65–97.

Giddens, A. (1984) *The Constitution of Society*. Berkely: University of California Press.

Gorard, S., Rees, G., Fevre, R. and Welland, T. (2001) 'Lifelong Learning Trajectories: Some Voices of Those in Transit', *International Journal of Lifelong Education*, 20(3): 169–187.

de Grip, A. (2008) 'Economic Perspectives of Workplace Learning', in W.J. Nijhof and L.F.M. Nieuwenhuis (eds), *The Learning Potential of the Workplace*. Rotterdam: Sense Publishers, pp. 15–30.

Gustavsson, M. (2007) 'Potentials for Learning in Industrial Work', *Journal of Workplace Learning*, 19(7): 453–463.

Hirschhorn, L. (1984) *Beyond Mechanization: Work and Technology in a Postindustrial Age*. Cambridge, MA: The MIT Press.

Karasek, R.A. (1979) 'Job Demand, Job Decision Latitude, and Mental Strain: Implications for Job Redesign', *Adminstrative Science Quarterly*, 24(2): 285–308.

Karasek, R.A. and Theorell, T. (1990) *Healthy Work: Stress, Productivity, and the Reconstruction of Working Life*. New York: Basic Books.

Klein, G.A., Orasanu, J., Calderwood, R. and Zsambok, C. (eds) (1993) *Decision Making in Action: Models and Methods*. Norwood, NJ: Ablex Publishing Corporation.

Kock, H., Gill, A. and Ellström, P-E. (2008) 'Why Do Small Firms Participate in a Programme for Competence Development?', *Journal of Workplace Learning*, 20(3): 181–194.

Lave, J. and Wenger, E. (1991) *Situated Learning: Legitimate Peripheral Participation*. Cambridge: Cambridge University Press.

March, J.G. (1991) 'Exploration and Exploitation in Organizational Learning', *Organization Science*, 2: 71–87.

March, J.G. and Olsen, J.P. (1976) *Ambiguity and Choice in Organizations*. Bergen: Universitetsforlaget.

March, J.G. and Simon, H.A. (1958) *Organizations*. New York: Wiley.

Marsick, V.J. and Watkins, K.E. (1990) *Informal and Incidental Learning in the Workplace*. London: Routledge.

Mezirow, J. (1991) *Transformative Dimensions of Adult Learning*. San Francisco: Jossey-Bass.

Miner, A.S., Bassoff, P. and Moorman, C. (2001) 'Organizational Improvisation and Learning: A Field Study', *Administrative Science Quarterly*, 46(2): 304–337.

Nijhof, W.J. and Nieuwenhuis, L.F.M. (eds) (2008) *The Learning Potential of the Workplace*. Rotterdam: Sense Publishers.

Nieuwenhuis, L.F.M. and van Woerkom, M. (2008) 'Rationales for Work-Related Learning', in W.J. Nijhof and L.F.M. Nieuwenhuis (eds), *The Learning Potential of the Workplace*. Rotterdam: Sense Publishers, pp. 297–310.

Norman, D.A. (1988) *The Psychology of Everyday Things*. New York: Basic Books Inc.

Olsen, S.E. and Rasmussen, J. (1989) 'The Reflective Expert and the Prenovice', in L. Bainbridge and S.A. Ruiz Quintanilla (eds), *Developing Skills with Information Technology*. Chichester, UK: John Wiley and Sons, pp. 9–33.

Rasmussen, J. (1986) *Information Processing and Human Machine Interaction. An Approach to Cognitive Engineering*. New York: North Holland.

Rubenson, K. (2006) 'The Nordic Model of Lifelong Learning', *Compare: A Journal of Comparative Education*, 36(3): 327–341.

Searle, J.R. (1980) 'The Intentionality of Intention and Action', *Cognitive Science*, 4: 47–70.

Schön, D.A. (1983) *The Reflective Practitioner: How Professionals Think in Action*. London: Temple Smith.

Skule, S. (2004) 'Learning Conditions at Work: A Framework to Understand and Assess Informal Learning in the Workplace', *International Journal of Training and Development*, 8(1): 8–17.

Svensson, L., Ellström, P.-E. and Åberg, C. (2004) 'Integrating Formal and Informal Learning: A Strategy For Workplace Learning', *Journal of Workplace Learning*, 16(8): 479–491.

Weick, K.E. (1979) *The Social Psychology of Organizing* (2nd edn). Reading, MA: Addison-Wesley.

Weststar, J. (2009) 'Worker Control and Workplace Learning: Expansion of the Job Demand-Control Model', *Industrial Relations*, 48(3): 533–548.

Young, M. (2004) 'Conceptualizing Vocational Knowledge: Some Theoretical Considerations', in H. Rainbird, A. Fuller and A. Munro (eds), *Workplace Learning in Context*. London: Routledge, pp. 185–200.

Zollo, M. and Winter, S.G. (2002) 'Deliberate Learning and the Evolution of Dynamic Capabilities', *Organization Science*, 13: 339–351.

Zuboff, S. (1988) *In the Age of the Smart Machine: The Future of Work and Power*. New York: Basic Books.

9

Towards a Meta-Theory of Learning and Performance

Darlene Russ-Eft

TOWARDS A META-THEORY OF LEARNING AND PERFORMANCE

No single theory of learning currently exists. Rather, a multitude of different theoretical positions emphasize different aspects of the individual or situation context. Furthermore, this situation has characterized the literature on learning and performance for a number of years. As Underwood (1964) wrote:

> There are many approaches which might be used to express the relationships among research findings for all forms of human learning. Undoubtedly, the most elegant way would be in terms of theory. A general theory of human learning ... is clearly an ideal solution. No such system is available (p. 48).

More recently, Merriam (2001) acknowledging this stated; 'What we do have is a mosaic of theories, models, sets of principles, and explanations that, combined, compose the knowledge base of adult learning' (p. 3).

Although no such comprehensive system or theory currently exists, there are many connections among the different learning theories. This chapter provides a meta-theory of learning and performance with an attempt to include many of the major theories. It begins with an overview of the major learning theories and their implications. It then presents a systems model of learning and performance in the workplace, along with implications for research and practice. As Senge (1990) stated, a systems model is 'a framework for seeing interrelationships rather than things, for seeing patterns of change rather than static "snapshots" ...' (p. 68–69).

Philosophical, historical, and theoretical background

Discussions concerning human learning began with the early Greek philosophers. Indeed, Reynolds, et al. (1996) provided an overview of the theories of the Greek philosophers, as well as current-day learning theories. They suggested that these approaches be positioned along a continuum from environment-centered (where all learning comes from stimulation outside the organism) to mind-centered (where all learning comes from manipulations within the mind of the organism). Such a classification helps to identify similarities and differences among the theories.

If we begin with the Greek philosophers, we see that Alcmaeon, Democritus, and Protagorus (Diels and Kranz, 1952; Diogenes Laertius, 1959; Royer, 2005; Taylor, 1999; Wachtler, 1896) held a view that can be labeled as 'environment-centered.' They suggested knowledge or learning comes only from the senses and what is observed. In contrast, Socrates (Brickhouse and Smith, 1994) rejected the notion that knowledge comes only from perception. He argued that knowledge comes from ideas, concepts, and reasoning. This can be labeled 'mind-centered.' Aristotle (Barnes, 1984) presented a compromise view in which sensations and perceptions combined with the organization of the mind to create higher-order concepts and processes. Thus, Aristotle provided what might be called an 'integrationist' view. Similar distinctions can be made of more current theories of learning.

Behaviorism

The behaviorist approach, derived from the British Empiricists (Locke, 1690, 1995; Mill, 1829) and popular from about 1910 until about 1960, held that all learning comes from behavioral responses to external stimuli. Thus, it provides an example of an environment-centered approach. Watson's seminal article (1913) stated, 'Psychology as the behaviorist views it is a purely objective experimental branch of natural science. Its theoretical goal is the prediction and control of behavior.'

Both Pavlov (1927, 1941) and Watson (1913) focused on classical or respondent conditioning. Pavlov introduced the principle of 'frequency' according to which the more frequently an unconditioned stimulus (e.g., meat powder) is paired with a conditioned stimulus (e.g., salivation) the greater is the likelihood that the conditioned stimulus (e.g., bell) will elicit a conditioned response (e.g., salivation). Watson added the principle of 'recency' indicating that the more recently a response has been made to a particular stimulus the more likely it is to be made again. The idea of reinforcement was added by Thorndike (1932). Specifically, the law of effect states that a connection becomes stronger or weaker depending on its consequences. Furthermore, the law of exercises states that, with practice, a connection will be strengthened, and, with no practice, the connection will be weakened. In addition, the concept of identical elements introduced the notion that transfer of training could be enhanced with greater similarity between the learning situation and the environment in which transfer of that learning is to take place. These ideas were further elaborated and codified through various mathematical equations by Hull (1929, 1943, 1951) and Spence (1956, 1960). Skinner (1938, 1953, 1968) refined these ideas to include various stimulus-response-reinforcement paradigms. According to this view, the learner is the passive recipient of knowledge. Information must be broken down into small units in order to maximize success (and provide reinforcement).

Gestalt/cognitive theory

Gestalt theory, with a focus on organization provided by the mind, posed certain dilemmas to the strict behaviorists. (See Koffka, 1935; Kohler, 1929; Wertheimer, 1912.) These dilemmas, such as response sets (Lashley, 1929), were easily solved by the behaviorists. However, Chomsky's work (Chomsky and Miller, 1958; Chomsky, 1959) represented a severe threat to the behaviorist approach – more specifically, his critique of Skinner's book (1957) on verbal learning. According to Chomsky, higher-order functioning, such as language acquisition and problem solving, could not be accounted for by stimulus-response-reinforcement. (For example, people would have to learn sentences at a rate faster than one per second for even small vocabularies.) The cognitive revolution led to the notion that humans are active processors of information. Furthermore, cognitive psychologists introduced the concept of mental representations and suggested a computational metaphor (with the computer). In this case, encoding specificity was introduced as the means by which transfer of learning took place (Baddeley, 1998; Thompson and Tulving, 1970). But, it should be noted that the metaphor of the computer still implied an external focus, given that data and instructions must be provided from outside the organism.

Schema theory

Schema theory emerged in reaction to the machine metaphor of early cognitive theorists. It falls close to the interactionist view but leaning toward mind-centeredness. Following the philosophical notions of Kant (1781, 1900) and Wittgenstein (1958), the mind frames perceptions and experiences, actively interacting with sensory information from the environment. Rumelhart and Ortony (1977) and Rumelhart (1980) suggested certain characteristics of schemas: (1) They have variables; (2) They can be embedded in each other; (3) They represent knowledge at various levels of abstraction; (4) They represent knowledge rather than definition; (5) They are active processors; and (6) They are recognition devices, determining the goodness of fit of the incoming information. Such schemas help to organize disparate bits of information into a meaningful system or network (Anderson, 1990; McVee et al., 2005). According to schema theory, the individual's background knowledge influences the processing of incoming information. Thus, trainee-centered approaches, such as strategy instruction, metacognition, and selective attention, are recommended.

Connectionist theory

Connectionism, unlike traditional cognitive models, focuses on nodes and networks. (See Bechtel and Abrahamsen, 1991; McClelland and Rumelhart, 1988; Quinlan, 1991; Rumelhart and McClelland, 1986.) In this case, cognition is the process of changing activation levels of interconnected nodes or neurons within the network. Knowledge is distributed among the nodes and connections. As with behaviorist notions, knowledge is acquired through contiguity and frequency. Back propagation allows for errors to be fed back through the system. Thus, this approach appears at the environment-centered end of the continuum. It emphasizes the importance of proceduralized knowledge, the automaticity of lower level skills, and parallel distributed processing. Rather than teaching isolated facts, network models suggest the importance of chunking information and proceduralizing and automating processes. Such proceduralization and automaticity reduce the cognitive demands or the cognitive load (Paas, et al., 2003). Recently, however, Kalyuga et al. (2003) found an 'expertise reversal,' such that techniques that reduce the cognitive load for novices may increase the cognitive load for experts.

Social learning or behavior modeling

Initial work on behavior modeling (also called social learning) began when behaviorism was pre-eminent. Bandura (1965a, 1965b) proposed, in contrast to the importance placed on frequency, that most human learning involves no trial learning. New responses are simply acquired by observing the behavior of other people (i.e., models). The person can, thus, learn new responses without ever having performed the task and without having received any reinforcement. Nevertheless, since observation of a model is critical to learning, this approach can be considered environment-centered. Sorcher and Goldstein (1972) reported on the first research on behavior modeling undertaken in an industrial setting. Goldstein and Sorcher (1973, 1974) reported on the use of such programs to reduce the turnover among 'hard-core unemployed' employees. Since then, over 50 published studies have examined various aspects of behavior modeling. (See Russ-Eft [1997] for a review of this research.) Elaboration of Bandura's original notions of 'no trial learning' tend to include the following steps as part of the learning or training process: (1) a description of the behaviors to be learned, (2) a model or models displaying those behaviors, (3) opportunities for learners or trainees to practice the behaviors, (4) feedback and social reinforcement following practice (Decker and Nathan, 1985; Robinson, 1982; Taylor et al., 2003, 2005, 2009).

Andragogy and self-directed learning

Merriam (2001) claimed that these two theoretical approaches formed the pillars of adult learning theory. Andragogy, introduced by Knowles (1968), characterized the adult learner as directing his/her own learning, using life experiences in learning, seeing changing roles as learning opportunities, focusing on the practical and immediate application of knowledge, and being internally motivated to learn. Houle (1961), Tough (1967, 1971), and Knowles (1975) explored self-directed learning. Such learning can lead to an increased capacity for self-directed learning, critical reflection and transformational learning (Brookfield, 1986; Mezirow, 1985), and social action (Brookfield, 1993). These theories seem aligned with mind-centered approaches, while recognizing the influence of the context.

Social perspective theory

In reaction to the cognitive approaches, a variety of theorists have begun to emphasize the importance of the social and cultural contexts. Given this emphasis on the social, cultural, and historical contexts, such theories fall near the environment-centered end of the continuum. These approaches have been labeled sociocultural perspective (Wertsch, 1991), social constructivism (Palinscar, 1998; Turner, 1995; Turner and Meyer, 2000), sociohistorical theory (Wertsch et al., 1995), and sociocultural-historical psychology (Cole, 1995). The development of cognition comes from an internalization of social interactions, and knowledge is constructed by and distributed among individuals and groups as they interact with one another. Thus, experiences are shared, and learning and knowledge emerges from participation in social interaction. Vygotsky (1979) suggested that learning occurs when a person internalizes the social experiences of interacting with another person; such internalization results in inner speech and thought processes. These theories point toward the importance of considering the training environment, the organizational context, and the broader social and cultural context. At the very least, such theories contribute to the notions of cooperative learning environments and contextualized activities.

Situated cognitive theory

Situated cognition arose from artificial intelligence and cognitive psychology (Brown et al., 1989; Clancey, 1993; Greeno, 1991, 1998; Winograd and Flores, 1986). Similar to Vygotsky, situated cognition results from reasoning that occurs when the individual interacts with the social and physical situation. In contrast to Vygotsky, this approach places greater emphasis on internal processes. Thus, knowledge is acquired through the internal processing of the individual as that person interacts with the situation. This theory seems close to an interactionist approach in that emphasis is placed on the mind, in the form of mental models, and on the affordances of the environment. This theory suggests that training should facilitate the development of trainee's mental models through problem-solving activities, particularly by using ill-defined problems. Anchored instruction means that the instructors or the medium must anchor or situate trainees in simulated contexts, situations representing life experiences, or apprenticeships in real life situations. Thus, not all learning involves the retrieval of stored propositions; rather the emphasis is upon providing rich contexts or situations in which learning can occur.

Organizational learning theory

Many of the learning theories focus on the individual, while organizational learning theory recognizes that larger groupings of individuals can solve problems and learn. Some definitions of organizational learning include 'a system that has embedded continuous learning processes and has an enhanced capacity to change or transform' (Watkins and Marsick, 1992, p. 387), 'processes within an organization to maintain or improve performance based on experience' (Nevis et al., 1995, p. 275), and 'the basic elements and processes of organizational development and growth' (Inkpen and Crossan, 1995, p. 301). Thus, the workplace can facilitate individual, group, and organizational learning by encouraging double-loop learning, which challenges basic assumptions and values, and possibly even the vision and mission of the organization (Watkins and Marsick, 1992). Although organizational learning dates to the work of Argyris and Schön (1978) and Simon (1969), most theoretical and research work began in the 1990s and continues today.

Summary of theoretical suggestions

Table 9.1 provides some training implications for each of the previously described theories. These implications describe how learners are viewed by the various theories, how learning is conceptualized, and how transfer might be achieved or enhanced.

Table 9.1 Training implications from specific learning theories

Learning theory	Training implications
Behaviorism	• Learners are passive recipients. • Information must be organized and broken down into small, simple steps for maximum success. • Learners should be encouraged to make observable responses. • Trainees should be encouraged to make these responses multiple times (frequency), and these responses should be rewarded (reinforcement). • Transfer of training can be facilitated through the use of identical elements (Thorndike and Woodworth, 1901).
Cognitive theory	• Learners are active processors of information. • Learners manipulate symbolic information. • Transfer can be enhanced through encoding specificity, meaning that the stimulus cues in the transfer environment must be encoded with the information being trained (Cormier, 1987). Perceived similarity, not actual similarity, appears to be most critical (Gick and Holyoak, 1980, 1983, 1987). • Providing a variety of examples can enhance transfer, leading to general rules.
Schema theory	• Trainees' background knowledge influences the interpretation of incoming information. • Active, involved trainees are critical to success in training. • Since schemata are procedures, strategy instruction, instruction in metacognition, and the use of selective attention are critical.
Social learning/ behavior modeling	• New behaviors can be acquired by observing the behavior of models and without actually performing the task and without receiving reinforcement. • New behaviors may, however, not be exhibited until and unless some reinforcement is provided. • Behaviors can be changed directly and do not require changes in knowledge or attitudes.

Table 9.1 Cont'd

Learning theory	Training implications
Andragogy/self-directed learning	• Individualized instruction is needed to match learners' needs and increase relevance. • Training should include individual tasks, group processes, and critical reflection to promote discovery, self-knowledge and self-direction.
Social perspective theories	• Training environment and social and organizational context shape individual learning, knowledge, and thought. • Trainees should have more opportunities to interact with peers and with those having more experience or more skill.
Connectionist theories	• Training should encourage the development of proceduralized knowledge rather than limit development to declarative knowledge. • Training should help to develop automaticity of lower-level skills. (Trainees who have developed such automaticity have more mental capacity available for other tasks.) • Training or trainers should support the development of trainee ability to check, proceduralize, or automate skills or processes.
Situated cognition	• Training should facilitate trainees' construction of mental models through problem-solving activities, particularly ill-defined problems (Brown et al., 1989). • Training should be 'authentic,' using realistic situations, leading to trainee's acquisition of the requisite knowledge and the condition for applying that knowledge (Sonntag, 1997). • Creating such mental models involves both individual and group construction. • Training should provide settings for group problem solving so that trainees can express their mental models to each other, improve their mental model, and use alternative mental models. (This can provide the 'Learning circle' or 'Lernstatt' [Sonntag, 1996, 1997].) • The trainer or the instruction materials should provide aid by identifying 'affordances,' such as easy routes, resources, or strategies. • Training needs to take place within rich contexts or situations (involving real-life tasks or using media to simulate such situations). • Trainees should be supported by 'coaching' or 'scaffolding' and should decrease over time ('fading')
Organizational learning theory	• Trainers or learning facilitators should identify theories-in-use that prevent learning. • Trainers and trainees should use ongoing processes and integrated systems to facilitate learning, growth, and change. • Trainers and trainees should engage in collegial sharing, collaborative experience, and reflection.

An inclusive meta-theoretical framework

This review of various learning theories helps to identify similarities and differences. Figures 9.1 and 9.2 depict a theoretical framework that combines the elements from the various learning theories. Figure 9.1 shows the learning and transfer for individuals, while Figure 9.2 indicates how individuals interact to create team and then these teams and individuals enact organizational learning. By connecting these theories, we can identify further practice and research implications.

Almost all of the learning theories, except perhaps for the behaviorist theory, recognize that learning takes place within a social and organizational context which, in turn, affects the training environment. Furthermore, this training environment leads to the use or non-use of such methods as coaching and fading. The effects of background and context are primarily emphasized in schema theories and social perspective theories.

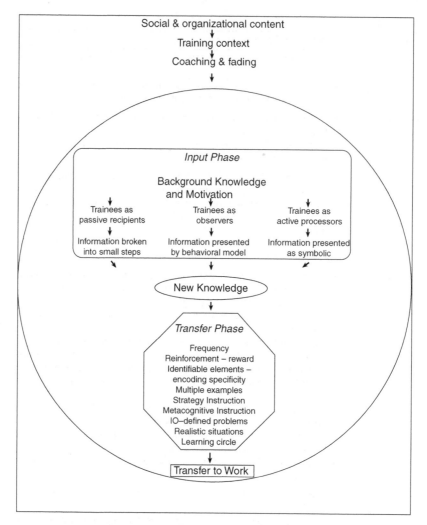

Figure 9.1   Theoretical framework derived from various learning theories

Critical differences among the theories seem to emerge in what might be labeled as the input phase of the learning process. Various theories possess different conceptions of the trainee and suggest different ways in which information should be presented. Thus, behaviorism posits that the trainee is a passive recipient of information, and therefore the information must be broken into small steps or small bits of information. In a similar way, connectionist theories emphasize the importance of automaticity of lower-level skills, presumably through repetition of procedures. With such automaticity, the learner can engage in higher-level learning, thinking, and problem solving. In contrast, social learning or behavior modeling suggests that the trainee is an observer and can learn simply by observing someone else. It may, nevertheless, require some form of reinforcement and feedback for the learner to display or perform the learned skill or task. Schema, cognitive, self-directed, and situated cognitive theories emphasize the importance of active, involved trainees. The theoretical framework presented in this chapter, however, recognizes that new knowledge can be developed and created through all of these different approaches.

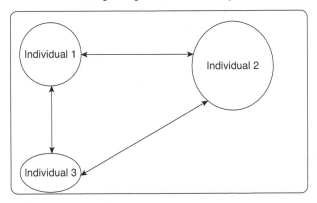

Figure 9.2 Model of team and organizational learning

Similarities also appear in some but not all of the methods suggested for the transfer phase. Common elements for the transfer phase include frequency, reinforcement or reward, identical elements (according to the behaviorists) or encoding specificity (according to cognitive theorists). Elements such as multiple examples, strategy instruction, metacognitive instruction, ill-defined problems, realistic situations, and learning circles appear in certain theories, such as the cognitive theories, and are missing in other theories, such as the behaviorist theories. Further discussion and exploration of the various elements critical in the transfer phase can be found in Russ-Eft (2002).

Furthermore, whatever the perspective on individual learning, these individuals can interact within the workplace to solve problems. This problem solving can yield immediate solutions (or single-loop learning) or can be found to appear intractable. When these latter problems result in questioning assumptions and standard processes, new learning and organizational can occur (leading to double-loop learning).

Research and practice implications

The theoretical framework presented above leads to certain implications needing further testing. The theoretical framework implies that trainees may need information to be presented in multiple ways. It may be that one approach or another may prove more effective for certain types of learners, certain kinds of information, and certain kinds of situations. For example, it may be that the features and benefits of a new product to be learned by salespeople in one day through an e-learning format is best conveyed in small bits of information. In contrast, using a behavior model may be the best method for instructing organizational consultants on new approaches to executive coaching. Alternatively, providing symbolic information and facilitating problem solving may prove most effective in training problem-solving skills to mechanics and computer programmers. These speculations need testing.

The theoretical framework assumes that alternative methods are equally effective in the input phase. Gagne (1970, 1985) and Gagne and Medsker (1996) argue that certain kinds of training may be more effective using a specific theoretical approach. More research is needed to determine whether alternative methods are indeed equally effective or whether certain approaches prove more effective for specific kinds of trainees, certain types of information, and specific situations. As another example, the framework indicates that social and organizational context affects the training environment and that the training environment affects the extent to which coaching and fading takes place. Some research efforts need to examine these relationships. Similarly, it is assumed that the social and organizational context, the training context, and the level of coaching and fading affect the input phase and the extent to which new knowledge is created during training. Again, these relationships need further examination.

If we remove some elements of the social and organizational context, what are the implications for the type of theoretical approach used for the input phase? For example, when uncertainty exists as to the support provided through the social and organizational context or the training context, do multiple input approaches or one particular input approach function better? Might it be that, using behaviorist or connectionist approaches, repetition and reinforcement would lead to learning and automaticity of the response? Such an implication needs further testing.

Various elements appear to affect the transfer phase (such as frequency, reinforcement, identical elements, and so forth). It is not at all clear whether each of these yields equivalent results. Russ-Eft (2002) provides a more complete taxonomy of elements affecting transfer. Research is needed to determine issues regarding the timing and use of these elements, particularly in relationship to the different types of input methods. For example, learning and transfer may not take place with the behaviorist approach of small steps and bits of information without using both frequency and reinforcement. In contrast, a social learning or behavior modeling approach, suggesting 'no trial learning' (Russ-Eft, 1997), may prove equally effective with or without reinforcement. In this case, the behavior or information may be learned but may not be performed without some reinforcement. Research is needed to distinguish between what is learned from what is performed.

Finally, research on individual, group, and organizational learning needs further investigation. To what extent is the individual learning different or the same as the group and organizational learning? Do the factors that affect individual learning and transfer also affect group and organizational learning? If not, what are the factors that affect such learning and transfer?

This chapter provides a review of multiple learning theories and presents an initial attempt to incorporate multiple learning theories into one inclusive theoretical framework. Implications from this framework can guide practitioners and researchers in future work to improve learning in the workplace.

REFERENCES

Anderson, J.R. (1990) *Cognitive Psychology and Its Implications* (3rd edn). New York: Freeman.

Argyris, C. and Schön, D. (1978) *Organizational Learning: A Theory of Action Perspective.* Reading, MA: Addison-Wesley.

Baddeley, A.D. (1998) *Human Memory: Theory and Practice* (Revised edn). Boston: Allyn & Bacon.

Bandura, A. (1965a) 'Behavior Modification Through Modeling Procedures', in L. Drasner and L.P. Ullman (eds), *Research in Behavior Modification.* New York: Holt, pp. 310–340.

Bandura, A. (1965b) 'Vicarious Processes: A Case of No-trial Learning', in L. Berkowitz (ed.), *Advances in Experimental Social Psychology* (Vol. 11). New York: Academic.

Barnes, J. (ed.) (1984) *The Complete Works of Aristotle: The Revised Oxford Translation.* Princeton: Princeton University Press.

Bechtel, W. and Abrahamsen, A. (1991) *Connectionism and the Mind.* Basil Oxford, UK: Blackwell Ltd.

Brickhouse, T.C. and Smith, N.D. (eds) (1994) *Plato's Socrates.* New York: Oxford University Press.

Brookfield, S. (1986) *Understanding and Facilitating Adult Learning.* San Francisco: Jossey-Bass.

Brookfield, S. (1993) 'Self-directed Learning, Political Clarity, and the Critical Practice of Adult Education', *Adult Education Quarterly,* 43(4): 227–242.

Brown, J.S., Collins, A. and Duguid, P. (1989) 'Situated Cognition and the Culture of Learning', *Educational Researcher,* 18(1): 32–42.

Chomsky, N. (1959) 'Review of *Verbal Behavior* by B.F. Skinner', *Language,* 35: 26–58.

Chomsky, N. and Miller, G.A. (1958) 'Finite-state Languages', *Information and Control,* 1: 91–112.

Clancey, W.J. (1993) 'Situated Action: A Neuropsychological Interpretation Response to Vera and Simon', *Cognitive Science,* 17: 87–116.

Cole, M. (1995) 'Socio-cultural Historical Psychology: Some General Remarks and a Proposal for a New Kind of Cultural-genetic Methodology', in J.V. Wertsch, P. del Rio and A. Alverez (eds), *Sociocultural Studies of Mind*. New York: Cambridge University Press, pp. 187–214.

Cormier, S.M. (1987) 'The Structural Processes Underlying Transfer of Training', in S.M. Cormier and J.D. Hagman (eds), *Transfer of Learning: Contemporary Research and Applications*. San Diego, CA: Academic Press, pp. 152–182.

Decker, P.J. and Nathan, B.R. (1985) *Behavior Modeling Training: Principles and Applications*. New York: Praeger.

Diels, H. and Kranz, W. (1952) *Die Fragmente der Vorsokratiker* (6th edn). Berlin, Germany: Weidmann.

Diogenes L. (1959) *Lives of Eminent Philosophers*. (translated by R.D. Hicks). Cambridge, MA: Harvard University Press.

Gagne, R.M. (1970) *The Conditions of Learning* (2nd edn). New York: Holt, Rinehart and Winston.

Gagne, R.M. (1985) *The Conditions of Learning and Theory of Instruction* (4th edn). Fort Worth, TX: Holt, Rinehart and Winston.

Gagne, R.M. and Medsker, K.L. (1996) *The Conditions of Learning: Training Applications*. Fort Worth, TX: Harcourt Brace College Publishers.

Gick, M.L. and Holyoak, K.J. (1980) 'Analogical Problem Solving', *Cognitive Psychology*, 12: 306–355.

Gick, M.L. and Holyoak, K.J. (1983) 'Schema Induction and Analogical Transfer', *Cognitive Psychology*, 15: 1–38.

Gick, M.L. and Holyoak, K.J. (1987) 'The Cognitive Basis of Knowledge Transfer', in S.M. Cormier and J.D. Hagman (eds), *Transfer of Training: Contemporary Research and Application*. New York: Academic Press, pp. 9–46.

Goldstein, A.P. and Sorcher, M. (1973) 'Changing Managerial Behavior by Applied Learning Techniques', *Training and Development*, 36–39.

Goldstein, A.P. and Sorcher, M. (1974) *Changing Supervisor Behavior*. New York: Pergamon.

Greeno, J.G. (1991) 'Number Sense as Situated Knowledge in a Conceptual Domain', *Journal for Research in Mathematics Education*, 22: 170–218.

Greeno, J.G. (1998) 'The Situativity of Knowing, Learning, and Research', *American Psychologist*, 53: 5–26.

Houle, C.O. (1961) *The Inquiring Mind*. Madison, WI: University of Wisconsin Press.

Hull, C.L. (1929) 'A Functional Interpretation of the Conditioned Reflex', *Psychological Review*, 36: 498–511.

Hull, C.L. (1943) *Principles of Behavior*. New York: Appleton-Century-Crofts.

Hull, C.L. (1951) *Essentials of Behavior*. New Haven: Yale University Press.

Inkpen, A.C. and Crossan, M.M. (1995) 'Believing is Seeing: Joint Ventures and Organization Learning', *Journal of Management Studies*, 32(5): 595–618.

Kalyuga, S., Ayres, P. Chandler, P., and Sweller, J. (2003) 'The Expertise Reversal Effect', *Educational Psychologist*, 38: 23–31.

Kant, I. (1900) *Critique of Pure Reason*. New York: Colonial Press (original work published 1781).

Koffka, K. (1935) *Principles of Gestalt Psychology*. New York: Harcourt.

Kohler, W. (1929) *Gestalt Psychology*. New York: Liveright.

Knowles, M. S. (1968) 'Andragogy, Not Pedagogy', *Adult Leadership*, 16(10): 350–352, 386.

Knowles, M. S. (1975) *Self-directed Learning*. New York: Association Press.

Lashley, K. S. (1929) *Brain Mechanisms and Intelligence*. Chicago: University of Chicago Press.

Locke, J. (1995) *An Essay Concerning Human Understanding*. New York: Prometheus (original work published 1690).

Locke, E. and Latham, G. P. (1990) *A Theory of Goal Setting and Task Performance*. Englewood Cliffs, NJ: Prentice-Hall.

Marsick, V.J. and Watkins, K.E. (1993) *Sculpting the Learning Organization: Lessons in the Art and Science of Systemic Change*. San Francisco: Jossey-Bass.

Marsick, V.J. and Watkins, K.E. (1999) *Facilitating Learning Organizations: Making Learning Count*. Brookfield, VT: Gower.

McVee, M.B., Dunsmore, K. and Gavelek, J.R. (2005) 'Schema Theory, Revisited', *Review of Educational Research*, 75: 531–566.

McClelland, J. L. and Rumelhart, D. E. (1988) *Explorations in Parallel Distributed Processing: A Handbook of Models, Programs, and Exercises*. Cambridge, MA: MIT Press/Bradford Books.

Mezirow, J. (1985) 'A Critical Theory of Self-directed Learning, in S. Brookfield (ed.), *Self-directed Learning from Theory to Practice*. New Directions for Continuing Education, No. 25. San Francisco: Jossey-Bass.

Merriam, S.B. (2001) 'Andragogy and Self-directed Learning: Pillars of Adult Learning Theory', In S. B. Merriam (ed.) *The New Update on Adult Learning Theory*. New Directions for Adult and Continuing Education, No. 89: 3–13.

Mill, J. (1829) *Analysis of the Phenomena of the Human Mind*. London: Baldwin & Cradock.

Nevis, E.C., DiBella, A.J. and Gould, J.M. (1995) 'Understanding Organizations as Learning Systems', *Sloan Management Review* (Winter), pp. 73–85.

Palinscar, A.S. (1998) 'Social Constructivist Perspectives on Teaching and Learning', *Annual Review of Psychology*, 49: 345–375.

Pavlov, I. (1927) *Conditioned Reflexes*. (translated by G. V. Anrep). New York: Oxford University Press.

Pavlov, I. (1941) *Lectures on Conditioned Reflexes* (Vol. I and II). New York: International Universities Press.

Paas, F., Renkl, A. and Sweller, J. (2003) 'Cognitive Load Theory and Instructional Design: Recent Developments', *Educational Psychologist*, 38: 1–4.

Quinlan, P.T. (1991) *Connectionism and Psychology: A Psychological Perspective on New Connectionist Research*. Chicago: The University of Chicago Press.

Reynolds, R.E., Sinatra, G.M. and Jetton, T.L. (1996) 'Views of Knowledge Acquisition and Representation: A Continuum from Experience Centered to Mind Centered', *Educational Psychologist*, 31: 93–104.

Robinson, J.C. (1982) *Developing Managers Through Behavior Modeling*. San Diego, CA: Learning Concepts.

Royer, J.M. (ed.) (2005) *The Cognitive Revolution in Educational Psychology (Current Perspectives on Cognition, Learning, and Instruction)*. Charlotte, NC: Information Age.

Rumelhart, D.E. (1980) 'Schemata: The Building Blocks of Cognition', in R. Spiro, B. Bruce and W. Brewer (eds), *Theoretical Issues in Reading Comprehension*. Hillsdale, NJ: Erlbaum, pp. 33–58.

Rumelhart, D.E. and McClelland, J.L. (1986) *Parallel Distributed Processing: Explorations in the Microstructure of Cognition*. Cambridge, MA: MIT Press.

Rumelhart, D.E. and Ortony, A. (1977) 'The Representation of Knowledge in Memory', in R.C. Anderson, R.J. Spiro and W.E. Montague (eds), *Schooling and the Acquisition of Knowledge*. Hillsdale, NJ: Erlbaum, pp. 99–136.

Russ-Eft, D. (1997) 'Behavior Modeling', in L.J. Bassi and D. Russ-Eft (eds), *What Works: Training and Development*. Alexandria, VA: American Society for Training and Development.

Russ-Eft, D. (2002) 'A Typology of Training Design and Work Environment Factors Affecting Workplace Learning and Transfer', *Human Resource Development Review*, 1: 45–65.

Senge, P.M. (1990) *The Fifth Discipline*. New York: Doubleday.

Simon, H.A. (1969) *The Science of the Artificial*. Cambridge, MA: MIT Press.

Skinner, B.F. (1938) *The Behavior of Organisms: An Experimental Analysis*. New York: Appleton-Century-Crofts.

Skinner, B.F. (1953) *Science and Human Behavior*. New York: Macmillan.

Skinner, B.F. (1957) *Verbal Behavior*. New York: Appleton-Century-Crofts.

Skinner, B.F. (1968) *The Technology of Teaching*. New York: Appleton-Century-Crofts.

Skinner, B.F. (1987) 'What Ever Happened to Psychology as the Science of Behavior?', *American Psychologist*, 42: 780–786.

Sonntag, Kh. (1996) *Lernen im Unternehmen*. Munchen: C.H. Beck.

Sonntag, Kh. (1997) 'Real-life Tasks and Authentic Contexts in Learning as a Potential for Transfer', *Applied Psychology: An International Review*, 46(4): 344–349.

Sorcher, M. and Goldstein, A.P. (1972) 'A Behavior Modeling Approach in Training', *Personnel Administration*, 35: 35–41.

Spence, K.W. (1956) *Behavior Theory and Conditioning*. New Haven: Yale University Press.

Spence, K.W. (1960) *Behavior Theory and Learning: Selected Papers*. Englewood Cliffs, NJ: Prentice-Hall.

Taylor, C.C.W. (1999) *The Atomists: Leucippus and Democritus: Fragments, A Text and Translation with Commentary*. Toronto, Canada: University of Toronto Press.

Taylor, P.J., Russ-Eft, D. and Chan, D. (2003) *The Impact of Alternative Rating Sources and Retrospective Pretests on Training Effect Sizes*. Paper presented at the Australian Industrial Organizational Psychology conference, June, Melbourne, Australia.

Taylor, P.J., Russ-Eft, D. and Chan, D. (2005) 'A Meta-analytic Review of Behavior Modeling Training', *Journal of Applied Psychology*, 90: 692–709.

Taylor, P., Russ-Eft, D. and Taylor, H. (2009) 'The Transfer of Management Training from Alternative Perspectives', *Journal of Applied Psychology*, 94: 104–121.

Thompson, D.M. and Tulving, E. (1970) 'Associative Encoding and Retrieval: Weak and Strong Cues', *Journal of Experimental Psychology*, 86: 255–262.

Thorndike, E.L. (1932) *The Fundamentals of Learning*. New York: Teachers College Columbia University.

Thorndike, E.L. and Woodworth, R.S. (1901) 'The Influence of Improvement in One Mental Function upon the Efficiency of Other Functions', *Psychological Review*, 8: 247–261.

Tough, A. (1967) *Learning Without a Teacher*. Educational Research Series, No. 3. Toronto: Ontario Institute for Studies in Education.

Tough, A. (1971) *The Adult's Learning Projects: A Fesh Approach to Theory and Practice in Adult Learning*. Toronto: Ontario Institute for Studies in Education.

Turner, J.C. (1995) 'The Influence of Classroom Contexts on Young Children's Motivation for Literacy', *Reading Research Quarterly*, 30: 410–441.

Turner, J.C. and Meyer, D.K. (2000) 'Studying and Understanding the Instructional Contexts of Classrooms: Using Our Past to Forge Our Future', *Educational Psychologist*, 35(2): 69–85.

Underwood, B. (1964) 'The Representativeness of Rote Verbal Learning', in A.W. Melton (ed.), *Categories of Human Learning*. New York: Academic Press, pp. 48–77.

Vygotsky, L.S. (1979) 'Consciousness as a Problem in the Psychology of Behavior', *Soviet Psychology*, 17(4): 3–35.

Wachtler, J. (1896) *De Alcmaeone Crotoniata*. Leipzig: Teubner.

Watkins, K.E. and Marsick, V.J. (1992) 'Building the Learning Organization: A New Role for Human Resource Developers', *Studies in Continuing Education*, 14(2): 115–129.

Watkins, K.E. and Marsick, V.J. (eds) (2003) 'Making Learning Count! Diagnosing the Learning Culture in Organizations', *Advances in Developing Human Resources*, 5(2), May: Thousand Oaks, CA: Sage.

Watson, J.B. (1913) 'Psychology as a Behaviorist Views It', *Psychological Review*, 23: 89–116.

Wertheimer, M. (1912) 'Experimentelle Studien uber das Sehen von Bewegung', *Zeitung der Psychologie*, 61: 161–265.

Wertsch, J.V. (1991) 'A Sociocultural Approach to Socially Shared Cognition', in L.B. Resnick, J.M. Levine and S.D. Teasley (eds), *Perspectives on Socially Shared Cognition*. Washington, DC: American Psychological Association, pp. 85–100.

Wertsch, J.V., del Rio, P. and Alverez, A. (1995) *Sociocultural Studies of Mind*. New York: Cambridge University Press.

Winograd, T. and Flores, F. (1986) *Understanding Computers and Cognition: A New Foundation for Design*. Norwood, NJ: Ablex.

Wittgenstein, L. (1958) *Philosophical Investigations* (3rd edn). New York: Macmillan.

10

Knowledge and Workplace Learning

Nicholas M. Allix

INTRODUCTION

From any general survey of the literature a researcher could conclude, not unreasonably, that workplace learning is a broad interdisciplinary, multi-perspective, problematic, and contested field of inquiry. Difficulties are wide-ranging and cover a plethora of unresolved issues. Problems begin at general levels, and narrow to more specific concerns.

At a general level the notion of 'workplace' is seen to be problematic, as is the nature of 'work', and therefore the focus on the workplace 'as distinct from other contexts' is questioned. In particular, terms and concepts in the field are purported to have 'become stretched' to the point of meaning different things to different researchers. Hence, the evident complexity and contested nature of the term 'workplace learning' may therefore 'no longer be useful' to researcher understandings (Fenwick, 2006: 268–9, 274). Contrastingly, the workplace is seen to be a legitimate learning space where activities and interactions are highly structured and regulated by particular powers and interests, and which, therefore, has pedagogical properties. In other words, workplaces as 'historically, culturally, and situationally shaped' are not 'imprecise and ill-focused' as environments for research (Billett, 2004: 312–13, 319). From critical and sociological perspectives there are explicit concerns with issues of power, inequity, whose particular interests are served in workplaces, and whether the personal needs and interests of workers as learners can be democratically accommodated in an organizationally civilized and sophisticated way (Axford and Seddon, 2006; Casey, 2003; Spencer, 2001).

At smaller scales a number of discrete conceptual and methodological issues crowd into the literature, which as such, are somewhat more tractable, though no less easy to settle, than larger and more general concerns. Questions arise about what workplace learning is for, and whether it is a component of a wider and more extended view of lifelong education, particularly in the context of a so-called learning society (Hager, 2004: 22). And, what is the connection between workplace learning and organizations and social institutions? Economic considerations suggest that workplace learning is important for 'enhancing productivity, innovation, and competitiveness', and is tied up with the notion of organizational learning. In other respects, it is seen to be 'instrumental in reducing stress and promoting healthier working conditions' and general wellbeing (Ellström, 2001: 421–2). For individuals, such learning in work and elsewhere may simply boil down to enabling 'the art of living' (Yeatman, 1996: 284) and a capacity to grow and adjust effectively to a ceaselessly changing environment (Hager, 1996: 236).

Despite such issues, there are nevertheless more specific matters that consistently arise in the literature, which, it will be argued here, are more amenable to conceptual and methodological analysis, and which may admit more systematic treatment, integration and resolution. Foremost is the overarching issue of the relationship between learning that is deemed formal in nature, such as that found in schools and universities, and learning that is viewed as informal, and something that is acquired through workplace experiences. Usually cast in the long-standing guise of a distinction between 'theoretical' versus 'practical' types of knowledge and learning, this dichotomy plays itself out in a number of ways in the literature, and the social sciences more broadly. From an educational point of view, the aptitudes required in the classroom are deemed to be anchored in formal intelligence, usually represented as a general factor known as g that is measured quantitatively and expressed as IQ, where a premium is placed on thinking and abstract problem solving. This is contrasted with what is recognized as the practical intelligence of doing in the everyday world. Both forms of intelligence are generally thought not to map well to each other, raising questions about the nature and role of formal modes of education, such as schooling, and its relationship with the world outside the school classroom (Resnick, 1987).

With respect to the world of work, formal education, whilst seen as important to professional practice, is often downplayed in favour of experience, or expertise derived from practical learning. As Schön (1995: 29) remarks, '... classroom knowledge is only part – and by no means the most important part – of what counts in practice'. Hence, in considering questions about the relevance of formal academic knowledge in relation to workplace know-how, the relationship between workplace learning and off-the-job education-based courses is seen to be 'problematic' (Hodkinson, 2005: 521). The perceived solution to this is for researchers to produce a better conceptual understanding of practice (Hager, 2004: 27), and a more integrated perspective, incorporating the two dimensions of theory and practice and explicit and tacit forms of knowledge, or an 'epistemology of practice' (Raelin, 1998: 280–1; Schön, 1995: 29).

The tension between formal and informal accounts of education is manifested in a variety of ways from an epistemological point of view. Although the concept can be 'slippery' (Fenwick, 2006: 270), clear epistemic distinctions are sometimes drawn between knowledge that is seen to be 'scientific' in kind, and practical knowledge, which is regarded as 'non-scientific'. Indeed, theory and practice are viewed as two distinct forms of knowledge, where it is claimed that the judgement and doing of practical knowledge 'obeys its own laws' (Yeatman, 1996: 285–7). Thus, with respect to educational delivery in the workplace, science is argued to be privileged as the 'foundation of all knowledge' and as the 'proper mode of knowing'. A long-standing focus has therefore been on learning as the acquisition of knowledge or skill as an outcome or product (Fenwick, 2006: 270), in which what is learned constitutes content, which is assumed will transfer to the site of work.

Opposed to this acquisitive view of knowledge and learning is the idea that learning is a process, and particularly a process of creativity, where learning occurs as it is being created (Engeström, 2001: 137–8), and where knowledge is something that is put to use (Fenwick, 2006: 271). In this respect, Torraco (1999: 249) notes that educational theory has not kept pace with evolutionary trends in the nature of work, and the skilled expertise needed to perform it, particularly in a context of significant ongoing change, where workers have to confront 'novel and ambiguous problems' that are difficult to identify, and for which it is difficult to specify educational solutions in advance. On this view, learning and problem solving is situated or grounded in social and physical contexts (Orr, 1998; Lave, 1991; Lave and Wenger, 1991). The situated view is thought to move toward overcoming the theory–practice dichotomy, for cognition is deemed to be spread and distributed over contexts, where mind, body and interactive activities are integrated (Hager, 1996: 239).

Given these distinctions and different views about the nature of knowledge and the contexts to which it is tied or seen to fit appropriately, it is not surprising therefore to find that conceptions of learning or processes of knowledge acquisition are similarly characterized by uncertainty and confusion. According to Hager (2004: 24, 28), the concept of learning 'is widely misunderstood', and that with the rejection in the field of a view of learning as product, 'theorists increasingly are searching for a better account of learning'. It is noted that learning is often not defined by researchers (Fenwick, 2006: 266), that little attention is given in the literature to explicating the meaning of the term, and that 'the concept of learning is taken for granted' (Ellström, 2001: 422). Where the notion of learning is articulated, there are very different meanings and understandings associated with the concept. Thus, it is argued that there is a need to focus and constrain the notion by returning to rigorous scholarship and 'conceptual basics' (Fenwick, 2006: 275).

Given also that it appears that 'little is known about processes of learning at work and the conditions that are likely to facilitate and constrain such processes' (Ellström, 2001: 422), it would seem that an appropriate theory-building strategy would be to address methodological questions and the adequacy of the conceptual and theoretical tools that are deployed in contemporary analysis and explication of the field. Methodological considerations are particularly important to theoretical developments because they furnish the epistemic resources that determine the content and structure theories can have in their particular domain of interest and application. This is because methodologies are underwritten by specific epistemologies or theories of knowledge which determine what counts as knowledge, how it is acquired, and how it is justified. To the extent that theories of knowledge specify these matters, they also implicitly specify a range of cognitive phenomena; that is, an epistemology implies a theory of mind, which explains how processes such as perception, memory, learning, representation, and cognition takes place. Thus, issues of knowledge, mind, and cognition, as specified by the methodological resources made available by an epistemology, have a direct bearing on many of the specific issues and problems which, as outlined here, concern workplace learning theory.

Therefore, it is argued here that an excursion into contemporary developments in epistemology will go some considerable way towards answering the kind of questions posed by Schoenfeld (1999), which neatly frame the central issues, as follows:

- 'Is it possible to build robust theories of how we think and act in the world – theories that provide rigorous and detailed characterizations of "how the mind works," in context?' (Schoenfeld, 1999: 5).
- 'Is it possible to build robust theories of learning – theories that provide rigorous and detailed characterizations of how people come to understand things, and develop increased capacities to do the things they want or need to do?' (Shoenfeld, 1999: 6).

In terms of providing a theory of learning mechanisms, which accounts for processes by which learning occurs, a central question is:

- 'How can we integrate brain research with research on human performance?' (Schoenfeld, 1999: 7).

These questions are addressed here, with the aim of providing a naturalistic basis and direction for future theory-building and research in the field of workplace learning. However, it is important to note that because of limited space, and the scope and complexity of recent developments, this account is not exhaustive. Rather, it is necessary to be selective, and to restrict discussion to an overview of those advancements that are of most importance to an understanding of current developments in epistemology and related philosophical and scientific extensions, and the corresponding relationships that these discoveries may have for issues and problems in workplace learning theory and practice.

EPISTEMOLOGICAL AND METHODOLOGICAL CONSIDERATIONS

Two dominant epistemologies and philosophies of science held sway for much of the twentieth century, and indeed still do today in many disciplines, particularly the social sciences. They are positivism and its more developed form known as logical positivism, as formulated by the Vienna Circle in the 1920s, and the later and most developed variant of these theories of knowledge, logical empiricism.

Logical empiricism

For logical positivism and logical empiricism, the media for knowledge were beliefs that could be justified as true. These were deemed to be expressed or represented in ordinary language statements, which could be shown directly through empirical observation, or indirectly by way of rules of logic, to correspond to some foundation of sensory experience. For logical empiricism beliefs in the form of statements or propositions about the empirical world were construed as synthetic, or contingently true, whereas beliefs derived from logical inferences or relations between ideas were analytic, or necessarily true. Beliefs that fell outside of these epistemic constraints were considered to have no empirical meaning or veracity, and were deemed to be metaphysical in nature, and therefore not part of scientific knowledge (see Ayer, 1975). Claims to knowledge that were not able to muster empirical support as required by logical empiricism's verification theory of meaning, such as ethical or value statements, were treated as little more than subjectively motivated theoretical claims of a non-cognitive nature that could not, in principle, be known.

Thus, logical empiricism created and maintained a clear division between observational and theoretical terms, and between facts and values. Furthermore, since a theory of mind is implied in an epistemology (Evers and Lakomski, 1991: 6, 8), logical empiricism provided little in the way of substantive methodological resources for articulating, explicating, and understanding value-laden aspects of mind, such as tacit knowledge and practical skills, and opened the way for behaviourism to prevail in the twentieth century as the appropriate scientific approach to advancing knowledge in psychology.

However, logical empiricism has over the past half century or more sustained considerable criticism concerning a range of philosophical and technical problems, associated particularly with the problem of induction (Popper, 1995: 33–65), and the so-called 'two dogmas of empiricism' linked with the verification principle and the related doctrine of reductionism, and the under-determination of theory by evidence (see Quine and Ullian, 1970; Quine, 1969: 79, 1951: 20–43; Duhem, 1953: 235–52). Arguably the most damaging assault on this epistemology, and at the same time the most renowned reconstruction of empiricism as an epistemological enterprise, is attributable to the work of American philosopher Willard Van Orman Quine.

Epistemology naturalized

Quine argued that the analytic-synthetic distinction which provided the logical empiricist framework for accepting a fundamental difference between observational and theoretical kinds of knowledge was unsound, because there were no unvarnished facts based on an incorrigible foundation of observation or experience, which constitute the indisputable truths of science and knowledge. Such notions, he argued, were empiricist dogmas. Quine (1951: 41) argued that the terms and statements that constitute our claims about the world face a 'tribunal of sense experience not individually but as a corporate body.' Thus, it is whole theories that constitute the basic units of meaning, and not individual terms and statements taken one by one. As theoretical wholes, all observations are *theory-laden*, and that what is observed is not privileged or incorrigible as a source of knowledge about the world. Because of this under-determination of theory by observational evidence, the appeal to empirical adequacy as a criterion for the justification of knowledge claims therefore collapses, and in its place Quine argued that claims to knowledge are a more holistic matter of evaluating a web or network of interrelated and interconnected beliefs (see Quine and Ullian, 1970), which do not neatly divide up into observational or theoretical statements, scientific and non-scientific beliefs, or facts and values (see Evers, 1988: 5–7, 10–11).

Philosophy, and epistemology in particular, were not, Quine argued, separate intellectual enterprises that stood apart from science, but were rather one and the same endeavour. Epistemology is not some prior or transcendent first philosophy functioning outside of science.

Thus, as an extension of science, philosophy employs the same methods of inquiry and standards of evidence as science itself in acquiring and evaluating claims to knowledge, including claims about knowledge itself. Since according to Quine (1969: 82–3) there is a reciprocal containment of epistemology in natural science, and of natural science in epistemology, when it comes to justifying what we claim to know, we use what we deem our best existing scientific theories to inform and assist with the tasks of evaluation, and bootstrapping our way to better theories about the world, and of our own place within it. Thus, on this view, the task of evaluating knowledge claims boil down to a more complicated affair of drawing on a much wider range of criteria over and above that of empirical adequacy alone, which together constitute so-called 'superempirical virtues' that are used to assess the global or systematic coherence of competing theoretical claims to knowledge in some domain or other (see Churchland, 1993: 146; Evers and Lakomski, 1991: 4, 37; Williams, 1980: 243–72; Quine and Ullian, 1970: 42–53). What an epistemology claims as knowledge is therefore as provisional and tentative as knowledge that derives from science. In light of these criticisms, logical empiricism, and its methods for acquiring and justifying knowledge, is generally accepted today as constituting an invalid account of science (see Churchland, P.S., 2002, 1992, 1987; Feyerabend, 1975; Hooker, 1975; Kuhn, 1970; Quine, 1969, 1951; Feigl, 1950).

With this process of naturalization, and a theory of mind as an implicit component, epistemology falls into place as a chapter of psychology, where we appeal to our best scientific theories of human learning and cognition to explain and justify how scientific knowledge is possible (see Evers and Lakomski, 1991: 8; Evers, 1988: 10; Quine, 1969: 82). This reconfiguration of knowledge and epistemology has been extended recently by the work of philosophers Paul and Patricia Churchland (see Churchland, P.S., 2002, 1992; Churchland, P.M., 1995, 1993), who have argued, against considerable conservative resistance (see Fodor and Lepore, 1996; Fodor and Pylyshyn, 1995; Fodor, 1993), that if work in philosophy and epistemology is to continue to advance, then inquiry must peer 'into the brain' (Churchland, P.M., 2006: 32) and be informed of developments in the brain sciences.

Neuroepistemology

The cluster of disciplines informing modern brain science, or what has come to be known as the 'new cognitive science' (Allix, 2003: 7; 2000: 284; Evers, 2000: 211), include fields of research as diverse as computational neuroscience, cognitive neurobiology, connectionist artificial intelligence, real-world robotics, artificial life, and computational neuroethology, to mention only some contributing scientific spheres. The development and application of tools and technologies in these disciplines provide effective means for investigating the structure and operations of the living brain, and for modelling these, as ways of uncovering its mysteries, and throwing light on ourselves as 'wild epistemic engines' (Churchland and Churchland, 1983). Developments have been such that the term 'epistemology' has begun to transmute into a newer and more naturalized incarnation called 'neuroepistemology' (Churchland, P.S., 2002: 270).

Although modern medical imaging tools allow scientists to look inside the functioning mind/brain, there are also powerful connectionist models that permit scientists to explore hypotheses concerning the structural and functional properties and workings of the brain and nervous system. Connectionist models are computer programs known as 'artificial neural networks' (ANNs), which are heuristic devices that function as analogues of real biological neural networks linking the microscopic level of neurobiology with higher systemic levels of cognition, and provides investigators with means for examining how intelligent properties emerge from the interaction of lower level neuronal components that do not have such properties. As such, ANNs are considered to be 'universal approximators' that can compute approximately any computable function (Churchland, P.M., 1998b: 41). This feature has helped researchers to develop new understandings of how the brain and nervous system may learn, and represent and process information. Thus, in a co-evolutionary manner, connectionist models are informed by neuroscience, and in turn also inform neuroscience (Munakata and McClelland, 2003: 423), and in this way connectionist artificial intelligence research furnishes new insights into the kinematics and dynamics of cognition and of the algorithms thought to underlie brain function (see Sejnowski et al., 1988: 1299–1301; Smolenski, 1998: 9–10).

Research with ANNs shows how networked structures such as biological brains can learn, and how they are able to retain or memorize this learning. As Kandel and Hawkins (1992: 53) explain, 'learning is the process by which we acquire new knowledge, and memory is the process by which we retain that knowledge over time.' Learning in connectionist models occurs through a steady calibration of the connection weights between the processing units or 'neurons' in a network. Activation through the network commences with an input stimulus that propagates from the input layer, through intermediate or 'hidden' layers, to the output layer of the network concerned. Driven by feedback from experience and the degree of error in the network output given its inputs, the weighted connections are gradually changed and adjusted by means of back propagation algorithms until network error is reduced or minimized, and settles down to produce a reliable output. This calibrated output can be acquired through either error-driven learning, or by self-organizing processes based on Hebbian learning principles, where units that fire together also wire together. This process of changes in connection weights from experience-driven feedback or self-organizing processes is the memory mechanism through which learning and development takes place. The learning or knowledge that has been acquired is located at no particular point in the system, but is distributed in the connections throughout the entire network (see Munakata and McClelland, 2003: 413–15; Evers, 1990a: 68–78, 2000: 211–15).

THE NATURE OF COGNITIVE REPRESENTATION AND COMPUTATION

Work in connectionist artificial intelligence and neurophilosophy has led to the emergence of a new account of how the brain deploys a conceptual framework during processes of perceptual recognition and practical action (Churchland, P.M., 1998a: 859). On this account the algorithms that underlie brain representation and computation are massively parallel and very high-dimensional pattern processing vectors, which are instantiated in variously weighted configurations of neuronal connections across large populations of neurons that comprise processing pathways in the nervous system. The vast matrix of layered connections in these various pathways determines the interpretive framework, or activated prototypes, by which the brain categorizes its experiences of features and phenomena in the world, and steers or guides the administration of practical action (Churchland, P.M., 1998b: 41). More specifically, for neural networks the representation of information about the environment is embodied in the connections between the sensory input layer and the 'hidden' or middle layers of a given processing pathway, and the computational capacity to use the represented information is embodied in the hidden-to-output connections of that pathway (Munakata and McClelland, 2003: 416). As such, processes of pattern or vector transformation in the form of category interpretation and appropriate learned response are functions that are typical of *theories* in general, in that they function to 'produce and steer well-tuned behaviour' or practical action in the world, which makes them thoroughly *pragmatic* in nature (Churchland, P.M., 1995: 90–1; 1993: 177).

Neuron populations in the brain define the axes of an abstract hyper-dimensional state space, where activity vector patterns represent positions or points in that state space and discriminative learning carves intricate hierarchical partitions across it, and where sequences of activity constitute trajectories through that state space. Dynamic trajectories through such state spaces can be linked in the brain so that, in turn, more complex sequences of such trajectories can be formed through learning (Churchland, P.S., 1998: 245). Through dynamic and non-linear vector-to-vector transformations, as cognitive processing proceeds from one population of neurons to another, and back again to earlier populations or layers in a processing pathway by means of recurrent processing (Edelman, 1989), the brain is able to alter and adjust in a flexible and fluid manner its own cognitive activities and actions. Importantly, these characteristics of brain functioning make it possible for the nervous system to make extremely fine-grained sensory and cognitive discriminations, and related highly contextual response adaptations, which in their subtlety and dynamism far outruns the analytic and descriptive capacities of language. Furthermore, this view of cognition accommodates and accounts for all five main modalities of sensory coding, and provides an explanation of computation as consisting of coordinate transformations from one state space to another, such as the guidance of cognitive or motor activity by current and recurrent sensory representations for instance, which is one of the most fundamental cognitive problems animate creatures have to face in their environments (Churchland, P.M. 1986: 220).

On this view of cognition, representation and computation are not regarded as consisting of symbolic or language-like processing. Rather, the brain's knowledge is understood to be instantiated in the configuration of weighted synaptic connections between the neurons in its various processing pathways. As such, this knowledge is *implicit* in the brain's structure, rather than explicit in the states of the neurons themselves (see Rumelhart, 1989: 135–6). Thus, the brain's epistemic system is sub-linguistic or sub-symbolic in nature (see Smolenski, 1988). From a connectionist point of view, human rationality is reconceived as being essentially skill-based, where inputs to computations are perceptual, and outputs are, in a broad sense, motoric (Clark, 2001b: 123).

On this causal account of cognition, knowledge does not appear to partition into categories of propositional and non-propositional, or explicit or tacit. Rather, scientific evidence suggests that for the brain and central nervous system knowledge appears to be a seamless and highly interconnected network of variously weighted neural interactions. From this perspective, symbolic/propositional language representation in the brain is consistent with other modalities of nervous system representation and computation, in being ultimately a practical matter of vector processing, where symbolic computation consists of patterns of activation and their trajectories through relevant interpretive, conceptual, and communicative state spaces. Thus, producing and communicating in language appropriately is a matter of knowing *how* to do this, and processes of learning the relevant conditions of language production can be understood in terms of *doing*, where gaps between learner expectations and experiences are gradually closed through feedback-driven steady weight adjustments to the networks of neurons involved in causing and guiding linguistic behaviour (Evers and Lakomski, 2000: 30). This conclusion fits with Quine's observations about the network-like nature of knowledge, and the reasoning of Ryle (1949: 55) and Polanyi (1997: 137) concerning the integrated nature of knowing, and the similarity of the underlying structure between 'knowing *that*' and 'knowing *how*', and theoretical and practical knowledge.

THE SITUATED NATURE OF COGNITION

Since the meditations of René Descartes (see Descartes, 1968) in the seventeenth century to the last decades of the twentieth century, inquiries into the nature of knowledge, mind, and thought and action, have mostly ignored questions about the role that the body and the surrounding environment plays in cognition. However, recent work in several scientific domains is now providing us with ever richer and deeper insights into the fundamental attributes and properties that make us what we are as cognitive creatures, and in the process is radically altering our standard and commonsense 'folk-psychological' (Stich, 1983) understanding of the nature of mind and cognition.

The embodied mind

Consistent with the motoric and pragmatic nature of cognition from work in neuroepistemology and connectionist artificial intelligence research, there is compelling evidence from recent empirical work utilizing medical neuroimaging techniques suggesting that the representation and activation of conceptual content occurs in modality-specific areas of the brain that correspond to various sensorimotor, functional, spatial, and other referential features and properties associated with the concepts concerned. Processes of representational integration are thought to occur across modalities by means of hierarchically organized association areas in the brain known as 'convergence zones' (see Barsalou et al., 2003: 84–91; Damasio and Damasio, 1996a: 167–8, 1996b: 20–1; Damasio, 1996: 100–5). Because of the sub-symbolic and sensorimotor nature of representation and computation, body and mind are also not sensibly seen as separate, as Descartes thought (see Descartes, 1968). Rather, cognition is viewed as intrinsically embodied and situated in the world, where the body and its sensorimotor machinery constitutes a frame of reference for mind, processes of cognition and reason, and for *feelings* of subjectivity and selfhood. Feelings, particularly, are deemed to furnish the sense of our biological self-concept, and to qualify our perceptions of the world, and through the causal interaction of our affective embodied mind with the world, generates our sense of situatedness in it. Importantly, this subjective sense or experience of situatedness is recognized as being crucial to the integrity of practical reasoning and action in the world, and our effectiveness in navigating the complexities of social and practical situations (see Dolan, 2002; Churchland, P.S., 1998; Clark, 1998; Damasio, 1999, 1996; Damasio and Damasio, 1996a, 1996b).

Ecological approaches to the study of embodied cognition in relation to the environment show that through processes of perceiving and acting, the boundary of the body, and *sense* of embodiment, can shift dynamically in interaction with affordances such as tools. As non-neural extensions tools dynamically alter and expand our perceptions of our own bodies and the environment, and as such constitute integral components of the perceptual system. This is only one of two different senses of embodiment, for we are also capable of *embodying*. Tools also become functional extensions of ourselves, as they alter our *effectivities* of perceiving and acting, and enable us to change and extend our capacities for action in relation to the environment. Consistent with multimodal representation and processing, perception of an object or tool, such as the key to a door for example, activates corresponding motor responses in the brain, for instance the appropriate hand shape for its use, as in the case of holding, inserting, and turning it (see Barsalou et al., 2003: 86). Hence, the 'body schema', and the representation of space, can be dynamically altered and re-mapped by tool use. Thus, organism and tool can be thought of as forming an extended and unified system of perception and action (see Maravita and Iriki, 2004; Kellenbach et al., 2003; Hirose, 2002; Maravita et al., 2001; Berti and Frassinetti, 2000; Lockman, 2000; Turvey, 1996). Of interest to the present context is how findings from these studies appear to mesh well with Polanyi's notion of 'indwelling', in that for something to function as a proximal term of tacit knowing, it is incorporated into the body, or the body extends in some way to include it, such that 'we come to dwell in it' (Polanyi, 1997: 141).

The embedded mind

Converging developments in research fields as diverse as real-world robotics, artificial life, computational neuroethology, and distributed and situated cognition, are generating a broader view of the nervous system beyond embodiment and embodying, which conceives of cognition as a process that is extended and *embedded* in the environment in various complex ways. From this perspective, adaptive behaviour of an organism is a function of the biomechanics of the body, the structure of the environment in which it is situated, and a continuous feedback loop between the nervous system, body, and environment. Thus, a close matching between nervous system and the environment creates both constraints and opportunities for the nervous system (see Chiel and Beer, 1997: 553–7).

Perception and action, and organism and environment, are regarded as tightly coupled (see Dobbyn and Stuart, 2003: 197, 200), and sensorimotor feedback from bodily movements and the embedding environment plays a vital role in generating, constraining, and shaping possibilities for adaptive behaviour. Hence, nervous system, body and environment together comprise a rich, complicated, and highly structured dynamical system, in which all interacting elements co-evolve over time, and where intelligent behaviour is an emergent property of the organism and its embedding environment. The representational strategy of the brain in this context also appears to be 'closely geared to the particular details of the body and world', where there is 'widespread use of task-specific, motor-oriented, and context-dependent encodings' (Clark, 1998: 275–6). Intelligent cognition is therefore viewed as 'an active, distributed, environment-exploiting achievement', in which the mind makes use of 'the structure of information in the environment' in solving problems (Clark, 2001b: 126, 130). The notion that cognition can be extended and distributed between humans, artifacts, and other external representational and computational media, explains how it is possible for human beings to create whole cognitive systems that produce knowledge. In doing so, some parts of the cognitive processes involved are 'offloaded' into the environment, and in turn parts of the environment function as 'scaffolds' for carrying out cognitive tasks (see Clark, 2008, 2001a, 1997; Giere and Moffat, 2003; Hutchins, 1996).

THE FUNCTIONAL ARCHITECTURE OF COGNITION

As the brain and nervous system are products of the particular evolutionary history of our species, the unique characteristic features and properties of our neurobiological makeup reflect the course of this developmental trajectory through time. This is particularly the case with respect to the brain's anatomical and functional organization. Although controversies and debates swirl around various aspects of ongoing research and theory building in this domain (see Reber, 2004, 1989; Sun and Zhang, 2004; Butler and Berry, 2001; Cleeremans et al., 1998; Dienes and Fahey, 1998; McClelland, 1998; Berry, 1997, 1997a, 1996, 1987; Dienes and Altmann, 1997; Manza and Reber, 1997; St. John and Shanks, 1997; Seger, 1994; Schacter, 1987), there is a converging consensus in cognitive neuroscience and cognitive psychology that information processing in the brain is organized into two broad and fundamental anatomical systems that appear to represent a fundamental psychological distinction, or division, in the way that knowledge is acquired and manifested. These systems are known by a variety of dual-process terms such as 'conscious-nonconscious', 'controlled–automatic', and 'systematic–heuristic' (see Bargh and Chartrand, 1999: 463, 476), and correspond to what is characterized here as 'explicit' and 'implicit' forms of learning and memory. Each system has separable goal structures and separate types of goal implementation mechanisms (see Stanovich, 2004: 31–79; Evans, 2003; Bear et al., 1996: 530; Squire, 1992: 209). The distinct properties of each will be outlined briefly.

Explicit learning and memory

Explicit memory, also referred to by terms such as 'declarative' or 'relational' memory, is involved in the association of *simultaneous* stimuli, such as the storage of a single event at a particular time and place, and stores consciously accessible facts and events, and does so relatively easily and rapidly (Kandel and Hawkins, 1992: 52). However, these memories are also more labile and easily forgotten. Most significantly, these memory systems have capacity for analytic processing (Stanovich, 2004: 36), for they not only store and retrieve information, but in conjunction with associated working and prospective memory systems, enable retrieved information to be accessed in relation to the current needs and goals of an organism, and integrated into coherent sequences of thought that lead to conclusions, decisions, or solutions to problems. A cognitive process that can defer or override immediate or more automated responses to incoming sensory information, and which can combine this information with retrieved memories and goals, confers great cognitive flexibility, particularly in complex contexts where novel associations need to be established between goals, sensory inputs, and long-term memories (see Stillings et al., 1995: 37–9). Thus, neurobiological machinery associated with explicit executive functions in the brain that make possible capacities for planning and for attending to the ongoing processing of recurrent contextual information facilitates cognitive properties such as foresight and the execution of goal-directed behaviours (see Curtis and D'Esposito, 2003: 415–23; Goldberg, 2001). Consequently, as the basis for *general fluid intelligence* or *gF* (Engle et al., 1999: 105; Cohen and O'Reilly, 1996: 267–95), explicit memory systems permit abstract hypothetical thinking (Evans, 2003: 454), free cognition and behaviour from the immediate imperatives of sensory stimuli and other cognitive processes, and are the engines of creativity and innovation.

Implicit learning and memory

Implicit memory, also known as 'procedural' memory, is an evolutionarily older system that stores skills or habitual behaviours that operate relatively autonomously and automatically (Stanovich, 2004: 37–44), and as a general rule cannot be consciously accessed (see Bear et al., 1996: 516). Thus, implicit skills can be performed without the need for conscious control, and only the products of its automatic and parallel streams of processing may be posted to conscious awareness (Evans, 2003: 454). Implicit memory also involves the association of *sequential* stimuli, and stores information about predictive relations between events. Significantly, it is characterized by 'improved performance on certain tasks without the subject being able to describe just what has been learned', since 'it involves memory systems that do not draw on the contents of the general knowledge of the individual' (Kandel and Hawkins, 1992: 54).

Thus, this type of learning entails the acquisition of a motor response in reaction to some kind of sensory input (see Bear et al., 1996: 516, 548). Implicit learning is also slow, requiring repetition and practice over many trial events to accumulate and form. Once formed, this type of memory operates in a reflex-like manner, and is highly robust and resistant to eradication or forgetting. Importantly, as a heuristic-based processing system that gradually extracts the underlying statistical structure of some stimulus domain during learning, the acquired memory or implicit knowledge gained by the system responds to the holistic properties of stimuli and relatively simple and easily retrievable cues (Stanovich, 2004: 36). In this respect, implicitly acquired knowledge is less manipulable and more context-bound than explicit learning, and appears to be tied to the surface characteristics of stimuli, which implies that it shows limited transfer or generalization to related tasks with the same underlying structure.

Implicit learning also produces a phenomenal sense of intuition, in that subjects respond the way they do because it simply 'feels right', or natural, in the particular context in which they find themselves (see Berry and Dienes, 1993). This phenomenological experience occurs because implicit memory systems not only respond directly and very rapidly to particular stimuli, but in the process also provide input to the relatively slower explicit or analytic memory systems, and in doing so serve to colour mental representations and to bias cognitive processing. In this manner, implicit or tacit knowledge precedes or paves the way to the experience of explicit conscious awareness and knowledge (see Stanovich, 2004: 52–61; Bargh and Chartrand, 1999). This 'primacy of the implicit' is consistent with the notion that 'the cognitive unconscious' and its biological machinery considerably antedates the evolution of conscious cognitive systems, which accounts for the dissociation between these systems, the greater resilience and robustness of implicit systems, and the independent operation of implicit perceptual and cognitive functions from consciousness (Reber, 1992, 1990).

The role of language and formal knowledge in the cognitive economy

Given this emerging view of knowledge, mind, and cognition, the question arises as to what place formal symbolic representations of knowledge have in the cognitive economy.

Language is the most widely used sociocultural symbolic currency and means of communication, and has long had a central role in education. However, if cognitive representations and computational processes consist, in the first instance, of distributed and dynamic non-symbolic sensorimotor neural maps, particularly in the form of vectoral patterns and their transformations, then our understanding of language and symbolically formulated theories and the roles they play in cognition come in for scrutiny and attendant pressures for conceptual revision.

On the view outlined here, language is dethroned from its central place in the cognitive economy and becomes instead a rather superficial and conventional representation of a way of understanding in some problematic domain, and can be better seen to function in the manner of *compression algorithms* and as means for condensing the rich multimodal coding strategy of activity vectors into sparser and more parsimonious semantic representations suitable for sociocultural intercourse (Evers and Lakomski, 2001: 505–7; 2000: 18, 1993: 145). As Hooker (1975: 217) explains, language may be construed as 'a surface abstraction of much richer, more generalized information processes in the cortex, a condensation fed to the tongue and hand for social purposes'. Nevertheless, language representation in the brain is consistent with other modalities of nervous system representation and computation, in being ultimately a practical matter of vector processing. From a neurocomputational perspective, understanding is not a linguistic expression, but rather shows itself to be a complex, hyper-dimensional, and massively recurrent situated *experience* for the individuals in which an activated vector, or prototype, is evoked. Thus, as Ryle (1949) and Polanyi (1997) noted, all 'knowing *that*' is just a form of 'knowing *how*', in that there is no principled difference between them as far as the brain is concerned.

Linguistic representations are appropriate things to exchange in complex institutional contexts, which are heavily dependent on external and public representations for sharing, extending, and enhancing theoretical and practical capacities, and as such, constitute just one, albeit highly important, valuable, and useful human devised cognitive technology (Clark, 2001a: 143; Churchland, P.M., 2002: 44–7, 1993: 224; Churchland and Churchland, 1996: 266). A primary function of language is to direct attention by *indicating* or *pointing* to the world (Hooker, 1975: 217). Hence, theories in explicit sentential or declarative form act as indicators of how prototypes are to be applied in any given context. Furthermore, as a way of understanding, language also functions to *activate* existing prototypes deemed appropriate to the comprehension of a local problem domain (see Churchland and Churchland, 1996: 263–4). Language also functions as a scaffold for action (Clark, 2008: 47–8) in facilitating the control of behaviour during the acquisition of new skills, and in overcoming obstacles and dealing with complex problems or aspects of situations that are puzzling (see Berk, 1994). In this respect, a common characteristic of complex explicit learning is that it may, with practice over time, progress to sensory-motor associations that are more or less automatic or habitual (see Merzenich and deCharms, 1996: 72; Anderson, 1982). Medical imaging evidence shows that matching neurobiological changes take place in the brain during such skill learning (see Raichle, 1994). Thus, when sufficiently practised, complex learning gradually becomes implicit, and is associated with the fluent kind of skills that characterize particular forms of expertise. Conceived of in this way, the grammatical, syntactic, and logic-like rules and structures embedded in human language may therefore be thought of pragmatically as a convenient assortment of codifications, guides, barriers, and signposts, which operate as heuristic rules of thumb in *steering* mental processes and behaviours during improvised action or learning (Bereiter, 1991: 15).

Language makes possible collective cognition, enabling humans to address and solve problems otherwise insoluble to solitary individuals, for the vocabulary of an inherited language constitutes an abstract template that narrows down an individual's search space during learning or problem solving (Churchland, 1995: 270). Language also reduces the complexity of conceptual structure by pulling together many notions under one symbol, each of which is a prototype vector that is highly interconnected with other associated prototypes, which makes it possible to establish ideas that are ever more complex and to use them to think at levels of abstraction that would otherwise be impossible (Damasio, A.R. and Damasio, H., 1992: 63). Thus, linguistic representations may be said to constitute human knowledge in an objective, independent, and collective sense, with which the knowing subject interfaces (see Hacking, 1975: 187). Spoken and written language is therefore a form of extrasomatic memory, through which the collective and accumulated learning of a culture can be passed on from one generation to another (see Churchland, P.M., 2002: 43–7, 1995: 270).

IMPLICATIONS FOR WORKPLACE LEARNING THEORY AND RESEARCH

From this survey of naturalistic research in the cognitive sciences emerges a picture of the nature and properties of knowledge, mind, learning, and cognition that is far more complex and multifaceted, and quite different from conventional understanding. The unfolding insights from this research have implications for significant issues that arise in the field, and suggest possible directions for theory-building and research. These will be identified briefly as matters for further inquiry.

The unity of content and process

From an empirical and methodological point of view, there is for the brain and nervous system no physical difference in the representation and computation of 'knowing *that*' and 'knowing *how*', or between theory and practice. As a prototypical skill, or ability, physically represented and computed in the brain's substrates, by means of elaborate network geometries and myriad synaptic connection weights and their associated transformations, all practice is profoundly theory-laden (see Evers, 1990a: 65–80). Similarly, all brain activity that appears to be theoretical in nature is also entirely practical, whether such activity be perceptual, deliberative, predictive, computational, manipulative, evaluative, comprehensive, or judgemental. Thus, from a naturalistic point of view, the dichotomous theory–practice and content–process view of cognition and learning finds conceptual unity.

This view reveals that the content of abstract and formal systems of symbolic knowledge is always dynamically interpreted and realized by the processes of a living cognitive system, in which representation is sub-symbolic, polymodal, and educated by an experiential history of extension and distribution through body and world in various complex ways. Such knowledge, when prototypically activated, is therefore inextricably intertwined with, and co-determined by a history, and/or a current (and recurrent) experience, of wider contextual processes of one kind or another, directly or indirectly.

Hence, abstract knowledge, conventionally understood as being of a 'theoretical' type, requires a *context* for both its evocation, and its corresponding application. This intimate inter-locking of abstract knowledge content with contextual processes therefore implies that distinguishing between 'scientific' and 'contextual' types of knowledge, or thinking and doing, finds no adequate justification.

Knowledge transfer

The unity of content and process suggests that where individuals have had no experience or exposure to particular situations that are communicated by formal knowledge, perceptual and practical understanding, and transfer to particular contexts, may be problematic. Unless there are situations where symbolic or linguistic compression algorithms are available that are developed enough to identify the essential features and processes of particular circumstances, and which are context invariant enough to generalize satisfactorily, attempts at transfer are likely to be disappointing or inadequate. Because knowledge cannot be readily separated from learning, the unitary nature of content and process implies that unless particular situations are sufficiently similar or identical in their empirical features and properties, transfer – whether from classroom to practice, or from one practical context to another different enough in a range of subtle ways to confound generalization – necessarily reduces to some or other process of learning.

Since much of what we know is implicit in its properties, and is tied to specific characteristics and features of particular environments and circumstances, the causal processes involved in conveying such knowledge and learning to other contexts are inevitably complex and often ambiguous as a consequence, and therefore will require recurring instances of temporally extended, embodied, and environmentally embedded learning and adaptation. Indeed, learning to make decisions that control performance in complex task contexts requires that such learning be tied to action for it to be most effective. Thus, to acquire such implicit skills effectively, it is necessary for learners to interact directly with the target task domain. Furthermore, where verbal information accompanies or is a component of such learning, learners should be encouraged to apply this knowledge (see Berry and Dienes, 1993: 129–31).

To extract the shared stochastic structure common to the environment in which learning takes place so it eventually generalizes satisfactorily, there is emerging evidence from connectionist modelling of explicit and implicit learning and memory systems that learning of complex skills may be best facilitated by *interleaved* processes of learning, rather than *focused* forms of learning, in which abstract formal knowledge is combined with exposure to situations (Richland et al., 2007: 557, 575; McClelland 1998; Anderson et al., 1996; McClelland et al., 1995). Interleaved learning allows new knowledge, from sources such as abstract formal knowledge, to incorporate itself gradually into more implicit existing knowledge structures in such a way that the consolidation of new knowledge does not interfere with the existing structure of knowledge acquired through prior experience with other related material (see McClelland et al., 1995: 433–8). While there is much still to be learned about how to structure and schedule such interleaved learning processes, research on implicit learning suggests that, as a general rule, and as a starting point, opportunities for implicit learning should perhaps precede exposure to explicit or symbolic formulations of learning, where this is possible (Berry and Dienes, 1993: 131). In this way, experiential structure provides a scaffold upon which the meaning and understanding of conceptual structure can more readily hang.

These considerations have implications for the validity of educational and training policies resting on assumptions that learning is generally best carried out by verbal or explicit instruction on the one hand, and that acquired skills and competencies are readily portable or transferable between various contexts on the other (see Berry and Dienes, 1993: 129–30).

CONCLUSION

It would appear from this survey of recent developments that learning is a process that is continuous and lifelong, and is not confined to learning in the academy or in the workplace, but is something that occurs in all contexts in which humans have to live and survive. It is also clear that, despite claims to the contrary (see Billett, 2004: 314–16), learning can be unconscious and passive; that is, it can occur implicitly and incidentally without thought, intention, or attention, and therefore what individuals acquire and come to show as habits and dispositions of mind and cognition can sometimes be just as unconstructively undesirable as they might be constructive and desirable. Thus, learning is not a neutral matter to be left to its own devices; it can, and *should*, be guided and managed when and where required. Hence, lifelong, and workplace learning as a subset of learning through life, presents educators – whether parents, teachers, learning and development specialists, knowledge managers, organizational leaders, and public policy makers – with social roles of significance and consequence for both individual and social wellbeing.

Learning is also a profoundly individual *and* social phenomenon. As individuals we have the capacity, and much occasion, to be both learners and guides to learning, where learning can be a mutually interdependent social process. Views of distributed and extended mind and cognition add to this by highlighting the importance of adaptive interaction with the world in which we live, in which solutions to the problems we face evolve *in situ* through iterative processes of trial and error (Robinson, 2002: 780), improvization and innovation (Brown and Duguid, 1996), and through more systematic processes such as action research (see Kuhne and Quigley, 1997) and project activities. Direct interactive involvement becomes an important methodological principle for those most affected by problems for which solutions are sought that have to be learned. Furthermore, the social and physical distribution of much knowledge, and the overlapping nature of many problem domains, suggests that learning experiences in such contexts must necessarily be collaborative. Long-, medium-, and short-term mechanisms such as (cognitive) apprenticeships, mentoring arrangements, establishing and developing communities of practice, and assembling work groups or project teams to address particular issues, are appropriate strategies to use to foster mutual and active systemic learning in the workplace and beyond. This general understanding justifies research interest and practice in the related disciplines of organizational learning and knowledge management. It is to these, and other matters yet to be perceived as scientific knowledge grows, that researchers must look, if our understanding of issues associated with learning in the workplace is to advance systematically.

REFERENCES

Allix, N.M. (2000) 'The Theory of Multiple Intelligences: A Case of Missing Cognitive Matter', *Australian Journal of Education*, 44(3): 272–293.

Allix, N.M. (2003) 'Epistemology and Knowledge Management Concepts and Practices', *Journal of Knowledge Management Practice*, 4. http://www.tlainc.com/articl49.htm

Anderson, J.R. (1982) 'Acquisition of Cognitive Skill', *Psychological Review*, 89(4): 369–406.

Anderson, J.R., Reder, L.M. and Simon, H.A. (1996) 'Situated Learning and Education', *Educational Researcher*, 25(4): 5–11.

Axford, B. and Seddon, T. (2006) 'Lifelong Learning in a Market Economy: Education, Training and the Citizen-Consumer', *Australian Journal of Education*, 50(2): 167–184.

Ayer, A.J. (1975) *Language, Truth and Logic*. London: Penguin Books.

Bargh, J.A. and Chartrand, T.L. (1999) 'The Unbearable Automaticity of Being', *American Psychologist*, 54(7): 462–479.

Barsalou, L.W., Simmons, W.K., Barbey, A.K. and Wilson, C.D. (2003) 'Grounding Conceptual Knowledge in Modality-Specific Systems', *Trends in Cognitive Sciences*, 7(2): 84–91.

Bear, M.F., Connors, B.W. and Paradiso, M.A. (1996) *Neuroscience: Exploring the Brain*. Baltimore, MD: Williams and Wilkins.

Bereiter, C. (1991) 'Implications of Connectionism for Thinking About Rules', *Educational Researcher*, 20(3): 10–16.

Berk, L.E. (1994) 'Why Children Talk to Themselves', *Scientific American*, 271(5): 60–65.

Berry, D.C. (1987) 'The Problem of Implicit Knowledge', *Expert Systems*, 4(3): 144–151.

Berry, D.C. (1996) 'How Implicit Is Implicit Learning?', *Implicit Cognition*. Underwood, G. (ed.). Oxford: Oxford University Press.

Berry, D.C. (1997) 'Introduction', in Berry, D.C. (ed.). *How Implicit Is Implicit Learning?* Oxford: Oxford University Press.

Berry, D.C. (1997a) 'Concluding Note: How Implicit Is Implicit Learning?', in Berry, D.C. (ed.). *How Implicit Is Implicit Learning?* Oxford: Oxford University Press.

Berry, D.C. and Dienes, Z. (1993) *Implicit Learning: Theoretical and Empirical Issues*. Hove, UK; Hillsdale, USA: Lawrence Erlbaum Associates.

Berti, A. and Frassinetti, F. (2000) 'When Far Becomes Near: Remapping of Space by Tool Use', *Journal of Cognitive Neuroscience*, 12(3): 415–420.

Billett, S. (2004) 'Workplace Participatory Practices: Conceptualising Workplaces as Learning Environments', *Journal of Workplace Learning*, 16(6): 312–324.

Brown, J.S. and Duguid, P. (1996) 'Organizational Learning and Communities-of-Practice: Toward a Unified View of Working, Learning, and Innovation', *Organizational Learning*. Thousand Oaks: CA: Sage.

Butler, L.T. and Berry, D.C. (2001) 'Implicit Memory: Intention and Awareness Revisited', *Trends in Cognitive Sciences*, 5(5): 192–197.

Casey, C. (2003) 'The Learning Worker, Organizations and Democracy', *International Journal of Lifelong Education*, 22(6): 620–634.

Chiel H.J. and Beer, R.D. (1997) 'The Brain Has a Body: Adaptive Behavior Emerges From Interactions of Nervous System, Body and Environment', *Trends in Neurosciences*, 20(12): 553–557.

Churchland, P.M. (1986) 'Cognition and Conceptual Change: A Reply to Double', *Journal for the Theory of Social Behaviour*, 16(2): 217–221.

Churchland, P.M. (1993) *A Neurocomputational Perspective: The Nature of Mind and the Structure of Science*. Cambridge, MA; London, UK: The MIT Press.

Churchland, P.M. (1995) *The Engine of Reason, the Seat of the Soul: A Philosophical Journey into the Brain.* Cambridge, MA; London, UK: The MIT Press.

Churchland, P.M. (1998a) 'Précis of The Engine of Reason, The Seat of the Soul: A Philosophical Journey into the Brain', *Philosophy and Phenomenological Research*, 58(4): 859–863.

Churchland, P.M. (1998b) 'Activation Vectors vs. Propositional Attitudes: How the Brain Represents Reality', in Paul M. Churchland and Patricia S. Churchland. *On the Contrary: Critical Essays, 1987–1997*, Cambridge, MA; London, UK: The MIT Press.

Churchland, P.M. (2002) 'Outer Space and Inner Space: The New Epistemology', *Proceedings and Addresses of the American Philosophical Association*, 76(2): 25–48.

Churchland, P.M. (2006) 'Into the Brain: Where Philosophy Should Go From Here', *Topoi*, 25: 29–32.

Churchland, P.M. and Churchland, P.S. (1996) *The Churchlands and Their Critics*, in McCauley, R.N. (ed.). Oxford, UK; Cambridge, MA: Basil Blackwell, Ltd.

Churchland, P.S. (1987) 'Epistemology in the Age of Neuroscience', *The Journal of Philosophy*, 84(10): 544–553.

Churchland, P.S. (1992) *Neurophilosophy: Toward a Unified Science of the Mind/Brain.* Cambridge, MA; London, UK: The MIT Press.

Churchland, P.S. (1998) 'Feeling Reasons', in Paul M. Churchland and Patricia S. Churchland. *On the Contrary': Critical Essays, 1987–1997,* Cambridge, MA; London, UK: The MIT Press.

Churchland, P.S. (2002) *Brain-Wise: Studies in Neurophilosophy.* Cambridge, MA: The MIT Press.

Churchland, P.S. and Churchland, P.M. (1983) 'Stalking the Wild Epistemic Engine', *Nous*, 17: 5–18.

Clark, A. (1997) *Being There: Putting Brain, Body, and World Together Again.* Cambridge, MA; London, UK: The MIT Press.

Clark, A. (1998) 'Where Brain, Body, and World Collide', *Daedalus*, 127(2): 257–280.

Clark, A. (2001a) *Mindware: An Introduction to the Philosophy of Cognitive Science.* Oxford: Oxford University Press.

Clark, A. (2001b) 'Reasons, Robots and the Extended Mind', *Mind and Language*, 16(2): 121–145.

Clark, A. (2008) *Supersizing the Mind: Embodiment, Action, and Cognitive Extension.* Oxford: Oxford University Press.

Cleeremans, A. Destrebecqz, A. and Boyer, M. (1998) 'Implicit Learning: News From the Front', *Trends in Cognitive Sciences*, 2(10): 406–416.

Cohen, J.D. and O'Reilly, R.C. (1996) 'A Preliminary Theory of the Interactions Between Prefrontal Cortex and Hippocampus that Contribute to Planning and Prospective Memory', in Brandimonte, M., Einstein, G.O. and McDaniel, M.A. (eds). *Prospective Memory: Theory and Applications.* Mahwah, NJ: Lawrence Erlbaum Associates.

Curtis, C.E. and D'Esposito, M. (2003) 'Persistent Activity in the Prefrontal Cortex During Working Memory', *Trends in Cognitive Sciences*, 7(9): 415–423.

Damasio, A.R. (1996) *Descartes' Error: Emotion, Reason and the Human Brain.* London and Basingstoke: Papermac.

Damasio, A.R. (1999) *The Feeling of What Happens: Body and Emotion in the Making of Consciousness.* A Harvest Book. San Diego; New York; London: Harcourt, Inc.

Damasio, A.R. and Damasio, H. (1992) 'Brain and Language', *Scientific American. Special Issue: Mind and Brain*, 267(3): 62–71.

Damasio, A.R. and Damasio, H. (1996a) 'Images and Subjectivity: Neurobiological Trials and Tribulations', in McCauley, R.N. (ed.). *The Churchlands and Their Critics.* Oxford, UK; Cambridge, MA: Basil Blackwell.

Damasio, A.R. and Damasio, H. (1996b) 'Making Images and Creating Subjectivity', in Llinás, R. and Churchland, P.S. (eds). *The Mind-Brain Continuum: Sensory Processes.* Cambridge, MA; London, UK: The MIT Press.

Descartes, R. (1968) *Discourse on Method and the Meditations* (translated by F.E. Sutcliffe). London: Penguin Books.

Dienes, Z. and Altmann, G. (1997) 'Transfer of Implicit Knowledge Across Domains: How Implicit and How Abstract?', in Berry, D.C. (ed.). *How Implicit Is Implicit Learning?* Oxford: Oxford University Press.

Dienes, Z. and Fahey, R. (1998) 'The Role of Implicit Memory in Controlling a Dynamic System', *The Quarterly Journal of Experimental Psychology*, 51A(3): 593–614.

Dobbyn, C. and Stuart, S. (2003) 'The Self as an Embedded Agent', *Minds and Machines*, 13: 187–201.

Dolan, R.J. (2002) 'Emotion, Cognition, and Behaviour', *Science*, 298(8): 1191–1194.

Duhem, P. (1953) 'Physical Theory and Experiment', in Feigl, H. and Brodbeck, M. (eds). *Readings in the Philosophy of Science.* New York: Appleton-Century-Crofts.

Edelman, G.M. (1989) *The Remembered Present: A Biological Theory of Consciousness.* New York: Basic Books, Inc.

Ellström, P. (2001) 'Integrating Learning and Work: Problems and Prospects', *Human Resource Development Quarterly*, 12(4): 421–435.

Engeström, Y. (2001) 'Expansive Learning at Work: Toward an Activity Theoretical Reconceptualization', *Journal of Education and Work*, 14(1): 133–156.

Engle, R.W., Kane, M.J. and Tuholski, S.W. (1999) 'Individual Differences in Working Memory Capacity and What They Tell Us About Controlled Attention, General Fluid Intelligence, and Functions of the Prefrontal Cortex', in Miyake, A. and Shah, P. (eds). *Models of Working Memory: Mechanisms of Active Maintenance and Executive Control.* Cambridge, UK: Cambridge University Press.

Evans, J.St.B.T. (2003) 'In Two Minds: Dual-Process Accounts of Reasoning', *Trends in Cognitive Sciences*, 7(10): 454–459.

Evers, C.W. (1988) 'Educational Administration and the New Philosophy of Science', *The Journal of Educational Administration*, 26(1): 3–22.

Evers, C.W. (1990a) 'Educating the Brain', *Educational Philosophy and Theory*, 22(2): 65–80.

Evers, C.W. (1990b) 'Schooling, Organizational Learning and Efficiency in the Growth of Knowledge', in Chapman, J.D. (ed.). *School-based Decision-making and Management*. London: Falmer Press.

Evers, C.W. (2000) 'Connectionist Modelling and Education', *Australian Journal of Education*, 44(3): 209–225.

Evers, C.W. and Lakomski, G. (1991) *Knowing Educational Administration: Contemporary Methodological Controversies in Educational Administration Research*. Oxford: Pergamon Press.

Evers, C.W. and Lakomski, G. (1993) *Exploring Educational Administration: Coherentist Applications and Critical Debates*. New York: Pergamon.

Evers, C.W. and Lakomski, G. (2000) *Doing Educational Administration: A Theory of Administrative Practice*. Oxford: Elsevier Science Ltd.

Evers, C.W. and Lakomski, G. (2001) 'Theory in Educational Administration: Naturalistic Directions', *Journal of Educational Administration*, 39(6): 499–520.

Feigl, H. (1950) 'Existential Hypotheses: Realistic versus Phenomenalistic Interpretations', *Philosophy of Science*, 52(17): 35–62.

Fenwick, T (2006) 'Tidying the Territory: Questioning Terms and Purposes in Work-learning Research', *Journal of Workplace Learning*, 18(5): 265–278.

Feyerabend, P. (1975) *Against Method: Outline of an Anarchistic Theory of Knowledge*. London: NLB; Atlantic Highlands: Humanities Press.

Fodor, J.A. (1993) 'The Persistence of the Attitudes', in Christensen, S.M. and Turner, D.R. (eds). *Folk Psychology and the Philosophy of Mind*. Hillsdale, NJ: Lawrence Erlbaum Associates.

Fodor, J.A. and Pylyshyn, Z.W. (1995) 'Connectionism and Cognitive Architecture: A Critical Analysis', in Macdonald, C. and Macdonald, G. (eds). *Connectionism: Debates on Psychological Explanation, Volume Two*. Oxford, UK: Cambridge, MA: Basil Blackwell, Ltd.

Fodor, J.A. and Lepore, E. (1996) 'Paul Churchland and State Space Semantics', in McCauley, R.N. (ed.). *The Churchlands and Their Critics*. Oxford, UK; Cambridge, MA: Basil Blackwell, Ltd.

Giere, R.N. and Moffatt, B. (2003) 'Distributed Cognition: Where the Cognitive and the Social Merge', *Social Studies of Science*, 33(2): 301–310.

Goldberg, E. (2001) *The Executive Brain: Frontal Lobes and the Civilized Mind*. Oxford: Oxford University Press.

Hacking, I. (1975) 'Why Does Language Matter to Philosophy?', *Why Does Language Matter to Philosophy*? Cambridge; London; New York; Melbourne: Cambridge University Press.

Hager, P. (1996) 'Professional Practice in Education: Research and Issues', *Australian Journal of Education*, 40(3): 235–247.

Hager, P. (2004) 'Lifelong Learning in the Workplace? Challenges and Issues', *Journal of Workplace Learning*, 16(1/2): 22–32.

Hirose, N. (2002) 'An Ecological Approach to Embodiment and Cognition', *Cognitive Systems Research*, 3: 289–299.

Hodkinson, P. (2005) 'Reconceptualising the Relations Between College-based and Workplace Learning', *Journal of Workplace Learning*, 17(8): 521–532.

Hooker, C.A. (1975) 'Philosophy and Meta-Philosophy of Science: Empiricism, Popperianism and Realism', *Synthese*, 32: 177–231.

Hutchins, E. (1996) *Cognition in the Wild*. Cambridge, MA: The MIT Press.

Kandel, E.R. and Hawkins, R.D. (1992) 'The Biological Basis of Learning and Individuality', *Scientific American*, 267(3): 52–60.

Kellenbach, M.L., Brett, M. and Patterson, K. (2003) 'Actions Speak Louder Than Functions: The Importance of Manipulability and Action in Tool Representation', *Journal of Cognitive Neuroscience*, 15(1): 30–46.

Kuhn, T.S. (1970) *The Structure of Scientific Revolutions*. (2nd edn, enlarged). Chicago: The University of Chicago Press.

Kuhne, G.W. and Quigley, B.A. (1997) 'Understanding and Using Action Research in Practice Settings', in Quigley, B.A. and Kuhne, G.W. (eds). *Creating Practical Knowledge through Action Research: Posing Problems, Solving Problems, and Improving Daily Practice*. San Francisco: Jossey-Bass.

Lave, J. (1991) 'Situated Learning in Communities of Practice', in Resnick, L.B., Levine, J.M., and Teasley, S.D. (eds). *Perspectives on Socially Shared Cognition*. Washington, DC: American Psychological Association.

Lave, J. and Wenger, E. (1991) *Situated Learning: Legitimate Peripheral Participation*. Cambridge, UK; New York: Cambridge University Press.

Lockman, J.J. (2000) 'A Perception-Action Perspective on Tool Use Development', *Child Development*, 71(1): 137–144.

Manza, L. and Reber, A.S. (1997) 'Representing Artificial Grammars: Transfer across Stimulus Forms and Modalities', in Berry, D.C. (ed.). *How Implicit Is Implicit Learning*? Oxford: Oxford University Press.

Maravita, A. and Iriki, A. (2004) 'Tools for the Body (Schema)', *Trends in Cognitive Sciences*, 8(2): 79–86.

Maravita, A., Husain, M., Clarke, K. and Driver, J. (2001) 'Reaching with a Tool Extends Visual-Tactile Interactions Into Far Space: Evidence From Cross-Modal Extinction', *Neuropsychologia*, 39: 580–585.

McClelland, J.L. (1998) 'Complementary Learning Systems in the Brain: A Connectionist Approach to Explicit and Implicit Cognition and Memory', *Annals of the New York Academy of Sciences*, 843(1): 153–169.

McClelland, J.L., McNaughton, B.L. and O'Reilly, R.C. (1995) 'Why There Are Complementary Learning Systems in the Hippocampus and Neocortex: Insights From the Successes and Failures of Connectionist Models of Learning and Memory', *Psychological Review*, 102(3): 419–457.

Merzenich, M.M. and deCharms, R.C. (1996) 'Neural Representations, Experience, and Change', *The Mind-Brain Continuum: Sensory Processes*. Llinás, R. and Churchland, P.S. (eds). Cambridge, MA: The MIT Press.

Munakata, Y. and McClelland (2003) 'Connectionist Models of Development', *Developmental Science*, 6(4): 413–429.

Orr, J.E. (1998) 'Images of Work', *Science, Technology, and Human Values*, 23(4): 439–455.

Polanyi, M. (1997) 'The Tacit Dimension', in Prusak, L. (ed.). *Knowledge in Organizations*. Boston: Butterworth-Heinemann.

Popper, K.R. (1995) *Conjectures and Refutations: The Growth of Scientific Knowledge*. London: Routledge.

Quine, W.V.O. (1951) 'Two Dogmas of Empiricism', *The Philosophical Review*, 60: 20–43.

Quine, W.V.O. (1969) 'Epistemology Naturalized', in *Ontological Relativity and Other Essays*. New York: Columbia University Press.

Quine, W.V.O. and Ullian, J.S. (1970) *The Web of Belief*. New York: Random House.

Raelin, J.A. (1998) 'Work-based Learning in Practice', *Journal of Workplace Learning*, 10(6/7): 280–283.

Raichle, M.E. (1994) 'Visualizing the Mind', *Scientific American*, 270(4): 36–42.

Reber, A.S. (1989) 'Implicit Learning and Tacit Knowledge', *Journal of Experimental Psychology: General*, 118(3): 219–235.

Reber, A.S. (1990) 'On the Primacy of the Implicit: Comments on Perruchet and Pacteau', *Journal of Experimental Psychology: General*, 119(3): 340–342.

Reber, A.S. (1992) 'The Cognitive Unconscious: An Evolutionary Perspective', *Consciousness and Cognition*, 1: 93–133.

Reber, A.S. (2004) 'Tacit Knowledge, Psychology of', *International Encyclopedia of the Social and Behavioral Sciences*, 15431–15435.

Resnick, L.B. (1987) 'Learning in School and out', *Educational Researcher*, 16(9): 13–20.

Richland, L.E., Linn, M.C. and Bjork, R.A. (2007) 'Instruction', in Durso, F.T., Nickerson, R.S., Dumais, S.T., Lewandowsky, S. and Perfect, T.J. (eds). *Handbook of Applied Cognition* (2nd edn). West Sussex, UK: John Wiley and Sons, Ltd.

Robinson, V.M.J. (2002) 'Organizational Learning, Organizational Problem Solving and Models of Mind', in Leithwood K.and Hallinger, P. (eds). *Second International Handbook of Educational Leadership and Administration*. Kluwer: Dordrecht.

Rumelhart, D.E. (1989) 'The Architecture of Mind: A Connectionist Approach', in Posner, M.I. (ed.). *Foundations of Cognitive Science*. Cambridge: MA; London, UK: The MIT Press.

Ryle, G. (1949) 'Knowing How and Knowing That', *The Concept of Mind*. Chicago: The University of Chicago Press.

Schacter, D.L. (1987) 'Implicit Memory: History and Current Status', *Journal of Experimental Psychology: Learning, Memory, and Cognition*, 13(3): 501–518.

Schoenfeld, A.H. (1999) 'Looking Toward the 21st Century: Challenges of Educational Theory and Practice', *Educational Researcher*, 28(7): 4–14.

Schön, D.A. (1995) 'Knowing-in-Action: The New Scholarship Requires a New Epistemology', *Change*, November/December.

Seger, C.A. (1994) 'Implicit Learning', *Psychological Bulletin*, 115(2): 163–196.

Sejnowski, T.J., Koch, C. and Churchland, P.S. (1988) 'Computational Neuroscience', *Science*, 241: 1299–1306.

Smolenski, P. (1988) 'On the Proper Treatment of Connectionism', *Behavioral and Brain Sciences*, 11: 1–74.

Spencer, B. (2001) 'Changing Questions of Workplace Learning Researchers', *New Directions for Adult and Continuing Education*, 92: 31–40.

Squire, L.R. (1992) 'Memory and the Hippocampus: A Synthesis from Findings with Rats, Monkeys, and Humans', *Psychological Review*, 99(2): 195–231.

St. John, M. and Shanks, D.R. (1997) 'Implicit Learning from an Information Processing Standpoint', in Berry, D.C. (ed.). *How Implicit Is Implicit Learning?* Oxford: Oxford University Press.

Stanovich, K.E. (2004) 'A Brain at War with Itself', *The Robot's Rebellion: Finding Meaning in the Age of Darwin*. Chicago and London: The University of Chicago Press.

Stich, S.P. (1983) *From Folk Psychology to Cognitive Science: The Case against Belief*. Cambridge, MA; London, UK: The MIT Press.

Stillings, N.A., Weisler, S.E., Chase, C.H., Feinstein, M.H., Garfield J.L. and Rissland E.L. (1995) *Cognitive Science: An Introduction*. (2nd edn). Cambridge, MA; London, UK: The MIT Press.

Sun, R. and Zhang, X. (2004) 'Top-Down versus Bottom-Up Learning in Cognitive Skill Acquisition', *Cognitive Systems Research*, 5: 63–89.

Torraco, R.J. (1999) 'Integrating Learning with Working: A Reconception of the Role of Workplace Learning', *Human Resource Development Quarterly*, 10(3): 249–270.

Turvey, M.T. (1996) 'Dynamic Touch', *American Psychologist*, 51(11): 1134–1152.

Williams, M. (1980) 'Coherence, Justification, and Truth', *The Review of Metaphysics*, 34: 243–272.

Yeatman, A. (1996) 'The Roles of Scientific and Non-scientific Types of Knowledge in the Improvement of Practice', *Australian Journal of Education*, 40(3): 284–301.

11

Rethinking Work-Based Learning: For Education Professionals and Professionals Who Educate

Karen Evans, David Guile and Judy Harris

INTRODUCTION

Work-based learning (WBL) is, at root, about relationships between the two fundamental human and social processes of working and learning. Different discourses about what these relationships can and should be are dominant at different times. The first challenge for professionals who aim to educate through the interplay of these two processes is to clarify the versions and values of WBL to which they subscribe. Any attempt to define the nature and scope of work-based learning brings oppositions, tensions and exclusions to the fore in ways that are far from resolution despite a burgeoning literature. This chapter argues that the relationships between work and learning have to be explored through the dynamics of different scales of activity: societal, organisational and personal.

At the heart of work-based learning lie the challenges of bringing together, at the point of use, different types of knowledge underpinned by different values and logics. Understanding how different forms of knowledge are 're-contextualised' as people move between sites of learning and practice in work, education and community settings provides new ways into longstanding and seemingly intractable problems of bringing together 'theory' and 'practice' in and through work-based learning.

RELATIONSHIPS BETWEEN WORK AND LEARNING

Among the different discourses about what the relationships between these human and social processes can and should be, neo-liberal, market driven versions have become dominant in the early twenty-first century. This dominance has been achieved in parallel with (and feeding off) moves towards economic instrumentalism as the dominant globalised discourse of 'lifelong learning'. So embedded are we in the dynamics of the 'here and now', that we sometimes lose sight of the powerful sources of alternative ideas and practices that endure over time and remain at our disposal. Rich philosophical antecedents of work-based learning in the work of Dewey, Rousseau and Gramsci are there for us to learn from. Yet the rich epistemologies of practice and work-based learning are accorded little intellectual respect in domains of higher learning, where they reside at the margins (Boud and Solomon, 2001) and go unrecognised, *incognito*, beyond them.

If the first challenge for professionals who aim to educate through the interplay of these two processes is to decide to which versions and values of WBL they should subscribe, the next challenge is to identify the spaces available that allow 'professionals who educate' to develop WBL practice in line with those versions and values. How far is it understood that versions that may be dominant now will not always be so and are far from immutable? Current discourses are always temporary settlements from which fields can and do move on.

THE NATURE AND SCOPE OF WORK-BASED LEARNING

The attempt to define and conceptualise work-based learning as a field opens up to scrutiny the oppositions, tensions and exclusions that remain far from resolution. A review of the field in 2009 has asserted that 'defining WBL is challenging as the literature is often vague and contradictory'(Burke et al., 2009). Similarly, researchers and practitioners complain of 'no agreed definitions' of workplace learning (see Jacobs and Park, 2009) a concept which overlaps with WBL, but which itself has different versions rooted in different paradigms. Some 'workplace' perspectives stem from Human Resource Development theories and perspectives, while others take social dynamics as their starting point underpinned by situated learning theories and Vygotskian traditions (see Sawchuk's themes in Chapter 12 of this volume). The latter distance themselves from positions that equate WBL with a 'class' of higher education programmes with particular characteristics (Boud and Solomon, 2001) by focusing on how work-based learning is embedded in production processes and the dynamics of the employee–employer relationship. Students on placement, and even some apprentices, have only a partial presence in these production and employment processes.

If, at their most expansive and foundational, both WBL and workplace learning are about the relationships between the human and social processes of learning and working, these relationships have to be understood both at the personal level and the organisational level (Barnett, 1999) as well as in wider societal terms. Both involve the interplay between highly complex individual and group processes and institutional practices, both recognise that 'learning is inherent in work and work in learning' (Jacobs and Park, 2009), but how these concepts are further developed and operationalised remains contested and often opaque. Attempts to construct competing conceptual frameworks have to be understood in terms of the underlying assumptions and priorities that are brought to the task in question. Where 'clarification of meaning' is sought, the purpose for which that clarification is itself being sought often introduces further sources of divergence and opposition in definitions and understandings, as different versions of the concepts are appropriated for different purposes. For example, the business and HRD purposes of using WBL as a means of 'managing employee competence' are fundamentally different from the purposes embedded in WBL frameworks for managing learning and assessment at higher education level. Different lenses lead us to different views; are these too often restricted by tunnel vision? (See Figure 11.1).

Furthermore, the debates between those who appropriate versions of WBL and WPL in order to manage learning processes according to particular contemporary sets of business or higher education interests often overlook the antecedents and traditions of learning in, for, and through work. The history of learning in and through work in apprenticeships and professional internships can be traced in accounts that go back through centuries. These portray the 'pride in practice' as well as economic exploitations that are associated with these forms of WBL. In a context in which dominant discourses are those of market-driven, economic instrumentality, ideas rooted in, for example, Gramscian celebrations of the aesthetics (see Coben, 1998; Mayo,

```
Different lenses ... tunnel visions?

'WBL'                                'Workplace Learning'

• As appropriated by HE/FE;         • HRD versions focus on
  family of programmes                'managing employee
                                       competence' – systems

• Acknowledges antecedents and      • Socio-cultural versions
  rich traditions (without            foreground learning in and
  building on them)                   through communities of social
                                      practice

• Strong focus on 'equivalence'     • New thinking at intersection of
  (for acceptance)                    industrial relations and
                                      'situated' theories of learning
```

Figure 11.1   Competing perspectives.

1999) dignity and morality of learning in work have been eclipsed but not eradicated. They co-exist and retain their power to influence and persuade, as we are reminded in the contemporary works of Sennett (1998, 2008).

EXPANDING WBL BEYOND CURRENT APPROPRIATIONS

When the origins of contemporary discourses are traced, it becomes apparent that the terminology of WBL entered the lexicon of higher education in the 1980s in the UK, and there are few instances of published work using this terminology in the English language before 1980. The same applies to 'workplace learning', of which there are few instances before Löfberg's 1989 contribution to Leymann and Kornbluh's book *Socialization and Learning at Work*. The concepts were taken up in higher-education policy discourses in the late 1980s and early 1990s with development most rapid in market-driven economies of the United States and Australia. In the UK, the Department of Employment defined work-based learning as 'The effective learning that can take place at the workplace, and not only in the formal academic setting of the lecture theatre and laboratory, and help individuals to learn through the experience of work itself' (Employment Department, 1988).

The idea that learning based on work activities could be integrated into, and possibly accredited within, academic programmes created further oppositions that are controversial both within higher education and employing organisations. The notion that such learning is 'valid and creditworthy' was, Guile (2006) argued, a clear departure from conventional higher-education thinking and practice. In the main, universities had retained the tradition of separating theory and practice and rarely offered accreditation for the latter within the structure of degree programmes (Barnett, 1994). These early debates about 'work-based learning' in higher education were centred, in the UK, on the potential and limitations of the National Council for Vocational Qualifications (NCVQ) concepts of work-based competence. Assessment became a preoccupation, with the subsequent search for equivalence through 'generic level criteria' shown to be far too narrow to embrace either the diversity of the forms of learning that occurred in workplace or to address the complex relationship between theory and practice (see for example Barnett, 1994, Evans et al., 2002, Rainbird et al., 2004). The search for wider conceptualisations of work-based learning began to focus attention on its value for organisational development as well as lifelong learning, of which the learning for 'employability' of new entrants is only one element. The European Commission Review of the state of research into 'work-related education and training (Brown and Keep, 1999) highlighted the need not only to "audit" the learning opportunities available, but also to evaluate the particular combinations of education, training, employment, and community contexts that can produce 'exceptionally rewarding learning environments' on the one hand, or 'sterility, where challenges and a series of mundane experiences lead to little learning' (p. 47). The need for deeper research-based insights into learning at, for, and through the workplace was also an important conclusion from the UK Economic and Social Research Council 'Learning Society' Programme, whose outcomes drew attention to significant gaps in knowledge and understanding of the key processes of learning as embedded in particular workplaces, in organisational structures and in specific social practices (Coffield, 2000).

'WORKPLACE' PERSPECTIVES – SCOPE AND LIMITATIONS

A first divergence between the university-appropriated conception of WBL and the concepts associated with 'workplace learning' stems from the extent to which the social dynamics of the workplace and the wider regulatory frameworks that govern the employer-employee relationship are taken into account. For 'workplace' perspectives that emphasise the social, cultural and political dynamics of workplaces, the lenses used bring into focus the work practices that other lenses sometimes miss, but can also produce 'tunnel visions' of a different kind. They distance themselves from WBL conceived of as a class of higher education programmes since such conceptions often disconnect the use of work as a resource for learning from the political realities and social relations of the workplace as experienced by employees. For those whose priorities are rooted in workplace learning, the 'work experience' or the 'placement' is seen as a source of learning which involves only a partial workplace presence. The workplace experience of the block-release or professional-year student does expose the learner to at least some of the wider aspects of workplace learning, either directly or by observation, but the placements do not embody many of the features of the employer–employee relationships that are so crucial in influencing workplace learning experiences.

In using socio-cultural lenses to focus on production, this family of approaches does reveal how learning at work is embedded in production processes and social relations. It can also offer insights into how these processes are affected by policy contexts beyond the workplace. But situated analyses of work and learning also often fail to make connections between the organised and planned (often termed 'formal') types of programmes that incorporate elements of work-based learning and the workplace learning that is embedded in 'everyday work' within the social dynamics of organisations; between the workplace and wider life–work relationships and the careers of workers as they move into and out of communities of social practice (and indeed participate in several simultaneously). When the analytic lenses of the social organisation of learning in the here and now of the enterprise are used exclusively, the learning individual is either out of focus or beyond the range of view.

A third set of perspectives attempt to find new connections that reflect fresh thinking about the nature of learning and different kinds of knowledge in the contexts of transformations of work and enterprises (Stern and Sommerlad, 1999). Can approaches which use theoretical concepts for analysing the constitution of practice as well as the problems that arise for people in their places of work, conceiving of practice as a resource to rethink theory, lead us towards a more inclusive set of understandings?

TOWARDS AN INCLUSIVE UNDERSTANDING OF WBL

Critiques of the narrowness of the early thinking about work-based learning, combined with growing interest of policymakers and providers in the field, have considerably broadened the way that thinking has subsequently developed in the UK and globally. This requires, as a first priority, the development of much better understandings of the ways in which people learn through everyday work practices. Higher education often approaches work-based learning by starting with the 'subject knowledge' and how this can be applied in work environments. Yet work-based learning usually starts in the work setting, through activities that derive their purposes from the context of employment. These activities generate the work-based knowledge that we all develop through everyday practice: intellectual resources from outside the workplace can be drawn on to deepen and expand understanding and practice. These are the processes that have to be modelled into work-based learning (together with the recognition that paid employment is not the only form of work that matters in work-based learning).

The second priority is to give renewed attention to the professionals in both the public and private sectors whose roles involve them in work-based learning. All education professionals, and professionals who educate, are engaged in their own continuing professional development, and many are responsible for supporting the work-based learning of others, through activities such as supervision, coaching and mentoring in workplace environments. This applies to professional trainers in companies; to programme leaders in NGOs; to teachers and lecturers who are workers in their colleges, viewed as workplaces; it applies to professionals and 'masterworkers' in all fields who model and share experience of practice.

The third priority is to understand better how work-based learning can be enhanced through the use of creative technologies. Drawing on new intellectual resources to deepen and expand our understanding and practice is made more possible, more feasible with digital technologies now available. 'Mobility' in learning has new meanings as the locations in which work is carried out diversify.

Can a rethought concept of WBL that goes back to the nature of these interlocking relationships break out of the narrow preoccupations with 'programmes' and 'standards' to accommodate the complexities of the social relations of production? In so doing can it offer an integrative way forward in a fragmenting field?

With the starting point that the workplace (whether in a hospital, business, voluntary organisation, school or college) is a crucially important site for learning and for access to learning, analytical perspectives on work-based learning have to take the social and organisational context of work and learning more fully into account. They also have to explore the intersection of work-based pedagogies that originate from research into how people learn in, for and through work with the further and higher-education pedagogies in which a subject-dominant starting point is applied to people at work.

The oppositions and exclusions that leave WBL weakly positioned as well as poorly defined are encapsulated in:

- tensions between participatory and acquisition views of learning;
- lack of engagement between work on learning processes and work on inequalities of access to learning;
- failure to combine organisational, individual, and wider socio-economic perspectives in much current theorising and practice;
- failure to recognise the combined significance of on-the-job, off-the-job, near-the-job learning as well as learning beyond the workplace.

These are aspects that have to be addressed in our search for ways to improve the relationship between learning and work. The relationships between work and learning have to be explored at different levels, 'zooming' in and out (to use a metaphor derived from use of an internet map or viewing tool) to gain an integrated view of the 'whole' and how the integral parts come together in ways that are best understood interdependently, holistically and in terms of location and cultural context.

An inclusive approach that expands and rethinks WBL rather than inventing yet another terminology is argued here to encapsulate:

- learning at work, for work and through work;
- .... that expands human capacities through purposeful activity;
- .... where the purposes derive from the context of employment.

This statement of scope has involved several expansions of previous positions.

At, for and through work

This is a statement of scope that expands the view of WBL as a class of programmes to encompass the 'situated' perspectives that foreground the context of employment. This expansion also has to take account of the diversity of people for whom WBL may be important and recognise that the impetus for WBL springs from many different sources.

In some conceptions, work-based learning is about 'placement' and experiences through which people coming from the world of full-time education are prepared for the 'real' world of work (see Brennan and Little, 1996). Objectives of 'graduate employability' quickly became dominant within the HE-appropriated versions of WBL, based on assumptions about disconnections between the worlds of education and employment. Yet increasing levels of paid work (to support rising costs) and unpaid work (internships/volunteering) are organised by students outside and beyond their courses, not only in the UK but globally – resulting in a generation of graduates who are better attuned to moving between contexts and settings than much policy assumes. School leavers and graduates have been deemed to 'need' work-based learning opportunities and this has become a driver for the development of work-based learning in national and international policy contexts. Yet this overlooks the main constituencies and purposes of WBL: work-based learning is 'for' people in work, at all levels of the workforce, at different ages and life stages. The purposes of WBL go far beyond those of assisting people into work by having some experience of the workplace to offer employers.

The UK Council for Industry and Higher Education (the body that promotes university–industry collaboration, with membership from both sides) opened a debate about work-based learning with a discussion paper (2005) that set out some of the challenges as its members saw them. While universities had been increasingly successful in developing new graduates for entry to employment, the engagement of universities in workforce development was portrayed as 'generally lacking'. Higher education providers, the authors argued, need to be much more focused on the learning of those who are already *in* the workplace, through development of work-based knowledge and skills, and learning undertaken *as part of* workforce development. According to whether the worker is a 'learner' preparing for work, a new entrant to work or an experienced worker developing supervisory or managerial responsibilities, learning takes place very differently depending on the specific context, on the status and role of the worker and his or her prior work and learning experience. Different types of worker-learner require different arrangements in the workplace and, where applicable, in the educational support provided beyond the workplace, to maximise learning.

Following on from the issue of 'whom is it for', is the question of whence the impetus for the work-based learning springs. WBL may start with shop floor activities that focus on 'health and safety' perhaps, or overcoming a technical problem – in which subject-based, procedural and personal forms of knowledge are utilised. The impetus may come from trade union membership or membership of a professional body. There are also aspects of WBL that are sectorally rooted. Each employment sector has its own history of policy and qualification development, its own culture of skills and practice recognition and improvement. Specific work-based learning *activities* such as projects, cases or problems can take their impetus from the job, the wider environment of work or the knowledge-base. For example, activities for a law student in an internship might start with subject knowledge and apply that to a 'real-life' problem, whereas CPD activities for a teacher or supervisor might start with a challenge encountered at work (developing a new curriculum or mentoring new staff). Finding ways of responding to unforeseen occurrences or new circumstances often engages groups and teams in specific, self-generated forms of in-company or intra-organisational WBL.

Expansion of human capacities through purposeful activity

WBL takes place individually and collectively in the workplace and beyond. One problem with value-free definitions is that they embrace the learning that the 'reasonable person' would regard as bad learning in workplaces, e.g. learning particular attitudes through cultures of institutional racism (see Allan, 2009). The literature of WBL does little to question prevalent assumptions in users of the terminology that all everyday learning at work is inherently good, despite the fact that this runs counter to the actual experience to most people who have ever participated in paid employment. Craig Johnson, in this Handbook, reminds us that there are 'negative as well as positive consequences, losers as well as winners' (see Chapter 34). An approach based on expansion of human capacities emphasises, very imperfectly, those aspects which a reasonable person would consider good. These aspects include, alongside familiar formulations of knowledge, skills and competences, the moral and aesthetic potential inherent in work, whose loss in modern day workplaces is bemoaned by writers such as Sennett in *The Corrosion of Character* (1998), and rediscovered in subsequent works such as *The Craftsman* (2008). Expansion of human capacity through purposeful activity begs the wider questions of which purposes are embraced by WBL and how these both position the learning involved and distinguish it in the broader spectrum of human learning?

The purposes of an expanded WBL, it is argued here, derive from the contexts of employment. These contexts themselves extend beyond the paid employment that is the focus for so much theorising and research, to the contexts of self-employment, contract-based employment and indeed unpaid employment in organisational contexts such as that of the voluntary or community organisation. Above all, the emphasis is on the learning that is inherent in work, and vice versa, not on the 'placement'.

The purposes that derive from the contexts of employment are:

- **Enculturation**
  – the purpose of 'learning how we do things here'. Whether in a leading blue-chip company, a local SME or NGO or a school, the impact of 'brands' and missions has made corporate enculturation processes more visible; shop floor enculturation may be compliant or resistant.
- **Competence, licence to practice**
  – the purpose of learning to achieve and perform to occupational standards, demands of increasing regulation, health and safety standards, introduction of new systems.
- **Improving practice, innovation and renewal**
  – practice improvement is a purpose that is often driven from the 'bottom up' in organisations; innovation is more often 'top down'. Increasingly employee-driven innovation is a focus of attention, with implications for knowledge flows and power relations between levels of the workforce. Learning to do what has not been done before involves significant WBL and occurs every time a new set of demands is introduced, particularly in the public sector.
- **Equity, ethics and social justice**
  – refers to the process of systematically reflecting on practice within a set of professional concerns about ethics, values, priorities and procedures. Theorising practice as a way of resolving professional concerns (Guile and Young, 1995) leads to the development and improvement of models and procedures. The organisation of learning through trades union structures and representatives foregrounds social justice; corporate social responsibility also embodies some of these purposes (see Quarter, 2000).
- **Wider capabilities**
  – This set of purposes may stem from the wider organisational context, from professional bodies or from the occupational field. It encompasses the development of professional and occupational capabilities; learning to 'do the next job' as well as the current one; learning to work in different cultures and environments. The impetus may come from the organisation or the profession as well as the individual's need for career development.
- **Vocational/professional identity development**
  – At one level, this purpose refers to new entrants 'thinking and feeling' their way into a vocation/profession and coming to identify with it and with others who participate in it. This purpose also extends to experienced workers who develop and reconstruct identities in and through work as positions, roles and contexts change (see Hodkinson et al., 2004).

The pursuit of all these purposes brings different types of knowledge (personal, procedural, ethical, propositional) with fundamentally different logics into play. At the heart of WBL lie processes of knowledge recontextualisation, as knowledge is put to work in different environments. A fresh approach developed by Evans et al. (2009) and Evans et al. (2010) concentrates on the different forms of knowledge involved, including those manifested in 'skills' and 'know how' and embedded in communities as well as in propositional knowledge. While research undertaken by Eraut (2004a, 2004b) has extensively typologised forms of knowledge used in a range of professional fields, our approach takes a different perspective. It focuses on ways in which different forms of knowledge have features and inherent 'logics' that are privileged and play out in different ways according to context. Understanding how different forms of knowledge are re-contextualised as people move between sites of learning and practice in universities, colleges and workplaces provides new ways into longstanding and seemingly intractable problems of relating 'theory' and 'practice'.

All knowledge has a context in which it was originally generated. Some knowledge is regarded as context independent, and ascribed higher status on that basis (see for example Young, 2007). Contexts are often thought of as settings or places, but contexts in our use extend to the 'schools of thought', the traditions and norms of practice, the life experiences in which knowledge of different kinds is generated. For knowledge generated and practised in one context to be put to work in new and different contexts, it has to be recontextualised in various ways that simultaneously engage with and change those practices, traditions and experiences. The starting point (Evans et al., 2009) is that recontextualisation is a multi-faceted, pedagogic practice. It refers to the idea that concepts and practice change as we use them in different settings. The research has drawn on (i) developments of Bernstein's idea that concepts change as they move from their disciplinary origins and become a part of a curriculum (Bernstein 2000; Barnett 2006), and (ii) van Oers' (1998) idea that concepts are an integral part of practice and that practice varies from one sector or workplace to another. Both of these notions have been substantially expanded in order to embrace the ways in which learners change as they recontextualise concepts and practices and the extent to which this process may spur innovation in workplaces as much as in educational contexts.

Chains of recontextualisation can be forged by practitioners, as they seek to understand and evolve practice. Four kinds of recontextualisation are significant (see Table 11.1).

Table 11.1 Four modes of recontextualisation

PKtW in the programme design environment: **Content recontextualisation**	PKTW in the workplace environment **Workplace recontextualisation**
PKTW in the teaching and facilitating learning environment **Pedagogic recontextualisation**	What the 'learner' (worker, manager, trainee. . . .) makes of it all **Learner recontextualisation**

Content recontextualisation (CR): putting knowledge to work in the programme design environment.

CR is the process by which 'codified' knowledge is selected and recast for particular learners, as part of programme design. In professional and vocational education it entails the selection and organisation of knowledge for the demands of professional and vocational practice.

Pedagogic recontextualisation (PR): putting knowledge to work in the teaching and facilitating environment.

PR involves the combination of disciplinary knowledge with practice-based knowledge and local company knowledge. PR takes place as decisions are made about organisation into learning activities, options, modules, for the purposes of teaching and learning. These decisions are never technical matters; they are influenced heavily by practitioners' assumptions about what constitutes good learning experiences and worthwhile outcomes

While the story often stops here for many forms of professional and vocational education and training, the workplace recontextualisation processes are both integral to and critical for work-based learning. Indeed, for in-house trainers and professionals who educate, the story usually starts with the work context:

Workplace recontextualisation (WR): putting knowledge to work in the workplace environment.

Workplace environments fundamentally affect how knowledge is put to work, and they vary in the nature and quality of learning experience that they afford. WR takes place through the workplace practices and activities that support knowledge development, and through the mentorship, coaching and other arrangements through which learners/employees can engage with and learn through workplace environments.

These practices and activities are fundamental to learners beginning to vary and modify existing workplace activities or to develop the confidence and capability to work with others to significantly change those activities. They allow us to see that we constantly 'progressively recontextualise' concepts in activity (for example, the concept of measurement takes many different forms in workplaces) hence pedagogic contextualisation requires a range of supports.

In the workplace, knowledge is embedded in routines, protocols and artefacts. The key challenges include learning: (i) to participate in workplace activities and use artefacts, and (ii) use work problems as a further 'test–bench' for 'curriculum' knowledge.

This is facilitated when workplaces create stretching but supportive environments for working and learning, and when learners take responsibility for 'observing, inquiring and acting'.

Learner/employee recontextualisation (LR): How the worker, whether new entrant or experienced practitioner, brings knowledge together from prior experience and from working with others to forge/reshape/develop identities.

Recontextualisation processes vary according to personal characteristics, group/cohort and the scope for action they have in any particular environment. Together with their prior learning and tacit knowledge, these may be unequally distributed (see Evans et al., 2004). Learner re-contextualisation takes place through the strategies workers themselves use to bring together knowledge gained through the programme and gleaned from working with more experienced people in the workplace. These strategies sometimes involve the creation of new knowledge, insights and activities.

Learner recontextualisation is critical to the development of a professional and/or vocational identity. For new entrants, it entails understanding and articulating the reasons for the constitution of their chosen occupation and their reasons for wanting to join it. It also influences their motivation and engagement with the other processes of recontextualisation. Learners come to self-embody knowledge cognitively and practically. For experienced practitioners, work-based learning in adult life can involve deepening experience, exploring perceived problems; drawing in new intellectual resources to rethink practice and vice versa; developing better ways of doing things; finding new directions; expanding horizons.

The dual challenge is to use knowledge as a set of resources to develop professional and academic identity together, using both curriculum and workplace knowledge as 'test-benches' for general principles and to meet academic requirements. Thinking and feeling one's way into a professional identity is facilitated by such practices as engaging in 'learning conversations' and hearing 'war stories'; voicing (articulating) developing understandings to others, being stretched through opportunities to work at the next level. Developing a professional identity evolves continuously as roles change, for example through redeployment or from front-line worker to management and to leadership or mentor roles.

Recontextualisation – putting different kinds of knowledge to work in different ways according to context – lies at the heart of WBL. Rethinking WBL in these terms moves beyond a preoccupation with 'transfer' from one setting to another. As Eraut notes elsewhere in this volume, the concept of transfer fails to recognise the higher orders of learning involved in putting it all together. In moving beyond typologies of knowledge (e.g. subject, personal, procedural, work process knowledge) towards strategies for putting different types of knowledge to work, the concept of recontextualisation allows us to:

- explain the ways in which all forms of knowledge are tied to context (settings where things are done);
- identify what actions assist people to move knowledge from context to context;

- identify how knowledge changes as it is used differently in different social practices (ways of doing things) and contexts;
- identify how new knowledge changes people, social practices and contexts;
- identify who and what supports recontextualisation processes.

The lens of *recontextualisation* focuses attention on processes involved in successfully moving knowledge between disciplines and workplaces via pedagogic strategies and through learner/ employee engagement. Some pedagogic strategies that facilitate these outcomes are 'smart' re-workings of longstanding pedagogic practices such as the 'gradual release' of knowledge and responsibility. Other strategies, such as the use of 'Industry Educators' – or 'professionals who educate' – supplement educational expertise while keeping academic requirements in view. The goals are best accomplished when a critical mass of compatibility is established between professional body, course and employer requirements.

A KEY PRINCIPLE: 'GRADUAL RELEASE'

The principle of 'gradual release' is not new. What is new is the way in which this principle can be deployed by practitioners in colleges and by workplace managers, supervisors and mentors to:

1 sequence the knowledge elements of a programme so as to develop learners' theoretical understanding iteratively with practice and development, rather than 'front-loading' the theoretical elements of the curriculum (Winch and Clarke, 2004);
2 sequence curriculum and workplace tasks along axes of time and predictability to ensure that gaps between theory and practice are surfaced and confidence is gained, rather than assume that learners will somehow 'connect' theory and practice (Guile and Young, 2003);
3 devolve responsibility to vary and eventually change practices in teaching and work teams to support their mutual development rather than assume that the workplace and curriculum are separate sites for learning (Beck, 2002).

ENACTING AND DEVELOPING NEW KNOWLEDGE

One of the biggest criticisms of the use of 'reflective' strategies in work-based learning programmes is that they are primarily designed to assist worker/learners to gain accreditation/ recognition for their existing knowledge, rather than to support them in generating and using new knowledge (Bradbury et al., 2009)

The 'learning conversation' approach offers a way to escape from this dilemma. Its key premise is that someone with extensive industry and facilitation expertise can design a conversational approach that not only recognises, but also expands employees'/learners' knowledge and puts it to work.

UTILISING ORGANISATIONAL RESOURCES

This is a generative pedagogic practice whereby company/organisational resources (documentary and human) are made available, illuminating and exploring company practices and developing learners' 'essential skills'. The following example from Evans et al., 2009 illustrates a 'double loop' in which an employee takes the company resource 'over the boundary' into college-based learning and then back into the workplace:

For one college assignment we had to present a problem in the workplace which had impacted on customer service and explain how we might resolve the issue. I selected a problem concerning a database which had many blockages. With the agreement of my manager, I was able to take screenshots of the database and collate user feedback in order to present the problem and some recommendations. Thereafter, my manager insisted that some of them be adopted; it was an excellent opportunity for me. It was a piece of work that I wouldn't have had the time to complete in the workplace but through investigation and concentration during college time I could complete the work successfully.

'USING INDUSTRY EDUCATORS AS KNOWLEDGE BROKERS'

Use of staff with up-to-date 'industry' experience as knowledge brokers goes far beyond the standard use of 'Visiting Lecturers' in programmes. Industry educators are acknowledged to make a difference when they have experienced the same (or similar) qualifying pathway as learners; they are aware of the challenges learners face and will face in future and they understand the working cultures and circumstances of the sectors and particular institutions.

Evidence demonstrates the power of learning from others' experiences, including mistakes. Industry educators, who can also be described as professionals who educate, gave examples of teaching and learning activities that helped to forge chains of recontextualisation. Drawing on knowledge of sector circumstances and the nature of financial markets in the present moment a lecturer with extensive experience in the banking sector as director of a transaction execution group talked about how, in a case study exercise, 'I might bring the theory alive by talking about things that have happened in companies – for example Northern Rock'. In another finance-sector programme, an industry educator injected a real-world perspective by recreating the thinking of the finance professional through visceral contextualisation and representation of interplays between forms of knowledge : 'I try and paint a picture – I want the students to be there in that company, feeling the anger of the dispute with the other person . . . the only way is to live it and get a sense of the reality within it. . . .' In the glass industry, an industry-educator based in the UK-wide employer organisation (GTL) facilitated learning conversations with managers as part of their management development programme. Experienced in the sector, fully conversant with the glass industry and highly qualified as an education professional, he ensured that industry life was at the heart of learning conversations that were rooted in a clearly articulated pedagogy: 'Every part of a learning conversation is steeped in company life – it has to be like that, or it won't work'. Industry educators, in short, use their experience to forge relationships between theory, sector-wide knowledge and the practices of particular organisations and particular people within those organisations. They become 'knowledge brokers'. Important as this is, it does not happen at the expense of academic and/or education-related qualifications and experience.

CONCLUSIONS

This chapter has argued for expanded, rethought versions of work-based learning embracing learning at work, for work and through work. WBL expands human capacities through purposeful activity where the purposes derive from the context of employment, including self-employment and unpaid work. These purposes range from enculturation and competence development to equity and social justice in and through the workplace; from practice improvement and innovation to the development of wider capabilities and professional identities.

At the heart of work-based learning lie the challenges of bringing together different types of knowledge underpinned by different values and logics. The longstanding language of 'transfer' hinders rather than facilitates such developments. It too easily conveys the impression that the hallmark of successful education-industry partnerships and work-based programmes consists of mechanistically transferring knowledge and practices between contexts. The concept of *recontextualisation* allows deeper insights into the processes involved. This fresh approach concentrates on the different forms of knowledge involved, going beyond the useful and illuminating work that has extensively typologised forms of knowledge used in a range of work contexts. This fresh lens focuses on ways in which different forms of knowledge have features and inherent 'logics' that are privileged and play out in different ways according to context. Understanding how different forms of knowledge are re-contextualised as people move between sites of learning and practice in universities, colleges and workplaces provides new ways into longstanding and seemingly intractable problems of relating 'theory' and 'practice'. A better purchase on these challenges is afforded by strategies such as 'gradual release' and use of industry educators, where these are planned in terms of knowledge recontextualisation and brokerage.

Moreover, WBL policies that place the emphasis on 'demand-led' education and training (E&T) and on 'skills needs' have to be supplemented by a focus on the quality and articulation of the relationship between supply of, and demand for, knowledge of different kinds in educational and workplace settings. Building such relationships is facilitated by dialogue at the local level. This has to involve stakeholders such as educational institutions, employers and employer organisations, professional institutes and employee representatives, if the wider purposes of WBL and those who engage in it are to be served.

REFERENCES

Aarkrog, V. (2003) *'The Coherence between Practice Situations and Ways of Transfer'*. Paper presented at the European Conference of Educational Research, Hamburg, Germany.

Allan, H. (2009) Negotiating supernumerary status: a new twist in the hidden curriculum in nursing? presented at the Learning to be Professional Conference, SCEPTrE, University of Surrey, Guildford April.

Allan, H.T., Larsen, J., Bryan, K. and Smith, P. (2004) 'The Social Reproduction of Institutional Racism: Internationally Recruited Nurses' Experiences of the British Health Services', *Diversity in Health and Social Care*, 1(2): 117–126.

Barnett, R. (1994) *The Limits of Competence*. Milton Keynes: Open University Press.

Barnett, R. (1999) 'Learning to Work and Working to Learn', in D. Boud and J. Garrick (eds), *Understanding Learning at Work*. London: Routledge.

Barnett, M. (2006) 'Vocational Knowledge and Vocational Pedagogy', in M. Young and J. Gamble (eds), *Knowledge, Curriculum and Qualifications for South African Further Education*. Cape Town: HSRC Press.

Beck, K. (ed.). (2002) *Teaching-Learning Processes in Vocational Education: Foundations of Modern Training Programmes*. Frankfurt am Main: Lang.

Bernstein, B. (2000) *Pedagogy, Symbolic Control and Identity: Theory, Research Critique* (revised edn). Lanham: Rowman and Littlefield.

Boud, D. and Solomon, N. (eds) (2001) *Work-Based Learning: A New Higher Education?* Buckingham: SRHE and Open University Press.

Bradbury, H., Frost, N., Kilminster, S. and Zukas, M. (2009) *Beyond Reflective Practice: New Approaches to Professional Lifelong Learning*. Abingdon: Routledge.

Brennan, J. and Little, B. (1996) *A Review of Work-Based Learning in Higher Education*. London: Department of Education and Employment.

Brown, A. and Keep, E. (1999) *Review of Vocational Education and Training Research in the United Kingdom* EUR 19243, COST Action A11, Luxembourg: European Commission.

Burke, L. Marks-Maran, D.J., Ooms, A., Webb, M. and Cooper, D. (2009) 'Towards a Pedagogy of Work-Based Learning: Perceptions of Work-Based Learning in Foundation Degrees', *Journal of Vocational Education and Training*, 61(1): 15–34.

Chambers, D. (2007) 'Is the Modern NHS Fit for Nursing Students?', *British Journal of Nursing*, 16(2): 74–75.

Council for Industry and Higher Education (2005) *Workforce Development and Higher Education*. London: CIHE.

Coben, D. (1998) *Radical Heroes: Gramsci, Freire and the Poitics of Adult Education*. Garland Reference Library of Social Science.

Coffield, F. (ed.) (2000) *The Necessity of Informal Learning*. Bristol: Polity Press in Association with the ESRC Learning Society Programme.

Davies, C. (1995) *Gender and the Professional Predicament of Nursing*. Buckingham: Open University Press.

Dewey, J. (1938) *Experience and Education*. New York: Collier Books.

Employment Department (1988) *Employment for the 1990s*. Norwich: HMSO.

Entwhistle, H. (1979) *Antonia Gramsci: Conservative Schooling for Radical Politics*. London: Routledge and Kegan Paul.

Eraut, M. (2004a) *Developing Professional Knowledge: A Review of Progress and Practice*. London: Falmer Press.

Eraut, M. (2004b) 'Informal Learning in the Workplace', *Studies in Continuing Education*, 26(2): 247–274.

Evans, K. (2009) *Learning Work and Social Responsibility: Challenges for Lifelong Learning in a Global Age*. Dordrecht: Springer.

Evans, K., Hodkinson, P. and Unwin, L. (eds) (2002) *Working to Learn: Transforming Learning in the Workplace*. London: Routledge.

Evans, K., Kersh, N., Kontiainen, S. (2004) 'Recognition of Tacit Skills: Sustaining Learning Outcomes in Adult Learning and Work – Re-entry', *International Journal of Training and Development*, Vol 8: 54–72.

Evans, K., Hodkinson, P. Rainbird, H. and Unwin, L. (2006) *Improving Workplace Learning*. Abingdon: Routledge.

Evans, K., Guile, D., Harris, J. (2009) *Putting Knowledge to Work*. London: Institute of Education, University of London (WLE Centre) www.wlecentre.ac.uk

Evans, K., Guile, D., Harris, J. and Allan, H. (2010) *Putting Knowledge to Work: A New Approach* in Nurse Education Today. Special Issue on Leadership in Learning , Vol 30: 245–251.

Felstead, A., Fuller, A., Jewson, N. and Unwin, L. (2009) *Improving Work as Learning*. Abingdon: Routledge.

Guile, D. (2006) 'Learning Across Contexts', *Educational Philosophy and Theory*, 38(3): 251–268.

Guile, D. and Young, M. (1995) '*Further Professional Development and FE Teachers: Setting a New Agenda for Work-Based Learning*', in I. Woodward (ed.) *Continuing Professional Development Issues in Design and Delivery*. London: Cassell, pp 235–268.

Guile, D. and Young, M.F.D. (2003) 'Transfer and Transition in Vocational Education: Some Theoretical Considerations', in T. Tuomi-Gröhn and Y. Engeström (eds), *Between School and Work: New Perspectives on Transfer and Boundary Crossing*. Amsterdam: Elsevier.

Hodkinson, P., Hodkinson, H., Evans, K. and Kersh, N. (2004) 'The Significance of Individual Biography in Workplace Learning', *Studies in the Education of Adults*, 36(1): 6–25.

Jacobs, R.L. and Park, Y. (2009) 'A Proposed Conceptual Framework of Workplace Learning: Implications for Theory Development and Research in Human Resource Development', *Human Resource Development Review*, 8(2): 133–222.

Larsen, J., Allan, H.T., Bryan, K. and Smith, P. (2005) 'Overseas' Nurses Motives for Working in The UK: Global Perspectives or Local Prejudice', *Work, Employment & Society*, 19(2): 349–368.

Löfberg, A. (1989) 'Learning and Educational Intervention from a Constructivist Point of View: The Case of Workplace Learning', in H. Leymann and H. Kornbluh (eds), *Socialization and Learning at Work: A New Approach to the Learning Process in the Workplace and Society*. Aldershot: Avebury.

Mayo, P. (1999) *Gramsci, Freire and Adult Education Possibilities for Transformative Action*. London: Palgrave.

Quarter, J. (2000) *Beyond The Bottom Line*. Westport, CT: Quorum Books.

Rainbird, H., Fuller, A. and Munro, A. (2004) *Workplace Learning in Context*. Abingdon: Routledge.

Rousseau, J-J (1979, original work published 1762) *Émile or, On Education* (translated by A. Bloom). New York: Basic.

Sennett, R. (1998) *The Corrosion of Character: The Personal Consequences of Work in the New Capitalism*. New York: Norton.

Sennett, R. (2008) *The Craftsman*. New Haven, CA: Yale University Press.

Spouse, J. (1998) 'Learning to Nurse through Legitimate Peripheral Participation', *Nurse Education Today*, 18: 345–351.

Stern, E. and Sommerlad, E. (1999) *Workplace Learning, Culture and Performance*. London: Institute of Personnel and Development.

van Oers, B. (1998) 'The Fallacy of Decontextualisation', *Mind, Culture and Activity*, 5(2): 143–152.

Whitehead, W. (2009) 'The Case of Commerzbank Presentation at the Putting Knowledge to Work'. WLE Centre, Institute of Education, London February 11.

Winch, C. and Clarke, L. (2004) 'Front-Loaded Vocational Education versus Lifelong Learning: A Critique of Current UK Government Policy', *Oxford Review of Education*, 29(2): 239–252.

Young, M. (2007) *Bringing Knowledge Back In*. Abingdon: Routledge.

Research and Practice

INTRODUCTION

An extensive and intense agenda for researching work, workplaces and the way individuals and organizations benefit and interact through this research work, has been built up internationally for over two decades with increasing vigour. The reflexive relationships between research and practice are yielding significant insights and development.

Section 2 explores this reflexive relationship by showing how international research themes and associated theories are reflected, contested and reconstructed in the ways in which people across the globe are investigating and developing practice at local/national levels. The contributions in this section have been selected to show how different social, cultural and organizational/institutional contexts of work and learning impact on the development of practice, and how the lessons learned from researching the diversity of practice are advancing concepts, understandings and theories of workplace learning at international level.

The section is introduced by two contributions that, respectively, map the research field (Sawchuk) and elaborate tools for enhancing the practices of workplace learning (Eraut). In Sawchuk's overview, the most influential 'lines of research inquiry' in the field are organized and critiqued under six headings: (i) cognition, expertise and the individual; (ii) micro-interaction, cognition and communication; (iii) mediated practice and participation; (iv) meaning, identity and organizational life; (v) authority, conflict and control; and finally, (vi) competitiveness and knowledge management. The conclusion that important gaps can be filled and insights deepened by open-minded dialogue underlines the intention behind the varied and diverse combination of contributions to this section as well as their connections to the volume as a whole. Eraut's contribution plays a crucial role in linking research directly to practice by showing how researching workplace learning can lead, through careful interrogation of practice into intellectual and practical tools for enhancing learning that have the potential to connect as well as to deepen lines of inquiry.

Overviews of priorities and trends in researching workplace learning from several continents lead into the selected examples of how contrasting theoretical frameworks and approaches are utilized in understanding and attempting to enhance practice in relating the two human and social processes of working and learning. North American perspectives reviewed in Marsick, Watkins and O'Connor's chapter 'Researching Workplace Learning in the United States' are problematized by Dirkx's 'paradigm shifts' and Fenwick's chapter on knowledge discourses, rooted in insights from Canadian policy and practice. Turning to another continent, the overview of Australian workplace learning research offered by Solomon and Boud argues for the superiority of particular lines of inquiry, while contrasting insights are offered by Clemans and Rushbrook and contributions by Australia-based authors in other parts of the volume. A mapping of European perspectives, which cover even more complex mixes of cultural contexts and competing traditions, is a challenge met by Harteis and Gruber in their discussion of a growing field of research and practice. The contribution by Sang-Duk Choi positions Korea in the wider Asian regional context and draws attention, in its focus on the development state, to the pitfalls of attempting wider regional generalizations.

The interrogation of programmes, policies and associated practices provides further insights into how people learn and develop in workplaces and around the notion of 'work', revealing cultural differences in each context, in what is assumed, emphasized and ignored. The sites include small- and medium-sized enterprises and larger organizations, with a focus on active programmes, directions and ideas in practice. Some of these throw into sharp relief the practice issues raised by globalized production strategies, for example, Mulder and Gulikers. The mix of papers combines hot topics such as virtual learning as presented by Brookshire, Lybarger and Keane as well as the enduring challenges of linking schools and workplaces addressed by Lakes. The section ends with new insights important for understandings of the social ecologies of workplace learning, and organizational practices are suggested by the Evans, Waite and Kersh chapter on workplace literacy learning, Beatty's view of workplace learning through an emotional lens, and Naegele and Walker's 'corporate age management' perspective on the challenges of older workers. These contributions engage with relatively under-researched topics and questions that will take their place in the 'researching work and practice' agendas of the future.

12

Researching Workplace Learning: An Overview and Critique

Peter H. Sawchuk

INTRODUCTION

The aim of this chapter is to build further awareness of the key conceptual themes of workplace learning research across the international scene. This aim brings with it many challenges. The challenges are rooted in the inter-disciplinary nature of the field, the ubiquity and multi-dimensionality of human learning that demands a plurality of approaches, and a range of subtle and not-so-subtle conceptual, epistemological and even ontological differences and preoccupations.

The chapter begins with a brief introductory 'assay' of the current research literature focusing on major perspectives in the field. It seeks to provide additional information to extend the introductory comments for the *Handbook* as a whole. For the remaining bulk of the chapter, I seek to profile the most robust 'lines of research inquiry' and key scholars associated with them. Six such lines of inquiry are discussed: (i) cognition, expertise and the individual; (ii) micro-interaction, cognition and communication; (iii) mediated practice and participation; (iv) meaning, identity and organizational life; (v) authority, conflict and control; and finally, (vi) competitiveness and knowledge management. Critical engagement with these ideas focuses on how they fill important gaps and deepen the intellectual value of workplace learning research as a whole. I conclude with comments urging (renewed) efforts at dialogue given the complexity, the multiple and sometimes conflicting vantage points, and importance of workplace learning to individuals, groups, organizations, governments and society as a whole.

ASSAYING RECENT WORKPLACE LEARNING RESEARCH: A STARTING POINT

The field of workplace learning research from the final quarter of the twentieth and into the twenty-first century has demonstrated an accelerated expansion of conceptualizations, dissection and even vivisection (by action and interventionist researchers). The multi-disciplinarity of the literature has seen a proliferation of identified skill types: from common notions of 'soft' and 'hard' skills, general education and vocationally specific skills, literacy, communication, comprehension, multi-tasking skills, procedural and declarative knowledge, through to somewhat more theoretically robust formulations of such things as work-related emotional skill, articulation skill, relational skills and aesthetic skill. And, the proliferation (helpful, rhetorical or otherwise) does not end there. Conceptualization of work-related learning processes has expanded as well. It is now common currency among researchers to recognize not simply individual, taught, self-directed learning, but that learning also includes formal, non-formal, informal and tacit aspects, experiential and incidental learning, reflective learning, legitimate peripheral participation, and learning 'activity' to name only a sampling. In turn, debate has moved in ever-widening circles from individual cognition to include emotion, biography, identity and meaning, power and resistance, social legitimacy and illegitimacy, and the social constructivist roles of communities of practice, meditational processes and participatory structures at the firm, sector, national and international levels. To make sense of the state of the field today, I begin with a brief introduction to what are often referred to in the literature as 'managerialist' and 'critical' perspectives as a necessary but likely insufficient means of orienting to the research.

Many managerialist perspectives on workplace learning emphasize the development of human assets, organizational commitment, flexibility and sustainable competitive advantage. In many instances these are matters of immediate economic survival for a firm, and in turn the workers, families and communities that have come to depend on them. But even from a managerial perspective, it is important to register that many workplace learning researchers recognize that workplace learning mediated by power relations (e.g. positional differences such as manager, supervisor, employee, as well as broader social differences across gender, race and disability and beyond). A good deal of this research has recognized the contradictory challenges of capitalist employment relations specifically, the way organizations both control and activate human capacities, freedoms and agency (Argyris and Schön, 1978; Coopey, 1996). Identified some time ago, a prominent goal in these terms is to have workers want to become flexible and agile human resources through processes such as reflective learning to generate the capacity to learn 'faster' than those in other organizations (e.g. Dixon, 1992). Likewise, Kochan et al. (1984) advise those firms adopting a 'mutual commitment' strategy to gain competitive advantage to make the necessary investment in their workforce and adopt concerns for lifelong learning (Bratton and Gold, 2003).

Other workplace learning researchers raise more fundamental concerns over arrangements of the contemporary workplace and seek to illuminate and analyze power relations, politics and conflicts of interest shape skill, knowledge and learning in a more radical way. Taking what is often called a 'critical approach', such researchers have developed sophisticated analyses of 'cultural control' through workplace learning (e.g. Legge, 1995; Solomon, 2001) and investigate how the training of 'competencies' can render work more 'visible' in order to be more controllable (e.g. Townley, 1994; Illeris, 2009). From this perspective, it is often argued that underpinning notions of 'high quality', 'flexible specialization', 'functional flexibility', 'information' or 'knowledge' work are presumptions that the present workforce lacks the relevant capacities to compete effectively (e.g. Livingstone, 2004). Critical studies reveal, however, that only a slim proportion of these worker learning capacities are effectively utilized in the labour process itself. And moreover, training and learning opportunities are unevenly distributed across social groups. That is, for example, 'peripheral' workers (as well as women, visible minorities, and young workers) tend to receive the lowest level of training (Ashton and Felstead, 2001; Livingstone and Sawchuk, 2004).

Leaving aside the distinctions between managerial and critical perspectives, some researchers have carried out careful reviews of thematic trends. A key example in this regard is found in the work of Fenwick (e.g. 2006, 2008).[1] Her review of research on the themes of work and learning reveals some important trends. For example, she shows persistent ambiguities in terms of 'learning as outcome', 'learning as process' and 'learning as experience', concluding in part that '... without better conceptual clarity, different researchers claiming to examine learning and its relationships with various contexts of work may be studying phenomena wholly different in kind, and generating more mutual confusion than enrichment' (2006, p. 266). Elsewhere Fenwick reveals that the individual as the point of analytic departure retains an important, foundational presence in the field (even when notions of communities and groups are considered), irrespective of the perceived onslaught of organizational, cultural or participatory approaches. A rough tabulation based on Fenwick's work suggests that approximately two-thirds of the research journal articles of the field take individualist approaches. She goes on to show that there remains a disconnection between learning and power relations within many research approaches, a tendency for instrumental orientations in network analysis, and a tendency for those interested in analyzing levels (individual, team, project, organization) to do so in static rather than dynamic ways. Most broadly, Fenwick suggests the tendency of self-referentialism with frequent calls for research in areas that are well-undertaken in other disciplines while at the same time 'theorizing subtle dynamics of learning processes, and drawing upon wide-ranging theoretical bases to do so' (Fenwick, 2008, p. 239–240).

However, I recommend that this basic recognition of managerial and critical perspectives on the one hand, paired with the type of thematic analysis on the other, can be further complemented. I suggest that this can be done by seeking to identify the most *robust* workplace learning research programmes.

CONTEMPORARY LINES OF RESEARCH INQUIRY

A comparison of themes and representative models

Based on a review of journals as well as edited collections and monographs that explicitly fixate on forms and processes of work-related learning and knowledge development below I identify several robust centres of research interest. I identify these based on several general principles. That is, they display the capacity to articulate *more whole rather than less whole* models of *both* work *and* learning; they *orient to broader theoretical positions* on the nature of the individual, the social and the institution of work and economy. Moreover, robust research is embedded in well constructed *empirical* programs which virtually always offer *a challenge to mechanistic view of reality*. That is, phenomena such as cooperation and conflict, human agency and freedoms, *as well as* determinations and structure, are each fundamental to reality, yet only in robust lines of inquiry are they both articulated. Most importantly, robust research tends to explicitly recognize the inherent *value-laden or political nature* of workplace learning. Such principles are of course relatively independent of topic and method choice, and thus my basic point here is simply this: under conditions of multi-focal and multi-disciplinary research there is much to be gained by moving beyond matters of topic and method. With these selection principles in mind, the following six themes offer what I believe to be the most robust, contemporary research programmes with something to teach us all.

Cognition, expertise and the individual

The themes of cognition, expertise and the individual remain key entry points for a great deal of workplace learning research as I have suggested. In this regard it is relevant to begin by noting the work of Michael Eraut, which is among the most widely cited workplace learning research today. Eraut outlines his work in another chapter of this *Handbook*, thus I need only to summarize its key aspects beginning with the fact that his work remains particularly central to analysis of professional development. He has offered an approach that incorporates many elements that make up the phenomenon of workplace learning based on extensive empirical exploration, testing and application to policy and practice. Conceptually, the strengths of Eraut's core set of models (e.g. 2000, 2004, 2008) is that they build on a number of inter-linked conceptual frameworks to produce an interactive typology of modes of learning, temporal trajectories anchored by an explicit epistemology of practice. His approach emphasizes levels of information processing from unconscious and implicit processing to conscious, goal-directed problem-solving, and demonstrates the many dimensions of workplace learning involving different functions of memory, reflection, discussion and planning (see Figure 12.1). Among other things, the work provides a key means of assessing the formal/informal continuum of workplace

Time of focus	Implicit learning	Reactive learning	Deliberative learning
Past episode(s)	Implicit linkage of past memories with current experience	Brief near-spontaneous reflection on past episodes, events, incidents, experiences	*Discussion* and review of past actions, communications, events, experiences
Current experience	A selection from experience enters episodic memory	*Noting* facts, ideas, opinions, impression; *asking* questions; observing effects of actions	*Engagement* in decision making, problem solving, planned informal learning
Future behaviour	Unconscious expectations	*Recognition* of possible future learning, opportunities	*planning* learning opportunities; *rehearsing* for future events

Figure 12.1   Eraut's typology of informal learning.
Source: From Eraut (2004, p. 250)

learning inclusive of its implicit and tacit aspects: i.e., 'the acquisition of knowledge independently of conscious attempts to learn and the absence of explicit knowledge about what was learned' (Eraut, 2000, p. 12).

It is worthwhile pointing out that as a key example of professional work and learning specifically, the topic itself demands the fore-fronting of matters of autonomy and creativity that are shaped by the normative character of these types of labour. Thus, in place of a framing of learning amidst conditions of structural conflict, alienation or resistance for example, we tend to see the challenges of workplace learning cast as barriers to professional development – a subtle but important distinction. It is in the professionalized work context that the distinctions between informal and formal knowledge and, specifically, the questioning of traditional modes of transmission of stable knowledge forms becomes a distinctively loaded concern. But what may be of particular interest in these terms is the prominence of various types of planning functions in Eraut's work. In fact, Eraut's approach recognizes that the goal of 'learning' in the workplace is regularly subsumed by other matters (outputs, professional socialization and so on; all of which could, in principle be extended to deal with a wider range of labour processes). This, I suggest, forms an important means of cracking the code of the mutually constituting relations across implicit, explicit, reactive or deliberative moments, and thus moves us closer toward an integrated model of formal/informal learning.

The work of many leading researchers complements and extends Eraut's typology of informal learning. In the area of professional development the work of Ellström (2001), Järvinen and Poikela (2001), Ericsson et al. (2006) as well as contributors within Boshuizen et al. (2004), for example, provide additional detail to the role of other cognitive dimensions of workplace learning including memory. Bauer and Gruber (2007) specifically draw on this research to explain, advocate for and extend what they refer to as a micro perspective on expert domains of work knowledge with special attention to script theory. The work of Beckett and Hager (2000, 2002) offer yet another complement (and in several ways a counter-point) to the basic themes of Eraut's work. They provide an alternative epistemology of practice, adding detail on the nature and role of judgement across conditions of contingency, practicality and the particularities of context addressing the embodied and holist nature of professional working knowledge.

Other, more general starting points for research within this theme involve a concern for learning transfer. In fact, stemming from a concern to re-establish a research focus on the individual learner against the perceived 'panacea' of contextual, social constructivist and participatory systems analysis, Cheng and Hampson (2008) provide an excellent updating of the case for sustaining research interest in learning transfer. Drawing on a theory of planned behaviour (which focuses on intentions and antecedents), these authors conclude with that skill use and transfer should remain the keystone measure of training *vis-à-vis* the individual.[2]

These and related approaches are, I suggest, a logical expression of both the cognitivist as well as the predominantly individualist approach that characterizes this first theme. These are hardly exhaustive of the interests relatable to the topic area of cognition, expertise and the individual. As the brief review of Fenwick's (2008) discussion of approaches to the individual and collective dimensions of workplace learning showed earlier, individual approaches retain a powerful place in the field, and I argue here that research into workplace learning would almost certainly be undermined were such concerns marginalized. There are, however, decidedly less individualized ways of approaching cognition and expertise. Among these is a tradition of workplace studies that focuses on micro-interaction.

Micro-interaction, cognition and communication

Quoting Harold Garfinkel, the originator of the field of 'ethnomethodology', Engeström and Middleton (1998, p. 2) tell us that 'there exists a locally produced order of work's things; that they make up a massive domain of organization phenomena; that classic studies of work, without remedy or alternative, depend upon the existence of these phenomena, make use of the domain, and ignore it'. Rawls (2008) draws a tight linkage between Garfinkel's work and workplace studies as the science of exploring the 'taken-for-granted methods of producing order that constitute sense – accompanied by displays of attention, competence and trust' (p. 701). While ethnomethodology is far from the only approach to interaction, cognition and communication, it does make for a fitting introduction to this brief section. Clearly, these are matters of potential interest to those researching workplace learning.

Within the fields of pragmatics, communications, ethnomethodology, conversation analysis, actor network theory, symbolic interactionism and an extended family of other approaches there is a range of researchers who have for several decades sought to pay careful attention to micro-interactional achievements that underwrite both work and learning processes. Importantly, they do not rely on survey, interview or other self-report methods. As is noted in Luff et al. (2000), this tradition focuses on strips of naturally occurring interaction and talk (e.g. Drew and Heritage, 1992). Roughly speaking, this field of studies has both a *language arm* emerging with a focus on talk and roots in discourse analysis, socio-linguistics, speech act theory, semiotics and conversation analysis,[3] as well as an arm exploring *material practices and interaction*,[4] the latter with roots in studies of science and ethnomethodology but covering a variety of forms of work.

Of these, the lineage that began with investigation of scientific workplaces specifically (e.g. Latour and Woolgar, 1979; Knorr-Cetina and Mulkay, 1983; Latour, 1992; Pickering, 1992) appears to have remained strong. But Suchman's (1987) ground-breaking study of human-machine interaction is just as seminal. And since then, robust approaches to work analysis of this type have included detailed studies of virtually any activity where quality recorded data of actual participatory events can be gathered or accessed. Much recent research has dealt with the role of work and technological design (e.g. Luff et al., 2000) including but not limited to research originating from human-computer interaction and computer-supported cooperative work. Such research asks how everyday environments shape communication and cognition; how, for example, the use, misuse and alternative uses of computer artefacts leads to reproduction as well as change in workplace cultures; how, for example, interaction at work is either organized or disorganized by changing goals and objects of work.

Analyses emerging from these types of methods have been able to detail the local invention and reproduction of 'mindful practice' (see Engeström and Middleton, 1998) at the individual and collective level, as well as the process through which expert practice comes about on an everyday basis. The collection edited by Pickering (1992) summarizes this general perspective with its focus on how 'practice' is actually carried out in ways not generally recognized by actors themselves addressing its implications for work organizations. A problem from the perspective of workplace learning research, however, is that such researchers tend to carry out analysis without reference to 'learning' *per se*. The suggestion here, however, is that this should not be viewed as a serious limit to workplace learning researchers. After all, it answers many questions. How exactly do we know 'workplace learning' when we see it? And perhaps in particular, what exactly is the nature of on-the-job and informal learning that seems to make up so much of the skill and knowledge development and acquisition process?

In relation to the goals of this chapter the distinctive origins and contributions of this cluster of approaches retains relevance. It links us to an alternative perspective on matters of cognition and mindful practice in the course of moment-by-moment micro-interaction, as an unfolding accomplishment. At the same time, however, not unlike the research discussed in the previous section, it tends to marginalize a number of important questions, such as the broader organizational context as well as the broader structures of participation and the many factors that shape or mediate the types of interaction that ultimately produce learning at work.

Mediated practice and participation

There are a variety of researchers that can be drawn on in order to illustrate this theme as well. However, if we wish to begin with a focus on particular researchers, two contributions stand out. The first is found in the work of Yrjö Engeström. Like Eraut, Engeström offers a profile of his work in this *Handbook*, so only a brief introduction is offered here. The key orienting theoretical school for Engeström (e.g. 1987, 1990, 2001, 2008) is what is known as Cultural Historical Activity Theory (CHAT). It is a tradition that builds originally on the Marxist-inspired research of the Russian psychologists L.S. Vygotsky, A.N. Leontiev and others, to make the claim that learning must be considered in terms of how external social-material relations of mediation and participation are inseparable from, but also functionally prior to, individual skill and knowledge capacity: a claim that provides a valuable complement (or counter-point) to the largely cognitivist and/or individualized approaches seen earlier. That is, what most people think of as skill and knowledgeability, in the conventional sense, may be seen as a by-product and currency of practice rather than a function of individualized cognitive processes.

Engeström's (1987) seminal work frames learning as a participatory structure defined in the CHAT tradition as *activity*. Activity composes a specific set of 'object-related' practices: broadly speaking, practices organized by broader collective purposes that define the individual, self-conscious and un-self-conscious, roles, operations and artefacts use of which it is composed. Thus activity is defined as the system through which individuals and groups engage in social action mediated by material things or tools, symbols/discourses, rules and divisions of labour taken together as an activity system is said to be the minimal, meaningful unit of analysis of human development at the workplace or elsewhere. Building on the founders' earlier work, Engeström's approach maintains that systems of activity include the broader social-structural *motives/objects* (e.g. the broader relations and forces of production), self-conscious *goals* and *action* (e.g. work tasks), as well as tacit *operations* (e.g. the local social and material conditions within which task are accomplished). Importantly, this transcends the boundaries of many approaches to the learning process which fixate on formal, informal, experiential, self-directed, reflective and tacit. Such a position loosely parallels aspects of a similar point offered by Billett (2002) that the distinction between formal and informal learning may in fact be unhelpful to researchers, if not altogether spurious.

Approaches to workplace learning that forefront participation are not limited to CHAT. The second major tradition within this theme is, of course, the pervasive theories of situated learning, legitimate peripheral participation and communities of practice. Situated learning approaches are typically associated with the work of Lave and Wenger (1991). In their seminal text, they draw on ethnographic materials inclusive of several workplace examples to provide a programme of inquiry into learning as a dimension of social practice generally.

Social practice is the primary, generative phenomenon, and learning is one of its characteristics. ... [It] is an integral part of a generative social practice in the lived-in world ... Legitimate peripherality is a complex notion, implicated in social structures involving relations of power ... [It] can be a position at the articulation of related communities. In this sense, it can itself be a source of power or powerlessness, in affording or preventing articulation and interchange among communities of practice (1991, pp. 34–36).

A host of researchers have drawn on situated learning and community of practice concepts, but among the most effective, recent examples are those emerging from a community of British researchers (see Fuller and Unwin, 2003; Evans et al., 2003; Fuller et al., 2005; Felstead et al., 2005; Evans et al., 2006; Felstead et al., 2007; Fuller et al., 2007; Kakavelakis et al., 2008) who have offered both conceptual expansion and effective application. While situated learning is not the only conceptual preoccupation of these researchers, they have effectively explored gaps in the tradition. Specifically, they pay close attention to the specific effects of economic context, mediations and relations specific to employment which are shown to be under-articulated in Lave and Wenger's original work. Notably, they build a deeper understanding of barriers and the definitions of communities from employee perspectives. In fact, this cluster of research offers a key example of the types of bridges that can be built across those researchers beginning from an interest in participatory structures on the one hand, and those interested in matters of conflict and control, and those interested in identity and meaning on the other.

As a whole, researchers associated with this theme seek integrated analysis. Whether it is artefacts or relational mediations by elements of a community of practice, we see exemplars of how individuals, groups as well as the many things that enable and shape their participation and learning are inseparable from one another (see Niewolny and Wilson, 2009). Though at the same time, in some criticisms of the approach we see claims that the individual herself, her identity and attempts to generate meaning are at times sacrificed. Whether this claim can be sustained or not, the fact remains that there are other researchers who take up these very issues as their core point of departure.

Meaning, identity and organizational life

Among these multiple projects, the themes of meaning, identity and organizational life have developed into a central set of concerns in the field of workplace learning research over the past two decades. Of the contemporary scholars who have developed robust lines of research inquiry in this area the work of Sylvia Gherardi stands out. In one sense, her work has taken a series of learning topics as grounded examples with which to flesh out dynamics associated with broader concerns over the nature of organizational life. Perhaps what is most impressive is the diversity of topics through which we see active concern for matters of subjective and objective reality, agency and structure and organizational change processes.

Among her goals is the broadening of the dimensions of organizational knowledge, its production/reproduction and its relationship to identity and meaning. Gherardi and colleagues seek to challenge the uni-dimensional and hierarchically ordered dimensions of organizational knowledge in these terms. In this sense, there is an implicit orientation to analysis of power relations in learning and work. For example, together with Nicolinia and Strati, Gherardi demonstrates a keen interest in balancing economic with subjective human needs in their research on 'passion ... expressive relations and attachment' (2007, p. 315). Analysis in Bruni, Gherardi and Poggio (2004) further strengthens the case for multi-dimensionality of organizational knowledge in relation to gendered/hetero-normative construction of entrepreneurial activity. Here the authors draw on feminist theory of identity among other traditions to study gendered identities at the level of interactions and discursive practices. Gherardi's research highlights the 'how' of the workplace learning process drawing on the subject's use of language to produce fine-grained accounts on the presentation of self and 'footing' in interviews, of a gendered 'dual presence', matters of legitimacy and more generally the importance that detailed empirical work provides of the divisional structures (male/female; homo-/hetero-sexual) and the spaces of organizational life 'breached ... negated', 'blurred, crossed and denied' (2004, pp. 423, 418–419). Gherardi's recent publication (Gherardi, 2007) offers an accumulation of earlier insights. Her preliminary discussion of the texture of workplace organizations, learning and 'knowing-in-practice' (2004; Gherardi and Nicolini, 2000) is further expanded. The empirical focus is on workplace safety as a learning process. In it safety is understood as a property emerging from the ordering of identities, technologies and knowledge in an organizational network, a specific form of knowing and organizational expertise. Again identity has a key role.

An important question that emerges in Gherardi's work concerns the degree to which it goes beyond an account of adaptation to organizational norms *vis-à-vis* work and learning processes. We find rich analyses of transgression (e.g. in her analysis of gender and sexuality at work) though in her latest work on safety, a concern for breakdowns, repairs, mending, darning, quilting practices appears inherently to orient toward a return to organizational normalcy of one type or another. In this sense, what becomes less clear is how these processes relate to forms of both organizational and broader social and economic change dynamics (cf. Gherardi, 2006; Gherardi and Nicolini, 2000; Gherardi, 2004; Gherardi et al., 2007).

In many ways, Gherardi's research speaks to the current status of organizational learning approaches generally. Organizational learning is, from this perspective, a process of 'knowing-in-practice' incorporating formalized, informal and tacit dimensions. Derived from this, organizational knowledge is seen as having the following characteristics: it is situational, relational, continually translated into practice, dynamic and provisional (Gherardi 2004, p. 62). Notably, these characteristics of organizational knowledge include attention to the role of memory. In these terms, there are a number of potential points of contact between Gherardi's work and that of Eraut or even several of the micro-interactionists discussed earlier.

Gherardi's work is obviously not alone in its concerns for these areas. Building on earlier work (e.g. Usher and Solomon, 1999) and incorporating scholars associated with the discursive and cultural turn in the analysis of workplaces in the 1990s (e.g. Anthony, 1994; Du Gay, 1996; Gee et al., 1996), Solomon (2001) offers another key example of additional workplace learning research in this area. She has shown that matters of meaning and the shaping of identities by organizational environments and managerial technique represent a crucial dimension of workplace learning:

> [C]ulture today has a privileged position due to its endeavour to structure the way people think, feel, and act in organizations. Although it may be tempting to accept and understand culture as a cliché or a fad, by doing so we would be overlooking its power as one of the key technologies for managing work and managing people (p. 41).

This link between identity, culture and control in workplace learning is further developed in the collection edited by Billet et al. (2006; see also discussions in Fenwick 2001, 2008). Among the most important advances here is not simply the recognition of the role of identity in processes of control, but, going a step further, its role in creative, subversive and resistant responses in the workplace, including the learning associated with self-invention. Thus, while work such as Gherardi and associates offers a leading, contemporary example of the development of meaning, identity and organization, we see in this theme area a concern for matters of power, conflict and control: a theme that is addressed in a somewhat different way in our next section.

Authority, conflict and control

To this point, we have seen that while questions of conflict and control have been entertained within several other theme areas, they are not typically the core focus, nor are they typically understood as inherent elements of workplace learning (or society) itself. In a series of articles beginning in the late 1990s driven by the need to understand the nature of informal learning in relation to other forms of learning and an interest in generating aggregate estimates of levels of activity, D.W. Livingstone established national networks of informal learning research focused

	Primary Agency	
	Learner(s)	*Teacher(s)*
Pre-established	Non-formal education Further education	Formal schooling Elders' teachings
Knowledge Structure		
Situational	Self-directed learning Collective untaught learning	Informal education Informal training

**Figure 12.2   Livingstone's agency and knowledge structure dimensions of learning model.
Source: From Livingstone (2005a, p. 981).**

on work in all its forms. Livingstone's conceptual framework specifically emphasizes the mutual roles of agency, structure, power and control. His model explicitly forefronts issues of human agency/freedom, and we see that from his perspective different forms of learning represent distinctive loci of agency (see Figure 12.2). In this approach, learning forms can express the standpoint of dominant institutional structures (e.g., through curriculum, organizational policy, teacher authority, teacher, trainer or corporate authority) while others can express the standpoints of the learner and their community (e.g., cultural forms, content, habitus, language codes). The model thus forefronts issues of authority, conflict and control in understanding learning and work which Livingstone has claimed is the 'missing link' in much workplace learning research (Livingstone, 2001). While authority, conflict and control are more easily recognized in organized forms of vocational education and training, for example, Livingstone has also shown their role in shaping informal learning and informal education as well. These are defined as either 'situational' or 'pre-established'. He includes in each both taught and untaught learning carried out in self or collectively-directed ways, or with the guidance of an expert other (e.g., mentor, teacher, coach). The social and economic context through which power is exercised is addressed in Livingstone's research as deeply shaped by the nature of capitalist society. Across Livingstone (2001, 2006; see also Livingstone and Stowe, 2007) we see significant social differences in terms of time spent on formal, non-formal and informal learning in relation to work, and indeed only in terms of time spent on informal workplace learning do we see a form of social parity across differences. This raises important questions about the nature of control and opportunity within these different forms of learning. The approach is further extended in terms of relations of formal education, labour markets and workplace learning in Livingstone (2004) which stands along with the work of Coffield (e.g. 1999, 2000) as one of the leading, contemporary criticisms of human capital theory.

These themes of authority, conflict and control are seen as politicized and inherent to work in capitalist society, and in several ways Livingstone's work has some important linkages with the research on workplace learning emerging from labour education, an important sub-field of workplace learning research. In most advanced market economies labour education research and practice has generated findings related to matters of how workers struggle to learn, represent themselves adequately in economic life, and/or seek to build a more democratic environment in workplaces through various forms of learning/education. From a labour perspective, adult education and training have long been viewed as a means of improving the quality of paid workplace experience and job security by developing job-related skills: formal, informal and tacit. The work of Cooper (e.g. 2006) has been among the most conceptually developed in terms of theorizing workplace learning and union development. Researchers in this area argue that the quality of work and the employability objective of adult education and training are made a reality by turning the workplace learning rhetoric back on management (e.g. Spencer, 1998). In this regard, Forrester (1999) argues that neglecting wider socio-economic conflict, control and the political nature of workplace learning might unwittingly make the 'brave new world of peda-gogics in relation to work and learning' (p. 188) a managerial tool for work intensification and control in the workplace. As Spencer (2001) warns, the rhetoric and enthusiasm for workplace learning, both from adult educators and some corporate leaders, can form part of a social tech-nology that masks 'new forms of oppression and control in the workplace that should be acknowledged in workplace learning research' (p. 33; see also McIlroy, 2008); a point raised in a different way by researchers of culture and identity such as Solomon discussed above.

Other researchers have explored related threads to these types of arguments. Tannock (2001) has looked at such matters for youth employment from a labour perspective. A variety of researchers have explored lifelong learning policy (e.g. Payne, 2001; Forrester, 2001; Coffield, 2000). Still others have looked at ongoing work practices (e.g. Nissen, 1994; Foley, 1999; Worthen, 2008; Sawchuk, 2001, 2003). Looking specifically at the United States, the work of Harris (2000) provides extended looks at workplace learning through the twentieth century with impressive integration of factors. Above all, issues of conflict and control in employer–employee relations remain central according to these analyses while it is demonstrated that some of the most progressive gains in work and workplace learning practice have emerged historically out of collective bargaining processes including quality of work-life/learning, paid education leave and the systematic linkages between continuing education and the workplace.

As useful as this research is, however, a significant gap remains regarding serious attention to the competitive pressures imposed by what many argue to be the reality of the emerging, globalized knowledge economy. Discussion related to these pressures in the first four themes I covered has been either presumptive or vague in this regard, while the research in this cur-rent section has tended to offer criticism of it primarily. Thus, in the material reviewed thus far there is virtually no discussion of the role of corporate leadership and the organizational strategies that in their own terms seek effectively to manage learning and knowledge produc-tion. This is a matter that leads me to my final theme of competitiveness and knowledge management.

Competitiveness and knowledge management

As Cheng and Hampson (2008) have recently remarked: '[a]s the idea that work has become increasingly knowledge based has taken hold, investing in intangible assets – especially human capital – has been regarded as a core strategy for competitive advantage' (p. 327). In many ways key contributions to understanding these concerns is found in the work of Ikujiro Nonaka. As distinct from traditional strategic management (e.g. Mintzberg et al., 1998), Nonaka and colleagues emphasize the pragmatic, practical (and even existential) dimensions of creating a truly knowledge-based firm. While hardly alone, Nonaka's work provides a key example in economic and managerial thought important for its comprehensive appreciation of epistemol-ogy, ontology, a concern to resolve the false dichotomy of objective and subject dimensions of reality, as well as its recognition of the importance of place. Nonaka and colleagues' work forefront active/tacit dimensions of learning and knowledge in the firm; it addresses interactive institutional places (or 'ba') whether these are found in departments, firms, sectors or related institutions such as the university. Here it is claimed that knowledge-generation emerges out of dialectical contradictions. In this sense his work provides a series of potential points of contact with several other themes discussed above.

The work most central to Nonaka's reputation is likely *The Knowledge-Creating Company: How Japanese Companies Create the Dynamics of Innovation* (Nonaka and Takeuchi, 1995). It represents a seminal publication from which much of his later work is drawn. In it he offers comparisons between American and Japanese management highlighting their distinct orienta-tions to knowledge and learning. Findings here suggest that North American management and the structure of American capitalism predominantly orients to formalized and explicit knowl-edge expressed in tendencies toward benchmarking and incrementalism. It is argued that this lies in contrast to Japanese management's concern for tacit, embodied, intuitive and construc-tivist notions of learning and knowledge as well as the larger role for state (as well as types of

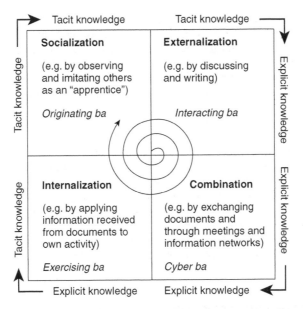

Figure 12.3   Nonaka's Elements of Knowledge Management (from Nonaka and Konno 1998).

cultural) regulation in Japanese capitalism/society. Nonaka and Takeuchi (1995) suggest that the latter produces greater potential for creativity and responsiveness to changing conditions emphasizing the value of the connection between production and top management *vis-à-vis* middle-managers and front-line supervisors who serve as the human mediators (making personal knowledge of employees available to the firm), the keystones of the transfer (both upward and downward) of innovation.

Later work expanded further on knowledge management and conceptual development of the concept of ba (e.g. Nonaka and Konno, 1998), and contradictions (e.g. Nonaka and Toyama, 2002); each useful for expanding thinking on the nature of the competitiveness of a firm beyond conventional management strategy. Noting its placement within concerns for the nature of management, strategy, as well as economic climates, Nonaka's work exemplifies a concern for learning processes which allows us to imagine certain bridges to themes discussed earlier. It seeks to represent the dynamic interaction of explicit and tacit workplace learning across specific, multiple places. It highlights what is referred to as the dialectic of internalization and externalization (see Figure 12.3).

It is from such analysis that Nonaka's approach to knowledge management (KM) emerges with its focus on the tacit-to-explicit learning transaction: the concern for transformation of previously invisible human capacities into manageable resources of the firm. In relation to KM specifically, Nonaka and colleagues have generally sought to theorize 'the cost of knowledge as inputs and the knowledge conversion rate' where firms are understood as 'a collection of knowledge assets' (Nonaka and Toyama, 2002, p. 996). His work goes on to problematize the difficulty of converting tacit knowledge to resources for the firm noting that, as yet, there are few effective way to for 'evaluating and managing knowledge assets' (p. 997). Nonaka and Peltokorpi's (2006) review of the KM field demonstrates that '[c]uriously, only a few scholars have discussed the nature of the knowers, humans' (p. 76), that if mentioned at all KM research has tended to produce highly 'deterministic or voluntaristic' (p. 77) portrayals of the learning process. The articulation of knowledge-creation at the level of the actor, including discussion in Nonaka et al. (2007) and Nonaka et al. (2002), where the focus is on knowledge creation process and practical wisdom (i.e. phroenesis), remains concerned with establishing conceptual reference points in these terms.

While the research of Nonaka and colleagues, as well as others in the KM tradition, provides effective outlines of how firms face competitive pressures through attention to learning, in fact there exist other traditions within this theme area that are well suited to speak to these same matters as well. A prime candidate for this is to be found in the field of organizational development (OD). A key example from this field is the work of Raelin (e.g. 2000, 2007). Raelin provides an applied model of new organizational forms and levels of cooperation required by a competitive, ever-shifting business environment. He draws on different theoretical perspectives than Nonaka and colleagues, though his work is equally broad. In terms of analysis of learning itself Raelin's work provides much of what Nonaka and colleagues may be missing. Raelin specifically identifies the need to increase forms of individual and collective reflection, and in this sense evokes the broad tradition of both reflective learning (e.g. Argyris and Schön, 1978) and self-directed learning (e.g. Knowles, 1975). Drawing on the work of Polanyi, in Raelin (1998) we see additional discussion of an epistemology of practice organized around recognizing tacit knowledge and then fostering the integration of tacit and explicit knowledge that parallels the interests of Nonaka. Here we also see some tenuous (and perhaps some contentious) points of contact with the work of Eraut on the one hand, and Beckett and Hager (2000, 2002) on the other, both discussed earlier in the chapter.

CONCLUSIONS FOR MOVING FORWARD

If one has come to be interested in the field of workplace learning enough to be reading this Handbook then it is likely in one form or another she will recognize the reality that was given voice by Barnett when he wrote a decade ago "work has to become learning and learning has to become work" (1998, p. 42). This statement has both a common sense as well as a startlingly challenging quality to it. It suggests that there are powerful forces at play here. This is so whether one subscribes to the view that such forces are naturally given to market competition that is intensifying with globalization and can potentially be ameliorated by problem-solving and the transformation of firms into knowledge-intensive organizations (e.g. Nonaka), or one subscribes to the view that short of significant transformation of power relations, and perhaps even democratization of work processes, these forces intensify inherent conflicts and contradictions (e.g. Livingstone). We may come to understand that the workplace is a site of identity, its constant re-construction and repair (e.g. Gherardi) or that it is a site in which even the most established and formalized knowledge forms (i.e. professional knowledge) come to be recognized as informal, tacit, planned and unplanned, situational and highly mediated rather than particularly stable. In all cases, the stakes for developing a better understanding of workplace learning are high for individuals, groups, units, firms, nations and beyond. All the more so when we remember that learning effectively defines the process of human change. Indeed, if one were to accept the notion that learning equates to change we are left with an interesting transposition within Barnett's claim which would read: *work has to become [change] and [change] has to become work*. This puts front and centre more than a few value-laden questions beginning with what kind of change and change in whose interests? In short, we likely have the stage set for a future of even more intensely political questions in the field of workplace learning; played out across myriad conceptual and methodological choices, topical preoccupations and explicit or implicit political beliefs and commitments.

Given that the aim of this chapter was to offer an opportunity for both a constructive and critical engagement with workplace learning research across the international scene, the initial assay of the field introduced the multi-disciplinarity and diversity of conceptual and topical preoccupations. The bulk of the chapter turned toward offering a profile of six key themes and a selection of key authors which exemplify them, outlining accomplishments, gaps and above all opportunities for dialogue.

What should be clear, however, is that a guiding thread of the discussion has been that balkanization of research communities into self-referential camps remains an important challenge.

It is a challenge that must be balanced against the creative potential that emerges out of sustained discussion that focused communities of scholars often produce. The simple message of this review is that no single thematic area of research can lay claim to any sort of definitive account of the multi-dimensional phenomena of workplace learning research as a whole. In this sense, some form of cross-fertilization across the types of robust lines of research inquiry that were explored will continue to prove useful.

NOTES

1 See different types of recent thematic reviews of the field of workplace learning research in Illeris (2003; Illeris and Associates 2004) and Tynjälä (2008) for example – both of which provide some orientations to research reported in (European) languages other than English.

2 For a contemporary review of work skills/competencies see Illeris (2009).

3 For a remarkable introduction to these approaches see Stubbe et al. (2003).

4 For a good, recent discussion of bodily interaction in relation to discourse in Hindmarch and Heath (2000).

REFERENCES

Anthony, P. (1994) *Managing Culture*. Bristol, PA: Open University Press.

Argyris, C. and Schön, D. (1978) *Organisational Learning: A Theory of Action Perspective*. Reading, MA: Addison-Wesley.

Ashton, D. and Felstead, A. (2001) 'From Training to Lifelong Learning: The Birth of the Knowledge Society?', (pp. 165–189) in J. Storey (ed.) *Human Resource Management: A Critical Text* (2nd edn). London: Thomson Learning.

Bauer, J. and Gruber, H. (2007) 'Workplace Changes and Workplace Learning: Advantages of an Educational Micro Perspective', *International Journal of Lifelong Education*, 26(6): 675–688.

Beckett, D. and Hager, P. (2000) 'Making Judgments as the Basis for Workplace Learning: Towards an Epistemology of Practice', *International Journal of Lifelong Education*,19(4): 300–311.

Beckett, D. and Hager, P. (2002) *Life, Work and Learning: Practice in Postmodernity*. London: Routledge.

Billett, S. (2002) 'Critiquing Workplace Learning Discourses: Participation and Continuity at Work', *Studies in the Education of Adults*, 34(1): 56–67.

Billet, S., Fenwick, T. and Sommerville, M. (eds) (2006) *Work, Subjectivity and Learning*. Netherlands: Springer.

Boshuizen, H., Bromme, R. and Gruber, H. (eds) (2004) *Professional Learning: Gaps and Transitions on the Way from Novice to Expert*. Dordrecht: Kluwer.

Bratton, J. and Gold, J. (2003) *Human Resource Management: Theory and Practice*. London: Palgrave.

Bratton, J., Helms-Mills, J., Pyrch, T. and Sawchuk, P. (2004) *Workplace Learning: A Critical Introduction*. Toronto: Broadview.

Bruni, A., Gherardi, S. and Poggio, B. (2004) 'Doing Gender, Doing Entrepreneurship: An Ethnographic Account of Intertwined Practices', *Gender, Work and Organization*. 11(4): 406–429.

Cheng, E. and Hampson, I. (2008) 'Transfer of Training: A Review and New Insights', *International Journal of Management Reviews*, 10(4): 327–341.

Colley, H., Hodkinson, P. and Malcolm, J. (2002) *Non-formal Learning: Mapping the Conceptual Terrain. A Consultation Report.* Available from: http://www.infed.org/archives/e-texts/colley_informal_learning.htm accessed 28.01.08.

Coffield, F. (1999) 'Breaking the Consensus: Lifelong Learning as Social Control', *British Education Research Journal*, 25(4): 479–499.

Coffield, F. (2000) *Differing Visions of a Learning Society, Volume 1*. Bristol: Policy Press.

Cooper, L. (1998) 'From "Rolling Mass Action" to "RPL": The Changing Discourse of Experience and Learning in the South African Labour Movement', *Studies in Continuing Education*, 20(2): 143–157.

Cooper, L. (2006) 'How Can We Theorize Pedagogy, Learning and Knowledge within Informal, Collective, Social Action Contexts? A Case Study of a South African Trade Union', in R. Edwards, J. Gallacher and S. Whittaker (eds), *Learning Outside the Academy*. London: Routledge. pp. 24–41.

Coopey, J. (1996) 'Crucial Gaps in the "Learning Organization" ', in K. Starkey (ed.). *How Organizations Learn*. London: International Thomson Business Press.

Dixon, N. (1992) 'Organizational Learning: A Review of Literature with Implications for HRD Professionals', *Human Resource Development Quarterly*, 3: 29–49.

Drew, P. and Heritage, J. (eds) (1992) *Talk at Work*. New York: Cambridge University Press.

Du Gay, P. (1996) *Consumption and Identity at Work*. Thousand Oaks, CA: Sage.

Ellström, P.E. (2001) 'Integrating Learning and Work: Problems and Prospects', *Human Resource Development Quarterly*, 12(4): 421–435.

Engeström, Y. (1987) *Learning by Expanding: An Activity-Theoretical Approach to Development Research*. Helsinki: Orienta-Konsultit.

Engeström, Y. (1990) *Learning, Working and Imagining: Twelve Studies in Activity Theory*. Helsinki: Orienta-Konsultit.

Engeström, Y. (2001) 'Expansive Learning at Work: Toward an Activity Theoretical Reconceptualization', *Journal of Education and Work*, 14(1): 133–156.

Engeström, Y. (2008) 'Enriching Activity Theory without Shortcuts', *Interacting with Computers*, 20: 256–259.

Engeström, Y. and Middleton, D. (1998) *Communication and Cognition at Work*. New York: Cambridge University Press.

Eraut, M. (2000) 'Non-formal Learning and Tacit Knowledge in Professional Work', *British Journal of Educational Psychology*, 70: 113–136.

Eraut, M. (2004) 'Transfer of Knowledge between Education and Workplace Settings', in H. Rainbird, A. Fuller and A. Munro (eds), *Workplace Learning in Context*. London: Routledge pp. 201–221.

Eraut, M. (2007) 'Learning from Other People in the Workplace', *Oxford Review of Education*, 33(4): 403–422.

Eraut, M. (2008) *How Professionals Learn through Work*. Surrey, UK: Surrey Centre for Excellence in Professional Training and Education.

Eraut, M. and Hirsh, W. (2007) *The Significance of Workplace Learning for Individuals, Groups and Organisations*, SKOPE Monograph 9, Oxford, UK.

Ericsson, K., Charness, N., Feltovich, P. and Hoffman, R. (2006) *The Cambridge Handbook on Expertise and Expert Performance*. New York: Cambridge University Press.

Evans, K., Hodkinson, P. and Unwin, L. (2003) 'Working to Learn: Transforming Learning in the Workplace', *International Review of Education*, 49(5): 546–547.

Evans, K., Hodkinson, P., Rainbird, H. and Unwin, L. (2006) *Improving Workplace Learning*. Abingdon: Routledge.

Felstead, A., Fuller, A., Jewson, N., Kakavelakis, K. and Unwin, L. (2007) 'Grooving to the Same Tunes?', *Work, Employment and Society*, 21(2): 189–208.

Felstead, A., Fuller, A., Unwin, L., Ashton, D., Butler, P. and Lee, T. (2005) 'Surveying the Scene: Learning Metaphors, Survey Design and the Workplace Context', *Journal of Education and Work*, 18(4): 359–359.

Fenwick, T. (2001) 'Tides of Change: New Themes and Questions in Workplace Learning', *New Directions for Adult and Continuing Education*, 92 (Winter): 3–17.

Fenwick, T. (2006) 'Toward Enriched Conceptions of Work Learning: Participation, Expansion, and Translation Among Individuals With/In Activity', *Human Resource Development Review*, 5(3): 285–302.

Fenwick, T. (2008) 'Understanding Relations of Individual-Collective Learning in Work: A Review of Research', *Management Learning*, 39(3): 227–243.

Foley, G. (1999) *Learning in Social Action: A Contribution to Understanding Informal Education*. London: Zed Books.

Forrester, K. (1999) 'Work-Related Learning and the Struggle for Subjectivity', *Researching Work and Learning: A First International Conference*. Leeds, UK: Leeds University, pp. 188–197.

Forrester, K. (2001) 'Modernised Learning: An Emerging Lifelong Agenda by British Trade Unions?', *Journal of Workplace Learning*, 13(7): 318–325.

Forrester, K. (2005) 'Learning for Revival: British Trade Unions and Workplace Learning', *Studies in Continuing Education*, 27(3): 257–270.

Fuller, A. and Unwin, L. (1998) 'Reconceptualising Apprenticeship: Exploring the Relationship between Work and Learning', *Journal of Vocational Education and Training*, 50(2): 153–172.

Fuller, A. and Unwin, L. (2002) 'Developing Pedagogies for the Contemporary Workplace', in K. Evans, P. Hodkinson and L. Unwin (eds), *Working to Learn: Transforming Learning in the Workplace*. London: Kogan Page.

Fuller, A. and Unwin, L. (2003) 'Learning as Apprentices in the Contemporary UK Workplace: Creating and Managing Expansive and Restrictive Participation', *Journal of Education and Work*, 16(4): 407–426.

Fuller, A. and Unwin, L. (2004) 'Expansive Learning Environments: Integrating Personal and Organizational Development', in H. Rainbird, A. Fuller and A. Munro (eds), *Workplace Learning in Context*. London: Routledge.

Fuller, A., Hodkinson, H., Hodkinson, P. and Unwin, L. (2005) 'Learning as Peripheral Participation in Communities of Practice: A Reassessment of Key Concepts in Workplace Learning', *British Educational Research Journal*, 31(1): 49–68.

Fuller, A., Unwin, L., Felstead, A., Jewson, N. and Kakavelakis, K. (2007) 'Creating and Using Knowledge: An Analysis of the Differentiated Nature of Workplace Learning Environments', *British Educational Research Journal*, 33(5): 743–759.

Garfinkel, H. (1986) *Ethnomethodological Studies of Work*. London: Routledge.

Gherardi, S. (2004) 'Translating Knowledge while Mending Organizational Safety Culture', *Risk Management: An International Journal*, 6(2): 61–80.

Gherardi, S. (2007) *Organizational Knowledge. The Texture of Workplace Learning*. Oxford: Blackwell.

Gherardi, S., Nicolini, D. and Suati, A. (2007) 'The Passion for Knowing', *Organization*, 14(3): 315–329.

Gee, J.P., Hull, G. and Lankshear, C. (1996) *The New Work Order: Behind the Language of the New Capitalism*. Sydney: Allen & Unwin.

Harris, H. (2000) *Defining the Future or Reliving the Past? Unions, Employers, and the Challenge of Workplace Learning*. (Information Series No. 380). ERIC Clearinghouse on Adult, Career, and Vocational Education, Washington, D.C.

Hindmarch, J. and Heath, C. (2000) 'Embodied Reference: A Study of Deixis in Workplace Interaction', *Journal of Pragmatics*, 32(12): 1855–1878.

Hodkinson, P. and Hodkinson, H. (2003) 'Individuals, Communities of Practice and the Policy Context: Schoolteachers' Learning in Their Workplace', *Studies in Continuing Education*, 25(1): 3–21.

Hodkinson, P. and Hodkinson, H. (2004) 'The Significance of Individuals' Dispositions in Workplace Learning: A Case Study of Two Teachers', *Journal of Education and Work*, 17(2): 167–182.

Illeris, K. (2003) 'Workplace Learning and Learning Theory', *Journal of Workplace Learning*, 15(4): 167–178.

Illeris, K. and Associates (2004) *Learning in Working Life*. Fredricksberg, DN: Roskilde University Press.

Illeris, K. (ed.) (2009) *International Perspectives on Competence Development*. New York: Routledge.

Järvinen, A. and Poikela, E. (2001) 'Modeling Reflective and Contextual Learning at Work', *Journal of Workplace Learning,* 13: 282–289.

Kakavelakis, K., Felstead, A., Fuller, A., Jewson, N. and Unwin, L. (2008) 'Making a Sales Advisor: The Limits of Training "Instrumental Empathy"', *Journal of Vocational Education and Training*, 60(3): 209–221.

Kazuo, I. and Nonaka, I. (eds) (2007) *Knowledge Creation and Management: New Challenges for Managers*. New York: Oxford University Press.

Knorr-Cetina, K. and Mulkay, M. (eds) (1983) *Science Observed: Perspectives on the Social Study of Science*. London: Sage.

Knowles, M. (1975) *Self-Directed Learning: A Guide for Learners and Teachers*. New York: Association Press.

Kochan, T., McKersic, R. and Cappelli, P. (1984) 'Strategic Choice and Industrial Relations Theory', *Industrial Relations*, 23(1): 16–39.

Kolb, D. (1984) *Experiential Learning as the Source of Learning and Development*. Englewood Cliffs, NJ: Prentice-Hall.

Latour, B. (1992) *Science in Action*. Cambridge: Harvard University Press.

Latour, B. and Woolgar, S. (1979) *Laboratory Life: The Social Construction of Scientific Facts*. London: Sage.

Lave, J. and Wenger, E. (1991) *Situated Learning*. Cambridge: Cambridge University Press.

Legge, K. (1995) *Human Resources Management Rhetorics and Realities*. London: Macmillan.

Livingstone, D. (2001) 'Worker Control as the Missing Link: Relations between Paid/Unpaid Work', *Journal of Workplace Learning*, 13(7/8): 308–317.

Livingstone, D.W. (2001) 'Expanding Notions of Work and Learning: Profiles of Latent Power', *New Directions for Adult and Continuing Education*, 9(2): 19–30.

Livingstone, D.W. (2004) *The Educational Jobs Gap*. Toronto: Garamond.

Livingstone, D.W. (2006) 'Contradictory Class Relations in Work and Learning: Some Resources for Hope', in P. Sawchuk, N. Duarte and M. Elhammoumi (eds), *Critical Perspectives on Activity: Explorations across Education, Work, and Everyday Life*. New York, NY: Cambridge University Press, pp. 145–159.

Livingstone, D.W. (2006) *Informal Learning: Conceptual Distinctions and Preliminary Findings*. New York: Peter Lang Publishing.

Livingstone, D.W. and Sawchuk, P. (2004) *Hidden Knowledge. Organized Labour in the Information Age*. Lanham, MD: Rowman and Littlefield.

Livingstone, D.W. and Stowe, S.L. (2007) 'Class, Race, Space, and Unequal Educational Outcomes in the United States: Beyond Dichotomies', in J.L. Kincheloe and S.R. Steinberg (eds), *Cutting Class: Socioeconomic Status and Education*. Lanham, MD: Rowman & Littlefield, pp. 97–119.

Luff, P., Hindmarch, J. and Heath, C. (eds) (2000) *Workplace Studies: Recovering Work Practice and Informing System Design*. New York: Cambridge University Press.

McIlroy, J. (2008) 'Ten Years of New Labour: Workplace Learning, Social Partnership and Union Revitalization in Britain', *British Journal of Industrial Relations,* 6(2): 283–313.

Mintzberg, H., Quinn, J. and Ghoshal, S. (1998) *The Strategy Process*. New York: Prentice-Hall.

Nicolini, D., Gherardi, S. and Yanow, D. (eds) (2003) *Knowing in Organizations: A Practice-Based Approach*. Armonk, NY: M.E. Sharpe.

Nielwolny, K. and Wilson, A. (2009) 'What Happened to the Promise? A Critical (Re)orientation of Two Sociocultural Learning Traditions', *Adult Education Quarterly*, 60(1): 26–45.

Nissen, B. (1994) 'Labor and Monopoly Capital in the Labor Education Context', *Monthly Review*, 46(6): 36–44.

Nonaka, I. (1994) 'A Dynamic Theory of Organizational Knowledge Creation', *Organization Science*, 5(1): 14–37.

Nonaka, I. and Konno, N. (1998) 'The Concept of "Ba": Building a Foundation for Knowledge Creation', *California Management Review*, 40(3): 40–54.

Nonaka, I. and Peltokorpi, V. (2006) 'Objectivity and Subjectivity in Knowledge Management: A Review of 20 Top Articles', *Knowledge and Process Management*, 13(2): 73–82.

Nonaka, I. and Takeuchi, H. (1995) *The Knowledge Creating Company: How Japanese Companies Create the Dynamics of Innovation*. New York: Oxford University Press.

Nonaka, I. and Toyama, R. (2002) 'A Firm as a Dialectical Being: Towards a Dynamic Theory of a Firm', *Industrial and Corporate Change*, 11(5): 995–1009.

Nonaka, I., von Krogh, G. and Voelpel, S. (2007) 'Organizational Knowledge Creation Theory: Evolutionary Paths and Future Advances', *Organization Studies*, 27(8): 1179–1208.

Payne, J. (2001) 'What Do Trade Unions Want from Lifelong Learning?', *Research in Post-Compulsory Education*, 6(3): 355–373.

Pickering, A. (ed.) (1992) *Science as Practice and Culture*. Chicago: University of Chicago Press.

Raelin, J. (1998) 'Work-Based Learning in Practice', *Journal of Workplace Learning*, 10(6/7): 280–283.

Raelin, J. (2000) *Work-Based Learning: The New Frontier of Management Development*. Addison-Wesley OD Series.

Raelin, J. (2007) 'Toward an Epistemology of Practice', *Academy of Management Learning and Education*, 6(4): 495–519.

Rawls, A. (2008) 'Harold Garfinkel, Ethnomethodology and Workplace Studies', *Organizational Studies*, 29(5): 701–732.

Sawchuk, P. (2001) 'Trade Union-Based Workplace Learning: A Case Study in Workplace Reorganization and Worker Knowledge Production', *Journal of Workplace Learning*, 13(7/8): 344–351.

Sawchuk, P. (2003) 'Informal Learning as a Speech-Exchange System: Implications for Knowledge Production, Power and Social Transformation', *Discourse and Society*, 14(3): 291–307.

Sawchuk, P. (2009) 'Re-visiting Taylorism: Conceptual Implications for Lifelong Learning, Technology and Work in the Public Sector', in D.W. Livingstone (ed), *Lifelong, Lifewide: Exploring Learning for Paid and Unpaid Work*. New York: Routledge.

Solomon, N. (2001) 'Workplace Learning as a Cultural Technology', *New Directions for Adult and Continuing Education*, 92 (Winter): 41–51.

Stubbe, M., Lane, C., Hilder, J., Vine, E., Marra, M., Homes, J. and Weatherall, A. (2003) 'Mutiple Discourse Analyses of a Workplace Interaction', *Discourse Studies*, 5(3): 351–388.

Suchman, L. (1987) *Plans and Situated Actions: The Problem of Human-Machine Communication*. New York: Cambridge University Press.

Tannock, S. (2001) *Youth at Work: the Unionized Fast-Food and Grocery Workplace*. Philadelphia: Temple University Press.

Townley, B. (1994) *Reframing Human Resource Management: Power, Ethics and the Subject at Work*. London: Sage.

Tynjälä, P. (2008) 'Perspectives into Learning at the Workplace', *Educational Research Review*, 3: 130–154.

Usher, R. and Solomon, N. (1999) 'Experiential Learning and the Shaping of Subjectivity in the Workplace', *Studies in the Education of Adults*, 31, 155–163.

Worthen, H. (2008) 'Using Activity Theory to Understand How People Learn to Negotiate the Conditions of Work', *Mind, Culture and Activity*, 15(4): 322–338.

13

How Researching Learning at Work Can Lead to Tools for Enhancing Learning

Michael Eraut

THEORETICAL FRAMEWORK

This chapter starts with the proposition that both *knowledge* and *learning* should be viewed through two lenses: the individual and the social. The *individual perspective* enables exploration of:

- what people know;
- what people can do;
- what and how they learn;
- variations in how different people interpret and use what they learn.

While a *social perspective* draws attention to:

- the social nature of most contexts for learning;
- the social origins of knowledge that is shared, passed on or developed by groups, networks or communities;
- the wide range of cultural practices and products that provide knowledge.

This leads to a useful distinction between *personal knowledge* and *cultural knowledge*. Within cultural knowledge, most attention is given to the *codified knowledge* presented in books, journals and their electronic successors. This knowledge domain is broader than positivist knowledge but still depends on peer review.

Codified knowledge is not the only form of *cultural knowledge,* so we need to consider the role of cultural knowledge that is not codified. Many would argue that this does not count as knowledge, but there is still a need for workers to be aware of their colleagues' or clients' customs and attitudes in order to do their own job properly. Socialisation, for example, involves mainly informal learning and even a kind of informal peer review. Although such *uncodified cultural knowledge* plays a key role in most work-based practices and activities, there is considerable debate about the extent to which it can be made explicit or represented in any textual form, and the evidence gathered so far suggests that its amenability to codification has been greatly exaggerated (Eraut, 2000). Whereas codified cultural knowledge is frequently discussed in terms of its truth and validity, uncodified knowledge is discussed in terms of its ownership, location and history. Who uses this knowledge, where and when?

This led Eraut (1997, 1998) to adopt the terms *personal knowledge* and *capability* for the individual-centred counterpart to cultural knowledge, defining it as 'what individual persons bring to situations that enables them to think, interact and perform'. The rationale for this definition is that its defining feature is the use of the knowledge, not its truth. This allows investigation of the effects of personal knowledge without necessarily being able to represent that knowledge in codified form. Eraut argues that personal knowledge incorporates all of the following:

- Codified knowledge in the form(s) in which the person uses it (Eraut, 1998).
- Know-how in the form of skills and practices.
- Personal understandings of people and situations.
- Accumulated memories of cases and episodic events (Eraut, 2000, 2004c).
- Other aspects of personal expertise, practical wisdom and tacit knowledge.
- Self-knowledge, attitudes, values and emotions.

The evidence of personal knowledge comes mainly from observations of performance, and this implies a holistic rather than fragmented approach to knowledge, because, unless one stops to deliberate, the knowledge one uses is already available in an integrated form and ready for action.

Eraut's model of practice is focused around three dimensions. The first dimension covers the context(s) and conditions where the practice is performed, which is discussed in depth later. The second dimension analyses performances by either individuals or groups in terms of four distinct but interconnected elements (Eraut, 2000):

- Assessing clients, and situations (sometimes briefly, sometimes involving a long process of investigation), and continuing to monitor them.
- Deciding what, if any, action to take, both immediately and over a longer period (either individually or as a member of a team).
- Pursuing an agreed course of action, modifying, consulting and reassessing as and when necessary.
- Meta-cognitive monitoring by individuals or collective monitoring within groups of the people involved, whether agents or clients, and the general progress of the problem, project or situation.

Each element can take many different forms, according to the context, the time available and the types of technical and personal expertise being deployed. Although analytically distinct, they are often merged into an integrated performance that is more complex than the simple sequence of assessment, decision and action advocated in many textbooks.

The third dimension is the time available, whether by choice or under the constraints of urgency or a heavy workload. Table 13.1 divides the time-continuum into three columns, whose headings describe the mode of cognition used by the performers. The *instant/reflex* column describes routinised behaviour that, at most, is semi-conscious. The *rapid/intuitive* column

Table 13.1 Interactions between time, mode of cognition and type of process

Type of process	Mode of cognition		
	Instant/Reflex	Rapid/Intuitive	Deliberative/Analytic
Assessment of the situation	Pattern recognition	Rapid interpretation Communication on the spot	Prolonged diagnosis Review, discussion and analysis
Decision-making	Instant response	Recognition primed or intuitive	Deliberative analysis or discussion
Overt actions	Routinised actions	Routines punctuated by rapid decisions	Planned actions with periodic progress reviews
Metacognitive engagement	Situational awareness	Implicit monitoring Short, reactive Reflections	Monitoring of thought and activity, reflective learning Group evaluation

Source: SKOPE

indicates greater awareness of what is going on, and is often characterised by rapid decision-making by professionals, who have sufficient experience to recognise what is needed because they have dealt with similar situations before. Decisions follow familiar routes when people know what is needed and how to check their understanding of what is happening. There may also be others who need to be briefed, clients who may be anxious, and some fine-tuning of the chosen pathway. As workers become more experienced, they acquire a wider range of precedents and recognise them more quickly and more accurately.

The *deliberative/analytic* column is characterised by explicit thinking by individuals or groups, possibly accompanied by consultation with others. It often involves the conscious use of different types of prior knowledge, and their application to new situations. These areas of knowledge may either be used in accustomed ways, sometimes with adaptation, or combined in novel ways that require a significant period of problem solving.

Professionals and technicians in training or recently qualified face a steep learning curve until a high proportion of their work has become sufficiently familiar for them to handle. Reaching that level is an emotional as well as a cognitive challenge, and that may continue if they seek, or are given, further challenging work. In many workplaces there is both complex and more routine work, and it is difficult to get the right balance. Hence the *relationship between time and cognition* is probably interactive, because shortage of time forces people to adopt a more intuitive approach as soon as possible, while the intuitive routines developed by experience enable people to do things more quickly. But, if those routines are less than effective because they cause workers to routinise too fast, the quality of the work will fall, or fail to achieve an appropriate target. Even when a group does have some time for discussion, its members may feel that their contributions have to be short and rapid. Then the meta-processes on the bottom line of Table 13.1 are limited to implicit monitoring and short, reactive reflections. Whereas, if more time becomes available, the role of meta-processes becomes more complex and expands beyond self-awareness and monitoring to include the framing of problems, thinking about the deliberative process itself and how it is being handled.

The greatest benefit of routinisation is that it reduces workers' *cognitive load*, enabling them to give more attention to monitoring the situation or communicating with clients and colleagues, hence becoming both more productive and more effective. We would not survive for long if we could not take for granted many aspects of what we see and do. Sometimes, however, routines do not derive from increased proficiency but from *coping mechanisms* developed for handling work overload with little regard for quality, and then a more evaluative perspective is essential.

The other disadvantage of routinisation is *inflexibility*. Routines are difficult to change, because they involve a period of disorientation, during which old routines are abandoned and new routines gradually developed. What 'change experts' fail to understand is that the disorientation of unlearning routines is more difficult to handle than the learning of new routines, precisely because they are routinised. Throughout this withdrawal period practitioners feel like novices without having the excuses, or discounts on performance normally accorded to novices. They lose control over their own practice, when tacit knowledge ceases to provide the necessary support and the emotional turmoil reduces their motivation. Hence more time and support is required than that normally provided (Eraut, 2004c).

THE TACIT DIMENSION OF PERFORMANCE

The role of tacit knowledge in *understanding people and situations* is a starting point, because people easily recognise the factors involved. Getting to know other people typically involves the absorption of a great deal of incidental information, acquired by being a participant observer on occasions when both are present but constrained by the normal conventions of politeness and sociability. While some of the knowledge gained may be explicit, much more will be gathered in the form of impressions of their character and behaviour or memories of episodes in which they participated. Both parties may also have acquired some secondary data in the form of stories about the person concerned. Such stories are normally regarded as an explicit form of communication, but they also carry implicit cultural and personal knowledge. Typically, we learn more about the people we meet than we are able to explain, and some of that knowledge may be so provisional that we are reluctant to make it explicit. Yet that knowledge may still be used when we interact with them, because we are unlikely to stop and think unless there is something problematic about the occasion. What influences our behaviour is our aggregated knowledge of that person, and that aggregation is usually a largely tacit process to which memories of incidents, encounters and episodes contribute in ways we cannot fully apprehend (Eraut, 2000).

Another factor is the way we tend to organise our knowledge of people: this affects how we perceive their behaviour as well as how we structure our memories of them; and neither is a fully conscious process. There is evidence that people use intensely personal constructs for categorising others, that early impressions affect later interactions and that we notice people's actions in groups only when they play a significant part. Moreover, managers have an additional problem, because their memories of occasions when they interacted with their subordinates are based on atypical samples of their subordinates' behaviour caused by their own managerial presence.

These factors contribute to the mixture of tacit and explicit knowledge which constitutes a person's knowledge of an organisation, context or situation. Many situations, for example, are largely characterised not only by the differing perspectives of the participants who are present, but also by the assumed behaviour of *'significant others'* off-stage, and knowledge of these perspectives depends not only on what people do and say but also on how their actions are interpreted by others in the context of what they already 'know' about the people concerned. While this assumption may often be valid, its further extension to people unknown can only be described as a case of unmonitored *tacit over-generalisation.* Thus tacit understandings or misunderstandings not only contribute to relationships and situational assumptions within an organisation but also to important transactions with external clients, customers, suppliers and stakeholders.

There are many professional *skills*, for which practice with feedback is essential for learning, but access to coaching is scarce and other feedback sparse. This is exacerbated by the tacit dimension in most skills, which limits the contribution of formal learning and codified knowledge. Several important work processes involve a combination of codified knowledge and skills of many kinds and their different contributions are usually highly integrated and interdependent. For example, a person's negotiating skill will affect the way in which they use their codified knowledge and even the choice of that knowledge. Another example would be interpreting what is going on beneath the surface of a business meeting. Simple well-defined situations might be analysed explicitly, but complex situations would be immensely difficult to portray or interpret. The technician trouble-shooting a piece of electronic equipment will draw on codified knowledge in a personal form which, being based partly on past experiences, suggests something about the likely nature of the problem. To learn to trouble-shoot a piece of equipment within a short period of time is probably best accomplished by going out with an expert with a varied caseload but enough time to talk, who can then show and explain what they are doing. Even this, however, may not always be successful, because trouble-shooting is often an intuitive skill by which people recognise patterns without being fully aware of the cues which prompted that recognition. Think how rare it is to find a computer expert who can come to your computer, sort out your problem, *and* teach you something about what was wrong and how to deal with it in the future. It is not just a lack of teaching skills.

The preceding section discussed the tacit nature of rapid intuitive *decision-making* in terms of situational recognition and prior experience. The research into naturalistic decision-making in less time-pressured situations, which allow some deliberation, suggests a pattern which relies more on the intuitive use of tacit knowledge when situations become more complex and uncertain. How does one decide what to say when asked for advice, when giving feedback and when being cross-examined in a meeting. In each case awareness of the interests and priorities of those being addressed, of the emotional dimension, and of the appropriate length of one's response is likely to guide any preparation, and the aim will be to reach a point where one feels that one has got it right, or can adjust one's plan in good time if what you say does not seem to be having the desired effect.

TRANSFER OF KNOWLEDGE BETWEEN CONTEXTS

Eraut's definition of knowledge transfer is '*the learning process involved when a person learns to use previously acquired knowledge/skills/competence/expertise in a new situation*'. This process may be simple if the new situation is similar to those previously encountered, but it is likely to be long and challenging if the new situation is complex and unfamiliar. In more complex situations the transfer process typically involves five inter-related stages:

1 The extraction of potentially relevant knowledge from the context(s) of its acquisition and previous use.
2 Understanding the new situation, a process that often depends on informal social learning.
3 Recognising what knowledge and skills are relevant.
4 Transforming them to fit the new situation.
5 Integrating them with other knowledge and skills in order to think/act/communicate in the new situation (Eraut, 2004a).

The stages are not simple, and rather than logical progression, there is usually considerable interaction between them.

Eraut et al.'s (1995) study of student nurses' and midwives' learning on placements found that the first three stages were beyond the knowledge of most students. Their placements were seen as a different world from that of academic programmes, and becoming accustomed to that new world and beginning to understand it was their priority. Formal knowledge no longer came to students' minds except with a short time interval, and the actions of qualified nurses and midwives were too routinised for appropriate connections to be made.

Salomon and Perkins (1998) made a distinction between forward-reaching and backward-reaching kinds of transfer. The *forward-reaching approach*, which anticipates that certain kinds of knowledge will be useful in the future, is most likely to occur in education and training contexts. Nearly all the taught components of professional and vocational education are intended for future use at work, but the evidence that this knowledge is used as intended is often disappointing. *Backward-reaching transfer* is required when one faces a new situation and deliberately searches for relevant knowledge already acquired. This is likely to occur with knowledge previously used in fairly similar contexts, when its relevance is quickly recognised, but committing time to searching for previously taught knowledge is rare without a promising starting point. The discourse and culture of the workplace are both so different from most education and training environments that persistent searching for what is perceived as *past knowledge* is very unusual. A major reason for this lack of commitment to exploring knowledge from one's past is a general failure to understand that transfer is a learning process, which often requires a lot more time than most people expect.

Learning in education or training settings cannot be substituted for learning in workplace settings. Practice components of programmes have to be authentic. However, learning to practise and learning to use knowledge acquired in education settings do not happen automatically. The conclusions drawn from the above discussion are that:

- Learning to use formal knowledge in practical situations is *a major learning challenge* in its own right – it is not a natural consequence of learning knowledge on its own, and trying to employ that knowledge in practice without critical questioning of its appropriateness and effectiveness will not meet the challenge.
- Such learning also requires both *time* and *support*. Learning programmes rarely allocate any time to this form of learning, but just assume (wrongly) that it will occur on its own.
- Not only has little thought been given to the kind of support needed for this kind of learning, but there is rarely any clarity about *who is responsible* for providing it (Eraut and Hirsh, 2007).

HOW DID THEY LEARN?

Evidence from the project on mid-career learning in business, engineering and healthcare was collected through two sets of interviews about six months apart: 120 respondents from 12 organisations took part in the first interviews and 88 in the second interviews (Eraut et al., 2000, 2002a, 2002b). Most of the learning described in the interviews was non-formal, neither specified nor planned. It arose naturally from the demands and challenges of work, when solving problems, improving quality and/or productivity, or coping with change involved social interactions in the workplace with colleagues, customers or clients. Much learning at work derives its purpose and direction from the goals of the work, which are normally achieved by a combination of thinking, trying things out and talking to other people. Sometimes, however, people recognise a need for some additional knowledge or skill that seems essential for improving the quality of their work, expanding its range or taking on new duties. Although this can involve some formal training being undertaken, it almost always requires learning from experience and from other people at work.

The most common form of learning from other people is consultation and collaboration within the immediate working group: possibly including teamwork, ongoing mutual consultation and support or observation of others in action. Beyond the immediate work environment, people sought information and advice from other people in their organisation, from customers or suppliers or from wider professional networks, often done on a reciprocal basis. Only a minority made frequent use of written or audiovisual materials like manuals, videos or computer-based training. The rest tried to circumvent materials by getting the information they needed from others. We also found that working for qualifications and attending short training courses were important for some people at particular stages in their career. But even then, work-based learning was still required for developing the ability to use what had been learned off-the-job. This was especially true for short courses, which have very little impact unless they are appropriately timed and properly followed up at work.

Finally, we found that the critical factors affecting the level and direction of learning efforts were: the micro-climate of the workplace, the self-confidence of the worker and the role of the local manager. The local manager influences both the climate and individual dispositions through proactive attention to social relationships, mutual learning and good feedback, and influences learning opportunities through organising work to provide the appropriate level of challenge and support for groups and individuals and to ensure participation in an appropriate range of work activities.

In the early career project, participants were observed at work, then interviewed and followed over their first three years' employment. There were 40 hospital nurses, 36 engineers and 14 accountants; with 20, 34 and 11 retained to the third year. Each participant was located in a different workplace. The detailed methodology (Steadman et al., 2005) enabled the development of a generic typology for classifying modes of learning at or for work. The first distinction was to classify learning processes according to whether their *principal intention* was working or learning. Most of the informal learning found in our previous project on mid-career learning (Eraut et al., 2000) occurred as a *by-product* of normal working processes, for which working was clearly the principal object. Although early career professionals were more likely to be involved in processes for which learning was the main goal, this still contributed only a small proportion of their learning. The second distinction arose from dissatisfaction with including processes, clearly bounded and relatively time consuming, in the same list as very generic and quite short actions, such as asking questions, observing or reflecting. When we separated these more generic, shorter actions from processes perceived as either working or learning, we obtained the refined typology used in Table 13.2.

WORK PROCESSES WITH LEARNING AS A BY-PRODUCT

These account for a very high proportion of the reported learning of people interviewed during the mid-career and early career projects, over 90 per cent for the engineers and nurses and over

Table 13.2   A typology of early career learning

Work processes with learning as a by-product	Learning actions located within work or learning processes	Learning processes at or near the workplace
Participation in group processes	Asking questions	Being supervised
Working alongside others	Getting information	Being coached
Consultation	Locating resource people	Being mentored
Tackling challenging tasks and roles	Listening	Shadowing
Problem solving	Observing	Visiting other sites
Trying things out	Reflecting	Independent study
Consolidating, extending and refining skills	Learning from mistakes	Conferences
Working with clients	Giving and receiving feedback	Short courses
	Use of mediating artefacts	Working for a qualification

Source: SKOPE

80 per cent for the chartered accountants, who were also receiving formal training for their professional qualification. However, the amount of learning reported varied significantly according to the available opportunities and the quality of relationships in the workplace. The majority of this learning through working involved learning from other people.

Participation in group processes covers both *team-working* towards a common outcome, and groups set up for a special purpose such as discussing a client, problem solving, reviewing some practices, planning ahead or responding to external changes.

Working alongside others allows people to observe and listen to others at work and to participate in activities, and hence to learn new practices and new perspectives, become aware of different kinds of knowledge and expertise, and gain some sense of other people's tacit knowledge. This mode of learning, which includes a lot of observation as well as discussion, is extremely important for learning the tacit knowledge that underpins routines and intuitive decisions and is difficult to explain. When people see what is being said and done, explanations can be shorter and the fine detail of incidents is still in most people's minds.

Consultations within or outside the working group, or even outside the organisation, are used to co-ordinate activities or obtain advice. The act of initiating a consultation, however, depends on the relationships between the parties, the extent of a worker's network and the culture of the workplace. For *newcomers* the distinction between a consultation and being mentored or supervised is not always clear, as part of a mentor's or supervisor's role is making oneself available for consultation.

Tackling challenging tasks and roles requires on-the job learning and, if successful, leads to increased motivation and confidence. However, people are less inclined to take on challenges unless they feel confident both in their ability to succeed as a result of previous experience and in the support of their manager and/or colleagues if they fail. Without such previous experience and support, challenges pose too high a risk.

Problem solving, individually or in groups, is not just talking, it may involve acquiring new knowledge before one can start, searching for relevant information and informants, imagination, persistence and interpersonal negotiation.

Trying things out is distinguished from trial and error by the intention to learn from the experience. It requires some prior assessment of risk, especially where other people might be affected, and may require special arrangements for getting feedback, as well as time for subsequent reflection and evaluation.

Consolidating, extending and refining skills are particularly important when entering new jobs or taking on new roles. It is sometimes supported by episodes of supervision, coaching or feedback, and is helped by informal personal support and some sense of an onward learning skills trajectory.

Working with clients also entails learning about the client, noticing any novel aspects of each client's problem or request and using any new ideas that arise from the encounter. Some workers have daily experiences of working with clients, but do not recognise them as learning opportunities. Some progress from less to more important clients, or from those with simple needs to those with more complex needs. There can also be a strong *emotional dimension*, either when a client arrives in a distressed state, is about to receive bad news, or when client contact gives the work meaning and value, thus enhancing workers' sense of collective purpose.

LEARNING PROCESSES AT OR NEAR THE WORKPLACE

The right column of Table 13.2 lists nine processes whose prime object is learning, listed in terms of their proximity to the workplace. Thus *supervision, coaching* and *mentoring* are at or near the learner's normal workplace; *shadowing* and *visiting other sites* are usually in other people's workplaces; *conferences, short courses* and *working for qualifications* are usually not in workplace settings; and independent study can be followed almost anywhere quiet (Eraut et al., 2002a,b).

For most workers the main influences of their *line manager* on their learning were through the *allocation of work, appraisal* and *support* for any *formal learning* requiring fees or time away from the job. New young employees were usually supervised by the person 'in charge' of the relevant work group.

Coaching and *mentoring* are provided mainly for newcomers, and occasionally for newly appointed managers. Coaching is often limited by managers not being prepared to release potential coaches from their normal work, and mentoring by lack of informal opportunities to develop an appropriate relationship. In many situations mentoring is provided by helpful others, who are not designated mentors, and this is usually best for mutual on-the-spot support and feedback.

Shadowing and *visits* to other sites are used for inducting some newcomers, for workers taking on new responsibilities and for improving cooperation between different sites. They could be very helpful for developing a *wider understanding* of projects, other work groups, suppliers and customers, a need often underestimated.

Conferences are more important for updating and networking than for direct learning, and *short courses* require further work-based learning to develop the ability to use what has been learned off-the-job.

Independent study may be supported by the provision of knowledge resources and/or agreed plans, such as lists of competences, learning projects or personal development plans. *Knowledge resources* such as manuals, reference books, documentation, protocols and an intranet were generally available to all workers, the engineers in particular using the intranet as their prime source of current information. Learners generally found it quicker to get information directly from more knowledgeable colleagues.

LEARNING ACTIVITIES LOCATED WITHIN THESE PROCESSES

The nine learning activities in the central column of Table 13.2 were embedded within most of the work processes and learning processes, and also found in short opportunistic episodes. The key issues for learning are the frequency and quality of their use.

Asking questions and getting information are important, proactive activities; and good questions and knowledge searches are appreciated in positive learning contexts. However, many novices feel diffident about asking questions of senior colleagues unless they are working together and the question is spontaneous. However, this does not apply to talking to peers or novices just ahead of them who still remember what it was like at their stage, and this should be considered when allocating and supporting newcomers.

Locating resource people is also a proactive activity requiring confidence and social understanding. Some early career professionals were proactive in seeking out and developing relationships with a wider network of knowledge resource people, while others gave it little attention, often because of not appreciating its potential value.

Progression routes to more ambitious tasks may depend on whom you get to know. Willingness to engage in routine work may earn you the right to access more challenging work.

Listening and observing activities are very dependent on what the observer/listener is able to grasp and comprehend; and comprehension depends on awareness of the significance of what has been said and/or done. Such awareness and understanding is developed through discussion and reflection. Much is learned through watching other people communicating with colleagues, clients or subordinates. However, it should be noted that the research encountered as much learning from bad examples as from good examples!

Learning from mistakes is possible in most working contexts, both from one's own mistakes and those of others, but opportunities for this activity are frequently missed. Consider also when it is better to be taught the right way and when it is better to allow people to learn from their mistakes.

Reflection is included because it occurs both on and off the job and often plays an important role in recognising and learning from mistakes. Schon (1987) argued that reflection lies at the centre of nearly all significant learning, but did not fully explore the range of reflective possibilities (Eraut, 2004b).

Giving and receiving feedback are both important, often vital, for most learning processes. We found four main settings for feedback:

- *Immediate comment* on aspects of a task or role given *on-the-spot* or soon after the event by a co-participant or witness.
- *Informal conversations away from the job* often convey indirect and/or unintended messages as well as intended advice, but second-hand messages are often misinterpreted.
- *Formal roles such as mentor or supervisor* involve some responsibility for a learner's short- to medium-term progress and an obligation to provide formative feedback on a regular basis, but this may not happen in practice.
- *Appraisal* is a process where designated appraisers are expected, but rarely succeed in, giving normative feedback on personal strengths and weaknesses and ascertaining views on learning opportunities and meeting expectations.

Although most learners need short-term, task-specific, feedback as well as longer-term, more strategic, feedback on general progress, the two are not necessarily found together. Good short-term feedback on performance was often accompanied by an almost total absence of strategic feedback, giving even the most confident workers an unnecessary sense of uncertainty and lowering their commitment to employers (Eraut, 2007b).

Most people at work get too little feedback, so being proactive can be very important. In the early stages it is best for newcomers to obtain some feedback from people just ahead of them. They can gain feedback by asking about their performance in particular situations, and it is more useful to them and easier for those asked if they seek advice on how they could improve.

Mediating artefacts need more explanation because they play an important role in structuring work and sharing information by mediating group learning about clients or projects in progress. Some artefacts in daily use carry information in a standard way that novices soon learn to understand. In both nursing and engineering, these include measurements, diagrams and photographs. For example, *patient records* cover temperature, fluid intake and output, drugs administration, biochemical data and various types of image. These refer to the immediate past and to plans for the immediate future, and salient features considered important are prioritised for the incoming shift at every handover. Understanding the thinking behind the handover rituals is essential learning for newly qualified nurses.

A mechanical engineer was observed regularly discussing her virtual design 'drawings' or digital photographs with distant colleagues, contractors and clients. A water-mains planning engineer and her colleagues all used her 'meterage' progress reports to decide whether to clean out a mains pipe, re-line or replace it, all with costings and timeframes.

Accountants learned how to interpret audit files and 'tests' for sampling clients' data, how to give priority to significant changes in accounts over time and how tactfully to find out how their client's business processes were represented in their accounts.

Finally, attention should be drawn to the use of textbooks, technical manuals and sets of data as mediating artefacts. They do not contain all the relevant knowledge required, because much of the practical knowledge does not reside in the artefact itself, but in the conversations that take place around the artefact. These conversations would be very difficult to develop without the artefact, which therefore plays an important role in sharing knowledge (Eraut, 2009).

THE DEVELOPMENT OF A TOOL FOR DESCRIBING WHAT IS BEING LEARNED

The research team developed generic coding systems for describing what is being learned, so it could be used across all the professions and specialties studied and easily understood by people outside those professions. This typology, presented in Table 13.3, covers a very wide range of knowledge and shows how many types of knowledge affecting professional work are given minimal or no attention. Another unintentional finding was that few categories appeared to describe endpoint learning. The possibility of further learning was always present. Moreover, many categories were more appropriate for lifetime learning than for a short period of early career or mid-career learning, so the team decided to call them learning trajectories, which are more mobile than *competences* and less pretentious than *categories of expertise*. Not all these

Table 13.3 A typology of 53 workplace learning trajectories

Task Performance	*Role Performance*
Speed and fluency	Prioritisation
Complexity of tasks and problems	Range of responsibility
Range of skills required	Supporting other people's learning
Communication with a wide range of people	Leadership
Collaborative work	Accountability
	Supervisory role
Awareness and Understanding	Delegation
Other people: colleagues, customers, managers, etc.	Handling ethical issues
Contexts and situations	Coping with unexpected problems
One's own organisation	Crisis management
Problems and risks	Keeping up-to-date
Priorities and strategic issues	
Value issues	*Teamwork*
	Collaborative work
Personal Development	Facilitating social relations
Self-evaluation	Joint planning and problem solving
Self-management	Ability to engage in and promote mutual learning
Handling emotions	
Building and sustaining relationships	*Decision Making and Problem Solving*
Disposition to attend to other perspectives	When to seek expert help
Disposition to consult and work with others	Dealing with complexity
Disposition to learn and improve one's practice	Group decision making
Accessing relevant knowledge and expertise	Problem analysis
Ability to learn from experience	Formulating and evaluating options
	Managing the process within an
Academic Knowledge and Skills	appropriate timescale
Use of evidence and argument	Decision making under pressure
Accessing formal knowledge	
Research-based practice	*Judgement*
Theoretical thinking	Quality of performance, output and outcome
Knowing what you might need to know	Priorities
Using knowledge resources (human, paper-based, electronic)	Value issues
Learning how to use relevant theory	Levels of risk
(in a range of practical situations)	

Source: Eraut et al., 2005a: 11

trajectories were active at once, because changes in the level and direction of a person's work cause discontinuities in learning. Hence, at any one time:

- *Explicit progress* is being made on several of the trajectories that constitute lifelong learning.
- *Implicit progress* can be inferred and later acknowledged on some other trajectories.
- Progress on yet other trajectories is *stalling*, or even *regressing* through lack of use or because new practices have not yet been adopted.

Trainees in most professions are allocated to a series of placements, through which they are expected, with suitable support, to acquire the specified level of competence. However, the learning affordances of each placement vary considerably according to the local context, and these differences affect what each trainee learns and the profile of their competence at the point of qualification. The use of learning trajectories addresses both variations in competence and continuity of learning by tracking aspects of trainee performance before, during and after qualification.

One problem was that most occupational activities require that several types of knowledge are integrated into a *holistic performance*. In practical environments people judge holistic performances, and in analytic environments they judge specific attributes of performances. Although these attributes may be called *competencies*, that would imply that the attributes are essentially the same in every performance and not affected by the other attributes involved, nor by the context in which the performance took place. The term *learning trajectory* allows the general concept to be similar while individual variations of it depend on specific holistic performances and their contexts (Eraut and Hirsh, 2007).

In practice, points on learning trajectories should be treated as windows on episodes of practice, in which therefore the aspect of learning portrayed by each relevant trajectory has played a significant part, and the evidence supporting the trajectory point has been sustained or enhanced. This could only be achieved if each window included the following information about the whole performance:

- The setting in which it took place, and features of that setting that affected or might have affected the performance.
- The conditions under which the performance took place, e.g., degree of supervision, pressure of time, crowdedness, conflicting priorities, availability of resources.
- The antecedents to the performance and the situation that gave rise to the performance.
- The other trajectories involved.
- Any differences from previously recorded episodes.
- Indicators of expertise in the domain of the trajectory having been maintained, widened or enhanced.

This last point draws attention to the complexity of learning and performance in professional work. It is unusual for a performance to use knowledge from only one trajectory, and the seamless integration of personal knowledge from several trajectories may itself be an important learning challenge that goes beyond progress in several separate trajectories. Within this overall framework it is still possible, indeed desirable, for different types of representation to be used for different trajectories and at different career stages. There is no one best way for describing complex knowledge in use.

LEARNING AND CONTEXT FACTORS

A distinctive aspect of the research was that much of the learning witnessed was not recognised by the participants until changes in their capability over time were discussed. This made it more difficult to find out more about factors influencing learning by using a grounded theory approach. The evidence suggested a range of possible factors, but careful discussion was needed to find out how these factors differed with the type of learning and the context. How did they interact with each other, and at what organisational level were the more significant features of the learning landscape determined?

One prominent finding on mid-career learning was the overwhelming importance of *confidence*. Much learning at work occurs through doing things and being proactive in seeking learning opportunities, and this requires confidence. Confidence arose from successfully meeting *challenges* in one's work, while the confidence to take on such challenges depended on the extent to which learners felt *supported* in that endeavour by colleagues, either while doing the job or as back-up when working independently. Thus there is a triangular relationship between challenge, support and confidence (Eraut et al., 2000). The contextual significance of the word 'confidence', used by respondents without elaboration, depended on which aspects of this triangular relationship were most significant for particular people at particular points in their careers. The dominant meaning for most mid-career respondents came close to Bandura's (1995) concept of *self-efficacy*, a context-specific concept, relating to ability to execute a particular task or successfully perform a role. For some mid-career respondents, however, confidence related more to *relationships* than to the work itself. Did they feel confident about the *support* and *trust* of their working colleagues, in more senior, more junior or parallel jobs? This depended on whether they perceived their more significant working relationships as mutually supportive, generally critical, faction-ridden or even overtly hostile. For early career professionals, this latter aspect of confidence was more prominent.

The early career project with observations over three years added greatly to the understanding and this led to a second triangle (Figure 13.1) and other new features. *Feedback, support* and *trust* have already been described as interacting learning factors, but they are less likely to develop if newcomers fail to show a sense of agency or seem unprepared to take any initiative. Feedback was especially important during the first few months of a new job, when it was often best provided by the person on the spot. This happened within the *'distributed apprenticeship'* approach we found in accountancy, and in other organisations where local workplaces had developed a positive learning culture of mutual support. In the longer term, more normative feedback on progress and meeting organisational expectations also became important.

Equally important for developing confidence after the first few months was the *right level of challenge*. Newly qualified nurses were over-challenged physically, mentally and emotionally by their sudden *increase in responsibility* and the unceasing *pressure of work* in most ward environments. The *value of their work* carried many nurses through their unnecessarily pressured start, because it had a major influence on *motivation* and *commitment*. This was strengthened in some contexts by their *social inclusion* in supportive teams.

Some engineers progressed through a series of challenging assignments with remarkable rapidity, went on site early on and regularly engaged with clients and other professions. However, many engineers were under-challenged, and those seriously under-challenged had little real experience of either teamwork or the nature of their product, because they worked entirely on-line, designing small components of complex products.

The role of *extrinsic motivation* is frequently discussed in the workplace, and is therefore not discussed here. But Thomas' (2000) analysis of intrinsic motivation is less well known. Under *opportunities* he puts *sense of choice* over work activities and a sense of the *meaningfulness* of their purpose, and under *accomplishment* he puts *sense of competence* in their work activities and a *sense of progress* in their purpose. This gives four kinds of intrinsic motivation, all of which affect personal choices.

The inclusion of observation in this study provided opportunities to focus on the allocation and structuring of people's work, their relationships at work and their level of participation in workplace activities, which led us to the extension of the first model to include a second triangle that focuses on the contextual factors that influence its learning factors.

The allocation and structuring of work was central to our participants' progress, because it affected: (1) the difficulty or challenge of the work; (2) the extent to which it was individual or collaborative; and (3) the opportunities for meeting, observing and working alongside people who had more or different expertise, and for forming *relationships* of *mutual trust* that might provide *feedback and support*. Our analysis of modes of learning in the workplace confirmed the importance of relationships by showing how many prominent modes of learning were dependent

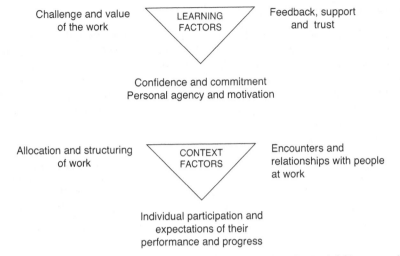

Figure 13.1   Factors affecting learning at work: the Two Triangle Model (Eraut et al. 2005, p2)

on good relationships with other people. These were not necessarily close relationships but required some mutual respect and a disposition to collaborate.

For novice professionals to make good progress a significant proportion of their work needed to be sufficiently new to challenge them without being so daunting as to reduce their confidence. Their workload needed to be at a level that allowed them to respond to new challenges reflectively, rather than develop coping mechanisms that might later prove ineffective. This usually worked well in the two accountancy organisations, but in engineering the appropriateness of the allocated work differed hugely according to the company and the specialty. Very few graduate engineers in electronics or computer science had sufficiently challenging work and nobody appeared to take any responsibility for addressing this problem. In nursing, the quality of learning was mainly influenced by the ward manager and her senior nurses, and some of the best and worst learning environments observed were in the same departments of the same hospitals. Eraut et al. (2005b) provide a more substantial account of these factors and their interactions.

We found that decisions affecting the structuring and allocation of work could be determined by any combination of the following factors:

1   *The nature of the work*, the way in which the organisation handled it and the discretion given to local managers in decisions of this kind. In all three professions studied, local managers had significant opportunities to facilitate learning through their allocation of work and support of novice workers.
2   *The quantity and urgency of the work* in hand. This was a major issue in hospitals where work overload almost overwhelmed novice nurses, while at the same time reducing the amount of support from more experienced colleagues, and was sometimes important in engineering, when a fallow period limited the supply of challenging assignments.
3   *Periodic decisions made by managers* in which learning needs might or might not have been considered. This was relevant when allocating novices to audit teams, nursing shifts or medium-term engineering tasks.
4   *Decisions made by more experienced colleagues* with delegated authority, who were currently working with the novice, and were probably best able to judge the appropriate level of challenge if they thought it important.

Whether these decisions benefited the learning of the novice professional depended on the disposition, imagination, competence (in making these kinds of decisions) and available thinking time of those who made them.

First-year trainee accountants

Figures 13.2a and 13.2b demonstrate the use of learning factors (13.2a) and context factors (13.2b) in chartered accountancy. The majority of the trainees' work was spent on audit visits, where tasks of increasing size and complexity were assigned. Providing appropriate and challenging work for most of the time increased trainees' capabilities; and this was seen as a good investment of their team-based attention to learning. Financially, this enabled them to pay their way after a few months, thus enhancing their sense of inclusion and their willingness to support the cohorts that followed them.

Key features of this learning were:

Challenge and value of the work
Good progression
Client variation
Audit is legal requirement
Value for clients is clear

LEARNING FACTORS

Feedback and support
Good on-the-spot feedback and support
Feedback on evaluation forms too late
Normative feedback weak

Confidence and commitment
Personal agency
Short-term confidence
Commitment to audit teams
Concerns about general progress
Less commitment to organisation
Range of career choices

Figure 13.2a   Learning factors for first year accountancy trainees (Eraut 2007a: 124)

1 Second- or third-year trainees were close by, often working alongside the new trainees.
2 Teams were generally small, and the object was a jointly constructed product – their client's audit report.
3 There were clear, usually non-negotiable, deadlines, and valuable time would be wasted if trainees caused delays, however small their own tasks.
4 It was normally possible for more experienced trainees to find a stopping point in their own task to answer a question or advise on a problem.
5 Helping new trainees was taken for granted by those in the same audit team, so novices felt able to ask silly questions to people, who still remembered their own recent experiences.

Trainee accountants also had a pass examinations to maintain a place in the profession. This involved extensive 'college work' and periods of study leave. They found most of their college work relevant to their work and valuable, although this was not always immediately apparent (Figure 13.2b).

The strong organisational culture in accountancy firms enabled them to share (1) their professional practices with help from a standard local approach to auditing accounts and (2) expertise in how to understand and represent their clients' accounts. The team has to treat the client's own their new set of accounts and the previous year's audit as important mediating artefacts, around which both discussion and reconciliation evolve towards a new audit that carries both legal status and notes for future issues to be considered the following year. Thus the work patterns of audit teams, continuity of practice across different audits of gradually increasing length and difficulty, and the structure of the audit documents themselves all provide strong scaffolding for learning (Figure 13.2b).

Accountants received immediate feedback quite often, because completed tasks were checked for the audit document. Undertaking increasingly complex tasks also indicated progress. However, good normative feedback on strengths, weaknesses or general progress was lacking, so trainees developed a stronger commitment to their work teams and colleagues than to their employing organisation. In their later stages, they reported that regular contact and increasing interaction with clients not only created awareness of the value of audits, but enabled them to gradually acquire the skill of connecting business transactions with accounts and to understand different types of businesses. This helped those trainees who

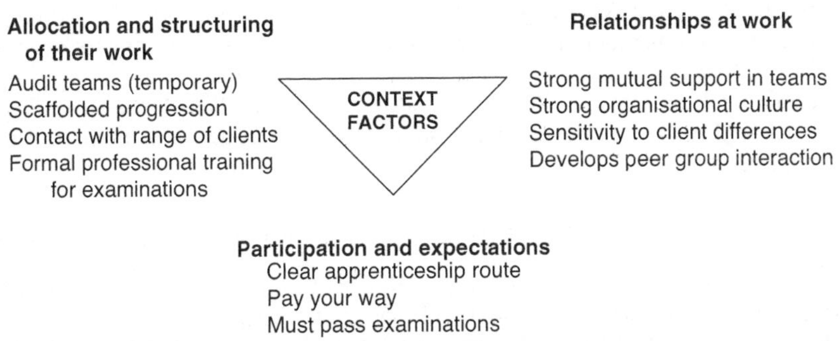

**Allocation and structuring
  of their work**

Audit teams (temporary)
Scaffolded progression
Contact with range of clients
Formal professional training
  for examinations

**CONTEXT
FACTORS**

Relationships at work

Strong mutual support in teams
Strong organisational culture
Sensitivity to client differences
Develops peer group interaction

Participation and expectations
Clear apprenticeship route
Pay your way
Must pass examinations

Figure 13.2b   Context factors for the learning of first year accountancy trainees (Eraut 2007a: 124)

were looking for other financial jobs after qualification, as well as those wanting to stay in accountancy.

THE ROLE OF MANAGERS IN SUPPORTING LEARNING

The typology of learning modes indicates how learning opportunities in the workplace depend on both the organisation of work and good relationships. This is an area where managers and supervisors can play an important role in promoting and enhancing the learning of those whom they manage, both individually and collectively (Eraut et al., 2002b). One major obstacle is that knowledge of workplace learning is conspicuously absent from most workplaces, even though the required behaviours are within most workers' capability and simple common sense. Moreover, much of what is needed can be done by people other than managers. The manager's role is not to provide most of the learning support themselves, but to set the climate and encourage others to take on this role as an integral part of their working responsibility.

To fulfil this role managers need to know that:

- Being over-challenged or under-challenged is bad for learning and morale. Providing an appropriate level of challenge is important for developing confidence and making good progress. Hence, this needs to be given attention by the relevant personnel when allocating and structuring the work of individuals and groups.
- The quantity and quality of informal learning can be enhanced by increasing opportunities for workers to consult with and work alongside others in teams or temporary groups. Therefore good opportunities are needed for working with others to develop mutual trust and cooperative relationships.
- They may need skills in conflict resolution and addressing bad relationships that threaten the group climate and/or achievement, and to consult others for advice if they themselves are directly involved.
- Support and feedback are critically important for learning, retention and commitment. Feedback is most effective within the context of good working relationships, and the rapid feedback essential for short-term learning is best provided by people on the spot. It is important for managers to develop a positive learning culture of mutual support between individuals and within and across work groups.
- More traditional feedback on progress, strengths and weaknesses, and meeting organisational expectations is also needed.
- Upsetting feedback, anxiety about one's status or performance, client behaviour, relationships or events outside the workplace can all influence the emotional dimension of a person's working life, and this may require ongoing attention for a period. The manager needs both to signal awareness of the situation and to check that they are receiving appropriate support.

Workplaces are complex inter-personal environments, where managers need to be well informed about relationships and personal or collective concerns without being unduly intrusive. They need to delegate and to work through other people as well as by direct action in order to support employee personal and professional self development. It is increasingly recognised that frequent informal conversations with individuals and small groups, listening to concerns, seeking advice, consulting, create good settings for preparing people for coming issues. Personal interests need as much attention as the collective interest, if workers are not to feel exploited.

The Institute for Employment Studies Report, Managers as Developers of Others (Hirsh et al., 2004), found that good development was delivered through a supportive relationship typically characterised as follows:

- Managers set a climate in which they are approachable, and where development is an important part of working life.
- They build developmental relationships with individuals in their teams, fostered by frequent, informal conversations about work, listening to concerns and offering positive support.
- Good development support is focused through a clear, shared analysis of development needs, frequent review and honest but constructive feedback.
- Development is delivered through a wide range of learning methods tailored to individual needs, such as informal coaching, formal training in the organisation, and the right kinds of experience both within and outside the job.
- They offer active career development and work to help individuals have a realistic sense of their own potential readiness for job opportunities. The individual's previous work experiences, interests and obligations outside work are also important.

These individuals reported increases in motivation and behaviour at work resulting from the increased sense of interest in work they obtained from the first two or three steps above. Attention to development can both improve the capability of individuals and improve their motivation and engagement.

Managers have a major influence on workplace learning and culture extending beyond most job descriptions. Doing nothing about learning and development will have a strong negative effect. Thus managers need to have greater awareness of the modes through which people may learn in the workplace, to recognise and attend to factors that enhance or hinder individual or group learning, and to take the initiative in the longer-term development of their staff. Preparation for this role should be given much greater priority in management development programmes, incorporated into qualifications for managers and supervisors, and included in the appraisal of all managers. The justification for giving this such high priority is that what is good for learning is also good for retention, quality improvement and developing the skills and people that will be needed in the future.

NOTE

I thank the Economic and Social Research Council for two grants within The Learning Society and Teaching and Learning Research Programmes, and to the commissioning of a monograph (with Wendy Hirsh) by the ESRC research centre on Skills, Knowledge and Organisational Performance (SKOPE). Both have substantially contributed to this chapter.

REFERENCES

Bandura, A. (1995) *Self-efficacy in Changing Societies*, New York: Cambridge University Press.

Eraut, M. (1997) 'Perspectives on Defining "The Learning Society"', *Journal of Education Policy*, 12(6): 551–558.

Eraut, M. (1998) 'Concepts of Competence', *Journal of Interprofessional Care*, 12(2): 127–139.

Eraut, M. (2000) 'Non-formal Learning and Tacit Knowledge in Professional Work', *British Journal of Educational Psychology*, 70: 113–136.

Eraut, M. (2004a) 'Transfer of knowledge between education and workplace settings', in H. Rainbird, A. Fuller and H. Munro (eds), *Workplace Learning in Context*, London: Routledge, pp. 201–221.

Eraut, M. (2004b) 'The Practice of Reflection', *Learning in Health and Social Care*, 3(2): 47–52.

Eraut, M. (2004c) 'Informal Learning in the Workplace', *Studies in Continuing Education*, 26(2): 247–273.

Eraut, M. (2007a) 'Early Career Learning at Work and its Implications for Universities', in N. Entwistle and P. Tomlinson (eds), *Student Learning and University Teaching*, Monograph Series 4, *British Journal of Educational Psychology*, pp. 113–133.

Eraut, M. (2007b) *Feedback and Formative Assessment in the Workplace*, presentation to TLRP seminar series on Assessment of Significant Learning Outcomes.

Eraut, M. (2007c) 'Learning from Other People in the Workplace', *Oxford Review of Education*, 33(4): 403–422.

Eraut, M. (2009) 'Understanding Complex Performance through Learning Trajectories and Mediating Artefacts', European Conference on Educational Research, Vienna.

Eraut, M., Alderton, J., Boylan, A. and Wraight, A. (1995) *Learning to Use Scientific Knowledge in Education and Practice Settings*. London: English National Board for Nursing, Midwifery and Health Visiting.

Eraut, M., Alderton, J., Cole, G. and Senker, P. (2000) 'Development of knowledge and skills at work', in F. Coffield (ed.), *Differing Visions of a Learning Society, Vol 1*, Bristol, The Policy Press.

Eraut, M. Alderton, J. Cole, G. and Senker, P. (2002a) 'Learning from other People at Work', in R. Harrison, F. Reeve, A. Hanson and J. Clarke (eds), *Supporting Lifelong Learning, Vol. 1 Perspectives on Learning*. Open University with Routledge/Falmer: London, pp. 127–145.

Eraut, M., Alderton, J., Cole, G. and Senker, P. (2002b) 'The Impact of the Manager on Learning in the Workplace', in F. Reeve, M. Cartwright and R. Edwards (eds), *Supporting Lifelong Learning, Vol. 2, Organising Learning*, Open University with Routledge/Falmer, London. pp. 91–108.

Eraut, M., Maillardet, F., Miller, C., Steadman, S., Ali, A., Blackman, C. and Furner, J. (2005a) *What is Learned in the Workplace and How? Typologies and Results from a Cross-Professional Longitudinal Study*. EARLI biannual conference, Nicosia.

Eraut, M., Maillardet, F., Miller, C., Steadman, S., Ali, A., Blackman, C. and Furner, J. (2005b) *An Analytical Tool for Characterising and Comparing Professional Workplace Learning Environments*. BERA Annual Conference, Pontypridd.

Eraut, M. and Hirsh, W. (2007) *The Significance of Workplace Learning for Individuals, Groups and Organisations*, SKOPE monograph. University of Oxford Department of Economics.

Hirsh, W., Silverman, M., Tamkin, P. and Jackson, C. (2004) *Managers as Developers of Others*. IES Report 407, Brighton, Institute for Employment Studies.

Klein, G.A. (1989) 'Recognition-primed Decision', in W.B. Rouse, (ed.) *Advances in Man-Machine Systems Research*. Greenwich, CT: JAI Press, pp. 47–92.

Salomon, G. and Perkins, D. (1998) 'Individual and Social Aspects of Learning', *Review of Research in Education*, 1–24.

Schon, D. (1987) *Educating the Reflective Practitioner: Towards a New Design for Teaching and Learning in the Professions*. San Francisco: Jossey-Bass.

Steadman, S., Eraut, M., Maillardet, F., Miller, C., Furner, J., Ali, A. and Blackman, C. (2005) *Methodological Challenges in Studying Workplace Learning: Strengths and Limitations of the Adopted Approach*. BERA Annual Conference, Pontypridd.

Thomas, K.W. (2000) *Intrinsic Motivation at Work: Building Energy and Commitment*. San Francisco: Berrett-Koehler.

14

Researching Workplace Learning in the United States

Victoria Marsick, Karen Watkins, and
Bridget N. O'Connor

RESEARCHING WORKPLACE LEARNING IN THE UNITED STATES

The term *workplace learning* is not used widely in the United States. *Workplace learning* is replacing the more narrow term, *training*. It is an appealing umbrella term because it helps us re-think the way we study how people learn for the betterment of themselves, their work groups, and their organizations. Workplace learning sits at the intersection of organization behavior – theories and knowledge about the workplace – and learning – theories and knowledge about how people learn, i.e., what causes learning, the nature of its facilitation, or what motivates learners. Table 14.1 offers a sampling of workplace learning definitions, illustrating terminology that US researchers have used in defining the term.

FOUNDATIONS

Whereas in other parts of the world, research in workplace learning has been led by academics as part of vocational or technical education research, here, research has often been led by business and industry and by professional associations in fields such as adult education, business and management education, training and development, organization development, and performance improvement.

Focus in the past has been on structured training and learning interventions appropriate to an earlier industrial era with emphasis on skill development. Changes in work have resulted in changes in learning as manufacturing has declined in the United States, jobs have been outsourced, jobs have moved increasingly toward what is often described as knowledge work or service industries, and all work has become more global. Organizations have become networked, decentralized, and focused on collaborative problem-solving, often in project groups and typically aided by smart technology.

CONCEPTUALIZING WORKPLACE LEARNING

In reviewing the literature, we were struck by the number of articles on the changing conceptualization of workplace learning. Harris (2000, in Altman, 2008) traces the historical shift over

Table 14.1   Sampling of workplace learning definitions

Author	Definition
Jacobs & Park (2009)	"The process used by individuals when engaged in training programs, education and development courses, or some type of experiential learning activity for the purpose of acquiring the competence necessary to meet current and future work requirements. The definition assumes the need to balance, though not always equally, the needs of organizations, which provide the context for the learning, with the needs of individuals who may undertake the learning to advance their own work-related interests and goals." (p. 134)
O'Connor, Bronner, and Delaney (2007)	"This vocabulary [workplace learning] reflects the reality that we have shifted from being dispensers of basic skills and information to being educational experts and business partners whose work is to make sure that learners learn, and not just that training takes place ... (p. x) ... all about creating an environment where learning can flourish" (p. xii)
Raelin, J. (2000)	"There are three critical elements in the work-based learning process: 1. It views learning as acquired in the midst of action and dedicated to the task at hand. 2. It sees knowledge creation and utilization as collective activities wherein learning becomes everyone's job. 3. Its users demonstrate a learning to learn aptitude, which frees them to question underlying assumptions of practice." (p. 2)
Resnick (1987) in Watkins (1998)	Learning in the workplace differs from schooling in that it is: a. focused on acquiring specific competencies vs. generalized skills; b. more social than individual with an emphasis on shared cognition; c. contextualized reasoning vs. symbol manipulation; d. tool manipulation vs. thought activities; e. the ability to see how the system works. (p. 57).
Watkins (1989)	Human Resource Development is the field of study and practice responsible for the fostering of a long-term, work-related learning capacity at the individual, group, and organizational level of organizations. (p. 427)

time from Taylorism in the 1970s and 1980s to interest in the learning organization, promoted by Senge's (1990) *The Fifth Discipline*. Harris describes organizational efforts to support learning as well as financial barriers, along with a rising interest by workers in their own learning. Fenwick (2008, pp. 19–20) traces a shift from learning as knowledge/skill 'acquisition'; to 'constructivist notions of workplace learning as sense making' with emphasis on 'reflective practice, self-directed learning, transformative learning, and learning style'; to the idea of the learning organization, along with a focus on communities of practice centered around the work of Wenger (1998). Fenwick notes the rise of complexity theory as a lens on workplace learning, recognizing the way in which individual learning and interaction is nested within other systems, that are in turn, part of larger systems, all of which interact and lead toward 'emergence' of new knowledge and ways of being and working. Both authors reflect a rising interest in understanding organizations as organic, living systems. Their focus is on individuals, but they underscore an increasing awareness that individuals learn collaboratively and in relationship with others.

The concept of the learning organization may have caused a revolution in how we think about how learning happens in the workplace. Later work by Watkins and Marsick (2003) extended this concept to focus on creating a learning culture. Adult learning research has moved beyond the behaviorist paradigm and increasingly centers on cognitive, constructivist, and social learning theory to understand how individuals solve problems, stop inequities in the workplace, and give power to marginalized groups in both organizations and adult education settings (Fenwick, 2008).

Illustrating these changes is IBM's technology-supported, three-tiered workplace learning architecture (IBM Learning Solutions, 2005) differently designed for: learning through structured modules ('work apart'); learning outside training that is triggered by work ('work enabled'), or incidental learning when focused on a task at work aided by performance support systems designed for that purpose ('work embedded'); IBM's re-conceptualization focuses on what learning is needed, when, by whom, and delivered in what best ways. IBM – which pioneered instructional system development in the industrial training era – has shifted its focus to a learning environment that suits today's knowledge era, one in which learning is supported close to the point of contact with a challenging task. This focus is also reflected in Raelin's (2000) concept of 'work-based' learning (vs. workplace learning), i.e. learning in and through work that is primarily experiential and informal or incidental and therefore contrasts with traditional training approaches.

Much training literature in the past looked at conditions and strategies to maximize transfer *after* training takes place (Baldwin and Ford, 1988; Burke and Hutchins, 2007). With a new focus on learner-centered development within the context of the task and organizational setting – as is the case with IBM's on-demand learning solutions – attention shifts toward support in real time for situated learning, including renewed attention to the learner's background and learning style preferences and to a rich learning environment.

The focus for this chapter, then, is on creating rich learning environments, and the appropriate preparation and supports by individuals, groups, and organizations both to help individuals to learn effectively, often through interaction with others around key tasks or challenges, and to help the organization maximize the benefit from this learning toward its own strategic goals.

In framing the chapter this way, we were struck by an article introducing an approach to child development at the Gazebo School, Esalen. George Leonard (1991, pp. i–v) tells the story of how the best minds in aeronautics competed for a highly-publicized $25,000 Raymond Orteig Prize for the person(s) who made the first non-stop flight from New York to Paris. Teams of experts worked with the view that the successful airplane would undoubtedly be 'a large plane having more than one engine, with a complete crew, including perhaps a navigator, radio man, and another pilot to spell the chief pilot . . . (with) sleeping quarters . . ., the latest in navigation and radio equipment, and nutritious food and drink, and life rafts with emergency provisions in case of a crash at sea.' Charles Lindbergh, 'an unknown airmail pilot' figured out the one critical ingredient needed for success: 'range'! Lindbergh designed 'a plane dedicated to range – streamlined, single-engine, single-piloted, with a huge load of fuel.' Lindbergh did not need highly refined, heavy, equipment; 'he (even) cut off and discarded the portions of his maps he wouldn't need, thus saving a few ounces of weight. *Range!*'

Leonard makes the connection to education, noting that 'The child comes to school well prepared for the journey, having just completed, with no formal instruction whatever, one of the most awesome feats of learning on this planet: the mastery of spoken language' (ibid, p. xx) – a feat attributed to a rich, interactive learning environment with many people and resources supporting the child's language acquisition. Leonard (ibid, p. xx) concludes: 'Clearly, the effectiveness of any educational experience depends upon the frequency, quality, variety, and intensity of the interaction between the learner and the learning environment.' We agree. In today's world, with the focus on learners taking charge of their development, with support from others and the environment, *interaction in a rich environment* is the equivalent of *aeronautical range*.

In Figure 14.1, we outline our model of workplace learning that frames our discussion of research on learning context, inputs, processes, and outcomes.

The learning context

Preeminent in any conceptualization of workplace learning is **context**. As shown in Figure 14.1, we describe levels of context that each of us inhabits at any given time in the workplace: individual, team, group, the organizational learning environment, and the global cultural context. The context is multi-level and multi-faceted. For example, in the case of

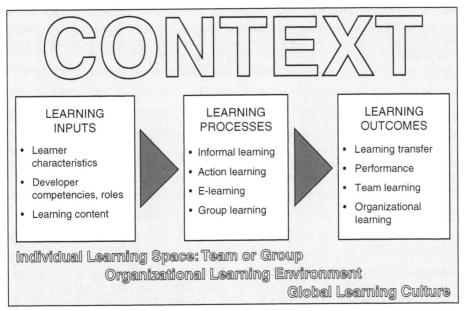

Figure 14.1   Workplace learning model

e-learning, the context includes the individual's learning space – are they working at home in their own time? on a computer workstation next to an assembly line? The learning environment is 'inside the box,' and potentially as well the organizational culture driving the need to learn. From a global culture perspective, the e-learning may be developed in Japan and delivered to a multi-national group of learners with cultural influences from both the developers and peer learners affecting what is learned. Context has long been important, e.g., early research by Scribner (1984) on contextualized reasoning, which contrasts school and workplace learning. Cseh et al. (1999) identified context as a critical driver of informal workplace learning as well.

Questions being asked about context include: What is a learning culture? What is it about the workplace environment that aids or hinders learning? How do race, gender, diversity, and power influence learning? What is it about the environment and the learners themselves that supports learning? What happens when one of these variables changes? One cannot work without learning – the line between 'learning' and 'work' is disappearing – so how can learning be best supported? In other words, what do we need to know, who knows it, and how best can others learn it?

Learning inputs

Inputs are similarly varied. The teacher was once the trainer, but increasingly could be a manager facilitating the learning of employees, a peer mentoring or demonstrating how to do something, a team learning their way through an ambiguous problem, or an employee directing his/her own learning. What learner motivation, cognitive or generational preferences, and characteristics are critical for learning? Where traditional training models assumed a universal learner, newer workplace learning models assume that learners vary and facilitators seek to provide just in time and just enough information.

What is learned, i.e. content, is also incredibly complex. Content in management training differs, for example, when pursuing a standard leadership curriculum – planning, organizing, developing/directing, staffing, coordinating, recruiting, budgeting – vs. action learning (O'Neil and Marsick, 2007) that develops leaders through working on real organizational problems chosen to 'stretch' capabilities. Researchers ask: Who decides what needs to be learned? Who is taking the lead in developing learning initiatives – the individual, work groups, managers, learning specialists? How have the roles of these groups changed?

Learning processes

With the advent of technology, globalization, diversity, and economic recession, the **processes** for learning are also necessarily more complex. They may be formal or informal; work apart, work-enabled, or work-embedded; static (training videos) or organic (learning management systems that evolve with learner input and critique), face-to-face or on-line, etc. Facilitators of workplace learning must work in multiple modalities, and be adept at diagnosing individual and organizational needs. What learning strategies (including classroom-based, e-learning, social learning, and action learning) work best in which learning environment?

Learning outcomes

Much has been written about **outcomes** of workplace learning. Kirkpatrick's (1994) model asked people to design training that moved from mere satisfaction with training to measurable organizational performance improvements. Baldwin and Ford (1988), and more recently Bates et al. (1997), among others, have focused on both learning transfer and organizational barriers that impede transfer from the learning setting to the workplace.

WORKPLACE LEARNING RESEARCH

Based on Figure 14.1, we reviewed research on North American workplace learning environments. The term 'learning environments' is primarily used in e-learning. We extend the term to include the context of what is being learned, where learning takes place, and the organizational culture, including issues of risk and power: inputs, processes, and outcomes.

To ensure a comprehensive review of U.S.A. scholars' research interests, we canvassed individuals who presented papers at the 2009 Americas' Academy for Human Resource Development, asking how their work, and that of other scholars, contribute to an understanding of the field. Respondents were a mix of academics and graduate students – many of whom have also been practitioners. In Table 14.2, we offer sample statements from U.S.-based scholars about workplace learning. In short, they suggested that:

- The boundaries between formal and informal learning are increasingly blurred, but research often focuses on one or the other, and should include both as complementary.
- Learning processes and approaches are greatly influenced by differences in workplace settings (health, education, business, non-profit, etc.) and context.
- Advanced technologies are revolutionizing our understanding of learning and how it is best facilitated.
- Learning is increasingly social and relationship-oriented, and thus, not a solo activity but one carried out in collaboration, often around real work tasks.
- Workplace learning, and its research, is global because that is the nature of work today; and thus, it is difficult to separate workplace learning in the U.S.A. from trends in other countries.
- Workplace learning research is shaped by many different disciplines, often in an eclectic, cross-boundary fashion with an eye toward improving practice.

We then reviewed published literature, turning first to selected peer-reviewed journals, including: *Academy of Management Learning and Education*, *Human Resource Development Quarterly*, and *Performance Review*. We searched databases using the key words 'workplace learning' and 'United States' – Proquest, JSTOR, ERIC, and Education Full Text. Though not peer-reviewed, we included popular journals, particularly the American Society for Training &

Table 14.2 Sample statements from U.S.-based scholars about workplace learning

Focus	Sample statements
Nature and focus of workplace learning	• "There is no solitary future for learning in the workplace. The topic will continue to morph and serve the changing nature of the workplace." (Gene Roth) • "The diminishing boundary between informal and formal learning in the context of the workplace . . . (due to) easy access to advancing communication and information technologies in and out of workplaces . . . (and to) generational difference." (Wen-Hoa David Huang) • "The concepts of organizational learning have made a huge contribution to understanding workplace learning in the US." (Barbara Daley) • "Brown and Duguid's work on canonical and noncanonical practice" along with Marsick and Watkins' work on informal learning have influenced focus on "types of activities that employees use to learn informally and the factors (environmental and personal) that influence engagement in those practices." (Margaret Lohman) • "HRD across organizations, industries, countries; action learning as an organization development intervention, HRD practices in IT, international HRD, gender diversity in workplace." (Yonjoo Cho) • "My thinking regarding workplace learning has evolved from focusing on content to also focusing on 'learning how to learn." (Consuelo Waight)
Key role of context	• "It became clear that how professionals learn and grow in their practice varies across professions and across context. . . . . I would hope that the future of workplace learning would include more in-depth work on the context in which learning occurs . . . ." (Barbara Daley) • "As a technical instructor (at a community college), we are always looking for the material that is the 'most relevant' to the local industry . . . . the college must understand what the local needs are in order to be able to create curriculum relevant to that." (Wayne Manchuaca)
Relevance to practice	• "I often think about how to transfer research to practice in a meaningful way and how to bridge the two." (Jessica Li) • "The most important (research studies) are those that can be practically applied in the workplace." (Irwin Horwitz) • "Provide practical guidelines for HRD in organizations" (Yonjoo Cho)
Eclectic research approach	• "Those who conduct research in workplace learning are 'mutts' who have migrated to this area of interest from different disciplines . . . depending on your frame of reference, you are likely to get a wide range of responses." (Gene Roth) • "Flexibility" is critical. "I do not see myself anchored to any single conceptual frame, but rather, find it more useful to keep current with . . . readings and allow for my research questions to flow" from that. (Irwin Horwitz)

Development's *T+D* since this journal reflects cutting-edge interests of workplace learning professionals. We sought articles that would provide insight into current definitions and understanding of workplace learning, including articles providing an historical perspective; reviews of literature and popular thinking about current trends; and illustrative research. Finally, we drew on our work and experience based on years of research, teaching, and practice in workplace learning at the individual, group, and organization levels.

Research on workplace learning context

Attention to context has increased because of rising interest in the virtual learning environment. Virtual learning environments are defined as 'computer-based environments that are relatively open systems, allowing interactions and encounters with other participants' and providing access to a wide range of resources (Wilson, 1996, quoted in Piccoli et al., 2001, pp. 402–403).

Because many U.S. companies are global, a very important set of contextual variables that also show up in individual characteristics and learning processes is global culture. Workman (2005) studied dimensions of culture in 436 virtual team projects over a 27-month period, 'selected for the naturalistic setting and ecological validity' in a 'transnational (high technology) organization serving in over 220 countries and territories covering more than 140 nationalities speaking 70 languages' (p. 443). Using Hofstede's seminal work on national cultures and his organizational culture framework (Hofstede et al., 1990), he looked at four dimensions hypothesized to affect virtual team performance: structure, relationships, primacy, and boundary delineation. 'This study indicates that virtual teams in which members formalize their process structures (means focused) outperform those in which teams concentrate on results (ends focused) in terms of both quantity and quality' (p. 453). Tighter control and management of process mediates cultural differences and controls for challenges to work and learning in less virtual environments, such as vying for power, potential conflict in group dynamics and development, and standardization of practices. Workman notes that 'indications of strong polarization among French, British, and U.S. nationalities' might have been overcome in face-to-face interaction but need to be controlled in other ways in virtual work.

Context becomes particularly salient when learning is taken out of the classroom and situated, instead, in natural work environments. The triggers, supports and barriers often reside in context. Ellinger (2005), in a qualitative case study, extends prior work on organizational factors that affect learning to identify organizational supports and barriers for informal learning. Ellinger cites Skule (2004) who identified seven critical learning conditions through a survey of businesses and public sector employees in Norway: exposure to change, exposure to demands, managerial responsibilities, extensive professional contacts, feedback, management support for learning, and rewards. Ellinger (2005) found that supportive leadership and management is key to success and a big barrier when not in place. Other factors that are a support when present and a barrier when flawed include appropriate work tools and resources, often technology centered; relationships with others through networks and interactions; and learning culture. Learning can be inhibited by physical and mental silos, time constraints, and magnitude of change.

A key variable is organizational climate and culture. Watkins and Marsick (1993, 2003), and Marsick and Watkins (1999), developed a diagnostic tool to measure changes in organizational learning culture based on their model, the *Dimensions of the Learning Organization Questionnaire (*the *DLOQ 1997)*. In addition, they developed measures of changes in financial and knowledge performance. The *DLOQ* has been tested and modified through numerous research studies across multiple languages, contexts, and cultures. The instrument captures the current status of an organization's culture relative to the dimensions of a learning organization. Results across several early studies were analysed using structural equation modelling by Yang et al. (2004). Findings indicated that four individual and group level learning activities – creating continuous learning opportunities, promoting inquiry and dialogue, encouraging collaboration and team learning, and empowering people toward a collective vision – had indirect but significant effects on organizational outcomes. These individual and group learning variables were highly interrelated. Three organizational level variables – connecting the organization to its environment, creating systems to capture and share learning, and providing strategic leadership for learning – were significantly correlated with organizational knowledge, financial and mission performance outcomes.

Research on workplace learning inputs

Inputs focus on the learner, the teacher/facilitator, and the learning content. Learners are becomingly increasingly self-directed in their learning, and organizations increasingly expect the same of their employees, in part because it is more cost-efficient, and in part because a more highly educated workforce is more in charge of their learning.

Early research by professional organizations focused heavily on the roles and competencies of trainers. Given the shift to learning through work rather than in the classroom, facilitators are often line managers (Ellinger et al., 1999). Facilitation increasingly is a blend of learning and organization development, and of work on real problems, sometimes called action learning. O'Neil and Marsick (2007) have begun to examine the role of facilitators of action learning.

Milton, Watkins, and Daley (2005, p. 8) studied virtual group facilitation and developed a model that integrated group management, group process, and group support interventions. They found that the online environment provided 'a unique opportunity for facilitators to be deliberate in how they intervene in a group, reflect on the results, and respond with flexibility to the group's needs.' Technology helped facilitators with 'modeling interventions so that participants have the opportunity to see, review, and then practice specific skills for their own professional development' (ibid.). They identified a future research need: peer facilitation. 'One goal of a facilitator, as a guide and co-participant, is to have a group take responsibility for facilitating its own learning and performance. The ability of the group to do this may be one indicator of the facilitator's success in fostering group performance' (ibid.).

Research on workplace learning process

Early studies of learning process focused on training design and delivery. Fenwick (2008) points out that the learning process prior to 1985 was understood as knowledge and skill acquisition. By 2000, constructivist understandings of learning as 'sensemaking' arose, along with new models of this learning process, e.g. informal and incidental learning (Marsick et al., 2008) based on learning that is experience-based, situated, reflective, self-directed, collaborative, and sometimes transformative.

A key shift is away from individuals learning on their own to relational learning via interaction with others around work challenges, i.e., through mentoring or coaching pairs, teams, groups, communities of practice, and networks. What, if anything, is different about this process? Hegstad and Wentling (2004) studied exemplary mentoring programs in 27 Fortune 500 companies. While acknowledging the immense growth of mentoring research and practice, they note that 'mentoring in the workplace has only relatively recently claimed recognition as a powerful HRD intervention that assists employees in career advancement, serves as a form of on-the-job training, and helps create learning organizations' (p. 423).

Kram (1985) pioneered the study of developmental mentoring. Kram originally conceived mentoring as multi-relational, 'including senior colleagues, peers, family, and community members' (Higgins and Kram, 2001) even though at the time, mentoring focused on a primary mentor, often older than the mentee, who shared the fruits of experience. While much research has been done on mentoring – e.g, on important individual factors such as 'locus of control' and gender/race of mentor-mentee pairs, as well as organizational factors such as culture, hierarchical structure and diversity (Higgins and Kram, 2001) – less research has focused on the informal learning process at the heart of such relationships. Higgins and Kram (2001) recently argue for re-conceptualizing mentoring as developmental networks, with a focus on 'network diversity and relationships strength' (p. 540). Development networks, they note, have increased because people move in and out of jobs, technology enables virtual mentoring, and increased diversity poses new challenges. Molloy (2005) reviewed research on interpersonal networks, utilization of network access, networks and career competencies, social capital and career success, and personality's role in development networks. Recent attention in this area also involves peer mentoring and coaching involving 'equal status of partners . . . ., focus on personal and professional development of both peers . . . , integration of reflection on practice to identify critical incidents for focus . . . , (and) emphasis on process as well as content that facilitates leadership skill development' (Parker et al., 2008, p. 490).

As technology increasingly mediates learning, we look at learning process via several recent studies of e-learning. A study by Kim et al. (2008) looked at emerging trends for blended learning. Learning processes considered standard and even state of the art were considered least used – lectures, discussion, role play, modeling – while emerging informal strategies were expected to be used most widely in the future – authentic cases and scenario learning, self-paced learning, problem-based and guided learning, mentoring and coaching, virtual team problem-solving. Emerging technologies expected to be used most widely for virtual learning were webcasting and video streaming, digital libraries, knowledge management tools, and on-line simulations. Employee performance on the job was the most likely outcome to be assessed in blended workplace learning.

In contrast, Paradise (2008) surveyed organizations to determine their use of a number of informal learning strategies and found that despite heavy reliance on informal learning strategies such as web-searching, Facebook, posting information on employee bulletin boards, etc., employees sought less technology – rich strategies as informal coffee clutches, voluntary mentoring, and personal e-mail to share knowledge. Mentioned by only 20 per cent of respondents was communities of practice (Paradise, 2008). Nevertheless, virtually every organization surveyed noted that informal learning was prevalent in their organizations.

Immersive learning via gaming, simulations, and second life is growing though less well researched. Jarmon et al. (2009), for example, point out that 'approximately 300 educational institutions . . . have established some kind of presence in Second Life' and that . . . 'by 2011, 80 percent of active internet users, including Fortune 500 enterprises, will have a "second life" in some form of virtual world environment'. Warburton (2009, p. 421) catalogues features that lend themselves to a new learning process, e.g.: 'extended or rich interactions,' 'visualization and contextualization,' 'authentic content and culture,' 'identity play,' 'immersion' via 'virtual embodiment in the form of an avatar and extensive modes of communication,' 'simulation,' 'community presence,' and 'content production.'

Research on workplace learning outcomes

Earlier training research focused primarily on individual learning outcomes, but given the above discussion about the shift to learning in collaboration with others, research is shifting toward a more complex understanding of learning at multiple levels that affect one another. Debates about whether learning or performance should be the primary outcome of focus still exist, but recent work also looks at both learning *and* performance.

Researchers remain interested in learning transfer. In addition to finding out whether or not individuals are able to use what they have learned at work, attention is being paid to post-training support for transfer. Brown (2005), for example, describes interventions oriented to Bandura's self-efficacy theory and to goal setting, which Brown then studied in a training program for Canadian government employees working on organizationally relevant tasks. Groups that set proximal goals did better than those only setting distal goals or expected to simply 'do your best.'

We are especially interested in the impact of workplace learning on organizational and employee performance. Rowden and Conine (2005), for example, studied the impact of informal, incidental and formal workplace learning on job satisfaction among employees in small banks. They demonstrated a significant positive relationship with all forms of workplace learning with informal learning accounting for 41 percent of the variance in overall job satisfaction, incidental learning for 35 percent and formal learning 26 percent (Rowden and Conine, 2008, p. 226). While job satisfaction is not job performance, it is nevertheless interesting to note that in this study, formal learning showed the least job satisfaction.

Sostrin (2008) examined barriers to workplace learning and performance, hypothesizing that reducing barriers would improve performance. Using factor analysis, Sostrin identified seven barriers related to: external environment, organizational structure and capacity, organizational culture, leadership and personnel, behavior, cognition, attitude and motivation, development, and finally learning (approach, design, and implementation).

Business in the United States has taken a pragmatic approach to learning with an emphasis increasingly on return on investment (ROI), an area of research that has been dominated by Phillips (2003). Russ-Eft and Preskill (2005) argue that ROI is not the 'holy grail'. Taking a systems approach, they point out that many organizational variables interact with training/HRD interventions to achieve results, and that 'most of the time, ROI is not necessarily what the client wants or needs, nor is it the best approach to answering the organization's evaluative questions' (p. 72).

Van Buren (2002, p. 63) argued that organizations increasingly understand 'workplace learning as an investment rather than a cost,' based on an American Society for Training and Development (ASTD) Future Search study conducted in June, 2001 with 65 'experts' made up of practitioners, researchers, senior managers, and learners at a time when the economy was experiencing a downturn. Van Buren (2002, pp. 69–70) cites, as well, a research report by ASTD (Bassi et al., 2000) that 'uncovered an extremely powerful connection between investments in workplace learning and financial measures such as total shareholder return.' Learning professionals in U.S. businesses do focus on justifying the costs of learning, and may do so all the more today given the global economic crisis.

CONCLUDING COMMENTS

Our selective review looks at workplace learning as the junction between organizational behavior and learning. Figure 14.1 helped us organize ways that researchers have defined and identified key variables to study contextual influences, inputs, processes, and outputs. Although many studies reviewed are exploratory and/or case study-focused, quantitative and mixed methods research has extended exploratory study insights. In today's world, ensuring that the workforce is prepared not only for existing jobs but able to adapt to global events and economies that impact us is of utmost importance. As academics, we continue to learn with and through our global business/organizational counterparts and our global network of scholars – to explore, challenge, explain, and predict ways to understand the workplace as a rich learning environment.

The authors express their thanks to Columbia University graduate student Stacey Robbins and graphic designer Peter Neaman for their assistance in developing this manuscript.

REFERENCES

Altman, B. (2008) 'The History of Workplace Learning in the United States and the Question of Control: A Selective Review of the Literature and the Implications of a Constructivist Paradigm', *Academy of Human Resource Development International Research Conference in the Americas*, Panama City, FL, Feb. 20–24. ED501676, ERIC.

Baldwin, T.T. and Ford, J.K. (1988) 'Transfer of Training: A Review and Directions for Future Research', *Personnel Psychology*, 41: 63–105.

Bassi, L., Ludwig, J., McMurrer, D.P. and Van Buren, M. (2000) 'Profiting from Learning: Do Firms' Investments in Education and Training Pay Off?' Research White Paper, American Society for Training & Development. Downloaded 6.18.09 from www.astd.org.

Bates, R.A., Holton, E.F. III, Seyler, D.L. (1997) 'Factors Affecting Transfer of Training in an Industrial Setting', in Torraco, R. (eds), *Proceedings of the 1997 Academy of Human Resource Development Annual Conference*, Academy of Human Resource Development, Baton Rouge, LA: 347–354.

Brown, K.C. (2005) 'A Field Study of Employee E-learning Activity and Outcomes', *Human Resource Development Quarterly*, 16(4): 465–480.

Burke, L.A. and Hutchins, H.M. (2007) 'Training Transfer: An Integrated Literature Review', *Human Resource Development Review*, 6(3): 263–296.

Cseh, M., Watkins, K.E. and Marsick, V.J. (1999) 'Re-conceptualizing Marsick and Watkins' Model of Informal and Incidental Learning in the Workplace', in K.P. Kuchinke (ed.), *1999 Proceedings of the Academy of HRD*. Baton Rouge, LA: Academy of Human Resource Development, pp. 349–355.

Ellinger, A.D. (2005) 'Contextual Factors Influencing Informal Learning in a Workplace Setting: The Case of "Reinventing Itself" Company', *Human Resource Development Quarterly*, 16(3): 389–415.

Ellinger, A.D., Watkins, K.E. and Barnas, C.M. (1999) 'Responding to New Roles: A Qualitative Study of Managers as Instructors', *Management Learning*, 30(4): 386–412.

Fenwick, T. (2008) 'Workplace Learning: Emerging Trends and New Perspectives', *New Directions for Adult and Continuing Education*, 119 (17–26). Wiley Periodicals, Inc., published online in Wiley InterScience (www.interscience.wiley.com).

Harris, H. (2000) 'Defining the Future or Reliving the Past? Unions, Employers, and the Challenge of Workplace Learning', Information series no. 380. ERIC Clearinghouse on Adult, Career, and Vocational Education.

Hegsted, C.D. and Wentling, R.M. (2004) 'The Development and Maintenance of Exemplary Formal Mentoring Programs in Fortune 500 Companies', *Human Resource Development Quarterly*, 15(4): 421–448.

Higgins, M. and Kram, K. (2001) 'Reconceptualizing Mentoring at Work: Developmental Network Perspective', *Academy of Management Review*, 26(2): 264–288.

Hofstede, G., Neuijen, B., Ohayv, D.D. and Sanders, G. (1990) 'Measuring Organizational Cultures: A Qualitative and Quantitative Study across Twenty Cases', *Administrative Science Quarterly*, 35: 285–316.

IBM Learning Solutions (2005) 'On Demand Learning: Blended Learning for Today's Evolving Workforce', Unpublished document downloaded from http://www-935.ibm.com/services/uk/index.wss/whitepaper/igs/a1022918?cntxt=a1006896 (accessed 18.06.09).

Jacobs, R.L. and Park, Y. (2009) 'A Proposed Conceptual Framework of Workplace Learning: Implications for Theory Development and Research in Human Resource Development', *Human Resource Development Review*, 8(2): 133–150.

Jarmon, L., Lim, K.Y.T. and Carpenter, B.S. II. (2009) 'Pedagogy, Education and Innovation in Virtual Worlds', *Journal of Virtual Worlds Research*, 2(1): ISSN: 1941–8477. Downloaded from http://jvwresearch.org (accessed 18.06.09).

Kim, K., Bonk, C. and Oh, E. (2008) 'The Present and Future of Blended Learning in Workplace Learning Settings in the United States', *Performance Improvement* 47(8): 5–16.

Kirkpatrick, D.L. (1994) *Evaluating Training Programs: The Four Levels*. San Francisco, CA: Berrett-Koehler.

Kram, K. (1985) *Mentoring at Work: Developmental Relationships in Organizational Life*. Glenview, IL: Scott, Foresman and Company.

Leonard, G. (1991) 'Introduction', in J. Lederman (ed.), *In Full Glory, Early Childhood: To Play's the Thing*. Big Sur: The Gazebo School Park Press, Esalen Institute.

Marsick, V.J. and Watkins, K. (1999) *Facilitating Learning Organizations: Making Learning Count*. London: Gower Press.

Marsick, V.J., Watkins, K.E., Callahan, M.W. and Volpe, M. (2008) 'Informal and Incidental Learning in the Workplace', in M. C. Smith with N. DeFrates-Densch (eds), *Handbook of Research on Adult Learning and Development*. Abingdon: Routledge.

Milton, J., Watkins, K. and Daley, B. (2005) 'Virtual OD: Facilitating Groups Online', in M.L. Morris and F.M. Nafukho (eds), *Proceedings of the Academy of Human Resource Development*. Estes Park, CO: Academy of Human Resource Development, pp. 1287–1294.

Molloy, J.C. (2005) 'Development Networks: Literature Review and Future Research', *Career Development International*, 10(6): 536–587. Downloaded 20.6.09 from Proquest (ABI/INFORM Global).

O'Connor, B.N., Bronner, M. and Delaney, C. (2007) *Learning at Work: How to Support Individual and Organizational Learning*. Amherst: HRD Press.

O'Neil, J. and Marsick, V.J. (2007) *Understanding Action Learning*. New York: AMACOM.

Paradise, A. (2008) 'Informal Learning: Overlooked or Overhyped?', *T & D*, 62(7)7: 52–54.

Parker, P., Hall, D.T. and Kram, K.E. (2008) 'Peer Coaching: A Relational Process for Accelerating Career Learning', *Academy of Management Learning & Education*, 7(4): 487–503.

Phillips, J.J. (2003) *Return on Investment in Training and Performance Improvement Programs* (2nd edn). London: Butterworth-Heinemann.

Piccoli, G., Rami, A. and Blake, I. (2001) 'Web-based Virtual Learning Environments: A Research Framework and a Preliminary Assessment of Effect', *MIS Quarterly*, 25(4): 401–426.

Raelin, J. (2000) *Work-Based Learning: The New Frontier of Management Development*. London: Addison-Wesley.

Resnick, L.B. (1987) 'Learning in School and Out', *Educational Researcher*, 16(9): 13–20.

Rowden, R. and Conine, C. (2005) 'The Impact of Workplace Learning in Small US Commercial Banks', *Journal of Workplace Learning*, 17(3/4): 215–230.

Russ-Eft, D. and Preskill, H. (2005) 'In Search of the Holy Grail: Return on Investment Evaluation in Human Resource Development', *Advances in Developing Human Resources*, 7(1): 71–85. Downloaded 20.6.09 from Proquest (ABI/INFORM Global).

Scribner, S. (1984) 'Studying Working Intelligence', in B. Rogoff and J. Lave (eds), *Everyday Cognition: Its Development in Social Context*. Cambridge, MA: Harvard University Press, pp. 9–40.

Senge, P.M. (1990) *The Fifth Discipline*. New York: Currency Doubleday.

Skule, S. (2004) 'Learning Conditions at Work: A Framework to Understand and Assess Informal Learning in the Workplace', *International Journal of Training and Development*, 8(1): 8–20.

Sostrin, J. (2008) *Establishing and Validating a Conceptual Framework of Barriers to Workplace Learning and Performance: A Q-method Study*. A Dissertation submitted to Fielding graduate university in partial fulfillment of the requirements for the Degree of Doctor of Philosophy in Human and Organizational Systems. UMI number: 3350581.

Van Buren, M.E. (2002) 'From Cost to Investment: Workplace Learning has New Significance', *Employment Relations Today*, 29(1): 63–70. Downloaded 18.6.09 from Proquest (ABI/INFORM Global).

Warburton, S. (2009) 'Second Life in Higher Education: Assessing the Potential for and the Barriers to Deploying Virtual Worlds in Learning and Teaching', *British Journal of Educational Technology*, 40(3): 414–426.

Watkins, K. (1998) 'Foundations for HRD in a Knowledge Era', in Stewart, B. and Hall, H. (eds), *Beyond Tradition: Preparing HRD Educators for Tomorrow's Workforce*. Columbia, MO: University Council on Workforce & Human Resource Education.

Watkins, K. (1989) 'Business and Industry', in S. Merriam and P. Cunningham (eds), *Handbook of Adult and Continuing Education*. San Francisco: Jossey-Bass.

Watkins, K. and Marsick, V.J. (1993) *Sculpting the Learning Organization*. San Francisco: Jossey-Bass.

Watkins, K. and Marsick, V.J. (eds) (2003) 'Make Learning Count!: Diagnosing the Learning Culture in Organizations', *Advances in Developing Human Resources*, 5(2).

Wenger, E. (1998) *Communities of Practice: Learning, Meaning, and Identity*. Cambridge: Cambridge University Press.

Workman, M. (2005) 'Virtual Team Culture and the Amplification of Team Boundary Permeability on Performance', *Human Resource Development Quarterly*, 16(4): 435–458.

Yang, B., Watkins, K. and Marsick, V.J. (2004) 'The Construct of the Learning Organization: Dimensions, Measurement, and Validation', *Human Resource Development Quarterly*, 15(1): 31–55.

15

Researching Workplace Learning in Australia

Nicky Solomon and David Boud

This chapter provides a snapshot of research in workplace learning in Australia from the perspective of some of its key players. Workplace learning as an interdisciplinary field covers a wide range of research and programme interests. This is exemplified in the diversity of journals that publish research on workplace learning (Fenwick, 2006). The range and complexity of the field contributes to its richness, but at the same time it presents interesting challenges in terms of making decisions on what is and what is not workplace learning. In order to identify and summarise the theoretical frameworks, conceptions and contributions to understandings of Australian workplace learning knowledge and practices we used an approach that focused on the researchers' own representation of their workplace learning research. At the same time we also recognise that as authors of this chapter we are making our own selection of what should be included within the scope of workplace learning research and we are re-presenting the researchers' representations of their work.

A brief picture of the broad socio-political context in Australia is provided in order to draw attention to features that influence research in workplace learning. We believe that the way research in workplace learning is undertaken and the nature and shape of its contributions to knowledge are a consequence of a dynamic relationship between academic researchers, institutional settings and government policies. The policies and settings provide both boundaries and opportunities, and the way these are enacted upon is influenced by a number of factors to do with the researchers – their disciplinary histories and professional trajectories, together with their institutional, national and international networks.

We begin the chapter by explaining our methodological approach. This is followed by a description of some of the features of the Australian research policy context of workplace learning. This leads into a section on the various understanding of workplace learning by Australian researchers in the field. Drawing on the submitted profiles we then consider the trajectories of the researchers and connect these to their contributions and their research methodologies. We conclude with some thoughts on the position of Australian workplace learning research and the conditions in which it has developed.

APPROACH

We identified main categories of workplace learning research in Australia based on our view of workplace learning. This view foregrounds *learning at work* and therefore does *not* include a focus on all those educational or institutional learning activities concerned with a preparation for work. The categories used were vocational education and training (VET), learning at work, workplace culture and worker identities, equity and diversity.

Within each category we identified prominent Australian authors. These represented not only authors whose work with which we were familiar but sought to include those from all the main centres of research activity in the area. Not all replied to our invitation and there are likely to be others we overlooked. While we acknowledge that this is not a comprehensive list, at the same time we suggest it is indicative of the Australian workplace learning research scene.

To help scaffold writing, we constructed a template for the researcher profiles in order to capture the areas that we, the authors, thought would usefully highlight the significant workplace learning contributions and the factors that have influenced their nature. Researchers were asked to address the following areas:

1   *Do you identify workplace learning as your primary area of research? If not, what is your primary area?*
2   *Your key contributions to problems/issues/knowledge areas in workplace learning.*
3   *Academic and professional trajectory i.e., the career, professional, institutional steps and stages that led to 'doing workplace learning research'.*
4   *Theoretical and conceptual resources for your research.*
5   *Factors that have influenced changes in research direction and focus, for example, peers, networks, international links, funding sources, institutional priorities.*
6   *Five to ten publications that characterise your research in workplace learning.*
7   *Is there something distinctive about workplace learning research in Australia (compared to other countries)?*

Finally we analysed submitted profiles in order to identify the various contributions – collectively and individually – and the various relationships between the researcher, their location, trajectory and theoretical framings.

AUSTRALIAN RESEARCH POLICY CONTEXT OF WORKPLACE LEARNING

Australia is a large country with a small population located in six states and two territories, that until the 1980s had exclusive responsibility for all matters to do with vocational education and training. Since that time, however, Australian research on learning and work has been dominated by national policy development in the area of vocational education and training. Influenced variously by the trade union movement initially and later by employer bodies, this agenda took a fragmented and disparate collection of qualifications and training provisions and aimed to create common frameworks for competency standards across the nation. The national training reform agenda sought to harmonise vocational qualifications across states and establish standards for all occupations (Knight and Mlotkowski, 2009). It grouped training into sectors with common features, involved expert practitioners in developing competency standards and moved away from a curriculum-driven model of provision to one based on 'training packages' that could be delivered and assessed within workplaces. It was less concerned with what was learned and how it was learned, and more concerned about how competence could be judged and by whom it was judged.

While the main features of this agenda did not appear to be influenced explicitly by research, considerable funding flowed accompanying this agenda and some was directed into commissioned research. The research supported was almost exclusively short-term (very few projects were longer than a year) and was directly aimed at supporting the immediate policy being implemented. University researchers successfully bid for funding, but a very large amount of it was directed to private consultants, often former senior employees of the VET sector, who were willing to provide what was wanted on the tight time-lines demanded. The overwhelming amount of research generated was reported in research reports rather than peer reviewed academic publications. The National Centre for Vocational Education Research in Adelaide took an increasingly pivotal role in organising and publishing this research and most of it was made available in the public domain for use within the sector. In volume, this work vastly outnumbers the academic research on work and learning in Australia. The publications arising from commissioned research by various Australian governments, along with other VET-specific publications, can be found in the VOCED database: http://www.voced.edu.au/

A few university research groups developed out of this funding, notably at Monash University, University of South Australia and University of Technology, Sydney (UTS), but it proved difficult to marry the exigencies of short turnaround, frequent reporting and often narrow agendas with wider conceptions of research. Some of this was possible and many of the researchers represented in this chapter either benefited directly from this kind of funding or were located in institutions that did.

Another source of development in this area were those higher education institutions that traditionally had responsibility within their states for the training of teachers for the public Technical and Further Education system (TAFE). After the major reorganisation of higher education around 1990, most of these institutions became part of universities and developed research interests of their own.

Research on workplace learning in Australia is dominated by research that arose from the changing VET context. While there has been research on work and learning conducted in business schools, the emphasis there has not been on learning *per se*, but on work and organisations. In summary, most researchers come from a background related to vocational education and training or have worked with co-researchers that have. However, in most cases they have broadened their interests away from what many of them experienced as a narrow and oppressive policy-driven approach to one that reflects a diverse range of interests that sometimes encompasses VET, but in many cases, may not. Formal vocational education and training acts as a counterpoint to the interests now developed, and, like the present authors, it has sometimes taken them into areas that are untouched and possibly untouchable by government policy.

In terms of outlets for workplace learning research, there is no Australian conference that covers the whole area of work and learning. However, the Australian Vocational Education and Training Research Association (AVETRA) has an annual research conference which focuses on research on the VET part of the field. Nevertheless, there is a great variety of relevant international journals based in Australia. These include *Studies in Continuing Education* (Taylor and Francis), edited by the authors of this chapter, the relatively new journal *Vocations and Learning* (Springer) edited by Stephen Billett, and the *International Journal of Training Research* (AVETRA) edited by Andy Smith. Until 2008 the *Journal of Workplace Learning* (Emerald) was edited from Australia by Darryl Dymock.

An interesting feature of the public policy agenda in Australia is that a lifelong learning discourse has not taken a strong hold. Indeed, only one of our respondents uses it in their own description of what they do. Unlike the European Union and the OECD that have strongly promoted the concept of lifelong learning, it has not been much mobilised in Australia. While it is not an unfamiliar term, it has not been commonly attached to government initiatives. Neither, unlike countries such as the UK and Sweden, has there been national or state policies, networks or communities that specifically relate to workplace learning other than the explicitly VET part of that area.

UNDERSTANDINGS OF WORKPLACE LEARNING

We know from the breadth of workplace learning literature as well as from some critical analyses of the workplace learning literature (Fenwick, 2006) that workplace learning means different things to different researchers. Indeed the researchers identified as workplace learning researchers for the purposes of this chapter confirm the diversity of areas and understandings. Importantly this is not simply a naming issue but reflects the fact that it is an emerging interdisciplinary field and one that is drawing on a range of theoretical traditions serving a range of academic and 'real world' purposes. This chapter is a site for making explicit the various practices around what can be described as workplace learning research.

The eighteen researchers surveyed described workplace learning as one of the following: a practice, a research context or site, a topic, a field, an emerging disciplinary area, an interdisciplinary area. Some locate themselves either as part of vocational education and training or a wider emerging area, while others place themselves outside the boundary of workplace learning research and see their contributions as part of a broader area. Nonetheless, such researchers still understand their work as contributing to workplace learning research.

Some of the researchers offer alternative names for workplace learning. For example, Devos names her work as learning related to/associated with work. Others foreground a disciplinary area, for example, Beckett describes his research as underpinned by the discipline of philosophy, as also does Hager who views philosophy of vocational education as an emerging sub-discipline. Seddon identifies primarily as 'a sociologist with a special interest in the historical sociology of education as a social institution and as a site of learning and working'. Other researchers seek to disentangle VET and workplace learning, while still others write as if VET and workplace learning are already interrelated. For example, Hawke describes his research as 'principally on vocational education and training with a more recent interest in workplace learning', while Simons and Harris describe workplace learning as a subset of VET reforms in Australia, and sits alongside interests in apprenticeships, competency-based training and building the capacity of VET organisations and their workforces. Reich captures the breadth and complexity of workplace learning research in her profile where she describes her research as in the 'becoming' interdisciplinary field (Fenwick, 2006) of workplace learning, which is 'an emerging field bounded by the fields of adult and vocational education, sociology of work, management/organisation studies, career development, human resource development, industrial/ employment/labour relations and innovation and technology studies'.

PROFESSIONAL TRAJECTORIES OF THE RESEARCHERS

The range of understandings of workplace learning is mirrored in the diverse academic, disciplinary and professional backgrounds of the workplace learning researchers in Australia, what Reich characterises as the 'long and windy road'. This variation of backgrounds in some ways accounts for the diversity of the workplace learning research. But importantly also, the diversity is symptomatic of the current nature of workplace learning as an area of research. As a relatively new area, it is not surprising that researchers' academic careers began in other disciplinary and professional areas. However, this may change as research activity in workplace learning continues and in so doing produce the next generation of workplace learning researchers. Devos and Reich are already examples of academics whose research interest in workplace learning began through their post-graduate and doctoral studies in the area.

For many of the researchers, their move into workplace learning has been triggered by education and research opportunities presented through changes in government and institutional policies. These policies are to do with a changing emphasis on learning in education institutions and learning in and through work, together with a growing appreciation of the value of learning at work. Importantly, while education institutions have become increasingly interested in work as a site of learning, organisations are also looking to education institutions to improve their own understandings of learning for work.

As described earlier, Australian national training and work reforms contributed to the development of the fields of adult and vocational teacher education in universities. The changing nature of work and the competency agenda were important drivers. The development of competency standards and competency-based training required different kinds of vocational curriculum for the VET sector, together with different kinds of knowledge and skills for VET teachers. Furthermore, changing work practices foregrounded communication skills and the language of learning. This had implications for government policy and workplace language and literacy programmes, which in turn provided an entry point for several of today's workplace learning researchers, such as Farrell, Scheeres and Solomon.

As vocational learning and teacher training programmes became increasingly connected to work and workplaces, the workplace as a site of learning and work as a source of curriculum knowledge became interesting to educators. For many of the researchers this was encouraged by teaching postgraduate courses, particularly in adult education, where students' work and professional experiences were part of the curriculum. Many of these students were workplace educators with training and development roles. Academic involvement in setting up or teaching in partnership programmes such as work-based learning degrees (Boud and Solomon, 2001), also helped to focus the research of some of the researchers on workplace learning.

Several researchers have drawn attention to the significant role their research students have played in their own research. This is nicely illustrated in the following quote: 'Over the course of this career, my involvement in teaching students drawn largely from trades and industry, and supervising their Masters and Doctoral studies, has meant that I have been able to give sustained attention to developments within fields such as workplace learning, vocational learning and HR. Many of the students I supervise presently are working in non-educational settings and researching aspects of knowing and learning in these settings. My commitment to workplace learning research is propelled, in part, by a need to successfully resource these supervisions. These students work in non-educational settings in learning and development sections of organizations' (Mulcahy).

Another factor that has led to a research interest in workplace learning is a theoretical one. A focus on workplace learning was a kind of 'natural' focus for adult educators drawing on experiential or situated learning (e.g. Boud).

The nature of workplace learning research is also influenced by the institutional location of the academics and the opportunities for collegial relationships within the same site. An example of this was at University of Technology, Sydney, during the 1990s and early 2000s when there was a concentration of VET/workplace learning research. However, at the same time collaboration does not only occur through co-location. At times, academics working across Australian universities form important research partnerships. For example Beckett and Hager, two philosophers with an interest in vocational education, describe their connection as a 'meeting of minds'. They met in the mid 1990s and continue to be co-authors.

International networks are also an important feature of the research work in Australia. The socio-political conditions that have led to a research focus on workplace learning in Australia exist in many OECD countries. While government policies may vary in detail, the economic imperatives to improve workplace and worker productivity has resulted in a shared concern with learning at work which in turn has resulted in many fruitful international connections. These are enhanced through participation in international conferences, taking study leave in a university in another country, co-writing relationships and involvement in international special interest groups. Invariably the researchers drew attention to their international connections. For example, Seddon notes European networks and programmes as key turning points in her research work (e.g. Seddon, 2007), and Farrell describes her sabbatical at Harvard as an important site of her focus on the economics of globalisation and workforce production. The usefulness and effectiveness of these networks exemplify the significance of global local relations in terms of the workforce and workplaces as well as of academic work. This is reinforced within some of the profiles, where the researchers wrote of their workplace learning research as focusing on universities as workplaces. In some ways this understanding disturbs the frequently invoked binary of universities and workplaces. This may partially explain the way the focus of some workplace learning research is on higher education.

The source of research funding is a significant factor in Australian workplace learning research. In the 1990s VET was relatively well resourced and university researchers were well placed to carry out both commissioned and non-commissioned research. However, while the National Centre for Vocational Educational Research (NCVER) continues to direct, manage and support VET research, academics are no longer the main researchers of policy work. Indeed the researchers' discussion of their research funding sources reveals a vulnerability of funding through universities.

CONTRIBUTIONS

In this section we describe the various contributions of the Australian workplace learning researchers. As we have indicated, the field is an interdisciplinary one and this is reflected in the diversity of areas of the researchers' contributions. Furthermore, given the range of professional and disciplinary trajectories of the researchers there is wide variation in the researchers' methodological approach – from philosophical analysis, to language and discourse analysis, to policy analysis, drawing on post-structural theories, Actor-Network Theory, critical theory, activity theory, and so on.

From the descriptions presented by the researchers in their profiles we have grouped the contributions of research in workplace learning in Australia around four categories:

- Vocational education and training (VET)
- Learning and work practices at work
- Cross-institutional relationships
- Workplace teachers and educators

These groupings capture the main areas within the field of workplace learning, although we recognise the categories are not discrete and in addition some of the researchers contribute over several of the categories:

Vocational education and training research

As suggested earlier, VET has been a major policy and practice area that has shaped a significant amount of research in workplace learning. VET in research terms is concerned with structured and unstructured learning, competence, competencies and assessment, generic skills and graduate attributes within the sector responsible for vocational qualifications. The focus of the research has changed over time in tandem with changing government priorities, policies and funding systems.

The early workplace learning contributions of Paul **Hager** (UTS) and David **Beckett** (University of Melbourne) were on the development and articulation of a holistic or integrated model of workplace/professional competence. This work was in collaboration with various others (Hager et al., 1994; Beckett and Hager, 2002; Hager and Halliday, 2006; Beckett, 2009). This particular focus has informed their work in the related areas of generic skills and graduate attributes (see Hager and Holland, 2006; Beckett and Mulcahy, 2006; Beckett, 2004) and lifelong learning (e.g. Hager, 2004). Their work has contributed to what they see as a fundamental reconstitution of Western educational epistemology in favour of experiential, practice-based lifelong learning (Beckett and Hager, 2002). For Hager, understandings of learning have been unhelpfully skewed by assumptions drawn from formal education arrangements, and this suggests a need to reconceptualise learning itself, as reflected in his recent work (e.g. Hager and Halliday, 2006; Hager, 2004, 2005).

The focus of Beckett and Hager's VET research focuses on questioning, and reshaping learning theory is complemented by others' research on VET systems, practices and relationships. For example, the early work of Geoff **Hawke** (UTS) used research to develop assessment policy and practices within NSW TAFE and then moved on to develop improved linkages between TAFE systems and key industry partners. Hawke led the team that established the first of the national competence standards in Australia, for metals and engineering, which in turn led to his appointment to establish the first National Industry Training Advisory Board in 1992. This early work provided a strong foundation for his research in the Research Centre for Vocational Education and Training at the UTS from 1995. Within this location and drawing on his work in competencies, assessment and VET policy Hawke's greatest contributions have been in linking key ideas from vocational education and training with key practices in workplace learning. In Hawke's view, to a large extent these two domains have developed independently (and often in contradistinction to each other). However, key educational notions such as those underpinning assessment practice within vocational education and training also have critical roles to play within workplace learning, and ideas about the situated nature of workplace learning have important ramifications for the ways in which vocational education and training is structured (see Chappell et al., 2003; Chappell and Hawke, 2008; Hawke, 2004).

The research of Leesa **Wheelahan** (Griffith University) provides a distinctive contribution to research in VET through her work on vocational knowledge. Her focus is on the relationship between vocational and academic knowledge, vocational and professional education, and the relationship between the Australian sectors of tertiary education – vocational education and training and higher education. Taking a social, 'distributive' justice perspective her focus is on democratic access to knowledge. She problematises competency-based training qualifications in VET in Australia arguing that competency-based training disempowers workers as it denies their access to disciplinary knowledge together with systems of meaning that are needed for knowledge to be under their control (Wheelahan, 2007a, 2007b, 2009a, 2009b). Her work is located within the emerging 'social realist' school of educational theorists and draws on the philosophy of critical realism and the sociology of Basil Bernstein. While recognising that knowledge is socially produced by communities of knowledge producers and is therefore fallible, her starting point is from a realist premise, finding the relativism of most constructivism and post-modern approaches to be problematic.

The work of Ann **Reich** (UTS, formerly of University of Western Sydney) is similarly distinctive in terms of its focus. Her research is driven by a theoretical and methodological approach, an analytics of governmentality, based on the later work of Foucault and other governmentality writers (such as Dean and Hindess, 1998; Dean, 1999; Rose, 1999; Rose et al., 2006). Her contributions have been in terms of providing approaches and ways of thinking about technologies of power, enterprise governance and liberal styles of government. Her contributions focus on the role of government in industry, industrial relations and in vocational education and training reforms. The use of an analytics of governmentality perspective allows Reich to focus on technologies of power which she believes is often ignored in the research about workplace learning and vocational education and training. Her contribution has been in raising this perspective in work and learning and vocational education and training research communities, particularly in its application to Australian contexts, since the late 1990s. She has used it to explore the ways in which the worker as learner, as a new subjectivity, was assembled in the industry, industrial relations and vocational education and training reforms (e.g. Reich, 2001, 2002). More recently she used the concept of technologies of training to explore the learning organisation and competency standards (Reich, 2008).

Key contributions made by Terri **Seddon** (Monash University) have been in the contextual analysis of VET reform, workplace learning and teachers' and managers' work. Her research uses the notion of 'context' to investigate the interface between policies and practices of educational work. This orientation opens up questions about social and cultural formations of work, learning and practical politics within working life. Her conceptualisation of contexts has always been a mix of political economy and discourse analysis, rooted in Marx's writings, elaborated through feminist analyses, especially those of Frigga Haug, who mobilised Foucault in critical ways in the 1970s. Building on these resources, Seddon approaches her research work historically, by locating contemporary developments in time (past, present, future) and, increasingly, in space (by recognising scales of practice and interscale agency). This gives her work a political edge because it steps outside local policy and everyday discursive frames and interrogates practice through translocal academic concepts (Angus and Seddon, 2000; Seddon, 1993). Most recently she has been developing a series of contributions that question current policy frames and emphasises the importance of expertise in educational work in VET, particularly in the context of increased global interconnectedness and mobilities (e.g. Seddon, 2009; Seddon et al., 2009).

The workplace learning research of Diane **Mulcahy** (University of Melbourne) grew out of research undertaken for the National Centre for Vocational Education Research (NCVER) in industry and enterprises, on competency-based training. Critically analysing discourses of competency that were circulating when CBT was introduced to Australian vocational education and training, this research involved investigating relations of competence, learning, and knowledge at work (Mulcahy, 1999; Mulcahy and James, 1999; Beckett and Mulcahy, 2006). Set within the interdisciplinary field of science studies, this interest assumes the form of tracing knowledge in action: investigating how disparate epistemic elements are transformed into knowledge and knowledge 'products' such as competency standards, professional teaching standards and their consequences and power effects. Mulcahy's contributions to the field of workplace learning concern an attempt to re-imagine working practices as power-knowledge practices and to explain workplace pedagogy as relational: a practice that moves between the institutions of work and education and promotes the idea of working across the disparate knowledge resources of each institution (e.g. Mulcahy, 2007).

Learning and work practices

A large proportion of the contribution by Australian workplace learning researchers has been in the area of learning and work practices where learning has nothing to do with qualifications. This echoes the significant place learning now has in settings outside educational institutions. The relationship of working and learning and of being a worker and a learner has in many ways dominated the research explorations, examinations and theorisations of many Australian workplace learning researchers. This in part is due to the fact that learning at work is now understood to play an important strategic role in organisations and to the fact that skills training is no longer considered to be adequate as a learning focus in organisations. There is now an emphasis on the complexities around the intimate relationship between learning and working (Beckett and Hager, 2002) and Australian researchers are concerned with new theorisations of learning that take on these complexities.

Stephen **Billett** (Griffith University) describes his contributions as both conceptual and procedural. His conceptual contributions cover a number of areas, and include: reconciling cognitive and socio-cultural perspectives (e.g. Billett, 1996); emphasising the socially-situated character of expertise Billett, 2001); elaborating inter-psychological processes (i.e. those between the personal and social) through the concepts of 'co-participation' and 'relational interdependence' at work (Billett, 2002a, 2006a, 2008); elaborating the duality between workplace affordances and individual engagement as explanatory concepts about leaning and remaking work (Billett, 2008); and conceptualising inter-psychological processes of socially isolated learners (Billett, 2008). His procedural contributions include identifying comprehensive accounts of the requirements for work practice (Billett, 2006b); how individuals learn these requirements through everyday activities (Billett, 2001); how guided learning can be promoted in workplaces (Billett, 2001); the development of a workplace pedagogy (Billett, 1996, 2006b); and models for the promotion of rich learning in workplaces through guided experiences in workplace activities and a workplace curriculum (Billett, 2001) and the role of personal epistemologies in learning through and for work.

The contributions of David **Boud** (UTS) to the field have shifted from a focus on the role of reflection in learning from experience, to reconceptualising reflection as a collective practice to be used within organisations and workplaces (Boud, 2006) to a focus on common issues and problem-solving around workplace challenges (Boud and Middleton, 2003; Boud, 2006). In addition Boud, together with Solomon, produced the first book internationally about emerging work-based learning practices in higher education (Boud and Solomon, 2001). While this focused on utilising workplace learning for higher education courses, more recent contributions are concerned with learning spaces and the opportunities for learning that occur when there are no teachers, trainers or staff developers involved in explicitly fostering learning (Boud and Solomon, 2003; Solomon et al., 2006; Boud, et al., 2009).

The research of Anita **Devos** (Monash University) seeks to address what she understands to be an under-theorisation of workplace mentoring. She has theorised how identity is shaped through mentoring and has begun to develop a political economy of mentoring in contemporary organisations, Devos, 2008, 2007a, 2007b, 2004a). Identifying as a feminist post-structuralist she has also contributed to the development of a gender analysis of workplace learning by linking feminist analyses of work and of learning, with post-structuralist readings of power that draw on the work of Michel Foucault and Judith Butler amongst others. Anita is interested in the relationship between changes to work, the regulation of the self at work and the formation of working identities. These relationships are critical as she sees it to understanding how and what people learn at work. Devos has also done critical work on professional development in universities. This includes, but is not limited to, a gender analysis of the role professional development plays in achieving organisational outcomes (Devos, 2004b, 2002).

Hermine **Scheeres** (UTS) describes her research as deliberately cross-disciplinary. She draws together theories of language, literacy and discourse, with theoretical approaches to organisations and organisational change and learning. She uses socially oriented language and discourse analysis that have roots in systemic functional linguistics and critical discourse analysis. These theoretical approaches are concerned with how language makes meanings in particular contexts and how it is structured for use across situations. She has turned to Foucauldian and post-structural work theorising knowledge, power and identity, particularly in relation to how discourses construct, maintain and permit particular knowledges and identities. Key contributions to workplace learning have been through using her disciplinary knowledge of discourse analysis in her investigations of work, workplaces and workers. For example, one area of research has been how the shift towards post-bureaucratic workplaces has produced new discourses, and how these discourses have been taken up in and as organisational practices (Rhodes et al., 2008; Scheeres, 2007). As an illustration, she explored the practices of multi-functional teams through a detailed analysis of team talk (more and more work is talk) and discussed how learning to be a team and learning to be a team member involve complex social interactions that implicate worker identity and positioning (Scheeres and Rhodes, 2006; Rhodes and Scheeres, 2004; Scheeres, 2003; Iedema and Scheeres, 2003). This kind of identity and discourse work emphasises the centrality of affect at work

Nicky **Solomon** (UTS), in conjunction with her research work with Boud (see above), has drawn upon post-structural understandings of discourse, to understand 'subjectivities of learners and workers' and 'work pedagogies'. She has focused on learning at work by examining the uptake of learning discourses by workers, and by identifying issues around the naming of work as learning and workers as learners (Boud and Solomon, 2003). In addition, given her interest in identity work her contributions have also focused on the construction of learner-worker identities through examining vocational and work pedagogies in a range of further and higher educational programmes (Chappell et al., 2003; Solomon, 2005). Her research has also contributed to understandings of the complexities of doing research in workplaces when identifying everyday learning at work.

The research of Margaret **Somerville** (Monash University) mainly draws on feminist philosophical analysis with philosophers of the 'body', such as Grosz, Probyn, Kirby and Butler. She has been heavily influenced by feminist post-structural methodological traditions such as in the writings of Lather and St. Pierre. More recently she has developed her own philosophical and methodological position as a post-poststructural and postcolonial hybrid. An important contribution has been her focus on workplace learning and safety. This work combines her interest in practical problems such as the high rate of accident and injury in workplaces such as aged care, coal mining and emergency services, and her 'post-poststructural' interest in theorising the body (Billett et al., 2006; Somerville, 2006, 2005; Somerville and Abrahamsson, 2003).

Cross-institutional relationships

The relationship between education institutions and workplaces, particularly the ways work is used for learning purposes, has been taken up by a number of workplace learning researchers. A key site of focus has been the recognition of prior learning (RPL), known in some other countries as the Accreditation of Prior Experiential Learning. For example, one aspect of Wheelahan's work has been on RPL, credit transfer and student articulation between vocational education and training and higher education. These contributions have added to understandings about the nature of sectoral relations, factors that inhibit or promote collaborative institutional arrangements and partnerships, and the consequences for students.

As RPL has been a strong feature of work-based learning degrees, some academics involved in the development and delivery of these degrees have focused their research on knowledge and learning that crosses institutional boundaries. Working within a social justice and social participation framework, the research of Regine **Wagner** (RMIT, formerly of University of Western Sydney) and Merilyn **Childs** (Charles Sturt University formerly of University of Western Sydney) has contributed to pedagogical practices in education institutions in relation to recognition of prior learning (Wagner, 2007; Wagner and Childs, 2006; Childs et al., 2002) and post-graduate work-based degrees (Wagner et al., 2001). They have also researched the nexus of work, learning and social change in industrial settings such as fire fighting (Childs, 2006, 2005), community service and private organisations. Central to their work is a questioning of the way higher education institutions act as gatekeeper and mediators of social, educational and labour market change. More recently they have focused on critical social pedagogy at the nexus of work and learning within the professional practice of university learning and teaching (Childs and Wagner, 2010). They define critical social pedagogy approach as 'the application of an inter-disciplinary action focus with the aim to balance power inequities and economic, social and political disadvantage'. This particular take on social pedagogy adds a cohesive critical theoretical framework to the activist and pragmatist traditions of social pedagogy in the nineteenth and early twentieth century.

Solomon's interest in researching workplace learning was linked to her teaching in and management of work-based learning partnership programmes (Boud and Solomon, 2001). In these programmes the curriculum was a three-way partnership between the university, an organisation and its employees, who were the learners. Through these experiences she sought to better understand the politics involved in inter-institutional partnerships, in the co-production of the curriculum and the learner identities that were being produced in such programmes. One of her earlier contributions to the field was on the 'identity work' of RPL pedagogies and the textual and language practices that learners used to make RPL claims (Solomon, 2005; Solomon and Gustavs, 2005; Chappell et al., 2003).

Workplace teachers and educators

Given that researchers are often also involved in conducting courses for those who educate in workplaces, it is not surprising that a focus on workplace teachers and educators can be seen in their research. The key contributions of Michele **Simons** and Roger **Harris** (University of South Australia) have been around the role of workplace trainers. These include those who as part of their work role assist others to learn in the workplace as well as those who for some part of their role as an educator are based in a workplace. Their studies rest on understanding these roles in terms of the ways in which they act to shape work and hence the learning that might be enabled in workplaces (e.g. Harris and Simons, 2000; Harris and Simons, 2001). While adopting a broadly interpretive perspective, they draw on post-positivist understandings to frame their work. Learning network theory and communities of practice have strongly influenced their thinking and writing.

Lesley **Farrell** (UTS, formerly Monash University) describes her area of research as language and social change and globalising workplaces. She has developed the concept of the textually mediated, globally distributed work*space* to describe how workers learn to produce and engage in the textual practices (overt and covert) that make economic globalisation happen. Her aim has been to examine the micro-processes of globalisation in order to identify 'points of vulnerability' where intervention could actually make a difference. A key dimension was the conceptualisation of workplace communication technologies as hybrid and available for co-opting (Farrell and Fenwick, 2007; Farrell, 2006; Farrell and Holkner, 2006; Farrell and Holkner, 2004). From this perspective she developed the idea of workplace educators as discourse technologists (following Fairclough) and looked at the roles of workplace educators as agents of globalisation (Farrell, 2003, 2001). More recently she has been involved in analysing the concept of the 'global workforce' and the role of workplace education in creating workers who can engage in global production networks. Farrell's early work drew on sociolinguistics but now she engages with a wide range of literatures and theories, including discourse theory, literacy studies, globalisation theory, economic geography and political economy, as well as in the 'various highways and byways' of socio-cultural activity theory.

Mulcahy's contributions to VET area is complemented by her current research investigating teaching standards *as* practice, that is, the actual contingent, situated process of performing teaching tasks. This investigation is set within a broader inquiry into the relationship between professional teaching standards and teacher professional learning. Mulcahy research in workplace learning has been guided largely by post-structuralist concepts and approaches. The theoretical lens of performativity, as exemplified in Actor-Network Theory (ANT), is used to examine how workplace learning and related practices such as working knowledge and innovation at work are assembled or come into being. ANT affords understanding that *realities* such as workers, workplace curriculum and workplace learning and *representations* of those realities (e.g. industry standards, curriculum material) are enacted or performed simultaneously.

AN AUSTRALIAN VIEW OF WORKPLACE LEARNING RESEARCH?

Research on workplace learning in Australia, as in any country, is a function of the conditions in which it operates and the circumstances that gave rise to it. These conditions relate to support for research, particularly the nature of funding available, the locations and environments in which researchers operate and the particular traditions and forms of research on which they can draw.

Research funding has been of two types: commissioned, short-term, immediate policy-related, and researcher-initiated studies. The former has represented by far the largest proportion of research funding, but very few large-scale studies have been undertaken and little of this work has travelled beyond Australia. The researcher-initiated studies that have been emphasised in this chapter are characterised by very low levels of funding and most have been necessarily small-scale. This feature has prompted a focus on innovations in conceptualisation and methodologies that are appropriate for in-depth, but not extensive studies. This work has travelled far and is well represented in international journals.

The locations and institutional environments of Australian researchers have also formed their interests. Many are co-located with colleagues in universities who conduct programmes for adult educators and vocational trainers who themselves are situated in workplaces. Some of them are engaged in commissioned research. They have been stimulated by the issues and problems their students encounter, by the issues that commissioned research ignores and by an awareness of the changing environments of work that they encounter in a variety of peripheral ways.

Research approaches have been particularly eclectic. Large-scale research and the kinds of methodology associated with it have been largely absent though, and the particular trajectories and interests of researchers have dominated. Very few researchers have come from a psychometric or other quantitative tradition. Many have combined a variety of methodologies in their own work, either as part of their own changing emphases or as a response to the need for multiple approaches to problems with which they have been confronted. While it is difficult to generalise from such a small sample, there is a general orientation towards the wide range of post-positivist methodologies. There is also probably a greater emphasis on post-structural approaches than might be expected and there is a thread of influence from those coming from a tradition of applied linguistics creating particular interests in language in workplace learning.

Collaboration is a strong feature, driven both by the exigencies of funding and from a desire to link with others. There is also now an increasing cohort of doctoral research students, many of whom have had and still have a substantial engagement with the world of practice, and these students are beginning to take their place in the academy as academic staff members. Those established in the field are increasingly reaching out into collaborations with colleagues in other countries and are well represented in international forums.

In summary, a small, but strong cadre of workplace learning researchers is established in Australia. They are working on a wide variety of issues with a range of different approaches. Their focus is on understanding the variety of practices and phenomena in the intersection of learning and work and they are responsive to new methodologies and new challenges. The boundary of the field of workplace learning research will continually be redrawn as it shifts to accommodate new interests and the politics of research.

REFERENCES

Angus, L. and Seddon, T. (2000) 'The Social and Organisational Renorming of Education', in T. Seddon and L. Angus (eds), *Reshaping Australian Education: Beyond Nostalgia.* Camberwell, Vic: ACER.

Beckett, D. (2004) 'Embodied Competence and Generic Skill: The Emergence of Inferential Understanding', *Educational Philosophy and Theory,* 36(5): 497–509.

Beckett, D. (2009) 'Holistic Competence: Putting Judgments First', in K. Illeris (ed.), *International Perspectives on Competence Development: Developing Skills and Capabilities.* Routledge: London.

Beckett, D. and Hager, P. (2002) *Life, Work and Learning: Practice in Postmodernity.* Routledge: London.

Beckett, D. and Mulcahy, D. (2006) 'Constructing Professionals' Employ-abilities: Conditions for Accomplishment', in P. Hager and S. Holland (eds), *Graduate Attributes, Learning and Employability.* Springer: New York.

Billett, S. (1996) 'Situated Learning: Bridging Socio-cultural and Cognitive Theorising', *Learning and Instruction,* 6(3): 263–280.

Billett, S. (2001) 'Reconceptualising Vocational Expertise', *Learning and Instruction,* 11(6): 431–452.

Billett, S. (2002a) 'Workplace Pedagogic Practices: Co-participation and Learning', *British Journal of Educational Studies,* 50(4): 457–481.

Billett, S. (2002b) 'Towards a Workplace Pedagogy: Guidance, Participation and Engagement', *Adult Education Quarterly,* 53(1): 27–43.

Billett, S. (2006a) 'Relational Interdependence Between Social and Individual Agency in Work and Working Life', *Mind, Culture and Activity,* 13(1): 53–69.

Billett, S. (2006b) 'Constituting the Workplace Curriculum', *Journal of Curriculum Studies,* 38(1): 31–48.

Billett, S. (2008) 'Learning Throughout Working Life: A Relational Interdependence Between Personal and Social Agency', *British Journal of Educational Studies,* 56(1): 39–58.

Billett, S., Fenwick, T. and M. Somerville (eds) (2006) *Work, Subjectivities and Learning: Understanding Learning through Working Life.* Springer: Dordrecht.

Boud, D. (2006) 'Combining Work and Learning: The Disturbing Challenge of Practice', In R. Edwards, J. Gallacher and S. Whittaker (eds), *Learning Outside the Academy: International Research Perspectives on Lifelong Learning.* London: Routledge, pp. 77–89.

Boud, D. and Middleton, H. (2003) 'Learning from Others at Work: Communities of Practice and Informal Learning', *Journal of Workplace Learning,* 15(5): 194–202.

Boud, D. and Solomon, N. (ed.) (2001) *Work-Based Learning: A New Higher Education?* SRHE and Open University Press: Buckingham.

Boud, D. and Solomon, N. (2003) '"I Don't Think I am a Learner": Acts of Naming Learners at Work', *Journal of Workplace Learning,* 15(7–8): 326–331.

Boud, D., Rooney, D. and Solomon, N. (2009) 'Talking Up Learning at Work: Cautionary Tales in Co-opting Everyday Learning', *International Journal of Lifelong Education,* 28(3): 325–336.

Chappell, C. and Hawke, G. (2008) *Investigating Learning Through Work: The Development of the Provider Learning Environment Scale.* NCVER: Adelaide.

Chappell, C., Hawke, G., Rhodes, C. and Solomon, N. (2003) *High Level Review of Training Packages: Phase 1 Report: An Analysis of the Current and Future Context in Which Training Packages will Need to Operate.* Australian National Training Authority, Brisbane.

Chappell, C., Rhodes, C., Solomon, N., Tennant, M. and Yates, L. (2003) *Reconstructing the Life-long Learner: Pedagogies of Individual, Social and Organisational Change.* Routledge Falmer: London.

Childs, M. (2005) 'Beyond Training: New Firefighters and Critical Reflection', *International Journal of Disaster Prevention and Management,* 14(4), 558–566.

Childs, M. (2006) 'Counting Women in the Australian Fire Services', *Australian Journal of Emergency Management,* 21(2): 29–33.

Childs, M. and Wagner, R. (2010) 'Liquid Learning – the "Life World" as De/Structured Learning Space', in M. Keppell, K. Souter, and M. Riddle (eds), *Physical and Virtual Learning Spaces in Higher Education: Concepts for the Modern Learning Environment*. Hershey, PA: IGI Global.

Childs, M., Ingham, V. and Wagner, R. (2002) 'Recognition of Prior Learning on the Web – a Case of Australian Universities', *Australian Journal of Adult Learning*, 42(1): 39–56.

Dean, M. (1999) *Governmentality: Power and Rule in Modern Society*. Sage Publications: London.

Dean, M. and Hindess, B. (eds) (1998) *Governing Australia: Studies in Contemporary Rationalities of Government*. Cambridge University Press: Melbourne.

Devos, A. (2002) 'Gender, Work and Workplace Learning', in R. Harrison, M. Cartwright and R. Edwards (eds), *Supporting Lifelong Learning: Volume 2, Organising Learning*. Routledge Falmer: London.

Devos, A. (2004a) 'Women, Research and the Politics of Professional Development', *Studies in Higher Education*, 29(5): 591–604.

Devos, A. (2004b) 'The Project of Self, the Project of Other: Mentoring, Women and the Fashioning of the Academic Subject', *Studies in Continuing Education*, 26(1): 67–80.

Devos, A. (2007a) 'Mentoring and the New Curriculum of Academic Work', *Journal of Organizational Transformation and Social Change*, (4)3: 225–236.

Devos, A. (2007b) 'Fashioning the Academic Subject', in L. Farrell and T. Fenwick (eds), *Educating the Global Workforce: Knowledge, Knowledge Work and Knowledge Workers*. Routledge: London.

Devos, A. (2008) 'Where Enterprise and Equity Meet: The Rise of Mentoring for Women in Australian Universities', *Discourse*, 29(2): 195–205.

Farrell, L. (2001) 'Negotiating Knowledge in the Knowledge Economy: Workplace Educators and the Politics of Codification', *Studies in Continuing Education*, 23(2): 201–214.

Farrell, L. (2003) 'Knowing a World in Common: Workplace Education and the Production of Working Knowledge', *Australian Education Researcher*, 30(1): 3–18.

Farrell, L. (2004) 'Workplace Education and Corporate Control in Global Webs of Production', *Journal of Education and Work*, 17(4): 479–493.

Farrell, L. (2006) 'Labouring in the Knowledge Fields: Researching Knowledge in Globalising Workspaces', *Globalisation Education and Societies*, 4(2): 237–248.

Farrell, L. and B. Holkner (2004) 'Points of Vulnerability and Presence: Knowing and Learning in Globally Networked Communities', *Discourse* 25(2):133–144.

Farrell, L. and Holkner, B. (2006) 'Making Language Work in Technologically Hybrid, Globally Distributed, Workspaces', *Studies in Continuing Education*, 28(3): 305–320.

Farrell, L. and Fenwick, T. (eds) (2007) *Educating the Global Workforce: Knowledge, Knowledge Work and Knowledge Workers. World Year Book of Education*. Routledge: London.

Fenwick, T. (2006) 'Tidying the Territory: Questioning Terms and Purposes in Work-Learning Research', *Journal of Workplace Learning*, 18(5): 265–278.

Hager P. (2004) 'Lifelong Learning in the Workplace? Challenges and Issues', *Journal of Workplace Learning*, 16(1/2): 22–32.

Hager P. (2005) 'Current Theories of Workplace Learning: A Critical Assessment', in N. Bascia, A. Cumming, A. Datnow, K. Leithwood and D. Livingstone (eds), *International Handbook of Educational Policy*. Part Two. Springer: Dordrecht.

Hager P. and Halliday J. (2006) *Recovering Informal Learning: Wisdom, Judgement and Community*. Springer: Dordrecht.

Hager P. and Holland S. (eds) (2006) *Graduate Attributes, Learning and Employability*. Springer: Dordrecht.

Hager, P., Gonczi, A. and Athanasou, J. (1994) 'General Issues about Assessment of Competence', in *Assessment and Evaluation in Higher Education*, 19(1): 3–16.

Harris, R. and Simons, M. (2000) 'The Role of Workplace Trainer: Implications for National Competency Standards and the Building of Training/Learning Cultures', *Australian Vocational Education Review*, 7(2): 15–25.

Harris, R. and Simons, M. (2001) 'Informal Workplace Trainers: Their Role in Building a Training Culture', in C. Velde, and T. Ghaye, (eds) *International Perspectives on Competence in the Workplace: Policy and Practice*. Kluwer Press: Amsterdam.

Hawke, G. (2004) 'Generic Skills in a Changing Work Environment', in J. Gibbs (ed.), *Generic Skills in Vocational Education and Training: Research Readings*, Adelaide: NCVER, pp. 124–135. http://www.ncver.edu.au/research/proj/nr2200.pdf

Iedema, R.A. and Scheeres, H.B. (2003) 'From Doing Work to Talking Work: Renegotiating Knowing, Doing and Identity', *Applied Linguistics*, 24(3): 316–337.

Knight, B. and Mlotkowski, P. (2009) *An Overview of Vocational Education and Training in Australia and Its Links to the Labour Market*. NCVER: Adelaide.

Mulcahy, D. (1999) 'Training for New Times: Changing Relations of Competence, Learning and Innovation', *Studies in Continuing Education*, 21(2): 217–238.

Mulcahy, D. (2007) 'Mobile Pedagogies: Spatially Producing the Learner-Teacher', in P. Jeffery (ed.), *Engaging Pedagogies*. Proceedings of the 36th Annual Conference of the Australian Association for Research in Education, 27–30 November, 2006, University of South Australia, Adelaide.

Mulcahy, D. and James, P. (1999) 'Knowledge-Making at Work: The Contribution of Competency-Based Training', *Australian and New Zealand Journal of Vocational Education Research*, 7(2): 81–104.

Reich, A. (2001) 'The Flexible Worker in the Learning Organisation', in F. Bevan, C. Kanes and D. Roebuck (eds), *Knowledge Demands for the Knowledge Economy. Proceedings of the 9th Annual International Conference on Post Compulsory Education and Training* (Vol. 2, pp. 137–143). Brisbane: Centre for Learning and Work Research, Faculty of Education, Griffith University.

Reich, A. (2002) 'Learning Organisations and Child Protection Agencies: Post-Fordist Techniques?', *Studies in Continuing Education*, 24(2): 219–232.

Reich, A. (2008) 'Intersecting Work and Learning: Assembling Advanced Liberal Regimes of Governing Workers in Australia', *Studies in Continuing Education*, 30(3): 1–16.

Rhodes, C. and Scheeres, H. (2004) 'Developing People in Organizations: Working (On) Identity', *Studies in the Education of Adults*, 26(2): 175–193.

Rhodes, C., Scheeres, H. and Iedema, R. (2008) 'Triple Trouble: Undecidability, Identity and Organizational Change', in C. Caldas-Coulthard, and R. Iedema, (eds), *Identity Trouble: Critical Discourse and Contested Identities*. Palgrave-Macmillan: Basingstoke.

Rose, N. (1999) *Powers of Freedom: Reframing Political Thought*. Cambridge: Cambridge University Press.

Rose, N., O'Malley, P. and Valverde, M. (2006) 'Governmentality', *Annual Review of Law and Social Science*, 2: 83–104.

Scheeres, H. (2003) 'Learning to talk: From Manual Work to Discourse Work as Self-Regulating Practice', *Journal of Workplace Learning*, 15(7/8): 332–338.

Scheeres, H. (2007) 'Talk and Texts at Work: Beyond Language and Literacy Skills', *Literacy and Numeracy Studies*, 15(2): 5–18.

Scheeres, H. and Rhodes, C. (2006) 'Between Cultures: An Ethnography of Core Values Training and Worker Identity in a Manufacturing Firm', *Journal of Organisational Change Management*, 19(2): 223–236.

Seddon, T. (1993) *Context and Beyond: Reframing the Theory and Practice of Education*. London: Falmer.

Seddon, T. (2007) 'The European in Transnational Times: A Case for the Learning Citizen', in M. Kuhn (ed.), *Who is the European?: A New Global Player?* Peter Lang: Bern.

Seddon, T. (2009) 'The Productivity Challenge in Australia: The Case for Professional Renewal in VET Teaching', *International Journal of Training Research* 7(1): 56–76.

Seddon, T., Henriksson, L. and Niemeyer, B. (2009) *Learning and Work and the Politics of Working Life: Global Transformations and Collective Identities in Teaching, Nursing and Social Work*. Routledge: London.

Solomon, N. (2005) 'Identity and Pedagogy: Producing the Learner-Worker', *Journal of Vocational Education and Training*, 25(1): 65–108.

Solomon, N. and Gustavs, J. (2005) 'Corporatizing knowledge: Work-Based learning at the University of Technology, Sydney', in E. Michelson and A. Mandel (eds), *Portfolio Development and the Assessment of Prior Learning*. Sterling, VA: Stylus.

Solomon, N., Boud, D. and Rooney, D. (2006) 'The In-between: Exposing Everyday Learning at Work', *International Journal of Lifelong Education*, 25(1): 3–13.

Somerville, M. (2005) 'Working Culture: Expanding Notions of Workplace Cultures and Learning at Work', *Pedagogy, Culture and Society*, 13(1): 5–27.

Somerville, M. (2006) 'Becoming Worker: Vocational Training for Aged Care Workers', *Journal of Vocational Education and Training*, 58(4): 471–481.

Somerville, M. and Abrahamsson, L. (2003) 'Trainers and Workers Constructing a Community of Practice: Masculine Work Cultures and Learning Safety in the Mining Industry', *Studies in the Education of Adults*, 35(1): 19–35.

Wagner, R. (2007) 'So Doctors Become Taxi Drivers: Tackling Professional Skills Recognition in Australia', *International Journal of Interdisciplinary Social Sciences*, 1: 155–162.

Wagner, R. and Childs, M. (2006) 'Exclusionary Narratives as Barriers to the Recognition of Qualifications, Skills and Experience – a Case of Skilled Migrants in Australia', *Studies in Continuing Education*, 28(1): 49–62.

Wagner R., Childs, M. and Houlbrook, M. (2001) 'Workbased Learning as Critical Social Pedagogy', *Australian Journal of Adult Learning*, 41(3): 314–333.

Wheelahan, L. (2007a) 'How Competency-Based Training Locks the Working Class Out of Powerful Knowledge: A Modified Bernsteinian Analysis', *British Journal of Sociology of Education*, 28(5): 637–651.

Wheelahan, L (2007b) 'What Kind of Curriculum, Pedagogy and Qualifications Do We Need for an Uncertain Future?', in M. Osborne M. Houston and N. Toman (eds), *The Pedagogy of Lifelong Learning: Understanding Effective Teaching and Learning in Diverse Contexts*. Routledge: London.

Wheelahan, L. (2007c) 'Blending Activity Theory and Critical Realism to Theorise the Relationship Between the Individual and Society and the Implications for Pedagogy', *Studies in the Education of Adults*, 39(2): 183–196.

Wheelahan, L. (2009a) 'The Limits of Competency-Based Training and the Implications for Work', J. Field, J. Gallacher and R. Ingram (eds), *Researching Transitions in Lifelong Learning*. Routledge: London.

Wheelahan, L. (2009b) 'The Problem with CBT (and Why Constructivism Makes Things Worse)', *Journal of Education and Work*, 22(3): 227–242.

16

Researching Workplace Learning in Europe

Hans Gruber and Christian Harteis

RESEARCHING WORKPLACE LEARNING IN EUROPE

For a long time, in European educational research, issues related to work almost exclusively focused on vocational education and vocational training. A powerful association of researchers co-operated in a number of ways, of which VETNET – the European Research Network on Vocational Education and Training (Lasonen, 1999) – deserves particular recognition, because it brought together researchers from a large number of countries. The VETNET group was, and still is, extraordinarily prominent at the European Conference of Educational Research (ECER), the annual conference of the European Educational Research Association (EERA), an organisation founded in 1994 aiming to foster co-operation between and among European associations and institutes of educational research, and international government organisations. Members of the groups involved in ECER actively searched for co-operation with psychological and sociological research groups; one example is the Priority Program 'Lehr-Lern-Prozesse in der kaufmännischen Erstausbildung' (Teaching-learning processes in vocational education; Beck, 2002), sponsored by the German Research Foundation.

Although some research groups analysed processes at the workplace, the first recognisable European association focussing on these topics was the Special Interest Group (SIG) 'Learning and Professional Development' of the European Association for Research on Learning and Instruction (EARLI), founded at the 1999 biannual conference in Gothenburg, Sweden. The SIG symbolises the growing interest in work-related research in Europe, as the increasing size of biannual SIG conferences shows (2002: Turku, Finland; 2004: Regensburg, Germany; 2006: Heerlen, The Netherlands; 2008: Jyväskylä, Finland). Soon after foundation of the EARLI SIG, European researchers started to more actively participate in the SIG Workplace Learning of the American Educational Research Association (AERA).

In this chapter, we describe research on workplace learning in Europe in some detail. We omit research on vocational education and vocational training, a broad field of research itself, but recognise that there is an overlap in research contents and research actors. Research on workplace learning received increased attention, because theories of work organisation substantially changed as the learning potential of workplaces was acknowledged and learning through work activities was considered to contribute to life-long learning. This perspective includes the notion that after vocational education and training, employees do not possess all capabilities and skills required for effective life-long work performance. Therefore, in the first section, we sketch the development of European work organisation and its educational implications as a base for researching workplace learning. In the second section, we analyse the growth of European research publication activities, both in journal contributions and in conference contributions. In the third section, we try to cluster European research activities by categorising them according to different metaphors describing workplace learning. A brief sketch of the historical development of the research involved in the fourth and final section helps to develop some perspectives for future research.

WORK-LIFE AND WORK ORGANISATION IN EUROPE

In Europe, as in North America, industrial understandings of work were based on Tayloristic ideas during the first two-thirds of the twentieth century. These ideas were in sharp contrast to handicraft conceptions based on individual development in apprenticeship relations from novice state to mastery. This Tayloristic perspective was more prominent, however, and in particular, it dominated mass production until the late 1970s, when European enterprises dreamed of fully computerised and automated production plants free from human workers (Waldner, 1992). The decline of Tayloristic work approaches in Western Europe began in the 1980 when Western enterprises adopted Toyota's idea of making use of employees' individual competences. Womack et al. (1990) argued that decentralisation of competences and responsibilities were the main new ideas. Decentralisation had counterparts in organisational concepts like the lean organisation or total quality management. The main potential for improvement of processes was no longer considered to be held at central steering and planning units, but rather at the operational level of individuals at workplaces. Responsibilities and decision making were transferred to blue collar workers to make smooth and flexible reactions possible on quickly changing market demands. Hence, motivation and competence of each individual employee became important for an enterprise's competitive qualities. Therefore, issues of workplace learning came to the attention of enterprises.

As economic and technological development progressed, the globalisation of markets and production intensified competition between enterprises and generated concepts of work organisation with flexible structures and temporary and partial co-operations and networks (Brafman and Beckstrom, 2008). For such practices of work organisation, competent employees who develop their competences not only in specially designed training settings, but also during their working activities at their workplaces are most important. As part of this perspective of organising work, workplace learning became a part of work activities. Since the 1990s, a number of theoretical accounts and practical means were developed to foster the development of individual competences during daily work. Most prominent are the strategies proposed by Nonaka and Takeuchi (1995) for explicating and exchanging knowledge between individuals within an organisation. Those considerations, developed in East Asia, quickly influenced Western Europe. The theoretical perspective on the relationship between organisation and individual changed accordingly. In early developments of workplace learning issues, the organisational origin of these changes could clearly be seen, for example, focusing on the analysis of competence supporting working conditions (Harteis and Gruber, 2004). Bauer and Gruber (2007) argued that this kind of analytic research has to be separated from research about individual attributes of excellence and successful work. Both kinds of research together form current European research on workplace learning in modern working organisations (Appelbaum and Gallagher, 2000):

- Workers have some degree of autonomy and control over job tasks and methods; thus, jobs are redesigned to enable employees to make work-related decisions.
- Workers are expected to participate in problem-solving and in improving production techniques; thus, they need professional expertise to identify problems and to communicate solutions to colleagues.
- The workplace is organised both around self-directed teams that are directly involved in the working process, and around offline problem-solving and quality-improvement teams that are not directly involved with regular working processes.

It would be exaggerating to claim that European industries developed homogeneously. Currently, the European Union consists of 27 countries, of which some underwent dramatic political and economical development in the recent past, and others have been stable for decades. The development of the work organisation described above mainly applies for those stable countries of the European Union, and even here between differences in the industrial development are to be observed. The Northern European countries (United Kingdom, Germany, The Netherlands, Scandinavia, Northern Italy) developed accordingly in the 1970, when Southern Europe began to change from rural and farming economies to industrial economies. Today, Southern Europe resembles the northern countries while the European Union countries of Eastern Europe still differ substantially. When in the West European industry the above-mentioned concepts of business organisation were developed, often driven through competition, the industry in Eastern Europe continued to follow planned economy. It was the political change in the 1990s which initiated changes in the industrial sectors of Eastern European countries. In 2004, eight of them entered the European Union (Czech Republic, Estonia, Hungary, Latvia, Lithuania, Poland, Slovenia, Slovakia), in 2007 two (Bulgaria, Romania); other countries are candidates (Croatia, Macedonia) or more or less loosely associated with the Union. The development of the economy and in particular of the industry in all these countries is still quite different from the development in the Western European countries, as wages and salaries indicate. As for example, wages in Romania are much lower than in Scandinavia, and manpower intensive work is increasingly transferred to Eastern countries. In these countries manufacturing and executive work still prevails, whereas in the Western part of Europe, knowledge intensive work prevails. Such patterns influence the role of research on workplace learning, leading to a different priority being given to issues of individual competence and learning across the European countries. The next section analyses these differences by describing contributions to research on workplace learning from different countries.

EUROPEAN RESEARCH ON WORKPLACE LEARNING: RESEARCH PUBLICATIONS

The most important indicators for research activity are contributions to the discourse in the academic community, be it in written form (journal publications) or in oral form (conference presentations). It is possible to identify the importance of research on workplace learning by counting contributions from different European countries.

Journal contributions

Currently, there is only one journal which is internationally acknowledged and which is exclusively dedicated to issues of workplace learning. The *Journal of Workplace Learning* is published by Emerald. In 2008, the journal *Vocations and Learning: Studies in Vocational and Professional Education*, published by Springer, was started. Since 2009, Sense will publish the journal *Empirical Research in Vocational and Educational Training*, which is also aiming at considering issues of workplace learning. All three journals are located in Europe. Tynjälä (2007) presented results of an analysis of publications in the *Journal for Workplace Learning* during the years 2000–2007. A total number of 251 contributions were published, with affiliations of first authors distributed among countries as shown in Table 16.1.

The major contributions come from English speaking countries; the Scandinavian countries and The Netherlands are the most productive in publishing in this journal from areas where English is a foreign language. The analogous analysis of affiliations of first authors of the contributions to the journal *Vocations and Learning: Studies in Vocational and Professional Education* is not yet as meaningful, because so far only 24 papers of original research have been published. Among these, however, 16 (66%) were contributions with first authors from Europe, three each from Finland, Germany and Sweden, two each from the United Kingdom and Denmark, one each from Belgium, Norway and Switzerland.

Table 16.1 Affiliation country of first authors in *Journal of Workplace Learning* publications

First author from	
United Kingdom	66
Australia	41
USA	34
Finland	24
Canada	21
The Netherlands	15
Sweden	11
Denmark	8
Others: 20 countries with one, two, or three publications	

Taking together both journals, it is plausible that the native English speaking countries provide the highest numbers of contributions, but there is also a considerable number of research published in these journals from European countries which are not English speaking countries. It seems that within Europe most journal publications on workplace learning stem from the United Kingdom, Scandinavia, The Netherlands and Germany. Researchers from these countries are most visible within the international discourse of scholars, and have, therefore, higher impact than colleagues from other European countries.

Conference contributions

The most important international conferences for research on workplace learning, to which European researchers contribute, are the following:

- Biennial conference of to the European Association for Research on Learning and Instruction (EARLI), in particular its Special Interest Group 'Learning and Professional Development'.
- Biennial conference of the Special Interest Group 'Learning and Professional Development' of the European Association for Research on Learning and Instruction (EARLI).
- Annual conference of the European Conference on Educational Research (ECER).
- Annual Meeting of the American Educational Research Association (AERA), in particular its Special Interest Group 'Workplace Learning'.
- Biennial conference on Researching Work and Learning (RWL).

A frequency analysis of workplace learning contributions of European affiliation countries of first authors to those conferences in 2007 and 2008 is presented in Table 16.2.

Table 16.2 reveals that five countries (Finland, Germany, The Netherlands, Sweden, United Kingdom) outweigh all others in the number of conference contributions on workplace learning. It is worth mentioning that European contributions are in the majority, even at the Annual Meetings of the AERA (SIG 'Workplace Learning'), as the lowest line in Table 16.2 indicates. Of course, numbers of conference contributions do not necessarily provide a valid and reliable measurement of research performance, but they indicate participation at the scientific community which itself is considered a valuable indicator of scientific importance (Palonen and Lehtinen, 2001). Without regard to the quality of the work involved, it is interesting to analyse the attention devoted in different countries to the discourse on workplace learning.

Regional differences

The summaries of journal publications and conference presentations clearly reveal a number of regional differences between the European countries concerning research contributions:

- Researchers from the United Kingdom are very visible in the interational scientific community. As English clearly developed into the *lingua franca* of educational research, one explanation of course is their native

Table 16.2 Affiliation country of first authors in contributions to conferences relevant for workplace learning

	EARLI SIG 2008	ECER 2007	ECER 2008	AERA SIG 2007*	AERA SIG 2008*	RWL 2008	Total
Austria			4				4
Belgium	1	1	2				4
Czech Republic		2	2			2	6
Denmark		3	4	1	1	3	12
Estonia		1	1				2
Finland	71	8	9	2	2	21	113
France		1	4				5
Germany	20	15	19	5	9	5	73
Greece	1	2	3				6
Hungary		1	1				2
Ireland		1	2				3
Italy					1		1
Lithuania		2	2				4
Malta						2	2
The Netherlands	22	11	3	3	3		42
Norway	4	2	1		4	3	14
Poland	1						1
Portugal	1	1	2				4
Romania		5					5
Russia	2		1				3
Spain		1					1
Sweden	1	2	6			23	32
Switzerland	3	3	8				14
Turkey						1	1
United Kingdom	6	11	14	6	6	40	83
Outside Europe	8		3	16	21	91	139

*The AERA SIG contributions were integrated in the full AERA conference. Counted are those contributions officially submitted via the SIG

command of the English language. International exchange obviously is easier for researchers from the United Kingdom. However, countries such as Ireland have the same advantage, but do not make a major contribution to the field of workplace learning. A second reason for the substantial activity in the United Kingdom is that educational research institutes at British universities most explicitly have to meet evaluation requirements with increased publication activity. Some educational journals were almost overwhelmed by British submissions. Third, as we will discuss below, there is a particular focus of research on the workplace which has developed in relation to the British industry and economy.

- There is a second group of countries with remarkable international visibility: Scandinavian countries (in particular Finland, but also Denmark, Sweden and Norway), The Netherlands, and Germany. Together with the United Kingdom, these countries represent those regions of Europe, whose industries have had the longest economic and technological development. Quite early in history, their economies turned to a knowledge-intensive organisation of the work-life. Thus, issues of work-related learning are well established and acknowledged in these countries. The relative eminence of Finland and The Netherlands within this group can be explained with the fact that these countries – similar to the United Kingdom – introduced evaluation systems in their universities quite early, with international visibility and peer-review publication being of utmost importance. In Germany, currently similar developments are occurring.

- It is a remarkable contrast that research about workplace learning from the Romanic countries (France, Italy, Portugal, Spain) is almost invisible. Traditionally, these countries bear a certain reservation towards the English language, which might explain reduced submissions to journals and conferences which communicate in English language. A second reason might be that those Southern European countries which joined the European Union in the 1980s (Spain, Portugal, Greece) are under-represented due to the fact that their industries began their development decades later than those in Northern Europe. The gap of research from France cannot be explained. Speculation might suggest that principal developments in the history were quite different in France; however, in natural science, such a particular role is not to be observed. Research into workplace learning has not developed strongly in France.

- Contributions from Eastern European countries occur only casually. As argued above, these countries' situation is different from the situation in other European countries in a variety of aspects. First, the swift change to a market economy occurred not longer than 20 years ago so that the importance of knowledge-intensive work is still relatively low. Second, it is still quite expensive for researchers from Eastern Europe to attend conferences and thus to get access to the scientific community. However, it seems that researchers from Eastern Europe currently are beginning to develop their integration into the international networks.

It is difficult to predict future development. The countries with major contributions to research on workplace learning have a long tradition of international exchange. It is an almost similar tradition that researchers from Romanic countries are under-represented in this exchange. It appears probable that this proportion remains more or less stable. However, it is plausible to expect an increase of Eastern European contributions as the economies and industries in these countries develop quickly and researchers from their universities try intensively to connect their work with the international scientific community.

This section aimed to describe regional differences and to identify major and minor European contributors to research on workplace learning. Hence, journal and conference contributions were distinguished by nationalities. The next section describes emphases of European research with regard to content.

CONTENT OF RESEARCH ON WORKPLACE LEARNING

National categories do not help to identify theoretical positions in European research on workplace learning. There are rather remarkable differences, however, within the most influential countries identified above in the dominant theoretical conceptions, research paradigms, and research methods, although all researchers agree on differences between learning within educational institutions (schools, universities) and learning at workplaces (Gruber and Palonen, 2007; Hodkinson, 2005; Tynjälä, 2008). In order to accentuate (and even deliberately exaggerate) differences between research perspective on workplace learning, metaphors for learning have been developed and applied (Sfard, 1998; Simons and Ruijters, 2008). These metaphors express explicit and implicit beliefs and assumptions about general mental processes shaping (workplace) learning, and thus they represent paradigmatic positions for analysing learning processes. 'As researchers, we seem to be doomed to living in a reality constructed from a variety of metaphors' (Sfard, 1998, p. 12). Hence, these metaphors facilitate a distinction of European researchers on workplace learning following their basic assumption and research paradigms. In the following, we attempt to discuss the focus of European research on workplace learning using such metaphors. We do not intend to mark these differences as 'nationally innate' or as stable, but rather as descriptions of academic origins and of current preferences.

Acquisition metaphor

The acquisition metaphor, which traces back to Sfard's (1998) seminal work, comprises a way of thinking in entities which are provided in learning settings or working settings and which can be acquired by the learners. This opens various perspectives. First, this metaphor incorporates the view of cognitive psychology with its focus on the storage and retrieval of information (Anderson et al., 1996). Entering a new workplace, for example, demands workplace learning in a sense of acquiring knowledge about tasks, methods, and limitations of responsibility. Second, European efforts include the generation of a competence framework for the certification of knowledge and competencies in order to enhance workers' mobility within Europe. The idea of certification implies that learning results fit within an external structure of capabilities. Such a certificate aims at indicating that an individual has acquired certain capacities of European acceptance. This perspective emphasises the fact of acquiring external standards rather than the fact of developing individual qualities. Third, the perspective of vocations as results of an apprenticeship interprets learning results as acquired capabilities to fulfil vocational tasks.

Vocational qualifications are comparable with attempts to certificate knowledge and competencies. A journeyman in a vocation is supposed to have acquired all necessary knowledge and capabilities to be able to execute his or her profession competently.

- An important strand of research on workplace learning follows the paradigm of expertise. The focus is on the analysis of knowledge structures which enable individuals to permanently perform on a high level. In this category there are conceptualisations of knowledge encapsulation (Boshuizen and Schmidt, 1992), which describe the embedding of conceptual knowledge in practical cases. Special attention is directed towards the role of experience (Strasser and Gruber, 2004), implicit knowledge (Eraut, 1994) and intuition (Harteis and Gruber, 2008) for enabling individuals to extraordinary work performance.
- There is a body of research which particularly focuses on various modes of knowledge acquisition during several work activities (Fischer and Boreham, 2004; Simons and Ruijters, 2004); in some cases this body of research distinguishes intentional and implicit learning processes (Eraut, 2004).
- A wide range of publications which were published in Europe and by European authors deal with issues of acknowledging and certifying individual competences which have been developed either in institutional curricula or in the experience of work practice (Griffiths and Guile, 2004; Rauner, 2004).

These three strands of European research activities reveal the broad scope of the acquisition metaphor. It covers narrow focused research on knowledge analyses as well as broadly argued positions aiming at a harmonisation of European educational policy in the field of vocational and occupational learning. Hence, European research on workplace learning covers mental analyses of individual workers as well as educational policy and labour market studies.

Participation metaphor

The participation metaphor refers to socio-cultural theories which understand learning as participation in cultural practices (Brown et al., 1989; Lave and Wenger, 1991). Workplaces in their social and material shape provide affordances and constraints for individual participation in workplace activities (Billett, 2006). Since individuals accept or reject circumstances at workplaces, they are actively involved in the generation and establishment of workplace practices. This describes the main difference to the acquisition metaphor, that individuals are not considered as recipients of external standards but necessarily as involved in the shaping of social practices. There are a number of research units in Europe which analyse workplace learning under the perspective of the participation metaphor. Some of these are described in the following (this list is not exhaustive).

- The Department of Lifelong and Comparative Education, University of London, United Kingdom: Members of this unit conducted quite large studies on workplace learning processes and how they are influenced by individual biography and experiences (Hodkinson and Bloomer, 2002) as well as social practices established and negotiated at the workplace environment (Evans, 2002). Central messages arising from their research are that (1) learning is an inseparable component of work and work activities and cannot be suppressed (Fuller and Unwin, 2004); (2) learning processes are relationally embedded in workplace activities and, thus, it is not possible to identify one single factor as crucially determining learning outcomes (Evans et al., 2006).
- The Faculty of Education and Institute for Educational Research, University of Jyväskylä, Finland. One of the main research programmes on workplace learning investigates challenges, constraints and dilemmas encountered in learning at work-life. Research in various domains explains the construction of professional identity under consideration of subjectivity (Collin et al., 2008; Eteläpelto and Saarinen, 2006) and influences on the utilisation of learning in training for workplace practice (Tynjälä et al., 2003).

Knowledge creation metaphor

This metaphor was introduced by Paavola et al. (2004) who refer to the theories of knowledge creation developed by Bereiter (2002), Engeström (1999), and Nonaka and Takeuchi (1995). The difference to the previous two metaphors, which were conceptually introduced by Sfard

(1998), is that learning under this perspective is a combination of individual and social processes. Here, learning is not considered in the sense of socialising people into an ongoing practice but as creating completely new knowledge. Several ways of learning exemplify this understanding: discovery learning, inspiration by reflection and observation, the moment of sudden insight (e.g. eureka effect). It is obvious that these ways of (workplace) learning do not occur independently from a social and material environment, but the individual is focused as locus of knowledge creation. Again, the following list of researchers applying the knowledge creation metaphor is exemplary rather than exhaustive.

- The University of Helsinki, Finland: Strong impact on the discourse comes from Center for Activity Theory and Developmental Work Research. Well equipped with resources, this group conducts several projects on the socio-cultural perspectives of generating new practices and new knowledge in work contexts (Kerusuo and Engeström, 2003). Also located at the University of Helsinki, Finland, there is the Center for Networked Learning and Knowledge Building which focuses on learning processes during collaboration at work within networks (Lallimo et al., 2007).
- There is growing interest in researching collaborative knowledge creation in networks. Thus, there is research on networking in workplaces from the United Kingdom (Brown et al., 2004), Finland (Hakkarainen et al., 2004), and Germany (Rehrl and Gruber, 2007). Such analyses provide insight in quality and quantity of group interactions and their influence on collaborative knowledge creation. An international co-operation study in this field (Rehrl et al., 2006) showed that the development of the EARLI SIG Learning and Professional Development can successfully be modelled as growing into an association marked by knowledge creation activities. It seems that both ontogenetic and phylogenetic developments of science can be well understood as processes of individual excellence within increased network activities and collaborative knowledge creation.

Even this brief classification of research about workplace learning in Europe indicates the variety of theoretical and methodological perspectives which are determined by institutional and collaborative contexts rather than by national contexts. Researchers conducting empirical field studies with selective perspectives rarely attempt to utilise a range of theoretical or methodological contexts. However, there is an increasing recognition of the necessity to combine quantitative and qualitative methods, and of attempts to relate individual and social influences on workplace learning (Harteis and Billett, 2008).

PERSPECTIVES OF INTERNATIONAL RESEARCH ON WORKPLACE LEARNING

It is remarkable that research on workplace learning became popular quite late historically. Learning during work activities has occurred as long as occupational work has existed, and medieval European occupational traditions (e.g. handicraft, trade guilds) established fixed schemes of becoming a member of an occupational entity by processes of work-related learning. Educational research did not even focus attention on workplace learning until the Sputnik trauma shook Western societies. This traumatic experience initiated research activities in the national educational systems, mainly focused on school education. It was this interest on school education, which prompted research on workplace learning. Billett (2008) distinguished generations of literature on workplace learning and introduced three categories of purposes for providing workplace learning experiences:

- Educational institutions which provide vocational degrees may integrate opportunities of practice experiences by (simulation of) workplace activities in order to secure or extent institutional learning.
- Enterprises offer workplace learning usually for all entrants from educational institutions in order to mediate all company-specific requirements. Workplaces are considered the only sources of learning experiences.
- Beyond all efforts of preparation for vocational activities, there is an increasing demand for permanent actualisation of knowledge and capabilities. By that, employees are supposed to cope with changing demands.

It is the situated cognition movement (Brown et al., 1989) that discovered workplaces as learning environments. Realising that institutional education in schools often fails regarding the applicability and transferability of knowledge, researchers focused on workplaces as areas where the development and flexible application of knowledge seem to be daily practice. Although this perspective eroded the exclusivity of educational institutions for preparing individuals, the main idea of the situated cognition movement has been to improve learning in schools. Substantial differences between learning in schools and learning outside schools were investigated (Resnick, 1987). The assumption that learning in workplace environments is completely different from 'typical' learning in schools or educational institutions is one of the basic paradigms that the researchers on workplace learning share across different research approaches and research strands. Two generations of researching workplace learning are to be distinguished.

First generation: Improvement of institutional learning

The most popular approach of situated learning, cognitive apprenticeship, seizes the principle of handicraft apprenticeship and applies this to mental learning processes. The basic idea of cognitive apprenticeship (Collins et al., 1989) is to provide experiential learning as masters provide opportunities for apprentices in order to improve the success of institutional learning settings. Similarly, the approach of anchored instruction (Cognition and Technology Group at Vanderbilt, 1997) aims at supporting the understanding of school learning issues by embedding the learning task into authentic problems. Both concepts aim at avoiding the creation of inert knowledge and try to use circumstances of workplaces (e.g. situated and social embeddedness) for improving school settings.

The late 1980s and early 1990s are the years when the constructivist view on teaching and learning became more and more acknowledged (Berliner, 1992; Mayer, 1992). Theories arose which explained inert knowledge by encoding processes which are too narrow to a specific situation and, thus, the recall of a cognitive skill only succeeds under very similar circumstances (Renkl et al., 1996; Ross, 1984). Even if there are European contributions to the debate on constructivist ideas of learning and instruction, the main impulses for the debate about situated learning did not come from European researchers.

Later generation: Workplaces as learning environments

Meanwhile, a broad range of research focuses on workplaces as learning environments in their own right. Whereas early research with anthropological backgrounds described processes and ways of workplace learning, for example, Lave's tailoring studies, more recent work also describes contents which people learn when they follow daily working tasks. Exemplary studies recently published focus on learning from mistakes in order to investigate how professionals take lessons learnt from insufficient incidents in the health-care system (Bauer, 2008) as well as in industrial work (Harteis et al., 2008). Guile and Okumoto (2008) describe the creation of new knowledge and activities of a novice but qualified employee who enters a workplace in the jewellery sector. Although the idea of practice-based learning has its roots in the medieval occupational contexts, workplaces as places of practice only recently have been interpreted as learning environment. Current research still differs widely in its scope. It is thus not yet possible to identify main strands of European research, because there are many ongoing developments.

EUROPEAN PERSPECTIVES FOR RESEARCHING WORK AND LEARNING

There are at least three main challenges for European research into workplace learning. First, the universities in Eastern Europe still have to gain on the field of research on workplace learning, as their economy will develop. Second, there is still much to be done to integrate Southern European researchers more extensively into the discourses. Third, existing research remains quite narrow in its theoretical and methodological scope.

The first challenge, it is assumed, will be influenced by the development of the Eastern European countries. Their development is underway, and so is the academics' development in connecting to the pan-European and worldwide discourses. The second challenge is more difficult to overcome, as only speculations as to the Southern European reluctance for research can be expressed. The third challenge is progress by active contributions. Currently, a tendency to cross-reference in the European literature on workplace learning is to be observed. This can be interpreted as an indication for an early stage of the development of a well-established international discourse. The growing of research communities actively contributing to conferences or publications and the foundation of additional publication platforms (e.g. journals and book series) are promising initiatives to bring forward European and international research on workplace learning.

REFERENCES

Anderson, J.R., Reder, L.M. and Simon, H.A. (1996) 'Situated Learning and Education', *Educational Researcher*, 25(4): 5–11.

Appelbaum, S.H. and Gallagher, J. (2000) 'The Competitive Advantage of Organisational Learning', *Journal for Workplace Learning*, 12: 40–56.

Bauer, J. (2008) *Learning from Errors at Work: Studies on Nurses' Engagement in Error-Related Learning Activities*. Regensburg: University of Regensburg.

Bauer, J. and Gruber, H. (2007) 'Workplace Changes and Workplace Learning: Advantages of an Educational Micro Perspective', *International Journal of Lifelong Education*, 26: 675–688.

Beck, K. (Ed.) (2002) *Teaching-Learning Processes in Vocational Education: Foundations of Modern Training Programs*. Frankfurt: Lang.

Bereiter, C. (2002) *Education and Mind in the Knowledge Age*. Hillsdale: Erlbaum.

Berliner, D.C. (1992) 'Telling the Stories of Educational Psychology', *Educational Psychologist*, 27: 143–161.

Billett, S. (2006) *Work, Change and Workers*. Dordrecht: Springer.

Billett, S. (2008) 'Emerging Perspectives on Workplace Learning', in S. Billett, C. Harteis and A. Eteläpelto (eds), *Emerging Perspectives on Learning through Work*. Rotterdam: Sense, pp. 9–26.

Boshuizen, H.P.A. and Schmidt, H.G. (1992) 'On the Role of Biomedical Knowledge in Clinical Reasoning by Experts, Intermediates and Novices', *Cognitive Science*, 16: 153–184.

Brafman, O. and Beckstrom, R.A. (2008) *The Starfish and the Spider: The Unstoppable Power of Leaderless Organizations*. Charlotte: Baker and Taylor.

Brown, A., Rhodes, E. and Carter, R. (2004) 'Supporting Learning in Advanced Supply Systems in the Automotive and Aerospace Industries', in H. Rainbird, A. Fuller and A. Munro (eds), *Workplace Learning in Context*. London: Routledge, pp. 166–182.

Brown, J.S., Collins, A. and Duguid, P. (1989) 'Situated Cognition and the Culture of Learning', *Educational Researcher*, 18(1): 32–34.

Cognition and Technology Group at Vanderbilt (1997) *The Jasper Project: Lessons in Curriculum, Instruction, Assessment, and Professional Development*. Mahwah: Erlbaum.

Collin, K., Paloniemi, S., Virtanen, A. and Eteläpelto, A. (2008) 'Constraints and Challenges on Learning and Construction of Identities at Work', *Vocations and Learning: Studies in Vocational and Professional Education*, 1: 191–210.

Collins, A., Brown, J.S. and Newman, S.E. (1989) 'Cognitive Apprenticeship: Teaching the Crafts of Reading, Writing and Mathematics', in L.B. Resnick (ed.), *Knowing, Learning, and Instruction*. Hillsdale: Erlbaum, pp. 453–494.

Engeström, Y. (1999) 'Innovative Learning in Work Teams: Analyzing Cycles of Knowledge Creation in Practice', in Y. Engeström, R. Miettinen and R.-L. Punamäki (eds), *Perspectives on Activity Theory*. Cambridge: Cambridge University Press, pp. 377–404.

Eraut, M. (1994) *Developing Professional Knowledge and Competence*. London: Falmer.

Eraut, M. (2004) 'Informal Learning in the Workplace', *Studies in Continuing Education*, 26: 173–247.

Eteläpelto, A. and Saarinen, J. (2006) 'Developing Subjective Identities through Collective Participation', in S. Billett, T. Fenwick and M. Somerville (eds), *Work, Subjectivity and Learning. Understanding Learning Through Working Life*. Dordrecht: Springer, pp. 157–177.

Evans, K. (2002) 'The Challenges of "Making Learning Visible": Problems and Issues in Recognizing Tacit Skills and Key Competences', in K. Evans, P. Hodkinson and L. Unwin (eds), *Working to Learn: Transforming Learning in the Workplace*. London: Kogan Page, pp. 79–94.

Evans, K., Hodkinson, P., Rainbird, H. and Unwin, L. (2006) *Improving Workplace Learning*. London: Routledge.

Fischer, M. and Boreham, N. (2004) 'Work Process Knowledge: Origins of the Concept and Current Developments', in M. Fischer, N. Boreham and B. Nyhan (eds), *European Perspectives on Learning at Work: The Acquisition of Work Process Knowledge*. Luxembourg: European Communities, pp. 12–53.

Fuller, A. and Unwin, L. (2004) 'Young People as Teachers and Learners in the Workplace: Challenging the Novice-expert Dichotomy', *International Journal of Training and Development*, 8: 31–40.

Griffiths, T. and Guile, D. (2004) 'Practice and Learning: Issues in Connecting School and Work Based Learning', in M. Fischer, N. Boreham and B. Nyhan (eds), *European Perspectives on Learning at Work: The Acquisition of Work Process Knowledge*. Luxembourg: European Communities, pp. 278–289.

Gruber, H. and Palonen, T. (eds) (2007) *Learning in the Workplace – New Developments*. Turku: Finnish Educational Research Association (FERA).

Guile, D. and Okumoto, K. (2008) 'Developing Vocational Practice in the Jewellery Sector through the Incubation of a New "Project-Object", *International Journal of Educational Research*, 47: 252–260.

Hakkarainen, K., Palonen, T., Paavola, S. and Lehtinen, E. (2004) *Communities of Networked Expertise: Educational and Professional Perspectives*. Amsterdam: Elsevier.

Harteis, C. and Billett, S. (2008) 'The Workplace as Learning Environment: Introduction', *International Journal of Educational Research*, 47: 209–212.

Harteis, C. and Gruber, H. (2004) 'Competence Supporting Working Conditions', in H.P.A. Boshuizen, R. Bromme and H. Gruber (eds), *Professional Learning: Gaps and Transitions on the Way from Novice to Expert*. Dordrecht: Kluwer, pp. 251–269.

Harteis, C. and Gruber, H. (2008) 'Intuition and Professional Competence: Intuitive Versus Rational Forecasting of Stock Market', *Vocations and Learning: Studies in Vocational and Professional Education*, 1: 71–85.

Harteis, C., Bauer, J. and Gruber, H. (2008) 'The Culture of Learning from Mistakes: How Employees Handle Mistakes in Everyday Work', *International Journal of Educational Research*, 47: 223–231.

Hodkinson, P. (2005) 'Reconceptualising the Relations Between College-Based and Workplace Learning', *Journal of Workplace Learning*, 17: 521–532.

Hodkinson, P. and Bloomer, M. (2002) 'Learning Careers: Conceptualizing Lifelong Work-Based Learning', in K. Evans, P. Hodkinson and L. Unwin (eds), *Working to Learn: Transforming Learning in the Workplace*. London: Kogan Page, pp. 29–43.

Kerusuo, H. and Engeström, Y. (2003) 'Boundary Crossing and Learning in Creation of New Work Practices', *Journal of Workplace Learning*, 15: 345–351.

Lallimo, J., Muukonen, H., Lipponen, L. and Hakkarainen, K. (2007) 'Trialogical Knowledge Construction: The Use of Boundary Object in Multiprofessional Negotiation', in H. Gruber and T. Palonen (eds), *Learning in the Workplace: New Developments*. Turku: Finnish Educational Research Association (FERA), pp. 157–184.

Lasonen, J. (1999) *EERA - Network 2 Programme: Network on Vocational Education and Training Research (VETNET) and Academy of Human Resource Development (AHRD)*. Jyväskylä: University of Jyväskylä.

Lave, J. and Wenger, E. (1991) *Situated Learning: Legitimate Peripheral Participation*. Cambridge: Cambridge University Press.

Mayer, R.E. (1992) 'Cognition and Instruction: Their Historical Meeting within Educational Psychology', *Journal of Educational Psychology*, 84: 405–412.

Nonaka, I. and Takeuchi, H. (1995) *The Knowledge-Creating Company: How Japanese Create Dynamics of Innovation*. Oxford: Oxford University Press.

Paavola, S., Lipponen, L. and Hakkarainen, K. (2004) 'Models of Innovative Knowledge Communities and Three Metaphors of Learning', *Review of Educational Research*, 74: 557–576.

Palonen, T. and Lehtinen, E. (2001) 'How to Illustrate Invisible Scientific Communities', *Higher Education*, 42: 493–514.

Rauner, F. (2004) 'Work Analysis and Curriculum Based on the Beruf Concept', in M. Fischer, N. Boreham and B. Nyhan (eds), *European Perspectives on Learning at Work: The Acquisition of Work Process Knowledge*. Luxembourg: European Communities, pp. 237–256.

Rehrl, M. and Gruber, H. (2007) 'Netzwerkanalysen in der Pädagogik. Ein Überblick über Methode und Anwendung [Network Analyses in Educational Science: An Overview on Method and Application]', *Zeitschrift für Pädagogik*, 53: 243–264.

Rehrl, M., Palonen, T. and Gruber, H. (2006) 'Expertise Development in Science', in H.P.A. Boshuizen (ed.), *Lifelong Learning of Professionals: Exploring Implications of a Transitional Labour Market* (CD-ROM. Proceedings of the 3rd EARLI SIG Professional Learning and Development Conference). Heerlen: Open University of the Netherlands.

Renkl, A., Mandl, H. and Gruber, H. (1996) 'Inert Knowledge – Analyses and Remedies', *Educational Psychologist*, 31(2): 115–121.

Resnick, L. (1987) 'Learning in School and Out', *Educational Researcher*, 16(9): 13–20.

Ross, B.H. (1984) 'Remindings and their Effects in Learning a Cognitive Skill', *Cognitive Psychology*, 16: 371–416.

Sfard, A. (1998) 'On Two Metaphors for Learning and Dangers of Choosing Just One', *Educational Researcher*, 27(2): 4–13.

Simons, P.R.-J. and Ruijters, M.C.P. (2004) 'Learning Professionals: Towards an Integrated Model', in H.P.A. Boshuizen, R. Bromme and H. Gruber (eds), *Professional Learning: Gaps and Transitions on the Way from Novice to Expert*. Dordrecht: Kluwer, pp. 207–229.

Simons, P.R.-J. and Ruijters, M.C.P. (2008) 'Varieties of Work-Related Learning', *International Journal of Educational Research*, 47: 241–251.

Strasser, J. and Gruber, H. (2004) 'The Role of Experience in Professional Training and Development of Psychological Counselors', in H.P.A. Boshuizen, R. Bromme and H. Gruber (eds), *Professional Learning: Gaps and Transitions on the Way from Novice to Expert*. Dordrecht: Kluwer, pp. 11–27.

Tynjälä, P. (2007, August) *Research on Workplace Learning: Approaches, Findings and Challenges*. Keynote lecture at the EARLI Conference at Budapest (Hungary).

Tynjälä, P. (2008) 'Perspectives into Learning at the Workplace', *Educational Research Review*, 3: 130–154.

Tynjälä, P., Välimaa, J. and Sarja, A. (2003) 'Pedagogical Perspectives into the Relationship Between Higher Education and Working Life', *Higher Education*, 46: 147–166.

Waldner, J.-B. (1992) *Principle of Computer-Integrated Manufacturing*. New York: Wiley.

Womack, J.P., Jones, D.T. and Roos, D. (1990) *The Machine that Changed the World*. New York: Rawson.

17

Initiatives in VET and Workplace Learning: A Korean Perspective

Sang-Duk Choi

INTRODUCTION

Studies of the 'East Asian Miracle' have shed light on the major role of education policies in the remarkable economic growth in East Asia between 1965 and 1996 (World Bank, 1993; Green, 1997; Ashton et al., 1999). During this period, while the average annual growth of GNP in the world level was 3.1 per cent, South Korea grew at 8.9 per cent, Singapore at 8.3 per cent and Hong Kong at 7.5 per cent (Castells, 1999: 206). As a result, the East Asian countries have been regarded as models to explain the important roles of the government in promoting economic development (Johnson, 1982; Amsden, 1989; Castells, 1992, 1999; Stiglitz, 2002). Moreover, East Asian skills formation systems have been regarded as among the main contributors to the rapid economic development (Ashton and Green, 1996; Ashton et al., 1999).

As in Korea, East Asian developmental states have been challenged by globalisation and democratisation since the mid-1980s. In particular, the economic crisis in Asian countries in 1997–8 ignited heated discussions on the implications of globalisation for the role of developmental states. Castells argues that the success of the developmental state in economic development has ironically contributed to its demise in East Asian economies because of the incompatibility of the developmental state with the global and informational paradigm (Castells, 1999). However, as he also has to admit, the pattern of economic development and crisis in the East Asian countries was 'dependent on the specific set of relationship between the state, economy and society' (ibid. p. 213; Henderson, 1998).

Japan shows how the developmental state came to an end throughout the 1990s because of its contradiction with global and informational capitalism. Castells points to three sets of factors as main causes of the demise of the Japanese developmental state (Castells, 1999). First, the financial system got out of government control under the conditions of the rapid globalisation of financial markets. Secondly, a transformation of the industrial development model toward 'global decentralization' undermined the 'systemic interaction between the developmental state and Japanese-based multinational networks' (ibid. pp. 235–6). Thirdly, the social structure based on patriarchalism was threatened by the rapid mobilisation of women through the increase of their participation in the political system as well as in the labour market.

By contrast, Singapore is an example which shows that global and informational capitalisation has been compatible with the developmental state. Since the 1990s, Singaporean economic strategy has changed, becoming more flexible and open under the challenge of globalisation (Mallet, 1999: 268–9). Its financial markets have been globalised and made transparent under state control. However, it is evident that a maturing economy and information revolution bring 'a more complex society' and multiply 'the number and capabilities of competing interests' (George, 2000: 198). This change increasingly requires a shift from a top-down, charismatic mode towards democratic and institutional mechanisms.

Taiwan shows a successful transition to democracy in response to globalisation. The consistent achievement of a 'soft landing' of Taiwan economy has been accompanied by political liberalisation since 1987. During the 1990s, the Taiwan government played a 'secondary role in the growing competitiveness of Taiwanese firms' while 'networks' of these firms in Taiwan and other countries found 'their own way out of the semiconductor slump' (Castells, 1999: 291). The largest reserves of foreign currency in the world could protect the economy from speculative attacks during the economic crisis.

China has become another example of the developmental state in that it has successfully transformed its economic system from socialism to capitalism under the strong control of the state. Its economic success has been remarkable even during the period of the Asian economic crisis in 1997–8. As a result, the 'Chinese economy is now the fourth largest in the world and its macro-economic performance remains strong' (OECD, 2008b). Therefore it is too early to predict the demise of the developmental state in China. However, it is also uncertain how long the Chinese Communist Party can keep control of China's economy without confronting political conflict.

In this chapter, the developmental state is defined as 'the state which focuses on economic modernisation as the primary means for nation-building or rebuilding at the expense of political freedom' (Choi, 2003). Developmental skills formation is defined as 'skills formation in which the state plays a major role in coordinating education, training and the labour market on the basis of central control and planning, with a stress on moral and social discipline' (Choi, 2003).

The Korean skills formation system has been recognised as a prototype for East Asian systems, which during the 1970s and 1990s may have provided the linkage between the rapid economic development and the remarkable expansion of education and training. For example, school enrolment rates for upper secondary and higher education dramatically changed, from 29.3 per cent and 9.0 per cent in 1970 to 89.8 per cent and 61.6 per cent in 1996 (Korean Education Index, KEDI, 1996: 32). However, after the Asian financial crisis in 1997–8, the remarkable levels of rapid economic growth plummeted. Castells, one of the best-known theorists of the developmental state, points to the demise of the developmental state and highlights the danger of global flows of capital and information (Castells, 1999: 66).

In this regard, this chapter will examine why and how Korean developmental skills formation has been moving toward the state-coordinated partnership model in response to globalisation and democratisation since the early 1990s, analysing an emerging framework of VET (Vocational Education and Training) and lifelong learning. In this chapter, the state-coordinated partnership model is defined as 'skills formation in which the state plays a major role in promoting the partnership between the state and stakeholders on the basis of the involvement of social partners in making and implementing policies'. These are viewed through an analysis of an emerging framework of VET and lifelong learning by examining new initiatives in VET and workplace learning. It will be discussed in three sections examining: changes in skills profile and requirements since the 1980s; transition from the developmental model to the state-coordinated partnership model in skills formation since the 1990s and continuing reform initiatives in VET and workplace learning in the early 2000s.

CHANGING SKILLS PROFILE AND SKILLS REQUIREMENTS SINCE THE 1980s

The rapid improvement in the skills profile has significantly contributed to the success of the Korean economy. As seen in Table 17.1, the rates of advancement into upper secondary schools and higher education increased from 84.5 per cent and 27.2 per cent to 98.5 per cent and 51.4 per cent, respectively between 1980 and 1995. In particular, as university enrolment quotas increased by 30 per cent in 1981, the progression rate to higher education suddenly increased from 27.2 to 36.4 in 1985. This change continued the academic drift towards mass higher education, while vocational education became marginalised.

By 2007, the rate of entrance into higher education was greater than 82 per cent, while more than 70 per cent of vocational high school graduates continued onto higher education (MOEHRD 2007a). Therefore, the nature of vocational high schools has changed, largely from preparation for work to preparation for higher education. Initial public training has also changed, from mainly training primary or lower secondary graduates to the level of vocational high school graduates to training upper secondary school graduates to the level of two-year college graduates.

Table 17.1   Rate of entering higher schools (%)

	1980	1985	1990	1995	2000	2005	2007
Lower secondary school	95.8	99.2	99.8	99.9	99.9	99.9	99.9
Upper secondary school	84.5	90.7	95.7	98.5	99.6	99.7	99.6
Higher education	27.2	36.4	33.2	51.4	68.0	82.1	82.8

Source: Ministry of Education & Human Resource Development, Statistical Year Book of Education

The expansion of higher education played a major role in narrowing wage differentials until the rapid economic liberalisation of the early 1990s (You and Lee, 1999: 14). In other words, the rapid growth of higher education graduates contributed to the decrease of the HE degree premium. However, this process is now reversing, as the demand for the highly educated, particularly in the financial and insurance sector, has increased under the process of economic globalisation (ibid., p. 14). The demand for finance, insurance, real estate and business services contributed to 30.2 per cent of the total increase in employment rate between 1992 and 1996, compared to 18.4 per cent between 1988 and 1992. Meanwhile, lower qualified labour became the main victims of the financial crisis. Therefore, priority has been given to VET policies to raise employability or to build a safety net for the unemployed or the vulnerable in the liberalised economy.

One of the most serious structural problems is that *Chaebols, or* family controlled conglomerates have exploited relatively low wages and union-free SMEs (small and medium enterprises) as a means to maintain competitiveness. As a result, the productivity differential between large firms and SMEs widened considerably, from 51 per cent to 38.9 per cent between 1981 and 1995[1] (You and Lee, 1999). According to You and Lee, the rate of subcontracting firms among SMEs drastically increased from 36.5 per cent in 1988 to 63.2 per cent in 1992.[2] This means that large *chaebol* conglomerates employed SMEs as a 'union avoidance strategy' under the pressure of active trade union movements since the Labour Movement of 1987 (ibid., p. 27).

The strategy was possible not only because trade unions are based on enterprises, but also because the influence and membership of trade unions are mainly dependent on the size of firms. For example, in the manufacturing sector, the unionisation rates of merely 0.9 and 5.4 per cent in companies employing 10–29 and 30–99 workers, respectively, starkly contrasted with the rates of 62.1 and 76 per cent in companies with 5,000–15,000 and more than 15,000 employees, respectively (ibid., p. 15). Within this context, the wide wage gap and unfair subcontracts between large enterprises and SMEs contributed to widening the productivity differential between them. You and Lee's study shows the productivity differential sharply declined, from 51.0 in 1981 to 38.9 in 1995 (ibid., p. 17).[3] The mobilisation of trade unions has significantly influenced the demand for skills as well as the nature of the labour market. The number of trade unions and union membership rate increased from 2,658 and 16.8 per cent in

Employees by Industry

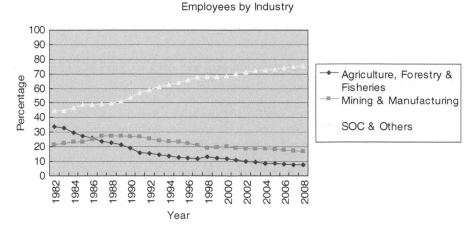

Figure 17.1 Composition of employment by industry

Source: **National Statistical Office, Economically Active**

1986 to 7,861 and 19.8 per cent in 1989 (MOL, *Year Book of Labour Statistics*). Moreover, the majority of trade unions, which had been subordinated to the state or employers, began to be replaced by independent or active trade unions, in spite of political repression.

Another change in the labour market had to do with the composition of employment by industry. As seen in Figure 17.1, the proportion of workers employed in manufacturing declined from 27.8 per cent to 20.2 per cent, whilst those employed in the services sector increased from 52.1 to 68.9 per cent during the period between 1989 and 2000.

The surge in trade union movements and the sharply increased wages of workers put pressure on employers to move towards skill-intensive manufacturing as well as subcontracting or outsourcing. With this increase in subcontracting, employers have tried to introduce new human resource management (HRM) since the late 1980s. This new approach focused on a shift from a seniority-based system to a merit-based one. A survey conducted by the Korea Employers' Federation in 1995 shows that 283 firms out of about 3,000 with over 50 employees introduced new HRM practices, and some of the remaining companies were considering introducing them (Bae, 1998: 95). The characteristics of traditional HRM, as Bae points out, have been 'seniority-based systems, rank-based grade systems, limited lifetime employment and confrontational employment relationships' (ibid., p. 93). However, the limitations of traditional HRM systems have been recognised, particularly by large companies, as both internal and external economic environments have dramatically changed with severe global competition and the rapid development of technology. Traditional HRM was not able to provide sufficient motivation for workers' skills development that is crucial in the move to value-added production. In this regard, large firms now emphasise the importance of further training rather than initial training. This change is also very important, because workers need more specialised skills and knowledge than ever before as well as continually updated skills under the flexible production system.

As rapid technological changes require the new HRM approach, recruitment policy is moving to an emphasis on individual ability in relation to skills and knowledge already acquired. Many Korean companies have started recruiting year round rather than once a year, focusing on job-related ability. These shifts imply that work experience and qualifications have become increasingly important. Such a trend, focusing on employees' flexibility and skills development, has already been seen in some large companies since the economic crisis in 1997. As even *chaebols* have become less committed to lifetime employment, lifelong learning policies are necessary to 'construct a systematic mechanism for this life-long learning for the emerging diversified learners' (Sakamoto-Vandenberg et al., 1998: 35). In other words, lifelong learning is increasingly important for upgrading skills as the labour market becomes flexible.

TRANSITION TOWARDS A NEW FRAMEWORK FOR VET AND WORKPLACE LEARNING SINCE THE MID-1990s

Since the mid-1990s, new initiatives in VET and workplace learning have been launched in order to introduce a new framework of skills formation that could empower workers to cope with the challenges of globalisation and a knowledge-based economy. Therefore, it is important to analyse the new regulations for VET and workplace learning through comparisons with former developmental skills formation, focusing on funding, a qualifications framework and the labour market. The new framework for VET and workplace learning will be discussed on the basis of explaining the transition from developmental skills formation to the state-coordinated partnership model of skills formation in the 1990s.

Direct state coordination of the supply and demand for skills ended with the replacement of the Economic Planning Board (EPB) with the Ministry of Finance and Economy (MOFE) in 1994. After the roles of the EPB were divided between the Ministry of Planning and Budget (MPB)[4] and the Ministry of Finance and Economy (MOFE), economic policy coordination by the MOFE was implemented separately from the budget control of the MPB. Since then, there has been no vertical coordination and education and training have enjoyed more autonomy.

In 1999, the Ministerial Meeting on HRD was established to promote Ministerial cooperation for HRD at the central government level. The Minister of the MOEHRD (Ministry of Education and Human Resources Development) became the Deputy Prime Minister for Education and the HRD Policy Bureau was established under the MOEHRD. However, as the Ministerial Meeting had not been granted the power over HRD-related budget allocation, its role was very limited. As a matter of fact, the government itself had little power to control the demand for and supply of skills within the emerging environment of economic liberalisation and political democratisation.

As a consequence of these developments, three significant changes in skills formation can be identified. First, the government almost abandoned the college enrolment quota system after 1995. Since then universities and colleges, excluding national universities and private universities in Seoul and the surrounding metropolitan area, have been allowed to determine their own admissions quotas (MOEHRD 2002). Secondly, the government also discarded its plans to expand the enrolment ratio of vocational high school students (Ihm, 1999: 315). The government invested more in junior colleges rather than vocational high schools in order to establish the lifelong vocational education system. Thirdly, with the increasing flexibility of the labour market, the focus of the vocational training system has changed, from initial to continuing vocational training, particularly since the economic crisis in 1997. Skills formation has also expanded from formal learning to informal learning in the light of the need for lifelong learning. More importantly, government intervention in VET and workplace learning has been changing from direct control based on standardisation to 'steering at a distance' based on diversification. The changes in VET and workplace learning will be discussed in detail below.

Changes in the funding system

The systems for funding vocational education and training need to be examined separately because their major sources of funding are different. The two major sources of public educational finance are governmental support and private contribution such as student tuition; these were respectively equivalent to 4.4 per cent and 2.8 per cent of the Korean GDP in 2004 (OECD, 2007). The major portion of the government budget for education and training depends on the general budget derived from taxation and from government-run funds, managed mainly by the relevant ministries. The governmental education budget, equivalent to 17.9 per cent of the government's total budget in 2007, is largely dependent on the government budget (MOEHRD, 2007a).

By contrast, the larger portion of the governmental training budget is derived from the Employment Insurance Fund (EIF). In 2007, only 29 per cent of the total funding originated from the government budget, whereas 71 per cent came from the EIF (KEIS, 2008; MOL, 2007). Allocation is normally defined on the basis of the specific purpose of funding and, therefore, the EIF resources are allocated only for training defined by the Employment Insurance Act. The funding mechanism, strictly divided between education and training, has contributed to preventing education and training from linking together.

Vocational education

Vocational education is provided by vocational high schools and junior colleges. Expenditure on vocational education in the governmental education budget was only 2 per cent of the total budget of the MOEHRD in 2006 (MOEHRD 2007b). This was a very small portion of the general account, compared to 80.1 per cent and 15.8 per cent, respectively on primary/secondary education and junior college/university education. More important, the number of vocational high school students rapidly decreased by 46 per cent between 1995 and 2007 while the number of vocational high schools also decreased from 762 to 702 during the same period (MOEHRD 2007a). Data show that 137 out of 148 junior colleges were private whereas only 289 out of 702 vocational high schools were private in 2007. Therefore, as junior colleges become the main providers of vocational education, this tends to be driven by the labour market rather than manpower planning or social partnership.

By 2007, 71.5 per cent of vocational high school graduates went on to receive tertiary education; the majority of them proceeded to junior colleges. Compared to 19.2 per cent in 1995, the rate of entrance to tertiary education is dramatically increasing (MOEHRD, 2007a).[5] Therefore, the role of vocational high schools is rapidly changing, from preparation for a job to preparation for tertiary education. This results in significant changes in VET and lifelong learning. As vocational education is moving towards the junior college level, initial vocational training is also moving from the vocational upper secondary to the junior college level. In 1999, 20 polytechnic colleges that had been among 40 public vocational training institutes under the Human Resources Development Service of Korea (HRD Korea), were allowed to award Industrial Associate Degrees as they had been placed under the Korean Foundation for Polytechnic Colleges in 1998. The other 40 institutes also provide training programmes, equivalent to the junior college level, with short courses.

In addition, eight vocational training institutes under the Korea Chamber of Commerce and Industry (KCCI) provide two-year public training programmes equivalent to the junior college level, and most of their graduates are awarded an Industrial Associate Degree with the support of these institutes. As the rate of entering upper secondary schools reached 99.6 per cent in 2000, it is very difficult for initial training institutes to recruit trainees for vocational upper secondary level programmes (MOEHRD 2007a). Even many public training institutes providing junior college level programmes no longer find it easy to recruit trainees for traditional manufacturing occupations although the programmes are free. Polytechnic colleges provide associate degree programmes for a fourth of the tuition fees of private junior colleges. They have gradually increased their tuition fees under pressure from their competitors.

Vocational training

As referred to above, there are two major sources of finance for training. One is the government budget, which is used mainly for the operational costs of HRD Korea and training for the unemployed amongst the uninsured. The other source is the Employment Insurance Fund (EIF) for initial training, further training and training for the unemployed amongst the insured. By 2007, the total amount of funding originating from the general budget was less than a third of funding from the EIF.

One of the most significant changes in the funding system for VET and workplace learning is the move from the training levy system focused on initial training for school leavers, to the

Employment Insurance System (EIS) emphasising further training for the employed or the unemployed. With the enactment of the Vocational Education and Training Promotion Act of 1997 and the termination of the Basic Vocational Training Act enacted in 1976; the training levy system was completely replaced by the EIS in 1999. Under the provisions of the Employment Insurance Act, the EIF pays for three different undertakings, namely employment stabilisation, vocational competency development and unemployment benefits, and is raised by way of social contributions (KRIVET and NCVER, 2000: 59–60). The contribution rate to the EIF differs with each category. For example, while 0.3 per cent of the payroll is allocated toward the Employment Stabilisation Fund, a varying per centage of the payroll, between 0.1 per cent and 0.7 per cent, depending on the size of the firm, is set aside for the Vocational Training Fund. These two payments are made by the employer only on behalf of the employed. By contrast, the employer and the employee share equal burden for unemployment benefits, each paying 1 per cent of the payroll. For employers, the total contribution rate of the three components adds up to a maximum of 2 per cent of the payroll, except in special economic circumstances, in which it can be increased to 3 per cent.

Compared to the levy system based on the Basic Vocational Training Act, the EIS based on the Vocational Education and Training Promotion Act has many significantly distinctive characteristics. First, the main focus of the EIS is to encourage employers and employees to undertake further training on a voluntary basis (KRIVET, 2000: 74). This focus reflects significant changes in the labour market. For example, the rate of graduates from lower secondary and upper secondary schools who advance to the higher school level dramatically increased, from 84.5 and 27.2 to 99.6 and 68.0, respectively, between 1980 and 2000 (*Statistical Year Book of Education, 1980, 2000*).

As a consequence, the demand for initial training in basic skills for early school leavers rapidly declined in the 1990s. However, while public training under the levy system focused on basic skills training for early school leavers without basic skills or qualifications, it lacked incentives 'for existing employees to improve their technical knowledge and skills to enabling them to attain higher-level technical certificates' (KRIVET, 2000: 73–4). By contrast, the EIS provides incentives for employers or employees undertaking training, as it gives them financial support in the name of the vocational competency development scheme (ibid., p. 75). As a result, the focus of training has rapidly shifted towards further training. For example, 98.8 per cent of employees who completed in-plant training in 1999 underwent further training (ibid., p. 25). Since then, workplace learning has been situated in the heart of the lifelong learning framework.

Secondly, particularly since the enactment of the Vocational Education and Training Promotion Act in 1999, the driving force of further training has shifted from public to in-plant training. The EIS assumes two forms of training, namely public and in-plant training, depending on the training institutions (ibid., p. 26). Public training institutions include the HRD Korea, Korea polytechnic colleges, the Korean Chamber of Commerce and Industry (KCCI), government agencies, autonomous local institutions and the Korea Employment Promotion Agency for the Disabled (KEPAD). The Korea polytechnic colleges are the biggest public training providers, with 40 local campuses, including seven regional colleges. By contrast, in-plant training conducted in three ways: independent training at an in-plant training institution, cooperative training with other employers, and commissioned training through a training institution run by a third party. While initial training is still driven by public training, further training has been mainly provided by way of workplace learning.

Thirdly, with regard to training for vocational competency development, the budget is mainly allocated to employers or employees rather than public training centres. For example, in 2007, 60 per cent of the vocational competency development budget from the EIF was allocated to employers who provided in-plant training, external education and training, and paid study leave for employees. In addition, when employers invest in training facilities or equipment they become eligible for a loan or subsidy from the government. Particularly in the case of SMEs, joint vocational training on the basis of close locations or similar occupations is encouraged. By contrast, only 20 per cent of the vocational competency development budget

Table 17.2 Annual outcomes and budget for vocational competency development (2003–2005) (Unit: thousand pers., 100 million won)

	2003		2004		2005	
	No. of Recipients	Amount	No. of Recipients	Amount	No. of Recipients	Amount
Initial training	32	2,435	38	2,368	33	2,874
Upgrade training	1,725	2,695	2,034	3,100	2,456	3,823
Training for the unemployed	113	2,663	109	3,116	117	3,070
Total	1,870	7,793	2,181	8,584	2.606	9,767

Source: MOL (2007). Korean Labour Statistics. Ministry of Labour, p. 70

was allocated to employees as training incentives and as tuition loans for studying at the level of higher education in 2000.

Fourthly, the system for authorising specific training providers was abolished and was replaced by a policy in which any education and training institute can now apply for 'approval' to provide government-sponsored training programmes on a project basis, if they are able to supply the required facilities and instructors.[6] That is, private training providers now have to compete with each other to provide programmes for the government or employers. In this context, some NGOs, such as the YWCA and the Citizens' Coalition for Economic Justice, have been providing government-sponsored training programmes. In particular, since the Kim Dae-Jung government came to power, an increasing number of NGOs have not only been allowed to provide various programmes for local residents or the unemployed, but to manage public training or welfare facilities with financial support.[7] For example, Women's HRD Centres are managed by several NGOs, including the YWCA, and the Korean Women Workers' Association, with support from central government.

As seen in Table 17.2, the Employment Insurance System, with the enactment of the Workers' Vocational Competency Development Act in 2004, has substantially contributed to a rapid increase in further training for employees. As a consequence, the VET system has become one of the main components of the lifelong learning policy framework, focusing on the establishment of a lifelong VET system.

Changes in the qualifications system

As a part of the the Presidential Commission on Education Reform (PCER) Report, a new vocational education system was proposed to ease the school to work transition on the basis of a new qualifications system. Three characteristics of the new qualifications system can be identified.

First, it is designed to build a lifelong learning framework for vocational school graduates or workers to enter tertiary education. In the new framework, vocational school graduates are given priority in entering junior colleges for a relevant field of study (KRIVET, 2000: 72). In addition, for industrial workers, polytechnic college graduates completing two-year courses have been granted industrial associate degrees since 1998. Those who hold associate degrees can either enter a university or enter the workplace.

Secondly, the system tries to link qualifications with formal education through the Academic Credit Bank System. National qualifications holders are given a limited number of credits for a bachelor's or associate degree (ibid., p. 34). For example, professional engineers, master craftsmen, engineers and industrial engineers are given 45, 39, 30 and 24 credits, respectively. However, the highest number of credits available through the acquisition of qualifications is 110 out of 140 for a bachelor's degree and 65 out of 80 for a two-year associate degree. Moreover, the Academic Credit Bank System has also contributed to recognising the value of work-based learning for lifelong learning because it has provided an alternative route to an associate or BA degree through the accreditation of informal learning. For example, since 1998, the number of degrees awarded has gradually increased and 12,254 learners were awarded diplomas in the first half of 2006 (Choi, 2007).

Thirdly, KRIVET, proposed by the PCER Report and established in 1997, has been the main institution to play a major role in building a new qualifications system and has overseen government-authorised private qualifications (GAPQs). Essentially, the government-authorised private qualifications aim to reduce the rigidity of the national technical qualifications system (NTQS) by challenging the monopoly of state qualifications. The NTQS focused mainly on technical occupations and has limitations in emerging or rapidly changing occupations such as those in the finance or IT sectors. In addition, while the NTQS was very effective for quantity-oriented manpower planning, it has shown serious limitations in raising quality and flexibility (KRIVET, 2000). Most important, the NTQS has not only been completely separate from vocational education and academic qualifications, but confined to technical qualifications under the responsibility of the MOL.

KRIVET assesses the government-authorised private qualifications every three years, and permits qualified awarding bodies to provide the certifications for an additional three years. Private qualifications awarding bodies can apply for government approval via related ministries. By February 2002, the government had approved 65 qualifications for 35 occupations with regard to eight ministries, including the Ministry of Finance and Economy, the Ministry of Labour and the Ministry of Information and Communications.[8] Compared to the NTQS, this resulted in significant changes in private qualifications. As government approval is regarded as a mark of quality, many awarding bodies are competing for recognition. As a consequence, this recognition has contributed to enhancing the reputation of authorised private qualifications. The effect seems to promote the role of the private sector in the national qualification framework and to affect national qualifications which reflect the demands of the workplace.

However, the new framework also resulted in another dual system of vocational qualifications. Whereas KRIVET oversees the government authorisation of private qualifications, HRD Korea is in charge of the national technical qualifications system. In an effort to coordinate the two, the MOEHRD legislated the Basic Act on Qualifications for 'an integrated qualifications framework' which includes both state qualifications and government-authorised private qualifications.

Changes in the labour market

Since the Asian financial crisis in 1997, the high rate of unemployment has been one of the most serious issues in Korean society. The unemployment rate soared to 6.8 per cent in 1998, sending shockwaves throughout the labour market because the rate had been less than 3 per cent for a decade. The most vulnerable victims were those with low levels of educational achievement. For example, the unemployment rate of those who were at least junior college graduates increased from 3.0 per cent to 5.7 per cent between 1997 and 1998, while that of low and upper secondary graduates increased more sharply from 1.5 and 3.3 per cent to 5.8 and 8.2 per cent, respectively. In addition, the need for flexibility in the labour market became a serious issue. The layoffs, that were delayed to take effect in 1999 after the labour struggle against them in 1996, were introduced soon after the crisis. Lifetime employment in large firms became a relic of the past. Workers in SMEs were the hardest hit by the financial crisis. In 1998, 'the average nominal wage in SMEs decreased by 2.5 per cent, whereas that in large firms was reduced by only 1.1 per cent' (You and Lee, 1999: 19).

The rate of temporary or part-time employment soared dramatically from 43.3 per cent in 1996 to 53 per cent in 1999 and this become a serious issue for social cohesion (Lee and Kim, 2001: 45). Temporary or part-time workers have frequently been discriminated against, in wages and welfare services provided by firms, and the majority of them have been excluded from the benefits of major social insurances (Shim, 1999). With the increased rate of unemployment since the financial crisis, however, the Employment Insurance was extended to temporary or part-time workers as well as to firms employing fewer than five employees in 1999 (op. cit. p. 45). Nevertheless, Employment Insurance still covered only 55.1 per cent of total wage employees in 2000. Therefore, training has been an important issue, particularly for the increasing numbers of temporary or part-time workers employed in large firms as well as for workers employed in SMEs.

As the issue of unemployment was put high on the political agenda, various proactive labour market policies were introduced to tackle the problems. For example, public training for the unemployed dramatically expanded until the rate of unemployment started to decrease. This paved the way for the rapid expansion of further training and lifelong learning. In addition, as social demand for a 'social safety net' rapidly increased with the increasing flexibility of the labour market, lifelong learning has been recognised as a means not only to prepare for the knowledge-based economy, but also to tackle unemployment issues in the name of 'productive welfare'. New approaches to skills formation were introduced under the framework of National HRD, which emphasises the coordination between ET-related ministries.

The establishment of the Korea Tripartite Commission (KTC) was a milestone in moving from developmental skills formation towards state-coordinated partnership, particularly in relation to the labour market and training. The KTC is seen as a distinctive example of the effect of changing relations between the state and civil society in the democratic transition. After the economic crisis, the KTC was set up at the behest of labour in order to empower workers to negotiate with government and management in return for allowing labour flexibility. In February 1999, labour, management and the government reached the first tripartite compromise on social agreement which was regarded as one of the major contributors to overcoming conflicts in industrial relations at the time. Also, at the request of labour, the Act for the establishment and operation of the KTC was promulgated on May 1999, and the tripartite system was legally institutionalised as the Presidential advisory body.

The KTC contributed to reaching agreements between labour, management and the government regarding the adjustment of the industrial structure and the labour market. At the same time, the KTC paved the way for the institutionalisation of trade unions' participation in making and implementing policy regarding industrial relations and training issues at the company and national levels. Although the mechanism is still vulnerable because some representatives of labour and management are suspicious of the KTC's role, it has reached a basic agreement on training. Under the provisions of the Workers' Participation and Cooperation Promotion Act of 1997, an employer is required to establish a 'Labour-Management Council' that has the power to make decisions on the 'basic plan for education and training and competency development for employees' at the company level. Therefore the agreement of the KTC on training can influence the contents of these training plans at the company level.

CHALLENGES TO VET AND WORKPLACE LEARNING IN THE 21st CENTURY

In the advent of a knowledge-based global economy in the twenty-first century, Korea faces challenges resulting from a rapidly changing work environment, declining birth rates and an ageing society. The main challenge to VET and workplace learning has been keeping VET institutions and workplaces relevant in a rapidly growing and changing economy. Therefore, continuing reform initiatives in VET and workplace learning seem to focus on building an 'innovative' skills formation system, emphasising the importance of coordination and partnership along with the trend in decentralisation and marketisation of government services. In this regard, the following section of this study will discuss continuing or new initiatives to establish a lifelong VET system promoting the involvement of stakeholders in the provision of VET and workplace learning, particularly for under-represented groups such as workers of SMEs, non-regular workers and the unemployed and low-skilled people.

Establishing a lifelong VET and workplace learning system

The Korean government has placed a high priority on establishing a lifelong VET system in response to rapid changes in the labour market. In particular, it is increasingly important to provide wide access to further education and training for a workforce less exposed to learning opportunities with strong connections between VET institutions and industries.

It is worth mentioning that the Ministry of Labour and the Ministry of Education, Science and Technology (MEST) have just launched two pilot activities to create individual learning accounts promoting lifelong learning. The Ministry of Labour seeks to provide financial support for jobseekers, workforce in SMEs, and non-regular workers. The learning account can be used for paying the costs of vocational training in the name of vocational competency development account (Ministry of Labour, 2007). It will provide increased training opportunities particularly for non-regular workers having been excluded from training. The MEST also intends to create lifelong learning credit account system, which define learning accounts not in financial but in educational terms (OECD, 2008a). The lifelong learning credit account is similar to a learning record which makes it possible for individual learners to accumulate learning credits based on various learning experiences, like the Academic Credit Bank System. It can provide alternative opportunities for people with low education to acquire academic certificates or qualifications by accumulating learning credits. The government seeks to combine the two pilot activities.

In addition, since the Ministry of Labour initiated an on-line training scheme in 1999, e-learning has rapidly expanded as a tool for the provision of vocational training in the workplace. The number of on-line training participants increased from 27,169 in 1999 to 740,365 in 2002. And the rate of on-line training also jumped from 2.8 per cent of all support funds in 1999 to 20.1 per cent in 2002 (Kim and Chung, 2005). It is worth mentioning that the expansion of e-learning has been possible due to the financial support given by the employment insurance fund.

Efforts to establish a Korean qualifications framework

The National Technical Qualification Act and the Basic Act on Qualifications were comprehensively revised in order to develop individual competencies by promoting lifelong learning. The revision of the National Technical Qualification Act in 2003 resulted in important changes in the national technical qualification system (Lee and Jung, 2005). First, the Ministry of Labour is responsible for drafting a basic plan for the development of the national technical qualification system. Second, the National Technical Qualification Policy Deliberation Committee and its sub-committees for each vocational field can play a role in reflecting industry demand, and industrial leaders or experts can give advice regarding standards and management of qualification examinations. Third, the testing service of a part of national technical qualifications can be commissioned to private organisations and institutions with expertise in certain qualification fields.

In 2007, the Basic Act on Qualifications was revised to establish a Korean Qualifications Framework (KQF) based on the Korean Skill Standards (KSS). It is expected to pave the way for a 'demand-oriented' and 'competency-based' qualification system. The main points of the revised Basic Act on Qualifications are as follows. First, government should develop the KSS in order to set standards for education and training curriculum, national qualification examinations, and authorisation of private qualifications. Second, the KQF has to be established on the basis of the KSS in order to promote an individual's vocational competency development based on connections between academic and vocational qualifications. Third, the ministry responsible should draw up the basic plan for the management and operation of the national qualification system. Fourth, private qualifications will be authorised through the deliberation of the Qualifications Policy Deliberation Committee.

With regard to setting occupational standards, the Sector Council was established to develop a demand-oriented VET and qualifications system in 2005. It has carried out coordination between the industrial demand for workforce and education and training programmes in ten industrial sectors under the responsibility of the Ministry of Commerce, Industry and Energy, which was renamed the Ministry of Knowledge Economy in 2008. It is mainly composed of industry leaders in HRD in order to encourage participation of industry in developing demand-oriented VET and qualifications systems.

Promoting training targeting SMEs

As the increasing productivity gap between large enterprises and SMEs has been recognised as a critical issue, the government launched several initiatives targeting SMEs. In particular, joint vocational training consortiums (JVTCs) for SMEs have been successful since it was introduced in 2002. This consortium has played a role in increasing training opportunities for SME employees by providing training designed to develop their vocational competencies (OECD, 2005). Large enterprises, public training institutes, employer organisations or universities can organise consortiums with SMEs to use their quality facilities or devices for training to provide basic or upgrade training. The costs of training programmes are covered by employment insurance and the budget for the JVTCs was increased more than five times between 2003 and 2007 (MOL, 2008). The JVTCs seem to be effective in providing tailored training programmes for SMEs when they are operated on the basis of cooperation between large enterprises and associated enterprises.

The government also initiated several projects targeting SMEs including subsidisation for SME employees' schooling, organised study at SMEs and training programmes necessary for better performance in core competencies at SMEs.

Building a partnership between labour, management and the government

As the importance of partnership in VET is growing, the central government is required to play a role in the coordination of relevant policies, and collaboration between stakeholders. The partnership between labour, management and the government has been recognised as an important issue, particularly since the legalisation of the Tripartite Commission (KTC). At the national level, there are also partnership bodies such as the Employment Policy Commission and the Vocational Education and Training Policy Commission. These operate mainly to promote the participation of stakeholders in collecting opinions in the process of forging vocational training policies (Chang and Chang, 2005).

As provided by the Workers' Vocational Competency Development Act, the government was given the mandate to offer financial support to promote the role of the 'Labour-Management Council' in developing vocational skills development plans at the company level after 2005. In this regard, it is increasingly important for the KTC to play a role in promoting partnership in VET and workplace learning at the company level.

Recognition of non-formal and informal learning

The Academic Credit Bank System (ACBS) is the distinctive system that recognises non-formal and informal learning in Korea. It embodies the idea of lifelong learning as it provides learners with an alternative opportunity to acquire associate or bachelor degrees when a sufficient number of credits are accumulated. Learners participating in the ACBS programme have been increasing since 1999; the total number of degree recipients reached 39,778 by the first half of 2006 as 12,254 learner were awarded in the first half of 2006 (Choi, 2007). On the other hand, the Bachelor Degree Examination Programme for Self Education (BDEP) system also provides an alternative route for the acquisition of bachelor degrees by passing examinations. For the BDEP, the number of degree recipients decreased from 755 out of 42,480 registered learners in 2001 to 610 out of 53,893 in 2005. The authority and responsibility for the systems belong to the Ministry of Education, Science and Technology (MEST), but the actual operation and management of the system is delegated to the National Institute for Lifelong Education, which became independent from the Korean Educational Development Institute as result of a merger between ACBS and EDBS in 2008.

Promoting partnership between higher education and industries

Directly connected with the shrinking population for higher education, provincial universities have great difficulty in attracting (talented) students and in securing employment for graduates. In response to this challenge, the government launched the New University for Regional Innovation (NURI) project in order to strengthen the innovative capabilities of junior colleges and universities located outside the Seoul metropolitan area (KRF, 2008). This project also aims to boost the building of a Regional Innovation System (RIS) through collaboration between universities and local governments, industries, research centres and NGOs (KRF, 2008).[9] Therefore, the regional development strategy needs to be implemented on the basis of partnership between universities and local governments and industries. With regard to collaboration between universities and industries, the project intends to enhance vocational competency development in universities, and encourage universities to provide employment support services for students (Chang, 2007).

CONCLUSION

Skills formation has moved through two different phases since the 1990s. First, during the Civilian (Kim Young-Sam) Government between 1993 and 1997, the government gave up manpower planning based on the quota system and encouraged diversity and competition between providers in the light of client-centredness, emphasising the transition from the developmental to the liberal skills formation system (PCER, 1997). Secondly, the Kim Dae-Jung Government, between 1998 and 2002, paved the way for state-coordinated partnership in tackling the Asian economic crisis. For example, the Tripartite Commission was established in response to the pressure of the IMF for the labour market flexibility. The Roh Mu-Hyun Government, between 2003 and 2007, served to strengthen the characteristics of state-coordinated partnership, emphasising balanced regional development based on the promotion of partnerships between civil society, local government, industry and higher education.

There are several implications of the transition from developmental skills formation to the state-coordinated partnership model for VET and workplace learning policies. First, with the dismantling of the EPB in 1994, the state-driven coordination mechanism for the supply and demand for skills was abandoned and the centralised system of education and training has gradually devolved to the local or institutional level. Second, with political democratisation, the oppression of the trade union movement was significantly weakened, and social partnership approaches to labour relations and training have started to be introduced. Third, the Employment Insurance System replaced the training levy system and the focus of training has shifted from initial vocational training (IVT) to continuing vocational training (CVT). Fourth, provincial or local governments have also considerably expanded the provision of training for the unemployed and of lifelong learning for their residents.

With regard to this transition in skills formation, some current issues arise. First, the division between vocational education/qualifications and the labour market prevents the implementation of holistic approaches to lifelong learning. For example, as the role of the MEST and the MOL is pivotal in promoting partnership between vocational schools and employers, a cooperative administrative system of VET is a prerequisite for this partnership. Second, after abolishing the Ministerial Meeting for HRD, it is still uncertain how best to coordinate the different ministries when their interests are in confrontation. Therefore, to secure a broad partnership across ministries' boundaries, the new mechanism replacing the Ministerial Meeting needs to have a means to influence each ministry. Third, with the rapid economic liberalisation after the economic crisis, social cohesion to overcome the increasing division between the rich and the poor has become a major issue in relation to skills formation and lifelong learning. Therefore, in building the framework for new skills formation, a comprehensive approach to lifelong learning needs to be emphasised because knowledge, skills and participatory citizenship all have to be recognised as essential for a maturing democracy as well as a knowledge-based economy.

The present (Lee Myung-Bak) Government, which came into office in 2008, has emphasised business-friendly and market-oriented approach to economic development. The government launched the Ministry of Education, Science and Technology (MEST) by merging MOEHRD and the Ministry of Science and Technology. The MEST faces the task of becoming a key engine for national development by incorporating the powers of education, science and technology. However, it is still unclear what kind of new horizontal mechanism for coordination will be successful in promoting the partnership between the government and other stakeholders in making and implementing VET and lifelong learning policies, particularly after the abolishment of the Ministerial Meeting for HRD. Time will reveal what the impacts of the new government policies on VET and workplace learning may turn out to be.

NOTES

1 The differential is an average labour productivity of SMEs as a percentage of average productivity of large firms employing 300 and more employees.

2 According to You and Lee, a subcontracting firm is defined as a company with 'more than 80 per cent of its total sales consisting of sales to other firms, with less than 20 per cent of its sales going to end consumers' (1999: 16).

3 Average labour productivity of SMEs as a percentage of the average productivity of large enterprises employing more than 300 employees.

4 When the EPB was abolished in 1993, the jurisdiction over planning and the budget was directly subject to the Office of the President. The Ministry of Planning and Budget was established when the Kim Dae-Jung government came to power.

5 See http://210.122.126.4/html/frame2.html (accessed 1.7.02).

6 For standard training, minimum requirements are more than 60 m² facilities and more than 20 hours training.

7 For example, in an interview, a staff member of People's Solidarity for Participatory Democracy mentioned that the organisation provided some programmes for civil servants for more than one year, with financial support from a local government.

8 http://www.krivet.re.kr/cgi-bin/nqual.cgi (accessed 5.9.02).

9 http://bnc.krf.or.kr/home/eng/nuri/aboutnuri.jsp

REFERENCES

Amsden, A.H. (1989) *Asia's Next Giant: South Korea and Late Industrialization.* New York: Oxford University Press.

Ashton, D. and Green, F. (1996) *Education, Training and the Global Economy.* Cheltenham: Edward Elgar.

Ashton, D., Green, F., James, D. and Sung, J. (1999) *Education and Training for Development in East Asia: The Political Economy of Skills Formation in East Asian Newly Industrialised Economies.* London: Routledge.

Bae, J. (1998) 'Beyond Seniority-Based Systems: A Paradigm Shift in Korean HRM?' In C. Rowley (ed.), *Human Resource Management in the Asia Pacific Region: Convergence Questioned.* London: Frank Cass.

Castells, M. (1992) 'Four Asian Tigers with a Dragon Head: A Comparative Analysis of the State, Economy, and Society in the Asian Pacific Rim', in R. Appelbaum and J. Henderson (eds), *State and Development in the Asia Pacific Rim.* London: Sage.

Castells, M. (1999) *End of Millennium* (Vol. 3). Oxford: Blackwell.

Chang, H. (2007) 'The Reform of the Korean TVET System for an Ageing Society', in T. Karmel (ed.), *Technical and Vocational Education and Training in an Ageing Society: Experts Meeting Proceedings.* South Australia: National Centre for Vocational Education Research.

Choi, S. (2003) *Changing Skills Formation and Lifelong Learning in South Korea*. Ph.D. Dissertation at the University of London, Institute of Education.

Choi, S. (2007) 'Recognition of Non-formal and Informal Learning in South Korea'. OECD Country Background Report.

Chung, J. and Chang, H. (2005) 'Partnership for HRD: Long-Term Policy in Lifelong Learning Society, in J. Kim (ed.), *New Paradigm of Human Resources Development: Government Initiatives for Economic Growth and Social Integration in Korea*. Seoul: KRIVET.

George, C. (2000) *Singapore: The Air-conditioned Nation*. Singapore: Landmark Books.

Green, A. (1997) *Education, Globalization and the Nation State*. Basingstoke: Macmillan.

Henderson, J. (1998) 'Danger and Opportunity in the Asia-Pacific', in G. Thompson (ed.), *Economic Dynamism in the Asia-Pacific: The Growth of Integration and Competitiveness*. London: The Open University.

Ihm, C. (1999) 'The Dynamics of Implementing VET Reform and Lifelong Learning in Korea', *Journal of Education and Work*, 12.

Johnson, C. (1982) *MITI and the Japanese Miracle: The Growth of Industrial Policy, 1925–1975*. Stanford: Stanford University Press.

KEDI (1996) *Hangug-ui gyo-yugjipyo [Korean Education Index]*. Seoul: KEDI.

KEIS (2008) *Goyongboheom Tonggeyyeonbo 2007 [Statistical Yearbook of the Employment Insurance 2007]*, Seoul: KEIS.

Kim, M. and Chung, T. (2005). 'Structural Transformation for Demand Oriented Vocational Training', in J.H. Kim (ed.), *New Paradigm of Human Resources Development: Government Initiatives for Economic Growth and Social Integration in Korea*. Seoul: KRIVET.

KLI (2000) *Jig-eobhunlyeonjedo-ui hyo-yulseong jegobang-an [A scheme to improve the efficiency of the vocation training system]*. Seoul: KLI.

KRF (2008) Korea Research Foundation BK21/NURI Committee, 2008. http://bnc.krf.or.kr/home/eng

KRIVET (2000) *Technical and Vocational Education and Training in Korea*. Seoul: KRIVET.

KRIVET and NCVER (2000) *Adult Retraining and Reskilling in Korea and Australia*. Seoul: KRIVET and NCVER.

Lee, J. and Jung, T. (2005) 'Vocational Education for National Competitiveness', in J.H. Kim (ed.), *New Paradigm of Human Resources Development: Government Initiatives for Economic Growth and Social Integration in Korea*. Seoul: KRIVET.

Lee, Y. and Kim, Y. (2001) 'Sahoebogjibaldal-ui Gyegeubjeongchi [Class Politics of Social Welfare Development]'. In Y.-H. Lee (ed.), *Hangug siminsahoe-ui byeondonggwa sahoemunje [Transition in civil society and social problems in Korea]*. Seoul: Nanum-ui jib.

Mallet, V. (1999) *The Trouble with Tigers: The Rise and Fall of South-East Asia*. London: HarperCollinsBusiness.

MOEHRD (2002) *2003 Self-Decision and Adjustment Plan of Enrolment Number in Universities and Industrial Universities*. Seoul: MOEHRD.

MOEHRD (2007a) *Analysis of Statistics on Education 2007*. Seoul: Ministry of Education and Human Resource Development and Korean Educational Development Institute.

MOEHRD (2007b) *Statistical Year Book of Education 2007*. Seoul: Ministry of Education and Human Resource Development and Korean Educational Development Institute.

MOL (2007) *Korean Labour Statistics*. Seoul: Ministry of Labour.

MOL (2008) *Jig-eobneungryuk Gaebalsaeob Hyunhwang [A Scheme of the Vocation Education Training System]*. Seoul: MOL.

OECD (2005) *Promoting Adult Learning*. Paris: OECD.

OECD (2007) *Education at a Glance: OECD Indicators 2007*. Paris: OECD.

OECD (2008a) *OECD RNFIL Country Note for Korea*. Paris: OECD.

OECD (2008b) *OECD Reviews of Innovation Policy*: China. Paris: OECD.

PCER (1997) *Education Reform for the 21st Century: To Ensure Leadership in the Information and Globalization Era*. Seoul: The Presidential Commission on Education Reform.

Sakamoto-Vandenberg, A., Green, A., Brown, P. and Lauder, H. (1998) *Japan's Human Resource Response to the Challenges of the 1990s (The High Skills project, Working paper one)*. London: ESRC.

Shim, S. (1999) 'Bijeonggyu Go-yong-ui Hwagdae-wa Nodongbogji [The Expansion of Atypical Employment and Labour Welfare]'. *San-eobnodong-yeongu [Industrial Labour Research]*, 5, 149–184.

Stiglitz, J.E. (2002) *Globalization and Its Discontents*. London: Penguin Books.

World Bank (1993) *The East Asian Miracle: Economic Growth and Public Policy*. New York: Oxford University Press.

You, J. and Lee, J. (1999, August) *Economic and Social Consequences of Globalization: The Case of South Korea*. Seoul.

18

Age Management in Organisations in the European Union

Gerhard Naegele and Alan Walker

INTRODUCTION

Work force ageing is an issue of vital importance to all Member States of the European Union (EU). As the world's oldest region and in the absence of mass migration, it is recognised that future economic growth, competitiveness and efficiency will depend increasingly on how effectively employers can utilise their ageing work forces. This necessity is accepted at the highest level in the EU and figured prominently in the leaders' summits in Lisbon (2000), Stockholm (2001) and Barcelona (2002). In Stockholm, an ambitious target was set to raise the employment rate among older workers classified as 50 years and over, from an EU average of 26.3 per cent in 2000 to 50 per cent by 2010. It is one thing, of course, for leaders to set EU targets, but their achievement depends on actions at lower levels, and, especially, by key actors within organisations, such as management, human resources management, supervisors, employee and works committees, medical officers and so on. These are the people who decide on the conditions of employment of older employees, and who are responsible for integrating older employees in the organisation. They will decide whether or not the employment outlook of this group will improve.

To achieve the ambitious EU goal, companies and management will need to abandon their former focus on youth in their personnel and employment policies and address changing work requirements and prospects of the shifting age distributions in the work force strategically. Most importantly, terms and conditions need to be created so that the extension of the working life is practicable and offers a genuine choice. Therefore concrete changes in working conditions need to be achieved so that it becomes possible to age positively in employment.

In spite of the high profile of this issue in the EU and the corresponding national government efforts, it is remarkable that the topic of work force ageing does not receive attention in many companies. For example, in every other German company there are no employees over 50 years of age (Frerich and Taylor, 2009). It is still the case that most companies discriminate against older employees. Based upon the findings of the German research network 'Demographischer

Wandel' und Arbeitswelt (Wolff, Spieß, K. and Mohr, 2001) this discrimination manifests itself in the following ways:

- age selective personnel hiring and recruiting policy;
- age spanned task assignment, with the common effect of reducing practical working possibilities;
- substandard attendance at operational organised continuing education;
- disadvantages in internal promotion possibilities;
- contempt of their know-how;
- short-term personnel decisions in relation to older workforce members.

There is an inconsistency in many EU countries' policies on older workers. On the one hand there are attempts to reduce retirement incentives but, on the other hand, there is a general failure to improve the working conditions of ageing workers. Economic incentives alone are insufficient when they are not accompanied by demographically sensitive conceptions of employment assurance and encouragement. These need to apply particularly to the operational level and then to the working conditions. The central connecting factor is the encouragement of the employability of the ageing working population. The employment must include dimensions which impact on the older workers' employability and work attendance, including state of health, qualifications, motivation and beneficial conditions. These aspects must be present in both working conditions and personnel policy (Ilmarinen, 2005).

One approach to changing operational age management in Europe is to establish guidelines of good practice. These need to be taken as a set of evidence-based guidelines aimed at enhancing the employment expectations and chances of older employees. Such guidelines must be supportive of policies and not be regarded as an alternative to constitutional arrangements such as legal action against age discrimination.

This chapter introduces such an instrument. The guide to good practice in corporate age-management in European Member States is evidence-based. It is derived from a major project funded by the European Foundation for the improvement of living and working conditions. The project focused on 130 longstanding case studies on employment initiatives for an ageing work force across 11 EU countries (Austria, Belgium, Finland, France, Germany, Greece, Italy, the Netherlands, Sweden, UK and Spain) and further information was gleaned from developments in this field across the EU including the new Member States (Mandl et al., 2005). It is a follow-up to the pioneering project in this field *Combating Age Barriers Employment*, also funded by the European Foundation for the improvement of living and working conditions, which produced the first guide to good practice in managing an ageing work force (Walker, 1999). The new guide updates and extends the earlier one (Naegele and Walker, 2006) and this chapter reports the main findings of the research.

The empirical data underlying this contribution and the guide were collected by national experts in the form of short-term case studies in each of the participating countries. Most of the correspondents (with the exception of the Austrian, French and Spanish contributors) were involved in the previous project. The short-term case studies were based on a questionnaire applied in all participant countries which interrogated different operational actors. The studies (Taylor, 2005) focused on the following objectives to:

- document measures in organisations (private and public) intended to improve the employment situation of older workers;
- identify factors influencing the evolution, success and sustainability of measures;
- consider the impact of initiatives on individuals and organisations;
- consider issues of life cycle and gender in measures;
- review lessons and devise guidelines for good practice in corporate age management.

The selection of the companies was based on current resources and information on established operational age management arrangements. By taking a longitudinal perspective, the project had an opportunity to assess how initiatives had been developed and evolved. For this purpose, the identification and selection of case studies was based with reference to the following sources:

- Combating Age Barriers in Employment: A European Portfolio of Good Practice (Walker and Taylor, 1998);
- www.arbeitundalter.at, an Austrian based website containing an international sample of good practice in age management; and
- Additional country-specific knowledge about longstanding measures contributed by the national correspondents.

Detailed information on each example of good practice on which this chapter is based can be accessed on the European Foundation's website: http://www.eurofound.eu.int/. This material is designed to be used to support the introduction of good practice.

WHY IS AGE MANAGEMENT NECESSARY?

There are four main reasons why age management is now considered by EU policy makers as an economic and social necessity.

The *ageing and shrinking of the EU work force* over the next two decades calls for a completely new approach to managing age at the workplace and in economic and social policy terms. Those aged 50 and over already represent one in five of the work force, and soon this figure will rise to one in four. As the influx of younger people abates, especially in the new Member States as a result of emigration, the challenge will be to retain and more efficiently utilise those older workers that European employers, in both the public and private sectors, have hitherto commonly encouraged to leave employment. In particular in competition with younger work forces in the USA and Asia, European employers will need to maintain the work ability and productivity of their ageing employees.

In the context of an ageing work force, *tackling age barriers and age discrimination* becomes an economic as well as a social necessity. The 2000 EU Employment Framework Directive reflects this necessity and creates a completely new legal context in most Member States. The Directive outlaws discrimination on grounds of age (among other things) in access to employment, self-employment and occupation; vocational training and guidance, and in the membership of organisations. Employers and policy makers need to work together to overcome age barriers in job recruitment, training and promotion as well as the ingrained negative stereotypes about older workers that underpin them.

Pressure for legislation to outlaw age discrimination in employment came from enlightened employers and human resources professionals, who recognised the need for *age diversity* in organisations (DfEE, 1999). Thus a work force with a mixture of youth and maturity, as well as diversity in other characteristics such as gender and ethnicity, is regarded as being best to respond to the rapidly changing circumstances associated with globalisation. By artificially limiting recruitment to so-called 'prime age' workers, many organisations have prevented themselves from maximising their recruitment potential.

The *public policy context* has created an imperative towards age management. In particular, widespread concern about the sustainability of some of Europe's public pension systems has led to a rapid closure of early exit gateways and the adoption of measures to encourage an extension of working life (Reday-Mulvey, 2005). Indeed, there is a remarkable consensus among the Member States about the need for active labour market and social protection policies aimed at raising employment levels among older workers and at postponing retirement. The EU has played a key role in raising the policy profile of this issue and, for more than a decade, it has promoted employment policies in favour of older workers and the sharing of good practice between the Member States. Since 2001, the EU has had a specific target to meet: an increase in the employment rate of older workers to 50 per cent by 2010 (European Council, 2001). The aim is to raise the effective retirement age by around five years by 2010 (European Council, 2002). Although the EU is already behind schedule in achieving these targets, they

Table 18.1   Employment rates of persons aged 55 to 64 years in the EU-15 in 2005

Country	Women	Men	Total
Austria	22.9	41.3	31.8
Belgium	22.1	41.7	31.8
Denmark	53.5	65.6	59.9
Finland	52.7	52.8	52.7
France	35.2	40.7	37.9
Germany	37.5	53.5	45.4
Greece	25.8	58.8	41.6
Ireland	37.3	65.7	51.6
Italy	20.8	42.7	31.4
Luxembourg	24.9	38.3	31.7
Netherlands	35.2	56.9	46.1
Portugal	43.7	58.1	50.5
United Kingdom	48.1	66.0	56.9
Spain	27.4	59.7	43.1
Sweden	66.7	72.0	69.4
EU-15	35.4	53.1	44.1

Source: Eurostat, Employment in Europe 2006

remain pressing on the Member States and, therefore, form part of the policy context within which organisations operate. The new central and eastern European Member States are starting to become familiar with this context, but it is no less urgent for them too. (see Table 18.1).

WHAT IS GOOD PRACTICE IN AGE MANAGEMENT?

As presented in the first European guide (Walker, 1999) good practice in age management can be defined as measures which combat age barriers and/or promote age diversity. These measures may consist of specific initiatives aimed at particular dimensions of age management and more general employment, or management policies that help to create an environment in which individual employees are able to achieve their potential without being disadvantaged by their age. Our data shows that the particular example of good practice may be isolated, transient and co-exist with bad practice. Only rarely is it part of a *comprehensive* human resources or employment policy of age management (Naegele, 1999). These organisations do not exemplify good EU practice.

Good practice, then, is not a once-and-for-all achievement but a range of possible interventions, from minor to major, that reflect the aims of age management to overcome age barriers and to promote age diversity. Good practice does not necessarily imply huge costs for organisations. On the contrary, many significant changes benefiting older workers can be implemented at low cost. The key questions are: is its effect monitored and, if it is beneficial, is it sustained? For organisations with little or no experience in age management the main point is to get started in the implementation of good practice, however small-scale that may be, and then to try to build that into a more comprehensive strategy. Most organisations do not start such initiatives and many of those that do fail to sustain them.

As well as operating at the organisational level, age management may also be aimed at the ageing work force as a whole in order to promote its labour market integration, increase or sustain its productivity, improve the quality of its work environment and increase its productivity. These objectives, micro, meso and macro, should not be seen as independent but ideally, as mutually reinforcing each other. Good practice in age management is the most important precondition for a substantial increase in the labour force participation of older workers and potentially creates a win-win-win situation for everyone involved: employees, organisations and public policy. In this chapter we focus on the organisational level.

THE ORGANISATIONAL DRIVERS OF GOOD PRACTICE

There are five main factors that trigger good practice within organisations. In most cases a combination of two or more factors is required to serve as organisational drivers and to help ensure a successful outcome in age management initiatives.

Sustaining the skills/experience base of the work force

Good practice in age management is introduced to ensure that the organisation's skill needs are met as precisely as possible. This goal can be reached by making new appointments as well as by investing in the skills and qualifications of existing older employees. Partly as a result of previous negative experiences with age-based redundancies, many companies have realised that the professional and social skills that older employees have acquired in their often long-lasting job tenure and/or broad industry experience represent a special company asset. New recruits and/or younger colleagues cannot fully replace these skills and experience and trying to do so will involve the companies potentially in high additional costs for the recruitment, vocational preparation or on-the-job training and education for the newly hired staff. The premature loss or non-replacement of skills such as accuracy, reliability and good communicative ability when dealing with customers and others, which distinguishes many older employees, often entails an economic risk for a company. As both practical experience and research demonstrate, older employees who are deployed in the right positions, given their individual skills prove to be highly productive. This is proven by the many successful examples of organisations with mixed-age groups or teams which successfully combine the specific skills and other attributes of different age groups in an optimal manner. Thus age management geared towards the promotion of the further employment of older workers is often regarded as an excellent instrument of intergenerational knowledge transfer.

Making necessity a virtue

The second driver for good practice in age management may be stimulated by the need to involve older workers in organisational restructuring or development. This may stem from the absence of younger workers with the necessary skills in the internal or external labour markets or because by being mandated by collective agreements. Thus employers may find themselves 'forced' into engaging with older employees, because there is no alternative, in a range of circumstances including the reorganisation or rationalisation of production or administrative processes and changes in market, demand or competition conditions. Where organisations make special efforts to ensure that their older workers are fit for the new challenges by introducing suitable age management measures, thereby raising the employability of the workers concerned, there is a good chance that older employees will not only adapt competently to the new circumstances but also, in the private sector, with considerable economic benefit. Indeed, in some cases, it may be preferable to employ increasing numbers of older workers rather than younger ones. This is true, for example, in those sectors with an ageing customer base or in which the demand is for age-specific products or services. Here well age managed older employees can be the best placed to respond to consumer needs and expectations, for example in the health services sector or the retail trade.

The prevention or reduction of age-specific labour costs

The third aspect of good practice in age management is triggered by the need to cut age-related additional expenditure and/or labour costs. If age-related increases in labour costs occur, for instance, higher sickness rates, due to the high average age or an unbalanced age profile of the work force, it is always advisable, according to our research experience, to check whether or not targeted measures to promote the health, skills or motivation of older employees are ultimately more sensible economically than laying off or pensioning older employees prematurely.

Investment in the economic employability of older workers can be shown by alternative calculations where, for instance, the costs of the (premature) retirement of older employees or of new appointments and their vocational training are off-set. Labour costs can also be lowered by making use of national support measures or public employment programmes, such as new appointments or on-the-job training and education.

Reactions to new external labour market conditions

Fourthly, in a number of cases, the need for organisational age management is created by changes in the general conditions for hiring older workers. This contextual shift may be in the form of legislative or regulatory changes in retirement ages or pension laws, public and collectively agreed principles and explicit sensitisation and promotion programmes for older employees. Examples of good practice include companies in Austria and the Netherlands utilising age management to promote older staff in reaction against early retirement programmes, in the UK there are regulations against age discrimination and, in Greece, as an answer to a national diversity campaign. Many companies also make use of the financial advantages of special public programmes for the promotion of the employment of older workers or the reintegration of older unemployed persons. This especially applies to Finland and its 2002–2005 Programme for Ageing Workers. German companies have in the past reacted to special programmes for the humanisation of the working life or, latterly, to the demographic sensitisation of companies a demography initiative of the German Ministry for Education and Research (Wolf et al., 2001). Other companies have begun with age management measures in the course of new collectively agreed provisions in favour of older employees taking effect, for example in Belgium and in Italy. However, experience also shows that isolated age awareness campaigns, on their own, cannot achieve much if they are not also linked to concrete 'incentives' for companies such as economic advantages or external regulations.

Regional and/or professional labour market bottlenecks

Finally, good age management practice, especially in the cases of new appointments of older workers or investments in the employability of existing older workers, is always successful if there are bottlenecks in the regional or local labour markets for qualified personnel. This research shows that in the cases in which the companies banked on older applicants in making new appointments, these proved their worth very soon after their appointment. This is because of their special motivation, the trust that was placed in them and, last but not least, the existence of suitable company support and promotion measures. Where prognoses suggest a future, demographically induced lack of labour or of skilled workers, organisations should react in good time with preventative investments in the employability of their ageing and older staff. Thus, should the occasion arise, they will be able to satisfy their employment needs.

In some of the new Member States, a special problem could arise in that many younger skilled employees are still migrating to the old EU Member States due to perceived better life chances and, therefore, are not available to their national labour markets. Also, in these states, the rapid change in the structure of the demand side is leading to bottlenecks, creating a need for investments in the qualifications and skills of older workers. Timely investment in older employees could be an important preventive measure here to avoid labour bottlenecks (Mandl et al., 2005).

THE DIMENSIONS AND BENEFITS OF GOOD PRACTICE

These dimensions reflect the most significant action fields identified in the case studies and represent individual measures aimed at specific aspect of an ageing work force. They can be oriented towards both prevention and compensation at the same time. The improvement of the employment chances of older employees and the expansion of their labour participation calls for a twin-track approach that aims at both (a) the preventive promotion of workers' employability over the whole working life as well as at (b) reducing and eliminating acute employment problems in its later phases.

Each dimension of age-management is discussed below with examples of initiatives and outcomes.

- job recruitment;
- learning, training and lifelong learning;
- career development;
- flexible working practices;
- health protection and promotion and workplace design;
- redeployment;
- employment exit and the transition to retirement;
- comprehensive approaches.

JOB RECRUITMENT

Good practice means ensuring that older workers have either equal or special access to the available jobs and that potential applicants are not discriminated against either directly or indirectly (Walker, 1996: 3).

Positive examples found in the research are:

- the waiving of age limits in job advertisements in order to encourage as much age diversity as possible;
- using specially qualified personnel for applicant selection and for job interviews with a selection process based on skills, competencies and experiences rather than age, as well as on the individual needs of older applicants;
- a close and co-ordinated, and if possible with regular site inspections, co-operation with local recruitment agencies;
- a good knowledge of public support programmes, e.g. wage subsidies or settling-in grants, and their competent utilisation;
- age-specific advertisement campaigns aiming particularly at older applicants;
- explicitly addressing those older applicants who are already in involuntary early retirement or unemployment, or who are threatened by dismissal.

The benefits that companies reported from hiring older applicants include:

- Older applicants, despite their greater age, often have skills superior to those of younger applicants and which are tailor-made for the companies.
- With the qualifications of the newly hired older employees, a general raising of the qualification level of the work force can be achieved. There are also benefits gained as the new recruits pass on their externally gained experience to younger colleagues.
- By virtue of the systematic linking of the newly acquired with the already available skills synergy effects can be produced so that a rise in the overall productivity and innovation propensity of the company can be achieved.
- The appointment of older workers positively affects the age mix of the work force as whole as well as individual teams.
- In certain age-sensitive trades and companies, newly hired older employees can, by virtue of their age, cater quickly to changing customer wishes and needs more authentically and can also achieve improved turnover.
- Recruiting older applicants can lead to additional external and internal corporate image benefits contributing to an improvement of the internal as well as the external corporate identity.
- Older applicants are seen to be a suitable solution to otherwise empty regional labour markets.

Such positive effects cannot be achieved without certain preconditions. In addition to an open-minded approach to job advertisement good practice presupposes 'age-neutrality'. This entails an exclusively occupational and task-related recruitment assessment and selection procedure and, if necessary, external support by specialist employment and consultancy agencies. Additional supports may be required. The offer of flexible working hours for newly appointed older workers is positive. Moreover, it is also important to make clear to the existing employees that they too will profit from the recruitment of older employees and, therefore, that they should not perceive the new appointments as competition but as an enhancement of the company's economic opportunities.

LEARNING, TRAINING AND LIFELONG LEARNING

Good practice in this field means ensuring that older workers are not neglected in training and career development, that opportunities for learning are offered throughout working life, that training methods are appropriate to older workers, and that positive action is taken where necessary to compensate for discrimination in the past (Walker, 1996: 4).

Although older workers frequently have important skills and qualifications that are difficult to recruit and that form a central element of the organisation's work; skills deficits are nevertheless considered to be a frequent employment risk associated with older employees. What is often overlooked is the self-fulfilling prophecy at work here: such skills deficits develop primarily because companies do not invest in their older workers, as is demonstrated by the low participation rate of older employees in company-organised further education and training.

There is a wide range of good practice dependent on the specific company context in this field. Some examples are:

- no age limits in access to company-organised learning and training opportunities;
- special motivation efforts, methodology and provision of support;
- systematic evaluation;
- specific company leave provisions;
- analysis of the skills needs of the company, matching these with the available skills and individual educational status of older employees and utilising them in the methodology and contents of training;
- continuous observance of the individual educational status;
- the conception of training opportunities as an integral part of career planning and not solely as job-specific, correlating training schemes to the life-course learning and development as part of the work organisation, e.g. within the framework of mixed-age teams and groups;
- using older employees and their special qualifications both as facilitators of further education for older and younger employees, and as an organisational 'knowledge pool'.

The benefits that companies reported include:

- In-company training and further education of older employees contribute to raising the qualification level and innovation potential of the work force.
- An enhancement of the motivation of younger staff as their own career perspective is reflected in older employees and, at the same time, respect for the job performance of the individual employee is witnessed. This is especially true for measures which involve different age groups as the intergenerational knowledge transfer and exchange can be advanced.
- Positive effects on the quality of a company's products and services.
- In many companies, the involvement of older employees is a guarantor of qualification maintenance, development and transfer within the company.
- For the older employees themselves, their participation in on-the-job further education and training entails an increase in their employability, most notably in the dimensions of flexibility, vertical and horizontal mobility readiness and motivation.
- Completing further education and training in earlier career phases raises the willingness to do so in later phases and thus overcomes participation barriers found among older age groups.
- Some older workers can be successfully deployed as mentors and teaching staff for both younger colleagues and those of the same age. This particularly applies to the solution of succession problems, where, for instance (older) job holders can familiarise (younger) job successors with their tasks.

In the light of the growing economic importance of qualifications and knowledge on the one hand and, on the other, the ageing of the work force, age-integrating and age-neutral on-the-job further education and training is an important organisational and executive function that carries high operational value.

The essential precondition for good practice and its benefits is the sensitisation of the persons in charge. Vocational education and learning in the workplace should be based on knowledge of current as well as future company skill requirements and on the educational status and potential of all employees. Also 'competence databases' have proven their value. In small and medium-sized enterprises learning and training is also feasible but, often, specific external support is needed, e.g. professional educational consultants, research institutions, chambers of commerce and industry, chambers of crafts or the benchmarking of good practice. Which method is suitable in each case and what the precise organisation of education and training should look like (e.g. individualised provision, specific programmes only for older employees, age-neutral methodology, on-the-job training, training in special institutions), can only be answered against the background of a company's specific needs. Nonetheless, there are two universally valid recommendations arising from our research: (1) job rotation in conjunction with on-the-job training is an extremely effective instrument, not only for older employees; and (2) working time releases should be facilitated, e.g. the combination of company education sessions with special working time arrangements such as partial retirement.

CAREER DEVELOPMENT

As with learning and training good practice in career development means ensuring that, rather than being neglected, older employees have opportunities to progress (not necessarily hierarchically), to maintain and enlarge their skills and knowledge and, where necessary, taking positive action to compensate for past discrimination.

Career development is an important instrument in preventive employment promotion and employment security for older employees. It involves structuring demands, incentives and stresses in the working life or job biography of an ageing employee in such a way that his or her motivation and performance are promoted and applied in the most effective situations. It involves the early counteracting of possible health risks due to working conditions. The matching of concrete job specifications on the one hand and, on the other, work-related performance changes typical of older age in the course of the career is a clear example of good practice in this field. Ideally employees should be able to perform those tasks in later phases of their working lives that harmonise with the special occupational experience and knowledge of older workers.

Good practice in career development that applies specifically to older employees is rare. Examples encountered in the research include the identification of individual career wishes and making plans relating to these, career planning that is tailored to occupational groups and systematic career consultation using specialist advisors.

The sorts of benefits companies reported from successful career development include:

- Career development reduces physical strains and mental stress, thereby contributing to the long-term maintenance of employability;
- Better utilisation of respective competencies and qualifications in the different career stages in the company is achieved;
- For the individual employee, irrespective of age, occupational perspectives become visible and can be planned, with positive effects on motivation, commitment, flexibility and productivity;
- Early retirements because of 'blind alley activities' or tasks of limited duration can be prevented and, therefore, operational employment periods can be prolonged;
- (Re)deployments which may nevertheless become necessary can be utilised more productively for the enterprise.

Career development for older employees is a demanding organisational function that calls for a number of measures on the part of the enterprise. These include detailed knowledge of qualification requirements and stress profiles associated with the work places, of the employability profiles of employees involved and of internal mobility opportunities. Successful good practice also depends on the systematic embedding of the measures in the company's education and training programmes, intensive employee preparation and, last but not least, concrete 'incentives' especially in the form of wage and tariff policies. Suitable company data and information systems are needed as well as managers who specialise in the areas of ageing and/or diversity. External business consultants and scientific institutions can also be utilised.

FLEXIBLE WORKING TIME PRACTICES

Good practice in this field means giving older workers greater flexibility in their hours of work or in the timing and nature of their retirement (Walker, 1996: 5) *and adjusting working time and other aspects of employment to reflect changes in the way people work and in family and caring responsibilities of the work force* (Naegele and Walker, 2002: 230).

The objective is not only a more productive alignment of working times and work (place) demands but also a better reconciliation of work with personal interests and commitments (work-life-balance) such as educational leave, the raising of children, or as is characteristic of many older employees today, family care responsibilities. Specifically, with regard to older workers, such working time flexibility may be an important instrument for retaining this group in employment.

Examples of good practice in this field include different forms of flexible working time practices, such as the adjustment of shift schedules, special measures of daily or weekly working hours reduction and flexible working for older employees, partial retirement, specific paid leave provisions, particular models of job rotation or relief for older employees from overtime and other extra work.

The benefits of flexible working time include:

- Flexible working time has positive effects on the state of health, motivation and off-the-job quality of life especially (but not only) of older employees.
- From the company's point of view, flexible working time leads to an optimal utilisation of labour resources. At the same time, good practice in this area accommodates the often complementary working time wishes of older and younger employees.
- Many enterprises report a fall in the number of staff sick leave and a decrease in work absences accompanied by a simultaneous rise in individual productivity. Especially in highly burdensome activities such as night shift work, flexible working time is an important instrument for the humanisation of the working life. A reduction in the number of early retirements/reduction in earning capacity pensions is proven.
- The individual work-life balance is improved. This particularly applies to (older) female employees who often have family elder care responsibilities.
- Under certain conditions the entry into retirement can be delayed by means of a more flexible working life.
- Flexible working time arrangements facilitate the implementation of other measures for the enhancement of the employability of all employees (e.g. training measures, career planning and knowledge transfer).
- Gradual retirement schemes ease the individual adaptation to retirement and, at an early stage, create scope for rehearsing post-job activities such as volunteering.
- A suitable offering of flexible working times not only enhances the social image of an enterprise, as for example, the 'family-friendly' company, but also its attractiveness in the labour market and this provides an important incentive for job seekers.

Special working time arrangements are often an expression of statutory or collectively agreed general conditions which facilitates their implementation. Sometimes they have also been developed as a return for specific workloads and as a compensation for extra effort (time instead of money). In fact, there are reservations concerning flexible working time arrangements, on the part of both employers (e.g. cost arguments, practical implementation problems, additional administration effort) and employees (e.g. loss of income and/or status, new workloads due to organisation changes). As a rule, however, these reservations can easily be overcome by means of a careful and participation-oriented approach to implementation. Employee participation and evaluation are basic requirements for good practice in this field. Special regulations which only apply to chosen, clearly defined, employee groups are often connected with discrimination and, consequently, with potential in-house status losses. Hence it is advisable to include as many employee groups as possible.

HEALTH PROTECTION AND PROMOTION AND WORKPLACE DESIGN

Good practice in health protection, health promotion and workplace design means optimising work processes and the organisation of work to enable employees to perform well and to ensure their health and capacity to work (Naegele and Walker, 2002: 230).

Good practice in this field, therefore, may take the form of preventive measures or measures intended to compensate for physical decline. There is an extensive range of ways in which work-induced illness or disability may be prevented by means of health protection and promotion measures, including ergonomics and workplace (re)design.

The most important good practices found in the research were workplace-related studies concerning health risks, company health reports, company health circles, external counselling of the enterprises by health experts, employee surveys, employee participation and schooling, regular health checks and preventive medical check-ups, the training of superiors and of key persons in the company, ergonomic workplace redesign, preventive redeployment as well as health-promoting working time arrangements (see above). A further important instrument in this respect is the establishment of mixed-age groups to ensure the optimal deployment of the different age-specific performance potentials and competencies.

The benefits of good practice in this field include:

- There are verifiable positive correlations between a fully developed system of occupational health and safety, health promotion activities and an above average health status of the work force, as measured by factors such as physical and mental stress, the number of staff off sick and health-related early retirement rates.
- The same applies to a high level of job satisfaction and motivation, a good atmosphere at work and a satisfactory quality of work.
- Companies can contain, to a large extent, the cost associated with work-related ill health such as absence from work.

Successful good practice in health promotion and protection aimed at older employees rests, first of all, on a systematic analysis and documentation of work places with health risks. This may take the form of a regular health bulletin.

External consultation with occupational health experts such as Occupational Health Services are useful. Preventive measures for specific risk groups, for example, regular health checks for night shift workers, have proven their worth. The appointment of key persons who are primarily responsible for the coordination and implementation of health promotion measures (e.g. disability managers) is another strategy.

As typical work-related illnesses have their causes in earlier phases of the work life ('career character') health protection measures should not be delayed until employees are older. An age-neutral approach is particularly appropriate. Furthermore, employee participation is indispensable, especially given the high degree of sensibility, experience and knowledge of older employees. Incentives such as bonus programmes, run for example by health insurance funds, in which health-friendly companies are rewarded with lower premium rates for health or accident insurance and vice versa, can also be helpful in creating a health-aware company culture. Health protection and promotion (for older employees) can only develop effectively in those enterprises in which health is acknowledged as a central guarantor for the productivity and achievement potential of its employees and in which its own responsibility, for whatever reasons, is recognised by management. Whether healthy ageing at work is an attainable goal depends to a large extent on whether the companies also do something in particular for the health of their (older) employees.

REDEPLOYMENT

Good practice in redeployment primarily refers to the right coordination of work place demands with the achievement potential of the older employees, that is, to the maintenance of work quality for the employees affected by the redeployments.

Redeployment may be considered a compensatory measure in response to existing perform-ance constraints but it can also, especially in relation to health protection or career develop-ment, have a positive impact. Good practice in redeployment, therefore, not only refers to the process of redeployment itself, to the choice and quality of the (new) workplace or to the care-ful preparation of the employees concerned but, also, to its long-term positive effects. So-called 'sheltered workplaces' should be avoided, likewise occupational dequalification processes and/ or company status loss. All of these have a demotivating effect on the employees concerned and, not uncommonly, lead to a premature 'inner retirement' and, last but not least, can also negatively affect the general working atmosphere. Good practice in this field is achieved if redeployments are regarded as a part of a preventative age management strategy geared to the maintenance of employability, especially as regards qualification and skill enhancement, and the maintenance of flexibility and health protection.

Good practice in redeployment has positive effects for both the employees concerned and the enterprises. For the employees, a reduction of workloads and monotonous work, a constant or higher work motivation, an increase in responsibility, the opportunity to continue to deploy occupational skills and qualifications, job security as well as new working opportunities, instead of dismissals or involuntary early retirement, are all important criteria for rating a redeployment as successful and the new workplace as suitable.

For the company, the rating of successful redeployment processes depends on individual productivity: is it maintained or can it be boosted? Absenteeism is an important factor. How succeeding cohorts of employees assess the redeployment practice of their companies with regard to their own later occupational development perspectives also has impact.

Important preconditions for good redeployment practice for older employees includes the participation of the employees concerned, a systematic approach towards redeployment (matching of individual capacities/competencies and working requirements/customer profiles), cooperation of the relevant actors (company physician, works council, personnel department, line manager, further external specialists), the consent of the union workplace representatives and of works councils, (if possible) provisions in company agreements to safeguard the employees against negative effects (especially to avoid income losses) as well as the integration of health promotion in the scope of redeployment. Of crucial importance for the acceptance of redeployments is the question to what extent the company decides to leave typically positive redeployment workplaces in the company and not to eliminate or source them out. This is not only a business decision but also reflects the specific company's age-awareness profile.

EXIT FROM EMPLOYMENT AND TRANSITION TO RETIREMENT

Good practice in this field means basing any redundancy decision on objective job-related criteria and ensuring that retirement schemes offer a choice of options and are fairly applied (Naegele and Walker, 2002: 232).

A problem for individuals, and society in general, is coping adequately with the necessity for early retirement. Even with the best possible corporate age management in place, redundancies and/or compulsory early retirements are frequently unavoidable. However, good practice is still possible. For many companies, actual cases of early retirement are also their first occasion for considering changes in their 'retirement culture'.

Examples of good practice in corporate exit and retirement policy range from preparatory measures for retirement at the corporate level, counselling facilities for former employees, assistance with the search for a new position, to opportunities for keeping in touch after final departure. Flexible forms of transition can enable employees to continue to be employed as relief or part-time staff on corporate tasks, or with tasks outside the company, such as community voluntary work.

Good practice in exit and retirement policies provides many benefits, such as making it easier to find successors and to familiarise them with the job; it can also enhance the internal and external corporate image. Companies can still draw on important skills and specialist knowledge of former employees, such as company history and customer contacts, even after these employees have retired. It is also possible to draw on former employees in times of staff shortages.

As is generally the case for age management measures, good practice in exit and retirement policy is dependent on the prevailing economic, labour market and legal context, over which enterprises have very limited control. Therefore early retirement should not be considered merely as a corporate adjustment to changes in economic conditions, but also as a means of improving the welfare of individuals and society by mitigating the social consequences of early retirement, with the reward of additional benefits for the enterprises themselves. Areas within the corporate sphere of responsibility include, in particular, the arrangement of flexible working hours to promote gradual transition into retirement, the provision of appropriate fields of employment for former employees, where expedient, either within or outside the company, or assistance to former employees in their search for such alternative employment. A positive attitude towards ageing within the enterprise is also helpful.

The prevailing external conditions governed by legislation and collective agreements are of particular importance, especially legislation concerning partial retirement and/or collective agreements and works council agreements based on this legislation. However, as in Germany, even these allow companies sufficient scope for action, to provide for gradual transition into retirement by making use of flexi-time in a way that is both effective for individuals and society.

COMPREHENSIVE APPROACHES

Organisations may want to take relatively small-scale initiatives in response to particular problems, such as skill shortages. However, the limitations of such actions must be recognised as must the problems that might be created when both good and bad HR practices towards older workers coexist. Therefore, specific measures to combat age barriers which focus only on one aspect of age management and/or the latter part of employees' working lives, as welcome as they are, should be seen as starting points towards a holistic HR strategy on age and employment (Walker, 1996: 11; Naegele, 1999).

Such a comprehensive approach to age management transforms the ageing issue into a quality gate for the entire range of HR policy measures, and it encompasses all aspects from recruitment to employment exit.

Good practice in comprehensive approaches can be characterised by:

- an emphasis on the *prevention* of age management problems;
- a focus on the whole working life and *all age groups*, not just older workers;
- a *holistic approach* encompassing all dimensions of age management; and
- in the short term, *remedial provisions* for older workers who are already touched by age-specific occupational problems such as skill deficits due to dequalification processes or bad health status due to heavy work loads.

In addition to such comprehensive strategies, a great variety of potentially integrated concepts exist in corporate practice. It is a matter of coordinating measures applied in various different areas. Thus, for instance, more flexible working hours can be combined with health care measures or readjustment of qualifications, or recruitment of young employees can be combined with knowledge transfer and preventive health care in a mentoring project, or an awareness-raising programme goes hand in hand with corporate advanced training and an optimisation of work organisation, or new concepts of working hour schedules and organisational structures are linked with the introduction of performance-based wages. The employment of older workers beyond the prevailing age limit cannot be achieved by financial incentives alone. An incentive mix is necessary, including, for example, personal motivation discussions, readjustments to work organisation and working hour schedules or opportunities for further education and training.

The benefits that (mostly larger) companies reported when applying comprehensive approaches include:

- Corporate flexibility in the area of age management can be increased.
- Comprehensive approaches can improve the effectiveness of individual age management measures.
- Integrated concepts can also be more easily incorporated in a general HR strategy than is possible with individual non-integrated age management measures.
- Individual age management measures are more readily acceptable to employees and executives if they are part of a comprehensive approach.
- Comprehensive approaches have a more lasting effect and promote more effectively the development of a corporate culture and policy that is sensitive to demographic changes and which is, consequently, sustainable.

The following prerequisites for success in good practice with comprehensive approaches were identified:

- The necessity for overall corporate integration.
- The approach should be part of a general corporate Human Resources management strategy, ideally an integrated corporate concept.
- Advanced training efforts are required for managers and supervisors in different age-related fields, such as capacities, changes, risks, possible interventions and unintended effects, and contradictions in isolated age-management measures.
- Company-wide age awareness campaigns are necessary.
- Commitment of both the corporate top management and the corporate staff representatives are essential.
- The approach should be part of a joint general strategic approach supported by corporate management and the trade unions.

CONDITIONS NECESSARY FOR SUCCESS AND SUSTAINABILITY

Good practice in age management in enterprises may be individual stand-alone measures or more comprehensive approaches combining a number of different measures. These may be compensatory but should be preventive as well. In many instances such measures take into account the position of individual employees in their careers as a vital factor determining which measures should be proposed and how they should be offered and organised. It becomes increasingly obvious that, apart from the *quality of work*, which concerns the actual workplace, the organisation of work, the working environment and the work content, that all have various effects on work ability, the *work–life balance* is also an essential factor in job satisfaction and the planning of lives and careers especially for ageing staff. In the development and introduction of age management strategies, and to achieve lasting results for the employees as well for the enterprise, a win-win situation, companies should always make a special point of considering the complex overall picture of wishes and expectations relating to the workplace among their ageing and older employees. With advancing age this context increasingly includes their personal lives outside working hours and independent from the company. The requirements for a successful and sustainable implementation of age management may be summarised as follows.

AGE AWARENESS

In order to develop a corporate climate sensitive to demographic change and a corporate culture with a positive attitude towards ageing, an awareness of this issue must be developed, especially by HR managers and staff representatives at all levels. The process of age awareness training, that is, imparting knowledge about the ageing process, serves to increase sensitivity towards the necessity and awareness of the advantages of a personnel policy that takes ageing into account, to disprove the traditional, mostly negative, stereotypes of ageing, and to consider ageing in employment in a more sophisticated and realistic manner. Moreover, regular training of managers concerning the background, requirements, opportunities and limits of age management is necessary to promote a well-informed approach to planning and implementation processes. Last but not least, it is also important to address the individual employee to create awareness of the process of his or her own ageing.

Smart planning and implementation

Care needs to be taken with conceptualisation and planning, for example, by introducing age management measures in stages as trial runs and pilot projects. Implementation should be kept open for possible changes, suggestions and criticism in the course of the process. Communication and participation, qualification, monitoring and evaluation need to be addressed at every stage.

Cooperation of all parties concerned

All parties involved within the company should be involved right from the beginning of the planning stage as well as in the implementation of age management measures, to ensure cooperation on the basis of equality. This applies particularly to the early commitment and participation of employees, staff representatives and trade unions. Any corporate measure or initiative involves some change and can therefore only be successfully implemented if readiness for change among staff already exists or can be developed readily. One way to accomplish this is to make the project participatory, which is to encourage active participation of employees in the project to increase their motivation. This will also win those employees' valuable practical knowledge for the project. Cooperation between management and staff representatives as well as other parties involved will contribute to success. The corporate institutionalisation of such projects, for example in the form of agreements with the works committee, is advisable. The development of effective relations between the social partners beyond the organisational level helps, as does the championship by top management. External counsellors or experts should be consulted if required.

Continuous communication

In addition to cooperation between all parties concerned, communication is a vital confidence-building factor in any process of change. Thus, open and continuous communication in connection with the project and in all stages of its implementation creates a solid basis of mutual trust, without which organisational change can be introduced only with difficulty. This can be accomplished by the use of works meetings, corporate magazines and other communication media. A culture of open discussion contributes to recognising and dealing with any possible problems, weaknesses or opposition.

Internal and external monitoring

Each organisation needs to collect data as to internal needs and external conditions of operation. Age management requires a systematic analysis of organisational data, such as age structure, qualification and personnel development needs, the status of employees' illness or work ability (for instance with the help of a work ability index). External data includes monitoring the regional development of the labour market, and consideration of the company's own needs as well as general conditions, such as amendments of the retirement pension scheme, labour market and wage policies. Knowledge of existing public assistance, for example for employment and health programmes and their application to individuals is useful. Other companies' approaches to age management are also of value.

Evaluation and assessment

The evaluation of measures serves more than one purpose. Evaluation during the process (formative evaluation) can contribute to uncovering possible weaknesses in conception or implementation, and pave the way for changes for more effective processes. This kind of evaluation leads to a corporate learning process. In addition to the learning effect, the benefits and success of such projects for the employees as well as for the enterprise can be demonstrated in connection with the final evaluation of the measure (summative evaluation), which can ultimately contribute to sustainability. Even though the success of such measures is not always easy to quantify, an evaluation of each project should be carried out by the company, its employees or staff representatives, to assess possible effects and results.

Towards an integrated age management strategy

While organisational initiatives to combat age barriers must be at the heart of any strategy to respond to work force ageing, the most successful outcomes are likely to occur within a context that is conducive. Age management should ideally embrace all responsible parties with all relevant actions and policies forming an integrated age management strategy. Integration involves not only the horizontal connection of measures within companies and beyond but, also, the vertical integration of policy and practice.

The essential ingredients of a strategy are:

- emphasising the long-term **prevention** of age management problems, such as the de-skilling of older workers and work-related health problems, rather than reactive problem solving;
- focusing on the **whole of the working life** and all age groups, not just older workers;
- ensuring a **joined-up approach** that brings together all dimensions and actors that contribute to effective age management;
- **changing attitudes** within organisations and in society as a whole to educate people about the need for age diversity;
- ensuring, in the short term, **catch-up provision** for older workers who missed out on specific skill training or whose health was affected adversely by employment;
- conducting regular strategic **evaluations** of age management policies and initiatives to assess their effectiveness.

If such a strategy were implemented it would help to eradicate the negative impact of ageing on various aspects of employment.

CONCLUSION

In all EU Member States, the issue of the ageing work force has gained in importance on the political agenda. After decades of early exit policies, a turnabout has taken place in labour market policy. The research on which this chapter is based is focused on how this new approach might be applied within organisations. The 130 case studies about the effective operational exercise of ageing management suggest many benefits from companies investing in older workers. It also demonstrated the huge scale of the challenge facing both the public and private sectors and, therefore, the need for a 'joined-up' policy approach spanning all levels of society. This chapter and the good practice guide that arose from the research are intended to add to the knowledge base about how to respond to ageing work forces, a big issue in Europe now, but one that will soon be global.

REFERENCES

DfEE (1999) *Age Diversity in Employment*. London: Department for Education and Employment.

European Council (2001) *Presidency Conclusions*. Stockholm 23–24 March. Brussels.

European Council (2002) *Presidency Conclusions*. Barcelona 15–16 March. Brussels.

Frerich, F. and Taylor, P. (2009) 'Ageing and the Labour Market – a Comparison of Policy Approaches', in G. Naegele, and A. Walker, (eds), *Ageing and Social Policy in Germany and the UK*. Basingstoke: Palgrave, pp. 46–81.

Ilmarinen, J. (1999) *Ageing Workers in the European Union. Status and Promotion of Work Ability, Employability and Employment*. Helsinki: Finish Institute of Occupational Health, Ministry of Social Affairs, Ministry of Labour.

Ilmarinen, J. (2005) *Towards a Longer Worklife. Ageing and the Quality of Worklife in the European Union*. Helsinki: Finish Institute of Occupational Health.

Mandl, I., Dorr, A. and Oberholzner, T. (2005) *Age and Employment in the New Member States*. Dublin: European Foundation for the Improvement of Living and Working Conditions.

Naegele, G. (1999) *Active Strategies for an Ageing Workforce*. Dublin: European Foundation for the Improvement of Living and Working Conditions.

Naegele, G. and Walker, A. (2002) Altern in der Arbeitswelt – Europäische "Leitlinien einer Guten Praxis" (good practice) für die Gleichbehandlung älterer Arbeitnehmer/innen in der betrieblichen Sozialpolitik, in Badura, B. et al. (eds): *Fehlzeiten-Report 2002*. Demographischer Wandel. Berlin et al.: Springer, pp. 225–234.

Naegele, G. and Walker, A. (2006) *A Guide to Good Practice in Age Management*. Dublin: European Foundation for Living and Working Conditions.

Reday-Mulvey, G. (2005) *Working Beyond 60*. Basingstoke: Palgrave.

Taylor, P. (2005) *Employment Initiatives for an Ageing Workforce in the EU 15*. Dublin: European Foundation for the Improvement of Living and Working Conditions.

Walker, A. (1996) *Combating Age Barriers*. Dublin: European Foundation for the Improvement of Living and Working Conditions.

Walker, A. (1999) *Managing an Ageing Workforce: A Guide to Good Practice*. Dublin: European Foundation for the Improvement of Living and Working Conditions.

Walker, A. and Taylor, P. (1998) *Combating Age Barriers in Employment: A European Portfolio of Good Practice*. Luxembourg: Office for Official Publications of the European Communities.

Wolff, H., Spieß, K. and Mohr, H. (2001) *Arbeit – Altern – Innovation*. Wiesbaden: Universum.

19

Work and Learning: From Schools to Workplaces

Richard D. Lakes

INTRODUCTION

This chapter on school-to-work transitions in the USA features the vocational charter high school and the career academy. The former is an institutional reform that utilizes the shared resources of state technical colleges governed through business and industry partnerships, whereby curricular decisions and instructional offerings serve the needs of cluster-based local area businesses. The latter is an older reform model integrating academics into high school career clusters noted for their small-scale learning communities. These two policy designs are viewed as part and parcel of the college and workforce readiness agenda, indicating to critics of vocational education that the field is serious about raising the graduation rates and college completion percentages, while helping firms strengthen their competitive edge with skilled knowledge workers.

THE POLICY PERSPECTIVE ON WORKFORCE DEVELOPMENT

Legislators in the state where I reside have just approved a plan whereby public school districts could convert to charter high schools to tailor educational programs for local communities. Charter high schools are state-sanctioned educational entities that receive public monies for a term of three to five years, whose plan of approval includes a documented improvement in student learning. Free of bureaucratic entanglements within the management of larger districts, charter schools are often viewed as sole business enterprises, whereby the educational leader has full authority to hire or fire teachers and contract for support services in operating and maintaining the school. Additionally, my state has levied $16 million dollars in the 2008 to 2009 academic year for five vocational charter high schools that would be positioned metro-regionally and partnered with a postsecondary technical college in the vicinity. Assignment of these academies will be matched to geographical targets identified by industry clusters in the state. Vocational charter high schools and career academies in partnership with postsecondary technical colleges are considered more likely to capture the local needs of businesses and industries by offering a larger pool of eligible students trained in high performance work. The vocational charters and career academies serve as communication networks, imparting information about future employment regulated through business and industry partnerships that determine the flow of human resources into area firms. The new policy focus in vocational education places greater emphasis on labor market needs *at the regional level*, with more cluster-based employers preferring their employees have a combination of real-world experiences and training credentials, as obtained in sub-baccalaureate programs offering degrees, diplomas or certificates at regional two-year community and technical colleges (Grubb, 1996).

Career and technical education (CTE) in the USA is facing more pressure by school reform policymakers to justify its position as an applied curricular offering serving secondary-level students up to age 18, many of whom are from underserved minority and at-risk populations. Few contest that academic intensification of the curriculum and ratcheting-up of student achievement standards will ready young people for work in a high-skills economy. In this policy environment toward more demanding core subjects, however, the continued relevance of secondary-level vocational education has been brought into question, evaluated and scrutinized by governmental leaders (Lakes, 2007). For example, President George W. Bush signed the No Child Left Behind Act (NCLB) into law in 2002, which was at the forefront of his educational agenda to tighten standards and improve options for parents of children at so-called failing schools – with an attempt to evaluate the effectiveness and quality of a school's instructional progress through high-stakes testing. The law required each state to create an accountability system of assessments, graduation rates, and other indicators such as teacher quality. U.S. public schools under NCLB mandates are modeled much closer to the British system of a national curriculum with regular report cards or league tables publicizing achievement assessments for comparative purposes, and market mechanisms are implemented that allow parents of failing schools a choice of transferring their children, if so desired. Recent reauthorization of federal funding for vocational education was steeped in the neoconservative language of accountability and standards fashioned tightly to align with college-preparatory curriculums, otherwise known as the college-for-all movement.

The largest lobbying group of vocational education professionals in the USA, the Association for Career and Technical Education, issued a policy paper in 2006, titled *Reinventing the American High School for the 21st Century* that responded to the college-for-all movement with a message of its own: 'In our view, there should no longer be an artificial split between academic coursework and CTE studies, nor should exposure to career- or interest-based coursework be delayed until late in high school or college' (Association, 2006, p. 4). In advocating what they termed career-focused interest-based areas in which students could pursue core academic courses while studying cluster-based occupations, CTE policymakers were on record as redirecting the field from its longstanding curricular function in preparing non-college-bound students for direct entry onto the shop floor with job-specific skills. To support that end, high school redesigns in vocational education under post-Fordism now utilize a template of career clustering in a number of pathways of study (there are 16 clusters altogether), organized under the broader all-aspects-of-industry approach in which jobs are grouped into families of related or nested occupations. For example, the health science cluster includes multiple pathways in therapeutic services, diagnostic services, support services, biotechnology research and development, and health informatics; the manufacturing cluster includes careers in production, process development, logistics and inventory, control maintenance, installation and repair, and health, safety and environmental assurance. The goal is to charge the CTE profession with the up-skilling of students in pathways to work or further schooling, while opening a talent pipeline in growth industries that are strategic to stimulating the employment base of a regional economy. The Association's (2006, p. 4) position rejects a monolithic one-size-fits-all formalism in high school studies, instead reinforcing the position that CTE assists young people in 'preparing every student for full participation in a spectrum of postsecondary education opportunities, meaningful work, career advancement, and active citizenship.' That being said, core courses have a place in schools as long as academic content is connected to an interest-based and relevant curriculum – and complement one another. Delivering academic skills within a broadened study of vocational clusters then has taken center stage in CTE curriculum reform.

Vocational students can gain favorable learning experiences via new reform models of schooling, resulting in successful program completions and leading to higher-paying jobs.

The crisis in workforce development is evident in a number of reports on American competitiveness in the marketplace. The largest lobbying organization of businesses in the country, the U.S. Chamber of Commerce, has weighed in on the issue as well. Their reports from the Institute for a Competitive Workforce advocate that stakeholders who drive education policy should identify and correct failures in student achievement, teacher quality, and school management (Archer, 2007). Yet a renewed commitment to workforce development, for example, has been touted in the latest findings by the National Center on Education and the Economy (2007), in a report written by a group of 25 panelists named the New Commission on the Skills of the American Workforce. These experts seek a broad overhaul of public schooling, primarily ending it after tenth grade by providing a series of state board qualifying examinations. Capstone tests would allow 16-year-olds who pass the first stage to proceed into further education such as postsecondary community and technical colleges and less selective state colleges. High-scoring students could stay in upper-secondary school for demanding academic preparation in rigorous studies for advanced placement or International Baccalaureate exams, readying them for entry into selective colleges. The first ten years of schooling are represented by a core of subjects emphasizing basic literacy skills in math and science, and students are expected to master this curriculum. No one younger than age 16 could leave school unless they were able to pass the first level of state boards. The idea that all students should be college-ready by the end of their sophomore years was derived from the crisis mentality of failed economic competitiveness in the technologically driven global workplace.

Pressure to heighten workforce development at home is due to a perception of competition abroad in countries such as China and India that produce greater percentages of work-ready graduates. The common wisdom is that a number of countries in the developing world have surpassed the USA in the past two decades in the percentages of working-age adults who complete high school. In order to maintain a higher standard of living for all Americans, given this scenario, workforce policymakers propose that the domestic pool of skilled labor be elevated and enlarged through educational reforms emphasizing math, science, engineering, and technical competence. A number of states are ratcheting-up diploma requirements and consolidating curricular track assignments. Proposed graduation rule changes and difficult exit exams, for instance, force incoming high school freshman to take a core in English, math, science and social studies, emphasizing basic skills preparation for work or college-bound pathways. High school students are being encouraged to take more difficult core academic classes that would ensure success in further education and in the workforce. Challenging course-taking is derived from a perspective that knowledge workers are employable, motivated and talented young people who will enter high-performance global workplaces and, more importantly, continue their work lives with a thirst for knowledge – a lifelong learning perspective that Field (2000) and others note has captured the attention of policymakers.

The two models of educational reforms detailed in this chapter – vocational charter schools and career academies – are favorable to workforce and economic development policymakers exactly because they promise to enhance young people's transitions into skilled jobs and increase the size of a home-grown pool of technically competent workers.

THE VOCATIONAL CHARTER HIGH SCHOOLS

The vocational charter high schools use the resources of a state's technical college system; allows articulation between both institutions no matter where students are physically enrolled (from three to four home schools); involves area employers in planning the school; and draws upon the state's charter school law to create a publicly-funded experimental form of educating children. This initiative in educational reform features a vocational charter school with both secondary and postsecondary facilities under one roof, one that awards advanced credits to high school students in technical subjects, offering a competency-based curriculum that uses state-of-the-art equipment and a small-scale learning community with dedicated teachers and motivated students who are taught work habits of industry. Employer representatives are formally folded into the governance structure (Lakes, 2003). Vocational charter schools also fit well with the neoliberal economic model of fiscal downsizing that all public institutions are faced with under new times – the erosion of operating budgets and cutbacks in state government. Neoliberals desire to minimize public funding for education, turning essential local services into a market economy, including privatizing public schools, and ending social security and other welfare benefits serving the aged, the poor, and infirmed. The major feature of running school as a model of business efficiency provides a rationale for school districts to curtail program duplications, reduce vocational course offerings, and relocate vocational teachers at a number of local high schools to one vocational center that shares facilities with a college. The delivery system offers customized training for existing or new firms relocating to the area, encouraging business partners to donate proprietary equipment and tools with the intention of tailoring instruction to specific manufacturing and assembly processes. Educational leaders can operate their programs as if business executives, circumventing seniority systems in the hiring or firing of teachers, and honoring the privatization of contractual services for running the schools. Yet the research evidence on charters and student achievement are uneven and inconclusive to date. Henig (2008, p. 7) suggested that 'the data and findings often provided weak and mixed pictures,' leading to a controversy among polarized camps of pro- and anti-choice advocacy and partisanship.

Federal charter school legislation began in 1994 with authorization for the next year of $15 million for state distribution to help fund start-up expenses. In 1998, Congress renewed the law and increased spending to $100 million for fiscal year 1999. By law charters are public entities managed by members of the community and free from many of the state and local regulations governing traditional public schools. Choice-conscious parents and other constituents quickly adopted a variety of entrepreneurial endeavors in schooling. Charters are tenured for periods anywhere from a short three years to an unusually long-term of 15 years, but can be renewed, depending upon state mandates (Lakes, 2003). One attractive feature of charter schools is scale, with median student enrollments only about 25 percent that of conventional public schools. This usually means a lower student–teacher ratio as well. Although unshackled from laws governing a host of operations (e.g., pertaining to teacher qualifications or the delivery of cafeteria meals), charters are accountable for improved student achievement, although school leaders must show evidence of measurable outcomes through timely evaluations. The vocational charter school model (also known as employer-linked charter schools) features a seamless educational experience for secondary students desiring to earn dual credits that apply to both a technical high school and the community college programs, but require articulation agreements between the two institutions in order to award certificates or degrees. Each school offers a variety of career clusters such as family, consumer and health sciences, business and information management, arts and communication, and engineering and technical services, among others. Students are positioned for jobs in childcare, computers, construction trades, electronics, graphic arts, health occupations, horticulture, video broadcasting, and welding. They are enrolled in vocational classes for one-half day daily, in two 80-minute periods scheduled in the morning or afternoon, and return to their home high school for additional course-taking requirements toward earning the high school diploma. Vocational charters feature additional credit-earning opportunities for students who are able to work 15-to-24 hours in weekly work-based learning assignments off-campus at youth apprenticeships, and paid or unpaid internships. Some community and technical college programs are available to students for advanced credits as in computer-aided drafting, computer repair technician, criminal justice, culinary arts, dental assisting, patient care technician, and welding certification. The charter high school closely monitors student attendance and tardiness, and uses a daily work ethic point system that is factored into end-of-term grades.

There is a four-stage model of development in the vocational charter high school (Chow, 2003; Lakes, 2008). First, a needs assessment and planning phase occurs where a taskforce of stakeholders are brought together to identity employment needs and technical knowledge.

Second, a design phase is required with identification of curriculum and courses, completion of articulation agreements, and arrangement of facilities and equipment. Third, an implementation phase is needed to begin the hiring of a school director (termed a CEO or chief executive officer), staff, and teachers, an in-service training for faculty in performance-based instruction, and delivery of courses. And fourth, an evaluation phase is implemented with the monitoring of instructional effectiveness and course content, and alumni follow-up on job placements and further education.

In the start-up year a group of stakeholders began the first phase planning in earnest several years before charter approval with a study of area employment concerns and analysis of data from the state department of labor, the area technical colleges, and national sources. The needs assessment survey is distributed to businesses and results tabulated with respondents noting clusters where job growth is expected to accelerate, among a number of findings about the future of economic development impacting educational services in the region. Survey results should indicate employers' attitudes about soft skills or personal workplace behaviors, such as tardiness, absences, poor teamwork, unsafe behavior, resentfulness of authority, conflicts with supervisors, cursing, theft, and so forth. The survey should note which potential course offerings employers might want to see provided by the vocational charter school. Then, stakeholders can move into the second phase of designing courses and curriculum, as well as securing a physical plant with laboratory space. Business partners are contacted for donations of training equipment, state-of-the art computers, and other customized installations at the school. The third phase of implementation requires the hiring of instructional staff, with a preference for teachers with extensive educational and professional experiences. The success of the school relies upon a visible and engaging principal, preferably someone from the business world, who reports directly to a board of directors bimonthly to decide on everything from busing schedules to resource allocations. One might surmise that a non-educator would have difficulties managing such a complex enterprise, but the charter school concept encourages flexible approaches to organizational design and leadership. 'The CEO's business pedigree helps bridge the chasm between public education and the private sector,' as MacAllum and Johnson (2002, p. 8) explained; 'He's fluent in both educational and business parlance and being from 'their' environment, he's trusted by business partners.' In the fourth phase of evaluation, the board must collect both qualitative and quantitative data on graduate placements and alumni satisfaction (Chow, 2003).

The vocational charter schools are expected to strengthen the quality of a cluster-based local workforce while providing employers with a pool of qualified candidates. Workforce development linked to vocational charters is a key to facilitating school-to-work transitions, especially under new economic conditions that require regional clusters find creative ways to attract businesses. Global business dictates cluster-based growth patterns in the states. Vocational education delivery systems integrated into business clusters are instrumental in attracting firms desiring to locate in the USA.

THE IDEA OF CLUSTER-BASED ECONOMIC AND WORKFORCE DEVELOPMENT

Under global trade policies that encourage capital flight overseas, nation-state borders are regularly crossed in the search for cheap labor and resources for manufacturing and assembly, and in off-shoring of information management services such as data collection and call centers, among others. Yet with shifting corporate interests from national to global, economic and workforce developers are forced to compete for jobs on a level plane regardless of location. Geographic regions nurture industry clusters to share resources and technical expertise and know-how in a global business environment. Cluster firms rely upon a pool of workers who are knowledgeable about the components of specialized production there. While businesses have always been integrated into the nexus of social partnerships in CTE, regional firms now expect a variety of customized services from public institutions including skill-based assessments and credentials for vetting future workers and for evaluating and monitoring those already employed. Transnational firms are attracted to the states because relocation packages offered by the economic development agencies deliver upon the promises of a ready-made supply of workers, up-skilled in the manufacturing and technical processes unique to that regional cluster, ensuring minimal disruptions in start-up. In addition, business decisions to relocate encounter few bureaucratic regulations or labor union contracts that might hamper human resource developments and job redesigns on-site.

Workforce training accommodates mobile capital in regions of industry growth. A flexible model of global production divides the core labor force into small and manageable business clusters of sub-contractors, suppliers and franchisees, noted as 'the new geography of capitalist activity,' in a report on management of higher education institutions published in 1999 by the Paris-based Organization for Economic Co-Operation and Development (OECD): 'Economic activity is dominated by interfirm relationships and 'collaborative manufacturing' which emerges at the regional level and allows both competition and collaboration to flourish' (1999, p. 18). Within the regionalization of economic activity there are a number of intermediate nodes as well, exhibiting interlocking networks of 'firms, chambers of commerce, government agencies, R-D laboratories, training and educational institutions including universities' (OECD, 1999, p. 18). For instance, a non-profit, state-funded model of workforce development, ranked one of the best nationally, is offered free-of-charge to new and expanding companies in one state. Each regional firm is partnered with an economic developer-trainer housed in one of the 34 technical colleges within strategic, industry cluster-based regions. The menu of services provided is comprehensive, including new employee orientations, pre-employment assessments, and a host of trainings on leadership and motivational skills, quality control measures, customer service and data processing, to name a few. In addition, the state's employers can search at no cost for talent using an online database uploaded with resumes from the state's technical colleges and research universities. The technical colleges are positioned as one-stop-shops for vetting future workers in cluster-based industries, and have enhanced their visibility by issuing a workforce readiness credential that assesses potential employees on cognitive knowledge and personal potential – both hard and soft skills. The National Governor's Association endorsed the cluster-based strategy as a policy tool in 2005, under what they termed best practices for aligning state workforce development and economic development initiatives (Troppe et al., 2005). CTE institutions are expected to be entrepreneurial in this neoliberal climate of strategic global advantage, encouraged to enter into public-private partnerships, and asked to manage costs with declining support from the taxpaying public (Levin, 2001).

Increasing reliance upon policy partners from the business-governmental-educational communities ensures that employers look to the vocational secondary or postsecondary school as a pedagogical space targeted to customize technical training for area firms. These programs prepare skilled youths for manufacturing positions nearby. Workforce developers ready students planning to enter clustered markets after completing technical education with degrees or certificates. The up-skilling of students is important to educational policymakers, according to Grubb (1996), because a majority of labor market entrants hold at least a high-school diploma but are unlikely to complete a four-year baccalaureate degree. Workforce developers suggest that investments in the labor force through education and training will result in improved earnings potential over a lifetime and benefit the country through greater productivity and economic growth.

THE CAREER ACADEMIES APPROACH

School-based reformers now want to fast-track high school students into postsecondary education and technical careers. This makes sense if one considers that in other countries formal schooling ends at age 16 (around tenth grade). Students lacking motivation or interest in their last two years of upper-level high school (grades 11 and 12) instead might be more focused and intent upon starting a career at an earlier age. Public policymakers desiring to prevent low-income and dropout-prone youth from leaving school early are encouraged by vocational programs that enable them to graduate on-time as well as transition to further education (Kazis et al., 2004).

Novel pathways are offered that integrate rigorous academics and technical education with access to postsecondary credentials – very appealing for young people with marketable skills who need the funds to pay tuition for college. Community and technical colleges in the U.S. generally attract non-traditional, working-class students earning associate degrees or certificates, who typically juggle part-time schooling with minimum-wage jobs just to raise families and make ends meet. Allen et al. (2004, p. 225) endorse an integrated model of secondary and postsecondary CTE because 'lower-performing students have too often been locked out of college-level technical courses, and high-end technical high school programs usually have very selective entry requirements.' Sometimes known as *early college*, these programs are designed to award advanced technical credit to high school students and help position them to reduce the amount of remedial education required in the first year of college. Remediation is costly and time consuming. Instructional support for under-prepared enrollees amounts to a staggering $3.7 billion, for instance, monies that are being used to divert faculty and staff from real college teaching, lost time spent on matriculation delays, and taxpayers waste to the tune of $1 billion a year to cover this redress (Alliance, 2006). A recent policy study on persistence in California's community colleges showed that about 60 percent of students dropped out or changed their plans to transfer to a four-year college shortly after the first semester of academic study (Driscoll, 2007). These young people were from underrepresented populations in higher education, often with educationally disadvantaged backgrounds, members of the fastest growing populations in the state. But success throughout college was dependent upon that critical initial experience at college. Early college programs 'do not foreclose options, rather, they open doors to higher-paying careers while keeping open the possibility of higher education' (Allen et al., 2004, p. 228). Advantages of the early college high schools are multifold and offer vocational students a way to bridge the divide between secondary and postsecondary levels.

The career academy is an early college model for high school students. It facilitates post-school linkages that help vocational students previously ill-served by the traditional route to academic and technical advancement. Although a much older reform initiative than vocational charter schools, the career academies are small learning communities within a larger comprehensive high school that are based upon all-encompassing occupational themes or career clusters (Mittelsteadt and Reeves, 2003). The academies function as schools-within-a-school that is a popular option in almost one-fourth of American high schools, particularly with cluster-based learning in information technology, health care, finance, and hospitality and tourism, among others. The academies hold anywhere between 50 to 75 students per grade level and 'foster a sense of community, personal attention from teachers, and constructive collaboration with peers' (Lerman, 2007, p. 53). Career academies are distinguished by their commitment to enroll at-risk students as well as high achievers, and feature block scheduling of classes that allow students to move together in groups as they sequence through several years of programming; a dedicated team of teachers; a rigorous college-preparatory curriculum; parental involvement; business support for work-based learning in job shadowing, internships, mentorships, and apprenticeships (Mittelsteadt and Reeves, 2003).

Career academies have been shown to curtail dropout-prone youth from leaving school, and these programs increase knowledge and skills (as reflected in grade-point-averages), which in turn increase the likelihood of graduating. There is a rich research base on evaluations of these programs. Studies on the earliest academies (beginning in 1985) using matching data found the high school dropout rate among the academy students was half of their counterparts. Students' testimony about the program and the mentors' evaluation was extremely positive with respect to their attitude toward school, and postsecondary articulation and employment rates were high. Maxwell and Rubin (2000) found career academy students dropped out at less than half the rate of non-academy students. Stern et al. (2000) cited ten studies with findings of higher graduation rates or lower dropout rates for career academy students than students in comparison groups. Kemple and Snipes (2000) found in a randomized study of career academies that for students at high risk of dropping out, the dropout rates were substantially reduced, while higher average attendance rates, and on-time graduation rates were substantially increased. And in the Manpower Development and Research Corporation longitudinal studies of career academies beginning in the 1994 to 1995 school year, evaluators analyzed ten career academies that had fully implemented the model (Kemple, 1997). The academies received twice as many applicants as they could accept. Half of the students were randomly selected into the study group while the others were placed into the control group. Students were categorized into subgroups based on whether they were high- medium- or low-risk of dropping out. Risk factors were: previous school attendance rates, credits earned in ninth grade, grade-point-averages, and rates of school mobility, whether a student was overage for his or her grade level, and whether he or she had a sibling who dropped out of high school. Kemple's (2004) subsequent evaluation *Career Academies: Impacts on Labor Market Outcomes and Educational Attainment* found positive and sustained labor market outcomes for young men – increased monthly earnings; no impacts on labor market outcomes for young women; substantial increases in employment and earnings for students who entered the programs at high or medium risk of dropping out of high school; and positive impacts in terms of number of months employed, hours worked per week, and hourly wages.

Both models of career academies and the vocational charters support the idea that students should begin college-level studies in their secondary school-going years. Beyond offering multiple pathways to advancement, the models try to stop 'the leakage in the education pipeline' among those most at-risk of academic failure, and offer possible 'traction for policies' that are based on solid research on what works (Steinberg and Almeida, 2007, p. 173). Educational reforms along these lines offer evidence that CTE students are less likely to drop out of high schools and more likely to undertake college-level work for further advancement. Workforce and economic developers alike advocate seamless educational transitions to credentials and careers.

THE FUTURE OF VOCATIONAL EDUCATION

Many states are ratcheting-up their diplomas and consolidating track assignments. Proposed graduation rule changes and difficult exit exams, for instance, force incoming high school freshman to take a core in English, math, science and social studies, emphasizing basic skills preparation for college-bound pathways but squeezing out room for art and music and foreign languages and career training credits. The State Scholars Initiative, a business and education partnership originally created in 2002 and funded by the U.S. Education Department, encourages students to take more difficult core academic classes that would ensure success in further education and in the workforce. Twenty-two states have participated in the program that features core requirements with a heavy emphasis upon English, math, science, social studies, and foreign languages. Challenging course-taking is derived from a knowledge worker perspective that assumes employability for motivated and talented young people entering high-performance workplaces. Initiatives along these lines are eagerly supported by the White House; the president's recently approved competitiveness bill passed in Congress and is touted as readying students for STEM pathways (science, technology, engineering, and math) in order to facilitate transitions into professional jobs and increase the size of our college-educated workforce.

Still, the high school in the USA will look quite different over time as the vocational and applied arts are slowly weeded out of the curriculum (Apple, 1998). These curriculums have fallen out of favor, replaced by seat-bound studies oriented to future professional workers attending a four-year college track. The U.S. public secondary education system was originally established to integrate socio-economic classes for community betterment. Yet in a matter of 40 years, according to Hammack (2004, p. 1), 'the comprehensive high schools has gone from praise to condemnation' due to a host of problems associated with underperforming youths. Massive changes in state-funded education have 'led to greater standardization and micromanagement of teaching and learning through tightened inspection systems, performance-related pay, and closely scripted curriculum reforms that severely reduced the latitude of teachers' pedagogical decisions' (Hargreaves, 2003, p. 5). The federal policy turn toward academic rigor in schools favoring high-stakes testing minimizes all that is considered valuable in postindustrial settings regarding learning-to-learn in social groups within communities of practice. Conservative views abound on the topic of what's wrong with the schools. One influential right-leaning think tank, for instance, charged policymakers to consider: 'If we're serious about improving academic performance we must encourage all our schools to focus on this core mission.' 'Everything else,' they continued, 'however worthy, is peripheral and secondary' (Finn et al., 1999, p. 10). The emphasis upon cognitive skills associated with subject-matter mastery is shortsighted, and policymakers falsely assume textbook learning holds transferability to work settings (Stasz, 2001).

Career-focused activities such as work-based learning have been shown in the research literature to complement academic course taking, and could 'serve a useful pedagogical role in improving how well students learn general academic subjects; making learning relevant to the concerns of students (including what careers they will pursue) can increase their motivation' (Lerman, 2007, p. 45). Students participating in real-life communities of practice find 'an authentic activity system in which actions and knowledge-use have real consequences.' Problem-solving processes have 'greater intensity and scope' through work experiences than in the classroom alone (Bailey et al., 2004, p. 166). Case study evidence from school-to-work program evaluations has shown that vocational learning enriches secondary-level academics, even facilitating the transfer function to postsecondary institutions (Castellano et al., 2004). Beyond technical skills training all students could benefit from experiential practices through career development, contextual learning and engagement in real-world activities that complement academics. High schools that honor learning differences should not have to conform to a procrustean one-size-fits-all agenda (see Rosenbaum, 2001).

Remove vocational education and see what happens to the educational attainments of low-income, marginalized youths. Participation in vocational education is highest in the poorest- to moderate-income-level schools, as measured by the percentages of students qualifying for federal free and reduced-price lunches (Silverberg et al., 2004, pp. 37–38). The most recent data, in 1998, indicated that schools with 50 percent of qualifying students earned 4.7 vocational credits; schools with fewer than 5 percent of qualifying students earned 3.2 credits. Greater participation in occupational programs overall is distributed along socioeconomic or social class lines. In addition, students with learning disabilities and other barriers to educational achievement such as limited English proficiency are disproportionately enrolled in vocational courses (almost 38 percent) and earned more credits in occupations (about six credits) than students without disabilities (Silverberg et al., 2004, p. 37). These so-called special needs students 'are more likely to graduate from high school, to be employed in higher-paying trades, or to enroll in higher education' (Gray, 2004, p. 132). Several researchers recommend that dropout numbers would be minimized if students could arrange their course schedules with a ratio of one-to-two: one vocational credit for every two academic credits during their high school years (Plank et al., 2005, p. 26). School-leaving decisions are impacted by 'relevance and attachment' in ways that students *experience* their education, they noted. Still, vocational education will change as states begin incorporating academic mandates and high-stakes testing. Ratcheting-up the academic curriculum without multiple pathways for career clusters will severely impact the attraction or draw among at-risk or underserved youths. Obviously the CTE community is worried about the future of secondary-level programming – perhaps summed-up by one policy wonk at an educational summit who titled his talk: 'Change or Die: The Challenge Facing Career and Technical Education Today' (see Kazis, 2005).

CONCLUSION

There is a noticeable policy shift in thinking about the mission of education under current times. Shrinking governmental support and rising competition from proprietary schools and electronic campus franchises has impacted the purpose of public postsecondary institutions (Jacobs and Dougherty, 2006). Perhaps conflicted in serving two masters – the universities, with the academic and transfer function for underserved and marginal students, and the business sector, with the vocational undertaking of economic development and job readiness – community and technical colleges continue to 'face new opportunities and challenges' (Bragg, 2001, p. 6). In their latest position paper entitled *Expanding Opportunities: Postsecondary Career and Technical Education and Preparing Tomorrow's Workforce*, the Association for Career and Technical Education affirmed that institutional seamlessness would enhance post-high school education and employment, and help solve the skills-gap shortage. 'CTE plays an important role in systems thinking,' the Association (2007, p. 3) reported, 'and can lead the way in building smooth transitions for students.' The vocational charter schools and career academies featured in this chapter give new purposes to CTE. In discarding older notions of partitioning students into silos separating by curricular tracks and age-graded levels, contemporary experiments in seamlessness just make sense for learning in the new economy.

REFERENCES

Association for Career and Technical Education (2007, March) *Expanding Opportunities: Postsecondary Career and Technical Education and Preparing Tomorrow's Workforce*. Alexandria, VA: Association for Career and Technical Education.

Association for Career and Technical Education (2006, January) *Reinventing the American High School for the 21st Century. A Position Paper*. Alexandria, VA: Association for Career and Technical Education.

Allen, L., Goldberger, S. and Steinberg, A. (2004) 'Pathways to Postsecondary Credentials: Schools and Programs that Blend Education and Employment', in R. Kazis, J. Vargas, and N. Hoffman. *Double the Numbers: Increasing Postsecondary Credentials for Underrepresented Youth*, Cambridge, MA: Harvard Education Press, pp. 221–229.

Alliance for Excellent Education (2006, August) 'Paying Double: Inadequate High Schools and Community College Remediation', *Issue Brief*. Available from: http://www.all4ed.org/publications/remediation.pdf (accessed 14.9.06).

Apple, M.W. (1998) 'Work, Power, and Curriculum Reform: A Response to Theodore Lewis's "Vocational Education as General Education"', *Curriculum Inquiry*, 28(3): 339–360.

Archer, J. (2007, February 28) 'U.S. Chamber of Commerce Grades States on Education', *Education Week*, 26(26). Retrieved from: http://www.edweek.org/we/articles/2007/02/28/26chamber_web.h26.html?levelID=1000 (accessed 7.3.06).

Bailey, T.R., Hughes, K.L. and Moore, D.T. (2004) *Working Knowledge: Work-Based Learning and Education Reform*. New York: Routledge Falmer.

Bragg, D.B. (2001) 'Opportunities and Challenges for the New Vocationalism in American Community Colleges', *New Directions for Community Colleges*, no. 115. San Francisco, CA: Jossey-Bass.

Castellano, M., Stone, J.R., Stringfield, S., Farley, E.N. and Wayman, J.C. (2004) *The Effect of CTE-Enhanced Whole-School Reform on Student Course Taking and Performance in English and Science*. Columbus, OH: National Research Center for Career and Technical Education.

Chow, A. (2003) *The Central Education Center: Research Report I (April-June 2002)*. Tallahassee, FL: Florida State University.

Driscoll, A.K. (2007, August) *Beyond Access: How the First Semester Matters for Community College Students' Aspirations and Persistence*. Policy brief 07–2. Berkeley, CA: Policy Analysis for California Education (PACE).

Field, J. (2000) *Lifelong Learning and the New Educational Order*. Stoke on Trent, UK: Trentham Books.

Finn, C.E., Jr., Kanstoroom, M. and Petrilli, M.J. (1999) 'Overview: Thirty-four Years of Dashed Hopes', in M. Kanstoroom and C.E. Finn Jr. (eds), *New Directions: Federal Education Policy in the Twenty-First Century*. Washington DC: Thomas B. Fordham Foundation, pp. 1–16.

Gray, K. (2004) 'Is High School Career and Technical Education Obsolete?', *Phi Delta Kappan*, 86(2): 128–134.

Grubb, W.N. (1996) *Working in the Middle: Strengthening Education and Training for the Mid-Skilled Labor Force*. San Francisco, CA: Jossey-Bass.

Hammack, F.M. (ed.) (2004) 'Introduction', in *The Comprehensive High School Today*. New York: Teachers College Press, pp. 1–5.

Hargreaves, A. (2003) *Teaching in the Knowledge Society: Education in the Age of Insecurity*. Berkshire, UK: Open University Press.

Henig, J.R. (2008) *Spin Cycle: How Research is Used in Policy Debates: The Case of Charter Schools*. New York: Russell Sage Foundation.

Jacobs, J. and Dougherty, K.J. (2006) 'The Uncertain Future of the Community College Workforce Development Mission', *New Direction for Community Colleges*, no. 136. San Francisco, CA: Jossey-Bass.

Kazis, R. (2005) *Remaking Career and Technical Education for the 21st Century: What Role for High School Programs.* Boston, MA: Jobs for the Future.

Kazis, R., Vargas, J. and Hoffman, N. (2004) *Double the Numbers: Increasing Postsecondary Credentials for Under Represented Youth.* Cambridge, MA: Harvard Education Press.

Kemple, J.J. (2004) *Career Academies: Impacts on Labor Market Outcomes and Educational Attainment.* New York, NY: Manpower Research Development Corporation.

Kemple, J.J. (1997) *Career Academies: Communities of Support for Students and Teachers – Emerging Findings from a 10-Site Evaluation.* New York, NY: Manpower Research Development Corporation.

Kemple, J.J. and Snipes, J.C. (2000) *Career Academies: Impacts on Students' Engagement and Performance in High School.* New York, NY: Manpower Research Development Corporation.

Lakes, R.D. (2008) 'The Vocational Charter School Model: A New Initiative in School Reform', *VOCAL: The Australian Journal of Vocational Education and Training in Schools,* 7: 2–6.

Lakes, R.D. (2007) 'Four Key Themes in Perkins III Reauthorization: A Political Analysis', *Journal of Career and Technical Education,* 23(1): 109–120.

Lakes, R.D. (2003) 'Employer-Linked Charter Schools: Origins of the Central Education Center', *Journal of Industrial Teacher Education,* 40(3): 46–62.

Lerman, R.I. (2007) 'Career-Focused Education and Training for Youth', in Holzer, H.J. and Nightingale, D.S. (eds), *Reshaping the American Workforce in a Changing Economy.* Washington DC: Urban Institute Press, pp. 41–90.

Levin, J.S. (2001) 'Public Policy, Community Colleges, and the Path to Globalization', *Higher Education,* 42, 237–262.

MacAllum, K. and Johnson, A.B. (2002) *Reconceptualizing Education as an Engine of Economic Development: A Case Study of the Central Education Center.* Washington DC: AED National Institute for Work and Learning.

Maxwell, N.L. and Rubin, V. (2000) *High School Career Academies: A Pathway to Educational Reform in Urban School Districts?* Kalamazoo, MI: W.E. Upjohn Institute for Employment Research.

Mittelsteadt, S. and Reeves, D.L. (2003, April) 'Career academies: Cutting-edge Reform or Passing Fad?', *Techniques,* 78(4). Available at: http://www.acteonline.org/members/techniques/

National Center on Education and the Economy (2007) *Tough Choices or Tough Times: The Report of the New Commission on the Skills of the American Workforce.* San Francisco, CA: Jossey-Bass.

OECD (1999) *The Response of Higher Education Institutions to Regional Needs.* Paris, FR: Organization for Economic Co-Operation and Development.

Plank, S., DeLuca, S. and Estacion, A. (2005, October) *Dropping Out of High School and the Place of Career and Technical Education: A Survival Analysis of Surviving High School.* St. Paul, MN: National Research Center for Career and Technical Education.

Rosenbaum, J.E. (2001) *Beyond College for All: Career Paths for the Forgotten Half.* New York: Russell Sage Foundation.

Silverberg, M., Warner, E., Fong, M. and Goodwin, D. (2004) *National Assessment of Vocational Education: Final Report to Congress.* Washington, DC: U.S. Department of Education, Office of the Under Secretary, Policy and Program Studies Service.

Steinberg, A. and Almeida, C. (2007) 'Creating Pathways for Struggling Students within a 9–14 System', in N. Hoffman, J. Vargas, A. Venezia, and M.S. Miller (eds), *Minding the Gap: Why Integrating High School with College Makes Sense and How to Do It.* Cambridge, MA: Harvard Education Press. pp. 167–174.

Stern, D., Dayton, C. and Raby, M. (2000) *Career Academies: Building Blocks for Reconstructing American High Schools.* Berkeley, CA: Career Academy Support Network, University of California, Berkeley.

Stasz, C. (2001) 'Assessing Skills for Work: Two Perspectives', *Oxford Economic Papers,* 3, 385–405.

Troppe, M., Crawford, S. and Simon, M. (2005, September) 'Aligning State Workforce Development and Economic Development Initiatives'. *Issue Brief.* 13 pgs. Washington DC: National Governor's Association, Center for Best Practices.

20

Competency-Based Training and Its Impact on Workplace Learning in Australia

Allie Clemans and Peter Rushbrook

INTRODUCTION

Competency-based training (CBT) is a workplace learning technology that focuses on the assessment of industry-specific standardized and observable skill outcomes rather than traditional course inputs or content. In Australia, skills standards are determined nationally by industry stakeholders, including peak employer groups and government bureaucrats. The agreed competencies are formally credentialed in stepped qualifications deemed appropriate to determined skills sets, ranging from shop floor operator to skilled technologist. Since the mid-1990s these skill bundles have been gathered together as 'Training Packages'. Qualifications are transferable across enterprises and are recognized in many industry areas not previously covered by traditional apprenticeship arrangements. This increased transfer, depth and breadth of national qualifications is considered to offer New Millennium workers more equitable opportunities for horizontal and vertical career movements, including those groups, such as women, migrants and indigenous Australians, considered disadvantaged by previous industry arrangements (Tovey and Lawlor, 2008, pp. 2–51; Goozee, 1993, pp. 116–117).

Over the past two decades CBT has been considered by some authors as '(a)rguably the linchpin, as well as the most enduring feature, of Australian training reform' (Harris and Hodge, 2009, p. 2), and 'in many respects the foundation of training reform in Australia' (Smith and Keating, 2003, p. 120). We agree with these remarks and seek in our chapter to locate and analyse the importance of CBT as a key signifier of latter twentieth century Vocational Education and Training (VET) transformation. Essential to understanding the apparent ease with which CBT was introduced from the late 1980s is an awareness of the way in which pre-existing forms of workplace and training policy and practice increased the receptiveness of industries and training authorities to the idea.

To account for, and assess the place of, CBT in Australian training and workplace practice we have considered four themes. First, we position CBT historically within the context of its intellectual origins and practice environments. Second, we map the evolution of CBT within the Australian context, including the necessary preconditions for its introduction and the tensions arising between the learning needs of the citizen and the workplace. Third, we present issues related to teaching and learning practice that have emerged through cases of competency-based workplace learning in Australia and highlight aspects of CBT that have been subject to critique for the ways in which they shape workplace learning. Fourth and finally, (as our conclusion), we close this chapter by signalling issues that hold potential to enhance competency-based workplace learning.

THE INTELLECTUAL AND HISTORICAL ORIGINS OF CBT

CBT is a member of the outcomes or objectives-based curriculum family (Harris et al., 1995). It also finds a home in the workplace systems engineering or industrial efficiency movement, which owes much to Scientific Management theory or Taylorism (Harris et al., 1995, p. 35). Drawing from the legitimated practice of these curriculum and workplace lineages, CBT expresses itself through specified workplace competencies based on observation of (best) practice translated into behaviourally measurable outcomes. While underpinning knowledge is acknowledged as important to understanding skill performance and occupational roles, it is generally employed using unproblematic and re-contextualized disciplinary knowledge rather than the problematized and socially critical theoretical systems found in higher education environments (Wheelahan, 2007, 2008; Stevenson, 1990). As such, CBT as a training technology is highly instrumental and suited to the immediate and pragmatic requirements of industries demanding a range of integrated yet discretely skilled occupational roles combined in an efficient and cost-effective manner. It is this nexus of transparent skills training and workplace utility proven over nearly a century of related practice that makes CBT attractive to workplaces and training organizations. A brief exploration of these intellectual and historical origins, particularly in relation to CBT's emphasis on behaviourally oriented workplace skills training, will better enable an understanding of its apparent timeliness for the flag-bearing role it rapidly assumed in Australian vocational education and training reform from the late 1980s onwards.

CBT's intellectual forebears are found chiefly in the innovative work of American behavioural psychologists such as Edward Thorndike and B.F. Skinner, workplace training and efficiency experts Frederick W. Taylor and Frank and Lillian Gilbreth (Braverman, 1974, pp. 173–183), and outcomes-based curriculum theorists John Franklin Bobbit, W.W. Charters and Ralph Tyler (Brown, 2003). CBT draws from Thorndike's fundamental insight, throughout his work in the early twentieth century, that learning is demonstrated from changes in observable behaviours, in particular through 'stimulus-response' activities. Learning is also considered to be incremental rather than insightful. Later in the century, Skinner reworked Thorndike's approach as the radical behaviourism of 'operant conditioning' and learning through positive rather than negative reinforcement. The behavioural approach was widely legitimized through such activities as Thorndike's WWI aptitude tests for American GIs and 'Word Books' to assist US teachers in teaching children to read and write as well as the popularity of Skinner's positive reinforcement ideas in education to counter traditional rote learning and punitive discipline regimes (Pinar et al., 1995; Harris et al., 1995, p. 39).

In the early twentieth century, Scientific Management claimed to develop a 'science of work' through the use of proven empirical data collection methods to break down tasks into their component parts and efficiently and cost-effectively re-design the workplace to achieve greater levels of productivity and profit. Workers were then matched and trained to perform and consistently repeat these narrowly defined tasks (Taylor, 1911). Taylor's systems approach was aided considerably by the work of Frank and Lillian Gilbreth whose 'time and motion' studies were used to determine the most efficient approach to achieve itemized tasks. Perhaps the most popular representation of Scientific Management was the assembly line, first used on a large scale in Henry Ford's production of the T Model (and the origin of Scientific Management's other pseudonym, 'Fordism').

Critics of Taylorism claimed the new assembly line process separated holistic craft knowledge from its itemized manufacture and privileged new industrial management systems over traditional trade control of the production process. Scientific Management, then, was considered as much a form of re-locating workplace power as it was a system of increasing industrial efficiency (Braverman, 1974).

In a complex interplay of Scientific Management workplace practice, behavioural philosophy, university-based curriculum research, school-based experimentation and media popularization, the period from WWI to the latter twentieth century produced a flowering of outcomes-based education as a preferred education model. A pioneer in the field and a contemporary of Taylor was John Franklin Bobbitt. Clearly a member of the efficiency movement, Bobbitt believed in breaking down broad fields of human experience into specific 'new industrial society' workplace functions after which learning objectives were derived to develop instructional programmes to assist students into their ascribed roles. W.W. Charters, another contemporary of Taylor, further developed this approach and influenced his promising student Ralph Tyler to develop the 'Tyler rationale' of setting instructional objectives, devising related instructional strategies and content, and organizing appropriate learning experiences and evaluation strategies, based on criterion-based testing, or evaluation against objectives rather than comparison or 'norm-referencing' with one's peers (Brown, 2003).

THE POST-WWII AUSTRALIAN WORKPLACE AND OUTCOMES-BASED LEARNING

The receptiveness of Australian post-WWII workplaces to a fusion of Scientific Management and outcomes-based education and training was shaped by the crucible of total war, together with the helping hand of government. The conditions of total war isolated Australia from its traditional sources of manufacturing supply in Great Britain and forced industry and government to work together on import replacement technologies (Spaull, 1987). The industrial war production line, however, was found lacking in quality, efficiency and output, for example, Australian enterprises could not produce parts of sufficiently accurate tolerances to fit the military equipment manufactured in the United States or England. To rectify the problem, the government established the National Standards Body in 1940 to define precise measurement systems and introduced Statistical Quality Control (SQC) as a precision-based manufacturing method. SQC was also able to monitor human performance, concluding that a skill broken down into its component parts and implemented in a scientifically managed production line setting, using workers trained in specific tasks, was a more efficient use of labour. With these systems in place, the marriage of industry production methods and government industry policy proved a successful partnership that carried over to the post-WWII economic boom (Mellor, 1958; Rushbrook, 2001).

The preconditions for formal workplace learning

The shift from workplace and non-credentialed training to credentialed vocational education and training was a slow process. In the 1950s and 1960s Australian capital remained reluctant to formally credential its workers, whether professional or non-professional, apart from trades-based apprenticeships in traditional metals manufacturing areas. Ironically, the initial push for formal vocational credentialing came in the late 1950s and early 1960s from the state and Commonwealth public services and statutory authorities related to the provision of gas, electricity and water. It was from here that professions such as engineering and architecture fought with employers and national wages bodies to recognize their status and pay them accordingly. A consequence of their successful campaigns was the creation of occupational 'gaps' between the profession and the trades that were eventually filled by technicians and a range of other credentialed paraprofessional or middle-level workers. The resulting occupational classifications were formed from traditional Taylorist analyses of public service workplaces, with professions at the apex, followed by technicians, tradespeople and operatives. Curricula for these credentials were developed by representatives from the public service and statutory authorities in partnership with post-compulsory vocational education colleges. The resulting courses formed the basis of outcomes-based curriculum experimentation that informed the eventual emergence of CBT as a form of public and private sector vocational credentialing (Rushbrook, 2007).

Economic crisis and skill supply

The quiet acceptance of credentialed training in the private sector, steered by the public sector and its state-funded vocational colleges, took place over two decades from the early 1970s. A variety of reasons encouraged the shift. First among these was the collapse of Australia's post-WWII economic 'long boom' in the mid-1970s. During these halcyon days Australia was indeed the 'Lucky Country' and its tariff protected economy easily warded off competition from often superior imported goods. But in 1973 the briefly lived reformist Whitlam Labour government (1972–1975) attempted an early flanking move to stave off economic disaster and slashed tariffs by 25 per cent. Australian capital was consequently encouraged to realign its industrial practices to more competitive global forces (Bolton, 1990). Skilled labour, too, became more difficult to source. Domestic labour supply also was hampered by an 'aristocracy of labour' that privileged male skilled workers in the dominant metals-based manufacturing industries. Potential domestic skill replacement through the use of women, unskilled migrants and mature age adults was consistently thwarted through organized labour's control of such traditional workplace skilling programmes as apprenticeships (Rushbrook, 2001; Hagan, 1981, pp. 317–319). A declining economy and a dearth of skilled workers, then, encouraged public and private partnerships to seek domestic solutions to skill supply.

With national inquiries and reports swiftly becoming the major tools of informing policy change and regulatory practice, the Tregillis report prompted swift political and bureaucratic action (Tregillis, 1969, p. 89). In a move that encouraged the tripartite participation of government, private enterprise and organized labour, a National Steering Committee on Training (NSCT) was formed, chaired by Peter Derham, General Manager of Nylex cable manufacturers. The NSCT established an enterprise-based train-the-trainer scheme and industry committees using Manpower Development Officers to assess training needs across 13 key industries. The NTSC and the later named NTC (by a Labour government in 1974) offered a model for tripartite cooperation that augured well for future workplace training reform (Derham, 1972).

A feature of this attempt at change was the involvement of the federal government in vocational education reform. With no constitutional authority over education, apart from the power to make occasional grants to students, the Commonwealth began at this time to flex its muscle and use its 1942 assumption of state income tax collection powers to hector, cajole, persuade and even blackmail the states to accept national education policy initiatives through the threat of withdrawal of Commonwealth monies.

A national role for public vocational education

With a tentative beginning in a national negotiating process that is now commonplace, the 1970s economic crisis fast-tracked both discussion and action. To a reforming social democratic government whose leader reflected that 'the most intense political debate during the 1960s was not about Viet Nam; it was about education' (Whitlam, 1985, p. 315) it was, then, perhaps surprising that vocational education was an afterthought following quick action on primary, secondary and university education. The vocational education sector was familiar with benign neglect over many years (Connell, 1993, p. 173). But persistent pressure from organized labour, including vocational education teacher unions and domestic employer groups, soon rectified this omission, particularly after politicians realized that the current crisis was not an aberration but a challenge for long-term management (Ford, 1983). And, perhaps economy recovery could be led by a vocational education revolution.

The tension between the then Labour government's commitment to radical social engineering and meeting the challenges posed by a declining economy, increasing unemployment and inflation, and its attempted resolution, was played out in its dealing with the emergent national workplace skills shortages. It was here that the last gasp of the 1960s education reform movement confronted the colder realities of 1970s 'manpower' (*sic.*) planning. Two belated but major vocational education national reports captured the mood, one now consigned to history's dustbin, the other valorized as the iconoclast of New Millennium vocational education provision. Both, however, remain shape shifters of workplace policies and practices and should be considered as seminal to the later emergence of CBT.

The first report was *Australian Labour Market Training: Report of the Committee of Inquiry into Labour Market Training*, chaired by Professor Don Cochrane of Monash University (Cochrane, 1974), the other *TAFE in Australia: Report on Needs in Technical and Further Education*, chaired by Myer Kangan, First Assistant Secretary of the DLNS (Kangan, 1974). The first inquiry considered labour market training as part of an 'Active Manpower' (*sic.*) policy that addressed the needs of capital and workplace skills shortages, the other the needs of the individual, his or her barriers to access, and opportunities to participate in recurrent or lifelong learning, within the reality of available workplace opportunities. The first inquiry's report gave rise to the raft of short-term, often uncredentialed, programme-based labour market skills training for the unemployed and disadvantaged workers that persist today, the other publicly credentialed vocational qualifications for full-time and part-time workers and students. Kangan, though, was aware of the possible clash between capital's demand for specific 'manpower' (*sic.*) and the choices made by individual citizens participating in TAFE programmes (Rushbrook, 1998). In a statement that has reverberated throughout subsequent years in debates about the nature of vocational education provision, Kangan expressed the view that the '*problem of reconciling personal and public advantage is complex and not easily solved. Its final solution will not be found in this report*' (Kangan, 1974, p. 9). Together, both reports shaped what today is considered to be the Australian Vocational Education and Training (VET) sector.

So, by the mid-1970s the essential preconditions had been established for the emergence of CBT as a national training approach in vocational and workplace training. Outcomes and industry-based training, even though non-credentialed, had been proven in the maelstrom of total war and boom-time economies, successful working partnerships had been established between employers, government and organized labour, and federal mechanisms were set in place for managing national vocational education provision. From here the quest for credentialed national course provision with appropriate curriculum modelling was regarded as the lodestone of vocational education unity.

The search for industry-friendly curricula

While many other government reports and inquiries emerged in later years to further refine the fundamental vocational education structures and relationships set in place by the Kangan and Cochrane reports, they are left relatively silent in this chapter except for foregrounding the role they played in attempting to resolve the remaining 'public and personal advantage' debate and its playing out in curriculum experimentation. A key outcome of policy shifts was a forced invitation to private and public sectors and national and state governments to work together on mutually acceptable training solutions.

From the late 1970s curriculum specialists within Australian state TAFE sectors began the process of determining a national approach. An early 1980s review of course provision (Broderick, 1982) discovered only one example of an attempt at national core curriculum – Queensland TAFE's electrical trades' programmes. Apart from this, most syllabuses were state based. According to Stevenson, the public vocational education sector search for industry relevance and responsiveness, as well as curriculum uniqueness in order to distinguish it from other education sectors, formed the basis of its approach to curriculum reform throughout most of the 1980s (Stevenson, 1990).

Economic rationalism and the national introduction of CBT

From 1986, more than at any other point in the history of vocational education, the national economy became a key factor in directing its future. A link between economic health and vocational training was provided through the re-invention of human capital theory, put simply as the investment in skills training for increased enterprise and national competitiveness, as a guiding philosophy underpinning micro and macro economic reform. For Australia to prosper it was required to move from reliance on traditional non-value-added commodities such as wool, wheat and ores to the manufacture of internationally competitive value-added products (Kelly, 1992; Pusey, 1991).

A key factor in the legitimation of the human capital approach to economic reform was the election of the Hawke Labour government in April 1983. The previous Conservative government, in spite of their austerity and tinkering with monetarism, had in fact departed little from prior Keynesian practice. With the failure of a predicted resources-led recovery in the early 1980s, mounting unemployment and industrial unrest, it was clear to incumbent powerbrokers that radical reform was required. National macro-economic decisions were about to exercise a profound effect on vocational education provision (Kelly, 1992).

Influential at the micro-economic level was the union movement which was prepared to sacrifice wage increases for economic stability. The most telling expression of organized labour's commitment to industrial change through training reform, union restructuring and management rapprochement was the report of a 1987 mission to Europe. Published as *Australia Reconstructed*, the ACTU/Department of Trade's mission's conclusions detailed work practices which demonstrated clearly the link between education and training, productivity, worker-management cooperation, and industrial peace. The mission's key spokesperson, Laurie Carmichael, former Communist Party member and a leading metals industry unionist, travelled the length and breadth of the land singing the report's praises and the need for radical change. He played a crucial role convincing employers, governments, unions and training authorities to work together with the common aim of reviving Australia's manufacturing system. He also recommended that 'consideration be given to, either through national vocational training legislation or appropriate mechanisms, the establishment of national competency standards for all skilled occupations and the introduction of nationally consistent final competency testing in such occupations' (*Australian reconstructed*, 1987; Harris et al., 1995, p. 51). Business, too, echoed the ACTU's sentiments (Carmichael, 1987).

Federal and state reforms to the training system were given national expression through the competency-based curriculum model used to deliver human capital's promise of increased productivity through human capital investment in vocationally relevant skills training. All states and territories were committed to develop a CBT system. Several final initiatives in the early 1990s collectively informed a 'Training Reform Agenda' that cemented the rapid progress made in the previous decade to align public vocational education with credentialed workplace training provision.

The effects of this period continue to inform New Millennium vocational education provision. In effect, TAFE's assumed monopoly of training provision was broken and repositioned as equal to other 'Registered Training Organizations' (RTOs), whether public or private. From 1997 this open market approach was reframed as 'user choice'. The separation of public TAFE providers from guaranteed government funding forced a renaming of the national training system, referred to from this time as the Vocational Education and Training (VET) sector. The National Framework for the Recognition of Training (NFROT) was established to create a national system of accredited courses and training providers as well as to standardize a CBT system. NFROT eventually evolved into the Australian Recognition Framework and the current Australian Quality Framework. From 1996 workplace competencies, their assessment and related qualifications managed through the AQTF were reworked as Training Packages endorsed by industry-based committees, from 2006 called Industry Skills Councils. An open and competitive training market was to be managed nationally by a new body created in partnership between the federal, territory and state governments. Named the Australian National

Training Authority (ANTA) it operated until 2005 when it was absorbed into the wider federal education and training bureaucracy (Harris et al., 1995, pp. 74–92; Smith and Keating, 2003, pp. 40–72; Tovey and Lawlor, 2008, pp. 6–46).

In the post-WWII decades through to the New Millennium, then, we have witnessed a slow, sometimes reluctant, acceptance of credentialed and competency-based workplace learning by Australian industry. Though receptive to funding training that promised immediate increases in productivity and efficiency, industry resisted credentialed learning offering generic education to its workers. This created a dilemma to public providers of vocational education who, since their foundation in the mid-nineteenth century, offered liberal education components within their programmes; to win the legitimacy of industry and their acceptance of credentialed course provision would require the sacrifice of this tradition. As with most matters related to education reform, however, the matter was taken out of the hands of industry and education providers and assumed by federal and state governments which created and enforced training reform based on their larger view of the realities of national economic survival. Within this context, the relationship between industry and vocational education was realigned. Competency-based training had forged a relatively smooth path to reach its central position as the nationally endorsed approach to workplace and vocational learning, upholding an orientation that emphatically favoured the needs of the economy over those of the individual (Rushbrook, 1995).

THE IMPACT OF COMPETENCY-BASED WORKPLACE LEARNING PRACTICE IN AUSTRALIA

Clearly, the historical trajectory through which national training reform has been realized in Australia, as narrated above, has had a marked impact on the way in which vocational learning has manifested in various learning settings, including workplaces. In this section, we turn our attention to the practice of competency-based vocational learning through Training Packages in workplaces. We focus specifically on the ways it has shaped teaching and learning in workplaces, drawing on literature to indicate the successes noted as well as ongoing considerations that require attention in order to realize the beneficial outcomes promised through the skill formation agenda.

The historical evolution of Training Packages, standing as competency-based national 'curricula' aligned to industry-based competency standards, has been described above. It should be clear at this point that publicly funded course delivery in the Australian VET system is currently based on Training Packages that exist and, in the case that they do not, upon industry endorsed standards. These packages comprise sets of competency standards, qualifications and assessment guidelines to support a model of training and assessment that is in accordance with the Australian Qualifications Framework (ranking all qualifications in relation across secondary schooling, vocational education and training and higher education sectors). Their purpose, according to Schofield and McDonald (2004, p. 14) is both to provide flexibility for learners, employers and training providers and regulatory insofar as they allow for national recognition of vocational qualifications. Their development was premised on the notion that industry could most effectively define current and future workplace requirements. In line with this, a predominantly industry-led system developed with responsibility for the articulation of the range of outcomes within these Packages.

Positive impact of CBT in workplace learning

Experiences that testify to the influence of CBT in workplace practice are mixed. At the positive end of the spectrum, CBT has been seen to have increased the legitimacy of workplace learning overall. This theme emerges both implicitly and explicitly in the literature, acknowledging that the process of rethinking skill formation and vocational education that transpired in the later part of the twentieth century resulted in greater recognition given to the workplace

'... as a site and source of legitimate work-related learning' (Johnston et al. 2002, p. 1). The use of Training Packages has been the predominant way in which workplace training has been undertaken since 1996. One of the few qualitative evaluations on their impact (Down, 2003) highlights the successes of Training Packages which include greater acceptance of these in large and medium enterprises, synergies between competency standards and workplace selection and appraisal processes and greater industry responsiveness in training practice (2003, pp. 4–5):

> These 'success stories' demonstrate that flexibility claimed as an advantage of Training Packages does, in fact, exist. The examples show that, innovatively implemented, Training Packages have the potential to provide gains in the effectiveness of vocational education and training (Down, 2003, p. 5).

Hellwig's (2006) assessment of the Australian training system reinforces the sense of overall receptiveness toward a competency-based approach as it has been broadly implemented. He similarly notes the sense of flexibility among learners and trainers in their experience of the system (p. 71).

Receptiveness to the structures surrounding the implementation of CBT has been seen to have also fostered positive changes to teaching and learning practices. Chappell (2004) discerned authentic changes in VET practice since the inception of training reform (and competency-based training) in the late 1980s which he characterized as becoming more learner centred, work centred and attribute focused (Chappell, 2004, p. 2). These changes in VET practices suggest that contemporary teaching and learning practices in vocational settings are driven less by behavioural (observable) and cognitive (learners' mental processing) approaches and more by constructivist approaches in which learners recognize the contexts that shape and give meaning to their worlds. Such shifts, Chappell argues, are responsive to teaching and learning as much as they are to the social and economic changes that gave rise to the training reform agenda in the first place – namely, the recognition that vocational learning best addresses holistic needs of workplace and social transformation; that continuous change demands learning that is not confined to traditional institutional providers, that workers are perceived as the originators of working knowledge as much as they apply it and that learning (rather than instruction leading to formal credentials) is the central educational driver in contemporary times (Chappell, 2004, p. 5). 'Indeed, perhaps the most important goal for VET today is to contribute to the construction of new worker-learners' (p. 5).

With time and experience, workplace learning practice shaped by CBT has then moved from what was initially perceived as a 'narrow' view of competency, solely concerned with achieving prescribed training outcomes, meeting minimum standards and equating performance with competence, to a richer view where the broader context in which working knowledge was located has been recognized and addressed in work place learning (Hackett, 2001; Wojecki, 2007). The growing sophistication around CBT and its impact on workplace learning reflects this evolutionary trend within workplace learning where competency-based training aspired to reach 'best practice' rather than to attain the minimum standards it initially aimed to realize. To achieve this, aspects of learning beyond technical and procedural knowledge (conceived often and narrowly as observable outcomes) such as theories, attitudes and contexts have been integrated into competency- based teaching and learning practices.

Beckett (2004) highlights the subtlety that is, or has the potential to be, incorporated in competency- based curricula through his analysis of CBT's capacity to make explicit the dimensions of practical judgement (knowing 'why') as much as knowing 'how'. By paying attention to the processes of learning as much as to the outcomes of learning, he positioned competency as having something concrete to offer workplace learning with a consequent positive impact on workplace performance.

Research by Johnston et al. (2002) presents a series of rich case studies detailing the ways in which workplace learning, underpinned by a competency-based training approach, was implemented in five diverse industry settings. Their study identifies some variability in work-based training and assessment practices in Australia, mediated by the nature of the industry settings, their respective understandings of work-based training as a method of organizational capacity-building and their institutional contexts which influenced their approaches to implementing workplace learning. Despite the variability that emerged across the differences within industry settings, Johnston et al. were able to discern three pillars that worked together to support an effective approach to competency-based workplace learning. They are (i) the existence of a set of performance standards to which training and assessment programmes are linked; (ii) the availability and expertise of support personnel within workplaces to assist learners through the process of work-related learning; and (iii) the connection between workplace learning and an enterprise system of reward and recognition (Johnston et al., 2002, p. 44).

These three pillars complement a set of criteria for developing 'good workplace learning' (NCVER, 2003) which suggest the following features as common to achieving this aim: (i) instilling an organizational culture of learning, (ii) the alignment of training and business strategy, (iii) the recognition of formal and informal learning, (iv) the customization of training to staff needs, and (v) the development of networks and, partnerships (NCVER, 2003, p. 11). Such research demonstrates that principles of effective workplace learning rest as much on training practice as they do on the broader organizational culture and human resources systems which support it. The system of competency-based training and the practices which flow from it establish learning as closely connected to organizational capacity building.

Undoubtedly then, CBT (which was ushered in on a platform of national training reform in the late 1980s after the prior laying of the ground work for its reception) has positively altered the workplace learning landscape in Australia. However, among the gains made sit issues which entrench weaknesses within workplace learning and its capacity to achieve the aims of local enterprise responsiveness and national economic competitiveness. It is to these that we now turn.

Troubling dimensions of competency-based workplace learning

Countervailing some of the enthusiasm and successes of a vigorous vocational system are a set of issues, often philosophical and ideological in nature, which hold implications for practice. Articulation of these issues is helpful in signposting features of a competency-based learning approach that stands to be more fully realized. One of these is the relationship between the knowledge encompassed within Training Packages and its capacity to express authentic workplace practice. This issue reconnects us with the unresolved struggle between the learning needs of citizenry and the workplace, raised earlier in this chapter when, from the 1970s onward, 'manpower' (*sic*) concerns took precedence over those of citizenship and an uneasy dichotomy between liberal and vocational oriented education/knowledge was established.

Competency standards have been seen to articulate descriptions of work that have been deemed an insufficient or unrealistic expression of contemporary experiences of work (Chappell, 2004; Wheelahan, 2007):

> Competency standards and Training Packages … tend to assume: descriptions of work can be generalised for particular jobs or occupations, a degree of stability in terms of the work skills required and consistency in terms of the requirements different employers demand of workers, vertical career mobility rather than horizontal mobility and standard jobs rather than non-standard jobs, the primacy of technical skills over generic employment skills and that the needs of enterprises and the needs of industry sectors are similar (Chappell, 2004, p. 6).

The capacity of competencies to adequately articulate workplace knowledge draws us into debates around the nature of knowledge and the distinction of various types of knowledge. In this vein, Wheelahan and Carter (2001) critique the rigidity of the Australian training reform system for placing too much attention on work-related knowledge to the exclusion of broader education. Such a position drew on significant criticism levelled against the initiation of a competency-based system in Australia dating back to the early 1990s in which the vocational reference point was perceived as becoming dominant. Training reform was seen to conflate vocational and general education (Marginson, 1991) such that knowledge of a more general, personal and social nature was only endorsed to the extent of its work-relatedness and capacity to yield productive citizens/ workers.

Wheelahan's later work (2007) deepened the critique around knowledge, positioning competency-based training as not only carrying the inheritances of a 'hand/mind distinction' (alluded to in the historical narrative of CBT above) but, undesirably separating disciplinary and embodied knowledges. The implicit rejection of disciplinary knowledge in the contemporary vocational education system, in favour of an approach which facilitates learners' construction of their knowledge of the work, has propped up a system in which, according to Wheelahan (2007, p. 648) '... a fragmented, atomistic and instrumental view ... ignores, to its peril, the need to understand ... the relationship between elements and how they are transformed in the context of such a relationship'. By focusing on the knowledge and skills to 'do' a job, Wheelahan argues that 'CBT assumes that outcomes can be achieved by directly teaching to the outcomes, and in doing so ignores the complexity that is needed to create capacity, and this goes beyond the level of experience in the contextual and situated' (Wheelahan, 2007, pp. 648–649). In this way, workplace learners are unable to transcend the particular context to which the training 'content' applies.

Significant questions have been posed around the nature of knowledge validated in a competency-based system. Calls to recognize the ways in which CBT had transformed the nature of workplace learning (and knowledge) in Australia were heard as early as 1990, as academics and researchers presented an opposing voice to the generally uncritical and rhetorically optimistic policy environment that consolidated training reform in Australia. Jackson's work (1994, 1995) was significant, not only as a critique of CBT but, for the implications her arguments held for training practice in the workplace. Contrary to the idea of competencies being defined to reflect the performance required in industries, she argued that, in fact, the competencies which guided vocational programmes (and by implication Training Packages) did not mirror the actual workplace performance required for competent workers to carry out their jobs and, as such, inadequately reflected the complex judgement and workplace performance that the CBT system was attempting to secure. Such analysis led her to conclude that this was not a weakness in the process of competency development itself but rather a product of a political process in which competencies were defined for the purpose of instantiating employer control. In this way, her work highlighted the connection between the initiation of a competency-based training system that was not just about educational transformation, designed to more adequately portray and achieve workplace performance, but tied to workplace, institutional and industrial reform with intentions that aimed far beyond pedagogical change.

Reinforcing the connection of competency-based training reform to broader forms of power and control, Edwards and Usher (1994) contributed a distinct voice in their critique of CBT. Drawing on postmodern ways of seeing, they argued that the definition of workplace competencies could be read as an act of 'discipline' – of both the learners whose lives and workplace action were defined by these standards, and of the educators, who subjected these learners and were subject themselves to the regulatory training practices of CBT.

Critique centred on the nature of knowledge captured by industry-led and defined competency standards asserts that while the competency-based system is well intentioned to create work-related and learner-centred practice, it precludes the kind of learning required for social innovation in the workplace and for healthy communities more generally (Field, 2000; James, 2000; Johnston et al. 2002; Stevenson, 2000). Questions around robust practice in CBT emerge particularly around the notion of generic skills (which began as the Mayer Key Competencies in the 1990s and in 2004 evolved into 'employability skills') which lay at the heart of the competency-based training system from its inception in the 1990s (DEST, 2005; Chappell, 2004; Cornford, 2006; Down, 2004).

Cornford (2000, 2006) offers an incisive and critical review of the ways in which employability skills are currently encapsulated in workplace learning and sends an urgent call for the need to pay more serious attention to workplace learning processes in order to genuinely realize these skills in practice. He highlights the general consensus that generic skills have not been successfully implemented in VET, with employability skills not sufficiently embedded within workplace learning practice (Cornford, 2006, p. 3):

> The focus of the Employability Skills, as the name suggests, is upon employability. But what is substantially missing is any really serious indication of how these desired qualities may be realistically taught.... What we are left with is a serious educational issue, namely that the business community, and those developing VET policy, have no real understanding of what generic skills really are or how they may be attained in any form (Cornford, 2006, pp. 3–4).

Cornford's work suggests that employers do not know enough about the transfer of learning and generic skills, nor fully comprehend their role in enacting learning around generic skills. He calls for policymakers and employer groups to go beyond 'simplistic interpretations' of the role of training in building national productivity and seriously attend to ways to facilitate the transfer of learning in organizational settings.

CONCLUSION

This chapter has highlighted the inheritances of CBT and mapped the stages of its incorporation within vocational education in general and in workplace learning in particular. Looking across the time period under review, it is clear that training reform and competency-based training has had the effect of raising the profile of learning and its relationship to work and organizational capacity building. There is limited empirical data to provide firm evidence that investment in training reform and workplace learning since the late 1980s has yielded commensurate positive economic and social outcomes (Cullen, 1997; Cornford, 2006). However, insights into competency-based training practice in workplaces demonstrate that it has worked well to initiate workers into workplace cultures, embedded career structures in workplaces to encourage workplace participation and commitment and instilled a sense of workplace belonging and professional identity. CBT has shown the effects of reducing staff turnover, of encouraging movement of staff within organizations to higher skill levels and, in some instances, of increases in workplace productivity (Johnston et al., 2002).

The historical narrative that began this chapter outlined the intractable national economic conditions to which competency-based training was designed to respond. Education and training was positioned as central to the economic ills of the nation and, likewise, was seen as the panacea to resolve them. Given the significance of this approach, CBT clearly was designed to not only rescue what was portrayed as a flagging vocational education and training system but, more importantly, to realign institutional and workplace relations with the goal of securing industrial efficiency. With such a mandate, it is not surprising that the learning dimensions of workplace training could pale in significance as a competency-based VET system was performing broader social and economic functions.

Interestingly, the most consistent and seemingly severe limitations to effective competency-based workplace learning emerging in the literature lie predominantly in the area of learning. It appears that over time, there has not been a forthright approach to building a robust orientation to learning that acknowledges the role of educators and trainers, the part they play in ensuring the transfer of competency into the workplace to positively enhance workplace performance and the nature of educational practice required to achieve this. CBT has seen much criticism for the way in which it was initiated without the inclusion of teachers (Gonczi, 1998; Jackson, 1994; Smith, 1999). The rationale for their absence was the reform of a system that was meant to be less about inputs and more about outputs, such that success was measured more by what learners could do rather than what teachers were able to teach. Obviously related, teachers' displacement from the process of conceptualizing the competency-based training system and the development of competencies and standards, was seen to be in line with a system where being able to do the job mattered more than the process of acquiring the capacities to demonstrate performance. Canvassing the literature, it appears now that it is this very issue – that is, the sidestepping of the significant pedagogical dimensions of CBT – that remains a point of weakness in the system itself.

A robust orientation to learning requires more than a set of competencies to guide workplace learning. It relies on an understanding of the relationship between teaching and learning and how this relationship is enacted to achieve workplace competence on the part of learners. It calls for explicit recognition of the role and capacity of the educator or trainer in designing learning tasks to develop learners' competence. Powerful work-related learning is shaped, too, by the articulation of workplace knowledge, defined as competencies, that express the complexity of vocational practice that underpins workplace performance and judgement. These aspects seem not to have been explicitly addressed in an Australian context.

CBT, as a central platform in the process of training system, has entrenched a powerful symbol of a living organizational and national commitment to workplace learning in Australia. The state of research and comment around CBT shows that teaching and learning, indeed the very dimensions that were perceived to be under attack since the inception of CBT – remain significant in mediating the success of the system and stand to more fully realize the potential of workplace learning to build competent and capable 'worker-learners'.

REFERENCES

Australia Reconstructed ACTU/TDC Mission to Western Europe: a Report by the Mission Members to the ACTU and the TDC (1987). Canberra: Australian Government Publishing Service.

Beckett, D. (2004) 'Embodied Competence and Generic Skill: The Emergence of Inferential Understanding', *Educational Philosophy and Theory*, 36(5): 497–508.

Bolton, G. (1990) *The Oxford History of Australia, Volume 5 1942–1988. The Middle Way 1942–1988.* Melbourne: Oxford University Press.

Braverman, H. (1974) *Labor and Monopoly Capital: The Degradation of Work in the Twentieth Century.* New York: Monthly Review Press.

Broderick, J.S. (1982) *An Investigation Into the Curriculum Development Processes in TAFE in Australia: A Comparative Analysis.* Adelaide: South Australian Department of Technical and Further Education.

Brown, M. (2003) 'Tracing the Ancestors of Competency Based Training', in Bowden, B. and Kellett, J. (eds). *Transforming Labour: Work, Workers Struggle and Change.* Proceedings of the Eighth National Labour History Conference, West End: Brisbane Labour History Association.

Carmichael, L. (1987) *'Perspectives on Education and Industry'.* Paper presented to working together: education and industry, an invitational seminar, Hotel Menzies at Rialto, 24 July.

Carmichael, L. (1992) *The Australian Vocational Certificate Training System.* Canberra: National Board of Employment, Education and Training.

Chappell, C. (2004) *Contemporary Vocational Learning: Changing Pedagogy.* Paper presented at the Australian Vocational Education and Training Research Association (AVETRA), Canberra.

Cochrane, D. (Chair) (1974) *Australian Labour Market Training: Report of the Committee of Inquiry into Labour Market Training.* Canberra: Australian Government Printing Service.

Connell, W.F. (1993) *Reshaping Australian Education 1960–1985.* Melbourne: Australian Council for Educational Research.

Cornford, I. R. (2000) 'Competency-Based Training: Evidence of a Failed Policy in Training Reform', *Australian Journal of Education*, 44: 135–154.

Cornford, I.R. (2006, November) *Making Generic Skills More than a Mantra in Vocational Education.* Paper presented at the AARE, Adelaide.

Cullen, R.B. (1997) 'Workskills and National Competitiveness: External Benchmarks, Report No. 2: Benchmarking Australian Qualification Profiles'. A project conducted by Performance Management Solutions for ANTA. Hawthorn, Vic.: Performance Management Solutions Pty Ltd.

Department of Education Science and Training (2005) *Training Package Development Handbook.* Canberra: DEST.

Derham, P. (1972) *The Task of the National Steering Committee on Training for Industry and Commerce.* Paper given to the Rotary Cub of Melbourne Seminar. St Kilda: Chamber of Manufactures.

Down, C. (2003) 'The Impact of Training Packages: What Might We Learn about Substantial Systemwide Change Processes', *International Journal of Training Research*, 1(2): 1–20.

Down, C. (2004) *Employability Skills: Revisiting the Key Competencies or a New Way Forward?* Paper presented at the Seventh Annual AVETRA Conference, Canberra.

Edwards, R. and Usher, R. (1994) 'Disciplining the Subject: The Power of Competence', *Studies in the Education of Adults*, 26(1): 1–14.

Field, L. (2000) 'A Framework for Understand Adult Learning and Education', in G. Foley (ed.), *Understanding Adult Education and Training* (2nd edn). Sydney: Allen & Unwin.

Ford, J. (1983) 'The Decision to Form the Kangan Committee – a Case in the Educational Policy Process', *Journal of Tertiary Educational Administration*, 5(2): 18–25.

Gonczi, A. (1998) 'The Potential Destruction of the Vocational Education and Training System', in F. Ferrier and D. Anderson (eds) *Different Drums, One Beat? Economic and Social Goals in Education and Training*. Adelaide, NCVER pp. 137–145.

Goozee, G. (1993) *The Development of TAFE in Australia: An Historical Perspective*. Adelaide: NCVER.

Hackett, S. (2001) 'Educating for Competency and Reflective Practice: Fostering a Conjoint Approach in Education and Training', *Journal of Workplace Learning*, 13(3): 103–112.

Hagan, J. (1981) *The History of the ACTU*. Melbourne: Longman-Cheshire.

Harris, R. and Hodge, S. (2009) *A Quarter Century of CBT: The Vicissitudes of an Idea*. Draft paper prepared for the AVETRA Annual Conference. Sydney, April.

Harris, R., Guthrie, H., Hobart, B. and Lundberg, D. (1995) *Competency-Based Education and Training: Between a Rock and a Whirlpool*. Melbourne: Macmillan.

Hellwig, S. (2006) 'Competency-Based Training: Different Perceptions in Australia and Germany', *Australian Journal of Adult Learning*, 46(1): 51–73.

Jackson, N. (1994) 'Rethinking Vocational Learning: The Case of Clerical Skills', in *Sociology of Education in Canada*. Toronto: Copp Clark Longman Ltd.

Jackson, N. (1995) 'These Things Just Happen: Talk Text and Curriculum Reform', in *Knowledge, Experience and Ruling Relations*. Canada: University of Toronto Press, pp. 164–180.

James, P. (2000) *Building Learning Communities in Industry: The Contribution of Competency-Based Training*. Paper presented at the International Conference on Post-compulsory Education and Training. Gold Coast, Queensland.

Johnston, R., Hawke, G., McGregor, C. and Johnson, G. (2002) *Changing Models for Changing Times: Learning and Assessment Practices in the Workplace*. Sydney: University of Technology.

Kangan, M. (Chair) (1974) *TAFE in Australia: Report on Needs in Technical and Further Education*. Canberra: Australian Government Printing Service.

Kelly, P. (1992) *The End of Certainty: The Story of the 1980s*. Sydney: Allen & Unwin.

Marginson, S. (1991) *Education and Public Policy in Australia*. New York: Cambridge University Press.

Mellor, D.P. (1958) *The Role of Science and Industry*. Canberra: Australian War Memorial.

National Centre for Vocational Education Research (2003) *What Makes for Good Workplace Learning?* Adelaide: NCVER.

Pinar, W., Reynolds, W., Slattery, P. and Taubman, P. (1995) *Understanding Curriculum: An Introduction to the Study of Historical and Curriculum Discourses*. New York: Peter Lang.

Pusey, M. (1991) *Economic Rationalism in Canberra: A Nation-Building State Changes Its Mind*. Sydney: Cambridge University Press.

Rushbrook, P. (1995) 'Straws in the Wind: The Construction of Technical and Further Education in Victoria 1945–1985'. Monash: PhD thesis.

Rushbrook, P. (1998) 'Technocrat or Visionary? Reflections on the Kangan Legacy', in F. Ferrier and D. Anderson (eds), *Different Drums, One Beat? Economic and Social Goals in Education and Training*. Adelaide: National Centre for Vocational Education and Research.

Rushbrook, P. (2001) 'Australia's First National Report on Vocational Education: The Commonwealth-State Apprenticeship Inquiry (The Wright Report) 1954', *History of Education Review*, 31(1): 60–74.

Rushbrook, P. (2007) 'Policy, Practice and the Construction of Paraprofessional or 'Middle-Level' Vocational Education Curriculum in Victoria, Australia, 1957–1975', *History of Intellectual Culture*, 7(1): 1–16.

Schofield, K. and McDonald, R. (2004) *Moving On: Report of the High Level Review of Training Packages*. Brisbane: Australian National Training Authority (ANTA).

Smith, E. (1999) 'How Competency-Based Training Has Changed the Role of Teachers in the VET Sector in Australia', *Asia-Pacific Journal of Education and Training*, 27(1): 61–75.

Smith, E. and Keating, J. (2003) *From Training Reform to Training Packages*. Sydney: Social Science Press.

Spaull, A.D. (1987) *Education in the Second World War*. St Lucia: Queensland University Press.

Stevenson, J. (1990) 'Curriculum and Teaching in TAFE', in J. Stevenson. *The Changing Context of Vocational Education: Selected Papers*. Conferences 1987–1993. National Qld: Griffith University.

Stevenson, J. (2000) *Codification of Tacit Knowledge for the New Learning Economy*. Paper presented at the International Conference on Post-compulsory Education and Training. Gold Coast, Queensland.

Taylor, F.W. (1911) *The Principles of Scientific Management*. New York: Harper.

Tovey, D. and Lawlor, R. (2008) *Training in Australia* (3rd edn). Frenchs Forest: Pearson Education.

Tregillis, B. (1969) *The Training of Skilled Workers in Europe: Report of Australian Tripartite Mission 1968–69*. Canberra: Australian Government Printing Service.

Wheelahan, L. (2007) 'How Competency-Based Training Locks the Working Class Out of Powerful Knowledge: A Modified Bernsteinian Analysis', *British Journal of Sociology of Education*, 28(5): 637–651.

Wheelahan, L. (2008) *Can Learning Outcomes be Divorced from Processes of Learning? Or Why Training Packages Make Very Bad Curriculum.* Paper presented at the AVETRA Annual Conference. Adelaide, April.

Wheelahan, L. and Carter, R. (2001) 'National Training Packages: A New Curriculum Framework for Vocational Education and Training in Australia', *Education & Training*, 43(6): 303–317.

Whitlam, G. (1985) *The Whitlam Government 1972–1975.* Melbourne: Penguin.

Wojecki, A. (2007) 'Crafting Youth Work Training: Synergising Theory and Practice in an Australian VET Environment', *Australian Journal of Adult Learning*, 47(2): 210–227.

21

Work-Related Learning in the United States: Past Practices, Paradigm Shifts, and Policies of Partnerships

John M. Dirkx

Education for work and other forms of workplace learning (what I refer to here as "work-related learning") have long occupied an ambivalent and, at times, somewhat uneasy location within the American psyche. Part of this uncertainty reflects changing conceptions of what Americans regard as "useful knowledge" (Kett, 1994) and what it means to be an educated person. Our approach to education has historically fluctuated between a curricular emphasis on general education, such as that represented by basic skills, classical education, or the liberal arts, and stress on more specialized forms of knowledge depicted in professional, vocational, and occupational education (Stark and Lattuca, 1997).

Despite growing recognition of the relationship of work-related learning to economic development, proponents of innovative vocational programs in the schools, even if they are sponsored by leading global corporations and promise high skills and good wages (MacAllum et al., 2002), struggle to convince parents that these programs are educationally solid. Concerned with the status and stigma possibly associated with such programs, parents prefer college preparatory programs for their children. In some community colleges, those deemed academically under-prepared for college need to complete remediation in basic skills before they are able to enroll for occupational-related courses. Institutions of postsecondary education that emphasize technical, industrial, occupational or career education are often seen as stepchildren to the more prestigious, four-year universities and liberal arts colleges. In some states, parole for inmates in prison is contingent not on obtaining an employable skill through vocational education but obtaining a certificate that reflects the equivalent of a high school education (Dirkx et al., 1999).

This notion of ambivalence with regard to what constitutes useful knowledge also works the other way. Leaders in schools of workforce development, as well as the students themselves, sometimes view general education requirements as more of a distraction or barrier than contributing to the overall preparation of students in occupational education. Training programs within the workplace must demonstrate a clear effect on individual job performance and organizational productivity (Swenson and Arnold, 1996) and anything that might smack of more generalizable skills, such as critical thinking or learning to learn tends to be marginalized or eliminated altogether from such programs. Participants in professional development and continuing education programs often eschew inclusion of theory and demand that facilitators focus on "what they can use on Monday morning." In many welfare reform programs, states place more emphasis on getting a job than on education or training (Martin and Fisher, 1999).

Work-related learning within the United States is highly decentralized and pluralistic, which may contribute to our feelings of ambivalence and uncertainty. Yet, recent developments and trends in policy, practice, and research within the United States suggest that this persistent world-view of the relationship of education and work may be shifting. Research and theory on how adults learn and the growing practice of collaboration across various sectors of the educational and business communities are contributing to what may be a paradigm shift in how we conceptualize and implement work-related learning in the United States. In this chapter, I will explore the basis for this claim and how this shift may be altering our conceptions of what it means to educate and train individuals for active participation in society and a global economy, in terms of current policy and practice. After first clarifying the various terms used to refer to work-related learning, I discuss trends in both formal education and training programs, as well as programs for incumbent workers. I also explore the role that technology is playing in reshaping our thinking and practice about work-related learning. I then look specifically at the formation and utilization of partnerships as one example of how this retheorizing is manifesting itself in both theory and practice. To be sure, this emerging vision of work-related learning remains tenuous and uncertain. Yet, within recent programmatic developments, curricular innovations, and state and national policy, we find signs of hope that work-related learning can represent a rich and fruitful context for preparing the educated person and for fostering lifelong learning within the general public.

To lay the foundations for this exploration, I first provide a brief overview of the various terms that have been used to refer to work-related learning. I then historically situate the evolution of our understanding of these terms within the United States, within formal educational institutions and programs and within workplace and continuing education.

TERMS USED TO REFER TO WORK-RELATED LEARNING

Work-related learning occurs within the United States in educational preparation programs apart from the workplace, in formal and informal learning within the workplace, and in continuing education and professional development programs offered outside of the workplace. Our understanding of these forms of work-related learning, demonstrated in the various terms used to refer to these phenomena, often reflects the particular historical contexts in which they emerge or have been used. For example, manual training in the late 1800s was a term that was often used to refer to a process of fostering "students" comprehension of the principles of science by first instructing them in the mastery of tools and mechanical processes' (Kett, 1994, p. 230). Manual training was concerned with preparing individuals for the crafts, but it also attended to a more general education than was evident in on-the-job training at the time. The idea of manual training, however, gave way to the emergence of vocational education in the late 1800s and early 1900s, a form of preparation for work that focused more specifically on specific trades and forms of work and less on the broader scientific or philosophical principles in which that work might be embedded. Recently, in an attempt to renew interest of the general public in work-related learning, the ideas of vocational or industrial education have given way to the term "career and technical education" or just "technical education." Rather than preparation for specific jobs, educators and policy-makers now talk about "career clusters" and "career pathways" as curricular avenues for individuals to consider.

The terms used to refer to work-related learning are also influenced by the particular social or organizational contexts in which it occurs. For instance, vocational education, industrial education, or career and technical education generally refer to programs associated with high schools, community colleges, or technical institutes, and they usually suggest forms of work-related learning that are pre-service. When work-related learning represents the primary focus of postsecondary education, such as in professional schools and career colleges, we often use the terms "occupational education" or "education for the professions."

On the other hand, a number of terms are used to refer to forms of work-related learning for incumbent workers that often occur in the workplace itself (Marsick, 1987), such as on-the-job training (Jacobs, 2001), human resource development (Gilley and Maycunich, 1998; Gilley et al., 2002), inservice education or staff development. Public schools sometimes provide continuing education for teachers within the schools and refer to these programs as staff development or "inservice education." Hospitals routinely provide continuing professional education and staff development for physicians, nurses, and other employees within the workplace. Colleges and universities also offer education and training programs for their teachers, under various umbrella terms such as faculty development, staff development, and HRD. Work-related learning is also reflected in terms used to describe activities that focus on incumbent workers but usually take place outside of the normal workplace, such as at conferences, workshops, and continuing education programs. In the United States, the terms "continuing education," "continuing professional education," or "professional development" are commonly used to describe this set of learning experiences. While trade apprenticeships were common during the colonial era (Kett, 1994), we now stress the importance of cognitive apprenticeships (Collins et al., 1991).

As one might surmise, these terms represent more than just different words to describe similar activities. Their differing meanings complicate discussions across different sectors of the community, challenging our quest for reform and quality. They often reflect complex historical, social, cultural, and political relations that help provide a deeper understanding to what these terms actually mean as a form of work-related learning.

WORK-RELATED LEARNING IN FORMAL PREPARATION PROGRAMS

In various forms, preparing individuals for the world of work has been a major purpose for education in the United States and an integral part of educational practices throughout its history. At times, a focus on work-related learning co-existed in a somewhat tense and indirect alliance with a broader, more general education focus. In some cases, as in apprenticeship training in the trades during the early parts of the eighteenth century, general education was less prominent. However, education for work was not necessarily divorced from the notion of the educated person. For example, Benjamin Franklin is well known for his emphasis on technical training, but he also created the junto as a means to provide general education for ordinary citizens (Kett, 1994). The junto was an educational activity that aimed at the mutual improvement of individuals and of society in colonial Philadelphia. It focused on debating issues of morality, politics, and natural philosophy.

In other times, a classical or liberal emphasis dominated approaches to education. According to Stark and Lattuca (1997), this emphasis on the importance of a general education suggests that "studying the liberal arts, including classic authors, improves students' ability to think, to appreciate knowledge, and to serve. These abilities, in turn, are believed to transfer to other tasks and settings, allowing graduates to serve society" (p. 48). During the colonial period, education reflected this general orientation and targeted the "elite" of society (Fuhrman, 1996). "Men of God" were considered part of society's elite and traditional study of the classics and the Bible was viewed as a means of preparing young men for the ministry (Kett, 1994).

However, within higher education, the idea that education should be practical and linked to preparation for work gained a strong foothold in the nineteenth century. This period saw the rise of industrialism and the need for trained and skilled workers (Kett, 1994). Occupations and professions emerged as a means to help address this need, and professional schools were established. Universities and colleges were called upon to provide a more practical education.

Vocational education emerged within the late nineteenth century and grew in stature through the early twentieth century (Kett, 1994; Kliebard, 1999). During this time, community colleges were established, with much of their mission initially grounded in a vocational orientation (Cohen and Brawer, 2008).

This practical orientation to education has evolved to the present-day, alongside the ebb and flow of a more liberal arts orientation. In the late twentieth and early parts of the twenty-first century, policy-makers stressed the growing importance of postsecondary education to the preparation of a skilled workforce and its importance for economic development. In recent years, education has been increasingly framed as an integral dimension of economic and workforce development (Moussouris, 1998; Sleezer et al., 2004). From the federal level to state and local governments, from presidents of major universities to superintendents of public school systems, policy-makers and leaders link the quality of the educational systems to our ability to prepare individuals to be economically competitive in an increasingly global economy.

During the 1980s and 1990s, a stormy period for American higher education marked by what is now referred to as the "cultural wars" (Graff, 1992), many scholars and policy-makers severely criticized the curricular movement in education that was said to be drifting away from the notion of a general education and a commonly held vision of the educated person. Critics such as Bloom (1987); Hirsch (1988); Cheney (1989); Bok (1974); and Boyer (1987) offered various suggestions for reform, mostly reflecting either a need to reassert the liberal arts curriculum or a return to the western "canon" that had traditionally characterized higher education curriculum (Stark and Lattuca, 1997).

Others, writing from a more critical or radical perspective, such as Giroux (1995) and Graff (1992) decried these conservative trends in higher education. No less enamored with work-related learning than their more conservative and establishment oriented colleagues, they warned of the consequences of such reforms to the disadvantaged and underprivileged, and attempts to honor diverse voices among our students. A few lonely voices, however, such as Fuhrman (1996) suggested that the development of educational thought within the twenty-first century would be marked by both an insistence on the value of a liberal education as the foundation for a higher education and that postsecondary institutions should also prepare individuals for productive employment.

While aspects of these curricular debates can be seen as a response to trends in specializing or vocationalizing the undergraduate curriculum, calls for reform within work-related learning itself were also evident during this time. The Carl D. Perkins Vocational and Applied Technology Act of 1990 and the School to Work Opportunities Act of 1994 provided strategy and support for a school-to-work transition process intended to help all students develop better connections between school and work. This legislation provided assistance to states for the development and operation of programs that linked that last two years of high school with the first two years of postsecondary occupational education or an apprenticeship program. Berryman and Bailey (1992) criticized what they referred as ineffective approaches to work-related learning and advocated for more contextual and integrated approaches. Using the stories of many community college teachers, Grubb (Grubb and Associates, 1999) helped us understand the complexities and challenges associated with work-related learning within these contexts and with these students. Writing from a more critical perspective, Kincheloe (1995) argued for the ideas of democracy and good work as guiding curricular visions in integrating academic and vocational education.

Education for the professions did not escape this reform fervor sweeping the country (Stark et al., 1986). The title of the book by Curry et al. (1993), *Educating Professionals: Responding to New Expectations for Competence and Accountability*, reflects the tenor of the times in which even the education of professionals was being subjected to scrutiny and calls for reform. For example, criticisms of medical education pointed to the disconnect between physician training and the needs of patients (Cantor et al., 1991). Many practicing physicians indicated they were not well prepared for various aspects of their practice (Baker et al., 1993). Critics charged that curricula being used to prepare accountants were too narrow and did not help students develop the ability to learn or address the uncertainties and ambiguities that characterized practice (Albrecht and Sack, 2000). In 1998, the Pew Health Professions Commission issued its final report, calling for a redesign of nursing education curricula to ensure that students acquire both general education skills, such as critical thinking, team work, and a commitment to lifelong learning (Bellack and O'Neill, 2000). Teacher education programs were accused of lacking rigor and intellectual challenge (Romanowksi and Oldenski, 1998). Collectively, these calls for reforms stressed the need for students to be active and engaged in their learning, and to work on problems that are ill-structured and reflect real world problems and concerns.

WORK-RELATED PROGRAMS FOR INCUMBENT WORKERS

Education and training programs for incumbent workers were also not immune from calls for change. A focus on increasing the nation's economic competitiveness drew attention to the need to enhance the basic skills of workers in many different contexts. The national workplace literacy program of the late 1980s and early 1990s provided for the establishment of adult literacy and basic skills education programs within the workplace (Carnevale et al., 1990), and called for the development of curricula and pedagogical strategies grounded in the context of the work and the workers' lives (Taylor et al., 1991). Many of these efforts reflected a kind of "back to the basics" movement that roughly paralleled criticisms of higher education, stressing the importance of basic skills in workplace learning programs. Other scholars of workplace literacy, however, provided more critical perspectives that sought to honor and give voice to the complexities of work, individuals, and the educational processes being used to enhance their literacy and performance levels (Hull, 1997).

In addition to workplace programs, basic skills instruction was also being offered through what we might broadly refer to as job training programs (Brokenburr, 2008). These programs, such as the Comprehensive Employment Training Act (CETA), the Job Training Partnership Act (JTPA), the Workforce Investment Act (WIA), and the Trade Adjustment Act (TAA) largely reflected national initiatives funneled through the states and often involved private–public partnerships. For the most part, these programs were targeted to low income adults (or, in the case of TAA, workers laid off through foreign competition) and intended to provide employability skills, including basic skills, if appropriate. Later, instruction in basic skills was connected with welfare reform, representing what some have called a transformation of adult literacy education (Hayes, 1999). In varying degrees legislation, such as the Personal Responsibility and Work Opportunity Reconciliation Act of 1966 and its associated Temporary Assistance for Needy Families system, the 1997 Welfare-to-Work program, and the Workforce Investment Act of 1998, served to limit access to basic skills instruction in favor of getting people back to work.

We can refer to many of these forms of work-related learning as "school-like." That is, they are often loosely modeled after formal learning settings that characterize teaching and learning in public schools and university and college classrooms. Several years ago, Watkins (1991) distinguished learning in the workplace from these more school-like forms of learning:

First, it is usually task focused. Second, it occurs in a social context that is characterized by status differences and the risk of one's livelihood (versus the risk of short-term grades). Third, it is collaborative, and often grows out of an experience or a problem for which there is no known discipline or knowledge base. Fourth, it also occurs in a political and economic context characterized by a currency of favours and pay for knowledge. Fifth, learning in the workplace is also cognitively different from school (p. 16).

Despite this distinction, learning in the workplace itself remains a complex and highly contested notion. One approach is to distinguish formal from informal conceptions of workplace learning. Aspects of formal workplace learning may resemble school-like work-related learning in that they often make use of workshop or seminar formats. Watkins (1991), Marsick and Watkins (1990) and others (Boud and Garrick, 1999; Garrick, 1998), however, stress the importance of more informal and even incidental forms of learning in the workplace. Some suggest, however, that labeling learning in the workplace as informal tends to marginalize it as inferior to other forms of learning that are more structured and intentional (Billett, 2001). Others argue that informal learning cannot be readily understood apart from the discourse in which it is embedded (Garrick, 1998). For the most part, this critical analysis of informal learning in the workplace reflects European, British, and Australian perspectives. Within the United States, the problematic nature of this concept is less apparent in research and theory on workplace learning.

The prevalent discourse within the United States is to view informal learning as occurring within the everydayness of experience in the workplace, often beyond one's level of conscious awareness. While the curriculum for school-like forms of work-related learning, such as career and technical education, education for the professions, and continuing professional education, is often explicit and clearly identifiable, in workplace learning the curriculum is more implicit and often emergent, arising within the specific contexts of work itself (Brockman and Dirkx, 2006).

This domain of work-related learning often falls within the fields of training and development (Dugan, 2003), and human resource development (Gilley et al., 2002; Rowden, 1996). As a form of workplace learning, Watkins (1991) differentiates human resource development from training, in that she sees the latter as "largely a short-term, skill-building, vocational function" (p. 16) while the former focuses more on the long-term development of both human resources and the organization. In these contexts, learning is facilitated rather than directly controlled and taught, as in more school-like programs. Because the workplace is constantly changing, the context for learning in the workplace reflects much higher levels of uncertainty and, at times, turbulence. Effective practice for these forms of workplace learning require much more attention to interpersonal skill than might be characterized by more school-like forms of work-related learning.

As Ellinger (2005) suggests, little is known about how informal learning within the workplace can be facilitated, developed, or encouraged, and we have much to learn in this area. While minimizing or ignoring informal learning in the workplace can and has occurred, however, recent research suggests a more central and important role for informal learning in both development of workers and performance improvement within the organization.

These different curricular visions are all helping to shape our collective understanding of work-related learning within schools, community colleges, and universities. While liberal arts currently enjoys something of a resurgence in some institutions, the importance of postsecondary education to the national economy and workforce development is being repeatedly stressed by leading policy-makers. Educators call for attention to the importance of attending to basic academic skills among students in higher education, while at the same time others argue for approaches to learning that are more active, engaged, contextual, and experiential – all qualities of effective work-related learning. Renewed attention is being paid to the importance of learning in and through work, while at the same time educators and policy-makers are stressing the importance of more formal preparation programs.

THE ROLE OF TECHNOLOGY IN WORK-RELATED LEARNING

Across all these various forms of work-related learning technology continues to influence who is learning, why they learn, where they learn, and how they learn. The rapidly changing nature and growth of knowledge in many disciplines, the need for retraining in new technologies, products, and services, and an increasingly global economy are exerting demand for continuous learning in many work-related areas (Harun, 2001). Learning mediated through or by the use of technology can be individual or collaborative, synchronous or asynchronous, formal or informal.

For example, video-conferencing, webcasts, podcasts, and e-learning modules are transforming not only the ways students learn in pre-service programs but also for learning experiences designed for incumbent workers. Simulations and computer games, such as Second Life, offer opportunities for learners to engage in life-like situations, including visual and audio cues that heretofore were either absent from case studies and problem-based learning scenarios, or only described in print. Medical students and residents in training carry with them on medical rounds in teaching hospitals smart phones that allow them to almost instantly connect with databases of information related to diagnoses of and treatments for their patients. Social networks such as Facebook allow individuals to interact around common areas of interest or work. Even retraining programs for dislocated workers are incorporating courses on computer applications to help former factory workers learn word processing and database programs, and to access the Internet. We now have international conferences on e-learning in the workplace (http://www.icelw.org/PROGRAM.htm, March 4, 2009).

Cursory surveys of the web suggest that the United States lags behind much of the rest of the world in terms of research and practice around the idea of work-related e-learning. As with the historical trajectory of work-related learning in general, work-related e-learning also demonstrates similar tensions regarding the nature of the educational experiences provided by these various forms of learning. For example, some question whether such forms of education or training are as rigorous as face-to-face settings. Others wonder about the *learning* part of e-learning, suggesting the lack of experiences that go beyond merely transmitting chunks of information to relatively passive learners.

In summary, the nature of work-related learning within the United States has evolved dramatically, from its early embeddedness in apprenticeship training within the trades to a rich mosaic of learning that reflects a wide diversity of content, contexts, and delivery methods. This evolution has been characterized by numerous tensions and debates that continue to characterize its discourse today. Recent research and practice on work-related learning within the United States, however, is increasingly reflecting several theoretical themes. In the next section, these themes will be developed. Then I will turn to how these themes are specifically manifest in the growing reliance on partnerships in work-related learning.

RE-THEORIZING WORK-RELATED LEARNING

In this section, I will sketch several theoretical developments within the United States that have influenced and shaped policy and practice in work-related learning. The overview on the historical trajectory of work-related learning has touched on some of these ideas and they will be developed here in somewhat more detail. As we shall see, these themes reflect paradigmatic shifts in how we are thinking about work-related learning, the influence of scientific research and especially brain-based research, a growing recognition of learning as socially and culturally situated, and a deepening awareness of the inherently subjective nature of work and learning.

The early history of work-related learning demonstrated an understanding of work-based knowledge that was grounded in an essentially rational understanding of the mind, knowledge, and how one came to know. That is, in the early years of this country, work-related learning was intimately bound up with the study of the classics, and critical knowledge related to the world of work was thought arise from a deep understanding of the great works and collective bodies of wisdom of the Western world. Skilled work reflected a developed and disciplined mind. As we became more industrial, work-related learning became somewhat decoupled from this rational worldview and more associated with an empirical perspective on the world and work. This perspective emphasized a more scientific and reductionist view, conceptualizing work comprising clearly definable sets of skills and knowledge. To learn and develop expertise in one's work involved acquiring and developing this skill and knowledge. To some extent, this view continues to be evident today in the use of job and task analyses (DACUM, 2001), and the emphasis in training and human resource development on performance improvement (Swenson and Arnold, 1996).

This technical and instrumental perspective on work-related learning within the United States, however, has been challenged by psychological and socio-cultural theories that reflect a more constructivist understanding of learning (Steffe and Gale, 1995). Admittingly, much of this theoretical work is occurring in other countries, and it is not easy to ferret out theoretical trends particular to the United States. Nonetheless, it is possible to chart certain forms of change taking place within work-related learning in an American context.

Arising from the work of Piaget (1955), constructivist views offer a quite different way of thinking about work-related learning (Aik and Tway, 2003). These approaches reflect a shift in understanding of knowledge and what it means to know, from one of knowledge "out there" and apart from the knower to one that understands the learner as intimately bound up with what it is that comes to be known, a learner that is an active creator and constructor of knowledge. Rather than seeing learning as receiving meaning transmitted from authorities, constructivist approaches to work-related learning regard meaning as constructed by the learner, based on the information and experiences they are having within the particular context in which learning is occurring.

Related to the development of constructivist understandings of work-related learning is the influence of schema theory and the notion of cognitive structures (Driscoll, 2005). Cognitive structures represent the ways in which learners structure or integrate bodies of knowledge. These structures reflect ways in which prior knowledge and experience has been organized and the means through which new knowledge is integrated into what we come to know. These theoretical ideas are further elaborated in the concepts of situated learning (Brown et al., 1989; Lave and Wenger, 1991) and cognitive apprenticeship (Collins et al., 1991) which undergird much of our contemporary thinking regarding work-related learning. The concept of situated learning suggests that learning reflects the activity, context, and culture in which it occurs or is situated. Situated learning stresses the social aspects of learning and that work-related learning occurs within the context of a community of practitioners (Wenger, 1998). For example, learning among frontline manufacturing workers occurs within the context of specific problems they are seeking to resolve and is mediated through their relationships with others in the workplace (Brockman and Dirkx, 2006).

Cognitive apprenticeship is another theoretical idea informed by the broader perspective of constructivism (Collins et al., 1991). While this idea obviously shares qualities with the earlier notion of trade apprenticeships, cognitive apprenticeships reflect the cognitive and constructivist dimensions of the learning and knowing that goes on within the context of authentic activity. In a sense it represents a continual interaction between the community of the trade practitioners and their knowledge, and the reflective activities typically ascribed to the academic community. Through this interaction, the student is thought to develop the cognitive processes and structures necessary to perform the work he or she is trying to learn. The idea of coaching, now quite popular among the professional development of school teachers and administrators (Kise, 2006) and business executives (Underhill et al., 2007), demonstrates the influence of the cognitive apprenticeship model on these particular forms of work-related learning.

Another manifestation in work-related learning related to the constructivist perspective is the emphasis now being placed on the socio-cultural contexts in which learning for and through work occurs (Fenwick, 2001). This idea of socio-cultural contexts ranges from a reference to quite broad structures and dynamics, such as the global market, international standards and technology, to the political and social relationships, beliefs, and values that constitute the contexts of particular workplace settings. Emphasis on socio-cultural contexts moves the consideration of workplace learning from the inner experiences of the individual to characteristics of the workplace, the way it is organized, and the various political and social processes that constitutes its relations (Fenwick, 2001). What is learned and how it is learned arises from a quite complex interplay of the inner life of the individual and the outer characteristics of the contexts for work-related learning.

Constructivist approaches to work-related learning have also given rise to considerations of self and identity and related notions of the emotional and spiritual dimensions of work-related learning. Again, much of this work seems to be occurring in other countries, but there are American contributions to the conversation around work-related learning and self-identity (Clark and Dirkx, 2000; Dirkx, 2005; Dirkx, et al., 1993; Steele, 2008; Wenger, 1998). While conceptions of the self within this discourse vary (Clark and Dirkx, 2000), scholars stress the intimate interrelationship between work, learning, and self-identity (Wenger, 1998), resonating with the broader, international discourse on work itself as a location for development (Welton, 1991) and self-formation (Chappell et al., 2003).

Related to the study of the self is emerging interest in the emotional (Ackerman and Maslin-Ostrowski, 2004; Bierema, 2008; Callahan, 2002) and spiritual (Geroy, 2005; Leigh, 1997; Mitroff and Denton, 1999) dimensions of work-related learning, and questions regarding the meaning of work (Dirkx, 2005; Pauchant and Associates, 1995). Both the emotional and spiritual threads manifest what some authors reveal quite different ways in which these aspects of the experience of work and work-related learning may be interpreted and approached. For example, Bierema (2008) indicated that, while consideration of emotion in the workplace may contribute to worker wellbeing and self-development, it also has the potential to be abused by management. Some suggest that considerations of the spirituality of work represent methods through which human resources exploit the worker's deeper yearning for meaning in life and work. Yet, consideration of both emotions and spirituality in work-related learning mirror how learning in and through work shapes one's sense of self, drawing attention to experience of the emotional and the spiritual within the workplace as a manifestation of developmental and biographical factors, as well as particular characteristics of the workplace itself.

Thus, much of the current American literature on work-related learning reflects movement away from conceptions of learning work as an apolitical and value-neutral, technical, utilitarian, and completely rational task in which learners acquire the specific skills and techniques thought to be required by certain categories of jobs. Rather, learning about, in and through work is seen as active, engaged, and deep expressions of human activity that are highly situational and contextual, and embedded in particular and specific forms of activity that characterize the particular socio-cultural environments in which it is occurring. Work-related learning is understood as a holistic expression of the worker connected socially and culturally with his or her immediate contexts but also with the socio-cultural, political and economic contexts of the broader society. In this line of research, the workplace represents a powerful location for learning and development of the worker, and work-related learning is understood as the realization of both rational and extra-rational dimensions of the human psyche.

To be sure, positivist, empiricist, and technical worldviews continue to influence and shape theory, practice, and policy around work-related learning in an American context. Job and task analyses continue to shape approaches to curriculum in many work-related programs and preoccupations with organizational performance (Swenson and Arnold, 1996) at times overshadow concerns for human development (Bierema, 2006; Dirkx, 1996). Yet, contemporary American scholarship increasingly demonstrates a portrait of work-related learning that is much more complex and multifaceted, and is becoming manifest in curricular practice and policy. Debates in higher education manifest renewed interest in the relationship of higher education to work. A more integrated curricular view of education and work, called for in the late 1800s and advanced by the work of John Dewey and the progressives of the early 1900s, is now being taken more seriously by policy-makers and practitioners at several different levels of education.

PARTNERSHIPS: COLLABORATION AMONG EMPLOYERS, EDUCATORS, POLICY-MAKERS

The historical and theoretical overview of work-related learning within the United States partnerships suggests that we have developed a more systematic approach to conceptualizing and implementing work-related learning programs. Among the key factors of this systemic view are broad contextual factors, the learning environment, and the nature of the work itself. However, partnerships between formal learning contexts and other entities have also played important roles in defining, theorizing, and implementing work-related learning. In the early parts of our country's history, these relationships were largely informal and often the learning environment and the partnership were one and the same, such as the trade apprenticeship (Kett, 1994).

As schools appropriated preparation for work, the preparation programs became increasingly disconnected from the locations or specific contexts of the work (Kliebard, 1999). Institutions providing vocational or technical education, such as high schools and community colleges, had to re-establish relationships that had become strained by this lack of connection between what students were learning and what they needed to know in the workplace (Kett, 1994).

In the last 40 years, however, these relationships have become increasingly central to work-related learning, especially those programs preparing individuals for work. But they have also evolved beyond informal partnerships and constitute a variety of connections between educational providers and industry, government, professional societies, community organizations, other educational institutions, and additional enterprises. Examples include articulation agreements between high schools and community colleges, and between community colleges and four-year institutions, which are helping to create more integration and cohesiveness in students' learning experiences. We are also seeing stronger connections between educational institutions and private businesses. These partnerships are fueled by the competitive nature of economic contexts, demographic changes, the technology and knowledge explosions, and the changing nature of work and the workplace.

Within the United States, partnerships reflect a variety of relationships and arrangements. The most common among these are those partnerships between educational institutions, such as high schools and community colleges, and specific industries and corporations. The School-to-Work Opportunities Act of 1994 provided funds and incentives to encourage such alliances among high schools and private industry. The Lansing Area Manufacturing Partnership (LAMP) is one of the more successful examples of such a relationship (Anonymous, 2002). This partnership involved the local school district and the United Auto Workers Locals 602 and 652, and the Lansing Car Assembly Center. The mission statement of LAMP reads:

> The UAW, GM and the LISD [Lansing Intermediate School District], in partnership with the public education community, will develop and implement a unique career preparation program, which prepares high school students to enter the workforce of the 21st century. This will be accomplished by providing an integrated curriculum (classroom instruction and work-based learning experiences) that equips students with lifelong learning skills, employability skills, and manufacturing proficiencies (Ingham Intermediate School District, 2008).

This program employed several of the conceptual ideas reviewed in the previous section, such as an integrated, employer-driven curriculum, project-based learning, team teaching, and opportunities for students and staff to establish ongoing interactions with employees in the plant (MacAllum, et al., 2002).

In developing and delivering work-related programs, community colleges are also actively involved in partnerships with private businesses. Often, these partnerships are two-way interactions, with the colleges providing customized training requested by businesses for particular employees, and businesses advising the colleges on the curricula and needed resources of their respective workforce training programs. In some states, such as Michigan, community colleges are represented on regional workforce development boards (Brokenburr, 2008). These boards are essentially led by business but also involve additional partners from the education, social services, and community sectors. They provide advice on regional policy issues related to workforce development and oversight for a variety of local programs involved in the Workforce Investment Act programs.

In other states, such as Colorado, community colleges are linked with a broader, state-wide system that focuses on economic development in the state by providing more effective occupational education programs (Raughton, 1998). Among the initiatives fostered by this partnership are programs designed to keep the state's workforce highly competitive by providing training for new or current workers that is designed to fit the needs of specific companies, accelerated career academies that provide adult learners with entry-level skills desired by new employers relocating into the area, and workplace learning programs that help connect students with what they are learning in the classroom with particular workplace contexts. Community colleges are also actively involved in the retraining of dislocated workers within particular areas of need designated by policy-makers within the state (Dirkx and Lan, 2009).

Partnerships are also contributing to the development or revision of work-related learning for incumbent workers, such as workplace literacy programs. As with many of the partnerships that characterize work related learning in the United States, workplace literacy programs arose from particular national legislation – in this case, the National Workplace Literacy Program. This program provided support for partnerships between private businesses and education organizations, which in turn collaborated on the development and implementation of literacy training for adults that related specifically to skills required in the workplace (Jurmo, 2004). While earlier efforts tended to rely on decontextualized approaches, more recent formulations emphasized a stronger role for the business partnerships and pedagogical methods that resemble those discussed earlier in the re-theorizing of work-related learning.

Private sources, such as the Mott Foundation, the Lumina Foundation, and the Gates Foundation regularly provide financial support for projects that aim at fostering professional development of teachers in schools, community colleges, and universities. Although these arrangements suggest a different kind of partnership, they nonetheless represent important ways in which educational institutions and private industry are entering into collaborative relationships for the purposes of enhancing and influencing the direction of work-related learning.

Whether these partnerships focus on work-related learning that is pre-service or involves incumbent workers, they have tended to strengthen the connection between what it is that individuals learn and what they need to know within the context of the workplace. In some instances, their processes focus on curricular issues. In other contexts, the stress reflects more of a concern with pedagogical methods that involve learners in more active, engaged, and contextual ways, and that emphasize higher-order thinking skills, interpersonal and team work competencies, and learning to learn as a lifetime disposition.

CONCLUSION

Since the early days of the trade apprentice during the colonial era, work-related learning within the American context has come a long way. Once maligned as undermining the integrity of what it means to be educated, it is increasingly viewed as integral to a more holistic understanding of the educated person. The context of work and the workplace has provided some of the most theoretically important advances in our understanding of human learning, leading to review and reform of curriculum in both general studies and occupational education. Such scholarship is also informing and changing the ways in which we think of the workplace itself as a location for adult learning and development, as well as our notions of what constitutes effective continuing education and lifelong learning. The emerging *rapprochement* between work-related learning and general education is mirrored by a growing reliance on partnerships between business and industry and educational institutions and agencies. While it is too early to suggest that America has worked through its ambivalence towards work-related learning, serious scholars and practitioners in a wide range of educational contexts understand this deep and necessary connection. For centuries, philosophers have been arguing for the importance of work to our lives and our happiness. Perhaps, American educators and policy-makers are beginning to understand what they meant.

REFERENCES

Aik, C. and Tway, D.C. (2003) 'Cognitivism, Constructivism, and Work Performance', *Academic Exchange Quarterly*, 7(3): 274–275.

Ackerman, R.H. and Maslin-Ostrowski, P. (2004) 'The Wounded Leader and Emotional Learning in the Schoolhouse', *School Leadership and Management*, 24(3): 311–328.

Albrecht, W.S. and Sack, R.J. (2000) *Accounting Education: Charting the Course through a Perilous Future*. Sarasota, FL: American Accounting Association.

Anonymous (2002) 'More Positive News on School-to-Career', *Techniques*, 77(6): 10.

Baker, L.C., Cantor, J.C. and Hughes, R.G. (1993) 'Preparedness for Practice: Young Physicians' Views of Their Professional Education', *The Journal of the American Medical Association*.

Bellack, J.P. and O'Neil, E.H. (2000) 'Recreating Nursing Practices for a New Century: Recommendations and Implications of The Pew Health Professions Commission's Final Report', *Nursing and Health Care Perspectives*, 21(1): 14–21.

Berryman, S.E. and Bailey, T.R. (1992) *The Double Helix of Education and the Economy*. New York: The Institute on Education and the Economy, Teachers College, Columbia University.

Bierema, L.L. (2008) 'Adult Learning in the Workplace: Emotion Work or Emotion Learning?', In J.M. Dirkx (ed.), *Adult Learning and the Emotional Self*. New Directions for Adult and Continuing Education, No. 120 (Winter). San Francisco: Jossey-Bass, pp. 55–64.

Bierema, L.L. (1996) 'Development of the Individual Leads to More Productive Workplaces', in R.W. Rowden, (ed.), *Workplace Learning: Debating Five Critical Questions of Theory and Practice*. New Directions for Adult and Continuing Education, No. 72, Winter. San Francisco: Jossey-Bass, pp. 21–28.

Billett, S. (2001) *Learning in the Workplace: Effective Strategies for Effective Practice*. Crows Nest NSW, Australia: Allyn and Unwin.

Bloom, A. (1987) *The Closing of the American Mind: How Higher Education has Failed Democracy and Impoverished the Souls of Today's Students*. New York: Simon & Schuster.

Bok, D. (1974) 'On the Purposes of Undergraduate Education', *Daedalus*, 103(4): 159–172.

Boud, D. and Garrick, J. (eds), (1999) *Understanding Learning at Work*. London: Routledge.

Boyer, E.L. (1987) *College: The Undergraduate Experience in America*: Princeton, NJ: Carnegie Foundation for the Advancement of Teaching.

Brockman, J.L. and Dirkx, J.M. (2006) 'Learning to Become a Machine Operator: The Dialogical Relationship between Context, Self and Content', *Human Resource Development Quarterly*, 17(2): 199–221.

Brokenburr, S. (2008) 'The Public-private Partnership: Community College Participation in Workforce Boards'. Ph.D. dissertation, Michigan State University, United States – Michigan. Retrieved 10.03.09, from Dissertations and Theses @ CIC Institutions database. (Publication No. AAT 3331877).

Brown, J.S., Collins, A. and Duguid, P. (1989) 'Situated Cognition and the Culture of Learning', *Educational Researcher*, 18(1): 32–42.

Callahan, J.L. (ed.) (2002) 'Perspectives of Emotion and Organizational Change', *Advances in Developing Human Resources*, 4(1).

Chappell, C., Rhodes, C., Solomon, N., Tennant, M. and Yates, L. (2003) *Reconstructing the Lifelong Learner: Pedagogy and Identity in Individual, Organizational, and Social Change*. London: Routledge/Falmer.

Clark, M.C. and Dirkx, J.M. (2000) 'Models of the Self: A Reflective Dialogue', in B. Hayes and A. Wilson (eds), *Handbook 2000 – Adult and Continuing Education*. San Francisco: Jossey-Bass, pp. 101–116.

Cantor, J.C., Cohen, A.B., Barker, D.C., Shuster, A.L. and Reynolds, R.C. (1991) 'Medical Educators' Views on Medical Education Reform', *Journal of the American Medical Association*.

Carnevale, A.P., Gainer, L.J. and Meltzer, A.S. (1990) *Workplace Basics: The Essential Skills Employers Want*. San Francisco: Jossey-Bass.

Cheney, L.V. (1989) *50 Hours: A Core Curriculum for College Students*. Washington, D.C.: National Endowment for the Humanities.

Cohen, A.M. and Brawer, F.B. (2008) *The American Community College* (5th edn). San Francisco: Jossey-Bass.

Collins, A., Brown, J.S. and Holum, A. (1991) 'Cognitive Apprenticeship: Making Thinking Visible', *American Educator*, 15(3): 6–11, pp. 38–46.

Corson, D. (1991) *Education for Work: Background to Policy and Curriculum*. Cleveland, England: Multilingual Matters.

Curry, L., Wergin, J.E. and Associates (1993) *Educating Professionals: Responding to New Expectations for Competence and Accountability*. San Francisco: Jossey-Bass.

DACUM (2001) DACUM: An Online Resource for Occupational Analysis. Available from http://www.dacum.org (accessed 1.3.09).

Dirkx, J.M. (1996) 'Human Resource Development as Adult Education: Fostering the Educative Workplace', in R.W. Rowden, (ed.), *Workplace Learning: Debating Five Critical Questions of Theory and Practice*. New Directions for Adult and Continuing Education, No. 72, Winter. San Francisco: Jossey-Bass, pp. 41–47.

Dirkx, J.M. (2005) '"To Develop a Firm Persuasion": Workplace Learning and the Problem of Meaning', in C. Elliott and S. Turnbill (eds), *Critical Thinking in Human Resource Development*. London: Routledge, pp. 155–174.

Dirkx, J.M. and Lan, T.D.N. (2009) 'From Factory to College: How a Community College Developmental Education Program Fosters a Learner Identity among Dislocated Workers', in J. Storberg-Walker (ed.), *Proceedings of the 2009 AHRD International Research Conference in the Americas*. Bowling Green, KY: Academy of Human Resource Development.

Dirkx, J.M. and Prenger, S. (1997) *A Guide to Planning and Implementing Instruction for Adults: A Theme-Based Approach*. San Francisco: Jossey-Bass.

Dirkx, J.M., Fonfara, T. and Flaska, K. (1993) 'Self and Not-Self in the Practitioner-Learner Relationship: The Problem of Boundary Awareness in ABE Practice', *Adult Basic Education: An Interdisciplinary Journal for Adult Literacy Educators*, 3: 51–68.

Dirkx, J.M., Kielbaso, G. and Corley, C. (1999) 'A Study of Vocational Education in the Michigan Department of Corrections'. East Lansing, MI: Michigan State University. ERIC Document Reproduction Service No. ED 430161.

Driscoll, M.P. (2005) *Psychology of Learning for Instruction* (3rd edn). Boston: Allyn and Bacon.

Dugan, L. (2003) *Approaches to Training and Development* (3rd edn). Cambridge, MA: Penguin Books.

Ellinger, A.D. (2005) 'Contextual Factors Influencing Informal Learning in a Workplace Setting: The Case of "Reinventing Itself Company"', *Human Resource Development Quarterly*, 16(3): 389–415.

Fenwick, T. (ed.) (2001) *Sociocultural Perspectives on Learning through Work*. New Directions for Adult and Continuing Education, No. 92. San Francisco: Jossey-Bass.

Fuhrmann, B.S. (1996) 'Philosophies and Aims', in J.G. Graff (ed.), *Handbook of the Undergraduate Curriculum*. San Francisco: Jossey-Bass, pp. 86–99.

Garrick, J. (1998) *Informal Learning in the Workplace: Unmasking Human Resource Development*. London: Routledge.

Geroy, G.D. (2005) 'Preparing Students for Spirituality in the Workplace', in S.W. Hoppe and B.W. Speck (eds), *Spirituality in Higher Education*. New Directions for Teaching and Learning, No. 104 (Winter), San Francisco: Jossey-Bass, pp. 67–74.

Gilley, J.W. and Maycunich, A. (1998) *Strategically Integrated HRD: Partnering to Maximize Organizational Performance*. Reading, MA: Addison-Wesley.

Gilley, J.W., Eggland, S.A. and Maycunich Gilley, A. (2002) *Principles of Human Resource Development* (2nd edn). Cambridge, MA: Perseus.

Giroux, H. (1995) 'Decentering the Canon: Refiguring Disciplinary and Pedagogical Boundaries', in J.G. Haworth and C.F. Conrad (eds). *Revisioning Curriculum in Higher Education*. ASHE Reader Series, Needham Heights, MA: Simon and Schuster, pp. 255–269.

Graff, G. (1992) *Beyond the Culture Wars: How Teaching the Conflicts Can Revitalize American Education*. New York: Norton.

Grubb, W.N. and Associates (1999) *Honored but Invisible: An Inside Look at Teaching in Community Colleges*. New York: Routledge.

Harun, M.H. (2001) 'Integrating E-learning into the Workplace', *The Internet and Higher Education*, 4(3–4): 301–310.

Hayes, E. (1999) 'Policy Issues that Drive the Transformation of Adult Literacy', in L. G. Martin and J.C. Fisher (eds), *The Welfare-to-Work Challenge for Adult Literacy Educators*. New Directions for Adult and Continuing Education, No. 83, Fall, pp. 3–14.

Hirsch, E.D. Jr. (1988) *Cultural Literacy: What Every American Needs to Know*. New York: Vintage Books.

Hull, G. (ed.) (1997) *Changing Work, Changing Workers: Critical Perspectives on Language, Literacy, and Skills*. Albany, NY: State University of New York.

Ingham Intermediate School District (2008) About LAMP. http://www.inghamisd.org/lamp/about.html (accessed 5.3.08).

Jacobs, R.L. (2001) 'Planned Training on the Job', *Advances in Developing Human Resources*, 3(4). Thousand Oaks, CA: Sage.

Jurmo, P. (2004) 'Workplace Literacy Education: Definitions, Purposes, and Approaches', *Focus on Basics*, 7(B).

Kett, J.F. (1994) *The Pursuit of Knowledge Under Difficulties: From Self-Improvement to Adult Education in America, 1750–1990*. Stanford, CA: Stanford University Press.

Kincheloe, J.L. (1995) *Toil and Trouble: Good Work, Smart Workers, and the Integration of Academic and Vocational Education*. New York: Peter Lang.

Kise, J.A.G. (2006) Differentiated Coaching: A Framework for Helping Teachers Change. Thousand Oaks, CA: Corwin Press.

Kliebard, H.M. (1999) *Schooled to Work: Vocationalism and the American Curriculum*. New York: Teachers College Press.

Lave, J. and Wenger, E. (1991) *Situated Learning: Legitimate Peripheral Participation*. Cambridge, UK: Cambridge University Press.

Leigh, P. (1997) 'The New Spirit at Work', *Training and Development*, 5(3): 26–33.

MacAllum, K., Yoder, K., Kim, S. and Bozick, R. (2002) *Moving Forward: College and Career Transitions of LAMP Graduates*. Findings from the LAMP longitudinal study. Washington, DC: Academy for Educational Development, National Institute for Work and Learning. ED 156, 475.

Marsick, V.J. (1987) *Learning in the Workplace*. London: Croom Helm.

Marsick, V.J. and Watkins, K. (1990) *Informal and Incidental Learning: A New Challenge for Human Resource Developers*. London: Routledge and Kegan Paul.

Martin, L.G. and Fisher, J.C. (eds) (1999) *The Welfare-to-Work Challenge for Adult Literacy Educators*. New Directions for Adult and Continuing Education, No. 83, Fall.

Mitroff, I.I. and Denton, E.A. (1999) 'A Study of Spirituality in the Workplace', *Sloan Management Review*, 40(4): 83–92.

Moussouris, L. (1998) 'The Higher Education – Economic Development "Connection" in Massachusetts: Forging a Linkage?', *Higher Education*, 35(1): 91–112.

Pauchant, T. and Associates (1995) *In Search of Meaning: Managing for the Health of our Organizations, our Communities, and the Natural World*. San Franscisco: Jossey-Bass.

Piaget, J. (1995) *The Child's Construction of Reality*. London: Routledge and Kegan Paul.

Raughton, J.L. (1998) 'Colorado Community Colleges: Full Partners in Economic Development', *Economic Development Review*, 15(4): 8–11.

Romanowksi, M.H. and Oldenski, T.E. (1998) 'Challenging the Status Quo of Teacher Education Programs', *The Clearing House*, 72(2): 111–114.

Rowden, R.W. (ed.). (1996) *Workplace Learning: Debating Five Critical Questions of Theory and Practice*. New Directions for Adult and Continuing Education, No. 72(Winter). San Francisco: Jossey-Bass.

Sleezer, C.M., Gularte, M.A., Waldner, L. and Cook, J. (2004) 'Business and Higher Education Partner to Develop a High-skilled Workforce: A Case Study', *Performance Improvement Quarterly*, 17(2): 65–81.

Stark, J.S. and Lattuca, L.R. (1997) *Shaping the College Curriculum: Academic Plans in Action*. Boston: Allyn and Bacon.

Stark, J.S., Lowther, M.A. and Haggerty, B.M.K. (1986) 'Responsive Professional Education: Balancing Outcomes and Opportunities'. ASHE-ERIC Higher Education Report No. 3. Washington, D.C. Association for the Study of Higher Education.

Steffe, L. and Gale, J. (eds) (1995) *Constructivism in Education*. Hillsdale, NJ: Lawrence Erlbaum.

Steele, J. (2008) '*Professional Identity and Professional's Workplace Learning: A Theoretical Perspective*'. Paper presented at the Academy of Human Resource Development International Research Conference in the Americas (Panama City, FL, Feb 20–24). ERIC Document Reproduction Service No. ED501709.

Swenson, R.A. and Arnold, D.E. (1996) 'The Purpose of Human Resource Development is to Improve Organizational Performance', in R.W. Rowden, (ed.), *Workplace Learning: Debating Five Critical Questions of Theory and Practice*. New Directions for Adult and Continuing Education, No 72, Winter. San Francisco: Jossey-Bass, pp. 13–19.

Taylor, M.C., Lewe, G.R. and Draper, J.A. (eds) (1991) *Basic Skills for the Workplace*. Malabar, FL: Krieger.

Underhill, B.O., McAnally, K. and Koriath, J.J. (2007) *Executive Coaching for Results: The Definitive Guide to Developing Organizational Leaders*. San Francisco: Berrett-Koehler.

Watkins, K. (1991) *Facilitating Learning in the Workplace*. Geelong, Australia: Deakin University Press.

Welton, M. (1991) *Toward Development Work: The Workplace as a Learning Environment*. Victoria, Australia: Deakin University Press.

Wenger, E. (1998) *Communities of Practice: Learning, Meaning, and Identity*. Cambridge, UK: Cambridge University Press.

22

Workplace Learning in East Africa: a Case Study

Martin Mulder and Judith Gulikers

In this chapter we describe a case study to discuss the relevance of and possibilities for developing work-oriented curricula in East-African countries, for the purpose of increasing the competitive strengths of businesses, the economic value of the country and the value of graduates.

The case study is of a capacity building project focusing on developing a curriculum for horti/floriculture in Ethiopia. This is grounded in the ideas of and research on competence-based education with a strong focus on workplace learning or, at least, workplace-oriented learning. In a close cooperation between partners from the Netherlands and teachers in Ethiopia, the competence-based curriculum development process, previously tried in many Western countries was utilised in the Ethiopian context.

The project, carried out from 2007–2011, is a partnership between Ethiopia and the Netherlands. The first phase of this project, which is described in this case study, focused on developing a workplace-oriented Master of Science (MSc), as the flori/horticulture industry as improvement of formal training at this level was set as top priority by the floricultural sector in Ethiopia. There is an immediate need for well qualified staff in this sector, as it has grown enormously, while the management is mostly done by foreign experts. Ethiopia offers education at the Bachelor, and only recently at the MSc level, but both only in horticulture with no trajectory for floriculture. An improved MSc trajectory that also focused on floriculture should educate highly qualified graduates that can function not only as researchers, but certainly also as managers and entrepreneurs in the horti/floricultural sector in Ethiopia.

Workplace learning has two meanings in the context of this project. Firstly, the curriculum had to be designed as a competence-based curriculum incorporating as much workplace (oriented) learning as possible. Secondly, teachers in Ethiopia are going through a 'professionalization' trajectory. At the project site teachers and educational developers who, through collaborating in this project, have learned and improved their educational competencies while working. Reflections about the effects and implications of both kinds of workplace learning will be taken into account in the discussion of the project in this chapter.

TOWARDS COMPETENCE-BASED AND WORKPLACE LEARNING

In Western countries, it is widely recognised that modern economy requires new skills from employees and employers. Professionals cannot get by anymore by simply being knowledge experts or trained routine workers. The labour market requires people to flexibly adapt to the fast changing world of work and generic competencies like communicative, problem-solving, and collaboration skills gain more attention, as they are crucial in all kinds of professions (see Wilson, Lizzio and Ramsden, 1997). Educational trajectories should be more oriented towards the requirements of the labour market and the types of jobs that students are required to do after graduation.

There has been an increase in workplace training in industries and businesses to support adult learners in their professional development and to help them keep up with labour market developments through training on-the-job (Cheetham and Chivers, 2001; Mulder et al., 2007a; Poell et al., 2004). Also in initial education (vocational, professional, and academic), in which learning and not working is the main focus, there is increased attention to relating learning to job tasks and professional fields. In this vein, the paradigm of competence-based education (CBE) is increasingly gaining attention in various countries (Mulder et al., 2007b) as it promises to bridge the gap between educational trajectories and working life (Biemans et al., 2004; Wesselink et al., 2007). CBE is a type of education that focuses on the requirements of the occupations or professional fields (i.e., job contexts, job tasks, job roles and professional competences needed for these jobs) and on societal needs in a more general sense (being flexible, self-responsible, learning oriented etc.), as the starting point for curriculum development. Students should be educated to handle the complex world of work, an array of job tasks, and flexibly adapt to work-related or societal situations. This requires *competences*, that is, an integration of knowledge, skills and attitudes needed to perform a certain job task or role (Mulder, 2001). CBE aims to stimulate competency development in students.

In essence, workplace learning deals with learning in the workplace. However, many studies show that the workplace is not automatically an effective learning environment (Smith, 2003), implying that simply placing students in the workplace does not guarantee effective learning. Competence-based education aims to incorporate elements from workplace learning in a more structured way into more formal educational trajectories, for example, by developing learning tasks that reflect professional tasks or allowing students to practice in authentic work contexts (Wesselink et al., 2007). In other words, competence-based education aims to bring the workplace into the school and the school, or formal learning, into the workplace (Smith, 2003).

CONTEXTUALIZATION: HORTI/FLORICULTURE IN ETHIOPIA AND THE NEED FOR WORKPLACE-ORIENTED EDUCATION

In African or, more generally, in developing countries there is still a strong focus on routine-based jobs and many people lack any education at all. With the globalization of the world, many of these countries could be strong competitors in many fields, for example, in horticulture and floriculture. These two export-oriented sectors in Ethiopia have been growing rapidly and form an important element in the country's efforts to expand and diversify the economy, raise export earnings and create employment. However, the floriculture sector is mainly ruled by international investors. The fast growing industry requires a growing supply of staff equipped with relevant and practical technical knowledge. All stakeholders in the sector acknowledge that there is an urgent shortage of technical and experienced staff at various levels: owners, managers, administrators, supervisors, and attendants. In Ethiopia, people are not properly trained for functioning at these different levels, certainly not in the professional field of floriculture.

Within Ethiopia, currently no floriculture industry specific practical training program exists. For instance, no vocational training institutes or higher education specialization deal with floriculture and at the higher education level the curricula are academic programs, focusing mainly on research instead of training students for the supervision or management tasks required at higher level jobs at flower farms. In response, many commercial flower farm companies, led by international investors, conduct or organize in-house training individually on an ad-hoc basis for their lower level staff. Unfortunately, these are often conducted with limited technical and practical know-how of the floricultural sector.

Higher level employees often aren't even available in Ethiopia and are recruited from neighboring countries. Initiatives from higher learning institutes such as at Jimma University College of Agriculture and Veterinary Medicine (JUCAVM), where BSc students in horticulture can go for a two month internship to a commercial flower farm are very much appreciated by the sector, but show the need for more practical and industry-oriented education at the higher education level. All stakeholders in the floriculture industry in Ethiopia emphasize the urgent need for the establishment of a sustainable, industry-led, practically oriented capacity building facility as a major prerequisite for the profitable and sustainable development of the industry in Ethiopia. This necessitated the NUFFIC capacity building project for setting up a workplace-oriented MSc curriculum in floriculture.

Partners and stakeholders in the NUFFIC project

Nuffic is a Dutch organization that sets up programs of international cooperation, mostly between institutes in the Netherlands and developing countries all over the world, to develop and share new knowledge. This Nuffic project is a collaboration between various knowledge institutes in the Netherlands with either expertise in horti/floriculture and or curriculum development and education (PTC+, LEI, ECS) and the JUCAVM university and exporters association (EPHEA) on the Ethiopian side. These institutes join forces to professionalize the staff at JUCAVM and (re)design a workplace-oriented, competence-based MSc curriculum for horti/floriculture. To assure the strong workplace orientation of the program, many stakeholders from the Dutch and Ethiopian horticulture and flower industries are involved as well as representatives of agricultural Ministries and policy makers. These stakeholders play a crucial role in several steps towards making the new curriculum workplace-oriented and competence-based, starting with collaboratively creating an occupational profile. This profile should appropriately represent the jobs in the horti/floricultural sectors in Ethiopia (see Table 22.1) and be the starting point of the curriculum (re)design. We will elaborate on this later on.

Workplace learning in the floriculture sector

There is no tradition of workplace learning or learning on-the-job in Ethiopia, except for some non-formal individual initiatives for lower level workers who are trained by more experienced personnel. Farm managers and supervisors, however, do have a lot of interest in workplace learning for three reasons. First of all, because the whole production process is very sensitive to problems and loss of profit, they want their employees to be very professional, punctual, and up-to-date with new developments. There is a tension between this goal and being able to let them leave the worksite for educational purposes. Second, the kinds of tasks for farm workers are very context dependent, and require the ability to work under pressure, and deal with a variety of growers with different requirements or exports to different countries with different rules and procedures. These tasks set high standards on knowledge and skills, but also strongly depend on professional attitudes, like accuracy. Being able to deal with all these pressing and varying variables in the farm context cannot be learned in isolation from practice (see Smith, 2003) and therefore, workplace learning should be an important element in educational trajectories in horti/floriculture. A third reason for farm managers' interest in workplace learning results from the job tasks of farm workers that are often characterized by a clear causal relationship (e.g. using this amount of fluid will have this effect on the plant). This offers opportunities for concrete practical training at the workplace.

In order to more systematically respond to the needs of the labour market and to upgrade the economical value of the Ethiopian horti/floricultural industry, EHPEA, as a training institute, decided to step in and implement a sector-oriented system of short practical courses, most of which are workplace learning courses. The core of this system consists of a quality assurance and improvement system to upgrade all farms in the sector. This system is focused on a code of practice, which is a set of standards with which a flower farm needs to comply. From an association point of view this code warrants minimum levels of quality on all aspects of flower production and handling realized by the farms, maintaining (and increasing) quality levels of work and production by training farm workers. Ideally, this code also prevents flower farms who cheat with international regulations on health and safety (spraying, for instance) to produce at a lower cost.

The first training courses were aimed at issues regarding safety and working conditions. Staff of nearly all of the (around eighty) associated flower farms have been participating in these courses. The next training programs handled various Code of Practice topics. Surprisingly, even though most courses focus on very practical topics and mainly on skills, the degree of workplace learning varies between courses. While some courses mainly involve workplace learning, other courses are taught mainly in class.

Thus, several actions are undertaken in Ethiopia to respond to the skill gaps of workers. However, while these workplace learning initiatives are mostly very practical, relevant, to-the-point and effective, they are often of a curative nature and only directed at the short term goal of increasing the practical skills of lower level workers. They are mostly related to the core production process of a flower farm and have no link to the flower farm as a business enterprise focusing on developing high-level workers (e.g. managers, supervisors) and facilitating the development of long term goals and strategies for the business.

To increase the economic value and survival of the Ethiopian horticulture and floriculture industry there is a need for more integrated learning programs for training people at *different levels* of the horti/floriculture industry. Certainly at the level of higher education there is a need to become more responsive to the labour market and train people to be more practical as well as economical and entrepreneurial oriented, instead of focusing mainly on research. Generic competences including communication, collaboration, entrepreneurship, presenting and convincing should have an important place in the learning trajectories, instead of content-only related topics, because these make graduates more employable in a broader range of jobs.

INTRODUCING WORKPLACE LEARNING IN A HORTI/FLORICULTURAL MSC CURRICULUM IN ETHIOPIA

As noted before, Ethiopia has prioritised the development of an MSc in horti/floriculture to train Ethiopian people to be able to become managers at a farm or create a new farm as an entrepreneur (the highest level in the hierarchy). Currently, JUCAVM has a long standing BSc trajectory and a recent MSc trajectory in horticulture and no program for floriculture. Moreover, these trajectories are too research-oriented. Graduates are directed towards research functions and do not get to the management level of farms, certainly not in the flower business. BSc students are allowed to enter the MSc program, guaranteeing a sufficient influx for the redesigned MSc curriculum. It is likely that the current BSc trajectory will be changed in a later stage to become more aligned to the new workplace-oriented MSc curriculum. In this chapter we further report on the methodology for the inclusion of workplace learning in the new competence-based MSc curriculum for horti/floriculture in the context of a capacity building project.

The methodology used in this project is based on a series of studies on competence development that show the relevance of starting at the workplace and what the workplace wants when developing a curriculum that should prepare students for the changed field of work. Brinkman et al. (2007) investigated the changing competence needs of agricultural consultants in Sub-Saharan Africa in a study revealing the importance of social competence, empathy, subtle personal and group interaction, understanding of cultural sensitivities and embarrassment and ways in which the consultants can handle these in practice. Mulder, Lans, Verstegen, Biemans and Meijer (2007) studied the way in which entrepreneurs in innovative horticulture develop their competence while working. They showed that the most important factor in the competence of an entrepreneur seemed to be 'having a learning orientation' meaning that the entrepreneur should constantly be focused on learning while working. These findings support the value of learning in and from the workplace and workplace experiences or observations. A study of Mulder, Gulikers, Biemans and Wesselink (in press) concluded that in higher education more emphasis on practical and work-related competencies is needed and often even wished for, but that this can be a struggle against the long academic, purely knowledge-oriented tradition of professors or institutions, certainly at the less occupationally oriented trajectories.

To facilitate the development of a workplace-oriented, competence-based curriculum, Wesselink and colleagues (2007) developed a matrix describing eight principles of competence-based vocational education (in which workplace learning plays an important role). This matrix described what characterizes a competence-based curriculum and how the workplace is represented in the whole curriculum. It is also a quality improvement instrument, and comprises four levels of implementation of the eight principles of competence-based education, ranging from traditional education in level 1 to fully competence-based education in level 4. Program teams can analyze their current curriculum and conclude were they are in the matrix, and where they want to go in the future. It helps to more precisely describe how competence-based the program currently is and to get their quality development priorities straight. Describing a curriculum and future plans in this matrix can also create a transparent description of the curriculum for external reviewers or assessors.

As this matrix is used in the capacity building project in Ethiopia and can be a valuable instrument for other comparable initiatives, Table 22.1 describes the eight principles in this matrix in more detail.

Table 22.1   Eight Principles of Competence-based Vocational Education (Wesselink et al., 2007)

Principle	Definition
The occupational profiles and competencies that are the basis for the curriculum are defined.	An occupational profile, aligned to the regional and local occupational sector, is put together with the participation of representative actors in the sector and occupations and this is frequently reviewed against the major trends and updated. This profile has to be used during the (re)design of the curriculum, as the core of the curriculum. An academic program often deals with various occupational fields, from research and management, to engineering, teaching and extension. The curriculum has to accommodate the variety of these occupational fields.
Vocational core problems are the organizing unit for (re)designing the curriculum.	The occupational profile is specified in core professional problems or essential responsibilities and tasks in the occupations. These feed the development of the learning and assessment tasks in the whole (new) curriculum.
Competence-development of students is assessed frequently (before, during and after) the learning process.	Assessment at the entrance of a program can help to accommodate the study trajectory for the individual student. Assessment during the courses takes place all of the time, and helps the teacher to fine-tune feedback and the next learning steps for the students. Assessment after the course is also taking place already, in the form of exams. Competence-based assessments, however, may be of a different nature than the traditional paper and pencil exams.
Learning activities take place in several authentic situations.	This principle means that learning activities take place in a diversity of authentic settings (in practice or at least simulations) as much as possible. This kind of practical learning increases the practical experience of students, which can increase their motivation significantly.
In learning and assessment processes knowledge, skills and attitudes are integrated.	As competence is an integration of knowledge, skills and attitudes, learning tasks should allow students to practice performing this integration and assessments should evaluate students' ability to integrate their knowledge, skills and attitudes into the performance of relevant job-related tasks.

(Continued)

Table 22.1   Eight Principles of Competence-based Vocational Education (Wesselink et al., 2007) (*Cont'd*)

Principle	Definition
Self-responsibility and self reflection of students is stimulated.	Students are responsible for their own learning process based on their own learning needs. Approaching students in this way as self-responsible adults, and stimulating them to constantly reflect on their performances will increase their ownership of the educational program and their motivation.
Teachers both in schools and practice fulfil their roles as coach and expert in balance.	Teacher roles change in competence-based education from stand-up deliverers of knowledge to being a coach of student learning. They should stimulate students to formulate learning needs and to manage their own learning processes based on careful reflection. This requires a change from teachers that research has shown is not easy.
A basis is realized for a lifelong learning attitude for students.	Competence development is never ending. Therefore, the curriculum should stimulate developing life-long learning skills. The diploma of an MSc, or BSc should not be perceived as the license to perform for a life-time, but that it is just the entry point for a further life-time learning itinerary.

BASIC STEPS IN THE DEVELOPMENT OF WORKPLACE LEARNING IN MSC HORTICULTURE

A determining factor in setting up a competence-based curriculum that focuses on what the workplace wants and aims to incorporate as much workplace learning as possible, is the active involvement of, and collaboration with, stakeholders from the sector in all steps of the curriculum development. This is strongly lacking in many countries and it is no different in Ethiopia.

In our curriculum development and capacity building project in Ethiopia, two starting points were crucial:

1   The workplace, job tasks and job roles, should always remain the starting point and frame of reference for the MSc curriculum.
2   Representative stakeholders from the Ethiopian professional fields in the horti/floriculture sectors should be involved in all steps of the curriculum development process.

In Ethiopian horticulture and floriculture, the most obvious field of work is the farms. Workplace learning in farms should not only focus on practical skills like cutting and storing flowers or plants, but also on running a farm, managing workers, writing business plans for the national and international market, etc. Certainly an MSc educational program that aims at educating farm managers and supervisors should pay a lot of attention to these higher-order competencies both in school and at the workplace. In addition, an MSc program should have a research component that should also have a clear link with research done and needed in the horticulture or floricultural tribal, regional, national and global market. Analysis of the needs for an MSc curriculum should consider this more broader perspective on the horticultural and floricultural professional fields and should select representative stakeholders (i.e., not only farm workers, but also supervisors, researchers and entrepreneurs).

With these assumptions in mind, the development of the MSc program was conducted using the following steps (based on Mulder, 1992):

a   Conduction of an informal curriculum evaluation with key representatives of the horticulture program that JUCAVM has been teaching. The previously described Matrix for CBE with its eight principles was used to review the curriculum and determine future plans. Several points of attention and suggestions for improvement were identified and documented.
b   Stakeholders of the new MSc curriculum were identified, such as producers, farm owners, the EHPEA, research institutes, universities, governmental bodies and NGOs.

c   Representative stakeholders were selected for site visits and interviews. We called this the *needs assessment*. Essentially, this is the inventory of future tasks and competencies of MSc alumni in the organizations these persons represent. This led to the identification of representative *job roles* with *occupational profiles* and belonging *job tasks* with *competence lists*. A labour market analysis was incorporated in this study.

d   Opinions of experts from research institutes, universities and flower farms (i.e., the main future employers of the JUCAVM MSc graduates) were collected via interviews and literature studies, and model practices were detected.

e   A further literature analysis of scientific as well as policy documents was done to see what is going on in the field of horti/floriculture training and development and the Ethiopian horticulture/floriculture market.

f   Based on the final occupational profiles (including job roles, tasks and competencies) courses were developed through filling in course formats developed for the purpose of this project (see Figure 22.1). The process is an iterative, collaborative and ongoing process between the teaching staff of JUCAVM and all other project partners, all bringing in their own expertise.

g   An invited curriculum deliberation was held to review the proposals (of the curriculum as a whole, and the courses described in the course formats in detail). with around seventy representatives of various stakeholder organizations.

h   Lastly, continuous interactive alignment with stakeholder needs and preferences is envisaged. This will be established by the staff of JUCAVM.

This model has been successful for our work. We now discuss an elaboration of these steps and their function in the curriculum development process in the Ethiopia project.

OCCUPATIONAL AND COMPETENCE PROFILES

Around twenty-five stakeholders in the horticultural sector have been visited in Ethiopia, many of whom are potential employers of MSc graduates in horti/floriculture. Among the stakeholders were heads of research institutes, researchers, trainers, and farm managers. They were interviewed about possible MSc-level occupations in the field of horti/floriculture in their organizations, the core tasks belonging to these occupations, and the core competencies that are needed for the occupations. Based on these interviews various occupational profiles were composed. For each occupation a short description and a list of core tasks and core competencies that are necessary to take along in the curriculum redesign process were developed.

In total eight different occupations were identified. These occupations have been aggregated in three groups; many of the tasks and competencies of these occupations were overlapping.

1   Group 1 are researchers, working in a variety of research institutes.
2   Group 2 consists of occupations that focus on sharing, spreading and co-constructing knowledge and/ or innovative policies and practices. These are trainers/teachers, extension agents, development workers, policy makers, and consultants.
3   Group 3 represents the occupations that strongly relate to managing a business. Identified occupations in this group are managers and private investors/entrepreneurs.

The occupational profiles contributed to the redesign of the curriculum. It focused on the alignment of the needs of the various occupations and allowed an identification of the gap between the current MSc curriculum and the reality of work. By actively involving several stakeholders from the sector in the curriculum redesign process, their commitment with the new MSc will hopefully increase. This kind of active involvement will enhance quality improvement of and trust in the MSc program and the respective graduates. Additionally, teachers of JUCAVM experienced the stakeholders' input as valuable for identifying the lacks in their current curriculum and giving them new insight with respect to the requirements for their graduates. This finding supports Gulikers, Baartman and Biemans suggestion that active involvement of multiple stakeholders in the evaluation of education can have a positive effect on quality improvement and a motivating effect on the teachers who have to improve or redesign their education.

COMPOSITION OF THE MSC CURRICULUM

Based on the occupational profiles, relevant courses were identified and sequenced. Next to identifying content-related courses relevant for the occupational profile, several new courses were identified to address generic skills like entrepreneurial skills or communication skills. The new MSc program comprises two years of two semesters. The first semester is a comprehensive semester for all students. The second semester is aimed at four specializations: flowers, fruits, vegetables or coffee. All courses explicitly address job tasks, roles and competences described in the occupational profiles and should include as much workplace learning (or at least workplace-oriented) learning as possible.

An additional link with the occupational profiles, and thus with the workplace component, is established by covering projects aiming at the three occupational groups. Each student should do three projects from the perspective of the three respective groups in the first year. In the second year, all students specialize in one of the three roles. A major part of the second year is allocated to a thesis that focuses on performing the chosen occupational role in a realistic and large project conducted in, or in collaboration with, the professional field. For example, setting up and delivering a training for farm workers on an innovative technique in the field (role: trainer/extensionalist).

For all courses, a fixed course format was introduced that was developed for the purpose of this project by educational specialists. Important components of this format that define the workplace component of the program are 'job tasks', 'competencies', and 'assessment'. Also, a variety of teaching methods, like practicals (practical assignments in the college setting, for example, in the greenhouse) and the field attachment (internship) give the full opportunity for workplace learning.

This course format 'forced' teachers to explicitly link their courses and course contents to the identified occupational roles, job tasks and competencies. Moreover, it required them to specify the kind of teaching methods they were going to use, including the kind and amount of workplace learning or workplace-oriented learning. The workplace component is integrated to varying extents, ranging from using cases from real practice, collaborating with professional practice, doing projects in the field, field attachments or short apprenticeships, excursions to the workplace, etc. In addition, the course format includes the assessment used to evaluate to what extent students developed the competences identified for the course. Also in the assessment part, JUCAVM teachers are stimulated to let students demonstrate their job related competencies in realistic, work-related contexts.

Below, an example of the course format is given from the course 'Entrepreneurship and Agribusiness Development'.

CONDITIONS AND CHALLENGES FOR A WORKPLACE-ORIENTED COMPETENCE-BASED MSC CURRICULUM IN ETHIOPIA

When it comes to workplace learning in an academic program like this MSc program, various changes need to take place. In the past, most of these kinds of programs were purely theoretical. Large classes were taught in plenary classrooms, and written tests were conducted to determine the mastery level of the course content. Practical training was sometimes impossible because of lack of materials such as soil, plants, chemicals, measurement instruments, greenhouses, irrigations systems, or even electrical power, computers, printers or water. One of the features of this capacity building project is that these materials are being provided, although in the long term viability problems related to operations and maintenance are known.

Moreover, changing towards competence-based and workplace-oriented education requires a conceptual change in all involved stakeholders (i.e., teachers, students and employers), a change that is not unique for this Ethiopian context, but that has turned out to be difficult in western countries as well (see Biemans et al., 2004). Everybody is used to a long tradition of traditional academic education, in which instruction focuses on transmission of knowledge,

Lecturer(s)	
Examiner(s)	
Contact person	
Mandatory prerequisite courses	Introduction to economics (at undergraduate level)
Course description	This course wants to stimulate an entrepreneurial attitude among students through confronting them with crucial aspects relevant for setting up their own horticultural business or selling innovative ideas, research findings, or products.
Core tasks performed in occupational reality, covered by this course:	Write a business plan Identify and analyse potential market opportunities to establish corresponding business Set up and run an agribusiness Check product and market price, and adapt price accordingly Undertake market research Promote products Search pro-actively to possibilities and information
Competencies necessary to be able to perform effectively, covered by this course:	Be able to work with customers, colleague entrepreneurs, and subordinates in any (agri) business Be able to commercialize ideas, products, and research findings Using knowledge of financial requirements and control Decision making skills Leadership skills Being able to recognize market potentials

Contact hours		
	Lectures	18 hrs
	Group paper	2 hrs
	Guided working class	2 hrs
	Problem-based learning	6 hrs
	Excursion	3 hrs
	Project education	3 hrs
	Exam-Assessment	3 hrs
Weight of practical component in the course		45%

Outcomes	Course components	Specification of content	Summative Assessment method
At the end of the course, the student should be able to: Work with customers, colleague entrepreneurs, and subordinates in any (agri)business; Commercialize ideas, products, and research findings; Estimate financial requirements and control finances; Steer and supervise subordinates; Recognize market potentials and ability to make related decisions.	1. Introduction to entrepreneurship 2. Introduction to (agri)businesses 3. Forms of business ownership	Entrepreneurs; entrepreneurship; economics and entrepreneurship; push and pull factors (lecture) Success, growth and failure; importance of business for economy; political, social and environmental aspects of business; advantages and disadvantages in Ethiopia (lecture) Sole proprietorship; partnership; corporation; cooperatives (2 taking different forms of businesses and identifying their adv. and disadv. and discuss in group on differentiating them from each other)	Continuous assessment Business Plan for a real farm and Presentation to workfield representatives (50%) Test (10%) Final exam: Test containing open questions and realistic cases (example question: discuss on the distinctive traits of entrepreneurs) (40%)

Figure 22.1   Course format for 'Entrepreneurship and Agribusiness Development'

Outcomes	Course components	Specification of content	Summative Assessment method
	4. Marketing in business	Product, price, promotion, place; market segments; market research; marketing strategies (3 hours for writing marketing strategy for some new product)	
	5. Develop a business plan	Do market research; choose purpose, business and format; write business plan (6 hours for collecting information and writing a business plan and I hour presentation)	
	6. Financing a business	Requirements; sources (2 lecture + 1 case analysis)	
	7. Business ethics and social and environmental responsibilities	Concern about consumer safety, care for environmental pollution in business (all time for lecture)	
	8. Risks and insurance	Definition; risk management; insurance forms (all time for lecture)	

Figure 22.1 *(Cont'd)*

learning is based on rote memorization and assessment is done through standardized, often closed answer, tests (Birenbaum, 2003). The teachers in Ethiopia, and as a result, students and employers, were unfamiliar with more activating teaching methods that allow interactive participation or questioning by students. There is also a very dominant hierarchy hindering this type of education: students are not meant nor used to speak up and ask questions to the teachers. And also the difference between BSc and MSc teachers is clearly visible. Learning in and out of the workplace was even more unknown territory. Alumni reported that farms did not allow students to practice various activities at their farms. Students were only given the opportunity to observe activities on the farm and students accepted this. Even though observation is an important form of learning, becoming a competent graduate also requires actually practicing relevant job tasks. These traditional conceptions and experiences should be addressed in a capacity building project as described in this chapter. Professional development of the teaching staff is therefore a crucial element in this project.

In the process of filling in the course formats, it also became clear that this required a whole new way of thinking from the Ethiopian teachers. Even though most teachers of JUCAVM were very enthusiastic about the course format and were highly in favour of creating close links between the courses and the professional practice, explicitly linking their courses, teaching methods, learning outcomes and assessment to the competencies and job tasks described in the occupational profiles turned out to be difficult. This required ongoing support from Dutch project members with expertise in competence-based education.

For the professional development of the Ethiopian staff involved, two Training of Trainer (ToT) groups (representatives of JUCAVM and the EPHEA) received intensive training in the Netherlands at the start of this NUFFIC project. The ToT groups focused both on technical training in horti/floriculture and competence-based or workplace-oriented curriculum development and activating teaching. These ToT groups were a kind of workplace-oriented learning for the JUVACM and EPHEA staff. We modelled competence-based education and activating teaching methods. ToT participants practiced job relevant tasks in Dutch greenhouses; they visited and interviewed representatives of the horti/floricultural sector; and we discussed the relevance and possibilities of transferring these learning activities to their Ethiopian curriculum. This directly confronted their traditional learning conceptions and we discussed creative solutions for practical or resource problems in Ethiopia. The teachers evaluated the ToT groups as very positive and eye-opening: 'This will have a huge impact on the way I teach and approach my students'. However, they all saw it as a big challenge to transfer their experiences to their colleagues back home. This indeed turned out to be challenging.

An additional crucial factor that was identified for implementing the workplace-oriented competence-based curriculum was setting up good communication channels between teachers, employers and students and communicating the responsibilities of all parties. The college needs to develop and maintain strong relationships with farms and research institutes, teaching staff should visit them regularly, and teaching staff should evaluate the workplace learning affordances in the thesis or apprenticeship organizations (Billett, 2001). On the other hand, farm owners should offer student more valuable learning environments and opportunities to practice and develop their competencies. Employers may regard this as counter intuitive in that they feel that teachers and students should be glad that students are welcome in the first place, irrespective of what they can do. However, for workplace-oriented, competence-based education to work, not only teachers and students, but also employers, should be willing to invest. In the end, better prepared and equipped graduates are favourable for all parties.

Other important possibilities for increasing the collaboration and cooperation between the university and the professional sector are, for example, that representatives of companies, research institutes, or NGOs are invited as guest lecturers and assessors. This way, the workplace is partly brought into the traditional school setting. These ways of cooperation allow all parties to learn to know each other better, and more facilities can be used to enhance the workplace learning of the students.

Obviously, the question about resources is a critical aspect. Our answer to this question is as simple as it is difficult. Also in Western societies educational institutions complain about resources, and often these complaints are justified. But rather than worrying about a lack of resources we propose to use creativity in exploiting the existing resources. In many cases, more can be done with less if the vision behind the innovation is clear and priorities are set right.

WORKPLACE-ORIENTED LEARNING IN AN ACADEMIC SETTING: AND ADDITIONAL CHALLENGE

This project illuminates an additional issue for implementing workplace learning: the battle between a research/academic orientation and the workplace orientation. This project focuses on developing a MSc curriculum, which obviously needs to incorporate research. Actually, research is one of the identified occupational profiles. A pitfall is to overemphasise research or academic-oriented courses in the program and use this as an argument for diminishing the workplace-oriented learning components. Although this is legitimate to some extent, and perfectly understandable, decision makers also have to realize that the social science and commercial components, regarding entrepreneurship, business development, business management, marketing, human resource management and development and communication are essential for MSc students. Given the differences of interest, proponents of the research-orientation and the workplace-orientation will have a conflict. In that sense, a way to combat workplace-oriented learning and learning at the workplace is needed, also for the betterment of the research-oriented faculty. In current research practice, generic workplace-oriented competencies become increasingly important. Research institutes are becoming more and more independent business units, and their managers are actually academic entrepreneurs, who can benefit a lot from high quality workplace preparation during their academic education. Moreover, next to this, the rise of evidence-based research (see Slavin, 2008) requires research to directly relate to what happens in the real world of work and feed back relevant and practical results into the real world. Thus, having actual workplace experience in the BSc and MSc programs is always an asset in the résumé of the graduate.

To conclude, this chapter described a NUFFIC project on capacity building in Ethiopian horticulture and floriculture education. This is done through (1) developing a competence-based MSc trajectory that incorporates workplace learning and workplace-oriented learning activities were possible. A characteristic of this development is the ongoing interaction and collaboration with all stakeholders in the project and in Ethiopia, including many representatives from the sector, and (2) professional development of the teaching staff of the local institutions, JUVACM and EPHEA.

The new MSc curriculum started for the first time in 2008–2009, with 15 students. The new influx for 2009–2010 is promising. In general, teachers and stakeholders are very positive, but they do experience serious challenges in actually changing the attitudes and approaches of students, teacher and employers. The actual effects and changes are still to be experienced. Additionally, the NUFFIC project continues with developing workplace-oriented programs or training to upgrade the skills of the Ethiopian population at different levels of the horti/ floriculture sectors. The BSc curriculum is redesigned in the same line as the MSc curriculum, and short practical courses are also being developed. Currently, the idea of certifying big companies as 'learning farms' to provide official certified on-the-job training is being considered.

The redesign of the MSc curriculum was just the start, but the workplace-oriented, competence-based approach is warmly welcomed by both the university and the sector.

REFERENCES

Biemans, H., L. Nieuwenhuis, R. Poell, M. Mulder and R. Wesselink (2004) Competence-based VET in The Netherlands: backgrounds and pitfalls, *Journal of Vocational Education and Training*, 56, (4): 523–538.

Billett, S. (2001) Knowing in practice: re-conceptualising vocational expertise. *Learning and Instruction*, 11: 431–452.

Birenbaum, M. (2003). New insights into learning and teaching and the implications for asessment. In M. Segers, F. J. R. C. Dochy and E. Cascallar (eds.), *Optimising New Modes of Assessment: In Search of Qualities and Standards*. Dordrecht: Kluwer Academic Publishers.

Brinkman, B., Westendorp, A.M.B., Wals, A.E.J. and Mulder, M. (2007) Competencies for rural development professionals in the era of HIV/AIDS, *Compare: A Journal of Comparative Education*, 37 (4): 493 – 511.

Cheetham, G. and Chivers, G. (2001) How professionals learn in practice: an investigation of informal learning amongst people working in professions, *Journal of European Industrial Training*, 25(5): 246–292.

Fenwick, T. (2003). Toward enriched conceptions of work learning: participation, expansion, and translation among individuals with/in activity, *Human Resource Development Review*, 5: 285–302.

Gulikers, J. T., M., Baartman, L. K., J., and Biemans, H. J. A. (in press) Facilitating evaluations of innovative, competence-based assessments: creating understanding and involving multiple stakeholder, *Evaluation and Program Planning*.

Mulder, M. (1992) *The Curriculum Conference: Evaluation of a Tool for Curriculum Content Justification. Dissertation*. Enschede: University of Twente.

Mulder, M. (2001) Competence development – some background thoughts, *The Journal of Agricultural Education and Extension*, 7 (4): 147–158.

Mulder, M. (2007) Competence – the essence and use of the concept in ICVT. *European Journal of Vocational Training*, 40: 5–22.

Mulder, M., Gulikers, J., Biemans, H., and Wesselink, R. (in press). The new competence concept in higher education: error or enrichment?, *Journal of European Industrial Training*, 33 (8/9).

Mulder, M., T. Lans, J. Verstegen, H.J.A. Biemans and Y. Meijer (2007). Competence development of entrepreneurs in innovative horticulture, *Journal of Workplace Learning*, 19 (1): 32–44.

Mulder, M., T. Weigel and K. Collins (2007) The concept of competence concept in the development of vocational education and training in selected EU member states: a critical analysis. *Journal of Vocational Education and Training*, 59 (1) 65–85.

National Skills Task Force (1999). *Delivering Skills for All. Second Report*. Sudbury: Department for Education and Employment/ Prolog.

Poell, R. F., Dam, K. van, and Berg, P. van den. (2004) Organising learning in work contexts. *Applied Psychology: an International Review*, 53: 529–540.

Smith, P. J. (2003) Workplace learning and flexible delivery. *Review of Educational Research*, 73: 53–88.

Weigel, T., M. Mulder and K. Collins (2007) The concept of competence in the development of vocational education and training in selected EU member states. *Journal of Vocational Education and Training*, 59 (1) 51–64.

Wesselink, R., H.J.A. Biemans, M. Mulder and E.R. van den Elsen (2007) Competence-based VET as seen by Dutch researchers. *European Journal of Vocational Training*. 40 (1) 38–51.

Wilson, K. L., Lizzio, A., and Ramsden, P. (1997) The development, validation and application of the course experience questionnaire, *Studies in Higher Education*, 22 (1): 33–53.

23

Policies for the Knowledge Economy: Knowledge Discourses at Play

Tara Fenwick

INTRODUCTION

This chapter examines diverse discourses of knowledge embedded in state policies set forth specifically to mobilize lifelong learning for the global knowledge economy. The discussion draws from the literature as well as examples of federal policy documents in Canada related to its Innovation Strategy launched in 2002. At least two broad policy directions have been at play in these policy documents. One continues to emphasize skill acquisition in a conventional deficit-oriented, individualist and universalist model of work education, where the educational goals are upskilling through control and measurement. The other urges innovation as the prime mover of the new economy, where the goals are formulating (and attracting) a 'creative class' through environments conducive to invention. It is suggested that, rather than creating the bifurcated skill economy that some have argued, these trajectories actually appear to create distinct but overlapping knowledge scapes or networks. These networks contain fundamental ambiguities and discontinuities about the meaning and value of knowledge in a knowledge economy, spaces which may open possibilities for educators.

The chapter proceeds in three sections. The first examines diverse notions of knowledge and skill that have proliferated in policies and critical responses linked to the knowledge economy discourse. The second discusses specific examples of federal policies in Canada that illustrate many of these currents. The third section discusses the ambiguities and tensions apparent in such policies, showing the play of knowledge discourses that invite openings for alternate conceptions of workplace learning and the knowledge economy.

KNOWLEDGE IN THE KNOWLEDGE ECONOMY

Since the 1996 OECD statement that "[k]nowledge is now the driver of productivity and economic growth" (p. 4), knowledge discourses have proliferated in economic policy documents of developed countries. These knowledge discourses tend to promote a generic and non-contextualized capacity to learn, to use tacit (know-how) knowledge to transform codified knowledge, to innovate with technology, and to form knowledge networks (Robertson, 2005). The focus has been on both defining knowledge for knowledge capitalism and determining the critical conditions for the production of knowledge. The goal is to articulate specific directions for human capital development (e.g. skills) on the one hand, and innovation (e.g. commercializable ideas) that will ensure a nation's competitive position in the global knowledge economy.

Innovation in particular has been frequently cast as a critical form of knowledge in the knowledge economy, with federal policies urging a focus on innovation in research and lifelong learning. For example, Canada's Innovation Strategy launched by the federal Human Resources and Development Commission in 2002 is similar to Australia's higher education reform announcing that "[r]esearch and innovation play a vital role in building Australia's competitive strength in a global knowledge-based economy" (Nelson, 2003, p. 31). A comprehensive national program of research funding in Canada, called Initiatives for the New Economy, simultaneously targeted four areas of education, lifelong learning, management and entrepreneurship. The program specifically invited studies that addressed questions such as: What conditions and factors stimulate innovation in firms and organizations? What business practices underpin innovation? What significant factors affect the relationships between innovation and organizational change? (INE, 2001). In 2002, the presidents of Canadian universities entered a framework agreement with the federal government to increase their funding through the Canada Foundation for Innovation in return for universities' agreement to double the amount of research for innovation conducted in their universities and triple their commercialization performance by 2010 (Briskin, 2002). As the Innovation Strategy declares: "Academic institutions have an essential role to play in strengthening Canada's innovation performance. They have acknowledged that they too must continue to strive for excellence and rise to the innovation challenge" (HRDC, 2002, p. 22).

Innovation is defined almost exclusively in economic terms, as "both the creative process of applying knowledge and the outcome of that process" (HRDC, 2002, p. 19). There is authority and inevitability in the statements that in "the innovative race to be run", we must measure "innovation outcomes" and "innovation performance" in the "innovation system" which connects learning, education, researchers, investors and entrepreneurs. The overall position is that "in today's knowledge-based economy, the importance of innovation has increased dramatically" (HRDC, 2002, p. 19). A diffusion of popular texts promoting innovation have accompanied such policy rhetoric. In North America for example, a particularly widely cited thesis was advanced by Harvard economist (recently recruited to the University of Toronto) Richard Florida in *The Rise of the Creative Class* (2002). In it, Florida claimed that economic growth depends on a 'supercreative core' of workers, about 30 percent of the labor force, who value creativity, individualism, difference and merit. He urged cities to create hip conditions attracting these elite innovators who want to be quickly accepted and participate culturally on their own terms.

While innovation appears to be the dominant preoccupation in such texts, an agenda of upskilling existing workers, particularly those considered to be vulnerable, continues to be emphasized as an urgent challenge in North America, Europe and Australia. Canada's Essential Skills Initiative (HRSDC, n.d.) stresses development of generic, 'soft' skills of communication, very similar to those promoted in the UK Core Skills Programme. The UK White Paper *21st Century Skills; Realising our Potential* (2004) focused on integrating government bodies, trainers, educational institutions and employment settings in a strategy to develop skills in communication, information technology, numeracy, working with others, and problem solving. Skill in these policies has, as Valentin (2005) points out, become increasingly flexible, social and transferable, more like personal traits than functional or industry-specific skills.

'Skill' is ubiquitous, the term being applied to such diverse phenomena as reading, writing, problem-solving, learning, team work, salesmanship, marketing, presentation, perseverance, motivation, enthusiasm, attitude, corporate commitment, customer-orientation, stress management ... skill means whatever employers and policy-makers want it to mean (Payne, 2000, p. 361).

The language of such documents invokes demands for both innovation and skill development, wedded with injunctions of continuous learning and success in a globalized economy – even weaving in social values of inclusion and equity – as though these are all naturally aligned and uncontested domains.

What counts as knowledge? Bifurcations and exclusions

Some educationists, according to Lloyd and Payne (2003), have responded enthusiastically to these knowledge-economy discourses. Their 'seduction' is the promise of a workforce that will be better educated and less hierarchical, as the deep-rooted divides between academic/vocational education and mental/muscle labour will supposedly dissolve in a post-Fordist knowledge-based workplace. Educationists, they show, are attracted to the possibility that all workers, across race, gender and class, can develop and exercise high-level skills of communication, analysis and creativity, and become involved in wider contexts of learning in which they take real responsibility for their learning. If this possibility becomes realized, then power relations governing workplaces would shift to reward those with intellectual skills rather than simply 'those at the top'. Other educationists have argued that, if decoupled from the economy, the vision of highly skilled, learning-oriented and creative citizens can lead to an actively democratic and socially just society (Avis, 2000, in Lloyd and Payne, 2003).

However, the emphasis on (technological) innovation and the fusion of learning/labor/education to innovate for economic growth has also spurred critique from many educational commentators. A common complaint has focused on the repressive effects of the continuous learning mantra, yoking human subjects to the market in a relentless, lifelong and lifewide human resource development project. Another critique focuses on problematic conceptions of innovation. In their analysis of Australia's innovation strategy for the knowledge economy, Kenway et al. (2006) point out its reliance upon a flawed techno-determinism: a Schumpeterian approach to innovation as preceding and 'driving' the economy. They argue that in this knowledge configuration, universities become tightly coupled with business in ways that repress the knowledge 'gift economy' where ideas flow freely. Knowledge workers are problematically configured as 'techno-preneurs': entrepreneurial subjects, networked and manipulating knowledge competitively for material gain.

Still others have argued that the emphasis on knowledge and particularly innovative knowledge, within an economy that continues to rely on low-skill labor, has created a high-skill/low-skill divide. Work organizations on the whole are still far from providing post-Fordist conditions of knowledge work, and still tend to segregate knowledge production work such as innovation from material production (Brown et al., 2001; Lloyd and Payne, 2003). A bifurcated economy has resulted, claim these commentators, where any changes in work organization or availability of high skill work has touched only a small minority of employees. Some argue that this bifurcation functions globally, and is reinforced by education provisions. Elite education of high skills development and social capital can increase integration and participation in global economy, but also promote worker migration to wealthy regions (Tikly, 2001). Basic education and low-skills training can improve conditions for the poor but also create wider exclusionary divides within and across regions. Education generally can legitimize an existing global order that, as Stiglitz (2002) claims forcefully, garners a disproportionate share of benefits for the West at the expense of the developing world, but education also fuels resistance by providing forum and focus for critical correspondence with the status quo.

Excluded from innovative work are those who may lack the tools, resources, environments and encouragement to have developed capacity to be sufficiently innovative. Florida's (2002) claim that a new 'creative class' is emerging which cities should entice and encourage suggests an ignored underclass – not just those relegated to jobs that suppress innovation, but also those whose skills and activity are not recognized as valued knowledge. Excluded, for example, are traditional and indigenous knowledges, and local knowledge in workplaces created through workers' everyday adaptations and translations – knowledge that is widespread and often invisible. Farrell and Fenwick (2007) urge critical analysis of how knowledge discourses that celebrate continuous learning, innovation and collaborative partnerships have become naturalized and assimilated into common notions of what counts most as work knowledge. These valuations subjugate other forms of knowledge such as embodied craft knowledge or collective ecological knowledge. The result of these pressures for continuous innovation, as Field (2000) notes, are widening inequality and exacerbating market assaults on fragile environments and communities.

Ambiguities: Innovation, skill and knowledge

Besides these problems of exclusion, inequality, economic bifurcation and techno-determinism produced by innovation-centric knowledge-economy discourses, there is another central issue at the heart of such policy rhetoric. That issue is the ambiguity about what exactly constitutes innovation and skill, and knowledge more broadly for the knowledge economy.

In organization and management studies literature, innovative knowledge and skill is granted central importance given the uncertain economy: "those organisations that prove to have superior abilities to manage exploration will be better able to adapt to changing circumstances" (McGrath, 2001, p. 119). Innovation tends to be conceptualized in two ways. First, as a process of research and development separated from everyday work processes, innovation is intended to develop the new products that ensure a competitive edge, or improve the efficient production and distribution of these commodities. Second, innovation as continuous ongoing improvement throughout the organization has been increasingly a central interest, with a focus in organizational learning strategies upon stimulating and supporting innovation, diffusing, integrating and institutionalizing it within everyday practice (Crossan et al., 1999). Writers advance theories about the processes of innovative learning, seeking ways of removing so-called barriers to innovation, and encouraging workers' experimentation, risk-taking, and variance- seeking (Crossan et al., 1999).

The larger enunciations and critical analyses of 'innovation' as being essentially the production of technological knowledge tend to overlook these embodied, situated forms of improvization and improvement that bubble forth in everyday work of the global economy (Farrell and Fenwick, 2007). In fact, the growing drift to implement international standards of operation often prohibits workers' improvizatory adaptations of routines. Workers tend naturally to engage in innovative activity all the time, or 'common knowledge' – precisely the sort of ongoing experimentation, adaptation, and local solutions required to make foreign tools and processes actually work in particular contexts.

Furthermore, argues Farrell (2006), the knowledge most promoted in many workplaces is not innovation but new textual literacies: mediating audit and management texts, communicating in self-directed work teams, and managing electronic texts that transports knowledge across contexts. Capacities such as image-management and self-presentation are often more evidently at play than knowledge generation in negotiating the multiple networks, virtual, social and material, that constitute everyday work activity (Thompson et al., 2001). These are arguably intellectual 'high skills', not the manual or standardized low-skill routines that critics have complained continue to dominate the available jobs in the so-called knowledge economy. However, these textual literacies are themselves routinized and highly regulated. They are not the improvizatory, free forms of creativity that innovation discourses gesture towards.

Recognition of knowledge and 'innovation' is a critical dynamic, particularly given the provisional, interactive and mobile nature of much innovative knowledge alongside certifiable vocational skill and codified scientific knowledge in workplaces. When does an invention become accepted and performed as an innovation in a given community, and in whose eyes? As Engeström (1999) pointed out, what is pronounced novel rests on community values, perceptiveness, historically shaped attitudes, expectations and desires. The uptake of innovations often depends less on the nature, quality or need for a new process or technology and more upon its complex and unpredictable mediating conditions. Recognition of skill, too, has long been understood to be a political negotiation that is gendered, racialized and classed. The emphasis on 'skill' development continues to label workers as categorically 'skilled' or 'unskilled', based on assumptions that the ability to perform certain activities can be standardized, measured and added where missing. The politics of who knows what is 'skill' becomes buried in such practices. This affects most profoundly not only those moving from one vocation to another as employment opportunities shift, but also the migrant professional workers seeking credentialization in host countries. Furthermore, as Sawchuk (2007) shows, alongside the press for workers to be 'upskilled' in technological competencies needed for the knowledge economy, the rapidly changing technologies have deskilled existing work beyond the point of recognition.

Against these more sedimented views of knowledge/skill as static and discrete, whether embedded in the body of a worker or in the product of scientific innovation, is the notion of the knowledge economy as a series of global networks. In the OECD (1996) statement, networks are represented as pipelines necessary to distribute knowledge efficiently, quickly, widely links across regions and sites of knowledge production – to encourage the emergence of innovation. This view conceptualizes differential global networks linking people with organizations and practices in distributed production and supply chains that make new demands on their capacity to produce new knowledge (Farrell and Fenwick, 2007). For example, using studies of concentrated knowledge production such as Silicon Valley, Brown and Duguid (2002) show that 'the networked economy is not just a technological network carrying digital information, but a social network supporting the creation of human knowledge' (p. 436).

A network metaphor can represent more entrenched, immutable and prescriptive networks as well as more open, diffused and exploratory linkages. But overall, a networked understanding of knowledge as mobile and uncontainable announces its distinction from other tradeable commodities in an advanced industrial economy. Olssen and Peters (2005) point out that, as capital, knowledge has increasing rather than decreasing returns, rather than becoming more scarce, knowledge grows through sharing and application. Furthermore, location doesn't matter given how knowledge travels through technology: knowledge 'leaks' and spillover (e.g., general principles developed along with specific innovations) make it almost impossible to protect or control. Similar knowledge has different value in different contexts, and some knowledge is easily produced and distributed while some remains embedded in local activity. In this sense, knowledge generation depends upon improvization, sharing and mobility, which depends upon social capital, conditions of trust and equity.

Yet these formulations are not easily reconciled either with the human capital/skills development orientation or with the drive to commercialize innovative knowledge production. Overall, while there seems to be almost universal agreement that the global economy is increasingly knowledge-based, there is no clear agreement about what constitutes 'knowledge', who or what participates in such knowledge, or how they make it or use it.

CANADA'S FEDERAL POLICIES FOR THE KNOWLEDGE ECONOMY

Turning to specific examples of policy, this argument will be developed through a discourse analysis of initiatives introduced by the government of Canada. In these we can see how policies for the knowledge economy embed discourses representing knowledge as flowing in relational collaboration alongside conceptions of knowledge as pre-determined and contained in discrete skills located within individuals. Innovation floats as both emergent and bounded, as process as well as property. Ambivalences open around program objectives, which tend to target skill deficits particularly of pre-identified populations of disadvantage, while announcing the need to foster conditions for creativity.

The analysis is premised upon documents circulated through three federally funded programs in Canada: the Essential Skills and Workplace Skills Initiatives, and the Innovation Strategy. These documents included web-based statements of the program's goals, rationale, activities and intended outcomes, as well as their calls for proposal through which program and research funding for workplace learning initiatives are distributed. It is important, particularly when examining ephemeral documents such as calls for proposal, to realize that while discourses are manifested partly through texts, that they are much broader and include social and cultural structures and practices that cannot be glimpsed through particular texts even though they inform textual production and consumption (Fairclough, 1992). However, texts are valuable artefacts of discursive practices, revealing particular signifiers and codes that influence social understandings and behavior.

Discourse analysis of policy documents

According to Fairclough (1992), whose methods of critical discourse studies appear useful for analysing policy documents that mediate knowledge production in the economy, everyday lives are increasingly textually mediated. Critical discourse analysis explores how different discourses work in these practices. Janks (1997) argues that close examination of texts and interactions in policy contexts is helpful in identifying prevailing discourses, how and by whom they are produced, taken up or resisted, interpreted, and acted upon and what results from discursive interactions.

In analysing diverse discourses involved in knowledge-mediating documents such as federal policy statements, then, one adopts what Patterson (1997) has called a "condition of doubt" to trace power relations evident in their interaction: which discourses are granted dominance, which are suppressed or nominalized, which become invisible, and which struggle for voice or resist. These tensions can be expected to occur within as well as between discursive formations. For Fairclough and Wodak (1997), the process of discursive negotiation involves not just conflict but also semiotic hybridity, intertextuality and identity flow. Identification of these dynamics proceeds through detailed analysis of semiotic features of texts and interactions, then examines how they draw in innovative ways on the 'orders of discourse', the shifting discourses and genres in particular relations.

The approach used here drew selectively from methods associated with discourse analysis in an iterative reading of specific aspects of the texts against one another and against their contexts of use, insofar as these are reported in available documents. Certain signifiers, linguistic structures, and associated meanings evident in these documents were analysed to explore the different discourses of knowledge that were being promoted, as well as the strategies used to legitimize particular forms of knowledge and particular ways of developing knowledge. Linguistic strategies such as foregrounding (emphasized concepts), backgrounding (omitted or marginalized concepts), and presuppositions (constructions and even appropriation of the reader's values, background knowledge, etc.) were examined (Huckin, 1997). It is important to situate such analysis within the contextual purposes and uptake of the texts. While these dynamics were not examined empirically in this analysis, consideration was given to the ways in which texts functioned within the contexts of federal expectations of knowledge outcomes, and the overall policy contexts such as federal social and economic objectives referred to by the texts.

The innovation strategy

Canada's Innovation Strategy (HRDC, 2002), announced in 2002, foreshadowed all of the initiatives discussed in the remainder of this chapter (the Essential Skills and Workplace Skills Initiative, and the Canadian Council for Learning). The Innovation Strategy was premised on the belief that:

> Increasingly, success in the knowledge-based economy requires individuals who are creative and who have highly developed problem-solving and communication skills ... By providing opportunities for all Canadians to learn and to develop their skills and abilities, we can achieve our commitment to economic growth and prosperity and demonstrate our social values of inclusion and equality (HRDC, 2002, p. 6).

This blurring of social inclusion commitments with human capital development was combined with emphasis upon innovation. Citations of literacy rates and productivity studies were linked to urgent imperatives in rhetorical strategies that invoked national insecurities: "Canada's innovation performance is weak, and this is affecting productivity levels and economic performance ... Canadians must become more innovative. Improvements in our innovative capacity are critical to productivity growth and wealth creation" (HRDC, 2002, pp. 21, 29).

The Innovation Strategy was presented in two documents. *Achieving Excellence: Investing in People, Knowledge and Opportunity* (Industry Canada, 2002) was broadly concerned with research capacity-building. *Knowledge Matters: Skills and Learning for Canadians* (HRSDC, 2002) focused on lifelong learning for work and human capital development. The dual positioning of these documents, argue Metcalfe and Fenwick (2009), reflected the bifurcated agenda argued by others (e.g. Brown et al., 2001) that separated 'skills' from 'innovation' while connecting both in a single knowledge production strategy.

Yet a closer reading of *Knowledge Matters* reveals both discourses at play, alongside rhetoric of social inclusion. On the one hand, it states injunctions that reflect acquisitional understandings of knowledge as a measurable, trainable skill that is accumulated and centered in the individual. The strategy's stated intentions are:

- to develop "individuals who are creative ... highly developed problem-solving and communication skills";
- to promote "*assessment and recognition* of previously acquired knowledge" and
- to "ensure Canadians have the tools they need to *participate fully* in today's knowledge economy" (with particular concerns stated for Aboriginal people, new immigrants and the "low skilled".

Innovation for national competitiveness also figures prominently in this document for workplace learning, although it is often framed as a bounded quality that is located in individuals. The injunction is to obtain individuals possessing this innovative capital:

- seeking "... a greater number of innovative people driving innovation, or applying innovations", and
- attracting and retaining "the highly qualified people required to fuel Canada's innovation performance."

However, the document also contains vocabulary-reflecting conceptions of knowledge as reliant upon conditions and structures of work that enable learning. Strategic directions include:

- "building learning infrastructure";
- promoting "networks to advance and disseminate knowledge"; and
- promoting "lifelong learning in the workplace."

This language steps away from viewing innovative knowledge as a pre-determined contained commodity and invokes conceptions of knowledge as networked and shared rather than individualist. Such notions gesture towards a sense of unpredictability, collectivity and perhaps emergence in knowledge generation that is distinct from the notions of specifying, measuring and controlling pre-determined knowledge.

'Essential Skills Initiative' in Canada

The Essential Skills Initiative, launched by the Canadian federal government for the stated purpose of "creating a more productive workforce" and attracting and retaining "the highly qualified people required to fuel Canada's innovation performance", is well-funded to drive research, practice and policy in workplace learning (HRSDC, n.d.a). Nine skill areas were declared essential in all work, such as document use, numeracy, 'working with people' and 'thinking' skills. All occupations, not just entry-level or low-skill work, are now in process of being 'profiled' to determine the precise mix of Essential Skills required. About 200 jobs in the National Occupational Classification index have now been profiled. An example might be Retail Sales Manager, whose necessary skills have been determined to be oral communication, problem solving, decision making and working with others on complexity levels of 2–3 (out of a possible 5). The profiles, accompanying tests and instructional materials are for use by teachers, career counselors and individuals "to know if they have the skills they need to do the jobs they want to do" (HRSDC, n.d.a). Colleges are now advertising their reconstituted programs, such as Bow Valley's "Building Workplace Essential Skills" classroom course for online delivery, complete with a database and individualized learning plans enabling instructors to track learners' success in mastering essential skills. Industry sector councils (30 in Canada including trades, resource sectors such as forestry, and certain professions) have participated in projects to assess individuals and develop their 'essential skills' as identified for specific occupations within their purview (HRSDC, n.d.a). Employers are reportedly employing the essential skills for recruitment, promotion, and assessment processes.

'Workplace Skills Strategy' in Canada

The 'essential skills' initiative has continued to be funded and supported while the workplace skills strategy (WSS) was launched in 2005 as the 'key pillar' program of the federal human resources department. WSS is a large multi-stakeholder-driven (business and labour, not educators or academia) set of programs to which the federal government announced a commitment of $3.5 billion over the next five years (HRSDC, n.d.b). The assumptions of the strategy are captured in the following statements from the HRSDC website:

> Canada's success, and the success of individual Canadians, relies on our economic productivity. And our productivity, in turn, is increasingly dependent on skills and learning ... To continue to prosper as a nation, we must develop value-added activities that focus on innovation, research, and worker skills and qualifications.

Here we see the clear links between learning, innovation and knowledge generation, all framed within a discourse of skills and human capital theory. The goals of WSS are stated to be promoting workplace skills investment, promoting skills recognition and utilization, *and* promoting partnerships, networks and information. Thus, alongside a continued focus on individual skills development and testing, there is now on the agenda at least a recognition that workplace environment and structures require attention too, and that inclusion is an issue that cannot be simply addressed through an individual's skill levels. So WSS mentions the need to improve apprenticeship opportunities and recognition of immigrants' credentials, remove barriers experienced by aging and disabled workers, and increase workers' access to learning opportunities (HRSDC, n.d.b).

The WSS funds projects that develop worker skills as well as innovative 'tools' for developing worker skills, through competitive bids submitted by partnerships that can include private and public organizations, research institutions, labour groups, etc. About $31 million was allocated to the first call for proposals; a second call closed on April 18, 2007 and a third call is in drafting process. In other words, significant resources have been made available to fund projects willing to frame themselves according to the HRSDC guidelines.

And what are these guidelines? According to the second and most recent call for proposal, priority will be given to proposals for applied projects that will "develop skills for workers" while demonstrating "lessons learned/best practices" that can apply across contexts (HRSDC, n.d.b). 'Impact' must be demonstrated – on employers, employees, stakeholders and workplaces. Projects must be 'promising', a term that is not defined. Purposes for the research are provided explicitly. Overall, projects are to develop solutions: "support the adoption, testing and sharing of promising tools and approaches for enhancing ..." skills of target groups (HRSDC, n.d.b). In this second call, the target groups were identified to be older workers, low-skilled workers, and newcomers to Canada: populations considered priority because underutilized in the labour market. The two-year timelines for projects are short, and must include realization of all knowledge development outcomes and full dissemination of innovative practices created.

Finally, 'partnerships' are emphasized: both for funding purposes (partners or applicants must provide 25 percent of the total project budget) and to 'secure expertise': applicants are expected to build upon or create new partnerships (HRSDC, n.d.b). However, the nature and meaning of 'partnership' and roles of 'partners' are not defined beyond these references. This creates an interesting ambiguity when the program is aimed at potential partnering participants across public and private sectors, industry and education, academic and vocationally oriented organizations.

DISCUSSION: TENSIONS AND AMBIVALENCES

These initiatives funded by Canada's federal government potentially can shape work-related knowledge in particular directions, depending on the degree to which educators and researchers take up their terms in order to solicit resources. The actual programs consist of funding available for projects that combine research with educational strategies to promote workplace learning for a knowledge economy. While this analysis does not examine the extent of this uptake, it is reasonable to assume that the funding available, in some cases in considerable amounts, would attract organizations seeking to increase training provision as well as workplace educators and researchers from universities, private agencies, or think tanks.

Project funding is obtained in a competitive application process submitted by partnered organizations. This hands-off strategy of distributing resources for workplace learning relieves the state from specifying and being accountable for any particular strategy for skill development and knowledge circulation. It also removes accountability for ensuring equitable assistance for the most vulnerable individuals and organizations. Projects simply must yield 'best' practices and knowledge that can be universalized, which may be defined in any terms by applicants. This discourse is based on a 'what works' perspective, in which a central assumption is that what *has* worked in the past, in a particular context with particular actors, corresponds to what *will* work in the future, across different actors in unpredictable contexts. As Biesta (2007) points out, this logic is legitimate as the logic of individual practice: that is, a practitioner continuously applies and adapts approaches recalled from past practice, but this application is particular, contextual and fluid. To apply such logic as a basis for knowledge development is to commit a logical fallacy, particularly in context of promoting innovation: what has worked cannot correspond to what will work, only to what might work in certain contexts. Further, what works is recognized very differently in various industrial, public sector, educational and other environments. The problem to be solved by 'what works' may be defined in ways that have little to do with innovative learning opportunities, broader knowledge circulation, workers' well-being, job enrichment, 'high skills' development, or any of the generative possibilities that educationists may have hoped for in a knowledge economy.

Against this 'best practices' discourse, which universalizes and centralizes knowledge, the networked knowledge discourse is about decentralization and circulation. The desire for certainty and control of developing best practices – both practices of material work and practices of learning material work – is thus asserted alongside discourses of knowledge as uncertain and emergent, implied in statements urging creativity and leading-edge innovation. Beyond these statements, little direction or allowance for innovation is provided. According to the terms of these initiatives, pursuits that might be linked to innovation are presumably not fundable: exploratory knowledge, workplace experimentation, forms of knowing that open new questions about existing systems, or knowledge that might reconfigure existing frames that continue to define problems and solutions.

Across these documents, certain common signifiers are positioned with emphasis but without much clear definition. Terms such as 'innovation', 'partnership', and 'promising' (that is, projects that indicate 'promising' tools or approaches will be given priority) are not clarified. 'Promising' can refer to projects that are most innovative, most viable, are most likely to have wide application, or that have the widest scope of solution. 'Innovative delivery' of education is encouraged, but also innovation in new solutions and new knowledge. Indeed the director of WSS admitted that the priority for 'innovation' was decreased in the third call for proposals because the HRSDC reviewing staff discovered that they had no clear or consensual meaning amongst themselves regarding what constituted 'innovative' projects (personal communication, March 23 2007). 'Partner' references, along with 'networks', provide no indication of how or why partnerships are to be created for knowledge generation, or what constitutes a 'partnership' beyond diversity (individuals/organizations, human non-human entities, public/private?). Knowledge generation within and across partnerships is left ambiguous – as long as it is linked to innovation and skill development.

A high skill/low skill analysis of these knowledge discourses might posit a separation of innovation from skill, where innovation is understood to be codifiable scientific research conducted and disseminated from knowledge-generating institutions, and skill is confined to discrete, low-level competencies in workplaces. But these policy documents do not actually reflect such clear separation. For example, statements of innovation appear, albeit conceptualized as both measurable human capital *and* fluid relational process, in skill documents of the WSS. The essential skills measurements embrace all 30,000 of the occupations classified in the national index, including professional sectors and knowledge producers, not just low-skilled or disadvantaged workers targeted for upskilling. Workplace and research institutions are expected to collaborate in projects without clear lines between knowledge producers and knowledge users, where results must be represented in terms of both codified new knowledge and 'knowledge mobilization' such as new skills developed among all partners.

Yet for all the emphasis on innovation and networks of innovation, the actual links of innovation to 'skill' are unclear. While Canada's overall innovation strategy emphasizes the importance of creativity, the essential skills initiative – claiming to spell out all the skills necessary for life and work – does not contain a single mention of creativity. No references occur to imagination or the arts. Nor are there references to skills in building networks and partnerships, creating and sustaining collaborations (e.g. for innovation), or the actual skills of generating knowledge. Surprisingly for an innovation strategy, skills of enterprise and entrepreneurism are not included – certainly nothing resembling the technopreneurial subject described by Kenway et al. (2006). Less surprising, skills of critical analysis and advocacy are invisible. But if such policies are intended to separate critical, innovation, scientific knowledge production from workplace 'low skills', it is important to note that material skills of work are also not mentioned, nor do any statements discuss embodied craft knowledge. Instead, most of the essential skills seem to focus on broad literacies such as document use and working with others. These skills are aligned with the new textual literacies discussed by Farrell and Fenwick (2007), which increasingly are required of all workers, the 'creative class' alongside skilled and low-skill workers, to be compliant with the knowledge standards circulating in the global economy.

CONCLUSION

In the language of policy documents promoting workplace learning for a knowledge economy, what becomes apparent are the diverse, even contradictory, meanings of knowledge playing across and within these documents. Innovation occupies a central rhetorical position, with claims that knowledge circulating in systems has higher inherent value than that locked in individual heads. Yet individual skills development is also a key value. Thus, the focus to identify and *reproduce* (and measure) pre-determined knowledge, as 'essential skills' is presented alongside a focus to *transform* through innovation. Human capital formation, conceiving knowledge as concretized and visible in distinct bodies, is entwined with commitments to promote innovation conceived as mobile, networked knowledge. The knowledge generation that is stated to 'fuel' the knowledge economy is associated with trust, openness and experimentation. These values are encouraged in networks that appear to co-exist with injunctions of performativity, accountability and surveillance fostered by the essential/workplace skills initiatives.

The projects and interventions sponsored by the skills initiatives focus on increasing discrete skills of disadvantaged individuals without apparent acknowledgement of the system constraints and enablers – both the socio-material relations in which skill/knowledge is performed as well as the 'learning infrastructure' of a workplace environment – that are stated to be so important to (innovative) knowledge generation.

Thus, rather than presenting a clear high skill/low skill dichotomy on the one hand, or a regulatory discursive regime on the other, knowledge discourses in such policy documents at best circulate in ways that create ambivalences. While there is pervasive rhetorical commitment to encourage a dynamic of innovation, it remains so ambiguous as to function as little more than an empty signifier. The concomitant discourses of skill are firmly focused upon control and containment of what is already known while gesturing fervently to the need for knowledge that is yet to come. However, the sorts of skills being targeted are so generic as to permit wide interpretation of what knowledge actually counts.

At the heart of these ambivalences in knowledge discourses are compelling uncertainties: uncertainty about the nature of knowledge and how to foster its development and circulation in a knowledge economy, and uncertainty about the forms of knowledge that are actually desired. There is little evidence of a clear ideological agenda from the state promoting particular forms of innovation or technopreneurship. Nor is there evidence of a regulatory regime beyond some diffuse pronouncements unsupported by policy levers or disciplinary technologies. Instead, what seems to have emerged in these knowledge discourses for the economy is confusion. Some may argue this to be evidence of the state's abdication of a responsibility to increase workforce skills. Others, following Žižek (2008), may insist that what is operating is 'everyday ideology' that, in a Marxist analysis, is ultimately creating a perfect equilibrium of high and low skills.

However, where there is uncertainty and ambivalence, there is space to manoeuvre. The vague categories of skill and innovation, and the contradictory meanings ascribed to knowledge, create spaces of possibility. These possibilities may include reframing the more repressive notions of a knowledge economy. They permit a redefining of workplace learning in any number of directions that may interrupt the bifurcated economic structures and promote greater equity, richer knowledge recognition, and wider freedom to participate in knowledge production. These possibilities also invite us to resist the compelling seduction of achieving some control over work-based knowledge, the sorts of control and need for certainty that are evident in the persisting discourses of skill specification and measurement. Instead, the ambivalences and disjunctures among these knowledge discourses beckon us to dwell within uncertainty – even undecidability – as a space in which to reconsider workplace learning and education. Uncertainty, undecidability, and risk, albeit uncomfortable, arguably are central conditions for generating new knowledge and fostering creativity – even, or perhaps especially, among educators.

REFERENCES

Avis, J. (2000) 'Policy Talk: Reflexive Modernization and the Construction of Teaching and Learning within Post-Compulsory Education and Lifelong Learning in England', *Journal of Education Policy*, 15(2): 185–199.

Biesta, G. (2007) 'Why "What Works" Won't Work: Evidence-Based Practice and the Democratic Deficit in Educational Research', *Educational Theory*, 57(1): 1–22.

Briskin, L. (2002) 'Faculty Expected to Triple Their Commercialization Performance', *CAUT (Canadian Association of University Teachers) Bulletin*. Toronto: York University.

Brown, J. S. and Duguid, P. (2002) 'Local Knowledge: Innovation in the Networked Age', *Management Learning* 33(4): 427–437.

Brown, P., Green, A. and Lauder, H. (2001) *High Skills: Competitiveness and Skill Formation*. Oxford: Oxford University Press.

Crossan, M.M., Lane, H.W. and White, R.E. (1999) 'An Organizational Learning Framework: From Intuition to Institution', *Academy of Management Review*, 24(3): 522–537.

Engeström, Y. (1999) 'Innovative Learning in Work Teams', in Y. Engeström, R. Miettinen and R-L Punamaki (eds), *Perspectives on Activity Theory*. Cambridge, UK: Cambridge University Press, pp. 377–406.

Fairclough, N. (1992) *Discourse and Social Change*. Cambridge: Polity Press.

Fairclough, N. and Wodak, R. (1997) 'Critical Discourse Analysis', in T. van Dijk (eds), *Discourse as Social Interaction* London: Sage, pp. 258–284.

Farrell, L. (2001) 'The "New Word Order" – Workplace Education and the Textual Practice of Economic Globalization', *Pedagogy, Culture and Society*, 9: 59–77.

Farrell, L. (2006) *Making Knowledge Common: Literacy and Knowledge at Work*. London: Routledge.

Farrell, L. and Fenwick, T. (2007) 'Educating a Global Workforce?', In L. Farrell and T. Fenwick (eds), *Educating the Global Workforce*. Abingdon: Routledge.

Field, J. (2000) *Lifelong Learning and the New Educational Order*. Stoke-on-Trent, Staffordshire, UK.

Florida, R. (2002) *The Rise of the Creative Class*. New York: Basic Books.

HRSDC (n.d.a). *Essential Skills*. Ottawa, ON: Human Resources and Skills Development of Canada. http://www.hrsdc.gc.ca/en/hip/hrp/essential_skills/essential_skills_index.shtml

HRSDC (n.d.b.) *Workplace Skills Strategy Overview*. Human Resources and Skills Development Canada. http://www.hrsdc.gc.ca/en/workplaceskills/overview.shtml (accessed 24.3.07).

HRDC (2002) *Knowledge Matters: Skills and Learning for Canadians: Canada's Innovation Strategy*. Ottawa, ON: Human Resource Development Canada (Document SP-482-02-02).

Huckin, T. (1997) 'Critical Discourse Analysis', in T. Miller (ed.) *Functional Approaches to Written Text: Classroom Applications*. Washington: US Information Service.

INE (2001) 'Initiative for the New economy, Guidelines for Applications'. Ottawa, ON: Social Sciences and Humanities Research Council of Canada. Available from www.sshrc.ca (accessed 25.9.01)

Janks, H. (1997) 'Critical Discourse Analysis as a Research Tool', *Discourse: Studies in the Cultural Politics of Education*, 18: 329–343.

Kenway, J., Bullen, E. and Simon, R. (2006) *Haunting the Knowledge Economy*. Abingdon: Taylor and Francis.

Lloyd, C. and Payne, J. (2003) 'The Political Economy of Skill and the Limits of Educational Policy', *Journal of Education Policy*, 18(1): 85–107.

McGrath, R.G. (2001) 'Exploratory Learning, Innovative Capacity and Managerial Oversight', *Academy of Management Journal*, 44(1): 118–131.

McKenna, B. (2004) 'Critical Discourse Studies – Where To From Here?', *Critical Discourse Studies* 1(1): 9–39.

Metcalfe, A. and Fenwick, T. (2009) Knowledge for whose society? Knowledge production, higher education, and federal policy in Canada. *Higher Education*, 57(9): 209–225.

Nelson, B. (2003) *Our Universities: Backing Australia's Future*. Canberra: Commonwealth of Australia. Also available at: www.backingaustraliasfuture.gov.au/policy_paper/policy_paper.pdf

OECD (1996) *The Knowledge Based Economy*. Paris: OECD.

Olssen, M. and Peters, M.A. (2005) 'Neoliberalism, Higher Education and the Knowledge Economy: From the Free Market to Knowledge Capitalism', *Journal of Education Policy*, 20(3): 313–345.

Patterson, A. (1997) 'Critical Discource Analysis: A Condition of Doubt', *Discource: Studies in the Cultural Politics of Education*, 18(3): 425–437.

Payne, J. (2000) 'The Unbearable Lightness of Skill: The Changing Meaning of Skill in UK Policy Discourses and Some Implications for Education and Training', *Journal of Educational Policy*, 15(3).

Robertson, S.L. (2005) 'Re-imagining and Re-scripting the Future of Education: Global Knowledge Economy Discourses and the Challenge to Education Systems', *Comparative Education*, (41)2: 151–170.

Sawchuk, P.H. (2007). Work and the Labour Process:"use value" and the Rethinking of Skills and Learning. In L. Farrell and T. Fenwick (eds), *Educating the Global Workforce*. London: Routledge, pp. 91–108.

Stiglitz, J.E. (2002) *Globalization and its Discontents*. New York/ London: Norton.

Thompson, P., Warhurst, C. and Callaghan, G. (2001) 'Ignorant Theory and Knowledgeable Workers: Interrogating the Connections between Knowledge, Skills and Services', *Journal of Management Studies*, 38(7): 923–942.

Tikly, L. (2001) 'Globalisation and Education in the Postcolonial World: Towards a Conceptual Framework', *Comparative Education*, 37(22): 151–171.

Valentin, C. (2005) '*Essential Skills and VET: Towards a Critical Role for HRD*'. Paper presented to the *Researching Work and Learning Conference*, University of Technology-Sydney, December.

Žižek, S. (2008) *In Defence of Lost Causes*. London: Verso Books.

24

Virtual Workplace Learning: Promises Met?

Robert G. Brookshire, Kara M. Lybarger, and Lynn B. Keane

INTRODUCTION

Virtual learning has become ubiquitous in the workplace as one of many modalities for delivering training. Companies around the world, large and small, provide training to their employees using computer technology. Indeed, the American Society for Training and Development found in a series of studies that 36 percent of all training programs in organizations were delivered by computer (Rivera and Paradise, 2006). As we will show, however, the impact of virtual learning has been decidedly mixed. Virtual learning can be efficient and effective, but it is not well suited for every subject, every employee, or every situation. At the same time, there are a variety of steps employers can take to maximize the probability of success in the implementation of virtual learning.

This chapter reviews recent research, from both corporate and academic settings, on virtual learning. Our objective is to explore the many complexities of virtual learning in order to help companies deploy it successfully. We also hope to make a small contribution to what has become a vast stream of research. We restrict our review primarily to works published since 2006. Tallent-Runnels and her colleagues provide an exhaustive review of the research literature prior to this date (Tallent-Runnels et al., 2006).

The chapter is organized into five sections. We begin by identifying, among the myriad definitions and terms associated with the use of computers in training, exactly what we mean by virtual learning. The second section reviews the benefits provided by virtual learning in the workplace. The third portion addresses the pitfalls and barriers to the success of virtual learning. The fourth part presents an examination of the success factors identified by research for virtual learning initiatives. Finally, we conclude with some observations about virtual learning.

WHAT IS VIRTUAL LEARNING?

It's a brave person who attempts to define the term 'e-learning'; there are many interpretations and many distinguished papers on the subtle nuances between definitions (Allison, 2007, p. 20).

The concept of virtual learning was born in the mid-1980s when Starr Roxanne Hiltz coined the term *virtual classroom* (Hiltz, 1986). The use of computers for instruction had begun practically alongside the development of computers in the 1950s and '60s, however, under the name *computer-aided instruction* (CAI). Reviewing the early history of CAI, Chambers and Sprecher (1980) distinguish between adjunct CAI, in which the computer supplements learning, and primary CAI, in which the computer substitutes for other modes of instruction. Primary CAI is the forerunner of virtual learning.

As virtual learning developed through the last few decades of the twentieth century, a variety of terms were coined to describe it. Technology-mediated learning, or TML, for example, "is defined as an environment in which the learner's interactions with learning materials (readings, assignments, exercises, etc.), peers, and/or instructors are mediated through advanced information technologies" (Alavi and Leidner, 2001, p. 2).

Another popular term, perhaps more widely used than any other, is *e-learning*. Broadly speaking, e-learning (sometimes *eLearning*) refers to "the process of learning from information that is delivered electronically" (Honey, 2001, p. 201) and is used by many authors to cover a variety of CAI technologies and techniques. It has even become established as part of the title of several journals and magazines, such as *The Electronic Journal of e-Learning,* the *European Journal of Open, Distance and E-Learning,* and *E-learning Age.*

As Tynjälä and Häkkinen (2005) note, terms such as distance learning, blended learning, and mobile learning have been used as synonyms for e-learning. Westbrook (2006) adds the terms online learning, Internet-based learning, and web-based learning. Aggarwal and Makkonen (2009) contribute the expressions asynchronous learning and networked learning. Servage (2005) provides a thoughtful review of the "e-nomenclature" problem and its implications for the way researchers, teachers, and organizations think and deal with the concept. Tynjälä and Häkkinen maintain, however, that e-learning is really more than just "delivering digital information and study materials to people through electronic media" (2005, p. 318).

As with e-learning, virtual learning is subject to multiple definitions. Stonebraker and Hazeltine have possibly the broadest conception:

> Virtual learning is defined as the delivery of learning through electronic mediation which bridges the gap caused when the instructor and student are separated in either time or place ... The range of electronic mediation includes voice, video, data, and print through such formats as radio, television, Web-based programming, and streaming audio and video, as well as a variety of recording technologies. (Stonebraker and Hazeltine, 2004, p. 209).

Most authors, however, restrict virtual learning to that which occurs only in a computer-mediated setting. Piccoli, Ahmad, and Ives, following Wilson, describe virtual learning as occurring in "computer-based environments that are relatively open systems, allowing interactions and encounters with other participants and providing access to a wide range of resources" (Wilson, 1996, p. 8; Piccoli et al., 2001, pp. 402–403). Likewise, Hornik, Johnson, and Wu write that in virtual learning, "learning processes, communications, shared social context and learning community are mediated through information technology" (Hornik et al., 2007, p. 25).

For the purposes of this chapter, we will use virtual learning to refer to learning that is delivered through information technology and that uses this technology to permit interaction among the participants, instructors and learners alike. Thus, as with Hiltz's original virtual classroom, computer technology creates a virtual environment in which learning takes place, rather than supplementing face-to-face instruction. This distinguishes virtual learning from other types of e-learning, such as computer-based training, in which the student works independently and interacts only with the computer. As Littleton and Whitelock write, at the core of virtual learning "is the facilitation of discourse for the purpose of building understanding" (2004, p. 173). Our conception is similar to computer-supported collaborative learning (CSCL), a term widely used among European researchers (see, for example, Tynjälä and Häkkinen, 2005). For similar definitions of virtual learning, see Weller et al. (2005) and Keller (2005).

THE BENEFITS OF VIRTUAL LEARNING

Large organizations in just about every field are utilizing eLearning through some of the latest and greatest technological advances. eLearning is helping them to fine-tune production, maximize sales and build the capacity of their workforces. They are gaining a competitive advantage that, in turn, encourages them to advance further along the eLearning adoption curve (Leary and Berge, 2007, p. 1).

The popularity of virtual learning in the workplace is due to its many benefits. The literature on virtual learning over the last 30 years has identified many advantages for businesses. In this section we review some of the most recent research findings and opinions.

Bell (2007) identifies the following advantages for businesses. It is easier and more cost-effective for training large numbers of employees in a short time span. Online content may be more up-to-date. Online training insures consistency across a global, diverse workforce. Online training can include automated auditing tools to insure compliance. Benefits for learners include flexibility and control over the learning experience, short periods of learning that do not interfere with work, the ability to take extra time with more challenging material, and a safer environment with less pressure than in classroom learning.

Like Bell, Schooley (2009) lists consistency as an advantage. Other advantages she identifies include faster learning; the ability to learn anytime, anywhere; reusability of content; and reduction in travel expenses.

A chief advantage of virtual learning is its adaptability for a variety of learning styles (Allison, 2007) and learning needs (Pearson and Koppi, 2003; Santos et al., 2007). The use of information technology allows material to be developed for almost any type of learner, "making it available both for on-demand, personal, consumption, as well as for group-based activities" (Allison, 2007, p. 21). Students can participate in group learning, and then return individually again and again to review materials at their own pace. Students' specific individual needs can be addressed (Santos et al., 2007) using virtual learning design (Pearson and Koppi, 2003).

Liz Falconer, of the University of the West of England, challenges the notion that tacit information cannot be transmitted or transformed using technology. Through an extensive review of the literature, she shows that, both empirically and theoretically, organizational learning can be enhanced through e-learning (Falconer, 2006). Jane Simmons (2006) makes a similar point from the perspectives of both employers and employees.

In the *British Journal of Educational Technology*, Allan and Lewis report the results of a four-year case study of a virtual learning community. The members of this community, composed of professional staff at a university, were able to increase their innovation and professional expertise through the support they derived from the learning community (Allan and Lewis, 2006).

Ward and Riley (2008) recommend virtual learning as a cost-effective strategy in a demanding economic environment such as 2008–2009. They say that virtual learning can provide expanded training at minimal cost, it can save time, and it can target training and learning on demand. Using computer systems allows more detailed tracking and reporting of training as well as different formats that match employee learning styles. As with Falconer and Simmons, Ward and Riley concur that virtual learning is useful for transferring organizational knowledge and keeping employees actively engaged in their jobs. Finally, they define well-designed virtual learning as that which can be used to attract and recruit new employees.

To summarize, then, virtual learning can have a variety of benefits that accrue primarily to the employees themselves, to the employers, and to both employees and employers. Benefits for the employees themselves include:

- Flexibility and control over their learning experience;
- The ability to take extra time with more challenging material;
- A safer environment with less pressure than classroom learning;
- The ability to learn anytime, anywhere; and
- Adaptability for a variety of learning styles and needs.

Benefits mainly for the employer include that virtual learning:

- Is easier and more cost effective for training large numbers of employees in a short time span;
- Can expand training at minimal cost;
- Can reduce travel expenses;
- Ensures consistency across a global, diverse workforce;
- Allows more detailed tracking and reporting of training;
- Can include automated auditing tools to insure compliance;
- Has reusable content;
- Enhances and expands organizational learning options; and
- Can attract and recruit new employees.

Finally, some benefits of virtual learning apply to both employees and employers, such as:

- More up-to-date content;
- Shorter periods of learning that do not interfere with work;
- Training and learning that are targeted and on demand;
- Employees who increase their innovation and professional expertise; and
- Employees who are actively engaged in their jobs.

CHALLENGES TO VIRTUAL LEARNING

> E-learning will not meet all requirements and the classroom training that has proved a mainstay for most organisations will not be swept away by this technology. Certain skillsets, such as leadership and project management, cannot be taught properly via a purely electronic format (Pancucci, May 28, 2002, p. 22).

Virtual learning is not for everybody, nor is it for every situation. Some kinds of learning seem better suited to face-to-face settings or other modalities. Even in cases where virtual learning is appropriate, trainers and designers must take into account the special requirements of the technology and the special needs of different types of learners (Pearson and Koppi, 2003). This section reviews research and opinion on the challenges to virtual learning.

As the introductory quote illustrates, not all subjects are well-suited to virtual learning. Those topics that require frequent close-range person-to-person interaction are in this category. In addition to leadership and project management, developing soft business skills such as negotiation or group facilitation, and creating personal or team trust are situations in which face-to-face instruction is more appropriate (Schooley, 2009).

Virtual learning requires special preparation to overcome workplace challenges. Simon discusses seven of the most common myths about delivering virtual learning. Workers may not take advantage of available learning materials. Rather than being carefully planned, assessments are often an afterthought. The learning environment outside the virtual learning space must be considered. The characteristics of the learning management system should be taken into account, especially the user interface. Trainers must make it easy to access the course materials and pay attention to the different hardware and software configurations of the users.

Alonso, Manrique, and Viñes examined 385 employees of the Spanish Administration who were studying the Java programming language in either face-to-face or virtual environments. They found significant differences in the amount of learning, satisfaction with learning, and the amount of time it took to complete the material based on the design of the learning modules (Alonso et al., 2009).

While virtual learning has the advantage of being potentially adaptable to different learning styles, if employees are presented with materials using a learning style different from theirs, results may be disappointing. In their study of 332 university students using a virtual learning environment, Hornik, Johnson, and Wu found that when there was congruence between learning style and the virtual environment, results were good. If there was no such fit, however, outcomes were significantly poorer. They conclude, "... the potential exists for organizations to waste large amounts of resources in their investments in their distributed initiatives and for employees participating in these initiatives to learn less, participate less, and ultimately have reduced skills and knowledge than if fit were considered" (Hornik et al., 2007, p. 38).

Attitudes toward computers can also impact employees' perceptions of virtual learning. Park and Wentling studied employees of a large construction and agricultural equipment manufacturer involved in virtual learning at work. They found learners who had positive attitudes toward computers viewed the virtual learning environment more favourably and were better able to transfer their learning to their jobs (Park and Wentling, 2007).

Using virtual learning with older workers can present different dilemmas than with younger workers. This may become more problematic as the workforce in developed countries ages. According to Githens (2007), organizations must work to eliminate stereotypes of older workers as unable to use technology, develop an appreciation for the advantages of older workers, and avoid situations where older workers could be embarrassed about memory loss. Older adults find some technologies easier to use than others, but accommodations may have to be made for vision problems and the slower rate at which older adults learn.

Not only is virtual learning different for employees of various ages, it is even different for employees in different parts of the same business. Gallaher and Wentling (2009) examined the rate of adoption of virtual learning across different professional groups in a large US company. They found finance and marketing professionals were the quickest to adopt virtual learning, followed by engineers and legal professionals. Surprisingly, human resource professionals were the slowest of the groups studied. Among the demographic factors they examined, only education and experience with the Internet affected the use of virtual learning.

Virtual learning is particularly challenging for smaller organizations. Birchall and Giambona (2007) write that employees in small and medium enterprises (SMEs) find it difficult to fit virtual learning into daily activities; SMEs often operate in relative isolation, and many do not have the infrastructure to support multimedia. Leary and Berge agree and point out that the economies of scale that help large companies justify virtual learning do not apply to smaller enterprises. In addition, smaller companies may lack professional training and technical staff, or even a learning culture. They may be too busy or unable even to identify their training needs (Leary and Berge, 2007). These conclusions are supported by Roy and Raymond's study of 16 SMEs in the Atlantic region of Canada. They found the need to develop an e-learning culture and the availability of technical skills and appropriate software were critical to the use of virtual learning in these companies, prerequisites that were often missing (Roy and Raymond, 2008).

The implementation of virtual learning in less developed countries may bring about a different set of problems. Ali and Magalhaes, comparing virtual learning in Kuwait to Western countries, found problems in Kuwait with access to technology, scalability, sharing of assets, measurement, and standards. They especially emphasize the failure of managers and management processes to appreciate and integrate technology into training. They write, "Although the potential for delivery [of virtual learning] at the global level is present, *actual* delivery is very much dependent upon local circumstances" (Ali and Magalhaes, 2008, p. 49).

With increasing security threats to online systems, technology managers have implemented additional security mechanisms. Tsiantis, Stergiou, and Margariti (2007) argue that many of the mechanisms are restrictive and autocratic, reducing dramatically the usability of online learning systems. Users resort to insecure behavior or suffer from low motivation. The answer is for designers of security procedures and software to recognize the special nature of virtual learning systems and to work with users to provide user-centered security. Ardito and colleagues present a framework for evaluating the usability of virtual learning systems that includes both software usability and pedagogical effectiveness (Ardito et al., 2006).

In her review of the virtual learning literature, Westbrook (2006) identifies problems such as collaboration fatigue, in which students feel overwhelmed by the demands of online collaboration; misunderstandings in the absence of verbal, body, and spoken cues; and irresponsibility among students in turning in assignments. In addition to student problems, teachers need additional training in order to be effective in the virtual classroom.

In summary, there are many factors to consider when implementing virtual learning that might negatively affect learning outcomes. We can group these factors into characteristics of the design of the training or training system, characteristics of the workplace, and characteristics of the learners themselves.

Among the characteristics of the training system or the training itself, we have the following:

- Topics that require personal interaction such as leadership training, negotiation, or group facilitation may not be appropriate for virtual learning.
- Assessments should be carefully designed.
- The learning management system's characteristics, including the user interface, can impact the effectiveness of virtual learning.
- Training materials must be easy to access.
- The technology available to the users must be considered in the design of the system.
- Security mechanisms must not interfere with the usability of the learning system.
- The pedagogical design of the training can significantly affect its effectiveness. In particular, there must be a fit between the learning style of the students and the style of the materials.

The characteristics of the workplace must be taken into account. These include:

- The physical learning environment must be appropriate.
- Adequate technical and professional training staff are required.
- An e-learning culture must be developed.
- Management support is critical.

The characteristics of the learners themselves may present challenges to virtual learning. Some of these include:

- Different types of workers approach virtual learning differently, including older workers and those with less computer experience.
- Systems must be adaptable to the physical needs of users.
- Overuse of virtual learning may induce fatigue with the system.
- Workers must be motivated to participate in the training.

CRITICAL SUCCESS FACTORS IN DEPLOYING VIRTUAL LEARNING

> It would be nice to think that a well-designed e-learning lesson will break through any obstacle in its way and will illuminate the light bulbs of all learners who touch it. The reality, however, is that many perfectly good e-learning lessons have wilted and died ... (Simon, 2009, p. 35).

In this section, we review the recent research on the critical success factors for the implementation of virtual learning. We examine not only quantitative research, but also qualitative studies and the informed opinions of business trainers and managers. There seems to be a general agreement on many of the important determinants of virtual learning success.

Luarn, Chen, and Lo, of the National Taiwan University of Science and Technology, surveyed 394 employees enrolled in e-learning through the Taiwan Knowledge Bank. The researchers identified six critical success factors for e-learning. These included factors that enhance learning performance, such as provision of courses that meet learners' immediate needs; provision of after-class services, including timely reporting of scores and interaction with instructors; and the maintenance of environmental quality, especially with regard to the equipment and learning space. Other factors were the establishment of an interactive mechanism, particularly with other learners; the provision of flexible learning, especially class times and the ability to work at the learner's own pace; and satisfaction of user needs, including the ability of learners to choose courses freely that meet their needs. They found that a feedback loop or "positive circle" was created with successful e-learning deployment, whereby enthusiasm for learning leads to greater participation, which increases the likelihood of success (Luarn et al., 2007).

Researchers Lim, Lee, and Nam surveyed 151 employees in three Korean firms who had participated in online training from one to six months. The researchers examined ten factors they hypothesized would influence the effectiveness of online training. Of these, they found eight were significant, including learning motivation, computer self-efficacy, the contents of the training program, ease of use, the support of supervisors, consistency in the learning environment, and face-to-face meetings between instructors and trainees. They found that e-mail communications did not seem to affect performance (Lim et al., 2007).

Roca and Gagné surveyed 174 employees of four United Nations agencies who had taken a virtual learning course offered by the United Nations System Staff College. They found the workers were more likely to continue using the virtual learning system when they felt autonomous and competent using the system. These feelings affected their motivation and their perceptions of the usefulness and playfulness of the system. When the employees felt supported and connected to their colleagues, they used the system because of the enjoyment they felt (Roca and Gagné, 2008).

Simmering, Posey, and Piccoli studied the performance of 190 university students in an online software applications course. They found that computer self-efficacy was positively related to learning, even after controlling for factors such as previous knowledge. In contrast to previous research, however, they found that motivation to learn was not related to learning (Simmering et al., 2009).

Birchall and Giambona looked at the use of virtual learning communities as a "way for SMEs to meet their training needs. They recommend the following to enhance success: "care in the selection of participants; early dialogue in the virtual community to encourage information sharing and to set the tone; appropriate use of technology for communications; the establishment of ground rules for behaviour within the community; facilitators providing a role model and also putting effort into maintaining momentum and energy levels" (Birchall and Giambona, 2007, p. 199).

Stonebraker and Hazeltine surveyed 338 participants in an online test preparation course at a large US company. They found a reduction in the social processes of learning such as interaction and sense of group cohesion. They also found that prior experience with the technology was the factor most closely related with course satisfaction and with completion of the course material. A combination of the students' perceptions of their levels of learning, the relevance of the material to their jobs, and their sense of cohesiveness explained a significant amount of variation in the levels of satisfaction with the course (Stonebraker and Hazeltine, 2004).

Based on interviews with companies and learning management system vendors, Claire Schooley, of Forrester Research, says that the critical success factors for an e-learning initiative are executive support, the learning staff, a mix of learning formats including face-to-face, engaging content, and easy-to-use technology (Schooley, 2009). Some of Schooley's recommendations are supported by the quantitative and qualitative research of Slotte and Herbert (2008). They studied 298 sales personnel and 37 sales managers participating in simulation-based virtual learning in Finland. They found that the blended learning design, accompanied by socially situated interaction, made the training much more successful.

Like Schooley, Aggarwal and Makkonen based their research on critical success factors on their personal experiences and the experiences of their colleagues, interviews with administrators and technical staff, and informal focus groups. They also received input from seminars, panels, and students. They grouped critical success factors for virtual learning into three categories. In the strategic category, they cite visionary senior management, planning for the initial investment, overcoming institutional resistance, and changing organizational culture. In the tactical category, they list building an e-learning team, realizing that one size does not fit all, developing a "custom-centric" approach, acknowledging that e-learning and e-teaching is not for everybody, and sharing knowledge through learning communities. In the operational category, they list creating an e-learning environment on the web, developing course content and management policies, thinking globally and acting locally, developing an e-learning infrastructure, and implementing an ongoing learning assessment process (Aggarwal and Makkonen, 2009).

Starke-Meyerring and Andrews managed a virtual learning project that included team members from different cultures. They recommend building interaction into all the instructional strategies, treating team members equally, and providing intensive mentoring, among other strategies. They also stress the use of appropriate technologies and strongly recommend at least one face-to-face meeting of the virtual team members (Starke-Meyerring and Andrews, 2006).

In a qualitative study of ten Hong Kong organizations, Chan and Ngai found the key factors influencing the adoption of virtual learning were the perceived benefits and costs, organizational readiness, and external pressure. They emphasize that success requires top management support, technically competent users, and the appropriate infrastructure (Chan and Ngai, 2007).

Many of the recommendations cited in this section seem clearly designed to counter the barriers or challenges to virtual learning identified in the previous section of this chapter. Many of the researchers agree on a number of strategies to help ensure the success of virtual learning. These include:

- The construction of a cohesive virtual community that provides interaction among the learners;
- A learning system that is flexible, customizable and adaptable;
- Quality content that meets employees' immediate needs;
- Appropriate technology infrastructure;
- Motivated employees with a sense of self-efficacy, competency, and autonomy;
- A learning environment that is easy to use;
- Managerial support;
- Good facilitators who can be mentors; and
- The inclusion of a face-to-face component in the training.

CONCLUSION

Overall, the conclusion is clear: Virtual workplace learning can be a successful technique for training employees in the twenty-first century. It has a number of benefits for both employees and employers. There are a variety of issues to consider when implementing virtual learning in the workplace, particularly in SMEs and less-developed countries. Research has identified, however, a number of factors that, if implemented, will contribute to the success of virtual workplace learning.

For companies, virtual learning can be cost effective, reusable, and provide consistency across a diverse workforce. It allows for more managerial control and accountability. It can enhance organizational learning and even be proffered as a benefit to prospective employees. Meanwhile, employees will find it adaptable to their needs, less stressful than a classroom environment, and offering great flexibility in time and place. Its content can be easily updated, taken in shorter bursts, targeted to immediate needs, and can increase employees' expertise, innovation, and engagement with their jobs.

At the same time, the characteristics of the learning systems, the workplace environment, and the employees must be taken into account when implementing virtual learning. Some important professional development topics may not be suited to virtual learning, the usability of the system must be maintained, and the pedagogical design of the training must be appropriate for the learners. Adequate technical and training staff must be available. The workplace must support virtual learning, both physically and culturally. Here, the support of key managers is critical.

Research has identified many critical factors that enhance the probability of successful virtual workplace learning. These include a vibrant virtual community, a flexible learning system with high quality content and appropriate technological infrastructure, employees who have the skills and motivation to use the system, good trainers, and the blending of virtual and face-to-face training. Here again, managerial support is vitally important.

Virtual workplace learning has not met every promise that has been made on its behalf; nor should it meet them. As with any tool, virtual learning has its appropriate uses. Just as traditional lectures are most efficient or effective to present some kinds of material while hands-on workshops are best for other types, so virtual learning has its place in the workplace training portfolio. As technologies such as simulation and virtual reality continue to develop, new varieties of virtual learning will appear that may broaden its reach. Employers willing to take care to implement virtual learning thoughtfully will reap its benefits, both for the company and the employees themselves.

REFERENCES

Aggarwal, A.K. and Makkonen, P. (2009) 'Critical Success Factors for Successful Globalised E-learning', *International Journal of Innovation and Learning*, 6(1): 92–109.

Alavi, M. and Leidner, D.E. (2001) 'Research Commentary: Technology-Mediated Learning – a Call for Greater Depth and Breadth of Research', *Information Systems Research*, 12(1): 1–10.

Ali, G.E. and Magalhaes, R. (2008) 'Barriers to Implementing E-learning: A Kuwaiti Case Study', *International Journal of Training and Development*, 12(1): 36–53.

Allan, B. and Lewis, D. (2006) 'The Impact of Membership of a Virtual Learning Community on Individual Learning Careers and Professional Identity', *British Journal of Educational Technology*, 27(6): 841–852.

Allison, S. (2007, September) 'E-learning in the Age of Multimedia', *e.learning age*, 20–21.

Alonso, F., Manrique, D. and Viñes, J.M. (2009) 'A Moderate Constructivist E-learning Instructional Model Evaluated on Computer Specialists', *Computers & Education*, 53(1): 59–65.

Ardito, C., Costabile, M.F., De Marsico, M., Lanzilotti, R., Levialdi, S., Roselli, T. and Rossano, V. (2006) 'An Approach to Usability Evaluation of E-learning Applications', *Universal Access in the Information Society*, 4(3): 270–283.

Bell, J. (2007) 'E-learning: Your Flexible Development Friend', *Development and Learning in Organizations*, 21(6): 7–9.

Birchall, D. and Giambona, G. (2007) 'SME Manager Development in Virtual Learning Communities and the Role of Trust: A Conceptual Study', *Human Resources Development International*, 10(27): 187–202.

Chambers, J.A. and Sprecher, J.W. (1980) 'Computer Assisted Instruction: Current Trends and Critical Issues', *Communications of the ACM*, 23(6): 332–342.

Chan, C.H. and Ngai, E.W.T. (2007) 'A Qualitative Study of Information Technology Adoption: How Ten Organizations Adopted Web-Based Training', *Information Systems Journal*, 17(3): 289–315.

Falconer, L. (2006) 'Organizational Learning, Tacit Information, and E-learning: A Review', *The Learning Organization*, 13(2): 140–151.

Gallaher, J. and Wentling, T.L. (2009) 'The Adoption of e-learning across Professional Groups', *Performance Improvement Quarterly*, 17(3): 66–85.

Githens, R.P. (2007) 'Older Adults and E-learning: Opportunities and Barriers', *Quarterly Review of Distance Education*, 8(4): 329–338.

Hiltz, S.R. (1986) 'The "Virtual Classroom": Using Computer-Mediated Communication for University Teaching', *Journal of Communication*, 36(2): 95–104.

Honey, P. (2001) 'E-learning: A Performance Appraisal and Some Suggestions for Improvement', *The Learning Organization*, 8(5): 200–202.

Hornik, S., Johnson, R.D. and Wu, Y. (2007) 'When Technology Does Not Support Learning: Conflicts between Epistemological Beliefs and Technology Support in Virtual Learning Environments', *Journal of Organizational and End User Computing*, 19(2): 23–46.

Keller, C. (2005) 'Virtual Learning Environments: Three Implementation Perspectives', *Learning, Media and Technology*, 30(3): 299–311.

Leary, J. and Berge, Z.L. (2007, Fall) 'Challenges and Strategies for Sustaining eLearning in Small Organizations', *Online Journal of Distance Learning Administration* 10(3). Retrieved February 6, 2009 from http://www.westga.edu/~distance/ojdla/fall103/berge103.htm

Lim, H., Lee, S. and Nam, K. (2007) 'Validating E-learning Factors Affecting Training Effectiveness', *International Journal of Information Management*, 27: 22–35.

Littleton, K. and Whitelock, D. (2004) 'Guiding the Creation of Knowledge and Understanding in a Virtual Learning Environment', *CyberPsychology and Behavior*, 7(2): 173–181.

Luarn, P., Chen, M.I.J., and Lo, P.K.Y. (2007) 'Critical Success Factors in Introducing E-learning', *International Journal of Information Technology and Management*, 6(2/3/4): 209–231.

Pancucci, D. (May 28, 2002) 'Finding the Right Blend', *Personnel Today*, 22–24.

Park, J. and Wentling, T. (2007) 'Factors Associated with Transfer of Training in Workplace E-learning', *Journal of Workplace Learning*, 19(5): 311–329.

Pearson, E. and Koppi, T. (2003) 'Essential Elements in the Design and Development of Inclusive Online Courses', *International Journal on E-Learning*, 2(4), 52–59.

Piccoli, G., Ahmad, R. and Ives, B. (2001) 'Web-Based Virtual Learning Environments: A Research Framework and a Preliminary Assessment of Effectiveness in Basic IT Skills Training', *MIS Quarterly*, 25(4): 401–426.

Rivera, R.J. and Paradise, A. (2006) *State of the Industry in Leading Enterprises: ASTD's Annual Review of Trends in Workplace Learning and Performance*. Alexandria, VA: American Society for Training and Development.

Roca, J.C. and Gagné, M. (2008) 'Understanding E-learning Continuance Intention in the Workplace: A Self-Determination Theory Perspective', *Computers in Human Behavior*, 24(4): 1585–1604.

Roy, A. and Raymond, L. (2008) 'Meeting the Training Needs of SMEs: Is E-learning a Solution?', *The Electronic Journal of e-Learning*, 6(2): 89–98.

Santos, O.C., Boticario, J.G., Fernández del Viso, A., Pérez de la Cámara, S., Rebate Sánchez, C. and Gutiérrez y Restrepo, E. (2007) Basic skills training to disabled and adult learners through an accessible e-learning platform, in *Universal Access in Human-Computer Interaction, Applications, and Services*. Berlin: Springer Berlin – Heidelberg. (pp. 796–805).

Schooley, C. (2009) The ROI of eLearning. Retrieved July 2, 2009 from Forester Research, Inc.: http://www.forrester.com/Research/Document/Excerpt/0,7211,53282,00.html

Servage, L. (2005) 'Strategizing for Workplace E-learning: Some Critical Considerations', *The Journal of Workplace Learning*, 17(5/6): 304–317.

Simmering, M.J., Posey, C. and Piccoli, G. (2009) 'Computer Self-Efficacy and Motivation to Learn in a Self-Directed Online Course', *Decision Sciences Journal of Innovative Education*, 7(1): 99–121.

Simmons, J. (2006) E-learning and earning: The impact of lifelong e-learning on organisational development, *European Journal of Open, Distance and E-Learning*. Retrieved January 28, 2009 from http://www.eurodl.org/materials/contrib/2006/Jane_Simmons.htm

Simon, M. (2009, January) 'E-learning No How', *T+D* 63(1): 34–39.

Slotte, V. and Herbert, A. (2008) 'Engaging Workers in Simulation-Based E-learning', *Journal of Workplace Learning*, 20(3): 165–180.

Starke-Meyerring, D. and Andrews, D. (2006) 'Building a Shared Virtual Learning Culture: An International Classroom Experience', *Business Communication Quarterly*, 69(1): 25–49.

Stonebraker, P.W. and Hazeltine, J.E. (2004), 'Virtual Learning Effectiveness: An Examination of the Process', *The Learning Organization*, 11(3): 209–225.

Tallent-Runnels, M., Thomas, J.A., Lan, W.Y., Cooper, S., Ahearn, T.C., Shaw, S.M. and Liu, X. (2006) Teaching courses online: A review of the research, *Review of Educational Research*, 76(1): 93–135.

Tsiantis, L.E., Stergiou, E. and Margariti, S.V. (2007) 'Security Issues in E-learning Systems', in Simos, T.E. and Marouis, G. (eds), *Computation in Modern Science and Engineering, Proceedings of the International Conference on Computational Methods in Science and Engineering 2007*: 959–964.

Tynjälä, P. and Häkkinen, P. (2005) 'E-learning at Work: Theoretical Underpinnings and Pedagogical Challenges', *The Journal of Workplace Learning*, 17(5/6): 318–336.

Ward, J.L. and Riley, M. (2008, August) E-learning: The cost-effective way to train in tough economic times, *Employee Benefit Plan Review*, 62(2): 12–14.

Weller, M., Pegler, C. and Mason, R. (2005) 'Students' Experience of Component Versus Integrated Virtual Learning Environments', *Journal of Computer Assisted Learning*, 21: 253–259.

Westbrook, V. (2006) 'The Virtual Learning Future', *Teaching in Higher Education*, 11(4): 471–482.

Wilson, B.G. (1996) *Constructivist Learning Environments: Case Studies in Instructional Design*. Englewood Cliffs, NJ: Educational Technology Publications.

25

Seeing Workplace Learning through an Emotional Lens

Brenda R. Beatty

The ubiquity of emotions in the workplace makes them an inevitable part of all workplace learning. Appreciation of this fact will someday be reflected in emotion's presence in every workplace learning chapter rather than in standalone chapters like this one. Nevertheless, as recently as fifteen years ago, emotion might not have found a place at all in a handbook such as the present volume. So we are making progress. This chapter is an invitation to consider emotion's place in learning at work. The first section explores the background to the depersonalised professional discourse that typifies so many organisations posing silent but deadly threats to workplace learning. The second section considers the role of emotion in learning theory with a focus on adult learning and development. The third section offers a discussion of some of the learning challenges facing workplace leaders. It presents empirically grounded findings and recommendations that position emotional meaning making as a powerful learning catalyst for these leaders, who, in turn, have a profound influence upon the social emotional conditions for learning experienced by all members of the organisation, including themselves.

SECTION ONE: RECOGNISING THE COST OF EMOTIONAL SILENCE: THE IRON CAGE OF BUREAUCRACY

The perspective on emotion's role in workplace learning in this chapter fits well with Antonacopoulou and Gabriel's (2001) three concepts of emotion: as a psychological state, as a perception of value or threat to something valued, and "… as transformation, i.e., an experience, an event which enhances understanding and provides meaning. Thus, emotion can be equated to thought, a way of seeing and reasoning described as a belief, a source of energy – a motivational phenomenon" (p. 436). Their treatment of an interweaving between social constructionist and psychoanalytical approaches to understanding emotion invites the reader to see learning as emanating from within, in response to social context cues in combination with embedded patterns of interpretation from psychological processing of life experience. For Antonacopoulou and Gabriel, "learning is a dynamic transformational process, continuously extended and re-defined in response to the context in which it takes place" (p. 439) involving release of knowledge and growth of the individual toward individuation. They note appropriately that learning is psychological work which involves tolerance for inevitable anxieties: "Learning represents a challenge and a threat to individuals, endangering some valued ideas, habits and beliefs about self and others and generating an unavoidable degree of discomfort and even pain" (p. 440). The agent of learning becomes critical here, as the mentor, teacher, guide is challenged by the need to create the safe place within which the adult may re-engage with the joy of learning. Love plays a role too: love of teacher, here or even oneself and ultimately the love of truth that "precludes any kind of sham or deception" (p. 440).

This framing of optimal conditions for learning in the workplace invite us to imagine the ideal; however, the reality is that organisational structures and processes often preclude the very conditions necessary for learning. In the typical processes of administering organisations the principle of precluding sham or deception could represent a confronting alternative to present practices of information control and perception manipulation typical of highly bureaucratic/hierarchical management protocols.

Weber's (1905) notion of the iron cage of bureaucracy demonstrates astute recognition that as organisations practise systematic depersonalisation to rationalise what goes on within them they become traps of our own creation. I go further to say that the depersonalisation and hyperrationalisation of policies and practices in bureaucratic organisations are denaturing and ultimately starving people and their organisations of critical opportunities for learning – from within themselves and with each other – learning that is required if we are to discover what we need to do differently *in place and in time*.

Bureaucratic hierarchies are ill suited for such learning responsiveness, characterised by sluggishness and a tendency toward retaining the status quo. Rischard (2008), argues that if we rely on bureaucracies to address global problem-solving, all will be lost. Instead we need flexible dynamic networks of acknowledged interconnectedness, that operate through the explicit recognition of the real experience of all living things, the whole planet, and the role of human organisations in maintaining or departing from the usual fare. If organisations are to reinvent themselves in light of the current realities that they both shape and reflect, they need to engender collective responsiveness to inner as well as outer crises such as climate change and conditions that make them vulnerable to global financial collapse. To be resilient and responsive to the need for change, organisations have to become workplaces that are collaborative learning communities, open to new learning at all levels, not rooted in bureaucratic stasis (Beatty, 2009a). The kind of change required, in contrast to the ways of thinking that created these problems, calls for new ways of seeing and being in the world. Workplace learning that builds on a foundation of acknowledgment for the lived emotional realities of the individuals within them can play a key role.

However, having institutionalised the self-denial of our own lived experiences, through the normative silence on matters of emotion, is it any wonder that acknowledgement of the interconnected nature of all systems remains well beyond the ken of most corporate organisations to date? We need new ways of thinking and feeling our way through to a more synergistic consciousness. This can only occur when sufficient trust develops so that people in new partnerships can embark on the learning journey together. We need to learn more about the deficits in former efforts as well as begin to establish new trajectories for a better future. By learning these things together, creating new socially and emotionally situated knowledge, members of any workplace can simultaneously, begin to make manifest the conditions for learning that are needed. To explore this approach, let us turn to our own lived experiences, and start by breaking the silence on emotion's place in the scheme of things.

Finding emotion's place

Emotions register within our embodied minds. They can remain private and hidden, even from the consciousness of the person experiencing them; be revealed inadvertently in body language, word choice or tone of voice; be deliberately displayed or "spill out", in spite of our efforts to suppress and hide them. In any case, emotions are experienced as a dimension of our internal state of mind and body.

Due to a phenomenon Denzin (1984) refers to as emotional infection, emotions can also be experienced collectively, as in crowd behaviour at rock concerts or riots, collective mourning at funerals or joyous celebrations of marriage. Collective emotions can also manifest in organisational/staff morale that reflects optimism, the opposite or something in between. The learning and sense of efficacy of groups are strongly linked and inextricably bound to the affective experiences of the individuals within them (Leithwood and Beatty, 2008).

It is this end, the collective learning life of organisations, that is the ultimate outcome of workplace learning research theory and practice. Yet all such learning also occurs within socially situated individuals alone and in connection with others. Emotions can be found, explored and understood by working at the individual level too. Since the learning and the emotions of groups, communities and entire organisations are experienced within the individuals that constitute them, this chapter focuses at this foundational individual level, where emotions dwell and where all learning begins (or fails to occur) and ultimately must manifest, one person at a time; this, with the caveat that it is the promotion of dynamic transformational learning throughout our organisations and our interconnected systems that is our ultimate goal.

One might hope for simplification through bifurcating the individual from the surrounding group and larger organisational milieu. In reality, however, it is important to accept that such separation is highly contrived. The individual – so called – is, in the phenomenological tradition, but one "object" among and inextricably linked to and shaped and reflected by many others. Thus when we speak of the individual or the self of an individual or the identity of an individual, of necessity we are at the same time speaking of a socially situated and socially constructed phenomenon. Perhaps this is making things more complex, rather than simpler, but such complexity needs to be acknowledged to make our way to the lens of emotion if we are to look through it to see workplace learning in new ways which are usually undiscussed and unconsidered.

Self-replicating, self-defeating mechanisms

Emotion is not regularly used to make sense of one's workplace or one's professional learning experiences, partly due to Western society largely ignoring emotional meaning making as a worthwhile endeavour, preferring the even more contrived and in terms of recent brain research misguided notion that emotion can be walled off from reason. The simple fact is we cannot have one without the other. Emotion has its root in the word 'emovere' to move. We cannot think without being moved to do so. Emotion provides motivation to do or not do anything at all. Emotion shapes how the lived experience is known, sensed or made viscerally evident to the embodied sensory awareness that is a dimension of our consciousness. Emotions are not optional; they play a continuously influential role in our consciousness, whether acknowledged or not. We also know from brain research that thinking and feeling occur simultaneously (Pert, 1998). The human mind operates through a continuously changing inner landscape (Damasio, 1997) that constitutes a seamless blend of thinking and feeling.

Most people learn quickly what is required of them in order to secure membership in their workplace organisations. Part of this largely incidental (Marsick and Watkins, 1991) learning involves the recognition of the local feeling rules (Hochschild, 1983) that define which emotional displays and attitudes will be rewarded and which ones punished. Despite an intuitive sense that thinking and feeling are hard to separate, this hasn't stopped us from developing and co-maintaining – socially constructing and co-constructing – our iron cage bureaucracies which are maintained through complicity with these norms and mores that respectively reward and punish compliance and departure from the organisational culture's expectations (Beatty, 2002). The emotional labour involved in perpetually masking and manufacturing emotions according to these expectations, ensures our continued organisational membership, something we desire or perhaps need in the sense as used by Maslow (1954).

Continuous emotional labour can also create a divided dis-integrated self, numb to its own health-regulating and health-restoring emotionality (Greenberg and Paivio, 1997). Gabriel (1993) has hypothesised that organisations themselves are merely constructions, ideas we use to stave off our existential anxieties (see also Fineman, 1993/2000). If remaining connected through emotional authenticity is important to our health, our collective survival and social evolution, the suppression of our actual lived emotional experience occurs at considerable cost. The vibrant relationship with one's real emotions also fosters our autonomous creativity. When personal autonomy is exchanged for membership that requires contrived denatured emotionality, fragmentation compromises the regenerative learning powers of individuals and collectivities. The image of a self-created iron cage is highly appropriate. A paradox of emotion and organisational membership lies in the dichotomy between the way people believe they must seem and the ways as highly functioning fully dimensional people, they need to be (Beatty, 2000a). It is important to distinguish between emotional control and the dangers of emotional numbness that can accompany it. To control the discourse within organisations, the threat of separation from lost membership is usually enough to silence the most independent. The costs of organisational membership can be high.

Workplace learning is susceptible to the same self-replicating pitfalls. Indeed if maintaining the status quo is the goal, it is probably better to avoid too much consciousness and certainly almost all references to emotion. A lack of consciousness about how our internal states are being negated and denied is critical for maintaining the constraints of compliance. Too much consciousness makes people wake up to the fact that they are occupying cells of their own creation. In contrast, workplace learning that is designed to promote renewal, regeneration, transformation and thereby, deeply creative organisational change, requires a level of consciousness, including emotional consciousness, that is anything but commonplace. This is workplace learning of a whole new dimension.

SECTION TWO: UNDERSTANDING EMOTION

We are our emotions. They are the lenses through which we experience the world. To understand emotions is to understand ourselves. As Hochschild argues,

> Emotion functions as a prism through which we may reconstruct what is often invisible or unconscious – what we must have wished, must have expected, must have seen or imagined to be true in the situation. From the colors of the prism we infer back what must have been behind and within it (Hochschild, 1983: 246).

The acknowledgement of the presence of emotion in all human endeavours makes intuitive sense. As Macmurray (1962: 75) argues, "The emotional life is not simply a part or an aspect of human life. It is not, as we so often think, subordinate, or subsidiary to the mind. It is the core and the essence of human life". Recognising the place of motivation, attitudes and feelings at the core of everything we do, Macmurray maintains:

> Any personal activity must have a motive and all motives are in the large sense, emotional. Indeed, an attitude of mind is simply an emotional state. The attitude of a scientist pursuing his vocation is, therefore, an emotional state. ... [If] the scientific state of mind were completely free of emotions, scientific enquiry could not be carried out. Further, if we identify this objective attitude with rationality, then it follows that rationality is itself an emotional state (Macmurray, 1962: 31–32).

According to Macmurray, emotion has a foundational role in the scientific state of mind, such that rationality itself may need to be reconceptualised. This has important implications for understanding all knowledge and thus all learning.

Exploring the professional silence on emotion

Workplace professionalism is often considered synonymous with being (or at least seeming) unemotional. While self-control and composure under stress remain critical capabilities, an attendant loss of connectedness with one's inner emotional meaning making processes and one's attunement to one's fellow organisational members can result. According to Hochshild's

(1983) study of airline attendants and bill collectors, the act of continuously engaging in the emotional labour of masking real feelings and projecting other emotions that one is not genuinely experiencing, causes emotional numbness. With emotional numbness, the rich resource of emotional meaning making can be rendered inaccessible. The unquestioning acceptance of a dehumanised/de-emotionalised definition of professionalism can also tear the fabric of the ethical self (Margolis, 1998). Without deliberate intervention to prevent it, a worker's integrated self is subtly but decidedly compromised (Kets de Vries, 1989).

> It seems clear that core organisational processes, such as communication, co-ordination, decision-making and problem-solving, entail both emotion and learning. However, many organisations systematically suppress emotion and/or block learning. It then becomes unacceptable to be seen to act in unpredictable or "emotional" ways or to admit to not knowing. Thus, some individuals can become what Kets de Vries (1993) describes as 'alexithmyc', denying all emotional experience or conflict and displaying a robot-like adherence to organisational routines which make them immune to any learning. (Antonacopoulou and Gabriel, 2001: 445).

How has this tradition of detachment, even shame (Scheff and Retzinger, 2000) about our emotional selves evolved? Historically the continuous processes of emotional inferencing have been denied and/or denigrated, despite their intrinsic relationship to the whole of human mind. Boler (1999) charts the history of this dichotomised relationship, claiming that reason and emotion have been separated in response to a deep-seated distrust of the receptive, intuitive dimension that is part of all human beings regardless of gender (see also Bem et al.,1976). Boler treats the artificial separation of reason and emotion generally as a multi-faceted manifestation of social control. Tracing its beginnings, she cites Bordo's (1987: 58) contention that the rejection of emotion is associated with the rejection of the feminine, resulting from the lost comfort of maternal "symbiosis and cosmic unity" that was enjoyed before the discovery that the Earth is not the centre of the universe. In Bordo's view, the resultant masculinisation of thought was a collective psychological response to separation anxiety and an attempt to regain control. As a consequence Boler (1999: 10) argues that today, "one finds the powerful Western confluence of femininity and subjectivity as a corruption to be transcended". This is a disturbing challenge which needs to be considered seriously. If the beginnings of the contrived separation between reason and emotion are themselves emotionally rooted then it is actually (emotional) denial that keeps the inherent importance of emotion's role unacknowledged and unconsidered! A reinforcing spiral of cause and effect emerges. Emotional reasons may have been responsible for emotion's relegation to the sidelines, then and now.

Woodward (1990: 3) also reminds us that even if we were to acknowledge them, "our vocabularies for the emotions are impoverished" asking, "If our language is so bizarrely truncated, what of our experience both in and out of the academy?" Further, what of our experiences in workplace learning, in theorising it, studying it, and practising it? With little proficiency in using language to describe our emotional lives, it is small wonder our understanding of its role in learning remains limited.

Ellis and Flaherty (1992) admonish the social science community for hierarchically positioning reason and objectivity above emotion and subjectivity. They argue this has created a distorted view of what we have and have not searched for and correspondingly, what we have and have not found. The repositioning of emotion as the complement of reason and a key ingredient in a different kind of meaning making, challenges us to acknowledge the inner realities of our experiences and to develop deliberately a legitimate place for the language of emotion in the workplace learning discourse, both in theory and in practice. Emotions in the end are epistemological, even if our institutions regularly filter out the acknowledgement of this way of knowing (Boler, 1999).

The denigration of emotion as feminine and/or inferior to, as well as separate from reason and/or masculinity, is also biologically misrepresentative. Recent brain research points to neurobiological evidence of an inherent error in the Cartesian dichotomising of reason and emotion. For Descartes, emotions happen to our souls, not to our thinking parts. His expression, "cogito ergo sum" or "I think therefore I am", depicted a separation of mind and body that has held the modern world in its grasp for centuries. Descartes' error lay in "the separation of the most refined operations of mind from the structure and operation of a biological organism" (Damasio, 1997: 250).

In contrast to Descartes' would-be separation of body and mind, reason and emotion, Damasio (1997: 144) describes the mind in terms of dynamic and interactive emotional processes, as "ceaseless change [in the] landscape of our bodies ... There are many maps coordinated by mutually interactive neuron connections". In effect, I would argue that one might just as appropriately declare, "I feel, therefore I am". Damasio's sequential, interactive model of emotion is a novel depiction of what goes on inside the "black box" of the human psyche:

> ... emotions and feelings may not be intruders in the bastion of reason at all: they may be enmeshed in its networks for better and worse ... feelings may be just as cognitive as other precepts (Damasio, 1997: xv).

No longer a question of mind or body: from this post-Cartesian perspective, even Western minds can begin to consider the body and mind as one. While the Western consciousness of this may be in its infancy, the wholeness of mind and body is foundational to Eastern philosophies and many indigenous peoples' perspectives. Research on human psychological and social processes, including theories of learning that acknowledge the importance of emotion, are ultimately not less, but more scientific. Perhaps now alternative pathways to understanding and exploring the lived experience of learning can take their place in workplace learning contexts.

Emotion's role in adult learning

Emotions are frequently considered unmentionable, despite the fact that they influence and even dominate what we do, see, learn and how we interact in the workplace. Seeing Workplace Learning through an emotional lens allows a better view of the learner in context and offers an improved way forward.

> Although emotion and learning can be studied as separate phenomena ... they are interrelated, interactive and interdependent, something that many organization and management studies tend to neglect.... Learning then is itself a deeply emotional process – driven, inhibited and guided by different emotions, including fear and hope, excitement and despair, curiosity and anxiety, organized in relatively long-lasting clusters (Antonacopoulou and Gabriel, 2001: 435, 444).

This is a vast topic. Learning in general is heavily dependent on emotion factors (Beatty, 2008). Considerations of emotional intelligence (Bar-On, 1988; Salovey and Mayer, 1990; Goleman, 1992) as a workplace factor, constitute a massive discourse itself. Ashkansky et al. (2005) and many others have now contributed extensively to establishing and extending the coalescence among studies in cognitive psychology and business. These studies deconstruct the inner workings of emotional patterns, tendencies and motivations to augment the arsenal of business tools for improved productivity. These discourses are not addressed *per se* in this chapter, although my commentary in this section crosses into this terrain at various points along the way. Rather, emotion's role in developing self, developing people, developing relationships and developing effective communication, all of which are profoundly important for fostering workplace learning among adults, is considered (Brew and Beatty, in press).

For over 15 years, organisations have been considered as emotional arenas and a focus for research and theory building by contributors like Fineman (1993/2000).

Organisational change is being considered in terms of emotion's influence on individual and collective openness to new learning (e.g., Antonacopoulou and Gabriel, 2001). Sociocultural theory which acknowledges the role of emotion in social process and interpersonal connectedness has begun to infuse our understanding of adult learning (e.g., Alfred, 2002; Fenwick, 2001). Workplace learning is also beginning to consider emotion's place in the scheme of things. For example, Tran (1998, p. 102) suggests that through the impact on organisational interactions, the emotional climate influences "idea generation and creativity, readiness and adaptability to change, and facilitation of learning processes. Hence it influences performance, both individual and organisational".

Merriam in, *A New Update on Adult Learning Theory* (2001: 1) revisits the traditional themes of andragogy, self-directionality, and the later transformational learning, characterising these and other advances in the field as an "everchanging mosaic". Since the establishment of Mezirow's (1991) transformational adult learning theory, the emphasis has shifted from what we know to how we know, and the importance of trusting relationships, feelings and context (Baumgartner, 2001).

Marsick and Watkins' (2001) model involving a progression of meaning making in practice that honours context and distinguishes among various incidental learning processes recognises informal and incidental learning. Hayes (2001) challenges patterns within essentialist gendered treatments of learning by proposing it is the learning situation that is gendered. Theories of situated cognition echo the context dependence of learning especially with respect to tools, and the qualities of social interaction that define communities of practice (Hansman, 2001). As Kilgore (2001: 54) explains, both critical and postmodern perspectives on learning define knowledge as taking form "in the eyes of the knower, rather than being acquired from an existing reality that resides 'out there'" even though critical theorists focus on political perspectives regarding systemic subjugation while postmodern theorists see all knowledge as "tentative, fragmented, multi-faceted, and not necessarily rational". The positioning of emotions and the images 'behind' them as fruitful for moving "toward a deeper, more conscious connection with these aspects of ourselves" (Dirkx, 2001: 69), echoes the call for deeper learning defined through qualitatively different kinds of engagement with the dynamic interplay among context, content and self. Such learning is fostered by the appreciation of recent research on the brain (Hill, 2001), somatic learning and the role of imagination in narrative learning or storytelling (Clark, 2001).

> Learning about one's emotions provides a useful starting point for recognising what causes these emotions and how they may be worked on, reconciled with and corrected. This in itself is the first step to freedom – moving out – to a new state of acting, behaving and being (Antonacopoulou and Gabriel, 2001: 445).

SECTION THREE: LEADING AND LEARNING THROUGH THE EMOTIONS

The emotions of the workplace and thus of workplace learning are as heavily influenced by leaders as by any other single factor. In order to improve capability and build the capacity of individuals and organisations, all persons in workplaces, especially leaders and managers, need to be or become open to acquiring new knowledge, skills and dispositions. The emotion factor is pivotal to achieving and sustaining such openness. What follows is a discussion of ways to optimise workplace learning by optimising the learning of the leaders. Such learning is essential. Leaders who experience the pressures of responsibility without the support and encouragement to work through the emotional processes involved in managing such pressures can become dangerously altered: dangerous to themselves, and dangerous to every member of their organisation (Mayer, 1993).

In a healthy emotional climate, people in organisations can experience connectedness in relationship with others. This is most likely to occur when individuals are able to retain at least a semblance of emotional connectedness with themselves. Deep understanding and self-acceptance extend far beyond skill sets and behaviours and well into a philosophical commitment to connectedness. Arguably then, a first step in workplace learning and development involves helping leaders become adept at reflective self-study in collaboration with others and through re-engagement with the complex, interconnected emotionally loaded web of their own experiential histories (Beatty, 2006).

Learning that occurs from and through experience represents one of four main sub-discourses of workplace learning identified by Garrick (1999). Emotionally challenging experiences are particularly important to re-experience, in order to learn and re-learn or to transform one's way of working. However, emotionally loaded sharing with professional colleagues about problematic experiences and moments of vulnerability is anything but typical. Even so, this is the sort of collaborative reflection that needs to occur. And it is particularly critical for leaders in order for them to discover the learning power of working through the lens of emotion.

Leaders who acknowledge emotion's power in their own professional lives are more inclined to make this possible for all organisational members (Beatty, 2007a). Only in acknowledging vulnerabilities do we discover these otherwise hidden portals for learning. Emerging here is the importance of emotionally safe spaces for such discoveries. Blackmore (1996) cautioned that fiscal reform jeopardised local school principals' former sense of safety for discussing their school concerns with each other due to changes in their educational market economy. Webber and Robertson (1998); Beatty and Robertson (2001) and Crawford (2001) have argued for the learning potential when leaders participate in electronically supported discussion groups. These views are consistent with Belenky et al.'s (1986/1997) argument for the transformational power of connecting and learning with peers. In their ability to bring peers together for shared meaning making, online discussion forums for groups of principals have supported emotional epistemological shifts from external to internal emotional knowledge authority (Beatty, 2002, 2005). This epistemological perspectival shift is a powerful part of the picture in considerations of workplace learning.

Workplace leaders need to facilitate successful face-to-face experiences within trusting collaborative learning communities. Workplace learning programmes can be designed to provide the structure and impetus for fostering these new ways of *learning with* others (Beatty, 2006). The concept of an emotionally safe space within which to come to terms with one's unfinishedness is particularly central to providing openings for new leader learning and genuine inquiry with others at all levels in the organisation. In essence, the leader needs to acquire a genuinely non-anxious presence (Friedman, 1985). Becoming a trustworthy leader is a critical part of the learning (Tschannen-Moran (2007). Leaders' attunement to worker issues such as satisfaction, morale, stress, anxiety is greatly enhanced by first-hand learning experiences with their own emotional meaning making patterns (Leithwood and Beatty, 2008).

While online environments can provide an anonymous and thereby much safer environment, conducive to transformation, if leaders are to re-culture their organisations with the people they encounter there, they also need successful face-to-face experiences within trusting collaborative learning communities. Workplace learning programs can be designed to provide the structure and impetus for fostering these new ways of *learning with* others (Beatty, 2006). The concept of an emotionally safe space within which to come to terms with one's unfinishedness is particularly central to providing openings for new leader learning and genuine inquiry with others at all levels in the organization. In essence, the leader needs to acquire a genuinely non-anxious presence (Friedman, 1985). Becoming a trustworthy leader is a critical part of the learning (Tschannen-Moran (2007).

Another part of what leaders and managers need to learn is what workers are experiencing. As Leithwood and Beatty discuss (2008), leaders need to learn about worker satisfaction and morale; stress, anxiety and burnout; individual and collective self-efficacy'; commitment and engagement. They need to appreciate the motivation to act and to learn with all of these things in mind. As explored in the final chapter of the book, leaders' attunement to these matters is greatly enhanced by first hand learning experiences with their own emotional meaning making patterns.

According to established learning organisation theory, all members of the organisation need to learn together and share in developing the organisation (e.g., Senge, 1990). From these collaborative experiences can emerge the next directions for learning and development of each organisational member and the organisation as a whole. As Vince (2001) suggests, however, individual learning within an organisation does not a learning organisation make. When managers block access between employees who serve different functions or in different departments, "then the organisation will not learn. These notions of employee involvement – now so central to thinking about increasing organisational performance – also turn out to lie at the heart of organisational learning" (Eraut and Hirsch, 2007: 63).

Once the work is redefined and more deeply understood in these ways, the discovery and exploration of new learning pathways usually calls for redesigning the organisation. Few leaders who do not understand their own emotions are likely to be able to 'get there from here'. The powerful self-replicating mechanism of bureaucratic hierarchy – that is the depersonalising 'professional' silence on matters of emotion – can undermine the best laid most elegantly conceptualised plans for workplace learning and organisational change (Beatty, 2000b). Leader learning can be fostered through a heightened awareness and understanding of their own internal states, especially their emotions, which represent the gateway to inner leadership, the place from which the most efficacious workplace learning for leaders, and therefore all others, begins.

Leaders, managers and workers who insist on the dignified entitlement to be a work in progress, can afford to share their fears, hopes and dreams and wonder aloud as they ask questions to which they do not yet know the answers. A critical aspect of workplace learning for organisational leaders then, is to establish a culture of inquiry within which workers are encouraged to wonder aloud, feel entitled to be imperfect, and thus safe to engage in critical self-reflection and collaborative explorations to generate new knowledge. Without experience in promoting no-risk innovative collaborations, it is less likely that persons in positions of authority will model such a view and create such safe learning spaces.

The provision of opportunities for learning to re-culture is a responsibility that leadership preparation and development programmes need to embrace. Leaders who are learning or re-learning their craft need to be supported in the emotional work required to understand and engage in the inner processes involved. Facing into and dealing with the anxiety associated with re-entering their own learning process is challenging for leaders whose insecurities have been buried and masked as part of their very professional identities. Consistent with theories of cooperative and collaborative learning is the recognition of interdependence within and among learners at all levels.

Learning about self and with others

Self-discovery is among the most critical pathways for developing and learning. Tools from psychology abound for understanding self and others. For instance, learning style inventories such as Kolb's (1986/1999) learning styles inventory; Myers-Briggs (1962) Jungian-based personality types; Salovey and Mayer's (1990) instrument to apply Reuven Bar-On's (1988) emotional intelligence, and many others, are used to provide lenses for learning about our similarities and differences. However, when such tools are used superficially, they can exacerbate the very conditions they are designed to address. When measurement and scoring are used to label and stratify, ironically, increased social emotional separation and fragmentation can result. Their apparent efficiency can tempt a managerialist, reductionistic usage, which can be counterproductive. When these instruments are used for building connections rather than creating further distances between people they can indeed be valuable and definitely do hold potential, especially for developing a shared appreciation for diversity.

Appreciation for diverse styles and perspectives can begin to slow down and unpack the knee jerk responses people tend to have to 'types'. Affinity for some and aversion to other (personality types) calls for deeper understanding, starting with one's own emotions. Ultimately, learning reciprocity is the ideal; that is, learning in an exchange of engagement and even caring, or what Noddings (1984) refers to as engrossment with the other. For open learning reciprocity to occur, again, we encounter matters of emotion.

In order to establish open learning reciprocity, one must be open to influence, to being emotionally "moved", to being vulnerable. All too often people move into illusions of self-sufficiency, control and power dynamics to manage the inevitable and often frightening experiences of vulnerability and movement into a power/control mode can lead to a relational pattern of entitlement, self pre-occupation, and failure of empathy in one person and accommodation, compliance and silencing in the other. While giving the appearance of connection, 'inauthenticity' and a deep sense of disconnection prevail. At its extreme, we see this pattern in many abusive relationships (Jordan, 1993: 1).

In typical hierarchical bureaucracies this cycle of distance and denial of vulnerability, or refusal to allow one's self to acknowledge actual vulnerability, can lead to the above noted cycle of abuse. Bullying that manifests from stonewalling to active aggression and open attacks is not uncommon among people in authority (see Blase and Blase, 2003). On the other hand, in organisational cultures where emotions are part of the official discourse, and respectfully integrated into the daily round, attunement to others' lived experiences and empathy for one's fellows foster attentiveness and active listening. In such receptive dispositions, much learning can occur. In my view, the importance of acknowledged vulnerability can hardly be overstated.

Leading the learning edge

Emotional meaning making creates common ground and universal entry points for learning no matter what one's beliefs, values, background or origins. The engagement of workers at all levels with issues of self-development and awareness of their inner ways of knowing is qualitatively different. Programmatic approaches to this terrain can be designed to engage different emotions, among them the rediscovery and celebration of joy in learning along with the acknowledgement of hurt, anger and shame. The willingness to embrace a pedagogy of discomfort (Boler, 1999) associated with facing into one's own fears (Beatty, 2006) is key.

For some time, images of self-awareness, self-discovery and personal transformation have been advocated for effective leaders (e.g., Bennis, 1989; Covey, 1990; Kouzes and Posner, 1993; Bolman and Deal, 1995; Bender, 1997; Loader, 1997; Gronn, 1999). Whether the personal journey is characterised in explicitly or implicitly affective terms this is emotional work, of the toughest kind. It takes courage to lead others by leading oneself in learning (Palmer, 1998). The engagement with learning for personal transformation requires emotional honesty and self-acceptance (Brill, 2000). Leaders who know themselves are far more likely to be able to listen to and learn with others in a non-defensive, non-aggressive way. Such leaders model a dynamic discovery learning process that is inherently transformational. Having faced their own anxieties and being fully aware of the normal presence of fear, leaders can, with the support of trusted colleagues, learn to face adversity and conflict with calm and self-acceptance. Furthermore, the non-anxious leader can access her/his own courage more readily when not fighting unacknowledged anxiety, shame and/or fear of shame (Scheff and Retzinger, 2000). It is in the acknowledgement of inner emotional realities and actual vulnerabilities that strength in self-awareness can be found. Leadership that goes beyond compliance management, the kind that dares to be creative, requires emotional awareness and connectedness with self and others (Bolman and Deal, 1995). Leaders who learn to learn in this way, are better prepared to create and maintain organisational conditions that foster workplace learning. The humility to resist the assumption that one knows what another is experiencing is part of a critical learning journey, for all members of highly functioning learning communities.

Without an expressivist discourse, a reigning 'culture of silence', on inner experiences can foster misrepresentations that confound connectedness and foreclose shared discovery with others. Learning about learning requires the valuing of internality.

By providing a conceptually 'bigger picture' of social and political patterns, within critical theory there are openings for adult learning that work through the lenses of social, economic and political identities. As Brookfield (2005: 5) notes, "theorizing is a form of meaning making, born of a desire to create explanations that impose conceptual order on reality, however artificial this order might later turn out to be." Brookfield links the power of critical theory in adult learning and teaching to Mezirow's (1991) theory of transformative learning as adults develop increasingly comprehensive and discriminating perspectives on how they see the world.

When a theoretical insight concerning hegemony (the process by which we embrace ideas and practices that keep us enslaved) helps us understand our practice in a new way, it often takes a great weight of potential guilt off our shoulders. There is no shame in admitting that we need theoretical insights to help us understand how the same destructive scenarios keep emerging in our lives, despite our efforts to prevent these. Without theoretical help, it is easy to see how many of our private troubles are produced by systemic constraints and contradictions (Brookfield, 2005: 5).

Emotional meaning making

Even though early experiences can inscribe our character types with emotional response patterns that are hard to change, by stepping around these patterns, and ignoring their significance, we may fail to engage with some of the deepest processes that influence all learning. Both psychoanalytic and social constructionist perspectives contribute to the understanding of ourselves as inextricably linked to our understandings and interpretations of others. The exploration of patterns in emotions and meta-emotions is worthy of explicit professional consideration as the quality of our relationships with ourselves and others relies upon it. Intellectual and emotional activities combine to create our views of ourselves and our world. Leaders need support in becoming emotionally prepared for their learning at work. There is an emotional development continuum that continues, or can continue throughout one's life. All workplace learning relies on the levels of emotional development of organisational members.

> Adults cannot be considered emotionally developed unless they understand the significance of emotion in representing their self-feelings, anticipate the effects of these feelings in a social context and identify and respond to feelings of others. Learning informs individuals of the ways they relate to others, allowing them to empathise and understand their emotions and enables them to take appropriate actions in pursuit of their aims. In effect, learning enhances understanding by allowing a reconsideration of one's emotional stance towards an issue and the opportunity to reconsider that emotion. Learning in the context of emotion implies a change in position, a reconstruction of one's way of perceiving and thinking (Kelly, 1955) (Antonacopoulou and Gabriel, 2001: 441–2).

Subconscious patterns in one's emotional responses tend to persist, resisting intellectual overrides to learned defences. However, as one's own emotional patterns become a source of curiosity and new learning, a greater range of choices emerges; about how to interpret situations, self and others. Thus, going through the emotions can release one from resistance to new learning. Adult development along a range of continua can continue throughout life, a shared understanding of which is very important for learning in the workplace (Glickman et al., 2009). Awareness of emotional choice is a kind of competence (Kolb, 1986).

Developing leaders who work through the lens of emotion

Theoretical points of departure can be helpful in promoting the re-examination of the role of emotion in working, learning and leading. For instance, the use of an emotional epistemologies theoretical framework within leadership preparation programmes has proven to be transformative (Beatty, 2002; Beatty and Brew, 2004; Beatty, 2006 and 2007b). The four-stance framework has been used implicitly and explicitly to make a range of perspectives apparent to learners: (1) the systemic prohibition upon the sharing and valuing of inner experiences (emotional silence); (2) the control and manipulation of behaviour through shaming and rewarding (emotional absolutism); (3) the discovery of potential for transcending disconnection and emotional numbness (transitional emotional relativism) and the deepening persistence in emotional ways of knowing (resilient emotional relativity). To explore ways of re-culturing organisations, one may simply change the feeling rules (Hochschild, 1983). By inviting emotional meaning making into daily workplace dialogues (Beatty, 2006) transitional emotional relativism is discovered and the continuous use of emotional meaning making becomes a way of being that fosters individual and collective resilience (Beatty, 2002, 2006). Emotional meaning making recognises that emotions need to be recalled, re-experienced, rediscovered and reflected upon. Assumptions about inferences made at the time of an emotionally memorable experience are revisited and questioned so that alternative perspectives on emotion's place in the intrapersonal, interpersonal and wider cultural spaces can emerge (Beatty, 2009b).

Ackerman and Maslin-Ostrowski's (2002, 2004) theory of the wounded leader elucidates the systemic likelihood of leaders being damaged in the act of disturbing the status quo. From their empirical work with school leaders, they present findings of a range of personal and professional impacts which help to make such events, and their results, transparent and shared. Findings are interpreted to suggest that the wound can become a potential opening for new learning, with sufficient support and attentive listening accompanied by caring feedback. This poses a transcendent opportunity inherent in emotional discomfort. Wounding is not confined to leadership. All workers have been wounded. Thus, while workplaces may be fraught with wounding events, by this theory, they are thereby also loaded with learning potential. By challenging the norm of silent suffering and permanent damage, and by deliberately creating a safe space for returning to the scene of the wounding, employees at all levels can connect with their colleagues' stories, and retrieve their own painful places. In sharing their stories with each other, the healing can begin, as a transformative process occurs. This is one of the ways that the personal professional and organisational dimensions of 'self' can be reintegrated (Beatty, 2000c, 2006).

Emerging theories that underpin the power of story in learning are fascinating. A brain-based approach provides the following explanation: When listening to a story, in the conscious, beta brainwave-emitting state, the language processing domain listens to the words, while the spatial visual domain fills in the pictures and affective material in a simultaneous and harmonious activity that blends thinking, seeing and feeling. Stories with multi-sensory detail are most easily remembered as they activate the fullest range of the brain's memory storage bases. As the story is told, and after, the mind searches for relationships, patterns and deeper meaning (http://storytelling.org.nz/spinoffs.htm). In sharing stories of inner experiences, all workplace learners can relearn how to listen and integrate new knowledge.

As in childhood, adults experience learning as an emotionally challenging process. Leaders who lead the learning in their workplaces need also to be mentors of a kind, people who confer upon learners Vygotsky's notion of the gift of confidence (Mahn and John-Steiner, 2002). Such leaders create conditions so that all adults in workplaces experience their surroundings as safe places to keep inquiring and continue developing, along the various adult learning continua. The leader attuned to this critical emotional dimension of her/his own learning and that of everyone in the organisation, can prioritise building trusting relationships and creating the conditions needed for continuous growth.

Our understanding of workplace learning is evolving. The reconsideration of shifts in epistemological perspectives on cognitive and emotional knowledge authority can assist in the discussion of leading edge redefinitions of workplace learning as dynamic inquiry and collaborative reflection (Beatty, 2009b and in press).

> … the need to encourage individuals within organizations to understand their emotions and to employ them constructively in their daily lives is one point on which psychoanalytic and other current accounts of emotions converge. Supporting individuals in gaining emotional understanding of themselves and others is seen as a vital part of organisational learning . . . the first step to freedom – moving out – to a new state of acting, behaving, being (Antonacopoulou and Gabriel, 2001: 445).

Both the human capital of individuals and the social capital of what individuals can learn and discover collaboratively, rely on relationships (Eraut and Hirsch, 2007). Relationships rely on emotions. Our understanding of workplace learning cannot afford to sidestep this critical connection.

REFERENCES

Ackerman R. and Maslin-Ostrowski, P. (2004) 'The Wounded Leader and Emotional Learning in the Schoolhouse', *School Leadership and Management*, 24(3): 311–328.

Ackerman, R. and Ostrowski, P. (2002) *The Wounded Leader: How Real Leadership Emerges in Times of Crisis*. San Francisco, CA: Jossey-Bass.

Alfred, M.V. (ed.) (2002) 'Learning in Sociocultural Contexts: Implications for Adults, Community, and Workplace Education', in *New Directions for Adult and Continuing Education, No. 96.* Winter, 2002. San Francisco, CA: Jossey-Bass. pp. 3–13.

Antonacopoulou, E. and Gabriel, Y. (2001) 'Emotion, Learning and Organizational Change', *Journal of Organizational Change and Management,* 14(5): 435–451. MCB University Press.

Ashkansky, N., Hartel, C.E. and Zerbe, W.J. (2000) (eds), '*Emotions in the Workplace: Research, Theory, and Practice*'. London, UK: Quorum Books.

Ashkansky, N.M., Zerbe, W.J. and Härtel, C.E.J. (2005) *Research on Emotion in Organizations: The Effect of Affect in Organizational Settings.* Elsevier/JAI series Volume 1.

Australian National Training Authority (2003) '*What Makes for Good Workplace Learning?'*, Adelaide SA:The National Centre for Vocational Education Research Ltd. http://www.ncver.edu.au/research/core/cp0207.pdf (Accessed 26/10/09).

Bar-On, R. (1988) The Development of a Concept of Psychological Well-Being, Unpublished Ph.D. dissertation. Rhodes University, South Africa.

Baumgartner, L. (2001) 'An Update on Transformational Learning', in *An Update on Adult Learning Theory,* Merriam, S. (ed.) Chapter 2: pp. 15–24. San Francisco, CA: Jossey-Bass.

Beatty, B. (2000a, Dec) *Emotion Matters in Educational Leadership.* Paper presented to the Australian Association for Research in Education, Sydney, Dec. 3–7, 2000. http://www.aare.edu.au/00pap/bea00445.htm (Accessed 26/10/09).

Beatty, B. (2000b) 'The Emotions of Educational Leadership: Breaking the Silence', *International Journal of Leadership in Education,* 3(4): 331–358.

Beatty, B (2000c) 'Teachers Leading Their Own Professional Growth: Self-directed Reflection and Collaboration and Changes in Perception of Self and Work in Secondary School Teachers', *International Journal of In-Service Education,* 26(1): 73–97.

Beatty, B. (2002) *Emotion Matters in Educational Leadership: Examining the Unexamined.* Unpublished Doctoral Dissertation, Ontario Institute for Studies in Education, University of Toronto, Toronto.

Beatty, B. (2005) 'Emotional Leadership', in *The Essentials of Leadership,* Brent Davies ed., Jan 2005. Corwin Press in the USA/ Paul Chapman Publishing UK: Sage.

Beatty, B. (2006) 'Becoming Emotionally Prepared for Leadership: Courage Counter-Intuition and Commitment to Connectedness,' *International Journal of Knowledge Culture and Change.* Volume 6.

Beatty, B. (2007a) 'Feeling the Future of School Leadership: Learning to Lead with the Emotions in Mind', *Leading and Managing.* 13(2): 44–65.

Beatty, B. (2007b) 'Going through the Emotions: Leadership that Gets to the Heart of School Renewal', *Australian Journal of Education,* 51(3): 328–340.

Beatty, B. (2008) 'Theories of Learning', in *International Handbook on the Preparation and Development of School Leaders.* G. Crow, J. Lumby, P. Pashiardis (eds), Erlbaum Publishers. pp. 136–162.

Beatty, B. (2009a) 'Toward an Emotional Understanding of School Success: Connecting Collaborative Culture Building, Principal Succession and Inner Leadership', Ch. 8 in *Australian Educational Leadership Today: Issues and Trends.* N. Cranston & L. Ehrich (eds), Australian Academic Press: 187–215.

Beatty, B. (2009b) Developing School Administrators Who Can Lead with the Emotions in Mind: Making the Commitment to Connectedness', Ch. 6 in *Canadian Educational Leadership.* Thomas Ryan (ed.), Detselig Enterprises Ltd. pp. 149–183.

Beatty, B. and Robertson, J. (2001, Apr) *Leaders Online: Emotions and Educational Leadership in the Context of Online Discussion Groups.* Paper presented at the Annual Meeting of the American Educational Research Association, Seattle, Washington, April, 2001.

Beatty, B. and Brew, C. (2004) 'Trusting Relationships and Emotional Epistemologies: A Foundational Leadership Issue', *School Leadership and Management,* 24(2): 329–356.

Belenky, M.F., Clinchy, B.M., Goldberger, N.R. and Tarule, J. M. (1997) *Women's Ways of Knowing: The Development of Self, Voice and Mind* (2nd edn). New York: Basic Books.

Belenky, M.F., Clinchy, B.M., Goldberger, N.R. and Tarule, J.M. (1986) *Women's Ways of Knowing: The Development of Self, Voice and Mind.* New York: Basic Books.

Bem, S.L., Martyna, W. and Watson, C. (1976) 'Sex Typing and Androgyny: Further Explorations of the Expressive Domain', *Journal of Personality and Social Psychology,* 34(5): 1016–1023.

Bender, P. (1997) *Leadership from Within.* Toronto: Stoddart.

Bennis, W. (1989) *On Becoming a Leader.* Reading, MA: Addison-Wesley.

Blackmore, J. (1996) 'Doing "Emotional Labour" in the Education Market Place: Stories from the Field of Women in Management', *Discourse: Studies in the Cultural Politics of Education,* 17(3): 337–349.

Blase, J. and Blase, J. (2003) *Breaking the Silence: Overcoming the Problem of Principal Mistreatment of Teachers.* Thousand Oaks, CA: Corwin Press.

Boler, M. (1999) *Feeling Power: Emotions in Education.* New York: Routledge.

Bordo, S. (1987) *The Flight to Objectivity: Essays on Cartesianism and Culture.* Albany: State University of New York Press.

Bolman, L. and Deal, T. (1995) *Leading with Soul.* San Francisco: Jossey-Bass.

Brew, C. and Beatty, C. (in press) 'Valuing Social and Emotional Connectedness among Learners at All Levels: Creating New Kinds of Conversations for Resilient Relationships', in R. Toomey & T. Lovat (eds), *Handbook of Values Education and Student Wellbeing.* Dortrecht: Springer Press.

Brill, R. (2000) *Emotional Honesty and Self-acceptance: Educational Strategies for Preventing Violence*. USA: Xlibris.

Brookfield, S. (2005) *The Power of Critical Theory for Adult Learning and Teaching*. Berkshire, UK: Open University Press.

Clark, J. (2001) 'Of Writing, Imagination, and Dialogue: a Transformative Experience', in P. Cranton (ed.), *Transformative Learning in Action. New Directions for Adult and Continuing Education*, No. 74. San Francisco: Jossey-Bass.

Covey, S.R. (1990) *Principle-Centered Leadership*. New York: Summit Books.

Crawford, M. (2001, April) *King John's Christmas: Developing Leadership Communities on Line*. Paper presented at the Annual Meeting of the American Educational Research Association, Seattle, Washington State.

Damasio, A. (1997) *Descartes' Error: Emotion, Reason and the Human Brain* (2nd edn). New York: Harper Collins.

Denzin, N. (1984) *On Understanding Emotion*. San Francisco: Jossey-Bass.

Dirkx, J. (2001) 'The Power of Feelings: Emotion, Imagination and the Construction of Meaning in Adult Learning', Ch. 7 in *The New Update on Adult Learning Theory*. No. 89 (Spring). S. Merriam (ed.), pp. 63–72.

Ellis, C. and Flaherty, M. (eds) (1992) *Investigating Subjectivity*. Newbury Park, CA: Sage Publications.

Eraut, M. and Hirsch, W. (2007) *The Significance of Workplace Learning for Individuals, Groups and Organisations, SKOPE Monograph 9*, Oxford, UK: Oxford University Department of Economics Economic and Social Research Council. 96pp.

Fenwick, T. (2001) 'Tides of Change: New Themes and Questions in Workplace Learning', in T.C. Fenwick (ed.), 'Sociocultural Perspectives of Learning through Work', in *New Directions for Adult and Continuing Education,* No. 92. San Francisco, CA: Jossey-Bass. pp. 3–18.

Fineman, S. (ed.) (1993) *Emotion in Organizations*. London: Sage Publications.

Fineman, S. (1993) 'Organisations as Emotional Arenas', in S. Fineman, (ed.), *Emotion in Organizations*. London: Sage Publications. pp. 9–35.

Fineman, S. (ed.) (2000) *Emotion in Organizations* (2nd edn). London: Sage Publications.

Fineman, S. (ed.). (2008) *The Emotional Organization: Passions and Power*. Oxford: Blackwell.

Friedman, E.H. (1985) *Generation to Generation*. New York: The Guilford Press.

Gabriel, Y. (1993) 'Organizational Nostalgia: Reflections on "The Golden Age"', in S. Fineman (ed.), *Emotions in Organizations*. Thousand Oaks, CA: Sage. pp. 118–141.

Gabriel, Y. (1999) *Organizations in Depth: The Psychoanalysis of Organizations*. London: Sage Publications.

Garrick, J. (1999) 'The Dominant Discourses of Learning at Work', Ch. 14 in *Understanding Learning at Work*, D. Boud and J. Garrick, (eds), New York, NY: Routledge. pp. 216–231.

Glickman, C., Gordon, S. and Ross-Gordon, J. (2009) *Supervision and Instructional Leadership: A Developmental Approach* (8th edn). New Jersey, NY: Prentice-Hall.

Goleman, D. (2006) *Social Intelligence: The New Science of Human Relationships*. London: Random House.

Greenberg, L. and Paivio, S. (1997) *Working with Emotions in Psychotherapy*. London: Guilford Press.

Gronn, P. (1999*) The Making of Educational Leaders*. London: Cassell.

Hansman, C. (2001) 'Context-Based Adult Learning', Ch. 5 in *The New Update on Adult Learning Theory*. No. 89 (Spring). S. Merriam (ed.), pp. 43–51.

Hayes, E. (2001) 'A New Look at Women's Learning', Ch. 4 in *The New Update on Adult Learning Theory*, No. 89 (Spring). S. Merriam (ed.), pp. 35–42.

Hill, L. (2001) 'The Brain and Consciousness: Sources of Information for Understanding Adult Learning', Ch. 8 in *An Update on Adult Learning Theory* S. Merriam, (ed.). pp. 73–82. San Francisco, CA: Jossey-Bass.

Hochschild, A.R. (1983) *The Managed Heart: The Commercialization of Human Feeling*. Berkeley: University of California Press.

Jordan, J.V. (1993) *Challenges to Connection. Work in progress No. 60*. Wellesley, MA: Stone Center Working Paper Series.

Kets de Vries, M. (1989) 'Alexithymia in Organizational Life: The Organizational Man Revisited', *Human Relations*, 42(2): 1079–1093.

Kilgore, D. (2001) 'Critical and Postmodern Perspectives on Adult Learning', Ch. 6 in *A New Update on Adult Learning Theory*, Sharan Merriam, (ed.). pp. 53–62.

Kolb, D. (1986/1999) *Learning Style Inventory, Version 3*. Boston, MA: Hay Group, Hay Resources Direct.

Kouzes, J. and Posner, B. (1993) *Credibility: How Leaders Gain and Lose It, Why People Demand It*. San Francisco, CA: Jossey-Bass.

Leithwood, K. and Beatty, B. (2008) *Leading with Teacher Emotions in Mind*. Thousand Oaks, CA: Corwin Press, Sage Publications.

Loader, D. (1997) *The Inner Principal*. London: Falmer Press.

Macmurray, J. (1962) *Reason and Emotion*. New York: Humanity Books.

Margolis, D.R. (1998) *The Fabric of Self: A Theory of Ethics and Emotions*. New Haven: Yale.

Mahn, H. and John-Steiner, V. (2002) 'The Gift of Confidence: A Vygotskian View of Emotions Learning for Life in the 21st Century', Ch 4 in *Sociocultural Perspectives on the Future of Education*. G. Wells and G. Claxton (eds), West Sussex, UK: Blackwell Publishing.

Marsick, V. and Watkins, K. (1991) 'Envisioning New Organizations for Learning', Ch. 13 in *Understanding Learning at Work*, D. Boud and J. Garrick (eds). New York, NY: Routledge. pp. 199–214.

Marsick, V. and Watkins, K. (2001) '*Informal and Incidental Learning*', Ch 3 in *The New Update on Adult Learning Theory*. S. Merriam (ed.), San Francisco: Jossey-Bass. pp. 25–34.

Maslow, A. (1954) *Motivation and Personality.* New York: Harper & Row.

Mayer, J.D. (1993) 'The Emotional Madness of the Dangerous Leader', *Journal of Psychohistory.* Volume 20: pp. 331–348.

Merriam, S. (2001) *The New Update on Adult Learning Theory.* San Francisco, CA: Jossey-Bass.

Mezirow, J. (1991) *Learning as Transformation: Critical Perspectives on a Theory in Progress.* San Francisco CA: Jossey-Bass.

Myers-Briggs, I. (1962) *The Myers-Briggs Type Indicator Manual.* Princeton, NJ: Educational Testing Service.

Noddings, N. (1984) *Caring: A Feminine Approach to Ethics and Moral Education.* Berkeley: University of California Press.

Palmer, P. (1998) *The Courage to Teach.* San Francisco: Jossey-Bass.

Pert, C. (1998) *Molecules of Emotion.* New York: Scribner.

Rischard, J. (2008) High Noon: The Urgent Need for New Approaches to Global Problem-Solving and the Role of Education Institutions. Keynote address ACEL *New Metaphors for Leadership in School.* Annual International Conference Melbourne Sept 30–Oct. 2.

Salovey, P. and Mayer, J.D. (1990) 'Emotional Intelligence', *Imagination, Cognition and Personality.* 9: 185–211.

Scheff, T.J. and Retzinger, S.M. (2000) *'Shame as the Master Emotion of Everyday Life',* Journal of Mundane Behaviour http://www.mundanebehavior.org/issues/v1n3/scheff-retzinger.htm (Accessed 26.10.2009).

Senge, P. (1990) *The Fifth Discipline.* New York: Doubleday.

Tschannen-Moran, M. (2007) 'Becoming a Trustworthy Leader', Ch 8 in *The Jossey-Bass Reader on Educational Leadership (2nd Edition)* (pp. 99–114). San Francisco CA.: Jossey-Bass.

Tran, V. (1998) 'The Role of the Emotional Climate in Learning Organizations', *The Learning Organisation,* 5(2): 99–103.

Vince, R. (2001) 'Power and Emotion in Organizational Learning', *Human Relations,* 4(10): pp. 1325–1351.

Webber, C.F. and Robertson, J. (1998) 'Boundary Breaking: An Emergent Model for Leadership Development [Electronic version]', *Educational Policy Analysis Archives,* 6(21). http://olam.ed.asu.edu/epaa/v6n21.html

Weber, M. (1905/2002) *The Protestant Ethic and the Spirit of Capitalism and Other Writings.* Trans P. Baehr & G. Wells. London, England: Penguin Books.

Woodward, K. (1990) 'Introduction (Special Issue on Discourses of the Emotions)', *Discourse: Journal for Theoretical Studies in Media and Culture,* 13(1): 3–11.

Young, I.M. (1997) 'Asymmetrical Reciprocity: On Moral Respect, Wonder, and Enlarged Thought', *Intersecting Voices: Dilemmas of Gender, Political Philosophy and Policy.* Princeton, NJ: Princeton University Press.

26

Towards a Social Ecology of Adult Learning in and through the Workplace

Karen Evans, Edmund Waite and Natasha Kersh

The ways in which adults learn in and through the workplace are rooted in educational trajectories and their complex intertwining with social institutions (of labour market, workplace, community) and social roles (of employee, citizen, family member) at different stages of the life-course. The usefulness of the social ecology metaphor is that it provides a way into understanding the complexity of factors that impact directly or indirectly on education and lifelong learning without losing sight of the whole. Every contextual factor and every person contributing or influenced is part of a complex ecology, a system of interdependent social relationships that is self-sustaining. Applications of ecological conceptualizations are found in studies ranging from macro-level analyses of organizations to ecologies of the inner workings of social groups. Recent applications to educational policy-making attempt to make visible the complexities of policy processes as interdependent and political, to incorporate 'the messy workings of widely varying power relations, along with the forces of history, culture, economics and social change' (Weaver-Hightower, 2008). According to Weaver-Hightower's overview, the four categories of *actors, relationships, environments and structures, processes* lie at the heart of social ecological analyses. These differ in the degree of significance that is accorded to personal agency, through which actors 'depending on their resources and power, are able to change ecological systems for their own benefit' (p. 156) Because ecologies are self-sustaining through interdependencies that operate without centralized controls, individuals and groups have spaces in which to exercise agency in ways that can influence the whole dynamic, through the interdependencies involved. While applications in policy studies sometimes focus on the ways in which resistance is exercised through the collective agency of (for example) teachers' unions or pressure groups, more often than not the account shows how agency is eventually 'squeezed out' through the power relations that operate over time in favour of those most powerfully placed.

Another family of approaches that has adopted a social-ecological metaphor starts with the 'learning individual' as the unit of analysis, in social psychological research (Bronfenbrenner, 1979) or, more recently, in the context of life-course research (e.g., Biesta et al., 2007). Biesta et al. argue that people do not act *in* structures and environments – they act through them. This resonates with conceptualizations of agency as bounded rather than structured (Evans, 2002). People's beliefs in their ability to change their situation by their own efforts, individually or collectively, are significant for the development of skills at work and beyond (Evans, 2002). These beliefs change and develop over time and according to experiences in the labour market and beyond. The ability to translate these beliefs into action is achieved rather than possessed (Biesta and Tedder, 2007) and capabilities are limited by bounds that can be loosened (Evans, 2002, 2007).

LEARNING AND DEVELOPMENT IN WORK ENVIRONMENTS

Fenwick's analyses (Fenwick, 2008a, 2008b and Chapter 23 in this volume) of learning and development in rapidly changing work environments argue for examination of the 'whole system at play': how employees interact and work together, how language is used and cultural meanings are constructed in and through organizational structures and how knowledge circulates within them. Hodkinson et al. (2004) have argued that individual agency is best understood when individual worker/learner perspectives are built into the dominant social–organizational view of learning at work. This perspective is integral to the central thesis of *Improving Workplace Learning* (Evans et al., 2006) which has revealed through an integrated programme of research that three scales of activity have to be kept in view. At the 'macro' level, wider social structures and social institutions can be fundamental in enabling or preventing effective learning from taking place. This includes the legal frameworks that govern employees' entitlements, industrial relations and the role of trade unions as well as the social structuring of business systems. In the latter, Whitley (2000) has shown how work systems in different countries contrast in the ways they structure and control how work is allocated and performed and rewarded: '… these systems are linked to the nature of firms, interest groups, and dominant governance principles or "rules of the game" in different societies, which in turn stem from different patterns of industrialization.' (2000: 88).

At the intermediate scale of activity, the nature of the learning environment in the organization can expand or restrict learning (see Fuller and Unwin, 2004). Establishing cultures that support expansive learning environments is problematic. For most employers, workers' learning is not a priority and a lower-order decision. As Hodkinson and Rainbird have noted, first-order decisions concern markets and competitive strategy. These in turn affect second-order strategies concerning work organization and job design. In this context, workplace learning is likely to be a third-order strategy (see also Keep and Mayhew, 1999). This means that improvements to workers' learning always have to be balanced against other priorities. The interdependencies of interests play out as senior managers exert influence over the culture of an organization and its approach to supporting workplace learning. These affect the expectations of managers, trainers, employees, and their representatives. However, corporate expectations are rarely transmitted into practice in large and complex organizations, as workforce development policies 'as espoused' at the top of the organization often depart substantially from workforce development as enacted by middle management and may be far removed from the development and support actually experienced by employees, particularly those in low-graded jobs.

For the individual worker, their past experiences, dispositions and present situation will affect the extent to which they take advantage of the opportunities afforded by their immediate work environment. These factors change over time. Professionals and other highly qualified workers are more likely to have access to continuing training and professional development than less-qualified workers (Aldridge and Tuckett, 2006) and are more likely to experience work environments that are rich in opportunities for learning, than workers in lower-level jobs. The challenge is to create the conditions in which all workers can take advantage of all these kinds of opportunities, as set out in Evans et al. (2006). One mechanism may be through entitlements to learning, established in law, through collective bargaining, or through the interventions of enlightened managers, trade unionists, trainers, and co-workers. Another mechanism is to build worker confidence through the recognition of tacit skills, discussed in more detail by Evans and Kersh (2006). One of the pitfalls of identifying these three scales of activity is that they become fixed levels of analysis. Instead it is more appropriate to keep the three scales in view in the same way that one might in 'zooming in and out' in internet maps, in ways that keep the interdependencies in view (see Evans et al., Chapter 11 in this volume). In this way, work on communities of practice can be understood in the context of the social relations of the workplace and the contradictory and antagonistic aspects of the employment relationship.

The ways in which employees can themselves, individually or collectively, influence their employment and life chances in and through the workplace environment have been documented through previous and current research. These have to be understood as part of a wider dynamic, keeping in view the macro organizational and policy environments and the interdependencies set up within and beyond the workplace. This has to include the recognition that workers are both part of the work system and have lives outside it; they are engaged in multiple overlapping structures and 'communities of social practice' that can themselves be analysed in terms of social-ecological interdependencies.

How adults at the lower end of the earnings distribution act through the environments of work and work-related learning is a theme running throughout this chapter. Starting from Economic and Social Research Council longitudinal research into the effects on individuals and organizations of workplace literacy programmes, this chapter aims to show how a social ecology of learning develops and can be supported with reference to three further sets of new evidence; first from motivations of adult learners in using technologies in work and in related learning; second, in research into adults' experiences of the interplay in formal and informal learning; third, in attempts to model interrelationships in ways that enable practitioners and learners to design interventions and plan for change.

THE WORLD OF WORKPLACE 'BASIC SKILLS'

The educational and labour market policy context in England has generated an unprecedented level of state support for workplace basic skills programmes as part of a national strategy. Substantial government funding, through the channels of the Learning and Skills Councils (LSCs), Regional Development Agencies (RDAs) and the Union Learning Fund (ULF) has given rise to a wide range of literacy, numeracy and ESOL provision across all sectors of the economy and public sector. These include discrete literacy, numeracy and ESOL courses in the workplace; literacy and numeracy embedded in IT, and in vocational and job-specific training as well as LearnDirect courses undertaken in online learning centres in the workplace. The absence of evidence about the effects on learners and organizations of participation in such provision prompted longitudinal research into 'Adult Basic Skills and Workplace Learning'[1] sponsored by UK Economic and Social Reseach Council from 2003. This research is now exploring (2009–11) the effects on individuals and on organizations of engagement in work-place basic skills programmes over time. It has been designed longitudinally to gain longer-term perspectives and deeper insights into both the trajectories of learners and the features of the organizations and workplaces than are possible through short-term evaluations.

Workplace basic skills courses successfully implemented under the UK national strategy in place from 2002 onwards have typically provided a standard, initial 30 hours of instruction in or near the actual work-site; have focused predominantly on literacy, are often built around the use of computers ('Laptops and Literacy' is a typical title) and use teaching material that is generalist rather than directly related to occupations. What happens to the employees that may be related to their learning experiences, and what happens in the company/organization that may be related to the existence of the learning programme? Quantitative analysis of a range of outcomes (measured progress in basic skills, employment, attitude inventory changes, etc.) have been combined with qualitative analyses of transcribed interviews and in-depth studies carried out in selected organizations. The rationale for employing in-depth interviews in addition to structured questionnaires[2] includes the need to collect more detailed, narrative-based biographical data, to allow for the analysis of more subjective aspects of the learning experience (e.g. effect of previous learning experience, motivation/confidence, stigma surrounding poor basic skills, social capital, etc.) and to pursue the broader organizational context in terms of organizational case-studies. The in-depth interviews add to the longitudinal dimension of the research in that they ask the respondent to think about past, present and future in their learning experiences and use of skills at work, and are themselves followed up periodically.

Findings have shown how adult employees' experience of learning is rooted as much in biographical experience as in the contexts of workplace activity and culture.

Many of the learners' experience of workplace learning can be described as 'compensatory' in nature in so far as they are frequently seeking to 'make up' for negative educational experiences in the past. The cases studied provide differing examples of how workplace courses can respond to employees' shifting attitudes to learning (Evans and Waite, 2009; Wolf and Evans, 2011). The combined data showed that:

- workplace programmes are successful in enrolling adults with very little or no previous experience of formal post-school learning;
- the most important general outcome of course participation, a year on, is an increase in learners' confidence: most noticeably in work, but also outside work;
- the outcomes which learners expect from courses are, more often than not, different from the outcomes they actually report afterwards.

BRINGING TOGETHER TWO DIFFERENT PERSPECTIVES

The research has brought together two different perspectives on the literacy levels of employees: the assessment scores which offer an independent measure of literacy as a set of skills, and the learners' own perceptions of whether they are coping or struggling with their existing skills. Indeed, several employees indicated they struggled to carry out aspects of their job as a result of poor literacy skills. Yet, as reported in Evans and Waite, 2009, 2010, we have also identified many examples of employees who have coped sufficiently in the workplace with their existing skills, in which case the literacy component of the course is often viewed as a chance to 'brush up' on their skills.

Workplace courses can play an important part in engaging individuals who would otherwise be intimidated by studying in a college. There are advantages and disadvantages of undertaking a course in the workplace as opposed to a college. From the learners' perspectives, the overriding majority of employees have emphasized such factors as accessibility, familiarity and convenience as being key advantages of workplace learning. Other factors of major significance include the differing environments for learning in different organizations (including diverse strategies for promotion).

Current research on adult literacy in the UK has tended to be shaped by differing epistemological approaches. Those who advocate the importance of researching literacy as a 'social practice' – emphasizing the social context of literacy usage – tend to employ qualitative methods framed by more relativist, hermeneutical perspectives. The concept of literacy itself is dissolved into a plurality of literacies shaped by differing contexts (see, for example, Street, 1995; Papen, 2005). These perspectives tend to contrast with UK government reliance on quantitative data on literacy that implicitly assumes an 'autonomous' rather than 'ideological' model of literacy (Street, 2001) in so far as literacy is perceived as a clearly defined set of technical skills the absence of which can impact negatively on an individual's economic and social opportunities. We viewed differing research perspectives on literacy that tend to coalesce around either quantitative or qualitative research methodologies as potentially useful avenues for exploring varying facets of literacy rather than as being the intrinsic components of sharply divided and irreconcilable epistemological traditions. The employment of mixed methods allowed for a more detailed exploration of how literacy is actually employed in differing contexts, putting the researchers in a position to take issue with assumptions underpinning the dominant 'Skills For Life' national discourse about the existence of large-skill deficiencies in literacy and numeracy that inevitably impact negatively on performance at work. This enabled the pursuit of a more nuanced approach that illustrates the diverse range of techniques that are employed in literacy practices whilst highlighting those cases where skills deficiencies exist.

The evidence yielded by mixed methods approaches suggests that it is more productive to think beyond the polarized conceptualizations of literacy and numeracy learning as either technical skills development or the expansion of social practices, towards a more ecological understanding of the phenomena observed. A 'social ecology' of learning in the field of workplace basic skills leads us to consider, with the three scales of activity outlined above in view (zooming in and out), the relationships between affordances of the workplace (or those features of the workplace environment that invite us to engage and learn), the types of knowledge afforded by literacy and numeracy learning (including knowing how and 'knowing that you can') and the agency or intention to act of the individual employee, reflected in their diverse motivations.

TRIANGULAR RELATIONSHIPS

These are triangular relationships and mutually interdependent sets of interactions. There are affordances for learning in all workplace environments. Some are more accessible and visible than others. The intention of employees to act in particular ways in pursuit of their goals and interests, whether in their jobs or personal lives, makes the affordances for learning more visible to them.

Shifting orientations to learning and efforts to compensate for early educational disadvantage allowed some employees to recognize and seize opportunities for learning within the workplace. The know-how associated with literacy practices such as report writing or finding better ways of expressing oneself, and the confidence of 'knowing that you can' often develop further as the person engages with the opportunity. For example, a caretaker involved in estate maintenance for a Local Authority experienced a surge of confidence in response to his enhanced capacity to cope with writing letters and reports at work, which provided enhanced learning opportunities through increased exposure to these duties. The process of making the affordances for learning more visible itself can generate some employees' will to act and use those affordances, and new knowledge results. In shifting orientations to learning, the changing levels of know-how and the confidence that comes from 'knowing that you can' both stimulate action and the seeking out of affordances within and beyond the workplace in the form of further opportunities. Literacy learners at work progressed to further courses, ranging from computer/IT training to creative writing courses. Some have accessed multiple online courses at company learning centres, which are indicative of an increased yearning for a wide - range of learning opportunities that have grown out of initial participation in workplace literacy and related programmes. Even where redundancy follows, as in several of the cases researched, the change in learning orientation is sustained, allowing the individuals to adapt to and enhance the quality of their life in these new circumstances.

These reflexive relationships, as the cases considered in this chapter illustrate, point the way forward in developing a better understanding of literacy learning as part of a wider social ecology of adult learning in workplace environments that foregrounds worker agency.

One particular framework is that of Eraut, summarized in this volume (see Chapter 13), regarding the factors that affect workplace learning. Based on a series of large- and small-scale projects investigating informal learning in the workplace, Eraut (2004) described the triangular relationships of learning factors and context factors. Of particular interest to this study is the interplay among confidence, challenge and support. In this context, confidence is linked to a view of agency not as a fixed attribute but as an orientation that changes as the individual successfully meets challenges in everyday work routines that require learning. At the same time, as Billett (2006) and Evans et al. (2006) have shown, the exercise of agency personalizes work by changing and shaping work practices.

However, this confidence to take on new challenges is dependent on the extent to which workers feel supported not only by a 'superior' but also through supportive co-worker relationships. As Eraut (2004) points out 'if there is neither a challenge nor sufficient support to encourage a person to seek out or respond to a challenge, then confidence declines and with it the motivation to learn' (p. 269). As opposed to identifying productivity gains relating to both formal and informal training it may be more advantageous to better understand employee job satisfaction and engagement with the workplace. A wider framework for understanding the organizational context also shows that interventions have to accommodate both employee and employer interests. The involvement of employee representatives contributes to the expression of employees' interests and can reassure them that business gains will not necessarily have a negative impact on jobs and conditions of employment (Rainbird et al., 2003). While learning needs to be seen as an integral part of practice rather than as something that is added on, attention needs to be paid to the environment as a whole; for example, the work environment affects how far formal learning can be a positive trigger for further learning and vice versa. A short-term timeframe and a narrow view of learning, dominated by measurable changes in performance, is unlikely to foster either engagement with learning or creativity. The affordances of the workplace (or those features of the workplace environment that invite us to engage and learn) are enhanced or limited according to the wider ecologies embedded and reflected in the employment relationship.

'USE IT OR LOSE IT': THE SIGNIFICANCE OF EMPLOYING LITERACY SKILLS IN THE WORKPLACE

The longitudinal dimension of 'Adult Basic Skills and Workplace Learning' has entailed undertaking literacy assessments at three intervals, as part of the tracking of longer-term impact of courses as well as the impact of shifting organizational structures on the uses of literacy and related work skills. Those learners whose literacy assessment scores have increased since engagement in the course have continued to use their literacy skills whether at work or at home. The work environment affects how far formal learning can be a positive trigger for the learning through day-to-day work and other social practices. The actual career events that can potentially follow on from engagement in learning can be categorized as progressive (e.g. promotion, planned move to a better job); upwards drift (gradual enhancement of work, overcoming difficulties, increased responsibilities); downwards drift; stagnation; interruption (see Evans and Waite, 2009).

Those learners interviewed in-depth who had made most literacy gains between the first and second literacy assessment[3] had generally continued to develop their literacy skills in the workplace and beyond. For example, in the case of a weapons manufacturing company, the learner whose level of literacy had improved most substantially in that organization had been promoted after the course and now actively used a wider range of literacy skills as part of a broader organizational shift towards the delegation of responsibility to lower-level employees. Whereas during the Time 1 in-depth interview he attached little significance to the literacy component of the course, at the Time 2 in-depth interview he retrospectively valued his participation in the course in the light of his recent promotion.

> I realise that it (the literacy component of the course) was quite an important part...before I wasn't really writing too much, and now obviously I use it a lot more, do more handwriting as well as on the computer.

Other learners we interviewed in this organization who had not benefited from these structural changes within the organization and had not been promoted and continued to engage in the same working routines (which entailed minimal use of literacy) made either no progress or negligible gains in their literacy scores. For example, Roger Taylor, who was doing the same type of job, continued to have minimal exposure to literacy practices and whose literacy score declined between Time 1 and Time 2 literary assessments, reported the following: 'I've never been particularly good at the English side of things ... I feel like I'd like to improve it but I don't find it necessary in what I do. I don't do an awful lot of writing.'

In our overall sample, learners have made modest literacy gains as a result of engaging in literacy courses. This finding is understandable in light of the short duration of the courses and their relatively light exposure to employment of literacy and numeracy skills in the workplace. Those learners for whom English was not their first language ('ESOL') made larger, significant gains in their measured literacy. This too is consistent with the 'use it or lose it' principle, since these employees are on a rather different 'learning curve' from native English speakers. They experience challenge and opportunity in practising their developing English language skills in everyday activities in rather different ways.

This underlines the fact that ultimately the development of such skills rests on their employment in practical work settings, a finding that is further substantiated in significant correlations[4] between growth in literacy scores and 'job change' found in the wider sample, where 'job change' refers to taking on new responsibilities or additional tasks within an existing role as well as taking on a completely new role at work.

UNDERSTANDING THE INTERPLAY OF LEARNING EXPERIENCES IN CONTEXT – BEYOND THE 'FORMAL' AND 'INFORMAL'

The examination of reflexive relationships as part of a social ecology leads as a next step into rethinking some existing frameworks for understanding the relationships between 'formal' and 'informal' learning at work. The majority of workers in the literacy programmes outlined above reported increased confidence as an outcome of participation in these type of courses (see for example, Evans and Waite, 2009; Tett and MacLachlan, 2007; Kell, 2009). Some of these employees drew on their newly acquired confidence, which arose out of participation in a course of structured teaching and learning activities, in order to seek out opportunities to embark on 'informal learning' in everyday work settings. This applied in different cultural settings, as shown by comparisons between UK and Canadian workplace programmes in the interplay of formal and informal learning and the uses of literacy at work (Taylor and Evans, 2009).

While there has been much definitional agonizing in this area, this has not significantly advanced understandings of learning in these different dimensions. Indeed, Jacobs and Park (2009) have argued that while the terms have their own validity and continue to have meaning, they represent 'incompatible levels of discourse' (p. 133) that unduly constrain thinking on the broader entity of workplace learning. This may explain why research itself tends to bifurcate, focusing either on social practices at work or on the processes and impacts of 'formal' training and courses rather than the interplay between these processes.

The Taylor and Evans 2009 study has provided new evidence on the nature and scope of 'training' activities for basic-level employees, highlighting the interplay of informal and formal learning by tracing the structuring of decision making and training characterized as 'informal' in nature as well as the significance of formal programmes in generating increased motivation for further learning through diverse channels.

Viewing workplace informal learning as part of the job (Boud and Middleton, 2003) can obscure the origins of the workplace skills and knowledge involved as well as the importance of their facilitation. Attempts to capture these elements have led researchers such as Ellinger (2004) to examine the concept of self-directed learning and its implication for human resource development. She acknowledges the benefits of self-directed learning in the workplace as relevant to both organizations and individual workers. Taylor and Evans (2009) show that SDL is a fundamental component of some types of informal learning: 'Searching Independently for Information' and 'Practicing without Supervision'. Ellinger suggests that integrating SDL into HRD requires that the teacher or trainer match the learner's stage of self-direction. For those learners who are relatively dependent, a more traditional approach to instruction is initially, to prepare learners for increasingly higher stages of SDL. Terry (2006), Livingstone (1999) and Livingstone et al. (2008) have also found that adults often require more learning support at the beginning of a structured learning opportunity, but self-direction gradually increases with confidence and engagement. Yet workplace informal learning is not limited to independent mastery of work procedures, but encompasses the relationships between employees (as learners as well as workers), context and opportunities. For example, Taylor and Evans (2009) found that informal learning can also result from "Mentoring or Coaching" as well as participating in "Focused Workplace Discussions" or committees, all of which entail the complex interplay of employee agency, workplace relationships and interdependencies and the affordances of the wider environment. These variables in some cases promote rich informal learning, for example, where 'doors are opened' to opportunities to expand and share knowledge and skills in supportive workgroups. In other cases, workplace discussions and mentoring/coaching can have unintended negative influences on learning, for example, where the interdependencies of the workplace are undermined by feelings of a lack of trust. Sociocultural understandings of ways in which knowledge and learning are constructed from social interactions in the workplace (see Billett, 2006; Fenwick, 2008a) problematize simplistic versions of 'self-directed' learning in ways that make visible the interdependencies inherent in workplace practices and environments. These observations add to the argument that, while learning needs to be seen as an integral part of practice, the practice is itself integral to organizational dynamics that limit or facilitate its richness as a vehicle for learning.

ADULT ENGAGEMENT IN WORK-RELATED LEARNING: HOW FAR DO TECHNOLOGIES ENHANCE AFFORDANCES FOR LEARNING WITHIN AN ECOLOGICAL APPROACH?

Many adults in work or seeking to re-enter paid employment want to sustain and develop their capacities to use rapidly changing IT and digital technologies. This applies to employees with varying levels of skills and qualification in the workforce. Turning to the experiences of adult learners aiming to improve their employment prospects through work-related learning,[5] both learners and the tutors recognize the potential benefits of capability with new technologies. They also notice that all types of the modern technologies need to be implemented carefully taking into account learners' individual interests and backgrounds. Some adults may need more training and support before they can actually feel confident to use the modern technologies (such as e-mail, Internet or Virtual Learning Environments) within their learning or workplace settings. Some need more time to get used to the new technologies. As noted by an adult learner who combined her studies with part-time work:

> I'm generally quite resistant to checking out new things, especially when they are technology. Also, when I get home I don't necessarily want to be looking at a computer screen, having done it for the day.

Our evidence suggests that if employees' interests and situations are not taken into account, the modern technologies may provide barriers to learning and, as a result, undermine motivation. Tutors' support plays an important role in the process of supporting people into using the technologies for the benefit of their learning.

Interpreted in terms of a social ecology of learning, important interdependencies become apparent. The motivational factors related to the use of new technologies are often contextually specific and they can take different roles in different learning or workplace contexts. The factors that could facilitate students' motivation in a college environment might actually hinder their progress in a workplace environment. These negative repucussions can occur as a result of a variety of factors such as restrictive learning environments, lack of supervisory support for the learners and poorly developed training materials on how to use a particular piece of software or electronic equipment. Such factors and conditions may combine to undermine the learners' motivation not only towards the use of the technologies but also in terms of creating adverse consequences for their general skills and competence development in the workplace. As Francis Green's work shows, increasing use of technologies in the workplace does not of itself drive up the levels of employees' skill and knowledge, the demand for which also depends fundamentally on workplace organization and the company strategy for employee involvement (Green, 2009).

Tutors may employ a number of methods and approaches to help adults to surface and recognize those capabilities that they already have and to reduce barriers to learning. Team work, one-to-one tutorial help and encouraging learners to help their fellow-learners have been identified as the methods that may help to uncover tacit skills and to enhance motivation. The provision of space and time to 'step' back and 'look at the things you do' are also important:

> What motivates me personally is I do enjoy learning, the process. And I do think it will be useful because [...] when you are in the working environment, you are very much coping with the day-to-day demand and you don't have time to step back and think about it. So seeing this, coming on this course, rather, gives you that insight, almost stepping back and looking at things you do at work more objectively (Interview with adult learner).

Interventions can and do support learning and motivation if the conditions and dynamics, personal and organizational, are right. That their impact is always uneven and their take-up often 'patchy' is unsurprising, given the complexity of workplace dynamics. Can interventions be designed in the context of the complex interdependencies of workplaces be anything better than 'hit or miss affairs'?

THE ACHIEVEMENT OF AGENCY THROUGH ENVIRONMENTS: CAN CONCEPTUAL MODELLING TOOLS FACILITATE IT?

In this section we turn to the question of how far interdependencies can be modelled in ways that can support the design of interventions. Interventions can range from input of resources for a new induction programme to a change in company policy. In this instance we focus on the relatively neglected area of interventions to enhance worker agency, with the wider social ecology in view.

So far, an ecological approach has been useful in describing chains of interdependencies that are set up when adults exercise their personal agency and motivations through environments and in relation to the human, technological and material affordances for learning. The tools available for designing approaches that aim to enter the chains of interdependency through the enhancement of worker agency are rather limited. They include 'self evaluation' check lists that are too often lists deficits that do anything but empower (see Evans and Niemeyer, 2004; Evans, 2009). They also include appraisal systems, some of which aim to institutionalize, in individualized ways, the spaces in which worker agency sometimes operates collectively and informally (e.g., in reciprocal feedback on performance of managers) or in resistance to planned changes.

An earlier paper (Evans et al., 2004) showed how conceptual modelling can be used as a research tool in carrying out systematic case comparisons in contrasting educational and workplace environments. These studies apply the Dynamic Concept Analysis modelling method (Kontiainen, 2002) for computer-assisted building of conceptual models[6] to give a comprehensive picture of how employee and workplace characteristics are likely to become interrelated. This method serves not only as a tool for research as shown in the 2004 study but can also be used as a tool that practitioners or tutors can use to plan interventions, assist workers and learners in evaluation of their personal or collective situation and assess the qualities of learning environments.

Kersh et al. (2008) have shown how this application can be used to plan interventions that focus on developing competences in the learning process itself. In consultation with an adult about her learning processes as represented in her personal model, hypothetical changes can be made when seeking directions towards more favourable outcomes. Learners can be assisted to self-evaluate their capabilities in the context of a specific activity, choosing attributes that best describe to what extent they feel they posses or can use particular competences in their work environments. In practice, the learner selected one attribute under each concept to characterize her own qualities. On the basis of students' responses, use of the tool builds models that graphically represent: (1) the extent to which learners possess certain skills or abilities; and (2) the ways the skills are related (or not related) to other skills or variables.

The models provide an illustration of the learners' level of use, recognition and development of competences, indicating links between various competences and suggesting how (through what activities/via what contexts) learners potentially may develop their capabilities. The modelling process enables learners not only to self-evaluate their own capabilities and attributes at a particular time but also to simulate various potential positive changes that can assist in their own development and that of their environment. Learners would use their individual models as a basis that would suggest: (1) the level (e.g. high, medium or low) of their skills and competences; and (2) through which activities or contexts they may use or develop their capabilities in desired directions. Taking the leading role in analysing and assessing their own models allows adult learners to uncover potential benefits and outcomes through a self-assessment process that they can themselves control and influence. For example, following interviews with a group of adult learners undertaking a course *"Women in Management"* *adults were asked to* evaluate their own skills and abilities in the context of "Discussion group" activity. Their responses were analysed and models were produced (see Kersh et al., 2009) reflecting their personal skills and defining interrelationships among the concepts.

As a first step, an adult student selects a combination of attributes to characterize her own central skills as related to a particular learning experience, in this case the 'Discussion group'. Secondly, a conceptual model for her combination of attributes is produced for interpretation and discussions with the student. Thirdly, if some changes seem to be needed in order to achieve more satisfactory results, a change of one or more attributes may be indicated. Simulations with new attribute combinations and new models may show new directions for change. Simulation involves changing, hypothetically, an attribute of a concept in a particular case (e.g. changing an attribute for 'listening' from 'medium' to 'high'). On the basis of the new data a simulation model can be produced that graphically represents how different qualities interact in a new model. Kersh et al. (2009) show how two different models can be produced for each case. Figure 26.1 below illustrates the initial model produced with an adult learner, and a simulation that shows how the model could change with a new attribute combination.

These methods aim to provide insights that can support learners in moving towards intentional evaluating of their personal competences and to reflect upon links and interrelations between their competences, experiences and the environments in which they are engaged. Self-evaluation of personal skills and competences in the context of the activities, tasks and environments has a number of practical benefits. Apart from enabling the learners to reflect upon their capabilities, it also provides them with the ideas of how (through what activities/ tasks/exercises) and with whose support they can develop these further. At the same time, self-evaluation in the context of activities may help the learners to understand better what particular attributes could be employed successfully to help them to succeed in a specific activity, task or environment. By demonstrating the possibilities for 'recontextualisation' (see Evans et al., 2009) of what is learned from a variety of experiences, such an approach can facilitate the learners into recognition and use of their tacit skills and personal competences.

As a modelling approach, this offers potential tools[6] for individual or collective self-evaluation, exploring links and relations in ways that allow development to be considered. The analysis can be adapted easily to personal, organizational or combined aims and goals and is best undertaken as a co-operative activity. The examples considered have demonstrated how these methods could be employed for different goals. Graphical representation of the self-evaluation of personal skills provides a visible illustration of learners' levels of skills' use, recognition and development, indicating links between various attributes, activities and environments and thus

Model 1: Modelling of an adult learner's case (pseudonym: Margaret Casey)

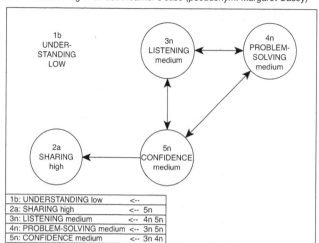

1b: UNDERSTANDING low	<--
2a: SHARING high	<-- 5n
3n: LISTENING medium	<-- 4n 5n
4n: PROBLEM-SOLVING medium	<-- 3n 5n
5n: CONFIDENCE medium	<-- 3n 4n

Margaret Casey describes her sharing skills as high (2a) in the context of this activity. As the Model 1 indicates, her medium confidence (5n) contributes to her high level of sharing skills (2a). While self-evaluating her personal competences in the context of this activity she argued that her listening (3n) and problem-solving skills (4n) reflect positively on her confidence (5n), thus contributing further to developing her sharing skills (2a). The model indicates that there are a number of links and interrelationship among her skills that enable her to develop her capabilities in this activity. However, the analysis of the model indicates that understanding of others is not fully used/developed in the context of the discussion groups activity. Her understanding within this activity is low (1b) and it appears isolated within this model. She admitted that she is not confident about understanding some terms used within the class discussion. The simulation with Margaret Casey's model (see Model 2) suggests that by developing her understanding skills from 1b (low) to 1n (medium) she will maintain and use further her listening and problem-solving skills. The simulation model shows that, potentially, her medium listening skills (3n) reflect positively on her understanding (1a). Understanding (1n) is now described as medium and it is better integrated into the model. The simulation of her model shows that her higher understating (1n) reflects also positively on her confidence (5n) and problem-solving skills (4n) thus contributing to her active participation in this activity. It focuses attention on how to improve understanding so that this change can be facilitated in practice.

Model 2: A simulation with MC's model – a potential change

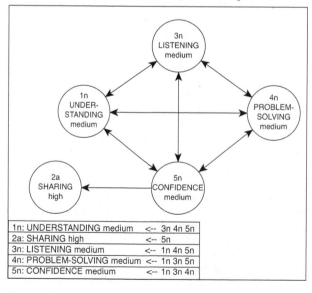

1n: UNDERSTANDING medium	<-- 3n 4n 5n
2a: SHARING high	<-- 5n
3n: LISTENING medium	<-- 1n 4n 5n
4n: PROBLEM-SOLVING medium	<-- 1n 3n 5n
5n: CONFIDENCE medium	<-- 1n 3n 4n

Figure 26.1 Conceptual models in use for self-assessment

suggesting how (through what activities) adult workers and learners may potentially develop in the direction they desire. For tutors and practitioners this could also be potentially beneficial in terms of planning and implementing changes to the employee support that is offered.[7] In these ways, making visible the links between personal skills and certain tasks, activities and environments may play an important role in facilitating the worker's agency in relation to the learning affordances of the workplace.

Evans et al. (2006) have noted that even the best individually oriented programmes for adult workers have only partial success, and this is a recognition of reality, not a cause for despair. Understanding and modelling 'what is facilitating what' in any particular environment is, at one level, a research process. Uncovering 'what (and who) is facilitating (or impeding) what' collaboratively with the actors in that environment is itself an intervention in the social ecology; in the contingencies of the workplace actors can influence the interdependencies in ways that can make particular desired outcomes more or less likely.

CONCLUSIONS

This chapter has presented several different scenarios in which a social ecological approach can help to elucidate the dynamics of learning in and through workplace environments and work-related experiences. These have focused on literacy learning, workplace practices and the uses of technology in enhancing work-related and earning capabilities. The potential of tools that can be used for conceptual clarification and for exploring the 'fuzziness' of interrelationships of workplace learning requires further work. Added to the practical uses of the expansive-restrictive continuum (see Unwin and Fuller, 2003) for assessment of the dimensions of workplace environments, tools such as Dynamic Concept Analysis can assist, in the exploration of any given workplace learning environment, to explore the interrelationships between attributes and qualities of that environment and the ways in which actors exercise their personal agency through that environment.[8]

As well as capturing the learning affordances and barriers that are active in work environments, a social ecological analysis has also to extend to factors beyond the workplace. For workplace ecology the interdependencies already mapped by Evans et al. (2006) in *Improving Workplace Learning* highlight the dynamics of three scales activity – macro-organizational, political, regulatory, cultural.

Ways in which agency can be achieved and exercised by 'ordinary workers' through the workplace environment have been documented through previous and current research. These have to be understood as part of a wider dynamic, keeping in view the macro organizational and policy environments and the interdependencies set up within and beyond the workplace.

While learning needs to be seen as embedded in practice, the wider environment and lives out-side and beyond work have to be kept in view. Keeping in view the three scales of activity – organizational, political, regulatory/cultural – while focusing on the agency, personal and collective of workers, leads us to see some social ecological possibilities for development. Although much of the policy debate assumes that what is good for business is also good for employees and for society, the pluralist framework of industrial relations (Rainbird et al., 2004), recognizes the conflict inherent in the relationship between workers and managers. This conflict, held to be inevitable, stems from different interests, trajectories and power bases. Achieving cooperation in the context of potentially conflictual relations requires active management (Edwards, 2003: 12) from middle managers who frequently find themselves in positions of having to foster creativity while controlling performance. In the positive view of active management, as identified by Geary (1995), strategies to win over employees' hearts and minds by fostering employees' wider involvement in the affairs of the enterprise can bring about new forms of work organization. Both Geary (1995) and Hyman and Streeck (1988: 4) view the assumptions that harmonious relations will be forged through these new structures of work with scepticism.

Yet the shift from 'training' to 'workplace learning' that itself involves locating learning in social relations at work does expand the spaces for the exercise of worker agency, as the strivings for 'hearts and minds' are played out. In the workplace literacy programmes, for example, managers were most interested in the potential of programmes to raise morale and strengthen the 'psychological contract' between firm and employee. Improving workplace learning means paying attention to what people want and need, and to the different expressions of interests that come from work groups differently located in the social landscapes of the organization and labour market. Employee voice plays a greater part in new management strategies, and can enable managers to bring about a better equilibrium of interests. In the end, however, expanding and improving learning at work in these ways involves evaluations of the balances of advantage involved in enhancing the qualities of the broader environment, recognizing that the organization's *raison détre* is the production of goods or services rather than learning *per se*. The benefits yielded by improving the workplace learning environment have to be balanced with consideration of the wider effects of such changes on other legitimate interests in the workplace. As Hodkinson and Rainbird (2006) have noted 'the eventual decisions about precisely how a particular learning environment can be improved will entail recognition of these different interests and whether mutual benefits can be identified' (p. 172).

In some of the scenarios discussed in this chapter, the balance of advantage in providing for workers at the lower end of the skills distribution had already been established, and these programmes tended to survive long-term. When no such balance had been identified or thought through, the programmes foundered as soon as short-term incentive funding became unavailable.

These social processes involve interdependencies in which workers can and do exercise an influence in changing the social ecology of the organization in ways that can potentially benefit both, yet the interdependencies involved extend far beyond the workplace both for the workers themselves and the organization. It is to further questions of the ways in which neighbourhood, labour market and community interdependencies play out in the life chances and livelihoods of workers and the trajectories of organizations that social ecological approaches will next have to turn.

NOTES

1 This research, part of the UK's Economic and Social Research Council's Teaching and Learning Research Programme (TLRP) and subsequently the ESRC LLAKES Centre programme (Award No RES-139-25-0120 and co-sponsored in its initial stages by the National Research and Development Centre for Adult Literacy and Numeracy (NRDC), has provided a framework within which the realities of adult basic skills learning accessed through the workplace can be explored longitudinally.

2 The research employs structured interviews with 564 learners (as well as managers and tutors) from 55 organizations in a variety of sectors. Between two and four interviews of subsamples have been conducted at intervals over a seven-year period. Each learner was assessed early in the course using an assessment tool that has been especially designed to take account of small changes in literacy development. We have also conducted in-depth interviews with a sub-sample of 64 learners from 10 of the sites.

3 Appearing in the 'top' quartile, indicating learners who had made improvements between Time 1 and Time 2 literacy assessments.

4 See Evans and Waite (2010) in press.

5 Included in an extension to the ESRC research, carried out through the WLE Centre, Institute of Education, University of London. Interviews were carried out.

6 The computer software developed by Seppo Kontiainen is available at http://www.edu.helsinki.fi/dca where it can be downloaded free of charge.

7 The potential has been identified (Kersh et al., 2009) for incorporation of the self-evaluation tool across various courses or training programmes. Tuition for groups of practitioners on how to use the method may assist practitioners in mastering the principles and the use of the associated computer software.

8 For example, the social dynamics in using or losing literacy gains through use in practice are being modelled through follow-on work in the ESRC LLAKES Centre by Evans, Waite and Kersh.

REFERENCES

Aldridge, F. and Tuckett, A. (2006) *Skilling Me Softly: A NIACE Briefing on Learning at Work.* Leicester: NIACE.

Biesta, G. and Tedder, M. (2007) 'Agency and Learning in the Lifecourse: Towards an Ecological Perspective', *Studies in the Education of Adults,* 39(2): 132–149.

Billett, S. (2006) *Work, Change and Workers*, Dordrecht: Springer.

Boud, D. and Middleton, H. (2003) 'Learning from Others at Work: Communities of Practice and Informal Learning', *Journal of Workplace Learning,* 15(5): 194–202.

Bronfenbrenner, U. (1979) *The Ecology of Human Development: Experiments by Nature and Design.* Cambridge: Harvard University Press.

Edwards, P. (ed.) (2003) *Industrial Relations: Theory and Practice* (2nd edn). Oxford: Blackwell.

Ellinger, D. (2004) The concept of self-directed learning and its implications of human resource development. *Advances in Developing Human Resources,* 6(2), 158–177.

Eraut, M. (1994) *Developing Professional Knowledge and Competence.* London: Falmer Press.

Eraut, M. (2000) 'Non-formal Learning, Implicit Learning and Tacit Knowledge, in F. Coffield, (ed.), *The Necessity of Informal Learning.* Policy Press in association with the ESRC Learning Society, Bristol.

Eraut, M. (2004) 'Informal learning in the workplace', *Studies in Continuing Education,* 26(2): 247–273.

Evans, K. (2009) *Learning, Work and Social Responsibility: Challenges for Lifelong Learning in a Global Age.* Dordrecht: Springer.

Evans, K., Hodkinson, H., Rainbird, H. and Unwin, L. (2006) *Improving Workplace Learning,* New York and Abingdon: Routledge.

Evans K. (2002) 'Taking Control of Their Lives: Agency in Young Adult Transitions in England and the New Germany', *Journal of Youth Studies,* 5(3): 245–269.

Evans, K. (2007) 'Concepts of Bounded Agency in Education, Work and Personal Lives of Young Adults', *International Journal of Psychology,* 42(2): 1–9.

Evans, K. (2006) 'Achieving Equity through 'Gender Autonomy': Challenges for VET Policy and Practice', *Journal of Vocational Education and Training,* 58(4): 393–408.

Evans,K. and Kersh,N. (2006) Chapter 3: Learner Biographies, Workplace Practices and Learning in Evans, K. et al. *Improving Workplace Learning*, Abingdon: Routledge

Evans, K., Kersh, N. and Kontiainen, S. (2004) 'Recognition of Tacit Skills: Sustaining Learning Outcomes in Adult Learning and Work Re-entry', *International Journal of Training and Development,* 8(1): 54–72.

Evans, K., Guile, D. and Harris, J. (2009) 'Putting Knowledge to Work', *American Educational Research Association Conference,* San Diego, April 2008.

Evans, K. and Niemeyer, B. (eds) (2004) *Reconnection: Countering Social Exclusion through Situated Learning.* Dordrecht: Springer.

Evans, K. and Waite, E. (2010) Stimulating the Innovation Potential of Routine workers through Workplace Learning, TRANSFER: *European Review of Labour and Research,* 16(2): 243–258.

Evans, K. Waite, E. and Admasachew, A. (2009) Enhancing skills for life? Adult basic skills and workplace learning. In J. Bynner & S. Reder (Ed.). *Tracking adult literacy and numeracy: lessons from longitudinal research.* London and New York: Routledge.

Evans, K. and Waite, E. (2009) 'Adults Learning in and through the Workplace', in K. Ecclestone, G. Biesta and M. Hughes, *Transitions and Learning through the Lifecourse.* Abingdon: Routledge.

Fenwick, T. (2008a) 'Understanding Relations of Individual-Collective Learning in Work: A Review of Research', *Management Learning,* 39(3): 227–243.

Fenwick, T. (2008b) 'Becoming an Ecologically Sustainable Organization: The Importance of Learning', *Development and Learning in Organizations,* 22(3): 28–30.

Fuller, A. and Unwin, L. (2004) 'Expansive Learning Environments: Integrating Organizational and Personal Developments', in H. Rainbird et al. (eds), *Workplace Learning in Context.* London, New York: Routledge.

Geary, J. (1995) *Work Practices: The Structure of Work,* in P. Edwards, op cit.

Green, F. (2009) Employee Involvement, Technology, Job Tasks and Required Education, ESRC LLAKES Seminar, 15th June, Institute of Education, University of London.

Hodkinson, P. and Rainbird, H. (2006) 'Conclusions: An Integrated Approach', Ch. 8 in K. Evans, et al. *Improving Workplace Learning*, Abingdon: Routledge.

Hodkinson, P., Hodkinson, H., Evans, K. and Kersh, N. (2004) 'The Significance of Individual Biography in Workplace Learning', *Studies in the Education of Adults,* 36(1): 6–25.

Hyman, R. and Streeck, W. (eds) (1988) *New Technology and Industrial Relations.* Oxford: Blackwell.

Jacobs and Park (2009) 'A Proposed Conceptual Framework of Workplace Learning', *Implications for Theory Development and Research in Human Resource Development,* 8(2): 133–150.

Kell, C. (2009) In-house Literacy, Language and Numeracy (LLN) Initiatives in New Zealand Workplaces: Interim Report. Auckland: Auckland University.

Keep, E. and Mayhew, K. (1999) The assessment?: knowledge, skills and competitiveness, *Oxford Review of Economic Policy*, 15, 1 pp. 1–15.

Kersh, N. and Evans, K. (2006) 'Recognition of Tacit Skills and Knowledge in Work Re-entry: Modeling of Learning Processes and Outcomes', in R. Edwards, J. Gallagher and S. Whittaker, (eds), *Learning Outside the Academy: International Research Perspectives on Lifelong Learning* Abingdon: Routledge. pp. 11–23.

Kersh, N., Evans, K., Kontiainen, S. and Bailey, H. (2009) 'Use of Conceptual Models in Self-assessment of Personal Competences in Learning and in Planning for Change', Working Paper of Centre for Excellence in Work-Based Learning for Education Professionals. London: Institute of Education.

Kontiainen, S. (2002) *Dynamic Concepts Analysis (DCA): Integrating Information in Conceptual Models.* Helsinki: Helsinki University Press.

Livingstone, D.W. (1999) 'Lifelong Learning and Underemployment in the Knowledge Society: A North American Perspective', *Comparative Education'*, 35(2): 162–86.

Livingstone, D., Mirchandani, K. and Sawchuk, P. (2008) *The Future of Lifelong Learning and Work: Critical Perspectives.* Rotterdam: Sense Publishers.

Papen, U. (2005) *Adult Literacy as Social Practice: More than Skills.* London: Routledge.

Rainbird, H. (1990) *Training Matters: Union Perspectives on Industrial Restructuring and Training.* Oxford: Blackwell.

Rainbird, H., Fuller, A. and Munro, A. eds (2004) *Workplace Learning in Context.* London: Routledge.

Reder, S. (2009) 'The Development of Literacy and Numeracy in Adult Life', in *Tracking Adult Literacy and Numeracy Skills.* New York: Routledge.

Street, B.V. (1995) *Social Literacies: Critical Approaches to Literacy in Development, Ethnography and Education.* Longman: Harlow.

Street, B.V. (ed.) (2001) *Literacy and Development: Ethnographic Perspectives.* London: Routledge.

Taylor, M. and Evans, K. (2009) 'Formal and Informal Training for Workers with Low Literacy: Building an International Dialogue between Canada and the United Kingdom', accepted for the *Journal of Adult and Continuing Education*, in press (2009).

Terry, M. (2006) 'Self-directed Learning by Undereducated Adults', *Educational Research Quarterly*, 29(4): 28–38.

Tett, L. and MacLachlan, K. (2007) 'Adult Literacy and Numeracy, Social Capital, Learner Identities in the Workplace', *Studies in the Education of Adults*, 39: 150–168.

Unwin, L. and Fuller, A. (2003) *Expanding Learning in the Workplace: Making More of Individual and Organisational Potential.* A NIACE policy discussion paper. Leicester: NIACE.

Weaver-Hightower, M.B. (2008) 'An Ecology Metaphor for Educational Policy Analysis: A Call to Complexity', *Educational Researcher*, 37(3): 153–167.

Whitley, R. (2000) *Divergent Capitalisms: The Social Structuring and Change of Business Systems.* Oxford: Oxford University Press.

Wolf, A. and Evans, K. (2011) *Improving Literacy at Work*, Abingdon: Routledge.

Issues and Futures

INTRODUCTION

Orville and Wilber Wright were successful aviators because they were the first to consider their problem a systems problem as they identified three interconnected facts of flight in their observations of birds. The Wright Brothers were the first to come to understand that before a bicycle could fly, you had to figure out how to:

1 Get it in the air.
2 Keep it in the air.
3 Make it go where you want.

Section III is all about creating environments in which learning can fly. In this section, you'll find some thinking by some serious scholar-practitioners who describe approaches and document opportunities and challenges related to understanding 'work' as a both a source of knowledge creation and the enabler of learning. There's a strong underpinning throughout these chapters that individuals learn through their day-to-day interactions with their environment, and that strategies to recognize and document the resultant learning is a challenge. Additionally, the role of technology in knowledge creation and dissemination is discussed here through chapters that describe the impact of technology on job structures and what constitutes knowledge. Throughout, too, the tension that exists between the role of the workplace and the university is apparent. How best can we create systems that blur the boundaries between our daily lives and the educational institutions that serve to create knowledge, ascertain that we've learned, or provided us with a credential? And perhaps most important, what is the responsibility of the organization to individual workers, to ensure that they become all they can be.

To begin, Harris and Chisholm make the argument that learning takes place in all aspects of life, and by creating structures for universities to provide credit for learning that is personally defined and directed (such as photography) would actually re-enable those who have been failed by formal education. Guile then describes an innovative apprenticeship model based on social capital theory through a case study of interns in a theatre production company. Costley continues the argument through a literature review of what is known about successful work-based learning programs in higher education; these programs, she says, are important for knowledge creation outside of academe as well as the development of workplace skills.

Through a conceptual framework of characteristics of corporate universities in the United States, Lui-Abel describes ways firms in the United States are structuring their learning and development departments to be more responsive to the needs of the learners as well as the organization. O'Connor and Lynch depict exemplary corporate/university partnerships in which emphasis was placed on the *who and what* of learning rather than the *where* of learning.

Regan and Delaney depict the workplace learning professional in the 'brave new workplace' who is operating in a technology-rich, knowledge-intensive, and learner-centered environment, where one of many issues is the organization's need to develop assessment strategies for learning outcomes, no matter where the learning takes place. Cheng, Son, and Bonk navigate readers through a discussion of technologies, including weblogs, Wiki, and podcasting, that support communication, help integrate knowledge, and the environmental characteristics that ensure their effective use.

Section III concludes with Johnson's vital reminder to us all that workplace learning has ethical dimensions; he discusses trends that could result in harm to individuals or their workplace when, for example, the needs of the corporation run contrary to the needs of the individual. Johnson brings us back full circle to the Wright Brothers; to an understanding that only those organizations that create environments to ensure to the interconnection of organizational needs and individual needs mesh (or fly!), will ultimately be successful.

27

Beyond the Workplace: Learning in the Lifeplace

Margaret Harris and Colin Chisholm

INTRODUCTION

Lifeplace Learning is 'Learning that encompasses knowledge, skills, behaviours and attitude acquired, being acquired or to be acquired throughout life, irrespective of when, where, why and how it was, is or will be learned' (Harris, 2008: 1). It is an all-encompassing view of learning and we believe it is the innovative, new approach needed for twenty-first century education. Although we readily recognize that there has been much progress in developing modern education, including interdisciplinary and multidisciplinary studies, lifelong learning, widening participation and social inclusion, it appears to us that most development is mainly based on traditional, on-campus, didactic systems with little formal recognition that such development could be underpinned by allowing accreditation of informal learning achieved in people's life places, such as the home and the community (Blair, 2005; Blair and Chisholm, 2006).

It would appear that the theoretical narrative that exists for valuing informal learning, and there is much of it, does not appear to materialize in practice and it is obvious that although '... learning takes many different forms among different groups of people, some forms of learning as well as ways of knowing, are valued more than others ...' (Williamson, 2002: 22).

This value aspect is clearly evidenced by the fact that traditional education is valued more than everyday life learning, evidenced by what is on the set curricula in schools, colleges and universities and in the academic elitism attached to various knowledge bases (Blair, 2005). This value aspect is challenged by our Lifeplace Learning concept, which places the value of the learning with the learners.

We believe our concept of Lifeplace Learning is a valuable process of, and topic for, learning and a valuable tool for recognizing and accrediting learning from life. It allows us to acknowledge all, and any, learning and encourages individuals to feel that knowledge gained through life is useful and valuable. From our work to date, we are convinced that this increases individual confidence levels, and a willingness to engage in more structured individual lifelong learning. In addition, the process of facilitating Lifeplace Learning brings benefits to the academic tutors. Our work also highlighted to us that the success of Lifeplace Learning depends on a fundamental change in attitude by society and academia as to what is considered valuable and credit worthy knowledge and skills and it requires recognition that learning can be valuable when done outside of academia, as well as in it, whether intentional or otherwise.

Most people already recognize that learning takes place in all areas of life: home, workplace, schools, colleges and universities (Rogers, 2004) and according to proponents of experiential learning, including Blair (2005) and Blair and Chisholm (2006), the experiences of life, irrespective of what they are, are the significant factors for real and authentic learning, and this should not be ignored. As Williamson states (2002: 29 and 189) '… people learn through their ordinary participation as citizens in the political and cultural life of their society' and through, '… dialogue with one another …'.

This, however, is not a new concept. In 1929, Yeaxlee (p. 155) stated that, 'Much adult education … will go on in clubs, churches, cinemas, theatres, concert rooms, trade unions, political societies, and in homes of the people where there are books, newspapers, music, wireless sets, workshops, gardens and groups of friends …'. This quote significantly underpins our core thinking on Lifeplace Learning, and we believe that in view of the array of learning situations available to us, we must move to a position where this learning is readily acknowledged, and where desired by the learner, is also assessed and accredited.

The Commission of European Communities (EC, 1995: 2) states that, '… the society of the future will be a learning society …' We believe this learning society can only be realized if new ways are considered to include those currently outside the traditional education system and a system is developed which allows learners to learn what they want in their own context (Williamson, 2002) and that is not restrictive and/or tied to outdated norms.

MOVING FROM WORK-BASED TO LIFEPLACE LEARNING

Work-based learning is already a well-established mode of learning, although still largely on the peripheral areas of full academic recognition. We recognize that this concept of learning utilization, and the accreditation of learning that is ongoing in a person's workplace and/or related to a work role, has strong justification as a learning mode in its own right, as it encourages people to become knowledge workers and engage in continuous learning. It values what is learned professionally outside of academia, providing such professional learning with some status.

Work-based learning is largely, but not exclusively, related to learning done from paid, voluntary or community work, that is, work which is in some way formal or organized. However, 'work-based' could be, and on occasion is, defined in a much looser context such as that relating to housework, parenting work or keeping fit. Lifeplace Learning extends this work-based idea of learning outside of the formal system while recognizing that the work-based learning model significantly contributes to our wider goal of accrediting any form of learning in any type of life learning situation (Chisholm and Blair, 2006).

What Lifeplace Learning adds is that the value of the learning becomes the concept of the learner and is not determined by employers, academic institutions or society's current value systems. Importantly, in a society that calls for qualifications as evidence of knowledge, skills and abilities (Blair, 2005), it also provides opportunity and becomes an enabler for individuals, so that they may prove that they have such required knowledge, skills and abilities. Of fundamental importance though, it also re-enables those who have been failed by the formal education system or who can't, or will not take part in it, to be recognized by society, highlighting that without the knowledge and skills gained from everyday learning, society would fail to operate successfully.

LEARNING ISSUES

A key element in our thinking is the recognition of previous, current and future Lifeplace Learning as valid learning, and of using such learning as a way of attaining accreditation and qualifications through reflective practice, thus using our learning lives more effectively (Blair and Chisholm, 2006). Lifeplace Learning includes processes that would permit people to utilize their everyday informal learning from TV, newspapers, the Internet, travel or general life experience and to analyze its value to them and to society.

This idea is supported by Coombs and Ahmed (1974: 8) who, in discussing informal education mention that, '... every individual acquires and accumulates knowledge, skills, attitudes and insights from daily experiences and exposures to the environment – at home, at work, at play: from the example and attitude of families and friends; from travel, reading newspapers and books; or by listening to the radio or viewing films or television ...'

In addition, according to Watanabe et al. (2001: 1), 'Without noticing, we are unconsciously learning ... learning automatically as we live our lives, whilst walking around and through subconscious learning we quite efficiently absorb knowledge and skill elements.' Again we agree and adhere to the idea of valuable unintentional learning.

Colley et al. (2002: 21) discuss and question the value of knowledge being gained in education; whether it is '... high status knowledge or not ...' and Williamson (2002: 14) states that '... all ideas, all claims to knowledge, all values need to be subjected to critical, open debate in an open society'. Once again we agree and are convinced that the real importance and status of knowledge is whether or not it is valuable to the learner. We therefore suggest that the academic community should not restrict the accreditation of knowledge and skills to those that are taught on campus when there is much being acquired from other valid sources.

It seems to us that the real issue is the interrelationship between types of learning. We need to change attitudes from assuming that specific learning can only be considered in specific settings, such as informal in informal settings and formal in formal settings and through the concept of Lifeplace Learning we can overcome the assumption that one type of learning is bad and another good and that pedagogic learning is better than individual, self-motivated learning. If we can make these changes in assumptions, then according to Colley et al. (2002) we can reduce the risk of setting a serious obstacle to better understanding of learning itself. We believe that this is critical not only to Lifeplace Learning but also to Lifelong Learning.

LIFELONG LEARNING

Lifelong Learning appears to be important within modern discussions about the continuing education for adults (Williamson, 2002). It certainly is in Scotland, where we are based (Gray, 2003), and generally in Europe (EC, 2001) but according to Kwon et al. (2000), Lifelong Learning is being torn between individual fulfilment and national progress. Lifeplace Learning could overcome this dichotomy of Lifelong Learning, as it has a clear, learner-led approach to learning that allows learners to develop into responsible and educated citizens, which we anticipate will support national progress.

Kwon et al. (2000) also proposed that people need equitable access to information channels and equitable access to adequate technologies. In other words, if we want people to engage in lifelong learning we should make it possible for them to do so. This theme is also to be found in the work of Williamson (2002) and Evans et al. (2002) who state that we have to be mindful of the inequalities and the gap between the powerful and the powerless, and that we have to break down barriers that exclude people from access to learning. Lifeplace Learning would contribute effectively to breaking down such power influences and barriers.

Smith (1996a) reminds us again of how old the concept of lifelong learning is, and Lindeman (1926: 4–7) also supports this suggesting that education is life and we must use the learner's experience in learning.

It would appear to us then that adult education is about life, that it should be built around student needs and interests, and that the resource of highest value in adult education is the learner's experience – yet our education systems barely recognize this. Smith (1996b) makes the point that these learner-centred issues conflict with the emphasis on employability competencies, economic issues and accreditation aspects currently in force within education, but link well with the thinking of current informal educators. Yeaxlee (1929) makes the point that learning in adulthood needs to be prepared for right from the start of our learning careers, particularly the encouragement of continuous education (see also Davis, 2002). He states (p. 28) that, '… adult education rightly interpreted is as inseparable from normal living as food and physical exercise. Life, to be vivid, and strong, and creative, demands constant reflection upon experience, so that action may be guided by wisdom …' The fact that some education systems do not encourage, and in some instances unwittingly discourage, this commitment to continuous learning is problematic. Lifelong Learning is supposed to provide appropriate access to education from birth and throughout life, but what it ignores is the recognition of value in the learning achieved (Blair, 2005). Williamson (2002: 1) suggests that, '… learning in adulthood is continuous and ubiquitous', and proposes that it should not be restricted to, or by, what is offered within the institutions of formal education. It should include a '… network of effective provision from childhood to old age, which is imaginatively conceived to be qualitatively different to all the existing educational provision.'

Our Lifeplace Learning model meets these criteria and offers this imaginatively conceived position. What follows are five brief examples of how.

Example 1: A learner involved in photography could build up in-depth knowledge of photography combined with an excellence in delivering art form photography. This example shows the potential for life learners to achieve success in a single discipline award as opposed to a broad-based study.

Example 2: A learner involved with a voluntary organization could build up a broad-based body of knowledge in the voluntary area, which, combined with the development of a range of knowledge-based skills, could lead to an award. This would involve learning in the community, their home and in the voluntary services environment.

Example 3: A learner at home could build an in-depth package of knowledge relating to a large range of subject-specific knowledge alongside developing a set of related knowledge-based skills in the modern home environment using a range of sources such as TV, radio, books, the Internet.

Example 4: A learner involved with life experiences. An example is a mother who for many years has cared for and managed a family in the home. The experiences could be wide-ranging and therefore the learning diverse but non-the-less important for her own 'workplace' (the home) environment. By using a reflective analysis of her life a mother could document activities and experiences and the learning from those activities and experiences, putting them into a context for accreditation and qualification.

Example 5: Individuals who work abroad could combine Lifeplace and work-based models if the person were determined to achieve a high level knowledge of the language, history, and culture of the country. The person would be in an ideal position to negotiate a learning agreement made up of goals and outcomes to be achieved in their lifeplace, whether work or socially related.

CONSIDERATIONS RELATING TO ASSESSMENT

Where assessment is required in Lifeplace Learning, the 'Know How' (learning derived from experiential knowledge and knowledge-based skills) needs to be addressed, as this is different from assessing traditional on-campus studies. The 'Know What', which normally relates to explicit knowledge, is also somewhat different in Lifeplace Learning studies, as there is more tacit and explicit knowledge integration than in on-campus methods, where tacit contribution is minimized or does not form part of the learning at all.

For Lifeplace Learning we need to focus assessment criteria around generic leaning outcomes defined by the learner, so assessment has to address a significant shift in the assessment approach. Lifeplace environments involve much greater amounts of autonomous learning, considerations of unconscious learning through in-depth reflection, and study based on learner negotiation with the facilitator using experiential situations.

Formative methods of assessment have proved highly successful in work-based learning (Boud, 2000) and we consider formative assessment an essential strategy for Lifeplace Learning. In our pilot studies formative assessment was employed and embedded successfully and we anticipate that as the model develops, learners will increasingly be able to have a role in their own formative assessment, producing learners who can truly understand the value of self-assessment and make critical judgements about their own learning. This means though, that we need enlightened educators who can mentor, facilitate and coach such learners and who have a belief in the value of Lifeplace formative assessment.

Self-assessment has implications for how Lifeplace programmes are designed, and we need to include as part of the learner outcomes, an approach that enables each learner to establish a set of formative criteria to achieve effective evaluation and judgement of their own learning.

A PERSPECTIVE ON LIFEPLACE LEARNING

What makes Lifeplace Learning different from other areas of learning, such as adult education; informal learning; independent learning; experiential learning; constructivist learning; and reflective learning is the recognition that Lifeplace Learning involves *all* learning that goes on throughout life and importantly, the student has the choice in where, why, when and how the topic is studied and whether it should be accredited. There is no restrictive delineation.

In order to evaluate the concept, we carried out two major studies during 2002–2005 and then during 2006–2008 (229823-CP-1-2006-1-UK-GRUNDTVIG-G1, 2008). The purpose of the initial study was to examine whether Lifeplace Learning was valid as a new, innovative and valuable concept of learning that could contribute to the range of existing paradigms of learning processes and to critically evaluate whether it could be appropriately integrated into the higher education curriculum in Scotland. We also evaluated the use that was being made of Lifeplace Learning within higher education in Europe, the US and Australia and to critically evaluate and make informed judgement on the importance of knowledge in the Lifeplace Learning environment.

Incorporation of this concept into an undergraduate degree programme was undertaken to enable us to understand the difficulties of including this within the higher education curriculum. This also allowed us to evaluate the tutor and student experience in terms of resources, pedagogy, assessment and curriculum issues, making informed recommendations as to how problems might be resolved. Our conclusions rested on providing a proposal for the integration of Lifeplace Learning into the Scottish higher education curricula (Blair, 2005). This work ran parallel with our studies involving work-based learning and the extension of the models of work-based learning into the much broader and inclusive Lifeplace Learning approach (Chisholm and Davis, 2005; Davis and Chisholm, 2005).

The second project involved us in testing the concept and model developed within the first project in three further European countries, Finland, Germany and Estonia, to provide us with information on how this concept could be transferred into other educational processes. In this latter project, independent evaluation was done by a partner from Spain.

RELATED CONCEPTS

It is worth discussing at this point the following concepts to provide some evidence upon which we have built our theoretical argument, as all five areas that follow are particularly apposite to the Lifeplace Learning model.

Constructivism

Constructivist learning theory is significant in what we are proposing. The theory, largely attributed to Bruner in 1960 (Kearsley, 2009) asserts that learning is an active process where learners construct new ideas or concepts based upon new information and its interaction with their own current and past knowledge, then making decisions based on that new information. This theory suggests that there is an individual and social construction of the meaning of information, and accordingly instructors should try to encourage students to discover things for themselves, present information in a format appropriate to the learner's current understanding and develop curricula to allow students to build upon what they have already learned.

According to Bencze (2008) constructivist teaching and learning principles should include recognition that learners have ideas and that these ideas often contradict those of teachers; that learners need 'first hand' experience and involvement with others; that students see what they want to see and are often not aware of what they know or don't know; that they need to know how to learn and be given the opportunity to determine their own beliefs.

Lifeplace Learning allows learners to use their own knowledge and new information and construct new ideas and attitudes which perhaps, lead to behavioural changes. It also adopts the constructivist learning process which we suggest is better for learning than a didactic approach that simply tells people 'what is' without allowing individuals any opportunity to challenge.

The modules developed to pilot our concept allowed students to self-direct their own learning, guided by a tutor who offered them the opportunity to test out new information and guide them towards better learning. It facilitated non-specific subject learning followed by reflection on new knowledge deriving from comparison with knowledge held by the person.

Reflection

Reflection is also at the heart of Lifeplace Learning since in order to put any learning into context the learner has to use reflection at some level and to some degree within the learning process. This applies whether examining a recognized discipline or examining his or her own life experiences. According to Schon (1983, 1987) reflection can be used to facilitate better and more useful learning. Both Schon's reflection-on-action and reflection-in-action can be used to identify learning achieved and evaluate how that learning experience can be used to improve ourselves mentally, or physically, and to model and shape our continued activities. Gibbs (1988) suggests that critical incident analysis is a good technique to aid reflection, and Tripp (1993) has suggested that critical incidents are produced by the way we look at a situation, an interpretation of the significance of an event.

Lifeplace Learning takes this further by allowing everything that we do to become a critical learning experience, large or small, consciously or subconsciously. Good reflective practice can involve any incident in our lives and analysis can be made of that incident to highlight to us what the learning was from it.

Phenomenology and ethnomethodology

We also touch on the qualitative, naturalistic approaches of enquiry: phenomenology and ethnomethodology (Cohen et al., 2002). Both of these approaches to enquiry are concerned with understanding experiences from our everyday lives. In phenomenology we look at our knowledge of people's behaviours and how we come to terms with our social reality which is shaped by our everyday experiences and varies from situation to situation. It is not shaped by external, objective and physically described reality (English and English, 1958). It questions the taken-for-granted assumptions of everyday life. In addition, ethnomethodology (Garfinkel, 1967) seeks to treat the practical things in daily life as topics of empirical study, giving small and commonplace activities the attention usually reserved for extraordinary events. Both ethnomethodology and phenomenology use a reflective element to examine experiential situations as does our Lifeplace Learning model. Our model uses a combination of the above, and additionally, allows the learner the control of what methods and to what extent the methods are used.

Tacit and explicit knowledge

We recognize that much of the world is still following traditional learning and teaching methods, and teachers still largely adhere to autocratic systems of control of what students learn. Lifeplace Learning, however, represents learning and knowledge that derives from the motivation and interest of the learner and involves learning which is achieved through learner negotiation with the educator. We believe that Lifeplace Learning offers a system that supports individual and societal growth and complements that achieved by conventional on-campus learning.

Our Lifeplace Learning concept goes well beyond our current understanding of distance or workplace learning as these in themselves are simply extensions of the on-campus approach. The education systems that we currently have put the emphasis on the formal, explicit, conscious learning done in a formal on-campus or formal off-campus environments. What Lifeplace Learning can capture is the 'other' knowledge; the type of knowledge that is sub-conscious tacit and which is not normally accepted as valuable learning; the conscious tacit which is not usually acknowledged or accredited; and the explicit, non-formal or informal that is not normally accredited.

This body of 'other' knowledge is what allows us all to function effectively within society and carry through life's activities that we gain through experience and practice, and/or the knowledge that we choose to learn for interest (Blair, 2005). This 'other' knowledge is well illustrated by Williamson (2002: 26) who states that:

> The study of lifelong learning has for too long been confined to the contexts of education or professional development in employment ... We need to learn how people become parents; how they learn to cope with the stresses of urban life and, most importantly ... how and what they come to know and believe to be true about themselves.

We have found that tacit knowledge has a significant role to play in Lifeplace Learning environments and that our model for Lifeplace Learning can effectively facilitate the integration of tacit knowledge with explicit knowledge, thus providing the learner with a more in-depth learning experience. For the integrative study to be effective though, we believe that tacit knowledge needs to be brought to a significant level of awareness within the studies.

Although it appears that little is understood about the transfer mechanisms and conversion of tacit knowledge to explicit knowledge, we feel that our lifeplace model does facilitate such transfer where relevant and that not all tacit knowledge requires to become explicit to facilitate integrative learning. In many situations the integrative learning benefits derived are from the tacit knowledge remaining tacit but blending subtly with the explicit to give an enhanced, synergistic, learning experience. We see the future development of the model as being about supporting the integrating of the two forms of knowledge.

Integrative development and adaptive flexibility

As most theories of enquiry are contested concepts in themselves there is none that is the optimal choice for our Lifeplace Learning concept. Kolb (1984: 209), however, says that the challenge of lifelong learning is that of integrative development, and he recognizes that professional specialization may inhibit development of an integrative perspective in individuals. His concept is in line with the argument that specialist knowledge taught within higher education courses inhibits real integrative learning. It has also been suggested that specialized technical experience or education is not critical for success in the workplace, where adaptive flexibility is much more important.

Illeris (2002) suggests that there is tension in contemporary learning theory between the cognitive, the emotional and the social. The gist of his conclusions is that all are needed within the learning process, but that the writers and researchers in these areas today write from standpoints of diversity and seclusion rather than from a complementary field.

He argues that looking at learning from a singular perspective is a flawed concept and, as Blair (2005) suggests, this is the dilemma that innovators face in trying to propose new learning paradigms to the experts. She found from her literature review that there is support for utilizing all of our environments for learning purposes, that all sources of learning could be used in the learning process, and in fact using all learning environments leads to greater motivation in learning (Smith and Spurling, 2003).

We believe from our foregoing analysis that reflective practice, constructivism, phenomenology, ethnomethodology, tacit and explicit knowledge recognition, along with adaptive flexibility and integrative development, all have a significant part to play in the Lifeplace Learning agenda.

ACCREDITING LIFEPLACE LEARNING

The first of our studies (2003–2005) involved students undertaking fully accredited modules of Lifeplace Learning in Scotland. The Scottish degree system consists of a four-year (level) Honours degree worth 480 credit points. Each level of the degree is worth 120 credit points and the increasing levels normally indicate greater depth and complexity of the studies. Each of the modules we developed for our project was worth 20 credits (one sixth of a level) and there was one for each level of the programme in order to provide the greatest student choice that we could within the academic and administrative boundaries of our institution. The modules ran a number of times over a period of eighteen months.

The format used was that of a generic module descriptor for each level, and then blank module descriptors, which students completed individually according to their own learning requirements, with guidance from, and through negotiation with, the tutor, essentially learning agreements. Students used either past, current or future learning to fulfill the requirements of the module, independently stated their objectives, what their aim was, what their research methodology would be, or had been, and how they wished to be assessed, thus attempting to incorporate and integrate experiential, independent and lifelong learning. The tutor's role in this process proved to be crucial to the success of the process and to the success of the students, as many students were unaware of academic protocols and the intricacies of completing module descriptors.

In students' being able to choose their own topic, learning style and assessment criteria, we believe that we were facilitating adult learning techniques and facilitating credit for non-standard subject content. In them being able to choose the learning resources and the learning environments, we enhanced and encouraged the personal and flexible learning concept. We ensured that standards were maintained in line with quality assurance procedures by utilizing the level benchmarks of the Scottish Credit and Qualifications Framework's flexible concepts (SCQF, 2002).

We evaluated using student questionnaires, a reflective log kept by the module tutor and comments from the external examiner. The evaluation from the tutor reflective log allowed the recording of a fairly intimate account of her own experiences. The extensive external examiner's comments throughout the project were useful for the practicalities of quality enhancement and assurance.

RESULTS AND CONCLUSIONS FROM THE STUDIES

The results of the first study (including the literature review) provided us with our working definition of Lifeplace Learning and some conclusions.

Our first conclusion was that Lifeplace Learning is a valid concept for learning both as a method of study and as the content of study and is able to be incorporated into the curriculum. It is able to be appropriately accredited and complements what already exists; it is not a substitution. Quality assurance of the model and the modules is easily achieved and work-based learning models can be adapted to facilitate it. It appears to open up learning opportunities and allow all learning environments and sources, including the self, to become valuable.

Secondly, Lifeplace Learning facilitates individual self-satisfaction, confidence building, autonomy and independent learning, encouraging wider learning providing choice and flexibility. Thirdly, students and tutors like Lifeplace Learning but it was acknowledged that training for, and development of, academic staff are vitally important.

This study, which required the examination of many strands of learning, education and pedagogic discussion, provided us with enough initial evidence to suggest that Lifeplace Learning could be important to educationalists, policy makers and the public, because it de-restricts us in acknowledging what learning is. This novel and innovative concept provided evidence that if the content is important to the learner, it *is* valid learning and should be able to be accredited. It could be used to bring more people into the learning arena and under this concept no learning need be excluded.

The second study (229823-CP-1-2006-1-UK-GRUNDTVIG-G1, 2008) was based on testing the concept in Europe, and on this occasion different models of Lifeplace Learning were developed to accommodate national regulation and protocol. The results of this second project not only reaffirmed our initial conclusions, but also highlighted other areas in need of exploration.

The results indicated that Lifeplace Learning is a viable and sustainable concept and that student and facilitator satisfaction was very high, particularly related to choice and flexibility. It provided added value to that offered by conventional courses and the facilitator/coach's role was highly valued and important. Facilitators could manage the flexibility of study and learning environments successfully without compromising academic integrity, and students were able to connect their different learning environments and utilize knowledge/skills arising from non-academic backgrounds.

Importantly, the wider the Lifeplace Learning approach, the higher the satisfaction levels and positive effect on students' learning. Unexpected learning, of both tutor and student occurred, relating to learning about themselves (skills, attitude and behaviour) *and* to the subject matter. Lifeplace Learning allows credit for things valuable to students as it allows informal learning to become visible. We believe it is important for social inclusion and could be used for developing current academic subjects, but time and strategies to foster Lifeplace Learning are essential.

The conclusions and recommendations of the internal and external evaluations carried out within this latter project strongly indicated that good understanding by the facilitators and students of the Lifeplace Learning concept is vital if it is to succeed and that the skills of the facilitator should not be underestimated. It was realized also that due to its very flexible nature, contact between students and facilitators should be regular, and both students and facilitators have to be proactive.

Interestingly, it was found that technology was not used to its best advantage and that this could be much enhanced to allow full participation by any person irrespective of where located and any accreditation requirements. Having tested the model in Scotland and Europe, we believe it could be effectively transferred to many other educational systems, with some minor adjustments.

CONCLUSIONS

There is growing recognition that learning outside of academia is a worthwhile area, that people should be able to get credit for experiential learning, that adult education should be about life, that self-directed and independent learning is good, that all resources can be used for learning, and that flexibility in learning and allowing everyone access to higher education, is to be commended.

Whilst it would appear that there is much talk of this within learning literature, and suggestions that it should be able to be captured within academic qualifications, it does not appear to be practised. What is recognized, and continues to be a growth area, is the learning done in semi-formal environments if related to a subject discipline. What was seldom found within the practice, was firstly the ability to have everyday life learning recognized, because it appeared not to be considered valuable enough for such consideration, or secondly to have the choice of study topic area. There was either the opportunity to study flexibly an already established academic discipline, or the opportunity to get accreditation for experiential learning if it was somehow related to work-based learning.

The way forward

Lifeplace Learning offers major expansion of the formalization of learning leading to a recognized higher education award (Harris and Chisholm, 2008). In addition, Lifeplace Learning environments provide the potential to considerably extend adult education, providing a radical positive shift in global lifelong learning for society. The nature and content of Lifeplace Learning is integral to everyday living in every sense and its development and operation in all Lifeplace environments (including the workplace and formal education environments) will have a profound effect on social inclusion by providing formalization of informal learning across all sectors of society and combining this with recognized formal learning in real transdisciplinary life environments.

Our research from 2002 to 2009 suggests that Lifeplace Learning complements the conventional on-campus, single-discipline and the work-based programmes. Its development will recognize formally, for the first time, all forms of informal knowledge which are currently lost to the educational system and society. Synergistic learning can be realized by having programmes based on a mix of work-based, Lifeplace and conventional on-campus learning. Lifeplace Learning requires a significant shift in pedagogical and didactical approaches to learning, as the learning environments could be much less structured, but the Lifeplace model offers greater flexibility and freedom of learning than traditional or work-based models. As Rogers (2004: 36) discusses from a theoretical viewpoint, '...acquisition learning and formalized learning need to be combined, to make for more effective learning'. He suggests that requests for bringing them together remain persistent and these should be acknowledged. We would agree with this.

Our research suggests that Lifeplace Learning will only succeed if on-campus tutors develop as mentors, facilitators and coaches, as opposed to traditional teachers/supervisors and appropriate assessment, and quality assurance procedures are developed. In addition, formative assessment modes, including self-formative assessment, are believed to be integral to a Lifeplace Learning system, and programmes should encourage and enable students to become effective in setting formative and summative criteria, and being able to make effective evaluations and judgements on their own learning.

In order to introduce Lifeplace Learning within education systems, there should be a critical re-examination of the current regulatory frameworks and quality assurance mechanisms in place for single-discipline, on-campus subjects to ensure that they are appropriate for the Lifeplace Learning model. We accept, though, that initially the introduction may have to be based on, and within, modified current curricula, quality assurance and pedagogical restraints, but its future development should be debated with a view to evolving a system that is more sympathetic to the philosophy of Lifeplace Learning. It would be a shame not to develop what the external examiner said was, '...a wonderful learning experience...a splendid piece of pedagogical design...and above all,...a truly developmental...learning experience...' (Cowan, 2005).

Of course, there were limitations to our original study. Although approximately 80 students undertook the modules over an eighteen-month period, and some took more than one Lifeplace module, these numbers were limited as far as a realistic sample is concerned. Other limiting factors were that the search area for the practice-based analysis was much too wide, and the term Lifeplace Learning was not readily recognized by others. A smaller, more focused study may have allowed greater depth of investigation, which might have revealed that our vision of Lifeplace Learning is hidden within another paradigm – but we doubt it.

To justify this concept of Lifeplace Learning there requires to be further research to ensure its relevance as a concept, to confirm its value to society and to assure in some fashion its standards because of society's current structure and philosophical standpoint to quality assurance and on what knowledge is considered valuable. Innovative teachers need to promote this and policy makers need to be convinced. This will not be an easy task but there are signs that there is some movement.

According to Blair (2005) in Australia a surfing qualification was added to the curriculum of a university in the early part of the century because students were missing so many classes to go surfing. Whilst some government education ministers thought that this was making a mockery of the educational system, Blair believed that this was making the most of it. We agree with her evaluation of this and again with the views of Williamson (2002: 7) who states convincingly that, '…Prevailing ideas about what it means to learn and to know and to claim to have knowledge need to be profoundly reassessed; for too often they reflect the dominant discourses of the powerful within existing institutions … The challenge, in fact, is to define radical alternatives to the status quo, for what currently exists is narrowly conceived, exclusive and deeply conformist…they fail to embrace all the other contexts in which adults learn…' We could not agree more.

Lifeplace Learning is novel, innovative and challenging, and does prescribe a new radical alternative. By breaking down the concerns that we see about accrediting non-standard academic knowledge, recognizing the value of learning environments outside the academy, allowing students to choose their own area of interest and allowing people to utilize the wide range of resources and tools available for learning, then we might truly create a learning society that is not scared to learn because their attempts at whatever they do and at whatever level they do it, will seem as valid and as worthy as any other. Perhaps then true lifelong learning might prevail, providing an equitable approach to knowledge and its value.

REFERENCES

Bencze, J.L. (2008) Constructivism (accessed 9/5/2009) at http://webspace.oise.utoronto.ca/~benczela/Constructivism.html

Blair, M. (2005) *Accrediting Lifeplace Learning (Including Work-Based and Work Place Learning) as Part of the Scottish Higher Education Curriculum*, Prof D Thesis, Glasgow Caledonian University.

Blair, M.S.G. and Chisholm, C.U. (2006) *Achieving Academic Qualifications Utilising Lifeplace Learning, Including Work-Based and Workplace Learning, as a Valid Part of the Higher Education Curriculum*. Refereed paper presented at The American Educational Research Association Annual Conference, San Francisco, USA.

Bruner, J. (1960) *The Process of Education*. Cambridge, MA: Harvard University Press .

Boud, D. (2000) 'Sustainable Assessment: Rethinking Assessment for the Learning Society', *Studies in Continuing Education*, 2: 151–162.

Chisholm, C.U. and Blair, M.S.G. (2006) 'Extending the Models for Work Based Learning into the Lifeplace', *World Transactions on Engineering and Technology Education*, 2(3): 172–176.

Chisholm, C.U. and Davis, M. (2005) *Extending the Model of Work Based Learning into the Lifeplace*. Presented paper at American Educational Research Association, Montreal, Canada.

Cohen, L., Manion, L. and Morrison, K. (2002) *Research Methods in Education* (5th edn), London: Routledge Falmer.

Colley, H. et al. (2002) Non-formal Learning: Mapping the Conceptual Terrain. A Consultation Report, Leeds: University of Leeds Lifelong Learning Institute, Accessed on 19/4/04 at http://www.infed.org/archives/etexts/colleyinformallearning.htm.

Coombs, P.H. and Ahmed, M. (1974) *Attacking Rural Poverty. How Non-formal Education Can Help*. Baltimore: John Hopkins University Press.

Cowan, J. (2005) *Excerpt from External Examiner Report to Team 2006*. Glasgow, Scotland: Caledonian University.

Davis, M. (2002) *Factors Affecting Student Retention in a Post 1992 Higher Education Establishment*, MEd. Thesis, Glasgow, Scotland, Strathclyde University.

Davis, M. and Chisholm, C. (2005) 'Integrating and Recognising Work, Life and Learning', *Proceedings of Conference on Researching Work and Learning*, Sydney, Australia.

English, H.B. and English, A.C. (1958) *A Comprehensive Dictionary of Psychological and Psychoanalytic Terms*. London: Longman.

European Commission (1995) *White Paper on Education and Training: Towards the Learning Society* Luxembourg: Office for the Official Publications of the EC.

European Commission (2001) Communication: Making a European Area of Lifelong Learning a Reality, Accessed on 5/6/05 at http://www.eu.int/comm/education/life/index.htm.

Evans, K., Hodkinson, P. and Unwin, L. (2002) *Working To Learn: Transforming Learning in the Workplace*. London: Kogan Page.

Garfinkel, H. (1967) 'Studies in Ethnomethodology', as cited in Cohen, L. et al. (2002) *Research Methods in Education* (5th edn). London: Routledge Falmer.

Gibbs, G. (1988) in Ghaye, T. and Lillyman, S. (1997) *Learning Journals and Critical Incidents: Reflective Practice for Health Care Professionals*. Quay Books.

Gray, I. (2003) 'Life through Learning through Life', *The Lifelong Learning Strategy for Scotland*. Scottish executive.

Grundtvig Project (2008) *Lifelearn*. European Project No (229823-CP-1-2006-1-UK-GRUNDTVIG-G1. Accessed 04/04/2009 at http://www.icll.gcal.ac.uk

Harris, M. (2008) *Lifeplace Learning*. 1st International Conference on Engineering and Business Education (ICEBE) Wismar.

Harris, M. and Chisholm C.U. (2008) 'Recognition of Learning through Work in Lifeplace Learning Environments: An Analysis of the Way Ahead', *Proceedings of the Work Based Learning Network Annual Conference* Cardiff, Wales. pp. 120–137.

Illeris, K. (2002) *The Three Dimensions of Learning*, Denmark: Roskilde University Press.

Kearsley, G. (2009) Constructivist Theory, accessed on 1/5/09 at *http://tip.psychology.org/bruner.html*

Kolb, D.A. (1984) *Experiential Learning: Experience as the Source of Learning and Development*. New Jersey: Prentice-Hall.

Kwon, S., Harreveld, B. and Danaher, P.A. (2000) *Individualising, Socialising and Globalising Knowledge: Approaches to Lifelong Learning in Korea and Australia*, 1st Lifelong Learning Conference, Central Queensland University, Australia.

Lindeman, E. (1926) *The Meaning of Adult Education*, New York: New Republic.

Rogers, A. (2004) *What is the Difference?: A New Critique of Adult Learning and Teaching*, Leicester: NIACE.

Schon, D.A. (1983) *The Reflective Practitioner*, New York: basic Books.

Schon, D.A. (1987) *Educating the Reflective Practitioner*, San Francisco: Jossey-Bass.

Scottish Credit and Qualifications Framework (SCQF) (2002) *National Plan for Implementation of the Framework*. Scotland, U.K.

Smith, J. and Spurling, A. (2003) *Understanding Motivation for Lifelong Learning*, Devon: Southgate Publishers for The Campaign for Learning and NIACE.

Smith, M.K. (1996a) Lifelong Learning, *The encyclopaedia of informal education*, accessed on 19/04/04 at http://www.infed.org/lifelonglearning/b-life.htm, (19/4/04)

Smith, M.K. (1996b) Non-formal education, T*he encyclopaedia of informal education*, accessed on 19/04/04 at http://www.infed.org/biblio/b-nonfor.htm

Tripp, D. (1993) *Critical Incidents in Teaching: Developing Professional Judgement*, London: Routledge.

Watanabee, T., Nanez, J.E. and Sasaki, Y. (2001) 'Perceptual Learning without Perception', *Nature*: 413, 844–848.

Williamson, B. (2002) *Lifeworlds and Learning: Essays in the Theory, Philosophy and Practice of Lifelong Learning'*, Leicester: NIACE.

Yeaxlee, B.A. (1929) *Lifelong Education*. London: Cassell.

28

Workplace Learning in the Knowledge Economy: the Development of Vocational Practice and Social Capital

David Guile

INTRODUCTION

This chapter provides an account of the development of a bespoke vocational training programme, indicative of the trends in workplace learning undertaken by specialist areas of endeavour, in this case, the creative and cultural sector. Similarly Mulder and Guliker in their chapter on training for the floriculture industry in Africa, identified the importance of the development of specialized programmes for niche industries. These programmes have been developed with a strong commitment to learning in the workplace. The major role of the creative and cultural (C&C) sector which contributes advertising, architecture, art and antiques markets, computer and video games, crafts, design, designer fashion, film and video, music, performing arts, publishing, software, television and radio in the global knowledge economy, has been acknowledged worldwide since the mid 1990s (Lash and Urry, 1994). Access to and development within the C&C sector, like other industrial sectors, has been conceptualised in neo-liberal terms by policymakers internationally as through the development of knowledge and skill as represented by qualifications (KEA, 2006). In this chapter, I adopt a radically different stance. The argument presented is that qualifications alone do not guarantee access to the C&C labour market. This sector is predominantly characterised by external labour markets, that is, freelance and contract-based work rarely advertised in a clear and transparent way. To secure such employment people have to demonstrate that they have developed the forms of 'vocational practice', that is, the mix of knowledge, skill and judgement that employers are looking for, and 'social capital', in this case, the networks of contacts to help them to secure employment. Moreover, to do so presupposes experience of working in the C&C sector.

The relation between the development of vocational practice and social capital is explored by drawing on research material used for a previously published case study of a bespoke apprenticeship programme was devised by the Birmingham Repertory Theatre (hereafter referred to as the Rep) and funded through the European Union EQUAL Programme (Guile and Okumoto, 2007).

Firstly, there is an identification of the forms of workplace organization, the mobilization of networks, and the forms of learning that facilitate the development of vocational practice and social capital to position people to enter the C&C sector, to provide a context for the discussion of the conceptual and policy implications of the Rep's apprenticeship model.

CONCEPTUAL FRAMEWORK: OBJECTS, LEARNING AND EXPERTISE

To do so, a new conceptual framework is employed. This framework is an integration of Nardi's (2005) notions of the 'formulation' and 'instantiation' of a new object of activity; Lave and Wenger's (1991) notions of the 'teaching' curricula with instruction into domain-specific knowledge, and 'learning' curricula, situated for the improvisational development of new practice; and Stone's (2001) notions of 'bonding', 'bridging' and 'linking' forms of social capital. The notion of formulation is used to identify the reasons that influenced the Rep's introduction of the apprenticeship, as an object, and the notion of instantiation to analyse the way in which different parties in the Rep had to enlarge their work roles to either take on a teaching role or to assist apprentices to develop a holistic understanding of the relation between the different occupational specialisms found in the Rep. The notions of teaching and learning curricula are used to identify at a general level the contribution of different types of knowledge and experience to the apprentices' development of vocational practice. Finally, the notions of bonding, bridging and linking are employed to deepen understanding of how immersion in different occupational specialisms within the Rep and within the wider field of theatrical work and live entertainment assisted the apprentices to move into their chosen occupational niche.

CASE STUDY: THE TECHNICAL APPRENTICESHIP AT BIRMINGHAM REPERTORY

Background to the Technical Apprenticeship

The Birmingham Repertory Theatre, established in 1913, has a long tradition of innovation. The Rep's mission is:

> To develop, produce and present a range of theatrical experiences of international quality that will entertain, enlighten and engage with the maximum number of people of all ages and communities from Birmingham and the surrounding region (Stuart Rogers, Chief Executive, interview, May 2005).

In pursuing its mission, one of the obstacles the Rep, in common with other repertory theatres, has faced had been 'a shortage of technical staff' (Stuart Rogers, Chief Executive, interview, May 2005). In an attempt to combat these skill shortages in theatre, broadcast media and outside events, the Rep agreed to participate in *The Last Mile* (TLM) Project that Birmingham City Council's Economic and Development Department had designed to support aspiring entrants move into the C&C sector. One of the attractions of TLM, for the Rep, was that it was funded through the European Union EQUAL Programme. This gave the Rep access to European Social Funding (ESF) and therefore the freedom to design a bespoke two-year apprenticeship, which reflected its interests and values rather than having to work within the strictures of the United Kingdom's Blueprint for apprenticeship. The occupational specialisms of wardrobe, wigs and make-up, lighting and electrics, sound, the stage technician and stage management were identified for the programme.

The Rep chose to formulate their own model of apprenticeship because they perceived that the national framework for apprenticeships in the United Kingdom:

> was more bounded by the rules of the education sector then by the rules of the industry... its inflexible time frame would not allow apprentices full immersion in theatre life (Stuart Rogers, Chief Executive, interview, August 2006).

In contrast, Stuart wanted to create a modern, culturally diverse and inclusive traditional craft apprenticeship, the Technical Apprenticeship (TA), that reflected the realities of the new work context in which the Rep and its staff operate. The nature of the production in the theatre industry has changed profoundly over the last 20 because there are:

> ...fewer reps and increasing co-productions. It's not about having a permanent company of stage management, actors or technicians. We are bringing in shows, co-producing or a show starts somewhere else or not building them all – shared-around. So, the need for having large numbers of permanent staff is no longer an option. Also, there are often less productions to build, you keep much less core technical staff within the building, and hire freelancers and casuals when required (John Pitt, Project Coordinator, interview, October 2005).

Thus, the Rep, in common with many other parts of the C&C sector in the UK (Bilton, 2007) and Europe (KEA, 2006) is characterised by a 'project culture'. This new work context means that it is extremely important to immerse newcomers into every aspect of mounting a production so they develop key aspects of vocational practice which do not necessarily surface again within the life span of a production. A 'multi-skilling' approach is regarded as desirable. It is also impractical to release apprentices to attend courses in Further Education colleges or private training providers that are based on educational terms or to stop and assess apprentices' competence in the middle of a production. To realize its vision, a Project Coordinator, John Pitt was appointed who had worked as Production Manager previously in the Rep as well as having extensive knowledge and experience in training and development.

Principles underpinning vocational practice development

The Technical Apprenticeship was embedded in the everyday 'work flow' of the Rep, that is, the logical sequence of activities that have to occur to ensure the success of a production (see Figure 28.1).

Stuart and John adopted this course of action because they both believed that 'vocationality', their term for the ability to grasp the reasons for and relationships between the production and directorial strategies, required the putting on of a production as well as the development of the specific forms of vocational practice so as to contribute effectively to that production. This makes 'apprentices employable as freelancers who aren't pigeonholed' (John Pitt, interview, October 2005). To do so, John had to negotiate with each Head of Department, (HoD) the people who officially received an apprentice into the organisation, to not only an enlarge their work role so they accepted responsibility for immersing apprentices into their chosen occupational field and supported their development throughout their period of apprenticeship, but also importantly their agreement to support other apprentices to be able to address the relationships between different occupational specialisms.

Following a recruitment process, the apprentices were immediately allocated to work with their HoD in their chosen occupational specialism. This provided the apprentices with an opportunity to establish a working relationship with their HoD and to begin to be immersed in that occupational specialism, initially through observing the work process and then through engaging with a gradually escalating range of demanding vocational tasks. The emphasis was entirely on learning on the job, learning in the workplace.

To support the learning process, John wrote, in conjunction with each HoD, what he referred to as 'learning outcomes'. These were designed to enable the HoDs and apprentices to gauge the development of the apprentices' vocational practice. The learning outcomes for the six vocational areas in the Rep, in contrast to the learning outcomes associated with the UK's national system of vocational qualifications (NVQs), were not part of a recognized national qualification. This approach was due to the Rep's concerns about the time-consuming nature of the NVQ assessment process. Moreover, the learning outcomes were kept as broad as possible and have general rather than detailed assessment criteria (see below for an example). This enabled HoDs to revise and alter the learning outcomes to reflect the knowledge and skill the apprentices were able to develop as they worked on different productions. This 'bespoke'

Flow of the Production Process

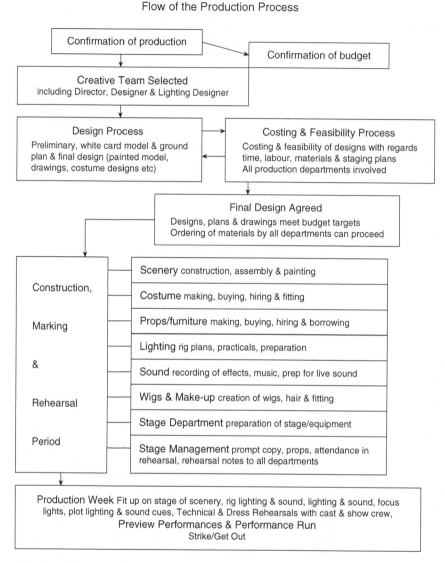

Figure 28.1 Flow of production process

training curriculum and programme addressed the specific and identified needs of the organisation.

TRAINING FOR WIGS AND MAKE-UP

As well as input from Department Heads and the apprentices, the job descriptions for the specific areas were used as a starting point for the development of the learning outcomes. The following example is provided from the wigs and make up specialism.

Hair-dressing to head dressing using wigs, and hair pieces, or perhaps face changes from clowns to animals to Munchkins! Wigs and make-up are the true companion to costumes in portraying a character whether as the result of days of patient wig knotting or a quick slap of face paint to accompany a quick costume change.

- An understanding of design and its interpretation into wig and make up production.
- A knowledge and understanding of the needs of wig making and make up.
- An awareness of how to select correct materials from a given design and how then to acquire those materials.
- A range of techniques in wig making to a varying degree of complexity.
- A range of techniques in make up to a varying degree of complexity.
- Be able to make alterations to existing wigs.
- Be able to dress and maintain wigs during a run of performances.
- Proficiency as a wig assistant and make up artist during a performance.
- Understand and demonstrate the organization and documentation for purchasing, hiring, borrowing and returning of wigs.

(Taken from Rep's job description for wigs and make-up, Birmingham, 2007)

From the outset, John and Stuart felt that the Rep's longstanding philosophy of 'duty-bound relationships', in other words, a commitment to the development of the diverse occupational traditions and long-standing collaborative ways of working, would provide a good underpinning for the development of vocational practice and social capital (John Pitt, interview, April 2006). These relationships serve a number of purposes. Formatively, they helped to secure the HoDs consent to enlarge their work roles by offering sensitive modes of coaching and mentoring to help the apprentices to develop their vocational practice. On some occasions this took the form of designated feedback sessions and on other occasions giving feedback during the work process. Summatively, the duty-bound relations underpinned the HoDs awarding of 'Certificates of Competence' (CoCs). These are the Rep's own certificates. Their status rests on the professional reputation of the HoDs who 'signed them off' and Stuart's reputation as a well-respected director of repertory theatres. Stuart and John authorized the HoDs to issue CoCs when apprentices are deemed to have reached the appropriate standard, so long as the HoDs felt that they could justify their decision that an apprentice has demonstrated appropriate skill development with respect to one of the learning outcomes to John, and by extension to their wider vocational community.

The development of vocational practice was supported by the Rep introducing a teaching and learning curriculum. In the case of the former, which was held during the 'dark periods' (i.e. down-time) between productions, John and the HoDs identified the content for the compulsory elements. One important element was the provision of health and safety courses. These courses often amount to little more than a list of 'do's and don'ts' in the workplace. In contrast, health and safety, for the Rep, is used metaphorically to refer to understanding the whole work context, the different specialisms required in the theatre, their relationship to one another, and the potential problems that may arise and how to avoid them occurring or to deal with them if do arise. The bespoke elements of the teaching curriculum were agreed after several months in a series of three-way meetings between an apprentice, the HoD and John. Prior to these meetings, the HoDs and John had gleaned important insights about the apprentices' learning and developments needs from a series of informal discussions that they had held with apprentices. Draft learning and development plans for each apprentice were drawn up by John, in consultation with HoDs and apprentices. The apprentices were either released to attend courses run by local Further Education Colleges or specialist trainers were invited into the Rep at times during the dark periods. These courses combined occupationally specific knowledge and skill with a broader engagement with the work process, as John observes, 'this was the bit they found useful – learning about some of the other areas', and the development of this wider understanding of apprentices' work role in relation to the other areas of work within a theatre 'is the basis of transferable skills' (Interview, October 2006).

In the case of the learning curriculum, the bonding of the apprentices and their respective HoDs and the cohort of apprentices and their respective HoDs created the conditions for all the apprentices to be 'legitimate peripheral participants' (Lave and Wenger, 1991) within their own department as well as 'boundary crossers' (Tuomi-Gröhn and Engeström, 2003) between departments. The Lighting apprentice clearly explains the benefit of the former arrangement:

If there is no communication, no show... if you do something wrong, they [the HoD and other members of the Department] just tell you – 'why are you doing that for? Think about it. What's going to happen? What does it look like?' Or, they will let you make a mistake, and ask, 'why did that mess up?' (Interview, September 2006).

The opportunity to bridge occupational areas also helped the apprentices to develop their confidence and capability to communicate with all professionals working in the theatre. As the stage management apprentice observed:

Books don't teach how to deal with people... the only way to sort things out when you've got actors and designers who are not happy is by involving other HoDs and people from their team (interview, September 2006).

The net effect was, as one HoD remarked, that the bonding and bridging processes that underpinned the learning curriculum helped to create a working environment whereby the apprentices became vocationally competent after 18 months:

I think after 18 months, we ended up relying on the apprentice within the Department... They become a part of the team. When they do other things, you miss them, although they need to have those experiences to do other things on their own (Head of Wardrobe, interview, February 2007).

The other feature of the learning curriculum was a programme of visits to other theatres and events across the country. Mobilizing their knowledge of networks within the theatrical and live entertainment sector, Stuart and John arranged for the apprentices to visit, for example, the Association of British Theatre Technicians exhibition, which exhibited lighting and sound equipment as well as front and back stage in other theatres and was attended by members of the industry who hired people for exhibitions, live events, and to visit a number of other reps during production and post-production periods. Because the UK's national system of repertory theatres is characterised by the type of strong mutually self-supporting networks, high levels of trust amongst all levels of specialism and seniority, the visits enabled apprentices to firstly, locate their understanding of vocational practice in a wider context and thus lay the foundation for them to develop the capability to transfer their knowledge and skill into other theatrical or live entertainment contexts:

I want to give them the widest scope possible – some transferable skills and to have the knowledge to be able to cope, as well as being a specialist in their own field. They will have some practice – the Lighting apprentice will go to Sound for two weeks to learn how it works. There is and will continue to be quite a lot of internal cross-fertilisation going on... Once apprentices gain the balance between practice and theories and between specialisation and transferability, they will be industry-ready as a freelancer with confidence (John Pitt, interview, April 2006).

Learning to transfer specialist knowledge and skill is a prerequisite for securing permanent or temporary employment in the contemporary theatre industry. This was affirmed by John:

the REP is one of the biggest producing theatres in the country. There aren't many places like it, which is why again, this recognition we have to give them through those transferable skills to be able to go into a very, very diverse industry from the start, i.e. television, exhibitions, events, small-scale touring, and theatres of course! (John Pitt, interview, October 2006).

And by HoDs:

I had to hire someone alongside my apprentice... This person was well-qualified. She didn't have much experience but had a right attitude. But when the show was up and running, it turned out that my apprentice was more confident and practical and had more knowledge and could adapt quicker (Head of wigs and make-up, interview, February 2007).

The visits also assisted the apprentices to make professional contacts by either being recommended by John to people in the industry:

The first time I heard it I couldn't believe it (Make-up apprentice, interview, February 2007).

or by linking themselves to a wider range of professional networks:

> The chance to tell people at event shows or in other reps what I've been doing is great. They then ask you whether you've 'done this or that' and if you have you can tell them about it and if not ask John what it is and can you do it (Make-up apprentice, interview, February 2007).

In conclusion, immersion in vocational practice and in theatrical and live entertainment networks resulted in all the apprentices being offered contracts for their services after they had completed the TA.

THE REP'S TA MODEL: THE INTERTWINING OF VOCATIONAL PRACTICE AND SOCIAL CAPITAL

The development of judgement

The TA is an attempt to design an apprenticeship based on holistic conception of the relationship between knowledge, skill and judgement. From the Rep's perspective, knowledge and skill, irrespective as to whether it is gained from the teaching or learning curriculum, are inextricably 'invested in action', rather than discrete entities that are learnt separately from one another and then applied to practice (Dunne and Pendlebury, 2002). By embedding the TA in the Rep's workflow, John and the HoDs created the conditions for the apprentices to firstly, call upon the different forms of knowledge that they were developing as they dealt with the 'here and now' situations which arose in the theatre. This principle of organisation assisted the apprentices to assess whether a situation is standard and typical and therefore similar to those ones that they have either learnt about or encountered previously, or whether the situation deviates in some significant respects and therefore is not covered by well-known and rehearsed procedures. Secondly, to ensure that apprentices encounter situations where they are able to take, under supervision, modestly acceptable risks in the workplace. Access to this type of situation helped the apprentices to gradually develop the personal resourcefulness to accentuate their knowledge and skill with relevance, appropriateness and sensitivity to context and, in the process, to gradually develop the judgement to decide what was or was not appropriate.

Clearly the notion of acceptable risk implies that access to workplace experience where it is less easy to predict the final result is central to the development of such judgement. This does not mean that the Rep is by any stretch of the imagination advocating that 'raw experience' is a sufficient condition to develop judgement. The provision of a teaching and learning curriculum, supplemented by John's role as mentor to the apprentices and by the HoDs, provided a rich range of support to assist apprentices to apply the different forms of knowledge that they have acquired through talking and working alongside their HoD, through their own self-directed learning, or from their boundary crossing within the Rep and into the wider fields of theatre and live entertainment that they had contact with.

Getting the balance right between these forms of support is crucial to the development of vocational practice because each practice field in the theatre has a specific texture of its own and is also intimately connected to other practice fields. The Rep used the learning and teaching to assist the apprentices to understand this relationship theoretically and practically. The learning curriculum enabled apprentices to see how decisions about appropriate courses of action in one field presuppose an understanding of the consequences of that action for people working in another field. Seeing connections between work areas and anticipating the implications of one's actions for other people working in the theatre presupposes the development of a mode of creative insight. The development of such creative insight requires apprentices to have, firstly, regular opportunities to boundary cross between different practice fields in order to appreciate the way in which a directors' vision inevitably influences the deployment of different facets of vocational practice to realise her/his artistic vision. Secondly, access to a teaching curriculum provides them with an opportunity to reflect amongst themselves and with John about how the different fields of practice cohere with one another in a successful production.

The development of the skill of transfer

The development of the skill of transfer is also, as we have seen, central to the Rep's approach to apprenticeship. The Rep's premise is that learning to transfer skill across theatrical or equivalent contexts such as broadcast media (i.e. television) and outside events (i.e. live productions) involves multiple interrelated social, cultural and organisational processes. Although widely used in the Rep and elsewhere in industry, the term transfer does not really capture what is involved in learning to deploy vocational knowledge and skill in different contexts. This is partly because transfer implies a rather 'atomistic', 'decontextualised' and 'reducationistic' set of assumptions about human activity (see *inter alia* Beach, 2003; Lave, 1988; Tuomi-Gröhn and Engeström, 2003). It is also partly because transfer is used as a 'folk concept' by practitioners to explain complex social and cultural and organisational processes (see John's comments earlier in the chapter). Given the Rep's strong emphasis on the holism of the process of learning vocational practice, the concept of 'recontextualisation' (Guile and Evans, forthcoming) offers a better way to clarify how the TA has supported apprentices to develop their vocational practice and move into their chosen occupational niches.

The concept of recontextualisation is based on a number of interrelated premises. The first premise is that the process of generalisation is central to the development of judgement, and that forming generalisations presupposes grasping the relations and processes that relate individuals' and their prior knowledge to the social organisation of which they are a part. From this perspective, as people begin to learn to recognise a situation and infer what follows they start to develop the capability to replicate or vary those cognitive processes and practical actions in another context. Translated into the context of the Rep, the pedagogic relationships and processes created between apprentices, HoDs and John Pitt established the context for apprentices to visualise, for example, how to hang lights in plays, pantomimes and musicals, and thus to begin to generalise about how to hang lights in other contexts.

The next two premises are related to one another: first, that as people begin to engage with the knowledge invested in practice and its associated artefacts, for example, different types of concepts that have informed the cultural-historical development of a practice such as wig making, they start to develop a specific vocational identity; and, second, the more people are able to move between different theoretical and practical activities in different contexts, the more likely they are to develop the capability to form broader and more encompassing generalisations about their field of practice and its relationship to other vocational practices. Once again, translated into the context of the Rep, as the apprentices communicated with members of other work teams, boundary crossed between occupational specialisms and other theatres, they gradually developed a better understanding of their own practice. This provided them with the basis to recontextualise, that is, to modify and vary their knowledge and skill in relation to the task-in-hand.

CONCLUSION

The chapter concludes with some conceptual and policy observations about the preceding analysis of the Rep's TA. In the case of the former, the chapter has developed one of the first attempts to integrate concepts from socio-cultural and activity theory – object of activity and learning and teaching curricula – with concepts from Social Capital Theory – bonding, bridging and linking – to explain how apprentices can be supported to develop their vocational practice, and to expand their network of contacts so as to position them to gain access to the performing arts' uncertain external labour markets. In doing so, it has been possible to show how the Rep created the organizational and pedagogic conditions to support the aforementioned goals by: (i) enlarging the HoDs work roles to immerse apprentices into specific occupational specialisms; and (ii) securing the support of all staff to assist the apprentices to develop a holistic understanding of their specialism in relation to other specialisms inside and outside the Rep. Specifically, the resulting integrated learning and teaching curriculum provided opportunities for apprentices to:

- immerse themselves in a formal programme of study to provide the background to their chosen occupational niche;
- participate legitimately, albeit, peripherally, with different theatrical technologies of practice in authentic settings and thereby begin to develop the forms of judgement that are integral to the development of vocational practice;
- bond, bridge and link internal networks with the Rep and external networks within the wider field of the theatre and live entertainments to develop the forms of social capital that will help them to gain access to the creative labour market.

This approach constitutes an embryonic, rather than a fully-realised, Socio-cultural and Activity and Social Capital conceptual framework of workplace learning to analyse the development of vocational and social outcomes. A number of issues require further consideration and refinement. They are: (i) the relation between the object of activity and the processes of bonding, bridging and linking. The chapter has used this relation schematically to highlight the way in which the Rep designed the TA to simultaneously enculturate apprentices into different fields of vocational practice and the networks that would support them to work as freelancers in the theatrical/live entertainment industry. Further work needs to be undertaken, however, to establish the principles for relating Socio-cultural Activity Theory and Social Capital Theory to one another, and why and how the notions of bonding, bridging and linking could enhance the pedagogic insights, such as legitimate peripheral participation and learning curriculum, that have been generated by the former theoretical tradition; and, (ii) the relation between the concepts judgement and recontextualisation. The former emanates from Aristotelian philosophy and is an attempt to define the nature of the expertise that arises from a process of vocational formation (Dunne and Pendlebury, 2002) while the latter emanates from Socio-cultural Activity Theory and is an attempt to explain how people deploy vocational expertise in different contexts (Guile, forthcoming). Up to now, little work has been undertaken to reconcile the insights from these two traditions, as a result, the coupling of the two concepts in this chapter is promissory rather than a fully realised accomplishment. This suggests that further work should be undertaken to explore how both concepts can contribute to a better understanding of the relation between the formation and continuing deployment of expertise. This would be enormously helpful in the field of workplace learning because there has been little work undertaken on the continuing development or reformation of expertise.

In the case of the policy issues, the TA is a far-sighted attempt on behalf of Birmingham Repertory Theatre to develop a model of apprenticeship that is appropriate for the type of project culture found in the modern repertory system and, arguably, elsewhere in small and medium size enterprises (SMEs) and micro-businesses which are increasingly a feature of national economies. These types of businesses constitute a difficult challenge for UK and EU policymakers. By and large they operate with 'Welfarist' notions of labour markets (i.e. that all employers will or can be persuaded to recruit regular numbers on an annually recurring basis), and 'Fordist' mechanisms of financial control (i.e. funding Vocational Education and Training (VET) on the basis of the recruitment of annually recurring volumes of apprentices). These assumptions about the labour market and this accountability and funding model are at odds with the growth of SMEs and project-work in the C&C sector in the UK and EU. This is because SMEs, on the one hand, are not necessarily financially and operationally in a position to commit themselves to recruiting volumes of apprentices, and, on the other hand, require bespoke models of apprenticeships that reflect the project-based nature of work in their sector.

The TA provides a number of principles that policymakers could use to sponsor the design of apprenticeships for project-based work contexts and to facilitate access into external labour markets. The principles are designing apprenticeships around, for example, the workflow as much as gaining a vocational qualification; the development of judgement as much as the accumulation of units towards a qualification; and immersion in networks as much as qualifications as a proxy measure for employment.

In advancing this claim, I am not implying that the VET curriculum and qualifications are no longer important, rather that they are only one part of the building blocks for apprenticeship. Based on the above analysis, it is apparent that policymakers should firstly rebalance their preoccupation with the outcomes of learning (i.e. qualifications) by paying more attention to the pedagogic processes that generate the 'social' and 'vocational' forms of expertise that actually assist people to secure employment in the C&C sector. Secondly, policymakers should pay more attention to the way that the webs of relationships and networks of trust amongst employers influence the process of employment. The existence of the latter amongst the UK's national system of repertory theatres meant that the mere knowledge that an apprentice was 'trained' at Birmingham Rep guaranteed their future employability as much as the possession of a nationally recognised qualification. All the apprentices were employed in the field of repertory/live entertainments (John Pitt, interview, October 12 2007). This role of networks reinforces the argument made in this chapter that apprenticeship should be viewed as the development of vocational practice and social capital, and that policymakers should fund models of apprenticeship accordingly.

NOTE

The author and publisher are grateful for permission to reproduce the following material in this book: Chapter 28 – David Guile

Generated Apprenticeship in the Knowledge Economy' *Journal of Vocational Education & Training* 59(4) (2007) pp. 551–574. Reprinted by permission of the publisher Taylor & Francis Ltd, http://www.informaworld.com.

REFERENCES

Beach, K. (2003) 'Consequential Transitions: A Developmental View of knowledge Propagation through Social Organizations'. In T. Tuomi-Gröhn and Y. Engeström (Eds.), *New perspectives on transfer and boundary crossing*. Amsterdam: Elsevier.

Billet, S. (2004) 'Learning through Work: Workplace Participatory Practices', in: H. Rainbird, A. Fuller & A. Munro (Eds.) *Workplace Learning in Context*. London: Routledge, pp. 119–125.

Bilton, C. (2007) *Management and Creativity: From Creative Industries to Creative Management*. London: Blackwell.

Birmingham Rep (2007) *Homepage*. Available online at: http://www.birmingham-rep.co.uk/ (Accessed 14 February 2007).

Boreham, N., Samurçay, R. & Fischer, M. (Eds.) (2002) *Work process knowledge*. London: Routledge.

Dunne, J. & Pendlebury, S. (2002) 'Practical Reason', in: N. Blake *et al* (Eds.) *The Blackwell guide to the philosophy of education*. London: Blackwell.

Evans, K. *et al* (2006) *Improving workplace learning*. London: Routledge.

Guile, D (forthcoming) *The Learning Challenge of the Knowledge Economy*. Rotterdam: Sense Publishers.

Guile, D. & Okumoto, K. (2007) 'We are Trying to Reproduce a Crafts Apprenticeship': from Government Blueprint to Workplace Generated Apprenticeship in the Knowledge Economy, *Journal of Vocational Education and Training*, 59(4), 551–575.

KEA European Affairs (2006) *The Economy of Culture in Europe*. Available online at: http://ec.europa.eu/culture/eac/sources_info/studies/economy_en.html (Accessed 1 March 2007).

Lave, J. (1988) *Cognition in Practice*. Cambridge: Cambridge University Press.

Lash, S. & Urry, J. (1994) *Economies of Signs and Spaces*. London: Routledge.

Lave, J. & Wenger, E. (1991) *Situated Learning: Legitimate Peripheral Participation*. Cambridge: Cambridge University Press.

Nardi, B. (2005) Objects of Desire: Power and Passion in Collaborative Activity *Mind, Culture & Activity* Vol 14 No 1/2 pp 5–22

Rowell, G. & Jackson, A. (1984) *The Repertory Movement: A History of a Regional Theatre in Britain*. Cambridge: Cambridge UP.

Stone, W. (2001) 'Bonding, Bridging and Linking with Social Capital', *Stronger Families Learning Exchange Bulletin*, 4, pp. 13–16.

Tuomi-Gröhn, T. & Engeström, Y. (2003) 'Conceptualising Transfer: From Standard Notions to Developmental Transfer', in: T. Tuomi-Gröhn & Y. Engeström (Eds.) *New perspectives on transfer and boundary crossing*. Oxford, Pergamon, pp.19–38.

29

Workplace Learning and Higher Education

Carol Costley

INTRODUCTION

In higher education (HE), workplace learning can become a part of a university's learning and teaching framework through a flexible and often negotiated curriculum provision. This is usually in the form of work-based learning (WBL) modules and programmes of study, foundation degrees, accreditation of learning gained from work, short courses, continual professional development courses, and other initiatives designated as workplace learning. WBL programmes and modules in higher education (HE) build on workplace learning by positioning the learner as bringing professional expertise and experience to the table of higher education programmes. For the purposes of this chapter work based and workplace are used synonymously.

The learning and teaching approaches used by workplace (or work based) learning practitioners in higher education institutions (HEIs) have broken away from conventional models used in higher education to educate and hence develop people in the workplace. Boud and Solomon (2001, 2003), for example, draw upon evidence from Australia and the UK to argue that workplace learning can be seen as 'one of the very few innovations related to the teaching and learning aspects of post-secondary education that is attempting to engage seriously with the economic, social and educational demands of our era' (2001: 1).

Workplace learning in Europe in higher education and training (HET) has involved a struggle in some member states because of reluctance to accept that learning can take place outside of universities. However, a European credit system for vocational education and training allows the possibility for universities to recognise vocational learning outcomes through the award of credit and for individuals to accumulate and transfer credit (ECVET) (www://ec.europa.eu/education/ecvt/work-en.pdf). The recognition of the value of knowledge creation and learning at work is central to issues of workplace learning and higher education. Other writers have gone further in understanding higher education and workplace learning in Europe to discuss issues such as political will and other important conceptual issues (Davies and Feutrie, 2008; Schmidt and Gibbs, 2009).

The broad area of workplace learning in higher education draws its academic focus from high-level practical knowledge and learning in a workplace context. In this formulation, the context of the learning lies outside the university, and this is a key feature of the field. Costley (2000) among others emphasise the importance of the learner's context and previous experience as the starting-point for the curriculum, with Boud (2001) noting that for individual learners the curriculum is essentially defined by the nature and context of their work.

The recognition of knowledge that emanates from work as a source of learning (Boud and Garrick, 1999) positions workplace learning students in their particular situated context rather than in disciplinary knowledge (though they may also draw on disciplinary knowledge). They often have insider knowledge, are primarily concerned with professional practice, and there is a deliberate focus on student autonomy and capability (Stephenson and Yorke, 1998), giving workplace learning a particular learner-centredness (Osborne et al., 1998).

Wider debates about the nature and creation of knowledge frequently refer to Gibbons et al.'s (1994) notions of non-disciplinary and transdisciplinary knowledge which are posed as being legitimate and recognisable by universities whereas the more codified knowledge of the disciplines has traditionally informed thinking and held sway for many generations.

PEDAGOGY

Introducing genuine workplace learning curricula has some significant implications for higher education. The power-balance between the university and the learner is changing more to one of partnership, and Lester (2002) comments on the need for universities to work through partnership or 'realisation' systems rather than through expert 'delivery systems'. Boud and Solomon (2001) describe workplace learning as a 'disturbing practice' that challenges the disciplinary structure of the university. Garnett (2007) states that it can sit uncomfortably with structures and procedures designed primarily to meet the needs of full-time undergraduates. Lester (2004) suggests that workplace learning can provide a platform for a university to develop expertise outside the traditional areas of teaching and research.

There is a broad approach to workplace learning pedagogy arising from UK and Australian universities that have significant numbers of students taking workplace learning modules and programmes and a distinctive approach to workplace learning pedagogy that uses particular learning strategies and assessment protocols through peer external examining. These HEIs focus on the development of a workplace curriculum and provide publications related to learning and teaching in the field. The work is supported by some of the research centres that specialise in Work and Learning, for example, the work of the Institute of Education, University of London, and the University of Technology, Sydney. There are increasing amounts of published work from these researchers, thus adding important pedagogical dimensions to the growing body of literature in this field.

Boud (2001) suggests that the wider process and pedagogic questions represented by a 'curriculum' is appropriate to workplace learning, not in the sense of defining a syllabus or programme but to capture the overall set of learning and pedagogic processes that make up workplace learning. See also O'Connor's (2004) ideas relating to a workplace curriculum.

There is agreement that university-level workplace learning needs to involve reflection that moves the learner beyond performative competence into understanding and judgement. There is generally also a consensus that to be valid in higher education terms, learners need to develop understanding that goes beyond the 'present and particular' (Brennan et al., 2006). Related to this is the now widespread use of generic level-based descriptors or criteria that are designed to accredit transdisciplinary or field-independent learning into qualification frameworks (Costley, 2000).

A workplace curriculum also draws in and builds on prior learning, often moving beyond a simple accreditation of prior e learning process to using learners' experience as a basis for reflection and further development (Armsby et al., 2006).

A more complete description of what can be termed a workplace learning curriculum is found in Boud and Solomon (2001) who use the learner's work as a starting-point, and emphasise the real-time, contested and transdisciplinary nature of workplace knowledge. They list seven key elements of a workplace learning curriculum: (1) a learning enterprise that is undertaken mainly at work while not being identical to work; (2) acknowledging the diverse range of knowledge and skills brought to the programme by learners; (3) locating learning outcomes in a framework of standards and levels of achievement; (4) a negotiated programme of activities; (5) supporting ongoing learning *in situ*; (6) encouraging critical reflection throughout; and (7) documenting learning in an assessable form relative to (3). Adding to this, Nixon et al. (2006) emphasise an experiential, learner-centred pedagogy where the curriculum is derived from the workplace context and the learners' knowledge and experience, and where learners agree outcomes through a learning contract that generally help them develop and broaden their understanding and ability to apply and develop theories and constructs in complex situations.

WORKPLACE LEARNING AS A FIELD OR MODE OF STUDY

Much in these descriptions of a workplace curriculum regard it as a *field* of study, rather than as a mode of learning within an existing disciplinary or occupational framework. This conception used at Middlesex University sees workplace learning as having its own set of principles and methodologies within which learners focus on their contexts and priorities rather than working within existing academic disciplines. Workplace learning can be used purely as a mode of study within a disciplinary framework, although this can potentially lead to tensions between the experience-based knowledge of learners and the propositional knowledge of academics.

Information and communications technology offering opportunities to improve dialogue and support has become a major feature of many workplace learning programmes. The introduction of the 'Learndirect' *Learning through Work* system (Saxton and Stephenson, 2005) placed initial programme planning and, in many instances, ongoing support is provided via web-based tools and learning environments; a wide range of approaches to on-line support ranging from simple learner–tutor interaction through sophisticated learning environments to simple provision of resources. Young and Stephenson (2007) found that learners are often very responsive to sustaining academic discourse on-line and this mode of support for workplace learning is highly effective provided that tutors adopt a facilitative rather than a directive approach while maintaining a focus on the academic parameters of the learning.

Where workplace learning 'departs substantially from the disciplinary framework of university study' and develops 'new pedagogies for learning' (Boud and Solomon, 2001) it needs to be supported by appropriate methodologies for assessment. Costley and Armsby, (2007) describe how inappropriate integration and assessment can undermine learning. This occurs both where workplace learning is used as a mode of learning but the type of knowledge that is generated from work goes unacknowledged, and where it is a field of learning in its own right but it is assessed through methods that are too closely tied to routine performance or 'appropriate' disciplinary knowledge. They conclude that workplace learning needs to be assessed against generic criteria based in a philosophy of reflective practice. Brodie and Irving (2007) broadly concur, seeing assessment as needing to reflect the interrelationships between understanding learning, critical reflection and the development of capability in the practice context. Harvey and Slaughter (2007) comment on the need to use assessment practices that are more reflective of the kinds of social, cultural and contextual knowledge used by practitioners in the workplace.

Eraut and Hirsch (2007) note that individuals judged on their performance need to know what improvement is needed, but they should also be offered ideas about how that performance might be achieved; in this way, the process shifts the focus from judgement to development.

The type of learner support needed on work-based programmes generally differs from that needed for taught courses (Boud and Costley, 2007) and conventional research degrees (Stephenson et al. 2006). It requires a different, if overlapping set of skills from those needed to teach courses or supervise research students, wherein an ability for advisers (teachers) to act in a more facilitative capacity is called upon. The relationship between adviser and learner ideally moves from one of expert 'delivery' to partnership 'realisation' (Lester, 2002), something that may not sit easily within the dominant culture of the university (Garnett, 2007).

Saxton and Stephenson (2005) identify several practical factors that make for good tutor support, whether provided on-line or personally. These include:

- advice at the time it is needed, mainly in response to queries;
- responsiveness to learner initiative and suggestions;
- support with generic issues relevant to programme procedures and success criteria;
- help in thinking things through;
- help to adjust to the (unfamiliar) culture of higher education;
- advice that helps learners to formulate, articulate and justify their achievements and intentions;
- constructive, confidence-building feedback;
- a focus on helping learners take themselves forward;
- sensitivity to changes in the learner's workplace.

Brennan et al.'s (2006) report to HEFCE on workplace learning strategies noted that, across the spectrum of higher education provision, many staff now had some experience of engaging with employers and their employees in negotiated workplace learning programmes leading to higher education awards. But they also noted that the distributed nature of workplace learning implied that different aspects of the learning process will need to be shared between different actors, and such a changing division of labour in supporting [such] learning 'will have implication for the roles of academic staff based in higher education' and of 'workplace' based staff (ibid.: 83). Further, they noted that the delivery of negotiated programmes required changes 'to the traditional role of academic staff (which might require new skills sets)' (ibid.: 83).

Learning agreements or contracts and partnerships

Stephenson and Yorke (1998), Anderson et al. (1996), and Garnett (1998) describe the use of learning agreements or contracts as a central part of the workplace learning curriculum, normally negotiated in conjunction with the learner's employer.

In workplace learning contexts learning contracts may be employed to support work towards predetermined outcomes such as the requirements of a syllabus or competence specification. Osborne et al. (1998) describe this type of workplace learning programme as being particularly valuable in more open curricula where the programme (or a significant part of it) is built around the experience, context and work focus or aspirations of the learner.

In the UK's Learning through Work (LtW) framework, an overall framework contract can be developed at programme level with specific detail being added for individual components as the programme progresses (Saxton and Stephenson, 2005). The LtW model broadly follows Stephenson's notion of a 'capability envelope' where a learning contract is drawn up at the outset of a programme and supported by ongoing review and tutor support, enabling changes and renegotiation to be incorporated as needed within the overall coherence of the contract.

In the workplace, learning contracts provide a means of formalising what is otherwise often an informal and sometimes ad-hoc process of learning. Many organisations are already using personal development plans or the equivalent as part of their employee and organisational development processes. Learning contracts can be seen as formalising self-managed workplace learning that focus employees on learning objectives that can be reported and reflected upon. These often do not have any links to formally accredited activity, although they do offer a common language and structure to bring together organisational, professional (including CPD), personal and academic objectives and requirements. Garnett (2000) discusses organisational involvement in learning agreements for university-accredited workplace learning programmes, and indicates that for the agreement to work properly the employer needs to be an active partner in the agreement. He also comments that the culture of the work organisation will have a significant effect on the learning agreement and the resulting programme, and this needs to be understood and managed by university staff.

Learning contracts/agreements may need to be better incorporated into wider processes. Nixon et al. state that quality assurance procedures and codes of practice 'will need to better reflect the breadth of approaches to flexible learning being adopted by HEIs so as not to stifle innovation in the future' (2006: 51). Williams proposes that, workplace learning 'frees higher education from the concept of physical borders and methods of delivery are without limit and the landscape is rich in opportunity' (2006: 191) and that 'these factors pose various challenges for effective quality assurance' (2006: 191). He echoes the issues made more forcefully in the QAA Code of Practice in the UK relating to work-based and placement learning (2007) which highlights concerns over the responsibilities of partners, the communication roles and the management of students, employers and universities.

Learning contacts could increase influence and impact on workplace development. An essential element to increase the impact of workplace learning on stakeholders is to ensure that learning opportunities are strongly linked to the learning needs of individuals and organisations within the framework of and context of 'future economic and technological changes'. This view is complemented by Garnett (2003) when reporting a case study on university–employer partnership. He suggests that the experience from this partnership illustrates the potential of a well-planned and implemented university–employer partnership workplace learning programme to challenge the deficit model of higher education that monopolises the supply of high-level and privileged knowledge to a model that recognises and extends the intellectual knowledge of employers and partners produced in the work context.

Nixon et al. (2008) found workplace learning graduates (from a variety of work based programmes) and their employers benefit from workplace learning programmes in terms of developing practice, building self-confidence and the appropriate skills to take on more challenging roles. However, one important lesson emerging from this study is the need for universities providing workplace learning to acknowledge the uniqueness of the process in its delivery, and to restructure in order to meet this uniqueness. Reeve and Gallacher (2005) pick on this 'structural fitness dilemma' to question the overemphasis of partnership in the development of workplace learning and work-related learning in higher education. They propose that there is limited evidence to suggest that employers are interested in the type of partnership promoted in workplace learning programmes partly due to the learning cultures embedded in different organisations and the quality assurance agenda of higher education.

Tasker and Peckham (1994) and later Barnett (2000) found that academic and industrial values are incommensurable, and that it is only by mutual respect that constructive collaboration can be fruitful. As Evans et al. describe it: 'the workplace is a site in which antagonistic relationships are expressed' (2006: 6). The focused and strategic development of learning agreements can act as a real attempt to bring the two worlds together to integrate and facilitate the learning experience. Yet despite its advantages, a learning contract may not offer the credibility required to give parity of esteem with traditional disciplined-based awards. There are continuing debates (in both the worlds of work and education) of what higher education is and how it should be evaluated. Pointing out such debates, Nixon et al. claim that quality assurance procedures and codes of practice 'will need to better reflect the breadth of approaches to flexible learning being adopted by HEIs so as not to stifle innovation in the future' (2006: 51).

Recognising informal workplace learning

A feature in the recognition of workplace learning is through the Accreditation or Acknowledgement of Prior Education and Learning (APEL). Although assessment and quality assurance processes for APEL are now becoming well-established (e.g. Johnson, 2002; QAA, 2004; Johnson and Walsh, 2005), its use and value is still a subject of debate in higher education.

Nixon et al. (2006) find that 'anomalies exist in the functioning of institutionally or regionally driven credit-based systems. For instance, the maximum amount of credit a student can achieve through APEL varies by institution and as such a rather arbitrary system seems to have emerged' (2006: 51). This challenge is particularly well covered by Brennan (2005) and Connor (2005).

As APEL practice continues to advance within workplace learning, the distinction between prior and planned learning, begins to blur. Chisholm and Davis (2007) challenge the standard practice in most universities that APEL should contribute no more than a proportion of an accredited programme, suggesting a model closer to the idea of the PhD by published work. Supporting and assessing APEL claims is sometimes thought of as a relatively costly activity for the HEI, and as APEL becomes more widely used, universities are seeking to improve the process and make it more efficient.

The accreditation of in-company training and learning by higher education institutions is now an established feature of the higher education landscape, having emerged particularly since the introduction of credit accumulation and transfer (CAT) systems in the 1980s, and given renewed impetus in recent government policy pushes towards increased employer engagement with higher education (see for example, Wedgwood, 2008). Initially the majority of this activity focused on in-house training courses, and to a smaller extent on full qualifications delivered in companies often with significant input from university staff. Subsequently accreditation has developed to include a much wider range of options that include customised or company-negotiated programmes and accreditation for individual experiential learning in-company.

University accreditation normally requires that learning demonstrates reflection, understanding and informed judgement and goes beyond performative notions of competence, and that it has wider applicability than within the host organisation alone (Brennan et al., 2006). Several authors indicate that there is increasingly common ground between the interests of the university and the workplace in this respect, with a trend for employers to see worthwhile benefits in developing the kinds of high-level abilities sought in higher education. In comparison, the use of higher-level National Vocational Qualifications in the workplace is declining.

Garnett et al. (2004) advocate a learning recognition and development perspective that is forward-looking, builds learning capacity and generates knowledge within workplaces, and adds to organisations' intellectual capital. These models may vary widely in the way that they partition responsibilities and activities between university and employer.

For universities, these partnership-based forms of accreditation point to changes in the way that universities engage with employers, in the way that they organise employer-facing provision, and in their epistemologies of practice.

For employers, there can be equivalent changes in culture and ways of working that occur as a result of partnership activity, particularly when this extends beyond the straightforward accreditation of in-house courses. The types of accredited activity that are appropriate is likely to depend on organisational culture (Garnett, 2000) and on the type of learning opportunities available within the workplace (Ashton and Sung, 2002; Brennan et al., 2006).

Practitioner-led projects

Practitioner research projects are a central feature of workplace learning programmes at university level (Boud and Costley, 2007; Rhodes and Shiel, 2007). They may take the form of a distinct project or investigation, or be an expansion of an activity that practitioners undertake in the normal course of their work (Costley, 2007) and in some cases activities that are already complete but can be used as the basis for reflection and further learning (Lester, 2002; Chisholm and Davis, 2007). Practitioner research within workplace learning provides both an academically valid approach to the study of issues arising in the workplace as well as being a developmental and change-oriented activity in organisations. As the field of workplace learning has developed in universities, improved understanding has emerged of how research works in practice-based contexts where the research is usually geared to affecting practice and where it is frequently cross-disciplinary in nature. At the highest levels the idea of the 'researching professional' (Bourner et al., 2001), or 'executive scholar' (Morley and Priest, 2001) has been used to distinguish between practitioner-researchers who are involved in researching within their own work situation, and professional academic researchers who are 'outside' the community being researched.

Ethical issues and tensions in practitioner research are explored in relation to confidentiality and researching with co-workers, and to manage tensions between themselves as researchers and practitioners, the needs and values of their organisation and those of the university (Costley et al., 2010).

The scale of projects involved range from small investigations that can be accommodated in a single module to major pieces of work that form the basis of doctorates and result in significant organisational or professional change.

Reflection and reflexivity

Two relevant strands relating to reflection are critiques of the concept of reflective practice in work and the professions, and the other practical guides to reflective activities within academic courses.

Boud et al. (2006) focus on reflection and informal learning at work and develop earlier ideas about the importance of social context. They suggest a new role for reflection in the context of organisational productivity. Opportunities for informal and collective reflection are created by the current trends towards organisational de-layering and devolving of management responsibilities to teams in the effort to remain sustainable. Conditions for effective collaborative reflection are discussed, such as the need for the workplace to be structurally designed to support reflective learning and also, in contrast, that un-designed, informal spaces are also made available, where group reflection through spontaneous dialogue can occur. An ethical dimension to reflection is also stressed, with discussion of the development of capacity for reflection as a means for the workforce to make sense of work and, by giving it meaning, contribute to organisational sustainability and excellence.

Moon (2004) provides a 'handbook' of reflective activities that can be incorporated into formal educational programmes. This practical focus is preceded by a discussion of reflection as an aspect of experiential learning. It is this that makes the book relevant to workplace learning. She argues that both reflection and experiential learning are relatively unmediated by teachers (in the sense that they do not rely on a formal taught curriculum), and thus their value extends beyond formal learning into the kinds of self-managed continuing professional development that may occur in the workplace. Other writers, such as Bolton (2006), base theories of reflection in discussion around reflexivity.

Different conceptualisations underlie different perspectives on reflection. There is sometimes interchangeable use of 'reflection' and 'critical reflection'. Moon (ibid.) distinguishes between 'reflective learning', 'reflective writing' and 'reflective practice' and characterises reflection in academic contexts as a process of re-organising knowledge with the purpose of achieving further insights about it, often with the view to then representing it in writing for assessment (which might change the nature of the reflection). In contrast, a definition of reflection highlights its relation to social context and how social dimensions and political functions are understood. This position clearly aligns with Boud et al. (2006) and confirms there is now a new focus on reflection as a collective activity.

The social context of reflection has relevance to organisational learning and practical educational use in group settings but there is a lack of consensus about reflection and of theorising about it, which may influence the effectiveness of its application. Since reflection is applied widely in workplace learning contexts, these are important considerations for future work in the area.

THE SOCIAL CONTEXT OF WORKPLACE KNOWLEDGE

The workplace itself is a crucially important site for learning and access to learning that needs a better understanding of the social nature of workplace learning and the economic and political frameworks which shape, regulate and drive policy in the area (Evans et al., 2006). The principle that workplace learning is concerned primarily with what Gibbons et al., (1994) term 'mode 2' knowledge is widely, although not universally, held, i.e. a socially distributed knowledge production system generated within a context of application. They were describing a new basis for the relationship between higher education and the wider economic, social and intellectual changes associated with a globalising and information-based society. The changes involve a move away from an elite form of higher education to a mass system that no longer seeks to reproduce a rigid class system.

Nowotny et al. (2001) highlight apparent contradictions between universities' scientific and social roles. The expanding field of workplace learning has enabled a wider access to higher education but has experienced difficulties within higher education systems because of its highly contextualised approach to knowledge outside of the university in the social sphere. The field of workplace learning has found that forming knowledge interests, alliances and regimes that define new kinds of knowledge outside the university (Bleiklie and Byrkjeflot, 2002) has led to new and innovative approaches to knowledge such as Mode-2 knowledge, horizontal learning, inter-connectivity, generic criteria, multidimensional and inter-professional learning.

Expansion in higher education is not only a matter of expanding curricula for a more diverse community of learners; HE also has to overcome a fairly unchanging model of knowledge creation, generation and use. However, issues and problems regarding many of the changes in the social context of knowledge do not seem to have made an impression on policy makers at all. This may be due to a lack of safe points of reference and uncertainty in the system concerning the development of new conceptual and policy matters. Perhaps as educators there is less common purpose in the belief that education should extend horizons, challenge assumptions, provide rigorous intellectual enquiry and promote a humanistic sceptical mindset (Taylor et al., 2002). Engaging the university with the whole community and not just an elite part of society, and bringing enquiry into the whole range of areas of importance to people, requires a closer relationship with communities outside academe. These factors are leading to a changing pedagogical role for universities: workplace learning in its ability to construct its own distinctiveness in an epistemology of praxis by developing new dynamic relationships between knowledge and values is opening up new possibilities. Such a field has been apparent in the prestige within which professional practice is held with its underpinning of ethical codes of conduct, and its a long history that dates back to the Workers' Educational Association, friendly societies and rekindling the relatedness of knowledge creation.

As well as being dependent on context, the field is concerned with the generic area of work, and knowledge content is transdisciplinary. Learning gained in, through and for work represents a significant proportion of what is counted as 'important knowledge' according to contemporary discourses relating to a 'knowledge society'. Multi-national corporations, the education sector, professional bodies, government departments and other agencies and communities are redefining their roles regarding access to and ownership of knowledge. Drawing on the spheres of the professional, the academic and the experiential, workplace learning can use instruments that approach knowledge that is not confined to discrete disciplines but focuses on the multidimensional nature of knowledge needed for understanding differing contexts of work.

Workplace learning fits very well into management philosophies of development and change and the way organisations are often now concerned with the development of new knowledge. The structure of workplace learning programmes is such that individuals or groups, in association with their organisation or professional area, can usually design a customised programme of study, which is responsive to the needs and aspirations of both candidates and their organisations.

Knowledge recognition, creation and use is likely to occur mainly at the stage of the work-based project that students usually undertake at the end of their programme of studies. Scott et al. (2004: 158) usefully point to how the 'co-production of knowledge has the potential to enrich the workplace'. They argue that for university awards (they are specifically discussing professional doctorates) it is 'the way universities understand and in the process construct relationships between academic and professional knowledge' (p. 42) that is important for workplace learners.

PARTICIPATION AND PROGRESSION

Workplace learning is widely regarded as increasing participation and progression in higher education, particularly for adult learners, but gaining reliable statistics on this is difficult because of differences in what are recorded as workplace programmes. Though there is some data on workplace learners accessing, and progressing through part-time higher education programmes, there is less on the effects on participation in workplace learning programmes and the backgrounds of workplace learners. And while, in principle, workplace higher education should provide opportunities for progression from apprenticeships and other Level 3 work-based programmes, there is little formal evidence of how progression is operating; there is also a lack of continuity and dialogue between 'post-16' versions of workplace learning and those used in higher education (Connor, 2005). With the advent of work-related foundation degrees (and renewed emphasis by government on apprenticeships in general) this situation may change in the future.

Nevertheless, there is clear evidence from universities that workplace programmes are attracting learners who would otherwise not have engaged with higher education or would have taken longer to do so. This occurs at all levels, although at postgraduate level the reasons may emphasise time issues and perceived relevance rather than confidence and issues about going 'to' university: for instance in research by Stephenson et al. (2006) a majority of the candidates interviewed had explicitly rejected doing a PhD before enrolling on a work-based doctorate.

CONCLUSION

Workplace learning requires a pedagogical understanding that relates not only to the teaching of adults but also to the acknowledgement of the existing experience and positionality of the student. It offers students the opportunity to develop themselves further because it is project-based, grounded in practice and tailored to the requirements of people at work. From current research, based on student interviews, we have found that an important reason why many practitioners select workplace learning is that it offers them a new and challenging transdisciplinary learning opportunity that will develop them further and provide a new challenge. Students are also particularly attracted to the way work-based projects are conceptualised in that it is, usually, directly related to their real-time work activities. Workplace learning is necessarily focused on the learners themselves within their particular organisation or professional area, not within the university but informed by the university. It formulates the possibility in which control of content, research method, context, assessment, and partnership between university and the profession lies with the participant within a generic framework of procedures and support offered by the university.

The construction of knowledge outside of the university means that learning takes place in a way that is associated more with self-direction of learning than being formally taught by teachers. Workplace learning is generated, controlled and used within a community of practice and brings new understanding to pedagogical principles as the role of the worker becomes also that of learner. The mode of learning enables students to work at a distance, using open learning techniques, as self-managed learners in their work-related context.

The profile of students of workplace learning in higher education is often that of self-managed practitioners capable of advancing their practice and operating effectively in environments of uncertainty and change.

Students might be individuals working in an organisation, community or voluntary organisation, or they might be part of a group who are undertaking an award as part of their staff development, sponsored by an employer or other funding source. Many workplace learning students in higher education are experienced practitioners who have developed the ability to learn autonomously and wish to improve themselves, their practice and their capability within the communities where they practice. Students often undertake the programmes for personal and/or career development. In workplace learning it is usually considered that effective practitioners are reflective people who are able to use current knowledge and ability to develop interests and become change-makers within their particular working contexts and sometimes also within their professional areas. The academic area of workplace learning has the capacity to acknowledge the interests of the student, the organisation/community and higher education academic interests. Workplace learning in HE is not without its problems. For example, there could be conflict of interest between the individual work based learner's benefit and organisational benefit.

Workplace learning programmes have moved from schools of education to business schools, from business schools to schools of education, and one from a central service to a school of education. We have also seen fairly well-established workplace learning programmes close down completely and workplace learning centralised in universities with a workplace learning unit (or named people) in each school or faculty, but mainly we have seen many programmes start up and proliferate within and across disciplines in mainly new universities (in the UK) but also in universities internationally.

Workplace learning, however, it is constructed, usually shares approaches to knowledge and understanding that are generated outside of the university in a context of practice. There is also a sharing of pedagogical approaches, where students are 'experts' in the sense that they are or have been in a particular work situation and have an understanding of its nuances, micropolitics and so on.

The flexibility in ways of approaching workplace learning programmes mean that a range of models of WBL can be offered. Partnership programmes, individual programmes, programmes that build opportunities for individuals to accredit some or all of their experiential learning, programmes that include taught modules from in or outside the university are all part of a negotiated flexible curriculum structure. Workplace learning programmes can be for people whose work is in paid employment, in their community or working in other communities on a voluntary basis. The widest range of models is possible where the awards have generic assessment criteria, are negotiated through learning agreements and where there is an holistic interpretation given to the term 'work'. Workplace learning can embrace these definitions and has the flexibility to meet the needs of many people who work and are ready to study at a higher education level. Universities' systems and structures need to be flexible and have a focus on learners who are work-based, often part time, learning at a distance with occasional visits to campus.

The story of workplace learning in a higher education setting needs to be told by those who are involved in its development. It does appear that, particularly at lower levels of workplace learning, a crude and worrying vocationalism exists that is not underpinned by a higher level approach to knowledge and to learning – and this needs to be addressed. Added to this, the focus by governments on meeting economic needs provides a rhetoric that is being accepted into the discourse of many workplace learning practitioners and other academics as well. Workplace learning is being funded in many instances because of its direct advantage for workplace performance and in turn its benefit to national economies.

Workplace learning can be seen as a result of changes that have focused on a shift from an elite to a mass model of higher education and have become more market retentive and reactive (Light and Cox, 2001). Although there is also a sense in which workplace learning can be seen as representing a conflation of what has hitherto been high and low aspects of intellectual culture, and in that sense it can be emancipatory.

REFERENCES

Anderson, G., Boud, D. and Sampson, J. (1996). *Learning Contracts: A Practical Guide*. London: Kogan Page.
Armsby, P., Costley, C. and Garnett, J. (2006) 'The Legitimisation of Knowledge: A Work-Based Learning Perspective of APEL', *International Journal of Lifelong Learning*, 25(4): 369–383.

Ashton, D. and Sung, J. (2002) *Supporting Workplace Learning for High Performance Working*, Geneva: ILO.

Barnett, R. (2000) *Realising the University in an Age of Supercomplexity*. Buckingham: SRHE and OU Press.

Bleiklie, I. and Byrkjeflot, H. (2002) 'Changing Knowledge Regimes: Universities in a New Research Environment', *Higher Education*, 44(3–4): 519–532.

Bolton, G. (2006) 'Narrative Writing: Reflective Enquiry into Professional Practice', *Educational Action Research*, 14(2): 203–218.

Boud, D. (2001) Using journal writing to enhance reflective practice, in L.M. English and M.A. Gillen (eds), *Promoting Journal Writing in Adult Education, New Directions in Adult and Continuing Education*, 90(9–18): San Francisco: Jossey-Bass.

Boud D. and N. Solomon (eds) (2nd edn 2003) *Work-Based Learning: A New Higher Education?* Buckingham: Society for Research into Higher Education/Open University Press.

Boud, D., Cressey, P. and Docherty, P. (ed.) (2006) *Productive Reflection at Work. Learning for Changing Organizations*. London: Routledge.

Boud, D. and Costley, C. (2007) 'From Project Supervision to Advising: New Conceptions of the Practice', *Innovations in Education and Teaching International*, 44(2): 119–130.

Boud, D. and Garrick, J. (1999) *Understanding Learning at Work*. London: Routledge.

Boud, D. and N. Solomon (eds) (2001) *Work-Based Learning: A New Higher Education?* Buckingham: Society for Research into Higher Education/Open University Press.

Bourner, T., Bowden, R. and Laing. S. (2001) 'Professional Doctorates in England', *Studies in Higher Education*, 26(1): 65–83.

Brennan, J. (2005) *Integrating Work-based Learning into Higher Education: A Guide to Good Practice*. Bolton: Universities Vocational Awards Council. Available at: www.uvac.ac.uk/downloads/0401_publications/int_wbl.pdfp.13 (accessed 14/10/09).

Brennan, J., Little, B., Connor, H., de Weert, E., Delve, S., Harris, J., Josselyn, B., Ratcliffe, N. and Scesa, A. (2006) *Towards a Strategy for Workplace Learning: Report to HEFCE by CHERI and KPMG*. Higher Education Funding Council for England, Bristol, UK.

Brodie, P. and Irving, K. (2007) 'Assessment in Work-Based Learning: Investigating a Pedagogical Approach to Enhance Student Learning', *Assessment & Evaluation in Higher Education*, 32(1): 11–19.

Chisholm, C. and Davis, M. (2007) 'Analysis and Evaluation of Factors Relating to Accrediting 100% of Prior Experiential Learning in UK Work-Based Awards', *Assessment & Evaluation in Higher Education*, 32(1): 45–59.

Costley, C. and Armsby, P. (2007) 'Methodologies for Undergraduates Doing Practitioner Investigation at Work', *Journal of Workplace Learning*, 19(3): 131–145.

Connor, H. (2005) *Workforce Development in Higher Education*. London: The Council for Industry and Higher Education.

Costley, C. (2000) 'Work Based Learning: An Accessible Curriculum', *Widening Participation and Lifelong Learning*, 5: 33–39.

Costley, C. (2007) 'Work-Based Learning: Assessment and Evaluation in Higher Education', *Assessment & Evaluation in Higher Education*, 32(1): 1–9.

Costley, C., Elliott, G. and Gibbs, P. (2010) *Doing Work Based Research*. London: Sage.

Davies P. and Feutrie M. (2008) 'University Lifelong Learning to Lifelong Learning Universities', *EUA Bologna Handbook*, Article B 1.6–9, Raabe Academic Publishers (Berlin).

Eraut, M. and Hirsch, W. (2007) *The Significance of Workplace Learning for Individuals, Groups and Organisations* 2007. SKOPE Research Centre: Oxford and Cardiff, UK.

Evans, K., Hodkinson, P., Rainbird, L. and Unwin, L. (2006) *Improving Workplace Learning*. London: Routledge.

European Credit system for Vocational Education and Training (ECVET): A System for the Transfer, Accumulation and Recognition of Learning Outcomes in Europe http://ec.europa.eu/education/ecvt/work_en.pdf

Garnett, J. (2000) 'Organisational Cultures and the Role of Learning Agreements', in *Work Based Learning and the University: New Perspectives and Practices*. Birmingham. D. Portwood and C. Costley (eds). SEDA Paper 109.

Garnett, J. (1998) *Using APEL to Develop Customised Work Based Learning Programmes at Postgraduate Level*. Beyond Graduateness, South East England Consortium for Credit Accumulation and Transfer, Page Bros.

Garnett, J. (2007) 'Employers and University Partnerships', in *Employers, Skills and Higher Education*, in S. Roodhouse and S. Swailes (eds). Chichester: Kingsham.

Garnett J., Portwood, D. and Costley, C. (2004) *Bridging Rhetoric and Reality: Accreditation of Prior Experiential Learning (APEL) in the UK*. Commissioned report for the Universities Vocational Awards Council (UVAC).

Gibbons, M., Limoges, C., Nowotny, H., Schwartzman, S., Scott, P. and Trow, M. (1994) *The New Production of Knowledge: The Dynamics of Science and Research in Contemporary Societies*. London: Sage.

Harvey, M. and Slaughter, T. (2007) 'Evaluation of an Access_Route to Higher Education through a Work-Based Assessment Strategy', *Assessment & Evaluation in Higher Education*, 32(1): 35–43.

Johnson, B. (2002) *Models of APEL and Quality Assurance*, Brentwood: Southern England. Consortium for Credit Accumulation and Transfer (SEEC).

Johnson, B., Walsh, A. (2005) SEEC Companion to the QAA Guidelines on the Accreditation of Prior Learning. London: Southern England Consortium for Credit Accumulation and Transfer.

Lester, S. (2002) 'Negotiated Work-Based Learning: From Delivery To Realisation', *Capability*, 5(1): 6–9.

Lester, S. (2004) 'Conceptualising the Practitioner Doctorate', *Studies in Higher Education*, 29(6): 757–770.

Lester, S. (2007) 'Professional Practice Projects: APEL or Development?', *Journal of Workplace Learning*, 19(3): 18–202. Accessed 14th December 2009 http://www.sld.demon.co.uk/projects.pdf

Light, G. and Cox, R. (2001) *Learning and Teaching in Higher Education: The Reflective Professional.* London: Sage Publications.

Moon, J. (2004) *Reflection in Learning and Professional Development: Theory and Practice.* London: Kogan Page.

Morley, C.L. and Priest, J. (2001) 'Developing a Professional Doctorate Business Administration: Reflection and the "Executive Scholar"', in B. Green, T.W. Maxwell and P. Shanahan, *Doctoral Education and Professional Practice: The Next Generation*, Armidale: Kardoorait Press, pp. 163–186.

Nixon, I., Smith, S., Stafford, R. and Camm, S. (2006) *Work-Based Learning: Illuminating the Higher Education Landscape.* Final Report for the Higher Education Academy (www.heacademy.ac.uk/researchpublications.htm).

Nixon, I. (2008) 'Work-Based Learning Impact Study', *Higher Education Academy.* York, Higher Education Academy. Accessed 14th December 2009. http://www.heacademy.ac.uk/assets/York/documents/impact_work_based_learning.pdf.

Nowotny, H., Scott, P. and Gibbons, M. (2001) *Re-thinking Science: Knowledge and the Public in an Age of Uncertainty.* Cambridge: Polity Press.

O'Connor, B.N. (2004) 'The Workplace Learning Cycle: A Problem-Based Curriculum Model for the Preparation of Workplace Learning Professionals', *Journal of Workplace Learning*, 16(6): 341–349.

Osborne, C., Davies, J. and Gamett, J. (1998) 'Guiding the Student to the Centre of the Stakeholder Curriculum: Independent and Work-Based Learning at Middlesex University', In J. Stephenson and M. Yorke, (eds), *Capability and Quality in Higher Education.* London: Kogan Page.

QAA (2004) *Guidelines on the Accreditation of Prior Learning,* The Quality Assurance Agency for Higher Education. Accessed 14th December 2009. http://www.qaa.ac.uk/academicinfrastructure/apl/APL.pdf

QAA (2007) 'Code of Practice for the Assurance of Academic Quality and Standards in Higher Education, Section 9: Work-based and placement learning', *The Quality Assurance Agency for Higher Education.* http://www.qaa.ac.uk/academicinfrastructure/codeOfPractice/section9/placementLearning.pdf

Reeve, F. and Gallacher, J. (2005) 'Employer–University "Partnerships": A Key Problem for Work-Based Learning Programmes?', *Journal of Education and Work,* 18(4): 221–235.

Rhodes. G. and Shiel, G. (2007) 'Meeting the Needs of the Workplace and the Learner through Work-Based Learning', *Journal of Workplace Learning,* 19(3): 173–87.

Schmidt, R. and Gibbs, P. (2009) 'The Challenges of Work-Based Learning in the Changing Context of the European Higher Education Area', *European Journal of Education.* 44(3): 399–410.

Saxton, J. and Stephenson, J. (2005) 'An Initial Evaluation of Participant Experiences of Ufl/learndirect's Online Learning through Work Programme Leading to Full University Qualifications', *Journal Industry and Higher Education.*

Scott, D., Brown, A., Lunt, I. and Thorne, L. (2004) *Professional Doctorates: Integrating Professional and Academic Knowledge.* Milton Keynes: Open University Press.

Stephenson J., Malloch, M. and Cairns, L. (2006) 'Managing Their Own Programme: A Case Study of the First Graduates of a New Kind of Doctorate in Professional Practice', *Studies in Continuing Education*, 28(1): 17–32.

Stephenson, J. and Yorke, M. (eds) (1998) *Capability and Quality in Higher Education.* London: Kogan page.

Sung, J. and Ashton, D.N. (2005) *Achieving Best Practice in Your Business. High Performance Work Practices: Linking Strategy and Skills to Performance Outcomes.* London: Department of Trade and Industry in association with CIPD.

Taylor, R. et al. (2002) *For a Radical Higher Education: After Postmodernism.* Buckingham: SRHE and OUP.

West, P.W.A. (2006) 'Conflict in Higher Education and Its Resolution', *Higher Education Quarterly*, 60(2): 187–197.

Wedgwood, M. (2008) Higher Education for the Workforce: Barriers and Facilitators to Employer Engagement. Dept for Innovation, Universities and Skills DIUS.

Williams, P. (2006) 'Quality Assuring Work-Based Learning: An Opportunity to Add Value', in S. Roodhouse, M. Bowley and C. McKevitt (eds), *Putting Work-based Learning into Practice. Proceedings of the University Vocational Awards Council Annual Conference,* York, Nov. 2006. Bolton, University Vocational Awards Council.

Young, D. and Stephenson, J. (2007) 'The Use of an Interactive Learning Environment to Support Learning Through Work', in *Work-based Learning Futures,* Young, D. and Garnett, J. Bolton: University Vocational Awards Council.

30

Identifying and Classifying Corporate Universities in the United States

Amy Lui-Abel[1]

Organizations have historically charged their training departments to ensure that workers possessed appropriate skill sets to do their jobs. Often, employees attended classes focused on specific job skills and did not necessarily understand how the content was connected to the organization as a whole. Training departments were typically reactive, tactical, organizationally disconnected, and focused on specific individual job skills (Meister, 1998). In the last few decades, however, the training department has changed and advanced. Once organized on a school-based model, where the focus of programs was on the instructor in the classroom, training departments have progressed to embrace a learner-based model, where the focus is on learner needs and outcomes, and operates whenever and wherever the learner needs to learn something. Representing this shift and focus on the learner, a new organizational form has emerged describing the function of learning and development – the corporate university. The corporate university has become the internal entity of an organization that is responsible for strategic employee development and workplace learning initiatives that would broaden the organization's competitive advantages. Notable examples of corporate universities are JetBlue University, Motorola University, MasterCard University, Harley-Davidson University, Disney University, and Intel University, to name but a few.

Despite the dramatic growth of corporate universities across all industries in the United States, they have been difficult to define in the literature and identify in practice as they have varying goals, serve and educate multiple audiences, implement different structures and operations, and rely on a wide variety of learning practices and delivery methods (Blass, 2005; Morin and Renaud, 2004; Rademakers, 2005; Shaw, 2005). An extensive review of supporting literature from academia and industry reveals a complex array of corporate universities' characteristics and dimensions. These characteristics and dimensions do not present a clear picture of what a corporate university is, thus neither help to operationalize the concept for researchers, nor create useful knowledge to assist managers in practice. To further our understanding of corporate universities, this chapter will introduce the corporate university phenomenon and present a summary of dimensions related to corporate universities. Then, a conceptual analysis of these dimensions will help define a corporate university. Finally, an empirical analysis will be presented to move forward to define and identify corporate universities. The analyses here are designed to offer insight into what corporate universities are and how this new organizational form is evolving. With a definition and a foundational base of what a corporate university is, further research can examine issues, differences, effectiveness, and performance related to corporate universities.

EVOLVING FORM OF CORPORATE UNIVERSITIES

As a relatively new organizational form, corporate universities have been described with varied definitions and characteristics. Jarvis (2001) defined a corporate university as "a strategic umbrella concept for the institution, created for developing and educating employees and the company's constituents in order to meet the corporation's purposes. [He noted that such institutions are] systems of teaching and learning rather than universities in the traditional sense" (p. 104). Corporate universities connect learning experiences for the learner and develop competencies that relate to organizational goals (Rademakers, 2005) and link learning with business results (Shaw, 2005). A corporate university assists companies in building a common culture and is a strategic partner in implementing change throughout an organization. A goal for the corporate university is to direct the learning and development of its members toward innovation and the strategic goals of the firm, which can spur superior competitive advantages.

The evolution of the training department to the corporate university is reflected across different aspects of the learning function. Even the name and language of this function and its related terminology has changed. The process of training is now often referred to as the process of learning, and the training department is now often called learning and performance, or increasingly, the corporate university. Employee students are referred to as learners, not trainees. Playing a strategic partnership role in the organization, the trainer is now referred to as workplace learning and performance professional (O'Connor et al., 2007). Of significant importance, the workplace learning professional with overall responsibility for the corporate university is often referred to as the chief learning officer, on par with other C-level management titles such as the CEO, CFO, and COO, which indicates a shift in an organization's understanding of the strategic importance of employee learning and development. These shifts in terminology are but one piece of evidence that the training department is transforming into a new organizational form.

More than simply changing the terminology that describes their work, corporate universities establish objectives that are aligned with strategic organizational goals, such as improving business revenues or changing the culture for innovation. In the corporate university, learning is viewed as a continuous process that supports employees to constantly learn new skills and improve existing competencies. Curricula are designed to connect learning initiatives not just for the job, but for the career trajectory of the employee. Corporate universities offer the ability to customize materials and content, use Internet and technology-enabled delivery of materials, address training demands with speed and flexibility, offer a broad and comprehensive range of content, and meet strategic needs by continuously improving the learning processes of employees (Nixon and Helms, 2002).

In the last two decades, the number of corporate universities has increased significantly. Some claimed that from 1988 to 2001, more than 100 four-year traditional colleges closed in the United States, while the number of corporate universities grew from 400 to 2000 (Meister, 2001). Corporate University Xchange, a consortium organization of industry members, asserted that over 1500 corporate universities existed in 2002 (Hilse and Nicolai, 2004), and that by 2010, the number can grow beyond 4200, exceeding the number of accredited for-profit and non-profit universities in the United States (Meister, 2006). Additionally, it is estimated that corporate training is a $60 billion market in the United States alone (Friga et al., 2003) and "there will be approaching 2000 corporate universities at the turn of the millennium and that the annual budgets in 1998 of each one was on average $10.7 million" (Jarvis, 2001, p. 104). The growth of corporate universities has been fueled by turbulence in the business and economic environment and demands from senior executives for greater efficiency and more measurable impact from their institutions' learning initiatives.

DIMENSIONS OF THE CORPORATE UNIVERSITY

From the literature and practice, dimensions of corporate universities can be documented; these dimensions include mission and strategy, governance and leadership, structure, stages of development, curriculum, learner population, evaluation and measurement, financing sources, technology usage, and partnerships with business line managers, human resources, external vendors, and academia. These 13 dimensions are the foundational clues that reveal what a corporate university is, and each will be explained and summarized.

Mission and strategy

The first dimension, a corporate university's mission and strategy, will determine the approach, leadership and reporting structure, resources available, and programs that will be utilized to execute the learning function. Successful corporate universities have learning strategies linked to business strategies. Learning strategies will determine how learning functions are designed and implemented. A corporate university's primary mission can be the firm-wide development and execution for the company's learning function based on the organization's goals and major initiatives. "The mission of a corporate university is diversified into achieving the corporate strategy objectives, conveying its culture, and providing a systematic curriculum" (El-Tannir, 2002, p. 77). A mission of a corporate university can also focus on objectives, such as, "to systemize the training function, maximize the investment in education … spread common culture and values, develop employability of the workforce and remain competitive" (Morin and Renaud, 2004, p. 297).

Governance and leadership

The second dimension, governance and leadership, may include a learning governance board where the top champions and business leaders of an organization collectively develop and support a shared vision for the corporate university. Senior executives who are committed to the learning function are key elements for the success of a corporate university. According to an industry benchmarking report, 67 percent of corporate universities have a learning governance board in place, and typical functions for this board include "identifying and prioritizing organizational needs, setting learning philosophy, and defining corporate university's mission and vision" (Todd, 2004, p. 46). The governance board includes members who are actively promoting corporate university capabilities internal and external to the company.

Many organizations have established a leader in charge of the corporate university function, the chief learning officer (CLO). Looking beyond training programs, chief learning officers are asked to manage human capital issues for the organization. These issues may include globalization of the learning function, reducing costs of learning delivery, decreasing time of learning for new employees, and "using learning as a strategic weapon to enter new business markets and geographies" (Meister, 2006, p. 70). From the *2006 American Society for Training and Development State of the Industry Report*, over 90 percent of high-performing learning organizations reported having a CLO position that was responsible for learning initiatives and had learning objectives as part of their own performance measures.

Structure

Structure, the third dimension of a corporate university, may range from centralized (focus of authority, decision making, and communication) to a decentralized (distributed and shared decision making). In a decentralized learning function, programs and initiatives are managed by disparate business units with little or no coordination of learning activities. Informal coordination of learning functions may be represented by distributed learning units throughout the company, and loose and informal coordination exist between the learning units, although there is no centralized coordination of learning activities.

In a formally coordinated learning function, distributed learning groups are managed with structured procedures and processes in place to coordinate efforts between the learning units. A federated model, such as this, can be represented as "business units having responsibility for their own training and are supported by a core team that manages some technology and corporate programs ... a shared services support unit may manage the learning technology infrastructure, set e-learning standards, establish uniform processes, and set program evaluation strategies" (Howard, 2006, p. 2). In a centralized corporate university, the learning functions are managed with strong centralized control (i.e., budgets, operational management) and coordination over most aspects of training and learning activities across the entire organization.

The structure of a corporate university may be a contributing factor in the support of learning functions. According to the *2006 American Society for Training and Development State of the Industry Report*, "standardization of the learning infrastructure, portfolio, and development process was identified as the most critical factor in successful global integration of the learning function," but organizations continue to grapple with issues of administering global learning investments to cost and allocations (Rivera and Paradise, 2006, p. 15).

Stages of development

The development of organizations, the fourth dimension, can be classified into phases of growth impacted by factors such as age of the organization, size, and rate of change internal and external to the organization (Greiner, 1972). Depending on the current phase of the organization, management would apply resources and efforts to different areas for encouraging creativity, management of controls and procedures, and deliberate collaboration and coordination. The stages of development of corporate universities, likewise, can be arranged as those institutions just starting to organize the corporate university function, those who have programs and operations running with participants beginning to recognize the benefit, those who are well established with many programs, processes, and procedures in place and well documented, and finally, those who are considered experts in the industry, defined by receiving industry awards and having frequent media citations and case study articles written about their corporate university.

Curriculum

A goal of many corporate universities is to instill and communicate the company's operations, values, and vision to all employees. This is operationalized through curriculum, the fifth dimension, by the corporate university. Similar to the role of academic universities that instill democratic values and national citizenship to its constituents, corporate universities perform the same function but are replacing this content with corporate values and cultural norms (Blass, 2001, 2005; Jarvis, 2001). Innovative human resources practices "are designed to improve organizational effectiveness by influencing employee attitudes and behaviors" (Tannenbaum and Dupuree-Bruno, 1994, p. 172). Common curriculum programs range in content from customer service, communication and team building, technical or business skills, and leadership capabilities. Curriculum programs can be designed for various competency-based job categories and career paths, instead of specific skills for a particular job.

Learning on the job and through experiences is an essential element of learning as adults (Merriam and Caffarella, 1999). Kolb (1984) conceptualized that learning from experience occurs in phases: willingness to learn, observe, and reflect upon what occurred and what was learned. With this new insight, the learner can then plan for a different course of action and carry out the necessary effort. In many companies, programs such as job-rotations are developed with the goal of increasing the experiential learning of employees. Programs such as mentoring and coaching offer employees valuable insight and assistance from another, typically more experienced, individual. A coach or mentor can aid the employee in reflecting and learning from what occurred in the workplace and how to do things differently to improve within the context and culture of the work environment.

Learner population

Corporate universities vary in their program offerings and curriculum offered to different learner population, the sixth dimension. Corporate universities may design programs to target specific groups, such as new hire employees, existing employees, and executive management development (Storey, 2004). This is especially important given the predicted demographic shifts in the population, current skill gaps, and the resulting lack of managerial talent (Friga et al., 2003; Kranz, 2007). The focus of corporate university programs is typically limited to employees within the company as the primary audience, although some have extended this reach to suppliers, external partners, and customers (Meister, 1998). One such example is Toyota University. In addition to training other non-automotive businesses on its expertise of continuous improvement, Toyota University has worked with Los Angeles Police Department and the Defense Department. Disney University also enrolls students who are not employees, including customers, suppliers, and even the public.

Evaluation and measurement

The seventh dimension, an important function for corporate universities, is the evaluation and measurement of learning programs. Training effectiveness and evaluation is a complex and difficult process for any organization to understand. Kirkpatrick's four-level model of training evaluation appears to be one of the most widely used in practice today (Alliger and Janak, 1989; Morin and Renaud, 2004). The first two levels include measuring initial reactions and satisfaction of the learner (Level 1) and testing the skills and knowledge attained (Level 2). The higher, and more difficult, two levels of the Kirkpatrick model attempt to measure actual transfer of learning to the job (Level 3) and impact of learning to the business (Level 4). While traditional training departments typically measure the two lower levels of evaluation, corporate universities are attempting to increase learning evaluations to Level 3 application of learning on the job and Level 4 bottom line business impact. A *2002 American Society for Training and Development Industry Report* found that most training organizations measure primarily Level 1 (78% of respondents) and Level 2 (32% of respondents) only. The more difficult levels to measure were found with less frequency (i.e., Level 3 with 19% of respondents and Level 4 with 7% of respondents).

In a qualitative study of four corporate universities and their evaluation methods, Kirkpatrick's Four Level Model was found to be the primary source in assessing effectiveness of their educational offerings (Allen, 1999). Using corporate and higher education's principles of evaluation, the study offered more insight into evaluation frameworks that corporate universities use to measure their own effectiveness. In another study, training evaluation within corporate universities examined four corporate universities (Bober and Bartlett, 2004). Using a case study approach, the results identified corporate universities that used training evaluation data and how the data were used to improve or influence training programs.

Financing sources

The source of funding, the eighth dimension, influences the strategy and day-to-day operations of a corporate university. Historically, training department funds were allocated exclusively by corporate budgets. While many corporate universities are still funded by this method, another model has recently appeared. Many corporate universities are moving toward self-funded models or a 'pay for service' strategy (Meister, 1998; Vanthournout et al., 2006). In essence, the corporate university operates as a profit center, similar to that of a product or service group. Business units are 'charged' for learning services rendered and funds are reallocated via internal budget distributions. Corporate universities in this model must remain profitable and fund their own expenses or expansion, rather than solely depending on corporate funds. The financing of corporate universities in the learning marketplace continue to evolve with multiple practices demonstrated.

Technology usage

Significant changes in the delivery of learning programs are made possible with the evolution of technology in the workplace, the ninth dimension. In contrast to traditional training departments, corporate universities view multiple delivery methods of learning programs as a key aspect to their success (Anderson, 2003). Programs can be delivered in many different methods, such as, classroom, online via the Internet, CD/DVD, video/VHS, pod-casts, web-casts, video-conferencing, etc. With the growth of online learning, organizations have been able to reduce training budgets and save money, while delivering training to more employees. Another benefit cited was the customization of content and delivery of training at point of need (Douglas, 2003). According to the *2006 American Society for Training and Development State of the Industry Report*, approximately 40 percent of learning programs were delivered with the use of technology amongst Fortune 500 companies and public sector organizations. "E-learning has reached a high level of sophistication, both in terms of instructional development and the effective management of resources" (Rivera and Paradise, 2006, p. 4). Corporate universities can offer courses from academic universities through the company website to employees' desktops (Pollitt, 2005), and "e-learning environments have the potential to support cognitive, social, motivational and affective processes of learning" (Tynjälä and Häkkïnen, 2005, p. 330).

One new and growing technology trend that is growing significantly in the learning industry is the use of learning management systems (LMS) to track, manage, and deliver learning programs to end-users. "A good learning management system (LMS) produces a practical environment in which learners can find the content they need, managers can develop their team to improve performance and the learning staff can evaluate training effectiveness" (Alvarado, 2007, p. 18). LMS applications give end users flexibility to manage their own training schedules, sign up for programs, and learn about upcoming mandatory or elective training sessions. The system also helps the organization track the participants of training sessions, manage and review costs of programs, and reduce administration overhead typically done by other personnel.

Partnership with business units

Corporate universities tend to have high involvement with business leaders in determining learning requirements and programs for business units, whereas in the past, many training departments would make assessments and develop learning programs with little assistance or interaction with their business leaders. The tenth dimension, partnering with businesses units, is valuable to assessment, development, and evaluation of learning programs (Meister, 1998; O'Connor et al., 2007). "Corporate learning functions must understand the business dynamics and propose how learning can drive significant improvements in revenue and speed to market" (Meister, 2006, p. 32). In aligning learning efforts, metrics of business values need to be taken into consideration. Business unit leaders are typically concerned with issues, such as, 'what is the revenue generated per employee?', 'how long does it take for a new hire to achieve the desired level of competency?', and 'what are the customer service indicators like?' (Ellis, 2002). Corporate universities that do not align well with business needs may face the danger of becoming a bureaucratic organization with little connection to senior management strategies. The value and connection to the business must remain the core focus of corporate universities.

Partnership with human resources management

In addition to employee development, the Human Resources Department typically focuses on processes such as hiring, conducting annual performance reviews, managing employee benefits and payroll, and termination of personnel. Corporate universities focus exclusively on processes related to the training and learning development of employees. Supporting the eleventh dimension, a recent benchmarking survey of corporate universities (Todd, 2004) reported that corporate universities typically work closely with human resources counterparts to improve employee performance. For example, corporate universities may analyze employee development needs from the human resources competency management system to create new learning programs, or develop reward systems with human resources to recognize employee learning accomplishments.

Corporate universities can also be viewed as a critical component to the development of human capital in an organization. Using an in-depth case study of one corporate university, researchers found that the corporate university's goals were linked to the strategic objectives of the organization overall in order to sustain competitive advantages. To create competitive advantages, "the management and development of human resources can be linked to the deliberate promotion of corporate universities as a catalyst for strategic human resource development" (Holland and Pyman, 2006, p. 20).

Partnership with external vendors/outsourcing

As the complexity of supporting the learning function has increased, corporate universities have realized that they cannot provide all services and programs alone. To be successful, corporate universities require the ability to develop and manage multiple relationships, internal and external, in order to successfully meet learning demands. Illustrating the twelfth dimension, many corporate universities outsource and partner with external vendors and institutions to bring content and delivery to learners to better serve the needs of their audience. Due to increasing focus on cost control and complex learning technologies in educating adults in the workforce, companies realize that in-house development and management alone are insufficient. Business units that require specialized training or expertise, such as leadership training or technical skills, may need to go to external vendors or programs (Storey, 2004). In fact, outsourcing needs for learning services are predicted to grow dramatically. "A recent study from IDC estimated the U.S. learning outsourcing marketplace was approximately $1.3 billion in 2005 (approximately 7 percent of the marketplace). The number is expected to increase over the next four years to $3.3 billion or about 13 percent of the total learning marketplace" (Meister, 2006, p. 70). An example is Avaya University, which outsourced 1800 product, technical, and business courses to Accenture consulting company in a high-priced, multi-year contract (Oakes, 2003).

Partnership with academia

As the complexity and diversity of training requirements have increased, corporate universities have partnered with academic universities, the thirteenth dimension, to deliver the appropriate content to learners (Thompson, 2000). These partnerships have resulted in greater customization of content from academic universities (Meister, 2003) and specialized degree programs, such as the adapted MBA program from Indiana University to General Motors employees, or specialized technology training to learners from Motorola University China. Babson College has partnered with Intel Corporation to offer an online MBA program (Anderson, 2003). Faculty exchange programs are another way for corporate universities to partner with a academic institution (Blass, 2005).

CONCEPTUAL ANALYSIS FOR DEFINING THE CORPORATE UNIVERSITY

Given the complexity and variety of these dimensions of corporate universities, no two corporate universities look exactly alike, thus making them difficult to define and identify. To reduce this complexity and attempt to define and operationalize the corporate university phenomenon, a conceptual look of the 13 dimensions is useful as grouping dimensions in a systematic manner can offer a descriptive lens that may help broaden our understanding of corporate universities in practice today. The following discussion will review existing literature of how learning functions are organized, and build upon this knowledge to present a new conceptual framework for defining corporate universities.

Management development, including training, can be defined as "any process whereby managerial knowledge and skills are attained from non-credit programs or on-the-job experiences" (Keys and Wolfe, 1988, p. 205). Organizations that focus on management learning and development have three critical aspects – the *content* that includes the delivery of ideas, concepts, or skills, the *experience* that permits the learner to apply the content in appropriate context, and the *feedback* that the learner receives as a result of the content and experience application (Keys, 1977). Content delivery, not necessarily content creation, relates to issues of selection of target populations (i.e., executive development or line managers), the competency-based programs or curriculum developed, and delivery mechanisms, including technology tools. Experience can be demonstrated by opportunities for learners to apply new content through case studies, simulations, on-the-job learning programs, mentoring, and other action learning techniques. Feedback is critical for the learner to understand the relationship between new content learning and the resulting performance. Assessment of the learner is a key part of the feedback dimension. These elements are similar to other learning models, such as Kolb's learning model of concrete experience, reflective observation, conceptualization, and active experimentation.

Prince and Stewart (2002) proposed a conceptual model for relating the processes of a corporate university. Based on concepts of knowledge management and organizational learning, a corporate university was defined as a learning system primarily concerned with four distinct processes. The first was *knowledge systems and processes*, which focused on the technology, databases, decision tools, other organization structures that support learning. *Network and partnership processes* related to the internal and external partnerships that a corporate university developed in support of learning needs. This element of a learning organization was crucial and "likely to increase as the trend to outsource training and development activities continues" (Prince and Stewart, 2002, p. 806). The third was *people processes*, which related to the ability for human resources management to enhance and execute learning processes with the goal of building shared meaning, culture, and skills across an organization. And last, the *learning processes*, which directed efforts at building a learning culture with programs, curriculum, and other training courses. These learning processes required commitment from leadership across the organization. The key function of a corporate university was the integration and coordination of these processes to support organizational learning.

Building upon Prince and Stewart's process model, a conceptual framework for defining corporate universities leads us to describe how the corporate university is organized and how it functions, which can provide an expansion to the definition of this emerging organizational form. For this view, the dimensions of corporate universities from the literature, research, and practice are grouped into four profile areas representing key organizational functions. The four profile areas, shown in Figure 30.1, are the *organizational profile* representing corporate university size, years in existence, structure, stage of development, governance and leadership, and

Figure 30.1   Conceptual framework for defining corporate universities

their strategy and mission; *learning delivery profile* representing curriculum offered, target learner population, and evaluation of learning programs; *operational profile* consisting of technology usage in learning and financing sources; and, *partnership profile* representing relationships with business areas, human resources, external vendors, and academic institutions.

Similar to other types of organizations, this framework provides a conceptual perspective in examining corporate universities. As an analogy, an organization focused on creating and selling a new product might have similar groupings in operations and functions. Instead of a learning delivery profile, the organization might have a *product development profile*, which would include functions of research and development, product testing, and product manufacturing. The *partnership profile* for this product group might include functions of marketing and product distribution. Corporate universities may demonstrate greater knowledge and expertise in one or more profile areas, while other corporate universities may demonstrate expertise in multiple dimensions across several functional profiles.

The functions of a corporate university grouped in this manner present a way to articulate the key attributes of a corporate university, and offers a sense of how they function and focus on their internal operations. Additionally, the conceptual framework suggests a foundational base and a systematic method to investigate, compare, and test different dimensions and profile areas across differing corporate universities.

EMPIRICAL ANALYSIS FOR DEFINING THE CORPORATE UNIVERSITY

These conceptual functional groupings assist in our understanding of what corporate universities do operationally; however, in varying degrees, all corporate universities exhibit capabilities in any or all of the dimensions, across the four functional profiles. For the casual observer, it is not readily apparent which dimension may be more significant or has been adopted by a vast number of corporate universities. For further in-depth examination, the following analysis highlights the dimensions that are significant in identifying corporate universities empirically.

To analyze these dimensions empirically, factor analysis research was conducted by this author, Lui-Abel (2008), in her study of corporate universities. Factor analysis aids in data reduction by taking a wide set of variables and eliminating those with high correlations to result in a refined set of composite elements that still retain the essence of the original variables. In this case, the factor analysis identified and emphasized five significant key component factors that serve to define corporate universities, all of which are distillates from the foregoing discussion. They are: strategy and execution with HR, developing skills to support business needs, evaluation of learning, partnerships with academia, and the use of technology to support learning initiatives. The five component factors represent 70 percent of the variance from the numerous original variables and empirically identify corporate universities in practice today. These component factors will be summarized further with corporate university examples provided as illustrations.

Strategy and execution with HR, the first factor, describes the overall corporate university's strategy and ability to execute learning efforts with the human resources department in support of the learning function. This factor represents functions such as having a well-defined strategy for executing the company's learning function; articulating a clear vision and mission for supporting learning performance in the organization; partnering with corporate human resources to analyze employee development needs for new learning programs; and creating learning programs aligned with corporate human resources talent performance appraisal processes.

Nestlé University, the food and chocolate company, worked closely with HR for key talent management initiatives the company had embarked on. To improve the leadership pipeline for the top 130 executives of the company, the corporate university, along with HR, implemented performance management processes, 360-degree reviews, and programs for succession planning. Having organizational processes in place for succession planning was viewed as a critical factor for the future success of the firm.

The second factor, *developing skills to support business needs,* emphasizes the collaboration with business units to focus on educating employees for specific job-related skills. Corporate universities working alongside business unit leaders help to identify those skills and knowledge that are the priority for the business unit's function. This factor represents tasks, such as, providing skill-based and/or job-based programs customized for specific business units; providing competency-based curricula for entry-level employee learning; developing programs for specific employee groups; and working together with line managers to determine requirements and design learning programs.

The machine manufacturing global firm, Ingersoll Rand University, worked closely with the learning governance to determine key learning initiatives that are aligned to specific business goals and skills. The learning governance board was composed of the CEO, executive business leaders, HR leaders, high-potential senior business leaders, and the Ingersoll Rand University team. Together, they set directives for learning programs around business objectives of customer intimacy, product innovation, strategic marketing, and lean six sigma for process improvement.

Evaluation of learning, the third factor, highlights the importance of measurement and evaluation of learning programs by corporate universities. The evaluation of learning programs continues to receive significant attention as companies allocate more resources to the learning function. Executives are demanding more 'proof' from the learning function that this allocation is well utilized (Bober and Bartlett, 2004; Philips and Philips, 2007). This factor looks at evaluating learning programs by measuring organizational-level results and/or impact to the specific business units; evaluating learning programs by measuring a Return-on-Investment for learning efforts; and evaluating the transfer of learning to the job role/tasks at some point following the completion of learning programs.

ManTech International Company, a software and support services company for US Government agencies, looks to measure financial and non-financial objectives for their learning initiatives.

For example, the chief learning officer developed a Return-on-Investment evaluation for every course that is delivered, which includes a post-training evaluation 30 days later, by the employee to reflect upon the impact of training on the job. ManTech also measures cost savings of learning programs by improving coordination of training efforts and leveraging their purchasing power with vendors for course discounts.

The fourth factor, *partnerships with academia*, stresses the need for corporate universities to supplement internal staff and their knowledge with external resources and expertise. Academic institutions are a likely source, especially for developing skills in specialized functions such as finance, accounting, technology, etc. Partnerships with academic institutions have grown in frequency (Meister, 2003) and many corporate universities now offer customized degrees available to employees, accredited by the academic institution (Anderson, 2003; Friga et al., 2003). This factor includes partnering with academic universities for customized design and/or delivery of non-credit learning programs, for credit and/or degree programs, and for faculty exchange and/or faculty development programs.

One example of a corporate university and academia partnership is the relationship between insurance company, MassMutual University, and the University of Massachusetts-Amherst. All managed by the corporate university, the two institutions have developed innovative programs such as "Evening University" and "University Without Walls" that permit employees of MassMutual to attain degrees or learn new skills. Additionally, the relationship offers internships to current UMass-Amherst students, as well as corporate sponsorships for university arts and athletic programs.

Finally, the fifth factor, *use of technology to support learning*, indicates the significant use of technology by corporate universities to extend the reach of their learning programs, especially across geographic locations (Douglas, 2003; Tynjälä and Häkkïnën, 2005). With the growth of online learning, organizations have been able to reduce training budgets and save money, while delivering training to more employees. Another benefit cited was the customization of content and delivery of training at the point of need (Douglas, 2003). This factor includes supporting learning programs via online (distance learning) technologies to employees and using a comprehensive learning management system to monitor, track, and administer learning programs.

The technology firm, Sun, discovered significant gaps in their sales force skills, which related directly to the department's performance. As a result, Sun Sales University realized the need for learning technologies to support their employee developmental efforts. One technology implemented was a learning management system to store, track, deliver, and report on learning activities by employees. A second technology adopted was a knowledge management platform used as a repository of key pieces of information, such as video recordings of successful sales presentations and how to maintain servers.

These five empirically derived factors are key defining criteria for corporate universities, and they can be used to distinguish corporate universities from other types of learning organizations. These factors identify differences between typical training departments and what corporate universities now allocate significant resources to. Managers of corporate universities can use these factors as criteria in developing their own learning strategy, and provide guidance on allocating resources. In specifying evaluation measurements per individual factor, managers can also assess their own performance over time in terms of operational efficiency of resource allocation and effectiveness of the learning function. For researchers, these component factors can be used to both measure and compare corporate universities in similar size or industry and over time.

CONCLUSIONS

Future research can draw upon rich sources of organization theory, strategy, and management literature to expand our knowledge and effectiveness of corporate universities and compare their differences and similarities to other types of learning organizations. This chapter presented a number of views for identifying and defining corporate universities. The conceptual framework provides a basis for drawing upon existing research to examine corporate universities, and empirical analysis presents another perspective to identify specific factors as variables for further analysis of corporate universities. The discussion presented here provides 'starting points' and can serve as a research base to developing our understanding of this evolving and exciting organizational form.

NOTE

1 The author would like to acknowledge and thank New York University Professor Emeritus Michael Bronner for his gracious counsel in helping her develop and refine this chapter, as well as his numerous editing reviews. His support is greatly appreciated.

REFERENCES

Allen, M. (1999) *Assessing Effectiveness in Four Corporate Universities.* Unpublished doctoral dissertation, University of Southern California.

Alliger, G. and Janak, E. (1989) 'Kirkpatrick's Levels of Training Criteria: Thirty Years Later', *Personnel Psychology,* 42: 331–342.

Alvarado, P. (2007, February) 'Effective Business Requirements for the LMS', *Chief Learning Officer,* 6: 18–21.

Anderson, L. (2003, March 24) 'Collaboration, Not Rivalry, Is Best Way Ahead – Corporate Universities v Business Schools', *Financial Times.*

Blass, E. (2001) 'What's in a Name? A Comparative Study of the Traditional Public University and the Corporate University', *Human Resource Development International,* 4(2): 153–172.

Blass, E. (2005) 'The Rise and Rise of the Corporate University', *Journal of European Industrial Training,* 29(1): 58–74.

Bober, C. and Bartlett, K. (2004) 'The Utilization of Training Program Evaluation in Corporate Universities', *Human Resource Development Quarterly,* 15(4): 363–388.

Douglas, M. (2003) 'Evolution at Corporate U', *Learning & Training Innovations,* 4(1): 36–41.

El-Tannir, A. (2002) 'The Corporate University Model for Continuous Learning, Training and development', *Education + Training,* 44(2): 76–81.

Ellis, K. (2002, September 1) 'Corporate U's: High Value or Hot Air? Corporate Universities Come in all Shapes and Sizes, but Only Those that Enable Business Objectives Earn the Highest Marks from Senior Management', *Training,* 39.

Friga, P., Bettis, R. and Sullivan, R. (2003) 'Changes in Graduate Management Education and New Business School Strategies for the 21st Century', *Academy of Management Learning and Education,* 2(3): 233–249.

Greiner, L.E. (1972) 'Evolution and Revolution as Organizations Grow', *Harvard Business Review,* 50(4): 37–46.

Hilse, H. and Nicolai, A. (2004) 'Strategic Learning in Germany's Largest Companies', *Journal of Management Development,* 23(4): 372–398.

Holland, P. and Pyman, A. (2006) 'Corporate Universities: A Catalyst for Strategic Human Resource Development?', *Journal of European Industrial Training,* 30(1): 19–31.

Howard, C. (2006) *Striking a Balance With Shared Learning Services: Scotiabank Establishes a Federated System for Global Learning* (Case Study). Oakland, CA: Bersin & Associates.

Jarvis, P. (2001) *Universities and Corporate Universities.* London: Kogan Page.

Keys, B. (1977) 'The Management of Learning Grid of Management Development', *Academy of Management Review,* 2(1): 289–297.

Keys, B. and Wolfe, J. (1988) 'Management Education and Development: Current Issues and Emerging Trends', *Journal of Management,* 14(2): 205–229.

Kolb, D.A. (1984) *Experiential Learning: Experience as the Source of Learning and Development.* Englewood Cliffs, NJ: Prentice Hall.

Kranz, G. (2007, June 11) 'Corporate Universities Getting Refresher', *Workforce Management.* 21–25.

Lui-Abel, A. (2008) *The Development of a Conceptual Framework and Taxonomy for Defining and Classifying Corporate Universities.* Unpublished doctoral dissertation, New York University.

Meister, J. (1998) *Corporate Universities: Lessons in Building a World-Class Work Force* (2nd edn). New York: McGraw-Hill.

Meister, J. (2001, February 9) 'The Brave New World of Corporate Education', *The Chronicle of Higher Education:* B10.

Meister, J. (2003, October) 'The Latest in Corporate-College Partnerships', *Training and Development:* 53–58.

Meister, J. (2006, March) 'Corporate Universities: What Works and What Doesn't', *Chief Learning Officer,* 5: 28–33.

Merriam, S. and Caffarella, R. (1999) *Learning in Adulthood.* San Francisco, CA: Jossey-Bass.

Morin, L. and Renaud, S. (2004) 'Participation in Corporate University Training: Its Effect on Individual Job Performance', *Canadian Journal of Administrative Sciences,* 21(4): 295–306.

Nixon, J. and Helms, M. (2002) 'Corporate Universities vs Higher Education Institutions', *Industrial and Commercial Training,* 34(4): 144–150.

Oakes, K. (2003, July 1) 'Will E-learning Be the Catalyst for Outsourcing?', *Training & Development,* 57: 17–21.

O'Connor, B.N., Bronner, M. and Delaney, C. (2007) *Learning at Work: How to Support Individual and Organizational Learning.* Amherst, MA: HRD Press.

Philips, J. and Philips, P. (2007) 'Next-Generation Evaluation', in M. Allen (ed.), *The Next Generation of Corporate Universities.* San Francisco, CA: John Wiley & Sons.

Pollitt, D. (2005) 'Heineken Toasts Successful Recipe for Management Training', *Training & Management Development Methods,* 19(2): 13–15.

Prince, C. and Stewart, J. (2002) 'Corporate Universities – an Analytical Framework', *Journal of Management Development,* 21(10): 794–811.

Rademakers, M. (2005) 'Corporate Universities: Driving Force of Knowledge Innovation', *The Journal of Workplace Learning,* 17(1/2): 130–136.

Rivera, R. and Paradise, A. (2006) *State of the Industry: Trends in Workplace Learning and Performance.* Alexandria, VA: American Society for Training and Development.

Shaw, S. (2005) 'The Corporate University', *Journal of European Industrial Training,* 29(1): 21–39.

Storey, J. (2004) 'Leadership Development through Corporate Universities', *Training & Management Development Methods,* 18(4): 41–49.

Tannenbaum, S. and Dupuree-Bruno, L. (1994) 'The Relationship between Organizational and Environmental Factors and the Use of Innovative Human Resource Practices', *Group and Organization Management,* 19(2): 171–202.

Thompson, G. (2000) 'Unfulfilled Prophecy: The Evolution of Corporate Colleges', *The Journal of Higher Education,* 71(3): 322–341.

Todd, S. (2004) *Corporate University Xchange Sixth Annual Benchmarking Report.* New York, NY: Corporate University Xchange.

Tynjälä, P. and Häkkïnën, P. (2005) 'E-learning at Work: Theoretical Underpinnings and Pedagogical Challenges', *The Journal of Workplace Learning,* 17(5/6): 318–336.

Vanthournout, D., Olson, K., Ceisel, J., White, A., Waddington, T., Barfield, T., Desai, S. and Mindrum, C. (2006) *Return on Learning.* Canada: Agate Publishers.

31

Partnerships between and among Education and the Public and Private Sectors

Bridget N. O'Connor and Doug Lynch

For the United States, or any country, to remain competitive, it needs individuals who can flourish—who can be strong, healthy, happy, and successful—in a rapidly changing global economy. Noted journalist and author Thomas Friedman (2005) remarked that we have been part of a global economy since the discovery of the new world, but that what constitutes success—effective competition—has changed. Early on, from 1492 to 1800, our country's success depended on how much muscle and raw horsepower we had, which he called 'Globalization 1.0.' From 1800 to 2000, success depended on how well we could take advantage of expanding options and declining costs in transportation, computing, and telecommunications, which he called Globalization 2.0. Today, in Globalization 3.0 (2000), success means being able to compete with capable individuals from all over the world. Individuals, Friedman said, are the current driving force, and communications technologies are their enabler.

Creating these capable individuals is the responsibility of three sectors: the K-16+ education sector, which can include both non-profit and for-profit; the public (non-profit) sector, which includes agencies at the local, state, and national levels; and the private (for-profit) sector. The entire education sector has a mandate to develop informed citizens capable and wanting to improve their quality of life by continuing to learn in successive educational and organizational learning programs. Additionally, education can be dedicated to preparing individuals for roles or jobs in particular disciplines and industries. Supporting this goal of an informed, capable, and motivated citizenry are government agencies that fund public and private education. This third sector, the private sector, spends more money yearly on learning and development than the entire K-16+ sector but is not fully integrated into any ongoing national strategy for workforce development and individual talent creation. The private sector is, in many respects, responsible for the remedial and continuing learning needs of its adult workforce, not just for the training and development of its workers in specific job roles.

Answering the question of "who benefits the most from learning?" the response is "individuals." Thus, by giving individuals control or options over what they learn, when they learn it, and how they learn it, the resultant outcome may be emancipation and independence—empowerment and engagement—rather than alienation or stagnation. Lindell and Stenstrom (2005) summed up this argument by saying that workplace learning efforts that attempt conformism, "can presume an almost religious dimension, where the most inner values and personal convictions of an individual, through learning, are being molded and occasionally replaced with stereotyped corporate values." (p. 195). An empowered, engaged individual is a productive individual; an alienated or stagnate individual simply doesn't care.

Thus, the responsibility for learning is too important to belong just to the education sector, and it hasn't for some time. Increasingly, the focus is moving beyond what schools can offer to what individuals need to survive in the new global economy. Rather than create new vocational-technical educational options, which have often not been successful in the United States, a distinctly global approach to labor market demands is to focus on the needs of the individual. That said, it is impossible to negate that the public and private sectors need a skilled, competent, engaged workforce, and the education sector can and must help. The solution? Partnerships.

Partnerships are the first steps in helping create a more integrated understanding of the roles and responsibilities each sector has in ensuring that we are a nation of engaged citizens/workers. The word 'partner' can be used both as a verb and a noun. Etymologically, the word comes from *parcener (co-heir)* and is rooted in the word *part*, which means *piece* or *portion* of a whole. In the various uses of the word *partnership*, a common theme of sharing emerges, whether between partners in an enterprise, a dance, or a competition. In games, *partnership* denotes players who are on the same side. In education, the American Council on Education (1997) notes that a partnership "includes informal relationships as well as more formal contractual alliances" (p. 2). In selecting exemplary partnerships that have addressed learning needs, we highlight cases where individuals were provided with access to learning resources, learned to share knowledge, and developed ways to favorably exploit cutting-edge technology. We conclude by suggesting that a national strategy centering on the development of individual abilities could work to better guarantee the talent that the workforce needs and ensure the self-fulfillment or self-actualization of the individual.

PARTNERSHIPS BETWEEN EDUCATION AND PRIVATE SECTORS

Partnerships between education and the private sector are rife with potential and are win-win options for both parties. Positive results for schools can include updated curricula, internship opportunities, research opportunities, and revenue streams. Positive results for the organization include the ability to tap independent knowledge bases, obtain new perspectives on issues, provide academic credits to employees, and establish positive public relationships with communities.

Either one or both of the authors have been involved in the cases described in this section, which include New York University's School of Continuing and Professional Studies (SCPS) partnerships with New York City-based organizations. Since the cases discussed here involve this division, we provide some background on the university and school for context. Each of the examples we provide demonstrates a unique approach, a different market and/or educational offering, and different outcomes.

New York University (NYU), established in 1831, is one of the largest and most selective private research universities in the United States. With its primary campus in Greenwich Village, professional schools (e.g., dental and medicine) in midtown New York City, and study abroad opportunities and campuses in 25 countries, NYU consists of fourteen distinct but interrelated schools, sometimes referred to as colleges. NYU's School of Continuing and Professional Studies (SCPS) characterizes itself as expert in delivering adult education and, as most offerings are focused on industry-specific credentials and content, professional education is one of its strengths. SCPS set up a division of Corporate Learning Services, whose mission was to leverage the resources of the school in a way useful to organizations. Following are three examples of NYU partnerships with American Express, WorldCom, and JetBlue Airways.

American Express and New York University

American Express (AMEX) is a successful marketer in its industry, an achievement based in part on its adroit use of information about cardholders' spending patterns. AMEX asked NYU for a tailored, online educational program that focused on marketing theory and international business relations for selected staff posted throughout Europe.

The curricular solution was to blend a graduate-level marketing curriculum taught at the SCPS Marketing and Management Institute with lessons on AMEX's method of doing business. About 50 percent of the courses' content was taken off the shelf from SCPS' broad curriculum, sparing both parties the expense of creating an entirely new program of study. This was delivered asynchronously, using SCPS' technology platform. The customized portion of the program was delivered synchronously.

The use of SCPS' technology allowed AMEX's sizable and geographically dispersed European workforce to take the lessons together, forming an on-line cohort, and it meant that no extra investment in technology was required. NYU did not have to recruit, enroll, manage, or support a cohort of highly qualified international students who were all fully funded by their employer. Moreover, AMEX paid the entire tuition bill for the cohort. Employees completing the curriculum received a Certificate in Direct and Interactive Marketing from NYU. This credential fastened their identification with their company, helped them better serve their clients, and advanced their careers.

JetBlue Airways and New York University

JetBlue Airways is a high-quality, low-fare, national airline. Its fundamental business strategy, since it flies the same routes as other, more established carriers, is to compete on customer service. Consequently, the company considers employee learning to be a core business strategy. The company wants employees to realize their full potential, whether they are recently immigrated baggage handlers or executives with degrees from prestigious American universities.

At the time of this partnership (2003–2007), JetBlue's geographically dispersed workforce of 6000 was growing by nine new hires a day. The partnership began with NYU helping JetBlue design and deliver assessment modules, as the FAA required assessments of pilots. Under the old system, pilots reported to one central location to take these modules, followed by paper and pencil tests which JBU then scored and forwarded to the FAA. Using NYU's technology and taking cues from NYU's team of instructional designers, JetBlue University (JBU) automated the process so that pilots could take the assessments on-line wherever they were. The resultant Learning Management System tabulated scores and developed reports that JetBlue could then forward to the FAA.

The next stage to the partnership, which both parties viewed as strategic, was to develop the instructional design and teaching skills of its faculty, who came from every level of the airline's ranks, and few of whom had formal backgrounds in the study of education. The goal was to develop cohorts of faculty who could transform existing learning programs to meet the needs of the rapidly growing, geographically dispersed employee base. We (Lynch and O'Connor) and JetBlue's Vice President and Chief Learning Officer, Mike Barger, jointly designed the program. The curriculum centered on the concepts and skills needed to create enhanced learning environments, develop strategies for transmitting knowledge and know-how, and implement program and individual learning evaluations. Its strategic goal was to motivate JBU faculty to become the best workplace learning professionals possible.

Before admission into the JetBlue/NYU Master Corporate Faculty Development Program, faculty candidates first demonstrated their expertise in their specialty by passing a JetBlue content examination. The program involved faculty from all five JBU colleges (Colleges of Flight, Inflight, Reservations, Customer Service, and Maintenance) and included activities that introduced them to learning theories, needs assessment approaches, instructional design, curriculum and materials development, and teaching and evaluation methods. These areas of learning were delivered by established NYU faculty through focused lectures, small group work, team projects, and a review of selected readings. Throughout the partnership, cohorts of twenty students learned a common vocabulary and further developed skills to support learning throughout the organization.

Faculty leading the program-assisted participants develop higher-order skills by helping them examine their workplace practices via action learning techniques. Thus, the program moved participants further into the articulation of theory into practice—and vice versa—and provided experiences that developed competencies transferable to the workplace.

A selling point of the program was that these JBU/NYU experiences could be applied as credits toward a master's degree, a career enhancement only a university can confer. Upon successful completion of Level I of the program, participants who met NYU admissions requirements were exempted from three credits in one of three advanced 36-credit SCPS programs: instructional/curriculum design, online learning, or advanced facilitation techniques. Graduates of these advanced programs were qualified to move into higher posts at JBU and other branches of the corporation. In addition to paying for Levels I and II, JetBlue provided partial tuition rebates to employees enrolled in these degree programs.

Through this partnership, JetBlue University faculty learned theory and best practices in transmitting workplace skills and corporate culture, as well as a sense of shared corporate purpose. Thus, this partnership not only elevated morale, but also helped strengthen JetBlue Airway's competitiveness and helped the company maximize productivity.

The University of Virginia, New York University, and WorldCom

Shortly after the Enron scandal in 2002, WorldCom also fell due to corrupt corporate governance. The Securities and Exchange Commission prosecuted the former WorldCom, now MCI, for fraud. As fallout from the scandal, a U.S. federal court ruled by permanent injunction that WorldCom's new leaders must provide training for their employees in ethics, finance and accounting, and corporate governance. The mandates required a course of action to change the corporate culture instilled by WorldCom's deposed, felonious management. WorldCom's incoming leadership was determined to foster a new, principled corporate culture for one of the world's largest communications technology companies. The company was poised to set and meet standards of business conduct even higher than compliance with the permanent injunction required. The senior managers of WorldCom were eager to restore public confidence in the company, raise morale among employees, and promote a climate of cooperation and trust within the company to improve operations.

Moreover, WorldCom's senior executives had concluded that merely complying with the permanent injunction would not adequately convey the depth of management's commitment to reform the company's practices and cleanse its reputation. Michael Capellas, WorldCom's new chief executive officer, declared that although the SEC gave no such order, insisting that all employees enroll in classes immediately was the right thing to do. He requested a proposal for a training program that would both satisfy the SEC and fulfill their own aspirations to transform a delinquent company. Both NYU and the University of Virginia's Darden School of Business responded to the call. The corporation asked the two universities to work together to build the program. Darden prepared the content for the classroom portion of the program, which was taught face-to-face to WorldCom senior executives at the University of Virginia's campus in Charlottesville.

NYU provided training both online and face-to-face in nine languages to more than 60,000 employees in every time zone around the globe. Every employee took a short, asynchronous version, while accountants took a much longer, synchronous program. The courses were both substantive and practical in terms of business goals, without being overly theoretical. WorldCom had also mandated that the courses be offered in multiple modalities; employees should be able to read, see, and hear what they were supposed to learn. In addition, senior executives needed to ensure that employees could critically apply what they learned in inventive ways to solve problems of graded difficulty. To do this, online instruction needed to be interactive, involving active participation on the part of the learner. NYU made sure that versions were complementary, accurate, and compelling. NYU also insisted that the caliber of online instruction be equal to the face-to-face teaching done at Charlottesville, New York City, and any of the corporate hubs around the country. Moreover, the classes delivered to senior executives were coordinated with the online programs, which were available in nine languages. In-depth training in finance and accounting was delivered synchronously to 1,500 employees in an eight-hour program. A 25-hour synchronous course on the same subjects was taught to 3,000 other employees, and an asynchronous, online ethics course was offered to yet another 58,000 workers. At one point, SCPS was enrolling 20,000 students a week in the program. Each day, the university published a list of people who had completed the courses.

In this partnership, pertinent relationships between subject matter and teaching methods are worth discussing. University faculty used case studies for face-to-face instruction and Internet seminars and discussions for synchronous online courses. In addition, they designed the asynchronous online courses to be self-directed, with employees learning at a time and place of their own choosing. As a result, this "campus" of teachers, libraries, and other facilities was as portable as the students' computers.

The four-course certificate program in ethics differed from other programs, in part, because it had first priority on WorldCom management's list. This ethics module offered a series of situations of increasing nuance and complexity that could arise in the workplace. Learners were required to respond to each ethical dilemma and decide what they would do. If an inappropriate response was given, the question would reappear until a suitable response was given. Only after a ethically proper course of action was chosen would the participant receive credit.

To address corporate culture at the management level, managers were held accountable for the performance of employees under their supervision. Moreover, each division's academic record was posted for everyone in the company to see. E-mail messages were sent to managers whose division failed to meet university standards. Similarly, publicizing each division's grades gave managers a powerful incentive to ensure their departments mastered the material.

No project of such magnitude and urgency could be expected to proceed without encountering some logistical problems. SCPS' technology could handle only 3,000 students at a time, so the system was initially hard-pressed to handle the approximately 10,000 WorldCom employees who called the Help Desk. Difficulties also involved technological glitches such as hardware and bandwidth that had to be promptly overcome. Also, hearing-and vision-impaired learners needed special materials. All of these problems were exacerbated by the limited time available for solving them, but the partners worked well together and solutions were rapidly found and delivered. Because of the success of this program, the corporation was out of bankruptcy, back in the bidding for government contracts, and in compliance with all 78 recommendations of the Corporate Monitor.

PARTNERSHIPS BETWEEN THE EDUCATION AND PUBLIC SECTORS

The cases that follow are based on partnerships between a university and a teachers' union; an educational consortium and a fire department; and a partnership between a university and a state health department. Each case is a unique partnership that demonstrates how partnerships can and often do reach beyond the grants for services that government, including the Department of Education, typically requests.

The City University of New York, the New York City Department of Education, and the United Federation of Teachers

The City University of New York (CUNY) is the nation's largest urban public university and includes eleven senior colleges, six community colleges, the CUNY Honors College, the Graduate School and University Center, the Graduate School of Journalism, the Law School and the Sophie Davis School of Biomedical Education. College Now, the University's academic enrichment program for more than 30,000 high school students, is offered at CUNY campuses and at more than 200 high schools throughout the five boroughs of New York City (CUNY, 2008).

In spring 2003, New York City's Department of Education issued new standards along with a mandatory curriculum for literacy education to be implemented almost immediately. Public school teachers in New York City needed to meet these new standards quickly so a teacher education program had to be up and running by the coming fall semester. Furthermore, the United Federation of Teachers (UFT) also wanted the courses to be credit bearing.

The UFT approached CUNY, and their request convinced CUNY to make a long-contemplated move—that of setting up a school with a flexible program development process and governance created specifically for employers and that maintained high academic standards.

Development would typically take a few years to accomplish at a traditional college, but a newly-created CUNY School of Professional Studies (SPS) worked with the UFT to develop curricula for a four-course "Literacy Leader" certificate program. SPS hired and trained course instructors over the summer and offered the first courses in fall 2004 in convenient locations around New York City, including public elementary and middle schools. These courses have been offered on a continuous basis ever since, and scholarship monies have been available for teachers.

In addition to gaining concrete skills to use in the classroom, teachers also received academic course credits, which could help them earn higher salaries under their union contract and could be applied toward master's degrees in education at several CUNY colleges. The course content, aligned with New York City and state education standards, prepared educators to teach the new literacy curricula in their own classrooms.

The Sloan Consortium and the Fire Department of New York

The Fire Department of New York (FDNY) employs the largest fire fighting force in the United States and is one of the largest in the world, with over 11,400 firefighters, 2,800 EMS workers, and 1,200 civilian employees. FDNY maintains one of the oldest fire department training programs in existence, established in 1869. Today, FDNY is an international leader in providing training and education for firefighters, and it has two major facilities in the New York area. It also is the most important trainer of volunteer firefighters for the state of New York.

The nature of fire fighting has changed dramatically over the years. Fire fighting and emergency services require increasingly sophisticated knowledge, including knowledge of hazardous materials handling, subway and tunnel response, high angle rescues, and major event response (e.g., terrorist attacks). While FDNY maintained training programs for most response situations, participation had been limited to face-to-face training at the FDNY's own academies. This mode of instruction and delivery limited access and effectiveness. Furthermore, the nature of shift work among firefighters—3 days on, 4 days off—creates timing conflicts with scheduled training courses. Ironically, on September 10, 2001, FDNY enacted a new policy linking education to promotion within the department, in part due to the increased need for college-educated individuals in its upper ranks. In a tragic turn of events, this need dramatically increased when a significant number of lieutenants, captains and battalion chiefs were lost or injured the following day.

The terrorist attacks of September 11, 2001, more than any other factor, highlighted the training needs of FDNY. The loss of over 1,300 active personnel to death and injury left the FDNY severely short-staffed. Personnel worked overtime, further limiting their ability to attend off-site training courses. Of the department's employees lost on September 11, many had the highest level of education and training available. Among these individuals were a significant number of qualified instructors. As a result, the FDNY training program suffered a brain drain and was short-staffed while facing a critical need for more sophisticated and accelerated training programs. New recruits responded immediately to vacancies within the FDNY, thus creating a higher demand for existing training courses, which effectively limited available courses for existing employees and volunteers, as well as stretching current FDNY training staff. In response, FDNY reached out to the Sloan Consortium.

Created with funding from the Alfred P. Sloan Foundation, the Sloan Consortium (Sloan-C) is the nation's largest association of institutions and organizations committed to quality online education. It is administered through Babson College and the Franklin W. Olin College of Engineering. Sloan-C helps organizations continually improve quality, scale, and breadth of their online programs so that education becomes a part of everyday life, accessible and afford-able for anyone, anywhere, at any time, in a wide variety of disciplines. Sloan-C encourages the collaborative sharing of knowledge and effective practices to improve online education in learning effectiveness, access, affordability for learners and providers, and student and faculty satisfaction (2006).

The Alfred P. Sloan Foundation partnered with NYU and FDNY to create FDNYU—the Fire Department's university. The pilot program, launched in January 2004, was a one-stop shop-ping source for FDNY personnel to access training. The program had two main parts: a virtual clearinghouse of higher education options and an internal database of FDNYU learning mod-ules. While housed under the same umbrella, both parts offered distinct learning opportunities for personnel.

Virtual Clearinghouse of Higher Education. The model for the clearinghouse is simple. Traditional full-time students each year select from an array of colleges the one that best meets their needs. Because working adults are often precluded from physically attending classes, FDNYU brings higher education to them. Using existing online programs from 80 accredited colleges, including 16 New York State institutions as well as the SUNY and CUNY systems, FDNYU offers over 500 programs to its firefighters. The institutions range from open access to highly selective. Many grant advanced standing to FDNY employees. Each of the educa-tional institutions invited to participate in this huge collaboration is a member of the Sloan Consortium. The sole criterion of membership is having demonstrated that one's online pro-grams are on par with traditional face-to-face programs offered by the college. In this way, FDNY employees can access the best of U.S. higher education whether in the firehouse or at home. The Council on Adult and Experiential Learning (CAEL) provided a framework, encouraging participating colleges to grant advanced standing for life experiences. In addition, CAEL built an online course so employees could learn how to present prior learning portfolios to colleges for consideration.

Internal Database of FDNY Modules. FDNYU's internal curriculum of 76 courses, which encompass 6,736 hours of instruction, breaks down into 2,798 hours of practical, hands-on application and 3,938 hours of lecture. FDNY personnel could either convert their own courses to online offerings, or the task could be outsourced. During the pilot phase, it was found that organizational culture and the extreme budget constraints made it more cost effective to outsource the conversion as the opportunity cost of internal conversion was too great. With outsourced conversion, the curriculum was quickly standardized and made accessible not only to FDNY personnel but to other firefighting departments trained by FDNYU. This model both improved standards and significantly decreased costs.

Now launched, the goal is to expand and institutionalize both the clearinghouse and the database. For the clearinghouse, the goal is to continue to recruit additional quality online-accredited education programs and to explore ways to provide scholarships to FDNY personnel. For the internal database, the goal is to convert nearly 4,000 hours of face-to-face classwork to online instruction, and this represents only the lecture portion. To explore tackling the 2,800 hours of practical training to see which of it is convertible (to, say, simulation) presents a more daunting task. Nonetheless, moving to an online format is compelling for both training and financial reasons.

Once institutionalized, the benefits will be enormous and self-evident. Training will move from an ad hoc, purely experiential approach to a designed learning experience based on the best learning approach. Training will be delivered consistently and at any time. Moving the appropriate components online will both reduce the time firefighters need to spend at FDNYU's training facilities and reduce the amount of training staff needed. Finally, since the infrastructure and systems are in place, by simply putting on a new shell, the organization can expand this program beyond the state within the fire services industry or throughout the state to serve other agencies.

More radical is the notion that one can pipe in higher education with all its wonderful diversity of institutional mission, programs, admissions standards and tuition fees as one symphony into an institution like FDNY. If successful in recruiting students, the benefits for companies are clear: access to a variety of programs allows individual employees to maximize their learning based on their interests and talents. Companies could also significantly reduce both cost and paperwork. For instance, the company need not negotiate individual agreements or figure out tuition reimbursements. Higher education gets access to qualified (and often fully funded) students without spending extra money recruiting. If this coupling of offerings is successful in this continuing education model, it brings the two worlds of formal learning and internal training together to create a seamless path for the learner.

Morehead State University, The Kentucky Department of Health Information System, and St. Claire Regional Medical Center

In 2004, President Bush issued a directive for the development of technology to support implementation of electronic medical records systems and health information exchanges. This system would operate regionally and ultimately become part of a National Health Information Network (NHIN). The overall goal was to create standards that supported the creation of health information databases, protect sensitive health data, and have data accessible to appropriate providers at appropriate times. Given this directive, the Department of Information Systems in the School of Business at Morehead State University teamed up with St. Claire Regional Medical Center to create a Regional Health Information Organization (RHIO) for eastern Kentucky.

Morehead State University, located in central Kentucky in one of the most rural and poorest areas of the state, is an exceptionally fine regional college that *US News and World Report* continues to rank as one of the top public universities in the South. According to its website (http://www.moreheadstate.edu/aboutmsu), MSU was the first institution in Kentucky to offer a completely online degree program, the Master of Business Administration (MBA). The university hosts graduate programs for nurse practitioners and physicians' assistants through the University of Kentucky. And for more evidence of its science and technology-savvy, MSU has a space tracking system in partnership with NASA as the first component of the Space Science Center. MSU is in no way an ordinary rural university!

A steering committee of faculty from MSU and health professionals from St. Claire studied RHIO models, researched alternative models, and began a partnership to address the government directive. MSU is serving as *neutral convener* in bringing together interested stakeholders. Two years of groundwork has been completed. Articles of incorporation and bylaws have been drafted, and the RHIO has been incorporated as a 501c3 non-profit corporation. Representation in the RHIO has expanded to Appalachian Regional Health, Fleming County Hospital, Primary Plus, MeadowView Medical Center, University of Kentucky HealthCare, Humana, Gateway Public Health District, the MSU Enterprise Center, East Kentucky Innovation Center, and Northern Kentucky Infrastructure Management Institute (Regan, 2008). In establishing the groundwork for this initiative, the steering committee has worked closely with state e-health initiatives to ensure that local direction will be consistent with state and national direction.

MSU faculty consulted with healthcare administrators and practitioners sharing their workflow reengineering expertise and information technology expertise. Together, they applied for grants. The partnership has led to expansion into healthcare curriculum in information systems, management, and finance, as well as opportunities for service learning and internships for both undergraduate and graduate students. Together, they explored organizational and political bottlenecks to developing an effective RHIO as well as the promises and limitations of current technologies. And together they view the development of the RHIO as a means to ensure the economic development of their region in Kentucky.

Pace University and the Westchester County Department of Social Services

Pace University is a private university in the New York City metropolitan area. Its mission is "to provide the best possible private education to a diverse and talented student body..." (Pace University website). Students attend classes at either Pace's urban campuses in New York City or its suburban campuses in nearby White Plains, Briarcliff, or Pleasantville. The University consists of six separate schools. Its youngest school, the Seidenberg School of Computer Science and Information Systems, holds classes at all but one Pace location, and it is in the forefront of not only rapidly developing technologies, but also in the use of innovative teaching and learning strategies. Its academic programs range from associate degrees to doctorates of professional studies. Moreover, nearly half of Pace's student body represents minority populations. With this as a backdrop, it is no surprise that when the Westchester County Department of Social Services chose Pace's Seidenberg School to develop and offer a vocational program in Office Technology for AFDC (Aid to Families with Dependent Children) recipients, the school accepted the challenge.

The resultant program, known as CLOUT (Computers, Literacy, Opportunity, University, and Technology) developed as its main offering a credit-bearing certificate in Personal Computer Applications for the Office Professional. Students who study full-time complete the certificate in two consecutive semesters (with each semester having two 7½ week terms) taking courses ranging from word processing, spreadsheet, and database applications to business communications and telecommunications. The program also includes a 140-hour, supervised internship. Thus, after 8 months of study, a student can have earned 18 credits transferable to an A.S. degree in Office Technology and be prepared for an entry-level office administration position. (Pace Department of CSIS website: http://csis.pace. edu/csis/clout/clout.html)

While some students are unable to complete the program because of its rigor or because of personal problems (e.g. child care, transportation issues), the retention rate is listed as 65 percent, and over 300 enrollees have completed the certificate or degree program. Moreover, 82.5 percent of those graduating were employed upon completion with starting salaries ranging from $20,000 to $47,000 (Pace University Department of CSIS website).

Because of its successes, the CLOUT student base has also expanded to referrals from other organizations, including the Yonkers Private Industry Council (YPIC) and the United Neighborhood Houses (UNH). These latter partnerships included funding for students from a variety of organizations and foundations, including The United Way, Citibank, Chase Manhattan Foundation, Helena Rubinstein Foundation, Sumitomo Bank Foundation, Independence Community Foundation, and William T. Grant Foundation (http://csis. pace.edu/csis/clout/clout.html). CLOUT continues to build on its successes, which are its ability to successfully prepare individual learners for the workforce. The myriad of public and private organizations that provide referrals and funding know that they are tapping into a professionally developed and successful program.

PARTNERSHIPS BETWEEN THE PUBLIC AND PRIVATE SECTORS

The public and private sectors seldom partner directly to support the learning needs of adult citizens in the workplace. Rather, they support individual learning in instances where tax credits are given to either employers or employees themselves or when specific job training monies are offered through competitive grants to the education sector and are targeted toward specific industries. Oftentimes, organizations provide supplemental funding to these grants, as well, and they are explicitly involved in their distribution and implementation. While examples abound, cases in point of each of these instances follow: first, the concept and pending legislation around Lifelong Learning Accounts (LiLAs) is discussed, followed by a brief discussion of the role of the Department of Labor in supporting job training. Both examples here depict ways the government can support *individual* learning.

Lifelong Learning Accounts

The Council for Adult and Experiential Learning (CAEL) describes itself as "a national non-profit organization that creates and manages effective learning strategies for working adults through partnerships with employers, higher education, the public sector, and labor" (http://cael. org/ June 3, 2008). CAEL has been at the forefront of efforts to promote the establishment of an IRA-type account, a Lifelong Learning Account (LiLA) in which an individual can save money that is matched (or contributed to) by his/her employer. While expenses related to job training are currently tax deductible, LiLAs are portable, pre-tax, interest-bearing accounts that can be tapped by the individual at any time not only for education and training related to a current job, but also to support an individual's job and/or career transition. Organizations' contributions are, likewise, tax deductible. Senator Maria Cantwell of the state of Washington originally promoted LiLAs in 2007, and Illinois Representative Rahm Emanuel reintroduced the bill, the Lifelong Learning Accounts Act, in May, 2008. Emanuel reported that LiLAs fill a much needed gap—that while parents can use 529 accounts to save tax-free for their children's education and 401(k)s to save for retirement, "between the ages of 18–65, you are effectively on your own when it comes to saving for additional education and training... Lifelong Learning Accounts will hopefully revolutionize the way that workers invest in their education and training" (Emanuel website)

As a pilot test of the concept, IBM put together a $60 million Global Citizen's Portfolio, which creates matching accounts for learning, a corporate service corps, and enhanced transition services. IBM is well out front in its understanding that an educated, socially conscious workforce is its most important asset. At the onset, IBM will offer matching contributions to workers with at least five years of service, and monies will earn interest. The company will establish a Corporate Services Corps to encourage a wider variety of leadership experiences for its employees. Moreover, for those who are transitioning out of the workplace, IBM will work to help place their employees to develop second careers (IBM Press Release).

Incentives and tax credits

Government agencies, including the Departments of Labor and Education at the federal and state levels and local agencies, help ensure that labor needs are met through partnerships with business and industry through a variety of incentives and tax credits. Such partnerships, which are often complemented by partners in the education sector, offer target grants in high growth sectors such as construction, health care, and transportation. Other foci are on support of remedial, literacy education. And yet other foci are directed toward individuals who can apply for Career Advancement Accounts that provide up to $3,000 per year over two years; these grant monies can be used to enhance current skills or develop new skills. (US Department of Labor website: http://www.dol.gov/opa/media/press/eta/eta20061877.htm October 1, 2008)

CONCLUDING COMMENTS

Reviewing the partnerships described here, it is easy to see that the case studies of AMEX, JetBlue Airways, WorldCom, and IBM are focused on enabling their employees to learn. The UFT, the FDNY, the KY RHIO, and the Department of Social Services focused on learning problems and opportunities that were best served by working with educational partners who had the expertise, technical infrastructure, or contacts to provide exemplary, creative solutions that would yield a win-win for every stakeholder, particularly the individual learner. These partnerships motivated lifelong learning by providing adult citizens a sense of control and multiple options to achieve their learning goals. Such results point the way toward a better future for everyone, as they ensure the talent needed to support the economic infrastructure of the country, create an informed citizenry, and ensure participation in Globalization 3.0.

Globalization 3.0, where the individual is the driving force, requires that we step back and take a more comprehensive approach to ensuring that the workforce can achieve its maximum potential. If we approach learning thinking about the *who and what* of learning rather than the *where* of learning, the potential for synergy and for economies of scale occurs. Opportunities exist for educators and educational institutions to form meaningful partnerships with the public and private sectors that prepare *individuals* for lifelong learning and their careers.

REFERENCES

American Council on Education (1997) *Postsecondary Partnerships with Business and Industry: Preliminary Results.* Washington, DC: American Council On Education (ACE).

CUNY Website: (http://collegenow.cuny.edu/whatiscn/history_philosophy accessed October 10, 2008.

Emanuel website: (http://www.house.gov/apps/list/press/il05_emanuel/LiLA08.html accessed 11/03/09.

Friedman, Thomas L. 2005 *The World is Flat: A Brief History of the Twenty-first Century.* New York: Farrar, Straus and Giroux.

IBM Press Release: (http://www-03.ibm.com/press/us/en/pressrelease/21937.wss, accessed July 18, 2009).

Lindell, M. and Stenstrom, M.L. (2005) 'Between Policy and Practice: Structuring Workplace Learning in Higher Vocational Education in Sweden and Finland', *Journal of Workplace Learning,* 17(3/4): 194–207.

Morehead State University website: http://www.moreheadstate.edu/aboutmsu, accessed September 23, 2008.

Pace University website: http://www.pace.edu/page.cfm?doc_id=9959, accessed June 2, 2008.

Pace Department of CSIS website: http://csis.pace. edu/csis/clout/clout.html, accessed June 3, 2008.

Regan, E. (2008) Personal communication with author, April 3, 2008.

US Department of Labor website: http://www.dol.gov/opa/media/press/eta/eta20061877.htm accessed October 1, 2008.

32

Brave New Workplace: The Impact of Technology on Location and Job Structures

Elizabeth Regan and Chester Delaney

The brave new world of work will be marked by a blurring of customary boundaries. Not only will distinctions between learning and work become increasingly blurred, but so will distinctions customarily associated with almost every aspect of work life. Distinctions in workplace, job roles, balance of work and personal life, career planning, performance management, training delivery, formal and informal training, and even between real and virtual experience, will all fade dramatically.

The effects of technology and globalization on the workplace are widespread and complex. The preceding chapters have discussed many aspects of the changing workplace. Organizations rely on technology more than ever before to deliver learning to an increasingly diverse, geographically dispersed workforce. Workplace learning and performance (WLP) professionals are experiencing the effects in every aspect of their roles as learning strategists, business partners, project managers, and professional specialists.

To help us better foresee how changing employment trends may likely impact WLP professionals, we will introduce Casey Callahan Melendez, a learning and performance professional, at her workstation in the year 2020.[1] Numbers in the picture of Casey at her desk (see Figure 32.1) match the numbered sections in this chapter. Each section explains a component of the picture. Taken all together, they add up to a prediction of work and the workplace in the future.

1. Introducing Casey@Work

Casey Melendez is a freelance learning and performance specialist working on a contract basis for the Human Development Corporation (HDC). HDC has a major, multiyear contract with The Zeta Group to implement Zeta's human resource development policies. Casey reports to Charlee Jones, HDC's account manager for Zeta. Charlee's contact at Zeta is Rabindranath Sumashekara (known as Sam to his colleagues). At Zeta, Sam is a senior officer, holds a seat on the enterprise's management committee, and is the firm's CLPO, chief learning and performance officer.

Under contract with Zeta, HDC provides a full range of workplace learning and performance services: talent management, succession and job mobility systems, career models, learning needs identification, individual learning plans, learning program design, learning and group process facilitation, knowledge sharing, and instructional delivery. As a matter of deliberate

Figure 32.1 Casey @ Work: Workplace environments of the future will become increasingly diverse, supporting work anytime, anyplace, anywhere.
Source: O'Connor, B. N., Bronner, M., & Delaney, C. (2007) Training for Organizations.
Cincinnati: South-Western Publishing Co. Reprinted with permission of the authors.

choice, Sam has the assessment of learning outcomes performed by Zeta's own internal auditors, and he purchases recruiting services from an HDC competitor.

2. The Electronic Workstation

Casey's desk, with all its devices, is connected through a secure WLP portal by high bandwidth communications infrastructure that provides worldwide access to the Internet and a wide variety of resources she needs to perform her job and provide a robust, multi-media learning and performance delivery system. Zeta, HDC, and Casey all subscribe to the network, and both Zeta and HDC provide a gateway to their private company networks and services for which Casey has been authorized. Access to each network is controlled by stringent security measures. Casey's subscription to the public net gets her a personal database "in the cloud," in addition to its usual messaging service and her choice of several information services (e.g., the ASTD Electronic Research Facility). Her memberships in ZetaNet and HDC's InfoMail are provided by the companies as tools for her work. Whenever Casey accesses the network at the office, at home, or on the go, she enters her personal identification code and password. The network recognizes the code and password as keys that unlock the electronic doors to all the data, software, and services that Casey owns or for which she is authorized.

Casey's workstation combines a computer, flat touch screen interactive smart panel, and real-time desktop videoconferencing. It provides access to all the resources she needs to do her job:

- Zeta's Learning Management System (LMS).
- Messaging, email, and productivity software.
- Databases and knowledge libraries.
- Network connection to a wide array of multi-media resources, RSS feeds, wiki's, blogs, social networks – such as LinkedIn and Facebook, virtual environments – such as Second Life, and other Internet and company resources.

3. The Learning Management System

Zeta's Learning Management System supports planning, design, scheduling, delivery, and managing learning resources for all Zeta's learning and performance professionals worldwide. It likewise serves the needs of all employees for training and learning resources, knowledge management, collaboration, work assignments, and performance assessment. It provides access to Just-in-time learning (JITL) – the training approach that makes context-sensitive learning material available online – in short omni-media modules, to be called up in real time, precisely when a worker needs to learn a specific something. A lot of training work goes into the design, creation, and maintenance of this just-in-time material. JITL has in fact become so much a part of the workplace that the acronym has entered the language: JITL materials are "JITLware" or "jittleware," and using them is "jittling."

The most recent addition to this delivery platform provides access to HDC's virtual learning environment, which has gradually expanded for use in recruiting, new employee orientation, multiple training needs, and change management projects. One of the benefits of Zeta Corporation's contract with HDC is access to this highly sophisticated and effective virtual learning environment. HDC has also helped Zeta establish an island on Second Life for recruiting and public relations as well as a number of highly effective simulations for training Zeta's global executives and knowledge workers. Through Second Life's simulated experience, Zeta has been highly successful in bringing new executives up to speed and helping them gain a deeper understanding of the complex operating dynamics of the company's global business requirements. One of the most critical, unanticipated benefits has been a significant improvement in the level of collaboration and creativity among Zeta's multi-cultural, geographically dispersed work groups. Zeta Group also uses its virtual environment on Second Life for prototyping new products, global team collaboration, and global management meetings.

4. Typical Daily Activities

Casey's sign-on this morning brought her a video announcement from the president of Zeta to all employees and associates worldwide concerning Zeta's acquisition of the Estes Park Ranch Resort in Loveland, Colorado. The announcement triggered an email message to Casey (return receipt requested) from Charlee, copy to Sam, to contact the Estes WLP department to begin the process of involving HDC in its internal and customer work. Casey's email and scheduling system sent Charlee the return receipt as soon as Casey read the message and, at the same time, set up a tickler for Casey to check completion. (Casey, of course, defines the priority levels for her mail and scheduling system.) Charlee selected Casey for this assignment because another specialty that Casey has been developing is the use of video-based groupware as a survey and discussion tool, a process she seems to have a knack for designing and doing in nonintrusive ways.

Later this week, the president is scheduled to hold his quarterly global workforce meeting in Second Life. After presenting the quarterly performance report, the president will lead a discussion on business strategy. The management team has found the virtual environment to be more effective than teleconferencing for meeting to discuss issues. Beyond giving participants a feeling of being with others despite physical distance, virtual worlds can make real work more efficient and effective. Meeting in a virtual environment generates a sense of cohesion, unlike most other non-real settings, that allows globally dispersed employees to congregate and analyze situations together, at the same time, regardless of physical location. Think about a group of executives studying a global business process, laid out in 3D along several virtual walls. Imagine the process integrated with actual back end data. Executives can manipulate the process in 3D to see how the data is impacted. These simulations – virtual to real and back – are hugely impactful and meaningful, particularly for top-level executives who are analyzing complex data, discussing concepts, and formulating strategies (Elchoness, 2009: 83).

Casey has given HDC's InfoMail a template of topics to watch for in certain publications. InfoMail's scanning software has spotted a report on the morning newswire concerning training for retirees interested in part-time work in bed-and-breakfast inns, child care, and family budget counseling. When Casey activated her workstation this morning, it notified her that one of her research interests had a hit, and she has pulled the report. Casey has made a specialty out of retiree retraining, and it is important for her to stay current with developments in this niche.

Also at this morning's sign-on, Casey's email messages included one from Dwight Feeley, an HDC employee. Feeley informed Casey that he has just completed a publicly available training program in air conditioning mechanics. This was a program of his own choice that he took on his own time via Internet links to his home computer, all at his own expense, and with no real connection to his HDC job as a customer service representative. Feeley asks Casey to certify that he has learned air conditioning well enough to enable him to be considered for posted air condition jobs at the HDC headquarters complex. (One of Casey's internal HDC assignments is responsibility for technical learning of all sorts.) The second half of Feeley's email asks Casey to assist him in evaluating advanced air conditioning training for his future use.

Casey has seen clear growth in this sort of client request – the certification of learning achieved and the evaluation and selection of training desired. More often than not, such requests pertain to situations where the learning specialist has played no part in the design or delivery of the training in question. This type of client need has grown dramatically as training programs of all sorts have proliferated in the virtually bottomless ocean of material that has become available through the growth of the Internet.

Casey also checks in on the progress of employees in her current online course module on managing culturally diverse project teams. The online course management component of HDC's LMS offers a wide variety of generic and custom designed course modules, which are scheduled based on demand and availability of online instructors. In the course module Casey is currently teaching, learners work asynchronously within scheduled timeframes. The current group of 20 employees in Casey's course has raised some interesting questions on the course discussion board. Casey takes time to respond and comment on some of the discussion points and also adds some questions of her own to bring out additional points. In the next assignment, enrollees will engage in a simulation game that will give them an opportunity to try their hand at managing a project team in a virtual environment. The course will culminate with a group project which will divide the employees into four project teams that will be required to plan a real or hypothetical project, including performing a cultural analysis and identifying the strategies that they will use to manage potential cultural differences in learning styles, leadership styles, and organizational practice. In making the group assignments, Casey will make each group as diverse as possible, taking advantage of the diversity of the geographically dispersed participants.

Still another activity on Casey's schedule for today is orientation for new employees. Casey will meet six new employees briefly in person before taking them to the virtual corporate welcome center on Second Life where they will meet several other new employees from different locations for a virtual tour of the company's global operations. Casey's avatar will be available to answer any questions that may arise as the employees tour. They will also meet various managers and employees at different venues around the globe as they tour. Zeta has significantly shortened the time needed to orient new employees to operations and the corporate culture, giving them a tremendous competitive advantage in today's fast-paced changing global environment. Zeta believes that through the use of virtual experience, they can bring new employees to a level of understanding in six weeks that used to take six months or more of travel and experience to acquire. From the trainer's perspective, Second Life allows them to provide a highly informative, consistent, and dynamic orientation experience for new employees with both breadth and depth not feasible in the past. The sense of personal interaction with knowledgeable company leaders is highly effective, yet doesn't repeatedly tie up the time of busy company leaders. Moreover, employees can easily go back and visit again if they need to reacquaint themselves for a new work assignment.

Another unanticipated use to which employees have put Second Life is communication with their families while traveling or on assignments in other countries when they elect not to relocate their families. Employees can sit down with their families for dinner – virtually through Second Life (Galagan, 2009: 37). They even help their kids with homework after dinner . . . *virtually*! The kids love it! And it helps combat the psychological isolation that an assignment away from home can mean. Casey got the idea from a conference presentation by NASA engineers who created an island on Second Life to link the astronauts in outer space back to their families, friends and co-workers on Earth.

5. & 6. Flat Panel Interactive Touch Screens

Casey has customized the flat panel display to provide easy access to the multiple resources at her command. A simple touch expands the display of an application to the forefront, where Casey can point and click to drill down into successive levels of detail. With a simple hand motion, Casey can easily zoom in or out to view details or show a broader view. Similar screens are available in the meeting rooms and training rooms here and at Zeta headquarters.

Casey has customized the flat panel wall displays to support a Focus Group on performance management and a Knowledge Sharing Initiative.

The Focus Group began as part of HDC's continuous learning needs analysis within Zeta. Casey created an electronic Focus Group to discuss the issues around performance management. The members of the group are mid-level managers who had reported problems in their units concerning this issue. The eight people on-line in this morning's session are physically located in four different cities, three in the U.S. and one in Switzerland. K.K. Cheung, Zeta's operations manager in Shanghai, is also part of the Focus Group but is not online now because of the 13-hour time-zone difference between himself and most of the group. K.K. will see and hear the entire Focus Group session at his desk when he logs on to the network tomorrow, and he will be able to add his thoughts at that time.

The group starts by looking at a summary of recent performance data. They then drill down into greater levels of detail, which quickly helps them focus in on problem areas. They have agreed at this point that the problems they have identified relative to performance management are not because of a skill deficiency on the part of their supervisory staffs. Thus, training will not solve anything. Rather, the problems are due to a weakness in Zeta's standards for performance feedback. They have each accessed Zeta's *Management Practices Manual*, part of the electronic library of manuals maintained online at corporate headquarters and have downloaded the three relevant pages of the manual into Zeta's word processing software. Using the shared editing and tracking features, the group has discussed the standard and made several edits to the copy. After reaching consensus on the change they think should be made, Casey offered to take responsibility for emailing the proposed policy changes to Zeta's corporate office for their approval.

The second purpose to which Casey puts these screens is to facilitate a discussion session for HDC's Knowledge Management (KM) Initiative. Casey is just one of numerous WLP professionals who have been assigned a target population to discuss processes and issues and document essential information to improve performance. The objective is to capture the rich depth of experience that HDC associates have and somehow make that experience accessible to others in useful form. "We would like everybody to make *new* mistakes," is the way Sam Somashekara has put it. In fact, "New Mistakes" has become the slogan of the entire KM initiative, which is a company-wide effort with sponsorship right from the Management Committee. Casey's group of professionals, 13 of them, are all HDC Financial Managers working in 11 different locations around the world. They represent collectively 203 years of experience in handling HDC finances, and the goal of the KM Initiative is to capture and share the specialized, irreplaceable knowledge that they represent. When Casey has all members of the group online at once, her screen filled with 13 little windows of talking heads, it takes all her facilitation and organizational skills to keep the discussion on track and productive. Difficult as it is, though, she is excited about the kind of information the group is surfacing and capturing. She has told colleagues that KM is going to be a major learning initiative for some time to come and that she wants to get more deeply involved in it.

On the shop floor at Zeta Group, workers have their individual wearable version of the touch panel. These iPhone-like devices are used to support the increasing complexity of assembly work. Operators receive clear, accurate and updated instruction. These devices provide the flexibility and adaptability needed to support extreme customer orientation and mass customization. They enhance speed and accuracy of information support for final assembly operators (Stahre, 2009).

7. Casey's Sweat Suit and Towel

Casey's contract contains a bonus clause for fitness maintenance. She is working assiduously to earn that bonus. If both she and her husband, Cruz – The Assistant Chief Administrator of a local municipal hospital – earn their incentive bonuses, they will have the money for a summer rental on a nearby lake.

Although Casey often dresses casually at the Workcare Center, she customarily wears more formal business attire when at headquarters or conducting face-to-face training sessions. Casey's avatar also wears business attire in Second Life and other simulated environments.

8. Doorway into the Next Room

Casey rents her desk by the hour at the Bartlett Workcare Center, a small office complex located in a campus setting about 15 minutes from her home. The center is a private business that provides (a) day care for children and elderly relatives, and (b) work facilities for knowledge professionals like Casey. Many of the elderly relatives serve as staff (some paid, some unpaid), helping with child care and office chores of various kinds. The center's office facilities include the electronic workstation at which Casey is sitting, as well as meeting rooms, classrooms, group videoconferencing facilities, full-scale graphics/printing capabilities, a gym, and a cafeteria. Casey, like most of her peers, works two or three days a week at home, where her personal workstation is a powerful but somewhat less fully equipped one than the center's, and two or three days a week at the Bartlett Center or others like it. At the center, Casey can also meet as needed with colleagues or clients from HDC, Zeta, or other companies with which she has contracts. The center's full-scale videoconference room, for example, has proved very helpful in Casey's KM assignment. It is only on relatively rare occasions – usually when she is delivering instruction – that she is physically present at HDC or client offices.

9. Wastebasket with "FEA" Brochure

Casey's HDC contract provides a Family Education Account (F.E.A.), a fund into which Casey contributes money tax-free and which HDC matches. The money in this account remains tax-free as long as it is used for educational purposes by Casey or the members of her family. Casey and Cruz are planning to use the money for their daughter's college education, less the funds used for Casey's mandatory annual program of 12 days of training. (Casey and her supervisor jointly select the content of that training.) Casey and Cruz each get a menu of possible employee benefits from their employers, some of them government-mandated, and they are able to select the mix from the two sources that best suits their family situation and lifestyle.

Casey's insurance plan also includes a Flexible Spending Account that allows her to allocate pre-tax dollars to cover unreimbursed medical expenses and dependent care. As a contract employee, her insurance plan is independent of her employer, but as part of her employment contract, HDC pays 60% of the cost of this portable plan. If Casey were to change employers, the plan would travel with her and she could negotiate with her new employer for a new cost share arrangement. This health insurance portability option has become fairly commonplace not only for contingent and contract workers, but with employers in many industries.

10. Electronic Clipboard

Last week, Casey traveled to HDC headquarters in South Bend, Indiana, for the company's annual learning conference, an event that is part education, part recognition, part personal network, part politics, and mandatory for all HDC WLP professionals Level XII and above. To handle the logistics of her trip, Casey called on a feature of her network's artificial intelligence, a software agent or knowbot. She gave the knowbot her trip parameters (destination, departure, and return dates), and the knowbot then accessed HDC's preferred online vendors and made all the arrangements – flights, hotel, car rental – all with Casey's dietary, seating, airport, and frequent flyer preferences taken into consideration. Today, with the trip over, the knowbot brought the trip expense report up on Casey's electronic clipboard. A light pen will allow Casey to fill in items by hand, with the clipboard doing the necessary calculations and verifying her signature. The completed form will be routed electronically to Charlee for her approval signature and will then travel by InfoMail from Charlee to HDC Accounting. Funds to reimburse Casey for her out-of-pocket expenses will be electronically deposited in the bank account Casey has specified, and the system will send her an email note to let her know that the deposit has been made.

As Casey prepares to leave for the day, she checks the arrangements for kicking off tomorrow's sales training session in HDC's virtual training environment.

This environment enables sales personnel to interact virtually with clients, marketing personnel, manufacturing reps, and government officials in various countries while learning product features and requirements. Sales representatives learn to deal with the challenges of global information exchange, currency conversion, and export regulations within the context of actual scenarios common to marketing and shipping Zeta products. By reducing the learning curve, the virtual sales experience has significantly shortened the training time required for sales representatives to become productive, thus enhancing their commissions, reducing attrition, and increasing company sales. While Zeta doesn't foresee virtual training replacing traditional learning events, it has revolutionized how employees learn at Zeta for a number of purposes. Games and simulations have become an integral part of Zeta's blended learning environment along with wiki-driven capabilities, blogs, and other social networking tools.

AN ENTERPRISE-WIDE BLENDED LEARNING INFRASTRUCTURE

Perhaps the most amazing fact about the foregoing scenario, is that most of it is already happening somewhere at innovative companies. Thus, in reality, it is more of a representation of the most innovative training scenarios of today rather than a look into a crystal ball of tomorrow. Certainly overall trends and issues are apparent in the scenario pictured here. Prior chapters described training efforts as strategic, informational, and operational. No matter what type of training is needed in the networked organization, everyone will be able to share a wide variety of learning resources and will be expected to be a learning resource to others. Communications technologies will allow change agents to respond to evolving forces and continually provide learning experiences that can help the enterprise grow. Powerful, versatile technology will provide an information infrastructure in support of the organization's constant need to manage change and learn. It will also offer a wide range of options as to where employees physically work and how they manage their personal and work lives.

Versatile information systems

With the constant growth in computing power and capacity to transport huge amounts of information, technology will continue to integrate into vast global networks with access for millions of people. Information will be increasingly available in varied and increasingly blended formats – data, text, voice, image, video – as well as three dimensional (3D) and virtual formats. Users of the computing resources of tomorrow will have networked, interactive, multifunction workstations and portable devices through which they function as processors, consumers, and transmitters of information. They will also have a wide variety of "information appliances" – such as notebook and tablet computers that slip easily into a carry case or purse and handheld devices, such as the Blackberry and iPhone, that fit in a pocket or belt clip. What all these systems have in common is their ability to connect to the Internet, making ubiquitous computing a real and universal possibility.

In the scenario pictured in this chapter, Casey's desktop device furnishes secured access to computing systems, telecommunications networks, databases, and the private, secure Intranets operated by her client companies. Her workstation provides any number of means to input and output information. Her access authority is tailored to her work and personal needs, ranging from knowing which databases are useful to her, to providing her a means to communicate with her clients, and enabling her to deliver training services to them. Her access rights travel with her wherever she may be – at HDC headquarters, at a client site, at home, at a public shared site – such as the Bartlett Workcare Center – or on her handheld device traveling anywhere in the world.

Blended learning environments

WLP will continue to experience a shift from event-driven training to blended learning environments that integrate a variety of methods and resources. Blended learning is defined as 'using the best delivery methodologies available for a specific objective, including online, classroom-based instruction, electronic performance support (knowledge management), paper-based, and formalized or informal on-the-job solutions among numerous others' (Hofmann and Miner, 2008). The key to blended learning is the *integration* of multiple methods, not a menu of delivery choices. And note the use of the term blended *learning*, not teaching or training. The distinction is that training implies an outside facilitator (either remote or face-to-face) is leading the learner experience whereas with blended learning, the experiences become more learner directed. Further, the focus is where it should be – on the goal (learning) rather than the means (instruction).

One highly promising aspect of blended learning is a shift to *immersive learning environments* that engage students more actively in the learning process. Immersive learning technologies include modest 2D casual games and simulations, robust 3D massively multiplayer games, and virtual worlds like Second Life. 'Proponents say immersive learning and other Web 3D technologies represent the biggest communications advance since the Internet was formed and promise they will revolutionize how people learn and interact' (Harris, 2009).

The scenario about Casey included a number of references to virtual learning environments, such as Second Life. While it is currently the dominant platform, Linden Labs' Second Life is just one among a growing number of virtual worlds. Whether it continues to dominate the virtual 3D world, or is eclipsed by others such as Active World, There, and Entropia Universe, or the next generation of 3D yet to come, early applications are demonstrating its use as a powerful tool for learning. Virtual environments offer a 'unique ability to engage and empower employees in ways that accommodate their digital and mobile lifestyles, adapt to their individual learning needs, and encourage collaboration' (Gronstedt, 2007). A quick Google search on 'Second Life' turned up over 16 million articles about these new virtual worlds, which are visited daily by millions of people.

Most proponents believe that we have barely scratched the surface on discovering the power of virtual environments and social networking tools for learning and performance. It's about being able to collaborate and share information at any time in a realistic setting. It enables companies to expand the learning toolbox rather than replace existing training methods. For example, a company might enhance existing instructional courses by adding virtual field trips that engage students in applying the instructional content. One of the biggest opportunities may be in collaboration. Training and collaboration will blur together as WLP professionals realize the many benefits of online virtual communication, which will make it easier to integrate access to formal learning from an LMS, combined with informal knowledge from wikis and blogs.

Following are some examples of innovative immersive learning applications currently being used in a variety of corporations.

- British Petroleum (BP) has begun using Second Life to train new gas station employees in the safety features of gasoline storage tanks and piping systems (Galagan, 2009: 36). 'In Second Life, BP built 3D renderings of the tank and pipe systems at a typical gas station. Trainees could "see" underground and observe the effect of using safety devices to control the flow of gasoline. They were able to observe the workings of a very complex system in a way they could never have done in real life, increasing compliance with safety regulations' (Galagan, 2009: 36).
- IBM has become one of the most aggressive corporate users of Second Life. CEO Sam Palmisano used Second Life to hold meetings with IBM's worldwide workforce (Galagan, 2009: 36). More than 6,000 IBM employees log into Second Life at least once a week for a whole variety of purposes. One interesting application is in the area of knowledge management (KM). IBM retirees come to chat about issues of the day and share institutional knowledge with current employees (Galagan, 2009: 37). These interchanges capture important information for increasing the value of the company's knowledge management systems.
- One New Jersey pharmaceutical company recently rolled out a program to demonstrate how physicians can expand their practices to offer vaccinations. 'By plugging in a CD, some 12,000 physicians can tour a virtual practice and "visit" various rooms and learn how to efficiently order and store vaccines, administer doses to patients, and bill for their services' (Harris, 2009: 45).
- 'Starwood Hotels used Second Life to learn from customers before building the first of its new line of hi-tech, loft-like hotels called Aloft. They designed and built a prototype hotel in Second Life where "customers" could walk through the hotel and give feedback' (Galagan, 2009: 37).
- Northrop Gruman Corporation, a $32 billion dollar global security enterprise with 120,000 employees, has entered the virtual world with a sophisticated five region presence in Second Life that they use to simply and inexpensively prototype products, conduct simulations, and train employees in environments that would be prohibitively dangerous, expensive, or even impossible in the physical world (Simulation, 2009).
- 'NASA owns an island in Second Life where a team of scientists is working on ways to link the astronauts who will go to Mars back to their families, friends, and co-workers on Earth. NASA thinks that the 3-D virtual world will help combat psychological isolation that the 800 day mission could cause' (Galagan, 2009: 37).
- 'Microsystems, a network services and solutions provider, instituted an open learning exchange called Sun Learning eXchange (SLX). It was created primarily for the purpose of giving leaders an alternative to formalized learning, taking advantage of expertise within the community and harvesting knowledge within the community. SLX is now a platform containing more than 5,000 pieces of informal learning, the majority of which are objects aimed at increasing productivity, aiding sales and technical support, and providing internal marketing. Any employee can contribute to the site, and the formats of learning bites includes PDFs, podcasts, and video. Moreover, their formal course curriculum leverages their informal content.... Their LMS provides a compendium of informal information including links to books and news, tag clouds, and media, much of which has been launched formally by being broken down into course-like structures. In doing so, Sun's learning team cut its program development time by 90 percent. Sun works to use the appropriate tools to solve the relevant problems, using 'a changing conception of learning to leverage what we are looking for, which depends on what the end user wants to accomplish' (Nancherla, 2009: 57).
- UPS makes use of virtual technology in its new Integrad Learning Lab in Landover, Maryland. Designed in conjunction with a $1.6 million Department of Labor grant, the new $5.5 million, 11,500 square foot learning facility revolutionizes how UPS trains its drivers. It offers many different delivery modes: online learning, 3-D models, podcasts, videos, along with traditional classroom methods and real-life simulations.

These examples represent just a few of several hundred organizations that currently have created places for learning in Second Life.

Putting trends and issues into perspective

To sum up the trends described in this chapter and the likely future to which they are leading us:

1　Your computing and networking services will be tailored specifically to your job and your interests, both professional and personal, and will be accessible from wherever you are physically working – at your employer's facility, satellite work center, at home, or on the go (mobile).

2　Learning Management System. Your computing and networking services will provide a rich matrix of learning resources and tools. The network will know you and the data and software for which you are authorized. Knowbots, research templates, online libraries, forms and manuals, knowledge management systems, wikis, blogs, data warehouses and analytics, video-conferencing, and virtual environments will be readily available and integrated. The desktop or laptop will be a major delivery vehicle for electronically based learning and reference resources. Touch screens will provide more flexible interfaces.

3　Greater collaboration. Electronic mail, electronic bulletin boards, groupware, wikis, blogs, twittering, and other social networking tools will enable you to contact and work with colleagues, customers, subordinates, bosses, and friends across the boundaries of organization, time, and geography. A general description for this network of knowledge work tools is "any to any." That is, on an any-to-any network, any one can use any workstation in any location to get at any data or any software or any applications for which he or she is authorized.

4　A diverse, multi-generational, geographically dispersed workforce. The workplace itself will be flexible and supportive of a very diverse workforce with a wide variety of needs in terms of how and where work gets done. Wellness will be explicitly encouraged in an effort to not only keep health expenses down, but also to keep productivity up. Reaching Generation X and Y employees requires different approaches to designing training than in the past. Moreover, companies today are under severe economic pressure. The challenge is 'how do you teach with didactic content and show learners how to apply their knowledge in the real world, and do so within a learning attention span of 45 minutes' (Harris, 2009: 45)? Immersive learning – games and simulations – are part of the answer.

5　Focus on performance and results. Training will become increasingly focused on learning outcomes and performance rather than training centric. It will be much more employee driven instead of instructor driven.

6　Learning organizations will become a reality. Workplace learning and performance will also become increasingly integrated with change management as enterprises are forced to adapt and evolve continually in the diverse, flattened workplaces of an increasingly competitive global economy. The frequency curve for change continues to climb, and its impact continues to widen. Since learning (and unlearning and relearning) is a key component of change, WLP professionals can expect to play an ever greater role in helping organizations effectively implement change initiatives. Thus, change implementation should be seen as one more competency required for the WLP professional of the future.

7　User-generated content. The focus of knowledge management can be expected to shift from data capture to shared learning. New technology environments such as wikis, blogs, and virtual environments provide new platforms for the collaborative creation of content.

8　Virtual environments will transform learning and performance in the workplace –providing geographically dispersed employees and executives a place to meet and learn together. Ubiquitous access to virtual environments, such as Second Life, will enable enterprises and WLP professionals to build custom immersive spaces and applications that increase productivity, creativity, and innovation while cutting travel costs and doing business in a more eco-friendly way. Hundreds of global organizations, including Fortune 500 companies such as IBM and Northrop Grumman, have already begun using Second Life to bring distributed teams together in a shared virtual workspace to collaborate, meet, learn, and prototype new products and services.

A myriad of driving forces for high-quality learning support

Significant forces in our world, including changing demographics, the globalization of work, and new technologies, have resulted in the requirement that all employees have learning opportunities to acquire or enhance the skills needed to maintain the company's and our society's competitiveness. Unions, as well as the federal government, are increasingly involved in ensuring continuing education options. The United Auto Workers, for example, won a $20 million retraining fund as Ford Motor Company revised its human resource management policies. The union agreement was later expanded to include managerial personnel (London and Bassman, 1989). Similarly, the federal government has considered legislation that would require all business organizations to invest a minimum percentage of total payroll in employee training.

Today, as well as in the near future, employees have any number of options available to them for continuing education. In the Casey Melendez scenario, Dwight Feeley had completed a training program completely outside the purview of his company's training resources. Casey's department did not deliver – or even know of – Dwight's training program. Nor did HDC! Casey was nevertheless expected to furnish competence measurement to certify that Dwight had indeed mastered specific skills to levels of proficiency required for certain jobs. Moreover, workers are increasingly less likely to be tethered to an organization for life. Individuals will therefore be taking fuller charge of their own learning needs, designing and managing their own careers. To do this, they will choose from a plentiful supply of learning options including, but not limited to, training furnished by their organizations. Other learning resources, such as programs on the Internet or on CDs, will be increasingly available. Also, courses at community colleges, universities, and private training companies – accessible either physically or through distance learning – will be available. Organizational training departments will continue to design and develop traditional training programs, but they will also work with individuals, unions, schools, and universities to become clearinghouses of learning opportunities.

CONCLUSION

This chapter offered a glimpse of a workforce learning and performance professional at work in 2020. Its premise is that in step with all the projected societal trends and new technologies, the job of the WLP professional will continue to focus on supporting learning and performance throughout his or her organization. Sophisticated information technologies, and especially the growth of virtual environments, will put required knowledge at our fingertips precisely when needed and help us deal efficiently with matters of administration. Computing competency will thus be an essential tool of the workplace, and this competency will be just a beginning. As has always been the case, the knowledge worker of the future, WLP professional or otherwise, will need to have an inquiring mind, will have to be a person ready to learn continually and adapt constantly to new knowledge and new ways of doing things. While specific skills and tools will be important, knowing what to do and why will continue to be as important as knowing how.

Just as organizational lines have blurred in today's flattened, multi-generational, global workforce, so have the lines between formal and informal training, real and virtual learning environments, and individual responsibility and collaboration. Advanced training technologies provide powerful new platforms for integrating learning and performance in the workplace. Blended learning environments will seamlessly integrate various delivery platforms and learning methods tailored to the specific objectives of the needed business solution at a given point in time. Learning, knowledge sharing, and performance support will be delivered just in time. The boundaries between individual learning and organizational learning will likewise fade as the need for continuous learning becomes a reality. Employees, likewise, are held accountable not only for their own learning but for contributing to the learning of others as well.

NOTE

1 This scenario is an update of a scenario originally published as Chapter 12 in O'Connor, B.N., Bronner, M. and Delaney, C. (2002) Training for Organizations. Cincinnati: South-Western Publishing Company. With permission.

REFERENCES

Elchoness, D. (2009) Your Path in 3D. *Training & Development Magazine*, January, 2009, 83. Active Magazine accessed 3/1/2009 http://e-ditionsbyfry.com/Olive/AM3/TDM/PrintPagesView.htm

Galagan, P. (2009) 'Second That: Could Second Life be Learning's Second Chance?', *Training and Development Magazine*, ASTD, February 2009, 34–37. Active Magazine accessed 3/1/2009 http://e-ditionsbyfry.com/Olive/AM3/TDM/PrintPagesView.htm

Gronstedt, Anders (2007) 'Second Life Produces Real Training Results: The 3-D Web World is Slowly Becoming Part of the Training Industry', *Training & Development Magazine*, August 2007, 1 & 44. Accessed 5/23/2009 http://e-ditionsbyfry.com/Olive/AMe/TDM/PrintComponentView.htm.

Harris, P.D. (2009) 'Immersive Learning Seeks a Foothold', *Training & Development Magazine*, January, 2009: 40–45.

Hofmann, J. and Miner, N. (2008) 'Real Blended Learning Stands Up', *ASTD Learning Circuits*, September 2008. Accessed 5/27/2009 http://www.astd.org/LC/2008/1008_hofmann.htm.

London, M. and Bassman, E. (1989) 'Retraining Midcareer Workers for the Future Workplace', *Training and Development in Organizations*, edited by Irwin Goldstein and Associates, San Francisco: Jossey-Bass: 357.

Nancherla, A. (2009) 'Knowledge Delivered in Any Other Form Is … Perhaps Sweeter', *Training and Development Magazine*, May, 2008: 54–60.

Nancherla, A. (2008) 'Technology 2020', *Training and Development Magazine*, December, 2008: 34. Accessed 3/1/2009 http://e-ditionsbyfry.com/Olice/AM3/TDM/PrintComponentView.htm.

—— (2009) 'Simulation Training and Prototyping in Virtual Worlds: Northrop Grumman in Second Life', Linden Labs Case Study. Pdf file downloaded 6/2/2009 from http://secondlifegrid.net.s3.amazonaws.com/docs/Second_Life_Case_NGC.pdf

Stahre, J. (2009) 'iPhone – the Work Tool for Sustainable Factories of the Future', *Chalmers News Summary*. #092546 Accessed 6/1/2009 at http://chalmersnyheter.chalmers.se/chalmers03/english/print.jsp?article=13608.

33

Technology and Knowledge Management

Jingli Cheng, Su Jin Son,
and Curtis J. Bonk

Knowledge has long been viewed as an asset that generates competitive advantages for today's organizations (Grant, 1996a, 1996b; Nonaka et al., 2000; Spender, 1996). Hence, the importance of managing knowledge and the need for organizations to build capabilities and capacities to do so are emphasized by many (Alavi and Leidner, 2001a; Murray, 2002). However, before long, people started to realize that not all knowledge can be captured, codified, and stored and the type of knowledge that is hard to articulate or document, what Polyani (1958) called tacit knowledge, may be more important for organizational success (Al-Hawamdeh, 2002; Bouthillier and Shearer, 2002; Brown and Duguid, 2001; Dougherty, 1999; Hildreth and Kimble, 2002; Hildreth et al., 1999; Lubit, 2001; Miller, 2002; Wilson, 2002).

We intend to examine in this chapter the complex relationships between technology adoption and knowledge management in the workplace. On the basis of examining previous knowledge management efforts using technologies, we analyze the underlying reasons why most knowledge management systems are faced with the challenges of underutilization or failure. We will then expound the proposition of a fundamental shift of our current knowledge management mentality from using technology to capture and codify knowledge to using technology to facilitate the creation, transfer, and exchange of knowledge. With a broadened understanding of "technology," we examine a sample of current approaches and emerging technologies being used to facilitate learning and knowledge transfer in the workplace and discuss their potential for knowledge management. Finally, we argue that the next wave in the knowledge management field will be characterized by a re-examination of our current knowledge mentality and the adoption of broader and new technologies and approaches that resemble how knowledge is truly created and transferred in the workplace.

KNOWLEDGE AS A SOURCE FOR ORGANIZATIONAL EFFECTIVENESS

Despite limited critiques (e.g. Foss, 1996a; Foss, 1996b), the knowledge-based theory of the firm is now a widely accepted approach to understanding the purpose and processes of firms in today's knowledge-based economy. This view of the firm holds that knowledge is the most strategically critical resource that generates economic rent and creates sustainable competitive advantages for organizations. However, despite the general agreement about knowledge and its strategic implication for firms, theories of the knowledge-based view of the firm vary greatly in terms of how knowledge is conceptualized. An understanding of the different views of knowledge is an important foundation for the discussion of knowledge management, because "theoretical developments in the knowledge management area are influenced by the distinction among the different types of knowledge" (Alavi and Leidner, 2001b, p. 112). While Alavi and Leidner's (2001b) discussion of different types of knowledge focused on distinctions between the multiple facets of this concept such as explicit vs. tacit and individual vs. collective knowledge, we focus our discussions here on two views of knowledge – (1) knowledge as an object, and (2) knowledge as a process.

Knowledge as an object

The knowledge-based view of the firm is deeply rooted in the resource-based view of the firm. The resource-based view sees the firm as a collection of resources that are utilized to achieve economic goals. It also argues that what gives a firm its competitive advantages are the types of resources that are rare, durable, of value, and inimitable. According to the resource-based view of the firm, knowledge, especially tacit knowledge, is an intangible form of resource that can help firms generate competitive advantage, because tacit knowledge only resides in the minds of a firm's employees (not public) and thus is inimitable by others (Barney, 1991).

Within the boundaries of a firm, the conversion of tacit knowledge into its explicit forms and the sharing of such knowledge among a firm's employees are seen as essential processes to the success of the firm. Knowledge, in this sense, is an object. Although intangible, it is viewed as an important organizational asset (e.g., Liebeskind, 1996) that in essence is not that much different from other more tangible corporate assets such as land and labor. Because knowledge is viewed as a "transferable commodity", management's focus must be on its "production, acquisition, movement, retention and application" (Spender, 1996, p. 48). Under this view, knowledge management focused on capturing knowledge and storing it (in the form of electronic documents, for example), and making it accessible for a wider audience within the firm.

Knowledge as a process

A different perspective views knowledge as a process. This view sees knowledge in the context of organizations and holds that "individual learning must always be considered in the context of the processes of the social entity that relies on that individual as its active agent" (Spender, 1996, p. 53). The organization's primary role is to integrate and apply knowledge in the production of goods and services (Grant, 1996b). The underlying mechanism of this process is the learning of the individuals in the organization and the interactions among them. Through this learning and interaction-based process, articulated knowledge (information) is converted from its tacit form to its more explicit form, detached from the individual, and communicated to others. As it is processed through the receiving individual's mind, the information is internalized and formed into (new) knowledge (Alavi and Leidner, 2001b; Liebeskind, 1996; Nonaka, 1994).

Cook and Brown (1999) use the term "knowing" to describe this process. Knowledge, in their view, is a tool for knowing. Using Dewey's notion of *productive inquiry* – "that aspect of any activity where we are deliberately (though not always consciously) seeking what we need, in order to do what we want to do" (p. 388) – they argue that "We must see knowledge as a tool at the service of knowing not as something that, once possessed, is all that is needed to enable action or practice." (p. 388)

This shift of view of knowledge from being an object to a process of integration and application has profound implications for knowledge management. First, the firm is viewed as "a system of knowing activity rather than as a system of applied abstract knowledge" (Spender, 1996). Knowledge is not simply seen as an object, an organizational production asset that needs to be captured, stored, and protected from appropriation or imitation by competitors. Rather, the emphasis is shifted to viewing the firm as an activity system that gives meaning to knowledge and provides the context for its integration and application. This is what essentially distinguishes the knowledge-based view from the resource-based view of the firm.

Second, the traditional approach of knowledge management focuses on knowledge as an object. In the shifted view of knowledge as a process, the focus of knowledge management is on the process, the activity of knowing. This is especially meaningful for contemporary firms where knowledge is decentralized and distributed across the system (Tsoukas, 1996), and employees, seen as active agents undertaking different activities to transform inputs to outputs (Spender, 1996, p. 46), need to continuously formulate and expand new knowledge through social interactions. The primary emphasis of knowledge management, therefore, is not to capture and store, but to facilitate the generation, transfer, and application of knowledge. Storing and providing access of knowledge only becomes secondary in this new approach to knowledge management.

TECHNOLOGY AND KNOWLEDGE MANAGEMENT: THE CHALLENGE

The recognition of the strategic significance of knowledge has led to the practice of seeking to "manage" knowledge. As is discussed in previous sections, seeing knowledge as an asset of the corporation underlies the knowledge management practice of "capturing knowledge and expertise created by knowledge workers as they go about their work and making it available to a larger community of colleagues" (Mack et al., 2001, p. 925). For this purpose, computer-based information and communications technology has especially attracted tremendous amounts of interest due to their capabilities to store, transfer, index, and search large amounts of information at high speed and relatively low cost, overcoming the barriers of time and space that are often considered as limiting factors in knowledge management activities.

Upon extensive review of technologies that are employed for knowledge management solutions, Marwick (2001) concluded that "the strongest contribution to current solutions is made by technologies that deal largely with explicit knowledge, such as search and classification" (p. 814). However, technology-based knowledge management systems that are aimed at collecting and disseminating knowledge typically face the challenge of employee's unwillingness to contribute their knowledge and underutilization of such technology platforms (Jian and Jeffres, 2006).

Ardichvili (2008), upon analyzing the motivating, impeding, and enabling factors of online knowledge sharing, found that technology-related factors such as the lack of ease of use can sometimes function as impediment for knowledge sharing. On the other hand, as those who have experience or enough exposure to the types of knowledge management systems that focus on the capturing and storing of knowledge would readily say, even if the technology platform has managed to collect and store some amounts of knowledge in the forms of videos, texts, etc., these often face the challenge of underutilization.

Here we would like to point out two primary reasons. First, complex knowledge is hard to represent well using text, image, sound or video, thus making what's captured usually not as useful. Second the content stored in these systems typically face the challenge of either having "too little" useful information, or having "too much" information that makes finding useful information a formidable and even impossible task.

TECHNOLOGY AND KNOWLEDGE MANAGEMENT: THE NEED FOR A CHANGED FOCUS

The underlying cause for the failure of knowledge management using technologies is not just the lack of usability of the technology. Many scholars have observed that effective knowledge management has to go beyond the narrow view of knowledge as objects that can be captured, stored, and retrieved when needed. The focus of these discourses (e.g., Alavi and Leidner, 2001b; Hildreth et al., 1999; Marwick, 2001) are largely based on the distinction between explicit and tacit forms of knowledge (see Polanyi, 1966) and the view of the knowledge generation and transfer process based on the inter-conversion between these two forms of knowledge (see Nonaka, 1994; and Spender, 1996). In this section, we expand this perspective by emphasizing on the important role of communication in the process of knowledge creation and knowledge sharing. The objective here is to highlight this key area where we believe information and communications technologies hold the most promise to contribute to the knowledge management effort.

Communication as key to intra-organizational knowledge management

As we have previously discussed, the process view of knowledge more accurately reflects how knowledge is created and transferred in organizations, and knowledge management efforts should focus on supporting this process. Considered from the perspective of contemporary thoughts on strategic management and organizational learning, this shifted view of knowledge as a process is even more significant. While the sharing and exchange of knowledge is desired by organizations for the purpose of increasing their competitive advantage, knowledge sharing and exchange even within the firm is shown to be easier said than done.

Organizations are faced with the challenge of employees unmotivated to contribute to organizational "knowledge repositories" (Subramanian and Soh, 2009). Szulanski (1996) used the term "internal stickiness" to describe the "difficulty of transferring knowledge within the organization" (p. 29). The origins of internal stickiness are analyzed from four perspectives: characters of knowledge transferred; characters of the source of knowledge; characters of the recipient of knowledge; and characters of the context. It is found that among others (such as causal ambiguity and unprovenness of knowledge, lack of motivation on both the source and recipient of knowledge, and lack of absorptive and retentive capacity on the recipient's part), an important factor that leads to the difficulty of knowledge transfer is the arduousness of this process. What this means, according to Szulanski (1996), is that transfer of knowledge, especially tacit knowledge, requires repeated exchanges between the individuals involved, and the success of such exchanges depends on two factors: "the ease of communication and the 'intimacy' of the overall relationship between the source unit and the recipient unit" (p. 32). Similarly, Hansen (1999) found that the transfer of complex knowledge across subunits in organizations requires a strong tie between the two parties. Such relationship relies on mutual understanding as a result of sustained communication between the parties.

Communication as key to integrating external knowledge

In the strategic management and organizational learning literature, the source of knowledge is viewed to exist not only within the boundaries of a firm, but it extends beyond the boundaries of the firm to other organizations. Such extensions might include strategic alliances with other firms as well as with individuals not necessarily affiliated with the organization, such as customers.

In fact, organizations increasingly rely on outside sources of knowledge. This cultural change is due to the fact that external knowledge is increasingly seen as an important source of innovation, which often requires higher amount of diverse information and more varieties of resources than a single organization may possess (Hienerth, 2006; von Hippel, 1988). For example, Anderson and Ejermo's (2005) analysis of the innovative performances of 130 Swedish corporations found that a corporation's innovativeness is positively related to its accessibility to external sources of knowledge, such as university researchers within the region of the firm's R&D staff. Similarly, Cassiman and Veugelers (2006) posit that innovation of a firm benefits from external knowledge sources such as universities and other research centers.

Individuals outside of a firm, such as customers, are also seen as important sources of external knowledge that can lead to innovation. For example, involving consumers in the design of a new product, especially in the earlier stages of the product cycle, is seen as vital to achieving innovative product design (Ciccantelli and Magidson, 2003). In addition, taking advantage of innovations from lead users is seen as a viable approach for development of commercially successful products by firms in computer software development (Jeppesen, 2004; Jeppesen and Frederiksen, 2006; Segelod and Jordan, 2004; von Hippel and von Krogh, 2003), the sports industry (Franke and Shah, 2003; Franke et al., 2006; Schreier et al., 2007), and even low-tech industries such as construction materials production (Herstatt and von Hippel, 2003). Obviously, the amount and diversity of information and the breadth and variety of resources that is typically required for innovation on the basis of external input can only result from significant amounts of repeated interactions with multiple external sources. Communication becomes central for integrating external sources of knowledge.

Conversation as the most fundamental mechanism for knowledge management

Interaction among individuals is a key mechanism that underlies the process of knowledge generation, transfer, and utilization both within and beyond the boundaries of organizations. Key to the interaction among individuals is the mechanism of communication and the most fundamental form of communication is conversations. For example, Thomas et al., (2001) discussed conversation as a social process and posited that "The social nature of talk is not an undesirable side effect, but rather the heart of it" (p. 871).

Conversation as a means of knowledge generation and transfer has been discussed by many scholars. Perhaps one of the most well-known is Orr's (1990) study of how photocopier technicians use story telling as a way of learning from each other. In this study, the technicians did not rely as much on the user manuals (stored knowledge) for trouble shooting the more complex problems with the machines. Rather, they relied on conversations with other technicians to learn the intricacies and nuances that helped with solving the technical problems. More recently, narratives and storytelling have been viewed as important mechanisms for knowledge generation and transfer. For example, Meyer (2004) found that narrative is a useful medium for knowledge transfer and exchange within the small teams he studied both in the private and the public sectors. Koivunen (2009), in building a theory of "collective expertise" to describe how professional experts work in organizations, found that narratives and storytelling are one of the factors that contribute to collective expertise.

By conversation we do not only refer to the voice-based conversation. We use it to refer to conversation-like exchanges that occur using any media as vehicles. With the advancement of technologies, conversations do not necessarily have to take the face-to-face or even voice-to-voice format as we know it. In fact, some of the most powerful technologies, as we will discuss later in this chapter, serve the purpose of enabling digital conversations. For example, email exchanges or discussions on a forum surrounding a certain topic, comments on a blog, short, quick exchanges on Twitter, video responses to an existing video on YouTube, etc., can all be considered as digital conversations.

Thomas et al. (2001) especially use the term "digital conversation" to describe "conversation within the digital medium" (p. 872). They argue that digital conversations are especially important for knowledge management purposes because electronic records can "persist". As they put it, "instantiated as text, whether typed in or spoken and recognized, [this capability of electronic conversation's] persistence expands conversation beyond those within earshot, rendering it accessible to those in other places and at later times" (p. 872). Similarly, Wagner and Bolloju (2005, p. ii) posit that digital conversations, "whether in discussion forums or other media, have been recognized as a useful medium for knowledge exchange and extraction". For example, Thomas et al. (2001) explained the Babble system as a "socially informed knowledge management system" on the basis of the importance of social factors for knowledge management. In discussing the social context and communication for knowledge generation and transfer, these authors view conversation as "essential" (p. 871). According to them, conversation is a fundamental social process that is key to effective knowledge transfer – "It is through conversation that we create, develop, validate, and share knowledge." (p. 871)

KNOWLEDGE MANAGEMENT AND TECHNOLOGY: A PEEK INTO THE FUTURE

It should be obvious by now that we take the position that knowledge is socially constructed and is highly subjective in nature. The creation, transfer, exchange, and application of knowledge, which should be the real focus of organizational knowledge management efforts, are most effective when considered in an organization's social context through interactions and engagement between individuals or groups. Knowledge, especially complex knowledge that is required for the success of organizations in today's knowledge-based economy, is too complicated and extremely difficult to be codified, stored, and transferred to be really useful due to their socially constructed and culturally embedded nature. Consequently, the previous strong emphasis on the explicit components of knowledge and the manner that information technology has been used to support the process of knowledge management is severely limited and constrained in today's organizational context.

We have proposed a different view and emphasis related to knowledge management on the basis of viewing knowledge as a process and organizations as entities that provide context for knowledge application. In this section, we discuss some emerging technologies and their potential for knowledge management. We do not intend to provide a comprehensive review of all emerging technologies, nor can we provide a definite prediction regarding this aspect, as these are beyond the scope of this particular chapter. The intention here is to provide some thoughtful comments in this regard that we hope will be useful for researchers and practitioners in the field of knowledge management.

Our definition of technology in this section is not limited to information technologies. Rather, it encompasses information technologies as well as organizational learning approaches such as informal learning and communities of practice, which we see as important approaches to knowledge management. The following discussion is based on the three basic premises which we have expounded in this chapter: (1) knowledge is a social process; (2) knowledge management should be focused on supporting knowledge as a process from its creation, transfer, and exchange to its application, rather than capturing and storing knowledge for access; and (3) capabilities to enable communication and conversations should be used as a measure for the adequacy of knowledge management technologies.

From knowledge management to knowledge networking: Communities of practice as an approach

The notion of communities of practice (CoPs) originated as a social learning construct but was widely adopted in the knowledge management field (Brown and Duguid, 1991; Lave and Wenger, 1991; Wenger, 1998; Wenger et al., 2002). Lave and Wenger (1991) originally defined CoPs as "an activity system about which participants share understandings concerning what they are doing and what that means in their lives and for their community" (p. 98). As a situated learning construct, it was used to examine how novices interact and learn from experts in a group. From this view, through growing levels of participation in the group's communal activities (a process that Lave and Wenger termed "legitimate peripheral participation"), novices become accepted as a member of the community.

As a powerful alternative to the dominant behaviorist view of learning, the situated learning theory and the communities of practice construct were immediately adopted by Brown and Duguid (1991). They used it in their analysis of how the Xerox copy machine technicians in the Orr (1990) study learn from each other's experiences and collaborate to solve problems at work. By shifting our view of working from conventional descriptions found in "manuals, training programs, organizational charts, and job descriptions" to that of a communities of practice perspective, Brown and Duguid argued, we can "reconceive of and redesign organizations" to improve working, learning, and innovation (p. 40). Wenger (1998) continued the explorations of the CoP's notion by way of studying in detail the dynamics through which clerks in an insurance claims processing office help each other learn job-related knowledge and skills. Through interacting with each other (mutual engagement), members of the community build a sense of togetherness (joint enterprise), and the language, routines, tools, and artifacts become the shared repertoire as a result of their interactions. In clearly linking to knowledge management, Wenger defines communities of practice as "groups of people who share a concern, a set of problems, or a passion about a topic, and who deepen their knowledge and expertise in this area by interacting on an ongoing basis" (Wenger et al., 2002, p. 4).

As the main concept of CoPs includes knowledge sharing, solving problems of groups and creating of a common knowledge repository as a by-product (Hislop, 2002), the approach is seen as effective to facilitate knowledge creation, transfer and application in organizational contexts. As Kimble (n.d.) puts it, CoPs "provide a useful social-cultural description of the process of the creation and reproduction of knowledge" (section 1, para. 1). In addition, Liedtka (1999) argues that the communities of practice metaphor create a larger context that supports what he calls an organization's "metacapabilities", which encompasses "learning, participative leadership, collaboration, strategic thinking, and total quality management" (p. 5). Lesser and Storck (2001) argue that communities of practice contribute to organizational performance by way of social capital and leads to performance outcomes including the decrease of new employee's learning curves, more rapid response to customer needs and inquiries, reduction of rework and prevention of the "reinventing of the wheel" phenomenon, and the generation of new products or service ideas.

Organizations should continue to explore communities of practice as an approach to both organizational learning and organizational knowledge management, as this approach focuses more on the social aspect of learning and knowledge, knowledge networking and community building through participation, dialogue, discussion, observation, and imitation among knowledge constructors rather than managing explicit knowledge. Several researchers have insisted that a significant amount of intense social interaction among knowledge constructors is strongly needed for the effective sharing of tacit knowledge (Brown and Duguid, 1991; Lave and Wenger, 1991; Leonard and Sensiper, 1998). Therefore, in order to build such communities and networks, supporting diverse collaborative ways of network and community building such as communities of practice, communities of interest which encompass people with shared interests will become more relevant in knowledge management (Brown and Duguid, 1991; Hislop, 2002; Lave and Wenger, 1991; Leonard and Sensiper, 1998).

Another important dimension of communities of practice or communities of interest is their potential to engage with external knowledge sources. The connections to external knowledge sources who do not typically have strong connections can be described using Granovetter's (1973, 1982) "weak ties" notion. As previously discussed, external knowledge is viewed as an important source for organizational innovations. Therefore, organizations should certainly not underestimate the strength of and potential of these weak ties (e.g., Anand et al., 2002; Constant et al., 1996)

Web 2.0 and social software

Several authors in knowledge management have highlighted the importance of informational technology in knowledge management (Hendriks, 2001; Hislop, 2002). The role of information technology in knowledge management has been dramatically changed during the past few years due to the different emphasis in the notion of knowledge. As the importance of the social aspect of knowledge keeps growing, emerging new information and communications technologies are used to facilitate the interaction and collaboration that benefit constructing and sharing of knowledge (Hendriks, 2001; Roberts, 2000). In this section, we will give a brief introduction of the new trend of information technologies in knowledge management including the concept of Web 2.0 and several social software such as weblog, wiki, and podcasting.

Web 2.0

According to Downes (2005), the concept of the Web is shifting over time from "being a medium, in which information was transmitted, into being a platform, in which content was created, shared, remixed, repurposed, and passed along" (section 3, para 4). The significantly important role of Web now is based on its interactive and collaborative features. This new generation of the Web has been referred to as "Web 2.0" (O'Reilly, 2005). Wagner and Bolloju (2005) have characterized Web 2.0 as "facilitating communication, information sharing, interoperability, user-centered design, and collaboration on the Web" (p. iii). In particular, the new concept of Web has led to the development and evolution of Web-based communities, hosted services, and Web applications such as blog, wiki, and other multimedia sharing services. Additionally, another major difference between old Web (which is called "Web 1.0") and new Web is the emphasis of the user's role. For example, in the new Web, users are enabled to participate directly in the creation, refinement and distribution of shared content. Thus, Web 2.0 applications are mostly used for creating and sharing knowledge effectively and securely rather than storing and transferring knowledge.

There are diverse forms of Web 2.0 applications, the so called "social software" (Lawley, 2004). According to Coates (2003), social software refers to "a particular sub-class of software-prosthesis that concerns itself with the augmentation of human social and/or collaborative abilities through structured mediation (this mediation may be distributed or centralized, top-down or bottom-up/emergent)" (section 1, para. 2). Boyd (2005) classified the three main elements of social software: (1) support for conversational interaction between people or groups, (2) support for social feedback, and (3) support for social networks. There are several examples of social software technologies including weblog, wikis, RSS, podcasts, multi-media sharing, and social tagging. In this chapter, we focus on weblog, wikis, and podcasting as some examples of social software that has potential for knowledge management.

Weblog

The term Web-log, or blog, was coined by Barger in 1997. It refers to a simple Web page created and arranged by the author in chronological diary form (Barger, 1997). Most blogs also allow visitors to add a comment below the author's own entry. The entries, usually called "posts", are displayed chronologically on the Weblog site. A post can be linked to other online articles, earlier discussions or related readings (Avram, 2005). One of the advantages of blogs is that it's easy to edit and publish content. In addition, the "conversation capability" of blogs – blog's archival, search, and categorization features – enables users to organize and retrieve the contents when they want to build knowledge logs (k-logs) (Wagner and Bolloju, 2005, p. iv).

The contents of blogs are diverse from personal diaries to professional knowledge repositories or networking instruments and often integrate the use of different multimedia such as photos and videos (Anderson, 2007). Due to blogs' highly subjective characteristics, they are considered a useful tool for users who wish to broadcast their expertise to a large public who have similar interests by sharing their personal stories and personal knowledge. Organizations can certainly take advantage of this capability to effectively use blogs to enable knowledge sharing and exchange both within and beyond the organization boundaries (e.g., Cheng, 2008).

Wiki

According to Avram (2005), Wiki was defined as a "composition system, a discussion medium, a repository, a mail system, a chat room, and a tool for collaboration" (p. 3) by the first wiki site, WikiWikiWeb. Simply put, a Wiki is known as a set of linked Web pages that allow users to add contents that can also be edited by anyone who is allowed access. Anderson (2007) has stated that "Wikipedia's popular success has meant that the concept of the wiki, as a collaborative tool that facilitates the production of a group work, is widely understood" (p. 8).

The most distinctive characteristic of Wiki is that most Wikis are open to the general public who can access the Wiki server to contribute to the collective content development. In other words, anyone who has access to a Wiki page can update and edit the existing content. In addition, different from blogs, Wikis generally have a history and rollback function which allows users to restore previous versions of the content. Given this premise, researchers have pointed out the prospect of the Wiki as an effective group working tool based on the ease of use, flexibility, and open access to users (Ebersbach et al., 2006; Lamb, 2004; Raman, 2006).

Wagner and Bolloju (2005) classified Wikis along with blogs and discussion forums as a conversational technology based on its capacity to enable knowledge creation and sharing through collaborative editing. In organizational contexts, many examples exist of local Wiki sites that are used to enhance communication between users and to support knowledge sharing from the collective work of the company (Raman, 2006).

Podcasting

Geoghegan and Klass (2005) defined podcasts as "audio content available on the Internet that can be automatically delivered to your computer or MP3 player" (p. 5). According to Felix and Stolarz (2006), originally, audio blog users initiated podcasting in order to add audio streams to blogs. As the use of MP3 portable players, such as the iPod, significantly increased, the process of creating and distributing audio/video contents became known as podcasting (Anderson, 2007). However, Podcasting is not only limited to iPod; it also includes other portable MP3 devices as well as traditional computers.

According to Ractham and Zhang (2006), more than 27 million iPods have been sold from 2001, and the free contents of podcasts are various, including music, sports, education, politics and science. Given the increasing number of users and the many positive aspects such as ease of use, significant time savings, and minimal search efforts, podcasting has been viewed as a useful knowledge management tool among users, researchers, and practitioners in academia and business (Ractham and Zhang, 2006). In particular, in organizational settings, podcasting can be used as a mechanism to push out short content to users because users can automatically receive updated content as long as they subscribe to the RSS feeds (Ractham and Zhang, 2006).

CONCLUSION

According to Grant (1996b), "A knowledge-based view of the firm encourages us to perceive interdependence as an element of organizational design and the subject of managerial choice rather than exogenously driven by the prevailing production technology. The general issue is devising mechanisms for integrating individual's specialized knowledge." (p. 114). In this chapter, we attempted to address the many aspects related to this issue of integrating knowledge in organizations. The traditional answer to this question was to capture and codify the knowledge in the person's head before he/she walks out of the company's door. Rather than this often futile effort, we believe that the focus should be on facilitating the sharing and transfer of individuals' knowledge while they are in the organization, so even though they leave the organization, some of their knowledge remains with others who are in the organization in the form of applied know-how.

We begun by clarifying our position on knowledge as a social process, as contrasted to the view of knowledge as an object. On the basis of establishing this perspective on knowledge, we proposed a shift of focus of knowledge management from codifying, capturing, and storing knowledge to enabling the social interactions that underlie contemporary views of knowledge creation, transfer, and application. With an expanded view on technologies to include not only "hard" information and communication technologies, but also approaches to organizational learning and knowledge transfer, we focused on a number of approaches and emerging technologies, including communities of practice, blogs, Wikis, and podcasts.

Our purpose was not to provide a comprehensive review of emerging technologies and their implications for knowledge management, but to use these as examples to illustrate our view of the potential promises that these social approaches and technologies hold for knowledge creation, transfer, and application in organizational contexts. We believe the future of knowledge management will be characterized by a stronger recognition of the social aspect of knowledge. As a result, technologies that possess the capabilities to facilitate natural and easy communication of knowledge through conversation-like interactions will find increasing acceptance and use.

Knowledge management has had a long interconnection with technologies, as information and communication technologies continue to provide capabilities to meet the knowledge management needs. Although technology has been the focus of this chapter, it is worth emphasizing that "knowledge management problems can typically not be solved by the deployment of a technology solution alone" (Marwick, 2001, p. 816), as there are other aspects, such as the organization's leadership and management, work environment, individual characteristics, organizational culture, etc. (Cheng, 2008) that are equally, if not more, important than enabling technologies.

It is our hope that this chapter will lead to more discussions about what knowledge management is today and what it can be tomorrow. Sousa and Hendriks (2006) expanded the definition of knowledge management to include "policies, strategies, and techniques aimed at supporting an organization's competitiveness by organizing the conditions needed for efficiency improvement, innovation, and collaboration among employees" (p. 318). As new work environments, organizational cultures, and Web 2.0 technologies for supporting new approaches to knowledge management make their appearance, the definitions and viewpoints of this will undoubtedly keep developing. As we embark on a broader understanding of knowledge management, it is time to embrace such environments and technologies and see what potential these hold for the field of knowledge management.

REFERENCES

Al-Hawamdeh, S. (2002) 'Knowledge Management: Re-thinking Information Management and Facing the Challenge of Managing Tacit Knowledge', *Information Research*, 8(1). Retrieved from http://informationr.net/ir/8-1/paper143.html

Alavi, M. and Leidner, D.E. (2001a) 'Knowledge Management and Knowledge Management Systems: Conceptual Foundations and Research Issues', *MIS Quarterly*, 25(1): 107–136.

Alavi, M. and Leidner, D.E. (2001b) 'Review: Knowledge Management and Knowledge Management Systems: Conceptual Foundations and Research Issues', *MIS Quarterly*, 25(1): 107–136.

Anand, V., Glick, W.H. and Manz, C.C. (2002) 'Thriving on the Knowledge of Outsiders: Tapping Organizational Social Capital', *The Academy of Management Executive (1993)*, 16(1): 87–101.

Anderson, P. (2007, February) What is Web 2.0? Ideas, Technologies and Implications for Education. Retrieved May 31, 2008, from JISC Technology & Standards Watch: http://www.jisc.ac.uk/media/documents/techwatch/tsw0701b.

Andersson, M. and Ejermo, O. (2005) 'How Does Accessibility to Knowledge Sources Affect the Innovativeness of Corporations? Evidence from Sweden', *The Annals of Regional Science*, 39(4): 741–765.

Ardichvili, A. (2008) 'Learning and Knowledge Sharing in Virtual Communities of Practice: Motivators, Barriers, and Enablers', *Advances in Developing Human Resources*, 10(4): 541–555.

Avram, G. (2005) 'At the Crossroads of Knowledge Management and Social Software', The Electronic *Journal of Knowledge Management*, 4(1): 1–10.

Barger, J. (1997) Robot wisdom weblog for December 1997. [Verified 6 June 2004] http://www.robotwisdom.com/log1997m12.html

Barney, J. (1991) 'Firm Resources and Sustained Competitive Advantage', *Journal of Management*, 17: 99–120.

Bouthillier, F. and Shearer, K. (2002) 'Understanding Knowledge Management and Information Management: The Need for an Empirical Perspective', *Information Research*, 8(1): Retrieved from http://informationr.net/ir/8-1/paper141.html

Boyd, D. (2005) 'The Significance of Social Software', Available at http://www.zephoria.org/thoughts/archives/2005/05/08/the_ significance_of_social _software.html

Brown, J.S. and Duguid, P. (1991) 'Organizational Learning and Communities-of-Practice: Toward a Unified View of Working, Learning and Innovation', *Organization Science*, 2(1): 40–57.

Brown, J.S. and Duguid, P. (2001) 'Knowledge and Organization: A Social-Practice Perspective', *Organization Science*, 12(2): 198–213.

Cassiman, B. and Veugelers, R. (2006) 'In Search of Complementarity in Innovation Strategy: Internal R&D and External Knowledge Acquisition', *Management Science*, 52(1): 68–82.

Cheng, J. (2008) 'How Macromedia Used Blogs to Build Its Developer's Communities: A Case Study', *Performance Improvement Quarterly*, 21(3): 43–58.

Ciccantelli, S. and Magidson, J. (2003) 'Consumer Idealized Design: Involving Consumers in the Product Development Process', *Journal of Product Innovation Management*, 10(4): 341–347.

Coates, T. (2003) 'My Working Definition of Social Software', Retrieved May, 8, 2003, from http://www.plasticbag.org/ archives/2003/05/my_working_definition_of_social_software/.

Constant, D., Sproull, L. and Kiesler, S. (1996) 'The Kindness of Strangers: The Usefulness of Electronic Weak Ties for Technical Advice', *Organization Science*, 7(2): 119–135.

Cook, S.D.N. and Brown, J.S. (1999) 'Bridging Epistemologies: The Generative Dance between Organizational Knowledge and Organizational Knowing', *Organization Science*, 10(4): 381–400.

Dougherty, V. (1999) 'Knowledge is about People, Not Databases' *Industrial and Commercial Training*, 31(7): 262. Retrieved from http://proquest.umi.com/pqdweb?did=115721259&sid=2&Fmt=3&clientId=12010&RQT=309&VName=PQD

Downes, S. (2005) E-learning 2.0. Retrieved October, 17, 2005 from http://www.elearnmag.org/subpage.cfm?article= 29-1&section=articles

Ebersbach, A., Glaser, M. and Heigl, R. (2006) *Wiki: Web Collaboration*. Berlin Heidelberg: Springer-Verlag.

Felix, L. and Stolarz, D. (2006) *Hands-On Guide to Video Blogging and Podcasting: Emerging Media Tools for Business Communication*. Massachusetts: Focal Press.

Foss, N.J. (1996a). 'Based Approaches to the Theory of the Firm: Some Critical Comments', *Organization Science*, 7(5): 470–476.

Foss, N.J. (1996b). 'More Critical Comments on Knowledge-Based Theories of the Firm', *Organization Science*, 7(5): 519–523.

Franke, N. and Shah, S. (2003) 'How Communities Support Innovative Activities: An Exploration of Assistance and Sharing among End-Users', *Research Policy*, 32(1).

Franke, N., von Hippel, E. and Schreier, M. (2006) 'Finding Commercially Attractive User Innovations: A Test of Lead-User Theory', *Journal of Product Innovation Management*, 23(4): 301–315.

Geoghegan, M. and Klass, D. (2005) *Podcast Solutions: The Complete Guide to Podcasting*. Berkeley, CA: Friends of ED.

Granovetter, M.S. (1973) 'The Strength of Weak Ties', *The American Journal of Sociology*, 78(6): 1360–1380.

Granovetter, M.S. (1982) 'The Strength of Weak Ties: A Network Theory Revisited', In N. Lin and P.V. Marsden (eds), *Social Structure and Network Analysis*. Beverly Hills, CA: Sage Publications. pp. 105–130.

Grant, R.M. (1996a) 'Prospering in Dynamically-Competitive Environments: Organizational Capability as Knowledge Integration', *Organization Science*, 7(4): 375–387.

Grant, R.M. (1996b) 'Toward a Knowledge-Based Theory of the Firm', *Strategic Management Journal*, 17 (Winter Special Issue): 109–122.

Hansen, M.T. (1999) 'The Search-Transfer Problem: The Role of Weak Ties in Sharing Knowledge across Organization Subunits', *Administrative Science Quarterly*, 44(1): 82–111.

Hendriks, P.H.J. (2001) 'Many Rivers to Cross: From ICT to Knowledge Management Systems', *Journal of Information Technology (Routledge, Ltd.)*, 16(2): 57–72.

Herstatt, C. A. and von Hippel, E. (2003) 'Developing New Product Concepts via the Lead User Method: A Case Study in a "Low-Tech" Field', *Journal of Product Innovation Management*, 9(3): 213–221.

Hienerth, C. (2006) 'The Commercialization of User Innovations: The Development of the Rodeo Kayak Industry', *R&D Management*, 36(3): 273–294.

Hildreth, P. and Kimble, C. (2002) 'The Duality of Knowledge', *Information Research*, 8(1). Retrieved from http://informationr.net/ ir/8-1/paper142.html

Hildreth, P., Wright, P. and Kimble, C. (April, 1999). *Knowledge Management: Are We Missing Something?* Paper presented at the 4th UKAIS Conference, York, UK.

Hislop, D. (2002) 'Mission Impossible? Communicating and Sharing Knowledge via Information Technology', *Journal of Information Technology (Routledge, Ltd.)*, 17(3): 165–177.

Jeppesen, L.B. (2004) Profiting from Innovative User Communities: How Firms Organize the Production of User Modifications in the Computer Games Industry: Department of Industrial Economics and Strategy, Copenhagen Business School, Copenhagen, Denmark.

Jeppesen, L.B. and Frederiksen, L. (2006) 'Why Do Users Contribute to Firm-Hosted User Communities? The Case of Computer-Controlled Music Instruments', *Organization Science*, 17(1): 45–63.

Jian, G. and Jeffres, L.W. (2006) 'Understanding Employees' Willingness to Contribute to Shared Electronic Databases', *Communication Research*, 33(4): 242–261.

Kimble, C. (n.d.) Communities of practice: Never knowingly undersold. Retrieved from http://www.comp.leeds.ac.uk/stellak/reading-group/Chris%20Kimble%20-%20Communities%20of%20Practice.pdf

Koivunen, N. (2009) 'Collective Expertise: Ways of Organizing Expert Work in Collective Settings', *Journal of Management and Organization*, 15(2): 258–276.

Lamb, B. (2004) 'Wide Open Spaces: Wikis, Ready or Not', *EDUCAUSE Review*, 39(5): 36–48. Retrieved November 2006 from http://www.educause.edu/pub/er/erm04/erm0452.asp?bhcp=1

Lave, J. and Wenger, E. (1991) *Situated Learning: Legitimate Peripheral Participation*. New York: Cambridge University Press.

Lawley, L. (2004) Blog research issues. Many-to-many. Retrieved from: http://www.corante.com/many/archives/2004/06/24/blog_research_issues.php

Leonard, D. and Sensiper, S. (1998) 'The Role of Tacit Knowledge in Group Innovation', *California Management Review*, 40(3): 112–132.

Lesser, E.L. and Storck, J. (2001) 'Communities of Practice and Organizational Performance', *IBM Systems Journal*, 40(4): 831–841.

Liebeskind, J.P. (1996) 'Knowledge, Strategy, and the Theory of the Firm', *Strategic Management Journal*, 17: 93–107.

Liedtka, J. (1999) 'Linking Competitive Advantage with Communities of Practice', *Journal of Management Inquiry*, 8(1): 5–16.

Lubit, R. (2001) 'Tacit Knowledge and Knowledge Management: The Keys to Sustainable Competitive Advantage', *Organizational Dynamics*, 29(4): 164–178.

Mack, R., Ravin, Y. and Byrd, R.J. (Writer) (2001) 'Knowledge Portals and the Emerging Digital Knowledge Workplace', *IBM Systems Journal*: IBM Corporation/IBM Journals.

Marwick, A.D. (Writer) (2001) 'Knowledge Management Technology', *IBM Systems Journal*: IBM Corporation/IBM Journals.

Meyer, E. (2004) *A Narrative Approach to Knowledge Management: An Investigation into the Use of Narrative as a Medium to Transfer Knowledge in Small Teams*. Unpublished Ph.D. Thesis, University of Southampton, England.

Miller, F.J. (2002) I = 0 (Information has no intrinsic meaning). *Information Research*, 8(1). Retrieved from http://informationr.net/ir/8-1/paper140.html

Murray, P. (2002) 'Knowledge Management as a Sustained Competitive Advantage', *Ivy Business Journal*, 66(4): 71–77.

Nonaka, I. (1994) 'A Dynamic Theory of Organizational Knowledge Creation', *Organization Science*, 5(1): 14–37.

Nonaka, I., Toyama, R. and Nagata, A. (2000) 'A Firm as a Knowledge-Creating Entity: A New Perspective on the Theory of the Firm', *Industrial and Corporate Change*, 9(1): 1–20.

Orr, J.E. (1990) *Talking About Machines: An Ethnography of a Modern Job*. Itehaca, New York: Cornell University.

O'Reilly, T. (2005) What is Web 2.0. Retrieved from: http://www.oreillynet.com/pub/a/oreilly/tim/news/2005/09/30/what-is-web-20.html

Polyani, M. (1958) *Personal Knowledge*. Chicago: The University of Chicago Press.

Polanyi, M. (1966) *The Tacit Dimension* (1st edn). Garden City, NY: Doubleday.

Ractham, P. and Zhang, X. (2006) 'Podcasting in Academia – a New Knowledge Management Paradigm within Academic Settings', *SIGMIS-CPR'06*, April 13–15.

Raman, M. (2006) 'Wiki Technology as a 'Free' Collaborative Tool within an Organizational Setting', *Information Systems Management*, 23(4): 59–66.

Roberts, J. (2000) 'From Know-How to Show-How? Questioning the Role of Information and Communication Technologies in Knowledge Transfer', *Technology Analysis & Strategic Management*, 12(4): 429–443.

Schreier, M., Oberhauser, S. and Prügl, R. (2007) 'Lead Users and the Adoption and Diffusion of New Products: Insights from Two Extreme Sports Communities', *Marketing Letters*.

Segelod, E. and Jordan, G. (2004) 'The Use and Importance of External Sources of Knowledge in the Software Development Process', *R & D Management*, 34(3): 239–252.

Sousa, C.A.A. and Hendriks, P.H.J. (2006) 'The Diving Bell and the Butterfly: The Need for Grounded Theory in Developing a Knowledge-Based View of Organizations', *Organizational Research Methods*, 9(3): 315–338.

Spender, J.-C. (1996) 'Making Knowledge the Basis of a Dynamic Theory of the Firm', *Strategic Management Journal*, 17 (Winter Special Issue), 45–62.

Subramanian, A. and Soh, P.-H. (2009) 'Contributing Knowledge to Knowledge Repositories: Dual Role of Inducement and Opportunity Factors', *Information Resources Management Journal*, 22(1): 45–62.

Szulanski, G. (1996) 'Exploring Internal Stickiness: Impediments to the Transfer of Best Practice within the Firm', *Strategic Management Journal*, 17: 27–43.

Thomas, J.C., Kellogg, W.A. and Erickson, T. (2001) 'The Knowledge Management Puzzle: Human and Social Factors In Knowledge Management', *IBM Systems Journal*, 40(4): 863–884.

Tsoukas, H. (1996) 'The Firm as a Distributed Knowledge System: A Constructionist Approach', *Strategic Management Journal*, 17: 11–25.

von Hippel, E. (1988) *The Sources of Innovation*. New York: Oxford University Press.

von Hippel, E. and von Krogh, G. (2003) 'Open Source Software and the "Private-Collective" Innovation Model: Issues for Organization Science', *Organization Science*, 14(2): 209–223.

Wagner, C. and Bolloju, N. (2005) 'Supporting Knowledge Management in Organizations with Conversational Technologies: Discussion Torums, Weblogs, and Wikis', *Journal of Database Management*, 16(2): i-viii.

Wenger, E. (1998) *Communities of Practice: Learning, Meaning, and Identity.* Cambridge, MA: Cambridge University Press.

Wenger, E., McDermott, R. and Snyder, W.M. (2002) *Cultivating Communities of Practice: A Guide to Managing Knowledge.* Boston: Harvard Business School Press.

Wilson, T.D. (2002) 'The Nonsense of "Knowledge Management"', *Information Research*, 8(1). Retrieved from http://informationr.net/ir/8-1/infres81.html

34

Workplace Learning: Organizations, Ethics, and Issues

Craig E. Johnson

The rhetoric surrounding workplace learning is overwhelmingly positive. Boud and Garrick (1999) declare, for example: "Learning at work has become one of the most exciting areas of development in the dual fields of management and education" (p. 1). Advocates promise that education on the job will promote economic prosperity, empower workers, foster collaboration, encourage lifelong learning, and reduce the need for organizational hierarchy (Fenwick, 1998). Government policy makers, human resource professionals, college administrators and faculty, employees, union officials, and executives all support corporate learning. Even the term "workplace learning" has positive connotations. This phrase makes older terms like "vocational education" and "training" appear quaint and outdated.

While supporters of work-related learning are upbeat, some observers offer a more critical perspective. They note that, as with any major international development, there are negative as well as positive consequences, losers as well as winners. Further, contemporary efforts to educate employees generate significant, but often unrecognized, moral dilemmas. These issues call for evaluative (ethical) judgments about whether educational practices are right or wrong.

This chapter draws from the critical perspective to highlight the ethical dimension of workplace learning. Learning situated at work has a potential "shadow side" that must be addressed by educators. The chapter is organized around five ethical issues identified by critics of workplace learning: the power of the economic paradigm, excessive corporate control, corporatism in the traditional university, exploitation of the knowledge worker, and fostering inequalities. Each of these trends threatens significant harm to individuals and/or institutions and organizations. For that reason, the description of each issue includes a critical response designed to counter its negative effects.

THE POWER OF THE ECONOMIC PARADIGM

As earlier chapters of this *Handbook* make clear, international economic developments are the primary forces driving workplace learning. In the capitalist global economy, national governments are increasingly focused on staying economically viable. They see knowledge as the key to regional prosperity (Boud and Garrick, 1999; Symes and McIntyre, 2000). At the same time, the nature of work has shifted from the production of goods to the production of knowledge. Workers in this postindustrial world increasingly labor with their heads, not their hands. Collectively, the skills and knowledge of the workforce are a form of economic capital. Human capital is now seen as the wellspring of economic growth, taking precedence over natural (natural resource based) capital and machine (equipment based) capital (Bouchard, 1998).

Within this economic framework, knowledge is treated as a valuable object or commodity like currency or precious metals (Butler, 2000; Garrick and Clegg, 2000; Myrick, 2004). Commodified knowledge is measurable, observable, recordable information that serves the needs of the organization (Fenwick, 1998). Objectified information is valuable because it serves a useful purpose, like increasing sales, efficiency and productivity. The task of individual learners is to acquire the data, skills and competencies, such as formulas, computer programs, accounting procedures, and service routines, that will equip them to help the corporation succeed.

Commodified knowledge can be standardized and offered in many different forms by a variety of providers, ranging from traditional academic units to educational consultants and corporate training departments. Content can be delivered to any location at any hour of the night or day via the Internet. Suppliers often divide up the educational process and assign its components to curriculum developers, trainers, technology specialists and others (Poon, 2006). Quality suffers, however, if curriculum developers and instructors have minimal pedagogical training and the primary objective is to keep training costs to a minimum (Muller et al., 1997).

Critics note that the economic paradigm privileges financial values over other important priorities, like promoting human freedom and social justice. Continuous learning is valued, not because it promotes personal development or reduces economic inequalities, but because it bolsters corporate profitability and regional development (Butler, 2000). When knowledge is treated as a commodity and learners focus on mastering specific skills sets, there is little room for self-reflection that encourages employees to consider their role in the organization and in society (Fenwick, 2001).

Not only does workplace knowledge privilege the needs of the organization over the individual, it may not equip employees to succeed in the contemporary workplace. Predicting which particular skills or knowledge will be needed in a rapidly changing global environment is difficult. Those with narrow training may be preparing themselves for jobs that will no longer exist. Consider how, for example, computer programming was once considered an essential skill for everyone, and even school children learned Fortran and other programming languages (Bouchard, 1998).

Critical response

Economic concerns will always play an important role in workplace learning, but they don't have to be the only or the most significant values. The international movement toward corporate social responsibility is a case in point. Socially responsible companies typically have values that extend beyond profit. The guiding principles of Starbucks, for example, include treating others with respect and dignity, embracing diversity, and contributing positively to communities and the environment (Starbucks, 2008). If Starbucks and other multinational companies hope to act as responsible members of the global community, their educational efforts will have to promote noneconomic priorities. Employees will need to learn about the environment, diversity, poverty, and other issues, and develop strategies for addressing these challenges.

Workplace learning's narrow focus on skills and competencies runs contrary to a long-standing tradition in vocational education in the United States. The earliest union education movements equipped members with critical skills to analyze class and social differences (Aronowitz, 1990; Taylor, 2007). Educational pioneer John Dewey (1916) argued that employees should learn about history, science, economics, civics and politics to help them deal with social problems.

> An education which acknowledges the full intellectual and social meaning of a vocation would include instruction in the historic background of present conditions, training in science to give intelligence and initiative in dealing with material and agencies of production, and study of economics, civics, and politics, to bring the future worker into touch with the problems of the day and the various methods proposed of its improvement (p. 318).

Dewey's vision promoted the creation of workplaces that value their employees and foster community. He wanted to empower workers to become active citizens who would transform businesses and other social institutions into functioning democracies. In contrast, the emphasis of modern workplace learning is on creating efficient, compliant workers (Butler, 2000).

Education for the whole person, such as that advocated by Dewey, appears to be better preparation for the demands of the modern workplace because it fosters critical thinking, analytical skills, creativity, and self-mastery (Mantsios, 1990; Caldwell, 2000). "Liberal" education has a long history in the academy. Training in the liberal arts is designed to better the life of learners; the subject matter may or may not have immediate application. However, through the study of the liberal arts, learners develop problem solving, self-reflective, and strategic thinking skills that can be applied in many different settings (Useem, 1989; Brown, 1994; Houston, 1996). Management guru Peter Drucker (2001) argued that the practice of management is a liberal art because managers utilize knowledge, wisdom, self-understanding and leadership to solve real-world problems.

EXCESSIVE CORPORATE CONTROL

Corporate control over work-related learning appears to be a given. After all, companies fund training programs and learning generally takes place in the workplace setting. Nonetheless, critics note that such control, particularly if it remains entirely in the hands of management, can have undesirable consequences. Training generally reinforces the organizational power structure rather than contesting it (Fenwick, 2001). Few organizations are willing to sponsor workshops that encourage workers to criticize excessive executive pay or to take issue with unfair promotion policies, for instance.

The development of corporate universities further extends management control over knowledge. Corporate universities bring together development and education functions under a "strategic umbrella" (Meister, 1998, p. 29). Such functions include formal classes and on-the-job training, leadership development, mentoring, career planning, professional certification, and e-learning (Hundley, 2002). Corporate universities are designed to further the goals of the organization by: (1) developing core competencies; (2) transmitting the group's culture; (3) promoting the corporate mission and vision; (4) recruiting members for organizational initiatives; (5) assigning learners to work on company projects; and (6) cutting product development times (Prince and Beaver, 2001; Jarvis, 2001; Hundley, 2002).

Workplace learning has also given short shrift to union input. Unions, despite shrinking membership and influence in some industrialized nations, remain "the most important and popular form of worker (or working class) organization in most liberal democracies" (Spencer, 2002, p. 11). In recent years, governments in Europe, Britain, Australia, and elsewhere have encouraged management and labor to form educational partnerships to promote economic development (Sutherland and Rainbird, 1999; Forrester, 2002a). While such partnerships can promote individual development, they are dominated by management and give priority to organizational development over the personal development of union members. Employers may fear that providing employees with transferable skills will increase turnover or that newly empowered workers will be hard to manage. Those workers who refuse to participate in training and development programs risk being punished. Participants may find that the greater job flexibility promised by workplace learning translates instead into greater job responsibilities requiring more intense effort on their part (Heyes, 1999; Sutherland and Rainbird, 1999).

Critical response

The promise of workplace learning cannot be realized unless employees are empowered to direct their learning. Workers need to be involved in program and course development, delivery, and evaluation. Unions and other employee organizations ought to function as true partners with management in collaborative educational efforts.

Critical (emancipatory, transformative) pedagogy is one strategy for providing learners with more control over their on-the-job education. Such pedagogy empowers employees to become equal partners in their organizations and to make their corporations more democratic. Gregson (1994) notes that critical pedagogy is marked by four values. First, it is participatory, involving students in collaborative group learning experiences. Working in diverse groups highlights the importance of collective learning and fosters responsibility for oneself and other team members. Further, such experiences diminish stereotypes of those of different backgrounds, enable participants to learn at their own pace, encourage significant encounters between group members, and help students develop communication and problem-solving skills that transfer to other settings.

Second, critical pedagogy takes learners from the known to the larger context. Students begin by learning job-related skills and information but then go on to examine how technology, knowledge, and work skills relate to the organization and society. Participants are also introduced to the historical setting. They explore such topics as the development of a product or industry and conflicts between management and labor.

Third, critical pedagogy engages participants in liberatory dialogue. They become equal partners in the learning process; the instructor serves as a guide, not as the final authority. Students might, for instance, reflect on their employment histories (their best and worst experiences at work) and develop possible strategies for organizational change.

Fourth, critical pedagogy makes learning experiences relevant by drawing meaningful connections between classroom content and students' lives both on and off the job. This can be done by basing discussion on student experiences and by tying activities to their problems and interests. At the same time, participants are involved in active citizenship, using their knowledge to serve others outside the educational setting.

Fifth, critical pedagogy makes topics problematic. Instead of filling participants with knowledge, instructors pose dilemmas that learners must solve. For example: How can employees gain more control over their working conditions? What role should technology play in organizational and societal change? Responding to these issues requires students to engage in critical, reflective thinking. Such thinking, which extends beyond technical matters to political, cultural, social and economic practices, can encourage students to change themselves, their organizations and the larger culture.

CORPORATISM IN THE TRADITIONAL UNIVERSITY

In the new world of workplace learning, traditional universities no longer have a monopoly on knowledge, but have been relegated to one segment of the educational marketplace (Garrick and Clegg, 2000). Learners are educational consumers who can choose from a smorgasbord of educational offerings, and often make their selections on the basis of cost and convenience. Competition for students and tuition dollars can be fierce. The largest proprietary schools in the United States, which include the University of Phoenix, ITT Educational Services and DeVry University, among others, enroll approximately 700,000 students (Donoghue, 2008). Institutional technology (IT) certification programs enroll over 2 million US employees who might otherwise attend traditional colleges and universities, and draw as many students from abroad (Kirp, 2003).

Traditional institutions are responding to the new realities of the educational marketplace by adopting corporate practices. Like their corporate counterparts, modern universities:

Downsize and outsource. Universities are cutting costs in order to stay competitive. Programs that don't generate enough tuition dollars are reduced or eliminated, including such disciplines as history and philosophy that are at the heart of the traditional liberal arts curriculum (Giroux, 2006). The number of tenured faculty in the United States has declined even as enrollments have increased (Lafer, 2001). Adjuncts and graduate students, who earn substantially less and often do not receive insurance benefits, are replacing traditional full-time faculty members. Contingent faculty members now teach an estimated 50–70 percent of all credit hours at US colleges and universities and the salaries of full-time faculty have barely kept pace with inflation (Lafer, 2001; Wilson, 2008). Women and minorities make up a large percentage of the contingent faculty workforce (Entin, 2005).

Develop new revenue streams. Entrepreneurial universities (in addition to raising tuition) are quick to jump into the lucrative niches in the market, identifying profitable new programs and locations. Technology is a key tool for cutting costs and reaching new audiences. No longer bound by geography, a growing number of universities offer courses wherever the market may exist. These schools adopt a variety of nontraditional delivery systems, creating on-line courses, satellite campuses, and evening and weekend programs for working adults. A number of research institutions are also signing lucrative contracts with industry. These agreements allow corporations to patent and market drugs, cell lines and other products created in university laboratories (Bok, 2003; Washburn, 2005).

Focus on the customer. To keep tuition revenues high, the university/corporation must please the customer. Consumer demand determines what courses are offered; customer feedback determines which faculty members are retained (Poon, 2006). Traditional colleges and universities are now more vocationally oriented, increasingly focused on preparing graduates for jobs.

Corporatism puts the university at risk. Some of the disciplines that help develop self-reflective citizens may be eliminated. The widespread use of contingent teachers undermines traditional collegial faculty governance, which relies on peer decision-making (Muller et al., 1997). Temporary workers generally do not participate in committees and are denied the job security that would allow them to express unpopular opinions. A more hierarchical model has emerged where university presidents act like corporate CEOS and administrators make decisions with little discussion and debate (Muller et al., 1997; Giroux, 2006). Faculty collegiality has been replaced by a caste system where a few core tenured faculty members enjoy the benefits of traditional academic employment while the vast majority of instructors labor with little hope of advancement (Entin, 2005).

Traditional universities competing in the educational marketplace are tempted to put profit above quality. When program directors are evaluated based on the revenue they generate, they find it harder to turn down marginal applicants or to remove failing students. Keeping the customer happy may tempt professors to reduce academic rigor and fuel grade inflation. Decisions about which faculty to retain increasingly depends on high student evaluations rather than on the quality of course content. This is despite the fact that students, who are often new to a discipline, are not the best judges of what they need to learn and how material should be delivered. Driven by a customer mentality, many students appear minimally concerned about learning. Instead, they are more interested in earning high grades and earning additional credentials (Muller et al., 1997).

Finally, corporate research partnerships threaten academic freedom. Those researchers receiving industry funding may not be free to disseminate their findings to other members of the scientific community. Instead, the knowledge they generate belongs to the corporate sponsor. Information about failed medical procedures and ineffective drugs may never be released to the public (Washburn, 2005).

Critical response

There is much to be said for operating in a businesslike manner. Good stewardship requires that resources be used carefully. Technology can enhance the learning process. Underserved markets should be provided with educational opportunities and the needs of students should be met. Yet, administrators and faculty at traditional universities ought to carefully consider which elements of corporate learning enhance the institution's mission and which detract from it. To maintain their heritage as centers of reflection, criticism, creation of knowledge and personal development, traditional universities will need to: (a) reduce the use of adjunct faculty and graduate student instructors; (b) resist the temptation to become knowledge factories serving industry; (c) focus on educational quality instead of profit; (d) be driven by mission and values rather than by customer demand; and (e) protect the rights of researchers to generate and disseminate information without corporate interference.

EXPLOITATION OF THE KNOWLEDGE WORKER

In a movement intended to empower workers, the individual is often rendered powerless instead. The premise of lifelong learning is that the individual is deficient and needs to continuously acquire new skills and knowledge to keep up. As a result, "Workers' lives become a human resource development project" (Fenwick, 2001, p. 12). Those who don't actively pursue additional skills may be terminated. As noted earlier, training is designed to benefit the corporation not the individual. In fact, participating in workplace learning may work against the individual's interests and reinforce inequitable corporate policies. Employees often end up taking on greater responsibilities and putting in more hours on the job with no increase in pay. Balancing work with family responsibilities becomes more difficult as more time is devoted to job responsibilities.

The nature of knowledge work also calls for greater commitment than other types of labor. Knowledge workers have to commit their minds as well as their bodies to the organization (Forrester, 2002b). The service industry, one of the most rapidly expanding sectors of the global economy, also demands the emotional commitment of workers. Service employees engage in emotional labor by managing their emotions and emotional displays to create positive encounters with customers (Hochschild, 1983; Leidner, 1993).

The utilitarian focus of workplace learning does not speak to the deepest needs of employees. As organizations assume a greater role in societies, more workers seek meaningful tasks and relationships that serve significant purposes. This desire for meaning and connection is behind popular and academic interest in workplace spirituality. Duchon and Plowman (2005) define workplace spirituality as "the recognition that employees have an inner life that nourishes and is nourished by meaningful work that takes place in the context of community" (p. 809). Duchon, Plowman, and others argue that employees have spiritual needs– which involve their core identities and values – and are motivated by more than material rewards. Workers want their employment to be fulfilling and to serve the greater needs of society. At the same time, members desire significant connections with co-workers that nurture their inner lives.

Workplace learning that ignores the inner life of employees has a fragmenting effect because it speaks to only part of the individual's identity. Employees are increasingly interested in pursuing a vocation or life calling, not just in qualifying for a particular position (Rayburn, 1997). Determining a purpose in life means identifying one's unique skills, abilities, and desires, and applying those elements both on and off the job. Those who live out their vocations are more satisfied, are more committed to their organizations, and are better equipped for service to others (Johnson, 2007).

Critical response

Adult educators should honor rather than diminish the worth of learner. They can do so by rejecting the notion that employees are deficient and by acknowledging instead that employees bring valuable knowledge and skills to the workplace and training setting. Human capital and human resources discourse ought to be replaced with language that acknowledges the strengths and importance of people. Some training content should promote individual development as well as corporate development. Those who upgrade their skills need to be rewarded, not burdened with additional responsibilities with no increase in pay. Corporations can encourage employees to maintain a balance between work and family responsibilities.

Organizations may also speak to the inner needs of workers by offering opportunities for spiritual development. In North America, meditation rooms and reflective gardens are found in a number of company headquarters and, according to one estimate, 4,000 chaplains are employed in secular organizations in the United States (Garcia-Zamor, 2003). While there are legal and ethical limitations to promoting particular beliefs in the workplace, spirit friendly corporations promote spiritual learning by studying spiritual materials, sponsoring spiritual discussion groups, and sending employees to workplace spirituality conferences (Johnson, 2009).

FOSTERING INEQUALITIES

To date, workplace learning appears to be widening, not lessening, the gaps between the powerful and powerless, the haves and the have-nots. Executives, as we've seen, control access to workplace education as well as its content, and the needs of employees and unions are subjugated to corporate interests. The gulf between tenured faculty and contingent faculty at traditional universities is growing.

Members of marginalized groups are often denied the benefits of workplace learning (Butler, 1999; Proubert, 1999). This includes women, ethnic minorities, immigrants, the disabled, and others. Marginalized employees are less likely to be approved for training, and face prejudice, stereotypes, lack of mentoring and other barriers to career development. As a consequence, they earn less and have little chance of advancement. Even when women and other diverse groups are included in training programs, there is a good chance that their concerns will be ignored. For instance, success in many jobs depends on following the traditional male role model – the worker who defines himself by his job. This model does not reflect the reality that women often bear a far greater responsibility for children and other family members (Proubert, 1999).

The benefits of workplace learning are distributed unevenly within postindustrial economies. Those in the professional-managerial elite have the most access to education and workplace learning. Workers providing symbolic-analytic services centered on problem-identifying and problem-solving (e.g., research scientists, software engineers, public relations executives, lawyers, real estate developers, investment bankers) hold the most lucrative, highly valued positions in the US economy (Reich, 1991; Samper and Lakes, 1994). This portion of the workforce is highly educated (generally college graduates) and majority male. Women are typically gender segregated, relegated to in-person service occupations like nursing and childcare where they are required to be pleasant and nurturing. Routine production workers (often recent immigrants) receive only minimal training, generally in basic literacy skills.

Workplace learning also contributes to global inequality. Education is less available in developing countries, giving an ongoing advantage to wealthier nations. Large portions of the population in Africa, Asia, and South America work outside the formal economy and have no access to training at all. Instead of equipping nationals to prosper in the local economy, Western groups typically fund educational efforts in these nations that prepare workers for labor in the global economy. Graduates often do not find local positions but are hired to work in industrialized nations, leaving their countries of origin at a further disadvantage (Farrell and Fenwick, 2007). Multinationals also engage in "knowledge extraction," taking information from poor nations while giving little in return. For example, data produced in clinical drug trials in less-developed nations goes back to company headquarters in Europe or North America. Weaker nations are given little support for their efforts to develop research facilities (Karim, 2000).

Cultural imperialism compounds global inequalities. Programs developed in the West generally promote individual development, which conflicts with the values of collectivist societies (Hoppe, 2004). Multinationals may offer training in English and ignore local educational practices.

In other instances, workers must adopt Westernized behaviors to succeed. Consider the case of workers at Indian call centers that support US businesses, for example. They are taught to develop an American or British accent, learning how to pronounce letters like "o" or "r." They mask their identities, adopting a "Western persona" to fool clients into thinking they are talking to someone in the United States. They must take abuse from irate customers who are racially biased (Mirchandani and Maitra, 2007).

Critical response

The inequalities fostered by workplace learning have to be addressed at both the organizational and societal level. Organizational leaders must create greater access for members of marginalized groups to training programs, mentoring initiatives, job sharing, and other efforts. They need to hire nontraditional instructors and provide nontraditional role models. At the same time, they ought to foster diverse organizational climates through diversity hiring and development initiatives, family friendly policies, flexible work arrangements, and diversity training, and by penalizing discriminatory behaviors and practices (racism, sexual harassment) on the job. Workplace educators should respect local values and practices when offering training programs in other cultural settings.

National and international leaders also have a role to play in promoting equality. They should encourage women and men to enter careers traditionally dominated by the other gender and equip workers in every sector of the workforce with skills that enable them to advance to better, higher paying positions. International organizations sponsoring educational efforts in developing nations ought to prepare citizens for local job openings. In addition, these sponsoring agencies should reach out to workers who labor outside the formal economy. Leaders in developed nations ought to limit the "poaching" of skilled individuals and knowledge extraction from developing countries.

CONCLUSION

Recognition that workplace learning has a shadow side serves as a reminder that "pedagogy is an inherently moral activity" (Myrick, 2004, p. 24). Workplace educators have ethical determinations to make about the nature and purpose of knowledge, competing values, balancing the needs of the individual and the organization, control over access to learning and curriculum, and their duty to either challenge or to support the social order. Further, they must make moral choices about the role of the traditional academy, their obligations to learners, and whether they have a responsibility to address inequalities.

Critics offer guidelines to educators faced with the ethical decisions described above. These tactics are rooted in concern for social justice, equity, quality, and inclusion. They promote democracy, education of the whole person (including the spiritual dimension) and learner empowerment, while fostering respect for individual dignity and diversity. Such guidelines will not be universally adopted. Proponents of workplace learning will likely disagree about the role of spirituality in the workplace, for instance, and the importance of educating the whole person. However, acknowledging the moral dimension of education on the job is an important first step. Only then can advocates begin to address the potential harm posed by learning situated at work, bringing the practice of workplace learning more in line with the positive rhetoric it generates.

REFERENCES

Aronowitz, S. (1990) 'The New Labor Education: A Return to Ideology', in S.H. London, E.R. Tarr and J.F. Wilson (eds), *The Re-education of the American Working Class*. Westport, CT: Greenwood Press. pp. 21–33.

Bok, D. (2003) *Universities in the Marketplace: The Commercialization of Higher Education*. Princeton, NJ: Princeton University.

Bouchard, P. (1998) 'Training and Work: Myths about Human Capital', in S.M. Scott, B. Spencer and A.M. Thomas (eds), *Learning for Life: Canadian Readings in Adult Education.* Toronto: Thompson. pp. 128–140.

Boud, D. and Garrick, J. (1999) 'Understandings of Workplace Learning', in D. Boud and J. Garrick (eds), *Understanding Learning at Work.* London: Routledge, pp. 1–11.

Brown, P.C. (1994) 'Liberal Education for Leadership', *Liberal Education,* 80(2): 44–48.

Butler, E. (1999) 'Technologising Equity: The Politics and Practices of Work-Related Learning', in D. Boud and J. Garrick (eds), *Understanding Learning at Work,* London: Routledge. pp. 132–150.

Butler, E. (2000) 'Knowing "Now", Learning Futures: The Politics and Knowledge Practices of Vocational Education and Training', *International Journal of Lifelong Education,* 19(4): 322–341.

Caldwell, P. (2000) 'Adult Learning and the Workplace', in H. Rainbird (ed.), *Training in the Workplace: Critical Perspectives on Learning at Work.* New York: St. Martin's Press. pp. 244–263.

Dewey, J. (1916) *Democracy and Education.* New York: Free Press.

Donoghue, F. (2008) *The Last Professors: The Corporate University and the Fate of the Humanities.* New York: Fordham University Press.

Drucker, P. (2001) *The Essential Drucker.* New York: HarperBusiness.

Duchon, D. and Plowman, D.A. (2005) 'Nurturing the Spirit at Work: Impact on Work Unit Performance', *Leadership Quarterly,* 16(5): 807–833.

Entin, J. (2005) 'Contingent Teaching, Corporate Universities, and the Academic Labor Movement', *Radical Teacher,* issue 73: 26–32.

Farrell, L. and Fenwick, T. (2007) 'Educating a Global Workforce?', in L. Farrell and T. Fenwick (eds), *World Yearbook of Education 2007. Educating the Global Workforce: Knowledge, Knowledge Work and Knowledge Workers.* London: Routledge. pp. 13–26.

Fenwick, T. (1998) 'Questioning the Concept of the Learning Organization', in S.M. Scott, B. Spencer and A.M. Thomas (eds), *Learning for Life: Canadian Readings in Adult Education.* Toronto: Thompson. pp. 140–152.

Fenwick, T. (2001) 'Tides of Change: New Themes and Questions in Workplace Learning', *New Directions for Adult and Continuing Education,* 92, Winter: 3–17.

Forrester, K. (2002a) 'Unions and Workplace Learning: The British Experience', in B. Spencer (ed.), *Unions and Learning in a Global Economy: International and Comparative Perspectives,* Toronto: Thompson. pp. 138–148.

Forrester, K. (2002b) 'Work-Related Learning and the Struggle for Employee Commitment', *Studies in the Education of Adults,* vol. 34(1): 42–55.

Garcia-Zamor, J.C. (2003) 'Workplace Spirituality and Organizational Performance', *Public Administration Review,* 63(3): 355–363.

Garrick, J. and Clegg, S. (2000) 'Organizational Gothic: Transfusing Vitality and Transforming the Corporate Body through Work-Based Learning', in C. Symes and J. McIntyre (eds), *Working Knowledge: The New Vocationalism and Higher Education.* Buckingham, UK: The Society for Research into Higher Education. pp. 153–171.

Giroux, H.A. (2006) 'Higher Education under Siege: Implications for Public Intellectuals', *Thought and Action,* Fall: 63–78.

Gregson, J.A. (1994) 'From Critical Theory to Critical Practice: Transformative Vocational Classrooms', in R.D. Lakes (ed.), *Critical Education for Work: Multidisciplinary approaches.* Norwood, NJ: Ablex. pp. 161–169.

Heyes, J. (1999) 'Workplace Industrial Relations and Training', in H. Rainbird (ed.), *Training in the Workplace: Critical Perspectives on Learning at Work.* New York: St. Martin's Press. pp. 153–171.

Hochschild, A.R. (1983) *The Managed Heart: Commercialization of Human Feeling,* Berkeley: University of California Press.

Hoppe, M.H. (2004) 'Cross-Cultural Issues in the Development of Leaders', in C.D. McCauley and E. Van Velsor (eds), *The Center for Creative Leadership Handbook of Leadership Development,* San Francisco: Jossey Bass. pp. 331–360.

Houston, G.R. (1996) 'Bury the Liberal vs. Professional Arts Debate', *Education,* 117(1): 12–16.

Hundley, S.P. (2002) 'Corporate Universities: Collaboration, not Competition', *Assessment Update,* 14(1): September–October: 1–2, 14–15.

Jarvis, P. (2001) *Universities and Corporate Universities: The Higher Learning Industry in Global Society.* London: Kogan Page.

Johnson, C.E. (2007) *Ethics in the Workplace: Tools and Tactics for Organizational Transformation,* Thousand Oaks, CA: Sage.

Johnson, C.E. (2009) *Meeting the Ethical Challenges of Leadership: Casting Light or Shadow,* (3rd edn). Thousand Oaks, CA: Sage.

Karim, A. (2000) 'Globalization, Ethics, and AIDS Vaccines', *Science,* 23 June, 21–29.

Kirp, D.L. (2003) *Shakespeare, Einstein, and the Bottom Line: The Marketing of Higher Education.* Cambridge, MA: Harvard University Press.

Lafer. G. (2001) 'Graduate Student Unions Fight the Corporate University', *Dissent,* Fall: 63–70.

Leidner, R. (1993) *Fast Food, Fast Talk: Service Work and the Routinization of Everyday Life.* Berkeley: University of California Press.

Mantsios, G. (1990) 'Worker Education: Developing an Approach to Worker Empowerment', in S.H. London, E.R. Tarr and J.F. Wilson (eds), *The Re-education of the American Working Class.* Westport, CT: Greenwood Press. pp. 35–49.

Meister, J.C. (1998) *Corporate Universities: Lessons in Building a World-Class Work Force.* (Rev. edn). New York: McGraw-Hill.

Mirchandani, K. and Maitru, S. (2007) 'Learning Imperialism through Training In Transnational Call Centres', in L. Farrell and T. Fenwick (eds), *World Yearbook of Education 2007. Educating the Global Workforce: Knowledge, Knowledge Work and Knowledge Workers.* London: Routledge. pp. 154–164.

Muller, H.J., Porter, J. and Rehder, R.R. (1997) 'The Invasion of the Mind Snatchers: The Business of Business Education', *Journal of Education for Business,* 72(3): 164–169.

Myrick, F. (2004) 'Pedagogical Integrity in the Knowledge Economy', *Nursing Philosophy,* 5(1): 23–29.

Poon, T.S. (2006) 'The Commodification of Higher Education: Implications for Academic Work and Employment', *International Journal of Employment Studies,* 14(1): 81–104.

Prince, C. and Beaver, G. (2001) 'Facilitating Organizational Change: The Role and Development of the Corporate University', *Strategic Change,* 10(4): 189–122.

Proubert, B. (1999) 'Gendered Workers and Gendered Work: Implications for Women's Learning', in D. Boud and J. Garrick (eds), *Understanding Learning at Work.* London: Routledge. pp. 98–116.

Rayburn, C.A. (1997) 'Vocation as Calling', in D.P. Bloch and L.J. Richmond (eds), *Connections Between Spirit and Work in Career Development.* Palo Alto, CA: Davies-Black. pp. 162–183.

Reich, R.B. (1991) *The Work of Nations: Preparing Ourselves for 21st Century Capitalism.* New York: Knopf.

Samper, M.D. and Lakes, R.D. (1994) 'Work Education for the Next Century: Beyond Skills Training', in R.D. Lakes (ed.), *Critical Education for Work: Multidisciplinary Approaches,* Norwood, NJ: Ablex. 95–107.

Spencer, B. (2002) 'Preface', in B. Spencer (ed.), *Unions and Learning in the Global Economy: International and Comparative Perspectives.* Toronto: Thompson. pp. 11–13.

Starbucks (2008) 'Mission Statement', viewed September 10, 2008, <http://starbucks.com/aboutus/environment.asp.

Sutherland, J. and Rainbird, H. (1999) 'Unions and Workplace Learning: Conflict or Cooperation with the Employer?', in H. Rainbird (ed.), *Training in the Workplace: Critical Perspectives on Learning at Work.* New York: St. Martin's Press. pp. 189–209.

Symes, C. and McIntyre, J. (2000) 'Working Knowledge: An Introduction to the New Business of Learning', in C. Symes and J. McIntyre (eds), *Working Knowledge: The New Vocationalism and Higher Education.* Buckingham, UK: Open University Press. pp. 1–13.

Taylor, J. (2007) 'From Union Education to Workers' Education: Workers Learning How to Confront Twenty-First-Century Capitalism', in L. Farrell and T. Fenwick (eds), *World Yearbook of Education 2007. Educating the Global Workforce: Knowledge, Knowledge Work and Knowledge Workers.* London: Routledge. pp. 65–75.

Useem, M. (1989) *Liberal Education and the Corporation: The Hiring and Advancement of College Graduates.* New York: Aldine de Gruyer.

Washburn, J. (2005) *University, Inc.: The Corporate Corruption of American Higher Education.* New York: Basic Books.

Wilson, R. (2008) 'College Too Pricey? Don't Blame Faculty Pay', *The Chronicle of Higher Education,* vol. LV, no. 11, 7 November. pp. A1, A10.

Index

Figures in **Bold**; Tables in *Italics*